The Cheshire Bantams

The Cheshire Bantams

Stephen McGreal

Pen & Sword
MILITARY

Dedicated to Frank McGreal,
The man I am proud to call Dad.

First published in Great Britain in 2006
reprinted in paperback in 2007
by
Pen & Sword Military
an imprint of
Pen & Sword Books Ltd
47 Church Street
Barnsley
South Yorkshire
S70 2AS

ISBN 1 84415 524 2

A CIP catalogue record for this book is
available from the British Library

Typeset in Palatino 10pt

Printed and bound in the United Kingdom by CPI

Pen & Sword Books Ltd incorporates the Imprints of Pen & Sword Aviation, Pen & Sword
Maritime, Pen & Sword Military, Wharncliffe Local History, Pen and Sword Select, Pen and
Sword Military Classics and Leo Cooper.
For a complete list of Pen & Sword titles, please contact
Pen & Sword Books Limited
47 Church Street, Barnsley, South Yorkshire, S70 2AS, England
E-mail: enquiries@pen-and-sword.co.uk
Website: www.pen-and-sword.co.uk

CONTENTS

INTRODUCTION
AND ACKNOWLEDGEMENTS

THREE DECADES AGO I made my regular visit to a nomadic unofficial street market in Liverpool; a forerunner of today's popular car boot sales. The offerings here were not the modern assortment of assorted junk and obsolete toys but objects of worth. For it was here that the good citizens of Liverpool were disposing of goods and chattels their relations had acquired since Victoria was on the throne. It was a period of happy hunting for collector and antique dealer alike, but you had to be there literally at the crack of dawn if you were searching for something special.

A sea mist had drifted off the Mersey, shrouding the sellers and their assorted wares strewn on the ground with a thin layer of condensation. The damp air seemed to permeate my bones as I glanced at my watch, it was now nearly eight in the morning, and the last couple of hours had for me been a waste of time. More in desperation than hope I enquired of one of the sellers 'If he had any thing military?' He replied, 'Try that wooden box on the floor mate'. I gingerly probed around in the box, searching for a medal or possibly a cap badge but to no avail, in the process I had decanted some of the items onto the floor. 'That's it,' the seller said as he pointed to a piece of dishevelled wet ribbon now lying on the ground. What an anti climax I thought as I picked a strip of faded purple ribbon up prior to gazing down upon a very small picture of Private J. Clarke on what transpired to be a marker for a missal or prayer book. Although it was only a modest buy, at least a purchase had been made, and there was always next week.

While heading back to my trusty Morris Oxford a friendly militaria dealer stopped and produced a World War Two, Fairbairn-Sykes commando dagger he had bought earlier for a pound or two. 'Have you had any luck?' he enquired. I fumbled in my pocket and produced the only buy of the day, fully expecting a hoot of derision. To my surprise he was impressed. 'You don't see much to the Cheshire Bantams,' said Mac, 'Do you want to sell it?' 'No thanks,' came my reply and I headed for home. During the drive home I pondered on the phrase 'Cheshire Bantams', who or what were they, as I had never heard of them before.

Returning home the new acquisition was gently cleaned and left to dry out, only then did the smaller print become more legible. The moving epitaph read:

In loving memory of Pte. J. Clarke,
15th battalion Cheshire Regiment.
The beloved husband of Nellie Clarke.
Who died of wounds in France,
On October 13th 1918, Aged 29 years.
He has fallen with others so noble and brave,
And peacefully sleeps in a soldier's grave,
Only those that have loved him are able to tell,
The pain that is felt in not saying farewell.

Following enquiries with the Commonwealth War Graves Commission they revealed 39930 Private Joseph Clarke of the 15th Battalion, Cheshire Regiment had resided in the St. Pauls' area of Macclesfield, where he also enlisted. On 13-10-18 he died of wounds, and is interred in grave II.D.2 at Ypres Reservoir Cemetery, Belgium.

The faded reminder has survived as a poignant reminder of the passing of the twenty-nine year old soldier; perhaps the item had been a cherished keepsake of Nellie, had it remained in her bible all those years? Could it have been that she had finally passed on to be reunited with Joe and her worldly goods had been sold off at the market, maybe her bible had been in that box on the floor? The answers we can only speculate on.

The search for information on the Bantams now began; long hours were spent thumbing through my assorted books on the Great War to no avail. Gradually a few details were gleaned from various sources, the general conception of the Bantams was that they were raised in Birkenhead, and were no taller than five foot three

Locally my quest proved to no avail. With the exception of the cenotaph, the town has no memorial to the soldiers of the battalions of which they had once been so proud.

Private J. Clarke 39930
15th Battalion, Cheshire Regiment
(Bantam Battalion).
Born St Pauls Macclesfield.
Height: below 5' 2"

Ideally this book should have been researched in the nineteen sixties when there may still have been survivors of the Cheshire Bantams available to interview; it is most regrettable that their passing has prevented the inclusion of their first hand experiences. From the outset of my research it became apparent that the small soldiers had all too frequently fought in small penny packets, where they fought and died attached to assorted battalions of infantry or laboured away fetching and carrying supplies to and from the line with all its inherent risks; these factors have made the research so much more difficult. Numerous letters forwarded to provincial newspapers throughout the country failed to generate any worthwhile response from their readers. My enquiries at the Cheshire Regimental museum were also unsuccessful, for apart from copies of the war diaries, a captured weapon and a battalion drum the museum advised they were bereft of Bantam documentation, photographs and artefacts. The trail of the Bantams was not simply cold, it was to all intents and purposes buried under a metre of perma frost.

The quest for Bantam information began with the first of scores of visits to the Borough Road, Birkenhead archive library, where the Great War newspapers were available on microfilm. This facility proved to be a gold mine of information that provided the foundation for this book.

Acknowledgements

Amongst my friends there are a number of dedicated Western Front amateur historians, who have gone out of their way to borrow, beg or photocopy material in any shape or form, which they considered may be of interest to me. Each snippet or photograph they have procured no matter how big or small has been of equal value to this project, and has often arrived during a period when I have despaired of completing my task; their fresh information and enthusiasm has usually spurred me on towards my goal. I can think of no fairer way to thank them for their contributions than to acknowledge them in alphabetical order. Ian Boumhrey who donated a postcard and more significantly a scarce book from his collection. Larry Clow for consistently searching for military postcards of the Cheshire regiment and related subjects. Kevin Core, a journalist at the Birkenhead News, whose fine article prompted several of his readers to loan material now reproduced in this project. Alan Gregson assisted greatly by combing the regimental magazine 'Oak Leaf' for information on members of the two Bantam battalions, also assisting with information for the soldiers died compilation, and the honours and awards. Ernie Ruffler for his patience while I photographed articles from delicate ninety year old newspapers, stored in the Wirral Museum, also Emma Chandler when I returned for more photos. During his research on the Wallasey war memorial Nick Simpson has acquired several Bantam photographs, which he has copied for inclusion in this project. A regular contributor to several books of this nature is my friend Peter Threlfall who has helped greatly with information on Birkenhead casualties so labouredly acquired during his research on the Birkenhead war memorial and also generously provided copies of postcards from his extensive collection. I also wish to thank fellow W.F.A. member Mark McGrath for making a pilgrimage on my behalf to the Ypres grave of Private Joseph Clarke, placing a Poppy Appeal memorial cross. Also to the members of the Birkenhead Historical Society for the use of their very scarce Bantam photographs. Finally the dynamic duo of Sylvia and Roni at Barnsley. Roni Wilkinson's good humour and advice has proved invaluable in the publication of this book. My long suffering family have tolerated my obsession with this project for over eight years, and have watched with some amusement my regular outpourings of annoyance aimed at my computer which appears to have a mind of its own. My daughter Gemma's computer skills have come to my rescue countless times, patiently redressing her Dad's errors, time after time as once again I blamed the infernal machine, yes I know a bad worker does blame his tools, but something has to take the blame for losing a long evening's work at the touch of a computer key pad. My two other daughters have also helped greatly; copious amounts of tea have magically appeared alongside the computer courtesy of Nicola. The Bantams' website has generated an enormous amount of emails from people who are tracing their family history; Stephanie has handled all the email correspondence and assisted greatly in searching the internet for sites containing anything relevant to this project. My lovely wife has been an absolute saint for cheerfully cutting the lawn and carrying out a million and one assorted tasks during these past eight years when I have spent precious spare time bashing away at the keyboard.

With their input this book and an extensive database of former Bantams have come to fruition and to them all I offer my sincere thanks for their generous assistance in this project.

Published sources

Allinson. Sydney. *The Bantams, The Untold Story of World War 1*. Howard Baker Press. London. 1981.

Bigland. Alfred. *The Call of Empire*.

Cave. Nigel. *Delville Wood*. Pen and Sword Books. 1999.

Chapell. Mike. *British Battle Insignia Vol. 1 1914-18*. Osprey Publishing Ltd. Oxford. 2000.

Davison. H.M. Lieut. *History of the 35th Division in the Great War*. 1926. Reprinted by Naval & Military Press. 2003.

Giblin. H. *Bravest of Hearts*. [Liverpool Scottish in WW1] Cromwell Press. Trowbridge, Wilts. 2000.

Gliddon. Gerald. *The Battle of the Somme*. A topographical history. Alan Sutton Publishing. Stroud.

Hallows. Ian. S. *Regiments and Corps of the British Army*. New Orchard Editions. 1994

Hart. Liddel. *History of the First World War*. Book Club Associates. London. 1979.

Haythornthwaite. P.J. *The World War One Source Book*. Arms and Armour Press. London. 1998.

Johnston. Harrison. *Extracts from an Officer's Diary*. Geo Falkner & Sons. Manchester. 1919.

Putkowski. J. & Sykes. J. *Shot at Dawn*. Wharncliffe Publishing Ltd. Barnsley. 1989.

Stedman. Michael. *Guillemont*. Pen and Sword Books. 1998

Stedman. Michael. *Manchester Pals*. Pen and Sword Books. 1994.

Wallace. Edgar. *Kitchener's Army & the Territorial Forces*. George Newnes Ltd. 8 – 12 Southampton St, Strand. W.C. 1920s.

Westlake. R. *Kitchener's Army. A Pictorial History*. Nutshell Publishing Co. Ltd. Kent. 1989.

Wyrall. *The History of the Cheshire Regiment*.

Birkenhead News Victory Souvenir of the Great War. Wilmer Bros. & Co. Ltd.

British Officer P.O.W.s 1914-18. Messrs Cox & Co's Enquiry Office. London. 1919.

Register of the Victoria Cross. This England Books, Cheltenham, Glos. 1997.

Sir Douglas Haig's Despatches. J.M. Dent & Sons Ltd. London. 1919.

Soldiers Died in the Great War. H.M.S.O.

War Illustrated. Vol X. The Amalgamated Press Ltd, London. 1919.

A Popular History of the Great War. The Amalgamated Press. London.

Periodicals and Journals

Birkenhead Advertiser. Birkenhead News. Wallasey News.
Illustrated War News. The. Part 53. 1915. 172 Strand. London. W.C
Lancashire Fusiliers' Annual 1917. Major B. Smyth. Sackville Press.
Findlater Place, Dublin. 1918.
Liverpool Daily Post and Echo.
Oak Leaf. The.
1918 Absent Voters' List for Birkenhead. 2 volumes.
The Saga magazine November 2001.
The Sphere Ltd. 8 June 1918. Great New St, London.
15th & 16th Cheshire Regiment War Diary. WO95/2487. The National
Archives. Kew. Surrey.

Libraries and Museums

The Wirral Museum. Hamilton Square. Birkenhead.
The Regimental Museum. The Castle, Chester.
The Williamson Art Gallery and Museum. Slatey Road. Birkenhead.
P.R.O. Chester.
Borough Road Reference Library. Birkenhead.
Liverpool Central Library.
Earlston Road Library, Wallasey.

Unpublished sources of information

'Memories of a Bantam Lancashire Fusilier' kindly supplied by Mr.
Somerville.

Grateful acknowledgements to:

Mr. Percy Harwood who was 97 years young when he contacted me
several years ago. Carole Ford for citation, paperwork and
photographs of Pte. R. Johnston. Mrs. Sheila Walker for providing the
photograph of Sgt. H. Fay D.C.M. The late Mr. Hal Giblin. Mr. Victor
Walkley for the providing the scans of the Souls brothers. The family
of R.S.M. Robert Lyon for kindly supplying copies of paperwork,
photograph and an extensive obituary. Cath Mitchelson for supplying

the photo of Bantams outside the cinema. Mr. Trevor Moffatt for supplying details of his grandfathers' war time experiences. Mr. John Noonan for the poignant documentation concerning his relation Sgt. J.H. Noonan. Mrs. Joan Smith for generously supplying a sepia photograph of Private Charles Smith. Robin Spencer who supplied a photograph and a letter written by Private J.N. Spencer. Mrs. Margaret Thompson for kindly loaning for copying several excellent photographs and paperwork relating to her father, a 16th battalion man. Simon Petrie and the members of the Birkenhead Historical Society for their help with my quest for photographs of the Bantams. Mary and Peter Formstone for kindly allowing the copying of her late mother's photographs taken in 1915 as the Bantams march by. The many Merseyside residents who contacted me with the odd snippet of information or the name of a former Cheshire Bantam to add to my extensive data base and nominal roll of former Bantams. To the scores of people who visited my web site www.cheshire-regiment.com and shared their memories of former 15th and 16th Cheshire family members.

CHAPTER ONE

Birkenhead Through the Years

LOCATED IN THE NORTH WEST of England lies the Wirral peninsula, whose boundaries are clearly defined by the geographical features of the industrial river Mersey, the opposite coast of the peninsula is bordered by the tranquil River Dee, both estuaries merge with the Irish Sea. The major town in Wirral is Birkenhead, which lies on the banks of the Mersey facing the renowned port and city of Liverpool.

The Norman baron Hamo de Massy is considered to have founded the origins of Birkenhead in the twelfth century, when he established upon the Mersey shore a small Benedictine priory. The monks provided hospitality and shelter to wayfarers, cultivated the land, whilst also providing the first reliable ferry service across the Mersey. In recognition of their charitable services King Edward the second awarded the monks two charters, the latter charter of 1330 included the perpetual rights to ferry passengers and goods from Birkenhead to Liverpool. For two centuries the priory prospered, the Prior gradually attaining the same rights and powers of a baron. The Priory flourished until King Henry VIII dissolved the monasteries in 1536, claimed all their properties and rights, and dispersed the monks. Today it is unknown if the monastery was wrecked or simply fell into ruin; the Chapter House was retained as a place of religious worship.

For centuries Wirral remained a tranquil rural retreat, while Liverpool expanded and prospered at a phenomenal rate. There was little development around the Birkenhead cluster of buildings until the dawning of the industrial revolution. By the early 1800s Birkenhead was gaining a reputation as a two-hotel riverside health resort whose further development was hampered by an inadequate ferry service, supplied by four oared boats, which carried a maximum of thirty passengers. The arrival of the steam paddle boat *Etna* circa 1820 offering a regular reliable cross river service from Tranmere to the Liverpool Queens Dock heralded the transformation of the Birkenhead shore line. Entrepreneurs now purchased the virgin countryside, which was now owned by the Price family and rapidly changed the area beyond recognition. The distinctive headland of birches or birchen head from whence the town derived its name was soon swallowed up under acres of docks and quays.

In 1819 Francis Price, the Lord of the Manor, financed the building of St Mary's Church, alongside the Chapter House, which was now too small for the larger congregation. The arrival of the Liverpool businessman William Laird set the area on the road to prosperity; he proposed to make Birkenhead an exclusive suburb for wealthy Liverpool merchants. Laird also established the Birkenhead Iron Works, this evolved into the shipyard which constructed Britain's first steel ship. The first iron ship seen in America named the *John Randolph* was built by the Laird yard in 1834. In 1833 royal assent approved an act for paving, lighting and improving of the township of Birkenhead. A market hall, beagle and night patrol was also established. The foundation stone for a new dock system was laid in October 1844, when a thousand navvies began converting a sector of the Wallasey pool into two docks, the nucleus of a modern port. As a result of the rapid industrialisation the population rose dramatically, for by 1846 the population stood in excess of 30,000.

The financiers of the new town suffered financial difficulties prompting the cancellation of all further developments; this coincided with a down turn in shipbuilding orders, as a result wide scale unemployment occurred. The rival port of Liverpool stepped in and purchased the Birkenhead dock system, gradually extending the facilities, although never in a style as grand as the system across the water. None the less the expansion brought welcome employment and by the turn of the century the population had trebled in size. The town offered a wide range of employment both skilled and unskilled in a variety of industries, which were predominately shipbuilding, stone quarrying, paint, and dock work.

In 1840 the Chester to Birkenhead railway line opened, four decades later the first railway tunnel under a river connected Birkenhead with Liverpool. After being rejected by Liverpool, American tram way pioneer George Francis Train set up Europe's first tram service in Birkenhead in 1860. The horse drawn trams trotted from Woodside ferry terminal to Birkenhead Park, which was Britain's first municipal park, and the inspiration for New York's Central Park. Yet another invention was the world's first steam driven submarine the *Resurgam* which was launched at Birkenhead in 1879. In conjunction with Laird an Edinburgh architect by the name of James Gillespie Graham embarked upon Europe's most ambitious town planning development. The layout is reminiscent of a typical American town system of blocks with intersecting roads. In close proximity to the Mersey underground station, affording easy access for Liverpool magnates wishing to escape from the overcrowded city of Liverpool, lies the town's centrepiece which is Hamilton Square

The square, which is named after the in-law family of Laird, remains today as an exceptional square of listed Georgian buildings. All face towards a central garden, originally intended as an exclusive garden for the use of the square's wealthy residents. One side of the

Charing Cross, Birkenhead.

The Mersey ferry **Daffodil** *in peace-time. She later participated in the 1918 raid on Zeebrugge.*

square is dominated by the borough's Town Hall, (now the Wirral Museum) which would later be the location for yet another unique Birkenhead concept.

The town planners had placed too much emphasis on the construction of grand stylish property, which spread throughout the leafy suburbs of Birkenhead. More modest properties were now required and by necessity row upon row of working class terraced housing in-filled the vacant street blocks. The crowded homes extended outwards to the very boundaries of the shipyards and docks where the majority of the populace earned their living. Within the first decade of the twentieth century Birkenhead established itself as a prosperous town, a hive of industry with the great shipyard of Cammel Laird shipbuilders and engineers at its very heart.

But Birkenhead's prosperity proved to be short lived, in the aftermath of two world wars the town, like so many others, went into decline. Large swathes of town centre terraced houses fell to the bulldozer; their occupants were relocated on modern housing estates on the town's boundary. One by one the docks and shipyards closed down, aided and abetted by a Tory Prime Minister who declared 'She wanted Britain out of shipbuilding'. In the 1990s European intervention funding brought about the gradual redevelopment of the area, and the town once again began to look like a town with a future.

Fledgling ship repair companies began to appear among the redundant dry docks, one company rose like a phoenix from out of the ashes, even purchasing the world famous Cammell Laird name from the administrators, before they too went into administration. Local historians are naturally proud of the area's rich heritage and the local newspapers regularly remind their readership of the town's past ground-breaking achievements. As the twentieth century drew to a close and the world looked forward to a new millennium, the press chronicled notable local events of the past century, yet one particular concept unique to Birkenhead appears to have slipped their notice. This historical omission is all the more remarkable, if one considers the interest which was once generated locally by the mere mention of 'The Bantams'. This is their story.

Royal visit to Cammell Laird's shipyard, 14 May 1917.

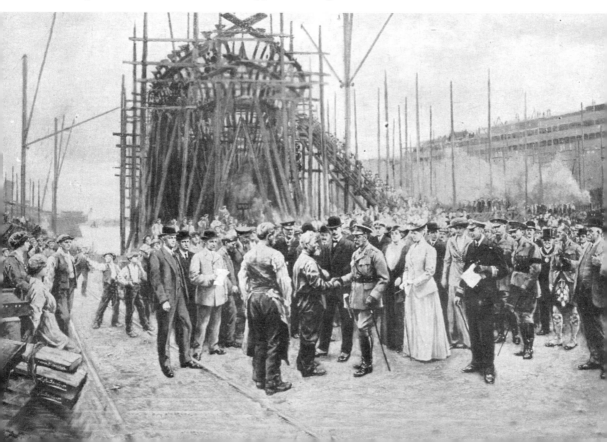

Chapter Two

Bigland's Birkenhead Bantams

Bigland's Bantams

'Where are you going to, my little man?'
'I'm going to France to fight if I can!'
'But you are too small to fight Germans,' I said,
'Just take off your coat and I'll fight you instead,'
'But what is your regiment if I may enquire?'
'The 1st Bigland's Bantams – a name to inspire
Those men who are longing to prove to the foe
That their spirits are right if their stature is low.'
'My eyes are as keen and my limbs are as strong
As all your crack Tommies with bodies as long;
I'm quick and I'm slim, and an excellent shot,
For all the world knows a small man's on the spot.'
'But what are you giving up, if I may ask?'
'Ah! Now you have set me an easy task.
I am giving up all, my country to serve,
As many men would had they only the nerve.'
'Your girl – what will she say when you come back?'
'Why, of course, she will marry me, I did not slack!
Now no time to waste, I must get on my way,
And when you're at luncheon just drink to 'Our Day'.'

Anon.   November 1914

A T THE OUTBREAK OF WAR Britain possessed an army similar in size to today's modern army. The professional army (excluding the Territorial force) numbered 186,400, a day after war was declared the nation called for a further 500,000 volunteers. The supplementary estimate of required manpower was swiftly amended to a call to arms of one million men. The county infantry battalions normally consisted of two regular battalions, one of which may be based for example in India while the other battalion remained on duty closer to home. In response to the European emergency of a war that would hopefully be over by Christmas, each line regiment was requested to raise at least one other battalion of 'New Army' troops to be raised only for the duration of the war. Men rushed to join the colours considering it to be their patriotic duty to defend Britain and her vast Empire on which the sun never set.

The Wirral peninsula lies on the outer fringe of the county of Cheshire (in 1974 political boundary reforms designated the area as Merseyside). 'Wirralian's' with military aspirations have always faced the dilemma of which of the two distinguished local county regiments to attest to should the need arise. The area has been part of the traditional recruitment area for the Cheshire Regiment and the King's Liverpool regiment for centuries. In Edwardian times it became the vogue for gentlemen to take up part time soldiering as part of the volunteer force, which was reformed in 1906 to become the Territorial Army. Prior to the outbreak of the Great War the Liverpool infantry regiment offered recruits the chance to serve in battalions such as the Liverpool Irish or the Liverpool Scottish, consequently persons with the slightest trace of Celtic origins frequently elected to serve in such units.

5th, 7th and 8th Territorial Battalions King's Liverpool Regiment.

The King's regiment fielded a total of forty-six assorted battalions in the Great War including four 'Pals' battalions, which offered workmates and friends the opportunity to serve with each other.

Whilst some decided to join the Liverpool regiment a large percentage of volunteers followed in their fathers' footsteps and joined the county regiment 'The Cheshires'. The regiment was raised in Chester in 1689 during the reign of King William III; in 1751 it became the 22nd Foot (later the Cheshire Regiment). The regiment had one regular battalion, and one volunteer battalion the 3rd. For three centuries the regiment served on Garrison duty throughout the Empire.

10th (Scottish) Battalion King's Liverpool Regiment.

While the regiment was serving in the Mediterranean area a detachment served at Dettingen. Legend has it that the 22nd Foot protected the King thus preventing his capture by the French. The King picked a sprig of oak from a tree and presented it to the Cheshires. This symbol of Royal approval is commemorated in their cap badge. The oak leaf is worn whilst parading for royalty and on special regimental occasions.

During the 18th century the capture of Louisburg in Nova Scotia was the regiment's most notable event, the Grenadier Company proceeded with Wolfe to the capture of Quebec. In remembrance of this event the regiment has an alliance with the 2nd battalion The Nova Scotia Highlanders (Cape Breton) of Canada. Following the Seven Years' War (1756-1763) the regiment went to the

8th (Irish) Battalion King's Liverpool Regiment.

Cheshire Regiment.

Cheshire Yeomanry post 1908.

Cheshire Volunteers.

West Indies, before travelling to New York for the American War of Independence.

After the first Afghan war, the Amirs of Scinde signed a treaty with the Indian Government to underwrite the costs of a combined British/Indian force in the Scinde. In order to protect the armies' lines of communications Sir Charles Napier's force was sent to Hyderabad to enforce the treaty, but the Amirs' Baluchi forces attacked the Residency there. Napier's 2,600 strong force including the only British battalion present, the 22nd Foot, engaged the Baluchis. After several hours fighting the Baluchis were driven off with considerable loss, the Amirs surrendered the following day. The 22nd Foot suffered eighty-one casualties. The two major battles in the campaign, at Meanee and Hyderabad, accomplished the complete rout of the armies of the Amirs of Scinde. The great battle at Meanee on 17 February 1843 is celebrated as the Regimental day. The regiment remained in India for most of the 19th century.

A second battalion was raised in 1814 for a brief while, disbanded and then re-raised in 1858, at the turn of the century the battalion fought in the South African war. At the outbreak of the Great War the 1st battalion took the brunt of the attack from two German Army Corps at the Belgian village of Audregnies near Mons. Their valiant stand saved the British Expeditionary Force from a disaster and is celebrated as a second Regimental Day on 24 August.

During the Great War the military strength of the Cheshire regiment stood at thirty-eight battalions of Professional, New Army, and Territorial, Labour, Reserve and Graduated battalions.

Birkenhead had a long affinity with the Cheshire regiment due to the 1/4th battalion volunteers who met at the Slatey Road drill hall. The idea of a service battalion of soldiers raised in Birkenhead was originally raised during the monthly meeting of the town's Chamber of Commerce, held on the evening of 1 September. Mr. A. W. Wilmer, president of the town's Chamber of Commerce remarked on Liverpool's success in raising a battalion of comrades (later known as the 17th King's Liverpool Pals) two days previously. The neighbouring borough of Wallasey took up this example, and attempted unsuccessfully to raise a Wallasey Pals battalion; the comrades later merged with other units and became the

Wirral Pals, the 13th Cheshires. While Mr. Wilmer acknowledged recruitment was vigorous, he wondered whether it would be possible to raise a Birkenhead battalion of the Cheshire regiment. He felt sure the Liverpool battalion would be keenly watched by the people of Liverpool, and that anything they did would be graphically reported in the local press. The remarks of Mr. Wilmer were simply noted as a suggestion for the authorities to act on and the Chamber agreed to take no immediate action.

The Houses of Parliament adjourned in September 1914, all members of the house too old to join the armed services, were urged during the recess to actively engage in the raising of volunteers for Lord Kitchener's army of volunteers. A suggestion was made that special consideration should be given to all matters concerning enlistment and the welfare of wives and dependants left behind, as frequently the dependants were enduring hardship due to incorrect completion of the paperwork by the erstwhile recruits. The member for Birkenhead East, Mr. Alfred Bigland M.P. resolved to do his utmost to assist in Britain's efforts to win the war.

Alfred Bigland wasted no time in forming a recruiting committee from amongst his peers, their headquarters were at the offices of Mr. Alfred Mansfield, 12 Hamilton Square, Birkenhead, who was the Hon. Secretary. The primary aims of the committee were to promote recruiting, and also to assist those who had already recruited, acting in conjunction with the military authorities, yet remaining independent of them. The committee aimed to keep in touch with those who had enlisted, and their relatives, in order to give them assistance should any difficulties arise.

The committee opened a recruiting office at the old corporation gas showroom, at number 109a, Grange Road, in the heart of the town's main shopping thoroughfare. The committee consisting of eminent businessmen and professionals was chaired by the town's Mayor, Alderman A.H. Arkle and Alfred Bigland M.P was the vice chairman. Other members were Messrs. Cecil Holden, J.M. Shuttleworth, G.J. Carter, J.W.P. Laird JP, T.C, Alfred Mansfield, A.W. Wilmer the man who first suggested the raising of a Birkenhead battalion; T.C, Alderman S. Vaughn, and Colonel Charles Brownridge, V.D. There were a further three sub-committees, as follows, Mr. Bigland being chairman of each – Grange Road sub committee, Messrs Shuttleworth, Brownridge and Vaughan. Meetings sub committee, Messrs Holden, Vaughn, Wilmer and Laird. Investigations sub

A. W. Wilmer,
Chairman of the
Birkenhead News.

committee, Messrs Carter and Brownridge.

The first notable cause taken up by the committee resulted in Messrs Bigland and Mansfield visiting Chester in the interests of the thousands of local recruits who had been despatched to Chester. The committee received reports that the accommodation provided was totally inadequate. A meeting was duly held with the General Officer in Command (G.O.C.) of Western Command where the deputation insisted on an immediate improvement to the system of billeting. As a result Mr. Bigland was able to report that 'While there had been some regrettable features in connection with the supply of requirements for the troops, the arrangements were now on a better basis, and he anticipated a very great improvement in the future'. His suggestions were in fact used throughout the duration of the war.

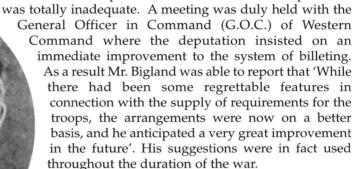

Alderman A. H. Arkle, Birkenhead Town Mayor.

The committee utilised the organised infrastructure connected with all the town's political parties for the purpose of the recruiting movement. Mr Bigland's initiative was to have as many small gatherings as possible, where questions could be asked and answered. Recruitment gatherings were also frequently held in working men's clubs, as a means of by passing the army regulations that insisted recruiting offices closed at 6-30 p.m. The committee later decided to open their recruiting office, at their own expense between the hours of 6-30 p.m. to 9-30 p.m. Three committee members attended the recruiting office every evening, to offer advice and answer the questions of potential recruits.

According to the *History of the Cheshire Regiment in the Great War*, in October 1914, four miners walked from Durham to Birkenhead in answer to the call for recruits for the Cheshire regiment. Upon being medically examined it was found these men did not come up to the required standard in height, although in every respect they were healthy sturdy men fired with patriotism. Their rejection on the grounds of lack of height was said to have inspired Alfred Bigland to raise a battalion of short men.

In 1922 Bigland published his memoirs in the book *The Call of Empire*, an entire chapter of which is naturally dedicated to possibly his greatest achievement, the raising of the Bantams, yet there is no mention of four Durham miners. He recalled how one morning Mr. Alfred Mansfield described a lively incident, which had occurred the previous night at the recruiting office. A young man preparing to enlist was asked by the sergeant to remove his hat, in order to be measured. Upon doing so the sergeant said, 'Nothing doing, you must get out', the rejected recruit demanded an explanation as he had tried at four or five recruiting offices but always with the same result. The sergeant retorted, 'Army regulation height is five feet three inches, you are only five foot two'. The young man then offered to fight any man in the room – he derided the idea that an inch in height precluded him from joining the army.

Though he ranted and swore the sergeant refused to give him the necessary papers and with great difficulty eventually got the young man out of the office. Mansfield commented 'this is a serious business, when we only wanted a small army a regulation height of five feet three inches might be good, but now every available man is wanted, and the subject should be reconsidered'.

The situation had presented itself to perhaps the one man in Britain who could envisage the utilisation of such an untapped source of manpower. Alfred Bigland then sought permission from Lord Kitchener to recruit men who were rejected due to lack of height but otherwise medically fit. He proposed a height of between 5ft. and 5ft. 3 inches., with a minimum chest measurement of 33 inches, which was an inch above the required chest measurement of taller men; this was to prevent men of a weak physical constitution from enlisting. Bigland could afford to be selective in the choice of recruits as he realised he had the entire male population of undersize volunteers to select from.

Within a few days Bigland was invited to visit Sir Henry McKinnon at Chester, where he was informed of the War Office's interest in the formation of a battalion of shorter men. Unfortunately the War Office had neither the time, nor the facilities to undertake the raising of such a battalion. However they

Lord Kitchener, Minister of War

were prepared to give authority to the Birkenhead recruiting committee to raise a special 'Bantam' battalion, this title originated in the dictionary definition of a small but pugnacious fighting cock. The War Office had a set of guidelines for specially raised battalions and was prepared to offer assistance. Regulations had already been drafted fixing a certain amount of finance for ration allowance, uniforms, equipment and billets. While the War Office was prepared to provide rifles, baggage wagons etc., all other matters had to be carried out by the persons raising the battalion.

Upon his return to Birkenhead, Bigland summoned his committee and reported on his meeting with Sir Henry McKinnon. The committee members declined to take financial responsibility for the proposed battalion, as the unknown financial liability may have proven to be considerable. Undeterred Bigland then approached the town Mayor, who in turn consulted the Town Clerk, who advised the situation was impossible, as the members of the town council would be personally charged if they voted to assemble the battalion and there was a deficit. No charge even if voted by the council, could be met from the ratepayers' pockets. At this juncture a lesser man would have conceded defeat and focused his attentions elsewhere, but Bigland was determined to raise his battalion. He carefully assessed the financial risk involved and decided with stringent housekeeping, and astute management the War Office financial aid may just be adequate.

Alfred Bigland, M.P.

Once again he visited Sir Henry McKinnon and assured him he alone would take the financial risk, McKinnon shrewdly agreed and gave Bigland permission to proceed. All necessary plans and estimates were then forwarded to the War Office for approval. The recruitment proposal was then officially cleared and Alfred Bigland and his recruiting committee threw themselves whole-heartedly into the work and arrangements for raising the new battalion.

The bi weekly local newspaper the *Birkenhead News* printed the following letter on 18 November 1914. (At least one major reference work erroneously claims this is the date when the battalion was raised.)

Bigland's 'Bantam' Battalion – Excellent Birkenhead idea
To the Editor of the Birkenhead News.

Sir,- Having been much impressed during a month of active recruiting work by the fact that men slightly under 5ft. 3ins. were rightly indignant that their country refused their services I appealed to Lord Kitchener for permission to raise a special battalion of men thoroughly medically fit, between 5ft. and 5ft. 3ins. in height.

I am pleased to say that his Lordship has courteously granted my request, and I desire through the medium of your valued paper to say that we are now ready to receive the names of men who are willing to join what it has been decided to call the 'Bantam Battalion', believing that a man is as good a soldier and as plucky a fighter at 5ft. 2ins., as at 5ft. 6ins. In proof of this I would point out that if Britain had fixed its standards for officers the same as for privates the Empire would have lost the priceless service of the Field Marshall who was lovingly dubbed by his men 'Bobs'[1] and whose death the nation now mourns; I therefore feel that men enlisting in this special battalion are passing a tribute of praise on the little great man in offering until the termination of the war their time, and maybe their lives, in the service for which he lived.

For the information of your readers I may state that the time of service, pay and separation allowances for wives and children and dependants are the same as in Kitchener's Army.

The Prime Minister's appeal for more men is proof that men are wanted, and if voluntary recruiting is not to break down under the strain of the present call every man possible must take his courage in his hands and VOLUNTEER.

Send in your name and address to Alfred Mansfield, Esq., 109a Grange Road, Birkenhead, and you will receive particulars where and when to enlist in the Bantam Battalion.

I wish to add that General Sir Henry McKinnon, General Officer, Commander in Chief, Western Command, Chester, heartily approves of the formation of this special Battalion, and is freely giving us his advice and support. Thanking you for granting me this opportunity of laying this subject before your readers. – I am, yours very truly,

Alfred Bigland. M.P. for Birkenhead.

The offer to command the proposed new battalion was accepted by Colonel W.H. Bretherton, who had retired as commanding officer of the 1/4th battalion of the Cheshire regiment ('The Greys'). He began his military service in 1877, when he joined the old 80th Lancashire Volunteer Rifles, as a private. Colonel Bretherton was described as a capable officer, one who inspired the rank and file with confidence. He was said to be a disciplinarian, but at the same time kindly, and was reputed to be a favourite with the newest recruit just as much as he was with his fellow officers.

Alfred Bigland had his commander, now he needed his promised battalion. Although the recruiting committee had the power to accept men from any part of the United Kingdom, it was originally anticipated sufficient recruits would have been available from the immediate neighbourhood of Birkenhead. The War Office appears to have dragged its heels setting the minimum standards of physique required for Bantam recruits.

The Bantams would eventually be involved in numerous battles but the first fight was with the army itself. Until the official measurement particulars were received the recruiting committee requested that men wishing to join the new battalion should send a

postcard to Mr. A. Mansfield, at 109A Grange Road. The names of those received by postcard were to have priority over those recruiting in the usual way.

The matter of Officers presented its own problems, as the war office was overwhelmed with requests for experienced non commissioned officers (N.C.O.s) and trained officers. The problem was further compounded, as the remainder of available commissioned officers were reluctant to become involved with an untried development such as a Bantam battalion. Bigland was invited to recruit his own officers who were to purchase their own uniforms, on the understanding that should they fail to satisfactorily complete a three-month trial they would be dismissed. Bigland then appointed treble the amount of officers he required in the knowledge the surplus officers would be taken up by other battalions. After three months' instruction at a training centre a competent staff officer successfully inspected all of Bigland's prospective officers, after which commissions were approved, and the new officers were then reimbursed by the war office for their uniforms. As all of the N.C.O.s and officers were recruited from men with previous military experience they all complied with pre Bantam army height requirements, and were not of conventional Bantam stature. On the parade ground this height variation was of no particular consequence, but on the battlefield enemy snipers soon learned how to differentiate who the officers were and aimed accordingly.

At every opportunity Bigland gave press interviews to publicise the Bantam initiative, he was keen to eradicate the misconception that he was raising a battalion of 'decrepits', but one of sturdy men who did not quite meet the height requirement. When questioned if he thought they would make good fighters, he replied:

Why shouldn't they, the average height of the Ghurkhas, perhaps the best fighters in our Indian Army is just over 5ft. What bantams lack in length they often make up in breadth, and are sturdy, if short. Such men in these days of trenches when little targets stand the least chance of being hit are preferable except, perhaps at close quarters to big men. A man's spirit has a great deal to do with his fighting value, and the little man whom we have hitherto had to reject will now have his chance to enlist. After all, some of the world's greatest warriors have been small men such as – Alexander, Napoleon, Wellington, and Roberts, none of these military leaders would have passed the British army height standard.

It was also pointed out that Julius Caesar was an epileptic and would have been turned away from the recruiting office with ignominy.

At this early juncture Bigland still thought his new Birkenhead Battalion later known as the 15th Battalion of the Cheshire Regiment, would be exclusively raised from the men of Birkenhead. Nonetheless, arrangements were made to issue notices to every recruiting office in the country stating that if men passed the local medical officer, and had a chest measurement of 34 inches (86.5cm.), a minimum height of 5ft. (152.5cm.) with a maximum of 5ft. 3 inches (160cm.) they would be supplied with a railway pass to Birkenhead, and could join the first ever Bantam battalion. To the great delight of the recruiting committee a new army order was about to be issued sanctioning similar battalions all over the country.

A suitable depot and billets now became a priority, without any red tape or delay the matter was swiftly resolved when the recruiting committee took over the agricultural show ground (now the site of the Oval sports complex, where the race sequences in *Chariots of Fire* was filmed) at Bebington, a district of Birkenhead. This was considered to be a splendid training ground, which could accommodate 1,000 men, had provision for dining rooms and stables for officers' horses. On 20

Members of the 15th Battalion on parade at Bebington Show Ground, taken early 1915.

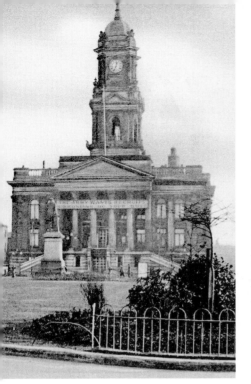

Town Hall, Birkenhead. A banner across the columns reads: 'The Army wants recruits, Birkonians do your duty'.

November Mr Bigland, M.P., accompanied by committee members, a military engineer and doctor, inspected the camp and the site was officially adopted. The Mersey Defence Engineers then commenced to convert existing structures, and other buildings were erected for the accommodation of the battalion. The entire transformation was not expected to be fully completed before 9 January, although the show ground itself could be used for drill purposes. The committee now urgently required a short-term alternative base, or the raising of the battalion would have to be postponed. As the recruiting committee were unable to find a building suitable for accommodating a battalion, they approached the town's Mayor with a view to using a school. The first choice of the committee was Rock Ferry School, but as evening classes were also held at the school, it was considered the use of the Mersey Park School would be less disruptive.

Yet another instance of civic cooperation was the Town Council's offer to allow the recruiting committee the use of the Town Hall for a recruiting depot, so that the work of enlistment could be done in comfortable conditions, also the building's central position would greatly facilitate recruiting.

The pre war infantryman was required to have a good physique, a clean bill of health both mentally and physically, and a minimum height of five feet eight inches. Faced with a tide of rising casualties, the minimum height was eventually lowered to five feet three inches. Although the war office had consented to a further reduction in height in favour of the Bantam Battalion, they were anxious that prospective recruits should still undergo a rigorous medical examination. Today's modern army, an equal opportunities employer, does not demand a minimum height from recruits, except for certain driving jobs where a minimum height of 1.58 metres or 5 feet 2 inches. is required. Candidates are now assessed in relation to their body-weight – height ratio (Body Mass Index). Nine decades after they simply faded away Bantam size troops are again on the march.

Volunteers for the new battalion were required to comply with the following war office specifications:

Height was to be not under 5ft (152.5cm.) and not to exceed 5ft. 3 inches. (160cm.). A minimum chest measurement of 33 inches was required with an additional 2 inches (5cm.) for expansion was required.

Height	Chest
5ft. 0 to 5 ft. 1 inch	33 inches
5ft. 1 inch to 5ft. 2 inch	33.5 inches
5ft. 2 inch to 5ft. 3 inch	34 inches (86.5 cm)

The new regulation was circulated to all recruiting centres. They were also advised that recruiting would begin on Monday 30 November 1914 until further notice. All men who passed the physical test and attestation, were given a rail warrant to Birkenhead, and instructed to report to the Town Hall, between 9 a.m. and 9 p.m., where they would be finally approved and given a regimental number. Married men were requested to bring their marriage certificate and also the birth certificates of their children. This was to facilitate the arrangements for payment of the separation allowance.

While recruits were accepted from all walks of life particular efforts appear to have been aimed at the recruitment of coal miners. These individuals were by the very nature of their employment physically tough, usually of a stocky build and short in height. A generation seems to have seized the outbreak of war as a means of escape from the six days of labour in the pits, while also doing their patriotic duty.

The tenacity of these born fighters is best summed up by a Doctor E.H.T. Nash who wrote:

The Lancashire miner is much the same type as the Welsh. They are sturdy and hard as nails, and better fighting and more quarrelsome men you could not find. The authorities could take 5ft. 2inch men from amongst this class and raise some of the finest battalions possible.

G. R.

Your

King & Country

Need YOU

I N the present grave national emergency men, and still more men, are needed at once to rally round the Flag and add to the ranks of our New Armies.

TERMS OF SERVICE.

Extension of Age Limit. Height Reduced to Normal Standard.

Age on enlistment 19 to 38. Ex-Soldiers up to 45. Minimum Height 5 ft. 3 ins.; chest 34 ins. Must be medically fit. General Service for the War.

Men enlisting for the duration of the War will be able to claim their discharge, with all convenient speed, at the conclusion of the War.

PAY AT ARMY RATES.

Married men or Widowers with Children will be accepted, and if at the time of enlistment a recruit signs the necessary form, Separation Allowance under Army conditions is issuable at once to the wife and in certain circumstances to other dependants.

Pamphlet with full details from any Post Office.

Notice the height restriction in the above public notice which debarred the little 'uns.

The recruitment headquarters had by now received scores of letters, highlighting how eager the under height men were to serve their country in its hour of need. The following are extracts from letters.

'I have tried my utmost to join the colours, but have been rejected because I did not reach the standards. I am willing to serve my King and country, I have two brothers serving at present'. – Burnham.

'I have been in a Canadian regiment 4.5 years – the 96th Lake Superior Regiment, Port William, Ontario – in which I hold the rank of corporal. I was the first to do so when the regiment volunteered for the front, but was refused solely on account of my height, being only 5ft. 1ins. in bare feet but well proportioned for my height'. – Bushey, Herts.

A recruiting officer at Burnley had written to say, 'That he could supply two or three hundred men if they could be put together in one company, so as to be like the 'pals". An assurance to the effect was given. Similar offers on a smaller scale were also received from Flint and Cheltenham.

Large numbers of postal applications flooded into the Birkenhead recruiting committees, one would-be Bantam walked all the way from Wigan. By 2 p.m. on Friday 27 November the exact number of candidates stood at 1,098, which was sufficient for a battalion. Unfortunately, the committee expected a significant amount of these men to be rejected, as many had applied prior to the exact physical standards being released. Consequently the committee continued to accept postal applications in the knowledge that the over spill of volunteers could serve in other Bantam battalions. Manchester had followed Birkenhead's leadership and was about to raise her own Bantam force, as were other industrial conurbations.

During the last few days prior to the enlistment day, there was a flurry of activity as final arrangements fell into place. The committee acquired from the White Star Line 1,100 single size mattresses; another source provided two blankets for each man. The vicar of St. Catherine's, Tranmere and the general secretary of the Y.M.C.A. offered the use of St. Catherine's Institute as a barrack room for the Bantams until the show ground was ready. The Institute, which was a two minute walk away from Mersey Park School, would provide the usual Y.M.C.A. comforts of tea, coffee, facilities for letter writing, and social enjoyment. The Tramways Committee promised an electric tram would be placed at the disposal of the Bantams on Monday to convey the new recruits to New Ferry, from which the show ground was a five minute walk away.

During the early hours of Monday 30 November (not the 18th, see note 2) the first of the prospective Bantams disembarked from the

Attestation at the Town Hall. Bigland towers over a prospective Bantam.

Birkenhead ferry-boats and the main line station at Woodside. The majority had travelled alone, some arrived with a friend but occasionally batches of a dozen to twenty men arrived from one town. Despite the autumn chill and the threatening rain clouds they were all in high spirits as they headed up the hill towards the Town Hall. In Brandon Street the Albert Industrial School Band played as the recruits formed an orderly queue and patiently waited through pouring rain for the doors to open at the arranged time of 9-00 a.m.

Inside the Town Hall long tables, piled high with attestation forms and manned by volunteer clerks were arranged in the assembly room. A committee room was used for medical inspections, which were carried out by Doctors Waugh, Wise, Davidson and Cross. Alfred Bigland had ordered a consignment of celluloid badges, decorated with a bantam surmounting B.B.B. in the patriotic colours of red, white and blue, which he intended to give to each new recruit. The recruits' badges were financed by Messrs B. Haram and Co, the proprietors of the *Birkenhead Advertiser and Guardian* newspaper; unfortunately the badges were not ready in time.

Artist's impression of the design for the Bigland's Birkenhead Bantam badge. This was not intended to be worn on a uniform. It was replaced with the standard WW1 Pattern Cheshire Regiment cap badge.

Also present were Mr Bigland, Colonel Bretherton, Major Allen, chief recruiting officer for the Western Command, Mr. A.A. Fisk in charge of general arrangements in the Assembly room. Lieutenant Strickland the recently appointed Adjutant of the new battalion was the recruiting officer, and a Colonel Carruthers acted as the approving officer.

At 9-20 a.m. forty of the men waiting outside were marched into the assembly room, where the Mayor greeted them with the following speech:

In the name of the town I am very glad to welcome you. I hoped every one of you will be able to join the battalion that was being raised – the first one of its kind in England. Things had been said about small men, but it was not height or size that made the soldier – it was quality, character, power in other ways (hear, hear) and they felt quite sure every one of them [the applicants] would do their duty, if they got into the firing line, at least as well as the men they had been reading about that morning in General French's despatch.[3] I do not think I can pay you any higher compliment than to hope you will do as least as good as they have done. They have done marvellous things, surely the Army never stood higher in the whole of its long history (hear, hear) and we think we can look to you with confidence to emulate and carry on its great traditions (hear, hear). As I have said it is a matter of character more than size.

Bantam recruits' presentation badge.
Courtesy of the Williamson Art Gallery and Museum.

The first Bantam to be enrolled, Robert Parker of York received the distinction, likely through postal application.

Quarter Master Sergeant Archie Sommerville. Turned down for the Cheshires he later joined the Lancashire Fusiliers.

In the name of the town I welcome you to Birkenhead and bid you, God speed, good luck and a safe return.
The speech received vigorous applause from the assembled audience.

Mr. Bigland then spoke to the first Bantam applicant, a sturdy young seaman named Alexander McKay. He had left his hometown of Fort George, Inverness-shire on the Thursday night, as he was unsure of the attestation day, and had been at the head of the Brandon Street queue since 6-30 that morning. He was especially keen to do his bit, as his only brother was serving in the front line with the Black Watch. Although he was the first Bantam to arrive at Birkenhead, the distinction of the first Bantam was awarded to Robert Stanley, of Market Wreighton, Yorkshire. It is assumed R. Stanley's postal application was the first to arrive.

The applicants then underwent a preliminary medical for chest and height requirements, several were rejected due to their chest measurement being too small. The chest test had been made severe for the Bantams as they would be expected to carry the same amount of kit as ordinary infantry, therefore good stamina and a robust build was required. A large number were either too small or too tall. During the first hour there were about forty rejections for chest deficiency, amongst these were several young men who looked as if they had just left school. So severe was the initial figure of rejections Alfred Bigland now feared for the raising of the battalion, he was not to know that one of the examining doctors a 'genial Irishman' was failing as medically unfit any volunteer in gainful employment. I have a copy of the unpublished memoir of a Bantam soldier, QMS Archie Sommerville, who was advised by the doctor to 'Keep out and stick to your civilian occupation' – he was then handed a certificate stating he was unfit to join His Majesty's Forces. The despondent volunteer was gratefully accepted several months later by another County Bantam battalion and served with honour for the duration of the war.

By midday approximately 200 recruits from all classes had been enrolled. Several remarkable chest measurements were re-corded; the largest was of an applicant from Halifax standing at only 5ft. 2ins. who had a chest of 39.5 inches normal. A group of fifteen sturdy men arrived from Chorley, where they had all passed the doctor, and had been sworn in. A further sixty young men from Bolton were in the process of enrolment. Behind them lined up thirty volunteers from Blackburn, part of a total of eighty-nine men from the town who were keen to enlist. There were plenty of football fans in the room. 'Play up Rovers', shouted some of the Bolton lads as their Blackburn rivals entered the Assembly Room. The room resounded with a wide range of accents mostly with a strong northern industrial dialect, at one stage in the proceedings, groups of twenty-five or so 'Owdham' lads mixed with thirty from Leeds, thirteen from Preston, seven from Lincoln and seven from Stoke on Trent. Later that evening fifty Londoners arrived adding cockney accents to the assembled group of volunteers gathered from throughout the length and breadth of the country. The successful Bantam applicants received their first papers and underwent a stricter medical, after which they were sworn in, and presented with their temporary badge.

A patriotically decorated tram car carrying flags, red white and blue draping on the side combined with coloured pictures of bantam cocks, all lit up by the novelty of electric light, ferried the men to the Bebington show ground where at one o' clock the recruits received a hot meal. By Monday noon approximately 200 recruits from all social classes had enlisted, by the following night the target of 1,100 recruits had been attained.

Against all odds Alfred Bigland and his committee had successfully accomplished the raising of the nation's first Bantam battalion. The new battalion was originally named the 1st Birkenhead Bantam battalion, which later became the 15th (Service) Battalion of the Cheshire Regiment.

Meanwhile the flow of recruits continued, recruiting officers throughout the kingdom forwarded telegrams advising of the imminent arrival of further recruits. Bigland and his team were now in a dilemma, Chester was telephoned and they in turn contacted by wire all the principal recruiting offices advising that the Bantam battalion was full. Three days after recruitment had begun, over 2,000 men had attested. As all the arrangements had been made to accommodate only 1,100 men, there were no facilities immediately available for the additional hundreds of recruits now arriving in Birkenhead. The immediate priority was food and sleeping accommodation. The Mayor allowed the men to stay overnight in the Town Hall, and 2,000 army blankets were promised from the army stores department at Burscough, Lancashire. The blankets were to be delivered to Liverpool by 8 p.m. and the battalion was required to make their own arrangements to collect them. Meanwhile bread, ham and cakes were

MEN WHO ARE FIGHTING TO-DAY ARE THE PEACEMAKERS OF TO-MORROW.

DAILY SKETCH

Telephones—Editorial and Publishing: 6676 Holborn.
Advertisements: 2972 Holborn.

BRITAIN'S BEST PICTURE PAPER.

LONDON: Shoe Lane, E.C.
MANCHESTER: Withy-grove.

Knitted garments for our fighting man may be sent for distribution to "Mrs. Gossip," "Daily Sketch."

BRISK RECRUITING FOR BIRKENHEAD BANTAMS—"QUALITY, NOT SIZE, WANTED."

R. S. Parker (York), the first to join.

A decorated tramcar taking the first of the day recruits to Bebington Camp for training.

A representation of the new battalion's mascot.

These seven miners came all the way from Barnsley to join.

Mr. A. Bigland, M.P. (Birkenhead), among yesterday's recruits.

Recruiting opened yesterday at Birkenhead Town Hall for the new "Bantam" Battalion, for the formation of which Mr. A. Bigland, M.P., has secured official sanction. Recruits came from all parts to join, and so be able to serve their King and country, and the Mayor, in welcoming them, observed that it was "not so much size as quality" that was wanted. Mrs. Bigland presented each accepted recruit with a badge bearing three "B's" and a bantam.

purchased locally, and the new arrivals were fed. To help while away the hours a concert was swiftly arranged, and many of the Bantams gave renditions of songs. The organisers spent several anxious hours before the arrival of the blankets at almost 11 p.m. They were distributed two to a man, soon after midnight the recruits settled down for the night, as no beds were available they simply slept on the floor.

Bigland urgently communicated with the War Office authorities and on the Thursday morning he formally received permission to raise a second battalion. This decision was just as well as Bigland already had 600 men for another battalion, and several hundred more had arrived that day. The *History of the 35th Division* states the War Office had initially stipulated a second battalion had to be raised to supply replacements for any losses incurred. Given Bigland's organisational skills this fact does look doubtful, as there were no arrangements made at all for an additional battalion.

By Thursday night a total of 2,200 men or the rough equivalent of two battalions of Bantams had been raised in a mere four days! Even so more men were still required as 1,100 men were not officially recognised as a complete battalion as thirty of that number must be officers, leaving 1,070 men. Then there must be a reserve of 250 men and six officers, making 1,320 men and thirty-six officers, or for two battalions, 2,640 men and seventy-two officers. The raising of the second battalion is regularly quoted as 3-12-14; this is ten days wide of the mark of the recruitment drive, perhaps it was the date when the War Office paperwork was completed.

Lord Derby visited the recruits of the second battalion and introduced their new commander, Major C.E.Earle.[4] The officer was a veteran of the South Africa campaign, where he saw service with the Royal North Lancashires, and after the war was

Lieutenant Colonel Earle.
Second Bantam's commander.

for several years on the army officers' reserve. He had recently been gazetted to the 3rd Lancashires and was now transferred to the 2nd Birkenhead Battalion, which was officially titled the 16th (Service) Battalion of the Cheshire Regiment. Any of the assembled recruits who had been a Cadet or a Boy Scout was immediately promoted to an N.C.O. This abbreviation for a Non Commissioned Officer will appear frequently in this text referring to any soldier from the rank of lance corporal to warrant officer first class who was usually a regimental sergeant major. The lowest ranking commissioned officer was second lieutenant.

Due to the unexpected success of raising a second battalion and there was now an accommodation problem, which resulted in hundreds of men bedding down overnight in the Town Hall. Once again the Mayor was approached, and he took upon himself the decision to make available Rock Ferry council school. The infants' department at the school was used for the men's meals and sleeping quarters, and accommodated 700 men and certain officers on Thursday evening. The local church workers stripped their own beds to provide hundreds of blankets for the little men. For the purpose of drilling the recruits, Derby Park was made available, and also an adjoining piece of ground belonging to the naval officer training ship *Conway*. By 8 December only 250 men were required to complete the full reserves for both battalions, known in military circles as depot battalions. The number was rapidly attained and the recruiting committee, having accomplished its task, began to direct men to the Bantam battalion being raised at Leeds.

Poster from Steepholm Island Museum near Weston-Super-Mare.

BANTAMS.

Did you ever see a Bantam in a fight?
No other Bird can "stick it"
Like a Bantam, or can "lick it,"
And you never saw a Bantam taking fright.
(From a new Song by Stephen West. Music by Edward Watson).

A 40 cm. x 13 cm. theatrical advertising poster for the latest Bantam song.

The early decades of the last century were the halcyon days of the musical variety theatres, where travelling artistes often adapted their satirical acts to suit the local populace. An absolute necessity in every performance was a catchy and cheery sing-song, which afforded the audience an opportunity to join in. In early December 1914 a new song was taken up throughout the nation's music halls, the 'Bantams song' composed by Messrs Stephen West and Edward Watson, and published by Ryalls and Jones, Ltd. of Argyle Street, Birkenhead. Mr. Alfred Bigland accepted the dedication of the song, which was said to have a good swinging chorus and would doubtless be a popular marching song of the day:

They've formed a new battalion the 'Bantams'
Did you ever see a bantam in a fight?
No other bird can stick it,
Like a bantam or can lick it,
And you never saw a bantam taking fright,
For a bantam's got the courage of a bulldog,
And a bantam's got endurance like an ox,
Quite a healthy sort of phantom,
Is your plucky little bantam,
When he's out to 'give em socks'.

Chorus
What can it matter then about the height,
Be it 5ft. 1 or 5ft. 10?
If the British heart beats right,
And is longing for a fight,
And the country asks for men.

Although the lyrics appear to be naïve, in reality the verse is no worse than the current offerings of today's latest boy or girl band. The success of this popular bantam song led to a spate of similar ditties and verses, composed by the townspeople of Birkenhead who had well and truly taken the Bantams to their hearts. The majority of Bantam recruits arrived in Birkenhead with a small bundle of clothes and very little money. Bigland asked one of the recruits where his kit was, only to be told the volunteer was wearing it all on his back. This encounter moved Bigland who later wrote 'Think of it, leaving home with no money, trusting himself absolutely without a care of those who called for his service'.[5] When the townspeople became aware of the plight of the majority of Bantams they made them especially welcome, providing clothing centres, concerts and a ready supply of the Bantams' favoured cigarettes 'Woodbines'. During both battalions infancy, Merseyside endured drenching storms. As few Bantams possessed overcoats, a public appeal was made for financial donations towards the purchase of policeman style capes. Messrs Bigland and Pollack had procured on account 500 of the Macintosh capes at the cost of £112.10.0. Each of the capes cost 4s-6d (22.5p) and a total of 1,000 capes were required. While several local gentlemen had donated £20 each towards the appeal the public was requested to forward donations to the appeal's Treasurer Mr. F. Pollock, 6, Castle Street, Liverpool. The fund raised £228, which covered the purchase of the 1,000 capes. The capes were equally divided amongst the two battalions, where they were allocated to the more needy recruits.

In response to Lord Kitchener's request for a 'New Army' of a million volunteers new battalions literally sprang up overnight; each new battalion immediately requested uniforms and rifles. Neither of these commodities was readily available, as the War Office was totally unprepared for a European war. In late 1914 a shortage of khaki material further compounded the problem. There was however a surfeit of blue serge, which was eventually utilised for military uniforms, the blue Melton uniforms were despised by the soldiers, as the uniform looked more like a postman than that of an infantry soldier. Enterprising local tailors produced army shirts, blankets and uniforms, which were purchased by the more affluent recruits. The less well off Bantams simply improvised by stripping the red upholstered seats of the Bebington show ground stands where they were quartered, this material was torn into strips and used as puttees on the legs of the civilian attired little men.

By mid December the 1st Birkenhead battalion had received 200 greatcoats, with the promise of a further 400 for the other battalion. The first batch of uniforms had arrived (believed to have been ex Boer War), and a further 400 suits a week were promised. A shortage in underwear had been solved and every man had received a shirt, underpants and socks. A thousand pairs of military boots had been distributed amongst the battalions; once again priority was given to those in most need. Naturally boots were in great demand, the Bantams' average boot size was a 6, a small size that had compounded the delay in outfitting the men. Both battalions were said to be steadily progressing with their drills, marches etc. all designed to knock them into shape as good soldiers.

The town's leaders' eagerness to proudly display their two new battalions to the military was fulfilled on 8 December, when General Sir Henry Mackinnon, accompanied by members of his staff visited Birkenhead to inspect the Bantams. The inspecting officer first paid a visit to the Mersey Park Council School, in the playground of which was the 1st Battalion. Sir Henry addressed the battalion. He congratulated them on their smart and soldier-like appearance, and said they were 'marked battalions', as the first that had been formed, and all England would keep their eyes on them, and see how they conducted themselves. They must go on with their drills, and be ready to go into action on the Continent if called upon. The party then proceeded to the Rock Ferry Council School, the headquarters of the 2nd Battalion. The Commander in Chief made a similar speech to the

Rock Ferry School, Ionic Street. Headquarters of the Second Birkenhead Battalion.

one given earlier to the 1st Battalion. A number of eminent ladies distributed Bantam badges to the assembled soldiers, (the 1st battalion had previously received theirs). The Mayor addressing the men said, 'It was indeed a proud day for him to be there at the inspection of Battalions of which Birkenhead was the originator; and when they got on the battle field they must uphold the honour of their country'.

The long dark hours after drill were filled by a visit to the Y.M.C.A. or the St. Catherine's Institute where home comforts, a relaxing atmosphere, and entertainment were provided for the servicemen. In response to appeals the public donated – patriotic gramophone records, up to date weekly periodicals, and cigarettes. Entertainers were also sought providing they could perform an act that was bright, good and thoroughly refined. In mid December the New Theatre Royal entertained 500 Bantams, upon entering the theatre each Bantam was presented with Woodbines. Special patriotic items were introduced into the musical comedy revue of 'Find the lady' and the whole house joined in with the singing of another Bantam song.

The Bantams
(To the men with small bodies but with large hearts)

They responded to the call.
Who the Bantams,
They came out to do their all
Who the Bantams.
When our M.P said one day,

'We should train them for the fray',
They're the lads, who wont say Nay,
Who the Bantams.

From the North and South they came
Who the Bantams.
They set Britain all aflame.
Who the Bantams.
They are little but they are tough,
They'll show Wilhelm fast enough,
How they deal with mealy stuff.
Won't you Bantams.

From the East and West they strolled.
Who the Bantams.
Into Birkenhead they rolled.
Who the Bantams.
Then before our gracious Mayor.
Each and all of them did swear,
That they'd do their blooming share.
Trust the Bantams.

Out to Bebington by car,
Went the Bantams.
Illuminated like a star.
For the Bantams.
They are training now like fun,
For their test match with the Hun,
Hark! A cock-a-doodle-do,
It's the Bantams.

You will show the world your pluck.
Wont you Bantams.
All Birkonians wish you luck.
Bravo Bantams.
Why should soldiers set a height?
Surely if a man's heart is right.
Shorts as good as tall in a fight.
Prove it Bantam.   *Cadet*

BOOTS V. SPURS.

(Sketched and contributed by a Young Correspondent).

First Bantam "The Bantams ought to be a cavalry regiment not an infantry".
Second Bantam. "Ows that".
First Bantam. "Well how can you expect a fellow to feel like a fighting bantam without spurs.

On Christmas day the 1st battalion based at the Bebington show ground began with a church parade. At the conclusion of the services the men were dismissed until 11-45, when they were paraded and marched to the dining room, which had been especially decorated for the occasion. Once the men were seated Colonel Bretherton addressed the men wishing them all a happy Christmas and complimented them in the progress they had made in their drills, during the past four weeks of training. He also proposed a toast asking all present to drink

"E" COMPANY. PLATOON N° 17.
COMPETING SECTION. MARCH 20ᵗʰ 1915.
WINNERS OF SWEDISH DRILL COMPETITION.

Compare the officer's height to that of the ranks of the Manchester Bantams. The Company is wearing the despised navy-blue Melton uniforms. They were considered to make the men appear more like bus conductors than proud soldiers of the King.

The newly recruited 18th Battalion Lancashire Fusiliers, all in civilian attire complete with flat caps.

to the 'Health of the King' followed by the 1st (Service) Battalion of the 15th Cheshires; this was followed by three cheers for the Colonel and three cheers for the King. The soldiers then enjoyed a hearty traditional Christmas roast dinner of roast beef, turkey, plum pudding, mince pies etc.

At tea time the men dined on bread and butter, cakes and apricots. In the evening the men visited various halls where much appreciated entertainment was provided by the locals. Both of the Birkenhead battalions shared similar arrangements for the Christmas festivities. The events were later overshadowed by tragedy. Amongst the men of the second battalion who enjoyed their feast at the Ionic Street school

Two unidentified Cheshire officers. As the photograph was taken in Rock Ferry it is most likely they were attached to the Cheshire Bantams.

was Sergeant John Brown, who was found dead on 26 December.

During the inquest into the death, 21169 Private Charles Mitchell, (who was later K.I.A. on 19-7-16) stated that he slept in the next bed to the deceased, at about 10-30 p.m. he noticed the deceased began to roll about in his bed evidently in great pain. However he made no noise, and soon after the witness fell asleep. Early next morning as Private Robert Johnson passed Brown's bed he noticed the deceased's legs were drawn up in a peculiar manner, upon examination he found the soldier was dead. The wife of the late soldier, Margaret Brown of 71, Kent St, Farnworth near Bolton, stated her husband enlisted on 30 November, and the last time she saw him was on 2 December. A post mortem revealed the deceased had died due to syncope consequent on embarrassment of the heart's action (heart attack) and the result of an overloaded stomach. The funeral of the unfortunate soldier occurred at Flaybrick cemetery, Birkenhead 30 December. His distressed comrades raised the sum of seven pounds to be donated to the soldier's widow. The Farnworth soldier has the dubious distinction of being the first service death amongst the Bantams.[6]

Grave of Sergeant John Brown at Flaybrick cemetery, Birkenhead.

Notes

(1) The November 12th edition of the *Liverpool Echo* reported the death of 81 years old Lord Roberts. While visiting Indian troops on the Western Front, he caught a chill that developed into pneumonia, and died. In his earlier years he had won the Victoria Cross, for the single-handed recovery of a standard, from Sepoys. He was interred in St. Paul's.

(2) The standard reference book *British Regiments 1914-18* gives the date of the raising of the 15th (Service) Cheshire Regiment as 18-11-1914. According to my research the battalion was actually raised on Monday 30-11-14; as this was the original Bantam battalion it is senior to all the others, the dates stated for raising all other Bantam battalions should be treated with caution.

(3) The British Commander in Chief's despatch included high praise for the troops and described the heroic deeds of the army since October, when it moved from the Aisne to meet the German danger in South West Belgium and Northern France.

(4) The *History of the Cheshire Regiment* states this introduction occurred on a cold bleak October day. As the battalion did not exist in October this is evidently incorrect. The arrival of Major Earle was first reported in the December 9th edition of the *Birkenhead News*.

(5) *The Call of Empire*. By Alfred Bigland.

(6) The early December suicide in a Wallasey outbuilding of Mr T. P. of West Bond Street, Cowenheath, Dundee is excluded. On his person he was discovered to have a railway pass from Dumferline to Birkenhead and an attestation form, but had not presented himself as a volunteer to join the Bantams.

CHAPTER THREE

The Raising of the First Bantam Division

THE RECRUITING CAMPAIGN for the Cheshire Bantams had proved to be a great success; the ensuing publicity prompted a surge in stocky volunteers. The authorities seized on this opportunity to enlist more men and the War Office instructed several regiments to form Bantam battalions with the overall target of supplying at least an entire division of the small men. This was a tall order (if you excuse the pun), for a Division then consisted of approximately 20,000 men. A Division is sub-divided into three Brigades each containing four battalions. This made a grand total of twelve battalions of Bantams per Division, requiring approximately 12,000 volunteers. The remainder of the proposed Division's soldiers would be employed in medical and transport services, artillery, and engineers; these men were all above the required Bantam height. In his book *The Call of Empire* Bigland recounts,

> In all 12,800 of these men enlisted, hundreds were recruited from the coal mines of Great Britain, and were therefore adept in the use of pick and shovel, being used to fatigue and working in strained positions. These men would prove wonderfully useful in modern warfare where digging mines, making and repairing trenches, crouching for hours waiting to deliver an attack, and dodging shells would become constant and daily necessities.

The overspill of volunteers for the two Cheshire battalions was directed by Alfred Bigland to the town of Leeds where the Lord Mayor, Mr. J. Bedford was raising a battalion 17th (Service) West Yorkshire Regiment, (2nd Leeds), recruited from shepherds, miners and wool workers from the West Ridings of Yorkshire. Today it is unclear why Bigland favoured the Leeds Bantams as closer to home numerous other battalions were in their infancy. Even today there is rivalry between Merseysiders and Mancunians; if it existed in those distant days, maybe it explains why Bigland failed to direct the surplus men to the City of Manchester, which is considerably closer than Leeds.

Inter-city rivalry spurred the elders of Manchester to follow the Liverpool concept of the Pals' battalions, formed from local social groups of men who often worked together in the same occupation. The city's recruitment drive was aimed at solely the middle classes who responded magnificently to the call of arms. In a surge in nationalism the city raised with moderate ease six City battalions, the seventh City battalion encountered problems in reaching full strength as the majority of potential recruits had already taken the King's shilling. The City fathers realised their target of two Manchester Pals' Brigades could not be immediately fulfilled and widened their horizons. Mr. D.E. Anderson of West Didsbury, who was a member of the Manchester branch of the National Service League, had commenced compiling a list of names of 1,200 under sized men willing to serve in the proposed Manchester Bantams. The War Office granted the City Mayor permission to raise the 23rd (Bantams) battalion resulting in the formation of the 8th City Battalion, and the completion of two brigades. This battalion contained a large number of miners from the pits in the Wigan area, also businessmen and office types from the Manchester offices. It would have been interesting to know what the tough working class miners thought of the blue collar office workers and vice versa. The Bantam battalion was separated from their fellow Mancunian Pals' when the battalion was placed in the 104 Brigade 35th Division. Another Pals unit the 24th Manchesters (Oldham Comrades) took their place in the Brigade. The Manchester regiment ultimately fielded a total of forty-four battalions during the conflict; only one of these was a Bantam battalion.

In the bustling towns of Lancashire cotton was still king, the vast mills stood high and proud above the uniform rows upon rows of two up and two down workers' terrace houses. Social conditions were grim and generations of poorly paid and under nourished mill workers produced a generation of stunted growth workers. When a committee of four M.P.s, Lieutenant Colonel George E. Wike and the Aldermen of Bury, Rochdale, Middleton and assorted district councils set about a Bantam recruiting campaign the response proved phenomenal. Launched in Bury at the beginning of January the campaign produced a Bantam battalion within five days; this became the 17th (Service) Battalion the Lancashire Fusiliers (1st South-East Lancashires). The new battalion moved to Ashton-in-Makerfield in April where the billets were huts in Garswood Hall Park. In mid January another Bantam battalion the 18th (Service) Lancashire Fusiliers (2nd South East Lancashires) was formed. The volunteers continued to present themselves and towards the end of March Mr. Montague Barlow M.P. and the Salford Brigade Committee raised in Salford another Fusilier battalion the 20th (Service) Battalion (4th Salford). The four above Lancastrian battalions later formed the 104 Brigade of the 35th Division.

The county of Yorkshire provided the nation's fourth Bantam battalion, this was recruited in Leeds in December 1914 by J.E. Bedford the Mayor of Leeds and the city elders. The Prince of Wales' Own (West Yorkshire) Regiment had raised a Leeds battalion a few months

*Private William
Boynton Butler,
Victoria Cross*

previously, consequently the latter battalion also carried the title 2nd Leeds. During the course of the war the West Yorkshire regiment earned four Victoria Crosses, one of these was awarded to a 23 year old Leeds Bantam soldier of the 17th West Yorkshires while attached to the 106th Trench Mortar Battery. On 6-8-17 east of Lempire, Private William Boynton Butler was in charge of a Stokes gun in trenches that were being heavily shelled. Suddenly one of the fly-off levers of a Stokes shell came off and fired the shell in the emplacement. Private Butler picked up the shell and shouted a warning to a party of infantry. He then turned and put himself between the party of men and the live shell, holding it until they were out of danger, when he threw it on the parados and took cover. The shell exploded, damaging the trench, but only contusing Butler.

Halfway through March 1915 the 19th (Service) Battalion (2nd County) Battalion of the Durham Light Infantry was raised at West Hartlepool by the Durham Parliamentary Recruiting Committee, of which the Earl of Durham was president. The other members of the committee consisted of C.R. Barratt, A.B. Horsley, J. Corrie, F.W. Stanley and T.W. Dawson. This Geordie battalion had a very strong element of miners from intriguing sounding pits like Esh Winning, Morpeth Main; there was also an exodus from the Sunderland and Gateshead shipyards. In 1914 the country employed 1.2 million miners, approximately 6% of the employed population, many of

The Bantams of the 23rd Battalion Manchester Regiment.

whom enlisted into the various Bantam battalions.

Prior to the outbreak of hostilities Lord Rosebury was greatly in favour of a peaceful settlement with Germany, a very unpopular opinion that he eloquently orated at public meetings. However once war was declared he used every means at his disposal to recruit for the armed forces. In February 1915 Lord Rosebury headed the Edinburgh based Royal Scots Recruiting Committee with the intention of raising a Bantam battalion for the senior British infantry regiment of the line. Over a thousand volunteers responded to the call by enlisting into the Royal Scots (Lothian Regiment), this battalion eventually became the 17th (Service) Battalion (Rosebury). The men were billeted in the city's St. Leonard's School, from here the raw recruits marched to King's Park where they were put through their paces by former soldiers. All attempts to procure uniforms for the men failed, the problem was solved by one of the Rotarians who converted his business premises into a tailor's factory and promptly manufactured sufficient uniforms to clothe the new battalion.

Nottingham was not to be out done and in February 1915 raised within ten days the 15th (Service) Battalion (Nottingham) Notts and Derby regiment from the area's miners and lace working population. The battalion's conception was greatly assisted when the city council authorised an allowance of £1,000 to raise a Bantam battalion. In common with all the battalions of this distinguished regiment the unit revelled in the title Sherwood Foresters, a hark back to the days of the legendary Robin Hood.

The mere mention of the name Highland Light Infantry conjures up the image of a feisty, kilt wearing highland crofter coexisting with nature on the mountainside. In reality the majority of these fighting men came from the tenements of Glasgow and other industrial conurbations. At the beginning of November 1914 the Lord Provost Sir Thomas Dunlop was approached by the Rotary Club to form a Bantam battalion. Permission was duly sought from Lord Kitchener, however it was not until March 1915 that permission was granted. Within a week the Lord Provost and city elders were proud to announce the city had raised yet another battalion, this later became known as the 18th (Service) Battalion (4th Glasgow) Highland Light Infantry. The City Corporation agreed to raise and equip the battalion; it was originally intended to equip the battalion with the kilt, but production difficulties would have delayed the equipping of the battalion to such an extent the idea of the kilt was abandoned. These spirited and somewhat aggressive recruits from the docks, shipyards and tough areas of Glasgow and Clydeside rapidly acquired for themselves another name – 'The Devil Dwarfs', a befitting title for the wee soldiers whose fists settled any arguments in the local hostelries. The original Commanding Officer of these tenacious men was Colonel John Shaunessey.

The West Country provided one Bantam battalion which was raised by the Bristol Citizens' recruiting Committee. On 22-4-15 the 14th (Service) Battalion of the Gloucestershire Regiment (West of England) was formed. The men were recruited in Bristol and also Birmingham.

The twelve Bantam battalions raised by the county regiments were all infantry regiments, the Artillery, Engineers and Pioneers still had to be raised. Three Brigades of the Royal Field Artillery (R.F.A.) were raised; once again each unit had a strong local connection to a specific town or city. 157 Brigade owed its existence to the activities of Sir James Taggart, the Lord Provost of Aberdeen and Lieutenant Colonel G. Milne, a prominent former commander of the Highland Territorial Artillery Brigade, who became the new unit's Commanding Officer. The Lancashire towns of Accrington and Burnley shared the honour in forming 58 Brigade, raised in February 1915 in response to a request from the War Office for an additional artillery unit. Captain Harwood the mayor of Accrington arranged the attestation, clothing, and equipment and perhaps more importantly to the troops their modest pay. The original commander was Colonel T.P. Ritzema. In June 1915 the Field Artillery unit relocated to the army camp at Weeton, outside Blackpool. 159 Brigade owes its origins to the Lord Provost and Corporation of Glasgow who agreed to form and kit out a Brigade comprising four batteries of Field Artillery, with Ammunition Column, and Reserve plus personnel. In March the City recruitment centres began their quest for volunteers, not the easiest of tasks in a proud City that had already provided a legion of patriotic volunteers. As April drew to a close the task was completed and an additional 943 officers and men had attested to the New Army unit. It was initially assembled at Ayr and when fully completed moved a few miles away to a camp at Dunoon. In command was Lieutenant Colonel W. Lamont, V.D. (Volunteer Decoration) a long serving territorial of the 3 Lowland Brigade, R.F.A. To complete the artillery the Mayor and

Two men from the 8th City Pals' 23rd (Bantam) Manchester Regiment.

Corporation of West Ham, London raised 163 Brigade of howitzers. The Division did not reach full strength until the following summer when three companies of Royal Engineers, a signal company and pioneer battalion arrived. This was the final division of Kitchener's New Fourth Army and was initially raised as the 42nd Division; however when the original New Fourth Army was dismantled in April 1915 the recently assembled division was renumbered.

CHAPTER FOUR

1915 – Birds of a Feather

IMMEDIATELY AFTER the conclusion of the New Year revelry the 1st Birkenhead Battalion faced a more sombre event. Private Robert William Hannan[1] regimental number 20114 of the 15th Battalion Cheshire Regiment died on 20 December 1914. The deceased Londoner left a widow and four children. This was the first member of this particular battalion to die, and he was interred with full military honours within Flaybrick cemetery, Birkenhead. As the Bantams were still lacking rifles, the funeral cortège through the streets of Birkenhead was led by a detachment of the 3rd Cheshires, with rifles reversed as a token of respect. At the conclusion of the graveside service a rifle volley was fired over the grave, the lament of the Last Post concluded the ceremony.

Long hours on the parade ground under the vigilant eyes of veteran soldiers transformed the clumsiest of civilians into credible soldiers. This was not an easy conversion and tried the patience of many an instructor excluding the R.S.M. who cajoled his men into shape with screams of 'You might have broken your mother's heart but you will not break mine'. Eventually the last of the uniforms had finally arrived and the two Bantam battalions were now resplendent in khaki. The Birkenhead Bantams wasted no time in marching throughout Wirral, these route marches broke in new boots, built up stamina, and displayed to the civilian spectators Britain's Lilliputian soldiers. In order to relieve the monotony of the long marches a drum and fife band accompanied the column, and the men sang along to popular songs.

Due to a now unknown alteration in the War Office conditions Mr Bigland was required to apply to the Borough Education Committee for an extension to the use of the schools. The Committee agreed to a compromise to the benefit of the school pupils and the military. From mid January the pupils at Rock Ferry School attended Well Lane School from 1-30 in the afternoon until 5p.m.; the Well Lane children were tutored from 9-00 a.m. until 12-30. The arrangements may not have been to the complete satisfaction of the Bantams but at least they still had a roof over their head.

On 6 February the Bantams trod the now familiar path to the vast Flaybrick cemetery for the internment of Private T.W. Ballard, a member of C Company of the 15th Battalion who had died of pneumonia at the Borough Hospital. Originally most of the WW1

Victorian Well Lane School provided a temporary billet for the Bantams. The building was demolished in the 1980s and replaced with a modern school.

soldiers interred at the then prestigious Flaybrick cemetery were placed in unmarked paupers' graves. When this disgraceful fact became public knowledge indignant Birkonians protested so strongly, that Birkenhead council agreed to cover the cost of the internments. The majority of out of town service men were interred in deep communal graves with a shared headstone, although there are also separate graves. They are all now cared for by the Commonwealth War Graves Commission.

Amongst the ranks of the 16th Battalion Cheshires was thirty three year old Sergeant Major Hugh Sloan, a native of Bolton. The Bantam

The final resting place of a dozen men, including three Cheshire Bantams: Privates Ballard, Hannan and Johnson.

N.C.O. was the World's champion long-distance walker. In 1907 he walked 2,250 miles in under 1,000 consecutive hours, a feat which required walking day and night for 1,000 hours maintaining an average pace of 2.5 miles an hour. At Manchester he walked 1,000 miles in twenty days. For a wager Sloan had also walked thirty miles with a wheelbarrow weighing a total of 50lbs, without once putting the barrow down. He completed a journey from Land's End to John o' Groats in twenty-one days. His many achievements were all the more remarkable, as they were all completed while wearing wooden clogs.

Bantam record walker, Sergeant Major Sloan.

The regimental walking record stood at seventy-four miles walked in twenty-four hours; this was held by a member of the Northumberland Fusiliers. For the honour of the Cheshire Regiment Sloan decided to beat the record, setting himself a target of eighty miles to be covered in twenty-four hours, only this time the champion walker would wear military boots. Due to inclement weather his first two attempts were unsuccessful. Finally Sergeant Major Sloan broke the regimental record by ten minutes, and exceeded the required distance by nine miles.

The New Army battalions adopted all the traditions of their regiments and shared their battle honours. Annually the Cheshire Regiment commemorated the Battle of Meanee (1843) and to mark the February event, the Bantams were awarded a half-day holiday. This allowed an opportunity for an inter-battalion football match which was played at Bebington. The match was keenly played and the First Battalion won by three goals to one.

In early February Lieutenant Lionel Irving Ferguson, 16th Battalion Cheshire Regiment, who resided at St. Aidens Terrace, Oxton, married Miss Kathleen Marjorie Hillis Forwood, the daughter of Mr and Mrs Forwood of Beach Cliff, Hoylake and grand-daughter of Sir William Forwood of Bromborough Hall. The ceremony was held on 2 February 1915 in the picturesque parish church in the tranquil village of Bidston, Wirral. The Oxton officer had Lieutenant Peter Forrester of the 2nd Battalion for best man. After the ceremony the bride and groom passed beneath a guard of honour from the church door to the lych gate, the bridegroom's fellow officers formed an archway of crossed swords. The regimental band struck up a tune as the happy couple drove away to a luncheon party held at the Adelphi Hotel, Liverpool.

Ferguson was originally a Territorial in the Liverpool Scottish (10th K.L.R.) with the regimental number 3045. He attained a commission on 5 December 1914 and is listed as an original 16th Battalion officer.

Bantams drawn up outside the Lyceum picturedrome 12 February 1915.

He later served as a company commander in the 13th (Service) Battalion Cheshire Regiment, known locally as the Wirral pals. By 1 July 1916 he was a captain. His battalion was held in reserve on the first day of the Somme. On 2 September 1918 he was wounded by a shell splinter, the next day he was operated on at Number 2 General Hospital. He was invalided home 17 September and saw no further service on the Western Front. He then served with the 3rd Battalion Cheshire at West Hartlepool until his demobilisation in March 1919.

The inhabitants of Birkenhead who had done so much to raise, clothe, equip, and provide entertainment for the Bantams longed for the opportunity to see them in full marshal array parading through the town. By the beginning of February the Bantams had finally been

Rare photographs of the Bantams marching through the town on review day.

16th (Service) Battalion Cheshire Regiment in Grange Road on review day.

issued with everything required, and the first public parade through Birkenhead was duly arranged. On Saturday 20 February at 2 p.m. the First Battalion left it's training depot at the Bebington showground, led by the Tranmere Gleam Silver Prize Band. At the same time the Second Battalion set off headed by its fife and drum band. Both battalions merged at the corner of Bebington Road and Church Road, Higher Tranmere, whereupon the combined battalions numbering 2,700 men set off for the Town Hall taking in a circular route, which covered a distance of six miles. The Bantams all in khaki with great coats rolled and strapped over their shoulders were received with great enthusiasm throughout the route along some of the town's busiest thoroughfares. The mass of troops impressive in bulk if not in stature, presented a smart, well trained addition to Kitchener's forces. Silent now the scoffing critics, who in the early days of the Bantams, had derided the idea of 'the little uns'. The Bantams were giving their answer to the sceptical.

The streets were lined with spectators as the Bantams marched by

53

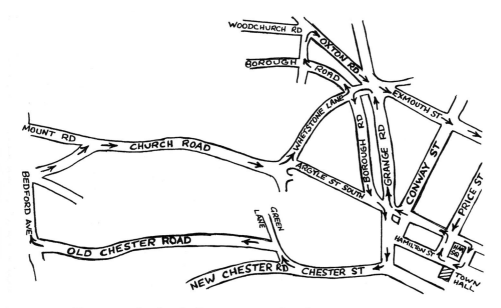

The route taken by the Bantams on review day.

accompanied by three bands playing lively martial airs. Birkenhead took advantage of the occasion not only to claim its parental rights in the Bantams but also to demonstrate its loyalty. At the principal points along the route there was a large display of bunting and flags of the Allied nations. On arrival at Hamilton Square the climax of the

Each company was headed by its officer commanding mounted on a horse. Spontaneous cheers greeted detachment after detachment of the small soldiers. Outside the Town Hall, Hamilton Square.

military spectacle was reached. Pouring out of Price Street the two battalions tramped along past the Town Hall until the foremost ranks were merged into the rearmost, drawing a striking military cordon. In front of the lower entrance to the Town Hall were assembled notable dignitaries. The battalions were then reviewed by Lieutenant General Mackinnon accompanied by General Theniller commander of 125 Brigade, Brigadier General Edwards, Captain Macindoe, Major Allen and Major McConachew.

Captain Phillips
Gloom was cast over the Second Battalion when, on 8 March, it lost one of its officers, Captain Phillips, who developed pneumonia. He had previously served with the Black Watch and had seen action in the Boer War. On Tuesday 12 March a section of Bantams served as escort when his coffin was conveyed to Liverpool Exchange Station. The funeral took place in his home city of Edinburgh.

Each company was headed by its officer mounted on a horse. Spontaneous cheers greeted detachment after detachment of the small soldiers. After the review Sir Henry Mackinnon congratulated the officers and men, remarking on the striking difference since when he last saw them a couple of months ago. Congratulations were also extended to the people of Birkenhead for their entire endeavour. Bigland announced,

Alfred Bigland MP

It is a proud moment in my life when I realise that the little effort I had made at the beginning had been rewarded by such a magnificent return, because not only in Birkenhead, but also in Bury, Manchester, Leeds, and other places the example had been followed. I am proud to think there were now 10,000 Bantams who are soldiers of the King. (applause)

After the review the men marched back to Bebington. Four days later the battalions repeated the exercise when they paraded through Liverpool. Upon arrival at St. George's Hall they paraded before Lord Derby and other dignitaries.

In late March Lord Kitchener arranged a brief weekend visit to Liverpool and Manchester, where both cities arranged a march past of troops to mark the occasion. Despite objections from religious leaders the military revue went ahead as planned on the Sabbath, this being the only day Kitchener did not attend the War Office. Approximately 100,000 spectators gathered to witness the occasion, which commenced at noon. Kitchener and his entourage assembled on the steps of St. George's Hall, Liverpool where 1,200 New Army troops in

The parade begins. The top-hat wearing Alfred Bigland is to the right of the saluting officer.

Some of the 12,000 locally raised soldiers . Ironically they are passing within a few yards of the site that would later be used for the impressive war cenotaph which would bear the legend, 'From the northern parts came a great army'.

Bigland, General Mackinnon and Lord Kitchener watch the Bantams go by.

full service dress paraded before them. The Bantams brought up the rear of the parade; when they appeared Kitchener's face broke into a smile and he turned to Bigland and shook his hand heartily.[2] At the conclusion of the parade Kitchener told Bigland that he was particularly pleased with the Bantams. They were the first he had seen, and he was more than surprised at their apparent efficiency. (Due to their uniformity of height the Bantams looked impressive on the march.) He also promised that they should have their full equipment without delay so they could take their place at the front.

Raising of the 40th Division

All of the martial pomp and splendour added to the increased social pressure on civilians to enlist and recruiting drives continued throughout the country. In September 1914 the Welsh National Executive Committee (W.N.E.C.) was appointed with the brief of raising a Welsh Army Corps under the same regulations as those units raised in Scotland and England. Whilst all avenues of recruitment were explored the W.N.E.C. attempted to raise as many Bantams as possible and they succeeded in raising four battalions of Bantam troops, enough to form a Brigade (later to be 119 Brigade, 40th Division). The other two brigades, numbered 120 and 121, were a combination of Bantam and regular-sized soldiers although the men were of mixed heights with a strong Bantam presence it was still considered to be a Bantam Division.

During the process of forming 119 Brigade the W.N.E.C. were able to select the Bantams with the finest physique and less well developed men found themselves in 120 and 121 Brigades. A significant amount of these volunteers who had bravely stepped forward to fight were considered to be underdeveloped and unfit for active service. Patriotic enthusiasm had swayed civilian examining doctors into turning a blind eye to the poor condition of the aspiring volunteers. Some of these recruits were schoolboys whose slight build had not been too evident while in attendance with other less built men. The military staff was quick to notice these weaklings and arranged a mass screening of the men, as a consequence of the examinations the 120 and 121 Brigades were thinned out so much that they each required two battalions to bring them up to war service strength. To rectify the matter those men deemed as fit for war service were re-organised into two battalions. The four battalions needed to make the two brigades up to strength were transferred from the 39th Division.

The twelve original infantry battalions constituting the 40th Division were:

119 Brigade
The first Bantam battalions raised by the W.N.E.C. were for the Welsh regiment; the 17th (Service) Battalion (1st Glamorgan) was raised in December of the previous year. An additional battalion, the 18th (Service) Battalion (2nd Glamorgan), was also raised for the same regiment.

17th Battalion the Welsh Regiment (1st Glamorgan) was raised in December 1914.

18th Battalion the Welsh Regiment (2nd Glamorgan) was raised in January 1915.

19th Battalion the Royal Welsh Fusiliers was raised in March 1915 by the W.N.E.C.

12th Battalion South Wales Borderers (3rd Gwent) was raised at Newport by the W.N.E.C. in March 1915.

120 Brigade
11th Battalion The King's Own (Royal Lancaster Regiment) formed at Lancaster as a Bantam battalion in August 1915. Absorbed into the 12th South Lancashire Regiment 2 March 1916.

13th Battalion The East Surrey Regiment (Wandsworth) was raised by the Mayor of Wandsworth on 16 June 1915. This was not a Bantam sized battalion.

14th Battalion, Highland Light Infantry was formed possibly at Hamilton about July 1915 as a Bantam battalion.

Men of the 17th Battalion Welsh Regiment Rhondda Bantams pose with their army boots which have just been issued to them.

14th Battalion Princess Louise's (Argyll and Sutherland Highlanders) were raised early 1915. They were not a Bantam battalion.

121 Brigade

12th Battalion, The Suffolk Regiment (East Anglia) formed at Bury St Edmunds in July 1915 as a Bantam battalion.

13th Battalion, Alexandra, Princess of Wales' Own (Yorkshire Regiment). Was raised as a Bantam battalion at Richmond in July 1915.

20th Battalion, The Duke of Cambridge's Own (Middlesex Regiment), (Shoreditch) was raised in Shoreditch, 18 June 1915, by the Mayor and Borough this was a non-Bantam unit.

21st Battalion The Duke of Cambridge's Own, (Middlesex Regiment), (Islington) raised in Islington by the Mayor and Borough on 18 May 1915. This was a standard height battalion.

40th Division badge.

The ambitious plan to raise an entire Corps from an area that had already greatly contributed to Kitchener's New Army was reduced to the more realistic aim of two Divisions, the 40th and the 38th (Welsh) Division.

The Gas Works Bantams

A prime source of heat and lighting in Birkenhead was the municipal gas works, which supplied gas to domestic and industrial customers as well as the town's streetlights. A day's gas supply for the town required the processing and handling of 180 tons of coal. The coal was laboriously broken up and conveyed to the furnace hoppers by coalers. In mid March they went on strike for higher pay. Alfred Bigland became a mediator between the two intransigent parties; the insensitive employers inflamed the situation by advertising for replacement workers. Amidst the Bantams' ranks were ex-miners and labourers whose stocky bodies were well used to a hard day's back-breaking graft. As Birkenhead was a defended port there was an abundance of troops in the town, various regimental contingents were used as labour at the Gas Works, including part of the 16th Battalion.

Two N.C.O.s of the Kings Liverpool Regiment with men from the 22nd Battalion Duke of Cambridge's Own (Middlesex Regiment). This unit was formed as a Bantam battalion at Mill Hill in June 1915. They served briefly in 121 Brigade, 40th Division until they were disbanded in April 1916. This unit never went overseas.

Number 3 Platoon, C Company, 16th (Service) Battalion, Cheshire Regiment.

The incensed Secretary of the National Union of Gas Workers contacted Lieutenant Colonel Earle with reference to the Bantams' employment in place of the striking men. Earle claimed the men were without a gas supply and could not cook food, consequently he asked the men to volunteer to make gas. He also claimed the Admiralty work at Cammell Laird's was suffering. This was not so as the shipyard produced its own gas. An un-named private soldier recounted how he and his pals had volunteered to work at the Gas Works.

A contingent of us were marched into a courtyard, and formed a line with our backs against the wall. Any soldier who did not wish to break the strike was ordered to take one step back, of course the wall prevented us carrying out this order.

By the end of March the strikers request for a wage increase equal to five shillings (25p) a week for men who worked a seven-day week was agreed. Those who worked a six-day week received an increase of four shillings. They returned to work on 3 April. Several months later questions were asked in the Houses of Parliament regarding the Gas Works Bantams and not for the reasons you might expect. The thirsty 'short uns' had managed to eat and drink their way through £70 worth of food and alcohol. A considerable sum of money at that time and the invoice was destined for the ratepayer hence the outcry. The account was discreetly settled by officers of the Cheshires.

The war was producing an ever-increasing amount of casualties. The fortunate ones survived the rigours of primitive field hospitals and were invalided back to Blighty. Hospitals throughout the United Kingdom were hard pressed to deal with the casualties of mechanised warfare, consequently auxiliary hospitals were established in any suitable buildings. Due to the shortage of such buildings in Birkenhead it was proposed to use the schools occupied by the Bantams.

While the 15th Battalion Cheshires remained at the Bebington show ground the 16th Battalion, quartered at the Rock Ferry school, prepared to relocate. In late April Bigland found a suitable camp site, near the rifle range at Meols, a small coastal village on the extremity of the Wirral peninsula. The site was a popular picnic area on a spacious field adjoining Park Road, convenient for the railway station. The field offered a few huts and a suitable area for a drill ground. Within a week 160 bell tents were erected in long rows. Large marquees were used as canteens, assembly rooms and also a branch of the Y.M.C.A. The men had everything they required including their own post office.

At 9 a.m. on the final day in April, approximately 1,300 Bantams departed from Rock Ferry, led by their fife and drum band. They marched through the principal thoroughfares of Birkenhead enroute for the sandy shores of Meols. The standard pace of the Bantams on the march was set at 140 to the minute. That was a fast, sharp pace, and

Comrades in arms. Men of the 16th Battalion, Cheshire Regiment, with some precious Long Lee Enfield rifles.

some of the little men felt as if they were almost running along. The men of the 16th Battalion were delighted with their new camp and a holiday atmosphere was said to prevail. When the men were not undergoing bayonet practice, 'square bashing', or a host of other training exercises, they enjoyed their seaside break. For many of the soldiers the experience was a complete novelty as some had never seen the sea before. The arrival of the Bantams at their new billets was met with heavy rain, after the first two nights all tents and contents were flooded, the situation was cheerfully accepted as a means of displaying their ability to rough it in the open. This experience on the low lying reclaimed land was a foretaste of conditions they would unfortunately experience for months on end while on active service.

As the sea was in close proximity it was considered unnecessary to provide bathing facilities within the camp, as the Bantams could bathe in the sea. While bathing in the tidal Hoyle-lake Private Leonard Taylor of C Company got into difficulties. His cries were heard by fellow C Company members Privates Arlott and Thomas, who went to his assistance. Due to the frantic struggles of the drowning man the rescuers found themselves being pulled under. They were unable to retain their grip and Taylor sunk beneath the waves. His body was

Officers of the 16th Battalion Cheshire Regiment, (Second Birkenhead Bantams).

NCOs of the 16th Battalion Cheshire Regiment taken at Meols, Wirral.

Rifle inspection for a platoon belonging to 16th Battalion.

recovered that evening by a fisherman named Jackson. The deceased was a single man, a former fitter's labourer from Worthley, near Leeds. His Union Jack draped coffin was conveyed to West Kirby station upon a horse drawn military wagon, escorted by Bantams with reversed rifles. As the cortège neared the station the brass band of the battalion struck up the 'Dead March'.

On 16 June, to stimulate recruiting, the fully equipped 15th Battalion Cheshires accompanied by their fife and drum band, marched from Bebington to Chester Town Hall. The Depot band from Chester Castle met the Bantams near the skating rink at the end of Liverpool Road. On the Town Hall steps were the Mayor of Chester, Sheriff, Dean of Chester and a large number of prominent citizens, as the battalion passed the Town Hall the officers gave the salute to Brigadier General Caunter in the absence of General Sir Henry Mackinnon. Afterwards the battalion marched to the racecourse where refreshments were served in Tattersalls, and shortly before 5.00 p.m. they marched to Chester station where they entrained for Bebington.

In mid June the War Office instructed Bigland to recruit a further 500 Bantams, in order to strengthen the reserve. Recruits were to report to their nearest recruitment office, undergo a medical, then receive a rail warrant to Headquarters at the Bebington showground. The two depot companies merged in August to become the 17th (Reserve) Battalion, Cheshire Regiment.

Notes

(1) His death is not recorded in Soldiers Died or the Cheshire regiment roll of honour.
(2) At the time of writing visitors to the Liverpool Kings Museum can see a movie reel clip of the Bantams marching by during this parade. It is mistakenly identified as members of the Liverpool Regiment.

DISCOVER MORE ABOUT MILITARY HISTORY

Pen & Sword Books have over 400 books currently in print. Our imprints include the Battleground series, Leo Cooper, Military Classics, Select, Pen & Sword Aviation and Pen & Sword Naval. We cover all periods of history on land, sea and air. If you would like to receive more information on any or all of these, please complete the form below and return. (NO STAMP REQUIRED)

Mr/Mrs/Ms ....

Address...

Postcode .... E-mail address ....

Please tick your areas of interest:

Ancient History ☐	Napoleonic ☐	Pre World War One ☐
World War One ☐	World War Two ☐	Post World War Two ☐
Falklands ☐	Aviation ☐	Maritime ☐
Regimental History ☐	Military Reference ☐	Military Biography ☐
Battlefield Guides ☐	Battleground Series Club *(free membership)* ☐	

Website: www.pen-and-sword.co.uk • Email: enquiries@pen-and-sword.co.uk
Telephone: 01226 734555 • Fax: 01226 734438

Pen & Sword Books Limited

FREEPOST SF5

47 Church Street

BARNSLEY

South Yorkshire

S70 2BR

CHAPTER FIVE

The 35th (Bantam) Division

THE 15TH AND 16TH BATTALIONS departed from the Wirral on Sunday morning 20 June, their destination was Masham, near Ripon, Yorkshire. At Masham camp in sectors known as Marfield, Roomer Common and Fearby, three infantry brigades of Bantam troops assembled. The Cheshires constituted half of 105 Brigade. On 5 July 1915 the 35th (Bantam) Division was officially formed, becoming part of Kitchener's New Fourth Army. The Bantams replaced the original three brigades of Kitchener's New Fourth Army resulting in twelve battalions being transferred to other army formations to form Second Reserve battalions. They consisted of 104 Brigade, 12th Battalion Royal Welsh Fusiliers, 9th Battalion South Wales Borderers, 12th Battalion Welsh Regiment, and the 9th Battalion King's Shropshire L.I.; 105 Brigade containing the 15th King's Liverpool Regiment, 16th Battalion King's Liverpool, 14th Battalion Cheshire Regiment and the 10th Battalion Prince of Wales' Volunteers. Finally, 106 Brigade had the 10th Battalion Bedfordshire Regiment, 11th Battalion Gloucestershire Regiment, 12th Battalion Essex Regiment, and the 13th Battalion Princess Louise's.

Each of these brigades usually contained four infantry battalions, of about a thousand men each. The entire Division numbered approximately twenty thousand men including artillery, engineers, medical and transport; it should be remembered that within the 35th Division only the infantry were of Bantam stature. At this time each division had a complement of 585 officers and 17,488 NCOs and other ranks. The Division was sub divided into three brigades each containing four battalions. Each battalion consisted of four companies containing 240 men; in the Cheshire Bantams these were labelled W, X, Y, and Z companies. These were subdivided into four platoons of sixty soldiers; finally these were sub-divided into four sections of fifteen men. The military strength of these units increased and decreased as the war progressed.

Lieutenant Colonel Charles Earle, the original commanding officer, had been in ill health for some time and when the battalion joined 105 Brigade at Masham, temporary Lieutenant Colonel Earle retired due to illness. Lieutenant Colonel R.C. Browne-Clayton, a retired officer formerly of the Irish Horse succeeded the forty-six year old officer in early August 1915. Exactly two years after his retirement Lieutenant Colonel Earle died of Cancer. He is interred in Highgate Cemetery, London.

The officers of the 16th Battalion Cheshire Regiment with Alfred Bigland M.P. Sitting next to Bigland is the new Commanding Officer R.C. Browne-Clayton.

The 35th (Bantam) Division was placed under the command of Major General Reginald John Pinney K.C.B. the former commander of 23 Brigade, 8th Division who returned from France to take up his new appointment. This experienced commander took up his duties on 4 July and from the outset fully appreciated the potential of the Bantams. He set about moulding his men into an efficient and well disciplined fighting unit. Unfortunately, all too many of his colleagues derided the midget soldiers. Visiting medical officers produced numerous adverse reports; one commented, 'It is impossible to expect undersized men to be useful as soldiers in the British lines at Flanders'. Another claimed, 'It is well known that such little men cannot bear the physical and moral load of modern warfare'. Pinney simply ignored the sceptics and established a programme of hard training. He was helped in this task by 106 Brigade's new Brigade Major, Bernard L.

Montgomery; a twenty-eight year old officer, formerly of the Royal Warwickshire Regiment. During the battle of First Ypres, 13 October 1914, he had led a platoon in an attack on the village of Moteren. During the action he was seriously wounded in the lungs by a sniper, resulting in a return to Blighty for recuperation. For his bravery in leading the attack he was promoted to Captain and was awarded the D.S.O., a rare award for such a junior officer. He later returned to the Western front serving as a Captain with 104 Brigade before moving up the promotional ladder in early 1917. To a later generation this man would be more familiar as Field Marshal Montgomery of Alamein.

The assembled New Army soldiers at Masham represented nine infantry regiments which had raised a total of twelve battalions. The 35th Division retained its original titles; new battalions were allocated as follows:

104 Brigade
   17th Battalion The Lancashire Fusiliers (1st South East Lancashire)
   18th Battalion The Lancashire Fusiliers (2nd South East Lancashire)
      raised at Bury.
   20th Battalion The Lancashire Fusiliers (4th Salford)
   23rd Battalion The Manchester Regiment (8th City)
105 Brigade
   15th Battalion Cheshire Regiment (1st Birkenhead)
   16th Battalion Cheshire Regiment {2nd Birkenhead)
   15th Battalion The Sherwood Foresters (Nottingham)
   14th Battalion The Gloucestershire Regiment (West of England)
   It was assigned the number 105 on 1-5-15.
106 Brigade
   19th Battalion The Durham Light Infantry (2nd County)
   17th Battalion The Prince of Wales Own (2nd Leeds)
   18th Battalion The Highland Light Infantry (4th Glasgow)
   17th Battalion The Royal Scots (Rosebury)

The 35th Division adopted a red cockerel as its divisional sign on transport etc. M. Chappell in his excellent book *British Battle Insignia 1914-18* reports, 'There is evidence that this device was worn on uniform also; an example exists in the Royal Army Museum in Brussels with a silver bullion rooster worked on a scarlet patch. The badges were discarded in early 1917 when they were replaced with an alternative design. Both designs are extremely scarce items unlike the 40th division badge of which I have seen several examples'.

I am Thinking of You at Masham

At Masham the 35th Division were put through their paces under the watchful eyes of veteran N.C.O. instructors. The men were introduced to simulated conditions representing the rigours of life on the Western Front; the long summer days were spent trench digging, honing musketry skills and participating in artillery co-operation exercises. Although the exercises took place at Masham the actual camp was at Roomer Common.

4th Platoon, A Company, 16th Battalion Cheshire Regiment at their Ionic Street School billet.

On 16 June the Division took another step towards completion when the Pioneer Battalion, the trench mortar batteries and machine gun sections arrived. The Pioneer Battalion was the 19th Battalion Northumberland Fusiliers who were raised in late 1914 by the Council of the Newcastle and Gateshead incorporated Chambers of Trade.

In late August the 35th Division infantry moved south to Perham Down on Salisbury Plain, Hampshire. Here the accommodation proved to be appalling, the camp's wooden huts leaked in the slightest of rains, as did the bell tents. The divisional artillery now became the responsibility of Brigadier General W. C. Stanley, who had recently returned from France where he was in command of 30 Brigade R.F.A. His first major challenge was to relocate the artillery to Bulford for gun practice; this was carried out with difficulty as the Artillery had insufficient horses to carry out the task efficiently. The guns and limbers were propelled by four-legged horsepower, a national shortage of equines due to unsurpassed demand combined with their slaughter on the field of battle, meant allocation was prioritised overseas. The Division's full complement of horses would not be received until December.

In late August the command of the 15th Cheshires altered when the aging Colonel Bretherton resigned on the grounds of ill health. Major Newell assumed command of the battalion, simultaneously rising to

Perham Down Army Camp near Ludgershall where the 35th Division was stationed in August 1915.

the rank of Lieutenant Colonel. In civilian life Newell was an engineer, who resided at 'Ciatra' Hill Road, Claughton, Birkenhead. He served as an officer in the Volunteer Force, was described as a promising athlete in his day, and a man of commanding presence. The previous August he enlisted as a private soldier, receiving a commission as Second Lieutenant on 23 December 1914, promoted Captain on 28-1-15, attaining field rank on 10 April 1915, promoted from Major to Lieutenant Colonel on 30 July 1915. A meteoric rise which few could equal. He was a specialist in musketry having won a first class certificate as instructor at the School of Musketry. At the time of his last promotion he was the First Birkenhead Battalion's musketry instructor.

As the war continued it became increasingly obvious that it would be a protracted one, as earlier expectations of a swift knock out blow to the enemy were dashed within months of the outbreak of hostilities. The rising tide of disabled and wounded servicemen provided visible reminders of the horrors of mechanised warfare, and as a consequence less and less volunteers were prepared to join the colours. By the autumn of 1915 the problem of maintaining a steady supply of recruits began to cause anxiety to the Government. The average infantry battalion was losing approximately fifteen percent of its manpower every four weeks, and to compensate for these losses at least 30,000 new recruits were required each month.

The continental armies were always raised by conscription, but in

Britain this was considered to be a loss of freedom, instead they relied on the concept of a volunteer army. Should the British Government decide to introduce compulsory military service they would face determined opposition from the champions of civil rights, no matter what peril the country faced. The sadly mistaken idea still prevailed that a volunteer was worth three conscripted men, but 2,000,000 single men kept well away from the recruiting offices. Although a significant percentage of these were involved in starred trades, a term for wartime production workers, the remainder were dubbed 'slackers'. The Government realising they were stuck between a rock and a hard place, as they were desperate for manpower, sought an amicable solution. At the end of September Lord Kitchener solemnly warned the Government that due to waning voluntarism, conscription was looking inevitable, without it Britain would be defeated. This announcement heralded months of political wrangling in the Houses of Parliament, and appeals for volunteers from the King.

In early October the Secretary for War requested Lord Derby to become responsible for recruitment. Lord Derby was effectively the King of Lancashire, a shrewd, plain speaking, hard working man who had used his considerable talents to raise the volunteer battalions of the Liverpool Pals. Immediately after Derby's appointment radical changes were implemented in the recruiting system. A national door-to-door canvas of non enlisted men of military age was organised, the door-stepped men were invited to volunteer. The initial response was favourable but the results of the campaign soon waned. A new canvas of six weeks' duration was launched; the results were again disappointing. In the final days of the canvas Lord Derby issued a final appeal; as a result 1,070,478 men attested to the colours and their attestation gave considerable encouragement to those in favour of the volunteer system. Unfortunately, a significant portion of the men turned out to be married men, over a million single men were still avoiding military service. Official figures, when allowing for starred or indispensable men, showed there still remained unaccounted for 651,160 single men.

The majority of the nation had now made up their own minds, that if the Derby scheme did not succeed, compulsion for the slackers must come. Opponents to conscription decided – better conscription than Britain losing the war. On 4 January the Prime Minister, Mr. Asquith, introduced in the Commons a bill for compulsory service – this excluded Ireland. All U.K. males and widowers aged between 18-41 years and without dependent children were to be conscripted. Over-zealous medical officers turned a blind eye to the physical conditions of the drafted men, they seemed to concentrate more on quantity than physical quality. The cream of the nation had already passed through the recruitment centres.

Second from left in rear row is Private J. Flowers who was KIA in 1917. Extreme right on front row is Private John Owen Williams. Both men served with the 16th Battalion.

Considering the problems with recruitment in general it is surprising that the 35th Division spent so much time kicking their heels in Blighty, as an explanation to the delay it appears the Bantams were literally detained for his Majesty's pleasure, as King George V had planned to inspect his unique Division of Bantams. The regular military training intensified to a much higher level of proficiency, as the troops would be required to march past the Monarch in review order, this is reputed to be a complicated manoeuvre. The Bantams rose to this new challenge rapidly adapting to the new form of square bashing. Unfortunately, whilst inspecting troops in France, the King fell from his horse and the royal inspection was cancelled. The review still went ahead with General Paget acting as a stand in for the King, this was very disappointing for all concerned as the absence of the monarch simply took away all the importance of the occasion.

On Salisbury Plain the Bantams watched enviously as less trained divisions were hastily despatched to the front line, they began to get the distinct impression their services were not wanted. This was indeed the case as the hide-bound military establishment were indeed reluctant to utilise the midget soldiers, no matter how bereft of manpower they might be. While the centre of gravity of the war may have been the Western Front, there was an abundance of sideshows which all demanded men. In December the 35th (Bantam) Division received orders to prepare to sail for Mesopotamia.

It was a bitterly cold December day when news spread around the camp like wildfire that they were heading for warmer climes to do battle with the Turks. Somehow it seemed most appropriate that the fighting Bantams would be engaged against the forces of Turkey. Full tropical kit was distributed, including incredibly baggy khaki drill shorts. They were so oversized the men clowned about walking two abreast inside one pair of short trousers. To complete the tropical uniform pith helmets were issued and when the Bantams wore them on parade they were said to look like overgrown mushrooms. But within weeks the order was cancelled and the Bantams now found themselves all dressed up with nowhere to go. Once again the Division would have to wait patiently for their day to come.

Meanwhile back at Bebington the 17th (Reserve) Battalion was required to carry out a recruitment march through Birkenhead. On 7 October, under the command of Major Austin, 876 reserve Bantams (two large drafts had previously gone to the parent battalions) assembled and following in the footsteps of the 15th and 16th battalions headed for the Town Hall, where they were inspected by Alfred Bigland. The occasion was one of their last public appearances

At their new camp the 17th Battalion formed part of 17 Reserve Brigade. On 30 November 1915 they celebrated their first anniversary of the formation of the Bantams.

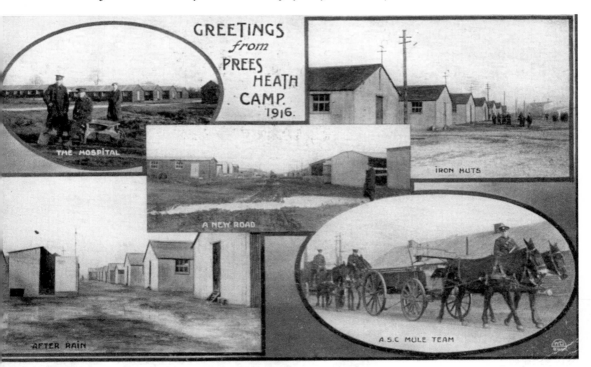

before moving to the recently constructed army camp at Prees Heath, Shropshire. The camp was established for training in trench warfare and ultimately 30,000 men would pass through it.

Amongst the new arrivals at the camp was Private J. Nelson Spencer who was assigned to Z company as an orderly clerk. He found the camp was commanded by officers mostly over six feet tall, the Commanding Officer, Battalion Sergeant Major, and Company Sergeant Majors were all former regulars who adhered rigidly to King's Regulations. It was an environment that suited Spencer who enjoyed military life for within a fortnight he had his Sergeant stripes. Some time later he attended a musketry course graduating as a marksman and musketry instructor, the majority of mornings he took troops to the firing range which entailed a five mile march through the Shropshire countryside. Lasting friendships were established with the civilians around Whitchurch and when the inevitable happened they thronged Whitchurch station waving off the troop train taking Nelson Spencer and his chums to the front, where Spencer joined the 15th Battalion.

The Cheshire Bantams spent Christmas in Blighty, for many of the originals this was to be their second Christmas away from home, and they had still not faced the enemy. One of the officers wrote home:

Christmas day passed off very happily for the men who had games, football and boxing throughout the day, then the usual big dinner at 5 p.m. followed by a good concert. The men seemed very happy and contented and for a time at least forgot they were on active service. The following evening the Officers had their turn and it fell to my happy lot to toast 'Absent friends'.

Unidentified Bantams at Prees Heath Camp in the winter of 1915.

74

Chapter Six

1916 – The Killing Fields Beckon

ONE OF THE FIRST TASKS of the New Year for the Bantams was to exchange the tropical kit for khaki standard issue; they were now destined for the Western Front. Lieutenant Colonel Harrison Johnson noted in his memoirs,

Paraded with everybody in full kit with all our Christmas tree decorations on. As we officers are only allowed to take one valise weighing thirty-five pounds, we all took as much as possible on our persons, luckily being mounted, my pack was on my horse. The men's total load including packs, uniform, two blankets, one inside the pack and the other protected by a waterproof sheet fastened outside the pack, a rifle, and one hundred and twenty rounds of ammunition each, averaged seventy pounds (5 stone). The men's weight stripped averaged one hundred and twenty pounds (8.5 stone).

While the loads seemed excessive the Bantams carried the same load in kit as other units, but on people of such short stature they gave the appearance of walking luggage racks.

> Oh clear the way, now clear the way
> We're on the line of march
> With rifles on our shoulders boys,
> Gay Bantams stiff as starch.
> We're off to the front boys,
> With hearts that are British made.
> So clear the way, now clear the way,
> For the Bantam 'Light Brigade'.
>
> Though not very tall we're not too small
> To make things hum to follow the drum.
> At the bugles call.
> So we're off to the front to try what we can do
> And we're all game, game, game.
> Cock-a-doodle do.
>
> Oh clear the way, now clear the way,
> And let the Bantams pass.
> Though small we are, our hearts are big.
> You'll find that we are class
> And when we go to meet the foe.

Their sausages we'll raid.
So clear the way, now clear the way
For the Bantam Light Brigade.

Oh clear the way, now clear the way.
We're off to Germany.
A warm place in the sun we'll give
The Kaiser, with rent free.
We'll make him straighten his moustache.
So when you hear the news.
Its 'Eyes front' 'Steady' 'Salute'
The cock-a-doodle doo.

For gootness sake H
der Bantams
are komi

The 17th Battalion, Lancashire Fusiliers, were the first unit of the 35th Division to leave for France. The following day, 29 January, the 15th Battalion departed by train from Tidworth to the port of Southampton where, after a ninety minute wait in dockside sheds, the majority of the battalion boarded the small but speedy HMS *Caesaera*. A dozen men from X Company remained behind under the command of Second Lieutenant McArthur to load up the steamers which were to carry W Company and the battalion's assorted transport. The 16th Battalion followed the next day and by the end of the month the complete Division had arrived safely upon the continental shore. Most of the Division crossed the Channel between Southampton and Le Havre, with the exception of the 15th Battalion, Sherwood Foresters, 23rd Battalion, Manchester Regiment and the 18th Battalion, Highland Light Infantry, which landed at Boulogne.

The strength of the 16th Battalion stood at thirty-four officers and 984 other ranks. The Commanding Officer was Lieutenant Colonel R. Browne-Clayton; Second-in-Command Major Worthington; Adjutant Captain C. Johnson; Quartermaster Hon. Lieutenant H. Halsall; Transport Officer Lieutenant T. Hare; Signalling Officer Lieutenant A.C. Styles; Company Commander's Captain S. C. Bacon; Major J. C. Bowe; Captain G. Playfer; Captain C. Sturla. Second-in-Command of companies were Captain E.F. Thurgood; Captain H.H. Hurst; Captain D. Burnett; Lieutenant H.D. Ryalls. Other officers were Lieutenants S.G. Hewitt; W.R. Batty; J.D. Hodgson; J.R. Dovener; R.F. Lawrenson; G.G. Earl. The second lieutenants were P.H. Jones; H. Halsall; S.G. Bowe; L. Millington; W.H. Findlay; J.B. Mennie; W. Wallace; R.P. Scholefield; R.D. Eccleston. The medical officer was Lieutenant F.N.

Stewart of the Royal Army Medical Corps.

Early on a beautiful evening the channel steamer *Caesarea* left harbour and set off across the channel which was as still as a mill pond. As she turned her bows towards the continent, a throng of Bantams congregated on the vessel's stern and pensively gazed at the sight of old England disappearing from view. As the harbour lights twinkled in the distance the leaving of England failed to dampen the volunteers' high spirits. But nonetheless there was a feeling of foreboding amongst the more thoughtful ones. However, even the most pessimistic of those assembled could not have imagined the destiny which awaited them.

Shortly before midnight the steamer berthed alongside the dock at Le Havre, her cargo of Bantams remained onboard overnight. Very early next morning the vessel's decks were alive with Bantams

An unidentified Cheshire Bantam.

hurriedly preparing to disembark. There had been no opportunity for breakfast and the Cheshires, attired in full marching order, were kept standing on the steamer's deck for two hours. Among the ranks, whenever the prowling NCOs were out of earshot, ribald comments were muttered and passed on through clenched teeth. The remainder of the battalion arrived and at 7-30 a.m. the Bantams gleefully passed down the gangplanks and smartly formed into ranks of four along the dockside. They found themselves facing a dockside hospital, outside of which were row upon row of head wounded men recumbent upon stretchers. A sobering reminder to the Bantams of the grim reality of war.

Upon the order 'quick march!' the Bantams set off through the the port of Le Havre towards Top of the Hill Camp. The French civilians gazed in amazement at these pint-sized troops, who were they, and had the mighty British Empire so early in the war been reduced to using these 'Piccaninni soldats' (small soldiers)? Surely these smartly turned out men would be no match for the army of the Kaiser? The troops marched proudly on through the roads lined with curious onlookers until they reached the imaginatively named 'rest camp' a few miles outside of town. The transit camp was sited upon the top of a steep hill and consisted of an inadequate number of assorted bell tents; a dozen men were allocated to each of the canvas shelters, while the company commanders occupied a tent each.

The Bantams had yearned for the opportunity to fight in France so imagine their disappointment when, so soon after arriving, three men from the 15th Battalion were declared as unfit for duty by the medic. For while attempting to prevent a cycle from falling Corporal Green of W company managed to break his arm. Lance Corporal Kelly and Lance Corporal Shea, both of X Company, also attended hospital. The former had developed pleurisy, the other a bad suppurating cyst in the neck.

On the last day of January the 15th Battalion entrained at Le Havre, the officers travelled in the 2nd and 3rd Class carriages while thirty-four men with full kit were crammed into each cattle truck, whose floor was carpeted in horse manure left behind by the wagon's previous occupants. Arriving at Blendecques the other ranks were more than pleased to disembark from their stinking trucks. Then they were faced with a twelve mile evening march through a moon-lit and frosty countryside. They arrived at Wallon Cappell at about 9 p.m. where a brief reorganisation of the various battalion components took place after having become mixed up during the Channel

An unidentified Cheshire Bantam.

crossing. This was an uneventful period until Saturday 5 February when a 15th Cheshire's sentry from Z Company fired his first shot in anger, following which he became the butt of many a joke. Upon hearing a noise in the still of the night the sentry had called out the appropriate challenge. As there was no response the sentry fired at the impending threat. His victim turned out to be a wandering mule which sustained a wound in the leg.

The recently arrived Division was scattered across the French countryside and had to begin to regroup. This concentration was completed by 5 February, and then training began in earnest. The 35th Division was now temporarily attached to XI Corps under the command of General Sir R. Haking. Within a week all of the units advanced towards the front line. 104 Brigade located to Wardrecques, replacing 106 Brigade which moved to Boeseghem. 105 Brigade containing the two Cheshire battalions relocated to Mollingham, near Aire.

A primary source of archival information concerning the 15th Cheshires is the book *Extracts from an Officer's Diary* by Lieutenant Colonel Harrison-Johnston D.S.O., published privately soon after the war. This account commences upon the battalion's arrival in France and gives an illuminating insight into the experiences of both men and officers of the battalion during its service overseas. Originally the Company Commander of X Company, Harrison-Johnston was unimpressed with the new surroundings at Mollingham. He refers to the abysmal countryside surrounding their new base, as 'very damp and intersected with a series of canals, ditches and waterways of stagnant water, a foul smell pervaded the entire area'. Fearing an outbreak of disease he had the entire camp treated with chloride of lime.

On 11 February the Division paraded near Aire for an inspection by Lord Kitchener and the G.O.C. of XI Corps. Despite the torrential rain the parade went ahead. A fair proportion of the infantry arrived far too early for the parade and stood in the wet and cold for over an hour before the hero of Khartoum arrived. While inspecting the ranks it is reputed that Kitchener remarked to a battalion commander 'They look very young, do you think they will be alright?' To this the Colonel replied with an emphatic 'Yes Sir'. Rumour had it that Kitchener had actually remarked, 'I don't know what the Germans will make of them but by God they frighten me'. The great man expressed his pleasure at the appearance and smart turn out of the Bantams.

In mid February the 35th Division became the G.H.Q. reserve; this required the Division to move nearer the front line. As a result on 21 February the 15th Battalion had completed two days of route marching and were in new billets at Locon, north of Bethune. The weather now took a decided turn for the worse, as the temperature plummeted to below freezing. Fur jackets were issued making the small soldiers look like teddy bears. The stagnant ditches were now covered in a thick sheet of ice capable of bearing the weight of a man.

The elements contributed to an unforeseen problem; the Cheshires' boots appeared to have been crafted from superb leather however a fault in the tanning process led to the boots falling apart while in use. Tallow candles were issued to the men to rub on their feet as some form of protection while wearing the leaky footwear, until new boots arrived. The remainder of the month passed relatively quietly, each evening two groups consisting each of a sergeant and eight men marched several miles to a designated position from where they launched patrols of two hours' duration.

The first recorded casualty to the 35th Division happened on 20 February when Private Caxton of the 17th Battalion, West Yorkshire Regiment, was killed in the trenches in the Neuve Chapelle region. His death was swiftly followed by five wounded to the 17th Battalion, Lancashire Fusiliers who acquitted themselves very favourably during a skirmish on their battalion front. As the first casualty telegram was despatched to the next of kin of Private Caxton, Bantam battalions throughout the Division began to compile listings of the dead and maimed. The haunting spectre of death gradually quashed the preconceived images of the great adventure.

At 6 a.m. on 27 February, reveille sounded for the 15th Cheshires and preparations for a move to Gore were carried out. Heavy snow was falling as the battalion struck camp at 10 a.m. By midday they were within half a mile of their destination when an explosion erupted within 200 yards of X Company. Fearing an attack by artillery or aircraft the men were hurriedly formed into platoons spaced at fifty yard intervals. It then transpired the bomb had been hurled from a trench catapult in an adjoining field where a bombing school was practising. The battalion marched to a huge château where 105 Brigade was held in reserve under orders of the 38th Division, while the remaining infantry of the 35th Division was attached to units for front line training. The battalion was now attached to 113 Brigade for instructions in the trenches at Givenchy with the Royal Welsh Fusiliers. The four companies were each attached to the 13th, 14th, 15th and 16th Battalions.

A Fusilier officer warily led the elements of the battalion along a muddy canal bank, each section set off maintaining a fifty yard distance from each other as the sector was under shell fire. Upon reaching a bridge they were met by another officer and four guides who led the Cheshires to their experienced instructors in the art of survival in the trenches. All of their training in the military establishments at home could not have prepared the men for the condition of the trenches, for the wooden duckboards within the mud lined trench were fixed to piles driven into the trench floor, but were still a foot below the water's surface. The short-legged Bantams found they were almost up to their knees in the putrid water, they were advised to tread carefully for if anyone came off the submerged duck board they plunged into three feet of vile water. The general conditions within these dank trenches were appalling. Company headquarters was established in an officer's dug out. To enter this smelly hole in the earth required crawling on all fours through a tunnel with a glutinous mud floor. No sooner had the Cheshires taken up residence than a trench mortar exploded outside the makeshift door; its blast buried alive three of the officers' batmen. Men raced to the scene of carnage, digging with whatever was to hand in a frantic effort to rescue their buried comrades. Their prompt actions recovered the shaken but still alive soldiers. Later that day during the regular interchange of small arms fire a stray bullet snuffed out the life of the first of the battalion's short soldiers.

The 15th Cheshires' battalion war diary entry contains the stark entry:

> *Gore. 28/2/16. Trenches. 1 man killed. 1 man wounded.*

The *Birkenhead News* expanded on the demise of the Bantam, although there is a discrepancy in the date.

> *On the 27th February Private Weightman became the first of the little men to be killed in action. Previous to enlisting he had resided with his mother and two younger sisters at 24, Whittier Street, off Smithdown Road, Liverpool.*

Lieutenant Colonel Newell wrote:

> *You might let Mr. Bigland or Mr. Cecil Holden[1] know that*
> *Private Weightman of Liverpool was the first Bantam to die*
> *for his country. We buried him in a little British cemetery*
> *quite close to the firing line, and we put up a cross with his*
> *name and regiment on and a Cheshire cap badge on the top.[2]*

Although the Bantams were far from home the population of Birkenhead were naturally still interested in the welfare of their Bantams. There were frequent appeals in the local press for items of the most mundane nature. Everyday articles that would normally be taken for granted became scarce commodities in the killing fields of France and Flanders. In order to alleviate the situation Mrs. Bigland and Mrs. Fred Newell opened the Bantams' Comfort Fund on 14 February 1916, Mrs. Bigland was President in charge of the sewing room, and Mrs Newell, vice president, treasurer and secretary. With the help of about twenty willing workers, two or more sacks of comforts were sent out each week. The work was generously supported by subscription from friends of the officers and workers.

While the 35th Division had been in training on Salisbury Plain they drew the attention of a wounded Canadian officer Major Frank Lindsay Burton. When rumours began of Canada's intention to raise a battalion of Bantams, Burton offered his services in the raising of such a unit and proposed himself as commander of the battalion. A fortnight later in mid February 1916 the Ministry of Militia authorised the raising of the 216th Overseas Battalion to be commanded by the recently promoted Lieutenant Colonel (Temporary) Burton. Shortly afterwards the title (Bantams) was included in the unit's name. The majority of volunteers were either Canadian or British immigrants; amongst their number was Billy Butlin who survived the war, settled in England and later established the legendary holiday centres.

As Canada had already provided legions of men for the Empire's fight against tyranny the availability of suitable recruits was limited. Eventually the unit came up to strength and received orders for departure overseas. The 216th Battalion arrived in Britain on 28 April 1917 and were almost immediately broken up and dispersed to artillery units, railway construction and labour units. The potential of Bantam Butlin was soon recognised by his appointment to lance corporal (unpaid). Unfortunately, a visit to his very hospitable mother's relations in the West Country led to Butlin overstaying his leave. On his return his CO reduced him to a private, as he considered Billy Butlin was unsuitable for a position of authority. While undergoing training at Sandgate camp, near Folkestone Private Butlin had a near brush with death. While learning how to deal with German hand grenades a detonator ignited in his face, temporarily blinding him; he spent an anxious week in hospital. After his recovery he was posted to France in a reinforcement draft to the dismounted 3rd Canadian Mounted Rifles.

Another dispersed unit were the 143rd British Columbia Overseas battalion (Bantams), after completing a journey of 6,000 miles they reached Blighty on 17 February 1917. As the war progressed and casualties began to mount the third draft of Canadian battalions were broken up on arrival in England. The 143rd Regiment were no exception. A large amount of the men were transferred to the 47th Overseas Regiment, while others joined the 2nd Canadian Mounted Rifles and the 3rd Battalion Canadian Railway Troops; the latter was a move to capitalise on the Canadians' skill and technical ability to construct railroads.

Trench warfare
During the first week of March, the three Bantam infantry brigades began to take over their sector in a quiet section of the front. The 35th Division took over a sector of the line from the 19th Division, although 105 Brigade who had been in Reserve was still undergoing instruction in the trenches of the 38th Division. The 15th Cheshires were in the trenches at Gore; on Thursday 2 March the opposing artillery heavily strafed each other's lines. During the onslaught there were cries of 'Stop it now Tommy' emanating from the Hun lines. Prior to the outbreak of war Britain's large cities provided employment for Germanic immigrants who rapidly learnt the English language; these workers had, prior to the outbreak of war, returned to the motherland. Whenever the lines were in close proximity it was not unusual for such an interchange to occur. Somehow or other the Germans always knew who was facing them. All too often the arrival of Bantams in the line was greeted by a chorus of crowing from across No Man's Land. The storm of steel continued, shells were bursting throughout the Cheshires' frontage sending searing hot fragments of jagged steel in all

directions claiming the lives of three of 15th Battalion and wounding another.

The weather now added to the misery of the trench occupants; during the first Saturday in March the normal morning sounds were muffled, for a thick blanket of snow coated the grim trenches, and snow was steadily falling. The snow compounded the misery throughout the line for the Bantams. Within the trenches they were frequently standing in areas where the now bitterly cold water sloshed about above their knees. The battalion left the trenches on the 8th for billets in the vicinity of Calonne; they now spent a week slithering around in the muddy fields removing redundant barbed wire entanglements.

On 11 March 1916 the entire division was paraded for inspection, despite it raining in sheets all day. The whole division just stood there drenched waiting for Lord Kitchener who arrived several hours later than expected. After the inspection the saturated battalions returned to billets before spending the evening hauling ammunition and supplies through the freezing rain and snow.

Eight days later they left their billets at Cornet Malo and set off for Epinette near Lestrum. They remained in their new billets until the 25th when the Division side-slipped to the north-east. In the final week of March they moved to Laventie where 105 Brigade relieved 23 Brigade, 8th Division. Here the following directive was continually repeated in the movement orders. 'Two sandbags per man for filling and placing on the fire step will be provided as parapets are not to be lowered.' This came about as the Bantams had a tendency to adapt the trench system to a height more favourable to their short stature. When average height troops took over the position they discovered the amended cover resulted in their head and shoulders appearing above the safety of the parapet making them an ideal target for an alert sniper. After three days in the mud-filled trenches they were relieved on the penultimate day in March 1916, by the 14th Battalion Gloucestershires. During the change-over the Cheshires handed over their steel helmets to the incoming Gloucesters. Steel helmets had been introduced the previous October, but were only issued to men in the trenches. By June every man within fifteen miles of the front had his own helmet resulting in a reduction in shrapnel wounds to the head.

The 16th battalion followed a similar pattern of moves as their brother battalion. On 7 March they marched from Robecq to Gorre for attachment to the 114 Brigade, 38th Division for instruction in trench warfare; companies were attached respectively to 10th, 13th, 15th, and 16th Welsh Regiment. The Bantams remained for eight days in reserve under the care of the old sweats of the Welsh regiment. Despite all the endeavours of the Welsh regiment to care for their new charges events took a turn for the worse when a mine explosion killed Private G.E.

Milne and wounded two others. The following day a rifle grenade exploded within the trench killing Privates J. Marsh and J. McCue; six more of the 2nd Birkenheads were wounded. The next twenty-four hours proved to be the unlucky 13 March as Corporal Adams of Z Company was killed and four men were wounded all as a result of rifle grenades. Private C. Reeder was mortally wounded and died of wounds several days later. In mid March the 16th battalion were released from the trenches and proceeded to rest billets at Calonne, moving on to billets at Pacaut and Estaires. On the twenty- sixth day of March they marched to Laventie where they relieved the 2nd West York's Brigade Reserve. Four days later under cover of darkness they filed into the line and relieved the Bantams of the 15th Sherwood Foresters, the following day Private Eastwood was killed and three men were wounded. Quietly and steadily the plucky little Bantams were being whittled down.

Over thirty officers and men from the 35th Division were killed in approximately two months on the Western Front before the Bantams officially engaged the enemy.

On April Fools' day we find the 15th Battalion in billets in reserve, at Laventie east. The trench systems required constant maintenance, whenever possible troops in reserve or worse still on a few days' rest were appropriated for this work and the Cheshire Bantams, like so many other battalions, would be called upon time after time.

Within the first few days of April Z Company of the Cheshires supplied a fifty strong working party to the 204th Field Company Royal Engineers (F.C.R.E.). The remaining force stood to during and after shelling of the enemy trenches, they rivetted the sides of trenches, built new fire steps, repaired others, and added sandbags to the parapet. At Dead End heavy enemy shelling interrupted their backbreaking labour work, but they still toiled on, cleaning billets and draining water from flooded trenches. On the evening of the 4th the 15th Battalion completed the relief of their fellow Bantams the 14th Gloucestershires.

The night in the trench at Laventie proved to be fairly hectic, two patrols were sent out to examine our parapet; upon their safe return, the Lewis gunners using hyperscope attachments permitting the weapon to be fired above the parapet without its crew showing themselves brought enfilade fire on Wick salient and a suspected enemy sniper's post. The following day there was artillery activity on both sides, our Lewis gunners did good work on an enemy loop hole, and a suspected sniper post was blasted with rifle grenades, this act may have been due to the death of 23089 Private J. Smith who was killed when a sniper shot him through the head. The shortage of sandbags on the parapet prompted frenetic activity as the height of the parapet was increased. If this was required for Bantam size troops it's

Don't be Alarmed,
the Cheshires are on guard

difficult to understand how other taller battalions managed. In close proximity was a mine excavation the spoil of which needed dispersing. From this source the Bantams filled 300 sandbags, before carrying them back to reinforce their position. Later a patrol was sent out to examine the enemy wire, over three hours later they returned reporting the enemy wire consisted of four distinct lines extending to sixty yards from the Hun parapet. On the 7th there were two slight injuries, one man sustained an accidental wound when a rifle grenade blew back, while another had a bullet wound in the thigh, one of those involved was 20003 Lance Corporal Holmes.

On 8 April several Bantams were at the bombing school, learning the effective use of the Mills bomb, which was a hand launched fragmentation bomb (better known as the hand grenade). Instruction was being given in a trench occupied by two officers, a private and Acting Company Sergeant Major W. Shooter. The unnamed private pulled the safety pin from a Mills bomb and accidently dropped it in the trench and then ran off without warning his companions. A couple of seconds later Sergeant Major Shooter spotted the bomb and picking it up, flung it out of the trench. The bomb exploded in mid air, wounding Shooter in the thigh. His heroic action undoubtedly saved the two officers from serious or fatal injuries. In recognition of his gallantry W. Shooter was later awarded the Albert Medal for lifesaving.[3] Prior to enlisting on 30 November 1914 he was a foreman stoker with the Bradford Dyers Association at Brighouse, Yorkshire. A year later he was again in the newspapers when it was reported,

The sergeant was again seriously wounded, and has now been in hospital for seventeen months. In the advance at St. Quentin a high explosive burst, in its descent it took away the bottom part of Shooter's jaw. So clean did the explosive do its work that it carried away all his teeth, one being split clean in two. Shooter is regarded as one of the miracles of medical science, for the hospital is rebuilding his jaw with marvellous success.

He was discharged from the army 26 November 1918.

Later that evening the battalion were relieved in the front line by the 14th Battalion Gloucesters. For the next few days working parties were supplied to the 204th F.C.R.E. and one platoon to the Divisional pioneers. W Company supplied a seventy-strong working party to carry coal at the Corps Coal Dump at Bac St. Arur. By now it must have seemed that the intention was to work the Bantams to death! Perhaps the experience had proved too much for 19599 CQMS J.M. Jones who was charged with drunkenness when on active service. The verdict of a Field General Courts Martial convened in mid April, saw him reduced to the ranks.[4]

Orders were now received for the Division to move southwards to the Ferme du Bois and Neuve Chapelle sectors. The 15th Cheshires were in rest billets at Sailly where they received orders for the relief of trenches on the left of the Ferme du Bois section. Although they had spent the majority of a wet rainy day working in the trenches, at 8 p.m. they left town and set off along a road ankle deep in slush, singing at the top of their voices the latest song, 'Pack Up Your Troubles'. After completing the late night relief of the 9th Battalion Royal Welsh Fusiliers, the following day proved to be routine with tit for tat activity by both sides. As darkness fell the enemy sprayed the Bantam parapet with machine-gun bullets. Fortunately, there were no patrols out in No Man's Land, as a bright moon prevented any patrol activity. The day's wounded consisted of 20066 Private Nethersole, 20108 Private Kidman and 19176 Private Miller hit by shrapnel from an enfilading German gun. Rifle bullets wounded 19513 Private Miller and Private Jackson. On 23 April the 15th Battalion was relieved by the 16th Battalion Cheshires. Once again while in billets the men were called on for ration carrying parties. They laboured away in the Richebourg St. Vaast sector for several days. There is no indication of what caused their injuries, but on their final afternoon whilst still in reserve 23008 CSM Legge, and 19725 Private Swain became casualties. That evening, 27 April, the 15th Battalion relieved the 16th Battalion Cheshires in the left sub section of the line.

The exchange of troops in the line was a lengthy procedure that had to be completed with the minimal amount of disturbance, to avoid alerting the enemy that a change over was taking place. In reality scores of soldiers trudged through crowded trenches, struggling to get past the outgoing troops; here and there their equipment snagging on the trench

Neuve Chapelle after the fighting had passed on.

sides, or a misplaced boot slipped off a duckboard, followed by a stream of profanities under stifled breath.

The 28 April was a beautiful warm day, the 15th Battalion, now in the line at Ferme du Bois, found themselves in a highly contested section sector. Despite all the lead flying around, at 12.15 a.m. a wiring party commenced repairing the British wire on the centre company's front, and another party built up the parapet. After midnight an intelligence gathering patrol was sent out into No Man's Land, they reported the enemy wire was in good condition and extended outwards from their parapet thirty yards; the wire stood three feet high and posed an impenetrable obstacle to any likely assault.

During the next couple of days in April both sides routinely strafed each other's front lines; assorted whiz-bangs, shrapnel and light high explosives spasmodically rained down on the Bantam positions. A troublesome machine gun continued to traverse the front parapet restricting movement so much that the only way officers and men could get from the position known as Pall Mall to the front line was to crawl on the duckboards to avoid being hit. Unfortunately, enemy action claimed the life of another Bantam, 22118 Private Thomas, also Privates 29660 Cotterel and 23128 G. Murphy were reported as being wounded.

Returning to April Fools' day we find the members of the 16th

Battalion in the line at Laventie. The following evening British trench artillery, trench mortars and grenades roared into life, accompanied by the rattle of machine guns firing at breaches in the Hun parapet. The enemy replied with machine-gun fire along our parapet and put up a barrage of artillery along our reserve line. A couple of days later they were relieved and moved to reserve billets at Laventie. They returned to the line on the evening of the 8th. Two days later a minor operation resulted in the loss of 21672 Private Hallsworth and 21672 Private Marsh who were interred at Royal Irish Rifles cemetery, another man was wounded. After being relieved by the 17th Battalion Royal Scots the battalion moved to Sailly in Divisional Reserve. Although they were technically out of the firing line only positions well behind the lines were considered to be safe from the average German artillery piece. A fact demonstrated on 16 April when the scream of incoming artillery shells prompted the inhabitants of the camp to take cover. Explosions erupted

If der 15th Cheshires
haf gone by, den I kan kom out.

all around; during the bombardment the members of Z Company had a lucky escape when their billet was hit by a shell, but there were no casualties. They later relieved the 9th Battalion Cheshires in reserve near Richebourg St. Vaast, remaining there for four days prior to relieving their fellow Birkenhead battalion. The month had almost passed with little consequence for the battalion with only a few men wounded, unfortunately their luck evaporated on 25 April when 29641 Private Duckworth was killed and another man wounded.

Opposing sides tirelessly strafed each other; on 27 April a retaliatory German bombardment on the Boars Head held by W Company of the 16th Cheshires resulted in the deaths of 21445 Corporal Tull, and two Birkonians; twenty-two year old 20525 Private Asher and 21845 Lance Corporal Hickman. Seventeen men were wounded including 15/19798 Private Dacy, and 21821 Private Malpas, who died of wounds at Number 7 Casualty Clearing Station. Later that day the battalion was relieved by the 15th Cheshires amid tremendous machine-gun and rifle fire. The last two days in April the 16th Battalion was in Brigade Reserve at Richebourg St. Vaast.

In a letter of condolence to Lance Corporal Hickman's widow CQMS F. Smith wrote:

The Germans were bombarding a part of our trenches on our right, and Bantam Hickman heard someone calling for help, and he ran to them. He rendered aid to eight men who had been hit. He carried one man out of the trenches, and was coming out with another when a shell burst above them, killing Hickman and a stretcher bearer, and wounding three others, one of whom passed away this morning.

On May Day the 15th Battalion was still in the front line at Ferme du Bois, keeping their heads down as our artillery shells flew overhead targeting the German front line and supports. The enemy artillery reply was swift and deadly, sporadic shelling continued throughout the day; at 12-35 p.m. two high explosive shells erupted close by, several shells also burst in the immediate vicinity of Bute Street. At 8-15 p.m. while the 15th Battalion was at stand-to three shrapnel shells burst simultaneously over the Strand killing and wounding the Cheshire defenders. As the day grew older the shelling sporadically continued; at 1300 hours a dozen high explosive shells rained down on the Rue de Bois, fortunately four of these were duds. The 35th Division replied to these bombardments by launching a series of night raids.

Late on the night of 2 May the 15th Battalion was relieved by the 16th Cheshires, amid the turmoil of the relief 20310 Private Jeffries and 29517 Private Jones were both wounded.

Despite all that was going on around them military discipline was constantly being asserted, for example a Field General Court Martial was convened when a Private of the 15th Battalion Sherwood Foresters was disciplined for being improperly dressed a distance away from barracks. A couple of days later a Cheshire Bantam faced a Field General Courts Martial, 19251 Private Hughes was sentenced to two years' imprisonment with hard labour; for the offence of absenting himself without leave knowing his battalion was due to go in the trenches. Early in June a twenty year old Edinburgh volunteer faced a court martial charged with desertion. During his trial Private James Archibald from the 17th Battalion Royal Scots was scathingly referred to as a 'typical slum product of poor intellect but a soldier of good character'. Although his life depended on a 'not guilty' verdict the young man was denied additional representation and defended himself with tragic consequences. The verdict was 'guilty' and the volunteer became the first 35th Division Bantam to face the

Lance Corporal Hickman. Although Joseph Hickman was over the military age limit his inherent sense of duty to his Country left him unable to resist the call for men. He enlisted in February 1915 and left behind his wife and four children. Arriving in France almost twelve months to the day he enlisted.

firing squad. The execution took place at dawn, 4 June 1916. He is buried in Beuvry Communal Cemetery Extension

The 15th Battalion moved from Richebourg St. Vaast to Croix-Marmuse where the rankers were billeted in two farms, spending the night on a barn floor lined with a thick layer of bean husks. This was an uneventful period spent in the now routine tasks of wiring parties and working parties. The monotony was broken by an inspection by the new commander of 105 Brigade Brigadier General A.H. Marindin, formerly of the Black Watch. He would remain in command of 105 Brigade until March 1918, when he was appointed as Divisional commander.

On Sunday 14 May, 1916, 105 Brigade relieved 104 Brigade in the Neuve Chapelle sector, the 15th Cheshires relieved the 17th Battalion Lancashire Fusiliers as Brigade Reserve Battalion, taking over billets at Croix Barbee, and garrisoning posts held by the 17th Lancashires. The following day two tactical working parties commenced a few days' work under the command of Royal Engineers officers, this work was not without danger. On 15 May the records reveal it was a soaking wet day as three platoons of X Company carried out work for the Royal Engineers at Euston R.E. Dump. Private Nicholas 19279 the company signaller who was described as a red headed ruffian was wounded by a rifle bullet through the neck.

The 15th Cheshires relieved the 16th Cheshires in the Neuve Chapelle sub section of trenches on the night of 18 May. Both sides knew when the exchange of sentries took place and would time their

War Diary for 1 May 1916 showing casualties to the 15th Battalion.

are contained in F. S. Regs., Part II.
aff Manual respectively.   Title Pages
pared in manuscript.

INTELLIGENCE SUMMARY

(Erase heading not required.)   15th (1) Bn T

Date	Hour	Summary of Events and Information
May		The following casualties occurred on the 1st May
		Killed
		No 19608 Pte TAYLOR J.W. 'Y' Coy
		" 19253 " HARGREAVES G.W "X" Coy
		Wounded
		" 19223 " HUNTER W.W.
		" 22121 Corpl WRIGHT J. } 'Y' Coy
		" 19253 Pte COOK W.C. "X" "
		" 19364 " RALPH J. "X" "
		" 19420 " ROSS J. "X" "
		" 19257 " SIRRS W. 'X' "
		" 19443 . MELLOY P. 'X' . (slightly still at du

strafes to coincide with the nocturnal activities. During this particular relief 19877 Sergeant Lowther of Z Company was shot through the head and killed while coming up through the communication trench. If the men of the 15th Battalion thought they were in for a torrid time, the unsuspecting 16th Cheshires marched into the camp at Croix Barbee to be continually shelled by accurate German artillery. Throughout the 15th Battalion's first night back in the line enemy machine guns were very active. At 2-50 a.m. the 17th Battalion Royal Welsh Fusiliers on the Cheshires' left commenced a short period of continuous rifle fire. The enemy retaliated by sweeping the Bantams parapet with machine-gun bullets. The Lewis gunners fired continually throughout the bright moonlit night on the enemy parapet and wire. Meanwhile a considerable amount of work was carried out improving snipers' loopholes, clearing machine gun dugouts and strengthening emplacements.

At dawn a heavy mist rose, before giving way to a day of brilliant sunshine. The officers took stock of the situation finding the condition of the breastworks generally good but required raising in some places, especially as German snipers were active. The barbed wire in front of this section was in poor condition urgently requiring attention. That night patrols and working parties entered No Man's Land to reinforce the wire entanglements. Enemy working parties had extensively reinforced their frontage, large amounts of new loose wire was laying about and the land was divided by ditches, making patrolling difficult; a successful advance in this section would prove to be near impossible. The recently erected Hun wire was described as looking like a blue haze, or a bank of bluebells.

Meanwhile work continued in the Bantam trenches forming a formidable defence, a short trench was now excavated connecting Highland Trench with the excellent water supply behind battalion headquarters. A reinforcement draft of seventy-two men arrived from the Cyclist and Pioneer battalions as replacements for battle casualties. These men were not Bantam size troops, who were proving increasingly difficult to replace. This draft signalled the beginning of the end for the unique concept of Bantam battalions.

A war diary entry for that day 20 May states,

The men of the battalion continue to display the fine qualities previously noted. Their keenness, attention to duty and good working in the trenches giving the utmost satisfaction to the officers, by proving that our confidence in these men, from the formation of the unit was not misplaced. The mutual confidence and affection of officers and men of the unit, compares very favourably with any troops whom we have yet come in contact with, during training and in France.

During the small hours of 21 May a five strong intelligence gathering patrol set off to examine at close quarters the German wire, two of the men were left mid-way as markers to guide their comrades back. The wire was reported in good condition, the main wire consisting of two concertinas three foot high and fifteen foot of low wire fixed on square wooded frames and the whole firmly picketed down. The patrol discovered that the enemy trenches were heavily manned. Sentries in pairs were positioned at twenty yard intervals. A considerable amount of noise and movement was emanating from the enemy trenches, indicating a relief was taking place.

Having accomplished their task the three Bantams attempted to locate the two men acting as markers, who would steer them back to their own lines. But as the three men had been gone a considerable time both markers had assumed the worst and gone back to the relative safety of their own lines. Consequently, Sergeant Britten, Corporal Tunstall and Private Urmston from X Company found themselves disorientated and unable to find their leaving point. As they drew close to a different part of the line Mills bombs were thrown from a British sap, wounding Sergeant Britten and Private Urmston. The latter took refuge until the bombing ceased, and then crawled away, returning to his own company frontage. The NCOs entered their lines and stretcher bearers carried away Sergeant Britten while Corporal Tunstall immediately organised a search party to find Private Urmston. An X Company officer, Captain Wolstenholme, also took out a search party to find the missing man. Unknown to the searchers Private Urmston had become entangled in our wire and had called out for help. Private R.H. Hughes climbed over the parapet successfully rescuing the trapped man. Both search parties were then recalled by a pre-arranged signal. Corporal Tunstall's good conduct was considered to be worthy of recognition and was reported; within a week he was made Lance Sergeant. The gallant 19251 Private Hughes had a two year sentence including hard labour hanging over his head (for absenting himself without leave, knowing his battalion was to go in the line) and it was hoped some of his sentence would be reduced in consequence of him going over the top to rescue his comrade.

Wiring parties were also active during the night; two additional Bantams were wounded, 29651 Private Sharkey and 19787 Private Berry, the latter's injuries were caused by a Very light. During their stint in the line the wiring parties had made good progress, one company erecting a double apron and fence for a continuous 105 yards in front of the existing wire on their company frontage. A trench behind Battalion H.Q. had been completed and also a new bomb store.

The weather near Neuve Chapelle on 22 May continued to be fine and warm, providing ideal conditions for each side to have an artillery duel. The shooting of Allied artillery was very accurate causing considerable damage. The enemy artillery's retaliation was swift, heavy and prolonged. The 15th Cheshires were unscathed, they were relieved during the night by the 16th Cheshires. The battalion carried out the usual working parties for the next five days, they returned to the Neuve Chapelle trenches late on 27 May.

Shortly before midnight on 29 May a trench raiding and covering party cautiously passed through the wire defences and crept out for a raid on the enemy frontage facing The Neb, and directly in front of Bois du Biez. They successfully crossed the drainage ditch in front of the wire by means of an eight-foot long duck board brought especially for the purpose, then lay out in the wastes of the neutral territory silently observing our Artillery shelling the distant front line. At midnight the parties advanced into the unknown, the leading group reached the intersection of two ditches. Meanwhile the covering party extended its flanks and in doing so encountered a covering party for an enemy working party. The enemy had become stranded in No Man's Land by our artillery bombardment and had taken shelter in a convenient ditch. The first the Bantams knew of their presence was a rustling noise coming from their right frontage, immediately followed by four grenades exploding around them. The Bantams scattered, then hurriedly reorganised themselves and bombed the enemy, wiping them out.

The CHESHIRES are "holding their own."

They continued on their mission crossing another drainage ditch, an earlier patrol had reported this ditch as impassable so they brought along the board which proved to be too short and some of the party had a ducking in the stagnant water. Upon reaching the far bank of the ditch the raiding party encountered another German patrol which they attacked and drove off. They were within thirty-five yards of his wire. Approximately twenty minutes after midnight the covering artillery fire ceased as arranged. They were unaware the progress of the raid had been delayed. Consequently the halt in the shelling allowed the enemy sentries a chance to check their frontages and at once they spotted the Bantam patrol. Immediately they reacted, unleashing a bombardment in the vicinity of the attackers. The Bantam raiders threw themselves down behind anything that provided the slightest bit of shelter and waited, with hearts racing, for approximately ten minutes as shrapnel burst all around them. A further seventy-five shells fell beyond the British support trench.

For the patrol a counter bomb throwing was out of the question as their supply of grenades was nearly exhausted. Lieutenants Frost and Wolstenholme gave the order to retire. They fell back in perfect order coming in as if on parade. Lewis gunners gave good covering fire, while the 15th Sherwood Foresters poured in rifle fire from the flanks, helping to keep the enemy's heads down. The first man over our parapet returned at 12-45 a.m.

Five soldiers from X Company were wounded, 20022 Sergeant Ferguson, 19341 Sergeant J.H. Armistead, 1493 Private Parr, 19305 Lance Corporal J. Hampson, 23162 Private Bates, also Private J. Bennet of W Company. The officers and men were extremely disappointed that the raid had to all intents and purposes been a failure, an assessment of the failed mission pointed the blame in the direction of the methods used by the artillery, as cooperation between infantry and artillery still left a lot to be desired. Although the Bantam raiders were short of Mills bombs the party would have penetrated the enemy's trenches if the artillery barrage had continued. The failure of the Trench Mortar and artillery bombardment to clear the enemy front line proved to be the final blow, as the raiders were fired on from the very trench they were intending to raid. If any of the raiders had the slightest feeling of failure it was soon dispelled by the arrival of a telegram from General Headquarters.

Congratulations to all concerned! The raiding party appear to have acted with great steadiness under difficult and unexpected circumstances and officers appear to have kept control. Better luck next time. The smallness of casualties is most satisfactory.

The 30 May, in the vicinity of Neuve Chapelle, began as just another day to the men in the trenches; snipers on both sides seemed to be having a contest in the amount of hits they could register. One sniper in particular seemed to be adept at successfully targeting the British trench periscopes. The hostile artillery remained ominously quiet until 7-25pm when the enemy laid an intense and comprehensive bombardment on the Bantam lines for over two hours.

The Royal Artillery responded immediately; after one or two short rounds they accurately targeted the enemy front line and supports. An assault was anticipated along the Divisional front and the battalions prepared to repel the attackers.

The Cheshire Battalion received orders to stand-to at 8 p.m., immediately they fired rifle grenades into the opposing trenches. The rifle companies, not to be outdone, poured rapid fire onto the usual targets. The Bantams were reported as being cheery and full of confidence. However, their situation was made worse when a combination of heavy fog and cordite-filled smoke drifted across the battlefield, offering ideal cover for advancing troops to emerge from. At 9-45 p.m. enemy machine guns raked the Cheshire Bantams' parapet. In reply their Lewis gunners swept the enemy line and No Man's Land throughout the night, expending over 3,000 rounds before dawn. With an attack imminent they stood-to most of the night, until at 3-20 a.m. the thick fog began to clear and the battalion was ordered to stand down.

Unidentified Cheshire Bantam.

The casualty report for 30 May lists the deaths of two Bantams 19038 Sergeant S.W. Davis from W Company, and also 19863 Private H. Churcher of X Company. A further eighteen men were wounded.

It later transpired that the German bombardment had in fact been the opening overture of a major raid as a counter-offensive to hinder Allied preparations under way for the Big Push. The main thrust of the attack had focussed on the front held by the 18th Battalion Lancashire Fusiliers, the heavy bombardment had cut the telephone lines and two runners were sent off to establish the situation on their flanks. They returned with news of the destruction of their neighbouring battalion the 15th Battalion, Sherwood Foresters who were completing a relief with the 14th Battalion, Gloucesters when the shelling began. Within minutes the British artillery began a counter-barrage. However, the enemy's bombardment had almost obliterated the Sherwoods' position. Scores of men were wounded, lay dead or were staggering around dazed and shell shocked. To spare further casualties Captain Ainsworth ordered his men to withdraw to the flanks thus leaving an undefended gap in the line of almost 200 metres.

A German field postcard of infantrymen posing with an artillery shell. The men belong to II Battalion K10 J.R.

The Germans quickly assessed the situation and stormed across the shell-pitted landscape to capture the thinly held line. They swept over the shattered parapet, bombs flying all around and ferocious hand-to-hand fighting ensued before the enemy withdrew. Units from the Lancashire Fusiliers plugged the gap and by 9-30 p.m. contact was made with the Sherwood Forresters and the line restored. The enemy had tried its best to break the 35th Division's line and failed. They had, however, taken almost forty Sherwood prisoners of war.

The Brigade was congratulated on its steadiness and sweeping fire which had, in the opinion of high authorities, staved off a big attack. The Divisional Commander is reported to have said that the bombardment while it lasted had been more intense than anything he had experienced. The discovery of hand grenades, rifles, picks and shovels indicated the German determination to remain, but as a result of the 14th Battalion Gloucestershire barrage of fire the Germans had hastily evacuated their new position. The 15th Battalion Cheshires received a personal commendation from the Corps Commander.

Who wished to convey his congratulations to the battalion in the way you held the Trenches during the night of May 30th. He considered it most creditable to all concerned.

The 16th Cheshires replaced the war weary 15th Battalion on the final day in May. The First Birkenhead Battalion returned to billets at Croix Barbee for the familiar routine of working parties, inspections, wiring parties and various courses of instruction. A week later they exchanged places with the 16th Cheshires and returned to the lines at

Neuve Chapelle.

The Bantams were becoming versed in the art of static trench warfare. They had learnt their lessons well: an old trench behind the position known as The Neb, a projection in the trench line was made to look occupied by the introduction of fresh sandbags and fires; the decoy trench tricked the German artillery into shelling the old trench. The nocturnal activities of British and German infantry in No Man's Land led to an increased level in casualties. For under cover of darkness the opponents continually probed the other's defences searching for an opportunity to break the stalemate of static warfare. One such raid occurred at 11 p.m. on the night of 11 June when the enemy attempted a bombing raid on the Cheshires' centre company. A raiding party of approximately a dozen or so men had advanced stealthily in the Bantams' direction, only to be detected by a covering party for one of our raids. They reacted with a flurry of Mills bombs causing the surprised Germans to turn back to their own lines after only slight resistance.

After two years of warfare the career of Lord Kitchener, the original driving force behind Britain's recruitment campaign, was in terminal decline. His autocratic manner created many enemies and the government was in a dilemma, for they dare not depose a man of his standing. The situation resolved itself when Kitchener boarded HMS *Hampshire* outward bound for a conference in Russia. While steaming past Orkney the armoured cruiser hit a mine, Kitchener (and over 600

Kitchener and over 600 others were lost when HMS Hampshire *hit a mine.*

Greater love hath no Man than this:
That a Man lay down his Life for his Friends.

Ruins of Neuve Chapelle.

others) were killed. At a stroke the Bantams had lost their greatest admirer. The nation mourned their great hero while the government breathed a sigh of relief at his passing.

The fine summer weather had given way to cold and rainy days. The trenches became ankle deep in rain water and the men in the line had now been soaked to the skin for two days, they had neither shelter from the incessant rain or facilities to dry out their soaking wet uniforms. Despite the inclement weather events continued as usual each night; listening posts and patrols lay out in No Man's Land hoping to make contact with enemy patrols. The Bantams were noted for their aggression on these missions, they even erected a telegraph board above their position displaying the level of Austrian and German losses.

Due to the frequent shelling of the lines there was a continual programme of maintenance to the trench fortifications and the defensive wire. Early on the night of the 12th, while repairing the wire, a Bantam working party was caught out in No Man's Land by an accurate barrage of shrapnel. That night the enemy machine guns had remained strangely quiet until 11 p.m. when a large number of guns were trained on the Bantam parapet and support trench, accurately sweeping the lines with a twenty minute stream of bullets. In reply rifle grenades were fired into the enemy trenches, casualties occurred as the plaintive call of the horn for stretcher-bearers was frequently heard in the German trench. The rifle grenadiers had now worked themselves up to an impressive fire rate of thirty-six grenades every four minutes. Their onslaught brought about a quick retaliation of heavier metal in the shape of trench mortars and .77 shells.

The raiding and counter raiding continued for the remainder of the tour of the trenches; none of the Cheshires were killed but two dozen were wounded including Lieutenant Colonel Newell wounded on the 15th day. The Lieutenant Colonel had sustained serious injury resulting in shell shock (this may be why there is no mention of his injuries within the war diary) and he was invalided home. After rest and recuperation he tried to return to his old command; instead his expert skills were utilised on railway construction works as Commander of Railways. He was the son of John Newell, the well known railway contractor. His decorations included an O.B.E., D.S.O., (L.G. 3 June 1919) M.C. The D.S.O. was awarded while he was with the Royal Engineers.

The battalion was relieved on the 16 June and now faced an eight mile march to their old billets at Croix Marmuse, but after standing ankle deep in water for several days the men's feet were swollen and soft and the march was completed with great difficulty.

The next day as part of a 35th Divisional infantry move the 15th Battalion left for Les Harisoirs. The men were in good spirits and had somehow managed to clean themselves up, this was rather fortunate because en route the battalion marched past the Divisional Commander. The Commander would have witnessed the procession of tenacious fighting men who had emerged from almost three tortuous weeks in the line. Their torn and dishevelled uniforms showed testimony to the countless skirmishes and artillery barrages of shrapnel that ripped apart anything in its path. Perhaps it was a coincidence, but the first day in reserve a kit inspection was held, new tunics and trousers were issued to a number of the men. This time the Cheshires had a more leisurely time in reserve; the days passed with opportunities for bathing, church services, training and even a whole day off for a water carnival.

On Friday 23 June the battalion set off on a half hour march to a field where a Brigade inspection parade was held before the First Army Commander, General Sir Charles Munro. During the inspection proceedings decorations for gallantry were awarded to a number of recipients. The following day Monro issued a congratulatory message to the G.O.C. of XI Corps.

To XIth Corps.

The G.O.C. First Army has great pleasure in forwarding a letter for your information, and in adding compliments for the gallant manner in which troops of 104 and 105 Infantry Brigades withstood intense bombardment and delivered an immediate counterstroke to drive the enemy back.

Signed, S.H. Wilson, Lieutenant Colonel G.S., First Army.

The main topic of conversation was now of the forthcoming offensive to be launched in the rolling landscape of Picardie, where the entire army seemed to be relocating in readiness for the Big Push that would finally break the deadlock of trench warfare. Towards the end of June the 35th Division became Army Reserve with orders to move at six hours' notice they began to prepare for a move to a new area, it came as no surprise to hear it was to be the Somme. From this point the 35th Division was no longer a part of XI Corps and came under the orders of XIII Corps.

During the night of July 2nd and 3rd the infantry brigades boarded trains for the Third Army zone, on the first day of the move the weather was hot and oppressive as the 15th battalion less transport entrained at Choques to meet with their fellow Cheshire Bantams at Sus St. Leger.

Notes

(1) Cecil Holden was a key member of the Birkenhead Recruiting Committee.
(2) Private Weightman 23045 of the 15th battalion was KIA. 27-2-16. He is interred in Guards Cemetery, Windy Corner, France.
(3) On 18-9-18 C.S.M. Shooter was awarded the Albert Medal by the King in the Quadrangle of Buckingham Palace. This award for saving life is no longer awarded; this has now been replaced by the George Cross. A controversial warrant of 1971 permitted survivors of the Albert Medal to exchange the medal for the George Cross.
(4) Private John Mortimer Jones was captured by the Germans and died 30 April 1918 in a prisoner of war camp.

CHAPTER SEVEN

The Battle of the Somme

T HE MUCH HERALDED BIG PUSH came about as a result of a conference held in mid February when the decision was taken to launch a Franco British attack on the Somme. The French General Joffre asked the British to relieve part of his troops in the north, thus freeing men for the defence of Verdun. Haig eventually agreed to the relief of the French Tenth Army located at Arras and wedged between his own First and Third Armies. Allenby's Third Army shifted to the north and the recently formed Fourth Army, commanded by General Rawlinson occupied the front between Maricourt and Hebuterne. The British now held a continuous eighty-mile front extending from Ypres to near the Somme. The German onslaught at Verdun continued for approximately seven months and in the process almost drained the French of its military strength, shifting the emphasis onto the British for an attack on the Somme. Originally France was to attack with forty divisions on a twenty-five mile frontage, and the British to use twenty-five divisions on a fourteen mile front. When the attack was finally launched the French frontage had shrunk to eight miles, their force evaporated from forty divisions to sixteen, of these only five attacked on 1 July. The main attack on a fourteen mile front from Serre to Maricourt was to be carried out by eighteen divisions of Rawlinson's Fourth Army, eleven were to spearhead the attack, while five divisions remained in close

With heavy fighting at Verdun General Joffre asked the British to relieve his troops in the north. Here French troops are moving up during the fighting around Verdun.

reserve, two more were held in army reserve. An additional two divisions of cavalry were also made available to take full advantage of the expected breakthrough! Also two divisions of the Third Army were to mount a subsidiary attack around Gommecourt.

The Germanic occupation of the French countryside was selective for they had chosen their positions wisely, taking full advantage of any topographical features. They had also been given sufficient time to transform the undulating Somme countryside into a fortified bastion. Innocent looking farms and villages were converted into defensive strong points. Benefiting from deep cellars, these provided safe shelter and were frequently interconnected by tunnels and trenches, all situated behind swathes of barbed wire forming an impenetrable barrier to the advancing infantry. The technology of the early 20th Century offered only one solution to breach siege warfare defences – artillery. This proved to be the attack's fatal flaw.

Haig's plan was fairly simple, as it relied on the Fourth Army's ability to capture the high ground of the Pozières Ridge and its surrounding area. The anticipated fifteen mile wide breach would allow the cavalry and infantry to sweep through into the open countryside. The details of the attack were left to the experienced General Sir Henry Rawlinson. He was aware that during the early phases of the German Army attack on Verdun the massive artillery bombardment unleashed on the French front line had almost won the battle. Rawlinson decided to use similar tactics on the Somme but with a larger concentration of artillery. The preliminary bombardment for the new offensive commenced on 24 June, in readiness for the attack on 29 June. The wet weather caused a postponement of the attack until 1 July; the artillery rounds were eked out with a consequent loss of intensity. Very few of the observers watching the onslaught expected any Germans to survive, but they were sheltering in deep bunkers, immune to only the heaviest calibre shells, sadly the British had very few land guns available capable of delivering such a heavy shell.

At 7-30 a.m., on a glorious sunny day, the British infantry rose from their trenches and marched as if on parade towards the German front line. Their orders were to advance steadily with arms sloped; each man was weighed down with sixty-six pound packs of equipment on their backs. As soon as the barrage lifted from the German front line the defenders emerged from their deep dug outs, quickly setting up their machine guns. The advancing British army had expected the Germans to be annihilated; instead it was they who were massacred by German gun-fire and a relentless hail of lead. Thousands fell, strewing No Man's Land with their bodies, before the German front line was even reached, hundreds of wounded men crawled into shell holes for cover, surrounded by the corpses of comrades draped on the mainly uncut barbed wire. Under such an onslaught the attack withered, but

Artillery moving up to the front in preparation for the Big Push.

the bulldog spirit remained and the survivors formed small groups and continued to press home their attacks often breaching the enemy defences. By the end of the day at least 57,000 men of the British army had fallen, 21,393 of these citizen soldiers were killed or missing presumed killed, without gaining a permanent foothold in the German territory except in the south next to the five attacking French divisions.

The Battle of the Somme would ultimately drag on for four tortuous months, like a moth to the flame scores of battalions duly arrived on the Somme, where the flower of the New Army withered and died. The 35th Division were not involved on the first day of the Somme, on the 1st of July [the 132nd day of the Battle of Verdun] the men of the 16th battalion found themselves at Hinges where they were held in reserve for XI Corps until Monday 3 July, when they departed for Sur St. Leger remaining here until 7 July. Two fresh drafts of Bantams now arrived consisting of men assigned to other battalions: 103 men came from the 11th Cheshires, the 10th battalion returned a further 61 men.

On 3 July 27 Brigade (part of the 9th Scottish Division) co-operating under the control of 30th Division, occupied the scorched and shattered assortment of tree stumps which was formerly Bernafay Wood. The wood was almost captured by the British on the 1st July, after Montauban village had fallen, later that day the Germans abandoned their front line trenches on the Montauban Ridge and several batteries along Caterpillar Ridge, Trones Wood and Bernafay Wood which lay three hundred metres away. German efforts to reclaim the area were defeated; on 2 July the 20th Battalion, King's Liverpool Pals sent a patrol into Bernafay Wood and discovered it was deserted. The following day two battalions occupied the wood, which was the cue for the Germans to continually shell it. A number of immensely fortified woods were scattered along the Bazentin ridge, each of these strongholds had to be wrested from the Germans if the allies were to gain territory; each of these German bulwarks would gain their own notoriety.

On 8 July the British gained a foothold in Trones Wood by fighting of a most violent sort. The British infantry, assisted by French artillery, advanced 1,000 yards into the dense wood. In the first five days fighting the 30th Division alone lost over 2,300 casualties. The fighting to capture the wood was essential to secure the right flank of the 9th Division's attack on Longueval. At tremendous cost in human life the wood was finally captured early on the 14 July. The retreating Germans ran desperately towards the protection of their secondary positions at Waterlot Farm and Guillemont.

Guillemont stands approximately five kilometres north of the River Somme, an unremarkable village in every sense except for its location and topography. The village

Clearing wounded on the Somme.

now guarded the south-eastern end of the Thiepval – Pozières ridge whose lesser hills run down through the Ginchy – Guillemont area gradually losing height as they run into the catchments area of the River Somme. The village also stood at the head of Caterpillar Valley as it threaded its way from Fricourt, past Mametz Wood, passing the northern extremity of Bernafay Wood into Trones Wood.

Following the capture of Trones Wood a few days elapsed before conditions were favourable for an attempt to seize Guillemont. Despite being only one thousand yards apart any attempt to capture the village would only have made more prominent a salient[1] in the Longueval – Waterlot Farm region. Any attempt to take Guillemont would be hampered by hostile fire directed from Delville Wood to the northwest. It became a necessity to take the portions of Longueval and Delville Wood, which overlooked Guillemont, prior to the attack on the village. British efforts on the Somme now concentrated against

104

Longueval and Delville Wood together with High Wood and the Pozières defences. Before an attack on Guillemont could be contemplated the left flank had to be secured at Waterlot Farm.

Six days after the opening of the Somme Offensive the 16th Cheshire Bantams marched to Beauval, south of Doullens where they transferred from the First Army to the Fourth Army, posted to VIII Corps. They billeted in the village of Beauval, possibly not the best psychological location for troops as it was used during the Somme battle as a medical centre for several Casualty Clearing Stations (C.C.S.). On the 10 July, they began several days of marching along the dusty French roads leading them to Grove Town, north of Bray it transpired to be nothing more than a railway siding, encircled by an assortment of tents and barbed wire prisoner of war compounds. On the 13th they marched to Billon Wood, finally after long days of marching the footsore men of the 16th battalion were granted two days' rest. The men of the 15th were less fortunate, they took over

Area centrered around Waterlot Farm, the scene of much bitter fighting.

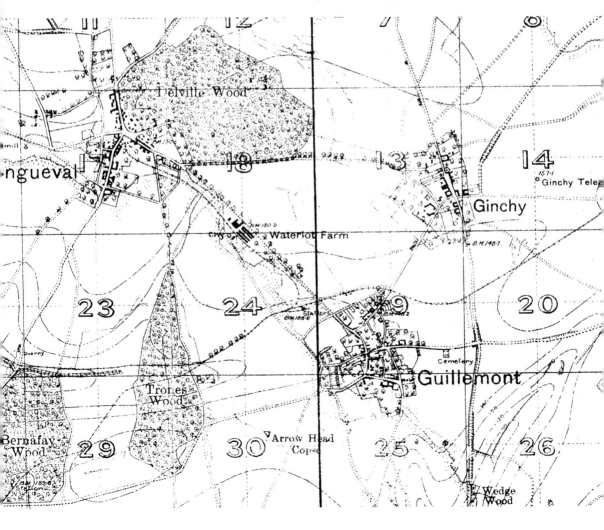

Result of British bombardment on a German position.

trenches in Bernafay Wood and provided carrying parties to the front line, an unpopular task for soldiers weighted down with fifty pound loads, complete with their own kit, rifle and helmet.

During the Somme battles the 35th Division rarely fought as a complete unit, brigades and separate battalions were utilised in various other brigades. The 105th Brigade came under the orders of the 18th Division and the 106th Brigade received its orders from the commanders of the 9th Division. The 105th Brigade were to relieve components of the 53rd and 54th Brigades in the front line stretching from the south of Trones Wood to the north of Bernafay Wood, an area heavily littered by grotesque corpses of both sides, a legacy of the bitter fighting for the woods.

After their short break the 16th Cheshires marched off early on the 16th July to take up positions in the line at Trones Wood, where repeated counter attacks by the Germans had been driven off by bayonet and shell. The move proved to be a wearisome task as they were carrying heavy loads in pouring rain through saturated communication trenches, where the ground had yielded into deep mud. The Bantams had wanted action and they now found themselves in the thick of it, hundreds of Bantams had previously earned a living with shovel and pick and they now put their skills to good use as Z and Y companies set about connecting by trench, a series of shell holes in front of Trones Wood. The Cheshires had no sooner established themselves in their now consolidated position when they received orders on the 17 July to take over at Waterlot Farm.

Meanwhile the 15th Battalion progressed through a succession of villages before briefly halting at Walroy Baillon, this respite gave the commanding officers in the Brigade the opportunity to travel ahead by motor transport to see at first hand the killing fields of the Somme. During the march from Walroy Baillon the battalion passed the 9th Cheshires fresh from their grim adventure in the Big Push. On they marched passing numerous guns, columns of wounded and prisoners of war. On the evening of 16 July the battalion [attached to the 53rd Brigade] relieved the 8th Essex from their position in Bernafay Wood captured two days previously. The Cheshires found themselves in an area devoid of adequate trenches and Lieutenant Colonel Newell was ordered to have trenches dug laterally to hold this recently gained ground. He advised his battalion that they would be shelled to death

FOURTH ARMY.

SPECIAL ORDER OF THE DAY.

The Commander-in-Chief desires that the following may be made known at once to all the troops :—

"The Russians are attacking in great force and with success on many parts of their front and have captured many thousands of prisoners and much war material in the last few days.

The Italians have pressed the Austrians back a considerable distance and are following up their advantage vigorously.

The French troops on our right have already gained brilliant successes and captured a large number of prisoners, guns, etc. They are pressing on steadily; their left flank co-operating closely with our right.

On the main front of attack our troops have broken, on a front of 12,000 yards, right through systems of defence which the enemy has done his utmost for nearly two years to render impregnable. We have inflicted heavy loss on him, capturing 8,000 prisoners and many guns, mortars, machine guns and other war material.

The enemy has already used up most of his reserves and has very few now available.

The defences which remain to be broken through are not nearly so deep, so strong, or so well prepared as those already captured, and the enemy's troops, exhausted and demoralized, are far less capable of defending them than they were ten days ago.

The battle is, in fact, already more than half won. What remains to be done is easier than what has been done already and is well within our power.

Let every attack be pushed home to its allotted objective with the same bravery and resolution as on the 1st July.

Let all objectives gained be held against all comers as British soldiers have always known how to hold them.

There is no room for doubt that steady, determined, united, and unrelenting effort for a few days more will definitely turn the scale in our favour and open up the road to further successes which will bring final and complete victory within sight."

Headquarters, Fourth Army.
    12th July, 1916.

H. Rawlinson, General,
Commanding Fourth Army.

Stretcher bearers take a rest near Waterlot Farm.

at daylight unless they dug themselves in. The Bantams were no strangers to hard graft; they immediately began to make themselves feel at home by digging themselves in. Despite intense and continuous shell fire the Bantams toiled away until the following evening they had not only dug the main trench but also minor trenches for cover.

The anticipated German artillery barrage began early next morning and after shelling the main trench heavily without any response then proceeded to attack. The Bantams were unscathed as none were in the main trench, and orders were not to move or fire until the Hun was within a few metres of the freshly dug T shaped trenches. In a later conversation with Alfred Bigland Colonel Newell proudly said:

> *You should have seen these little fellows fight when the word was given— they were over the top like cats and bayoneting the enemy ranks before the Boche realised what had happened. The Germans retreated and the Bantams were quickly back in their shelters. The repulsed German troops reformed and charged again, with the same result – after the second repulse the Germans shelled the ground so heavily that no support or rations could be brought up for many hours, but the Bantams held the ground gamely and were highly commended by the Brigadier General for their conduct.*

Thanks to their deep cover the Cheshires' casualties were kept to a minimum, and the wood held under the heavy shelling. A large Jack

Johnson shell struck the front lip of number 5 Platoon's trench at its intersection with a former German rail track. The explosion blew several men off their feet, killed three of the Bantams, wounded three more and another was found to be suffering from shell shock. Communications with the companies and 53 Brigade was a source of great anxiety to the 15th Cheshires' commanding officer; the stress combined with a lack of sleep contributed to his breakdown from shell shock on the afternoon of the 18th. The command of the battalion was taken over by Major C.C. Shaw, one of his first difficult decisions was to ignore the request from the heavily shelled 16th Cheshires (who were holding Trones Wood) until permission was granted from Brigade (53) for two companies to reinforce them. Although the telephone lines were being repeatedly cut by the shelling communications remained almost constant with Brigade due to the exceptional gallant work of the linesmen, two of whom were recommended for decoration. With the lines of communication open the C.O. was granted permission to send one company to the assistance of their brother battalion. This was carried out at 5 p.m. on 18 July and the second at 2 p.m. next day. In the afternoon an attempt was made to reinforce the battalion in Trones Wood while doing so twenty-three year old Second Lieutenant G.F. Austin was killed[2].

Fighting continued in Trones Wood, Delville Wood and Longueval intermittently throughout the 19th and 20th; the fighting in these areas was not too severe, although Bernafay Wood remained under constant shell-fire. The battalions holding Longueval and Delville Wood were so weakened in numbers they could not afford to send men to the rear for water and ammunition. In nearly every case assistance was rendered. The route to Longueval had a barrage put on it very often during the day and the men of the carrying parties displayed great gallantry in the manner in which they faced this danger. The companies in the East and North East of the wood were either working or standing to all day and night owing to the repeated attacks which were taking place on Trones Wood between midnight and dawn. Frequent reports were received of Germans massing near Guillemont. All the activity kept the battalion constantly on the alert and for the ninety-six hours they were in occupation neither officers nor men in the trenches had any chance of sleep. The battalion was relieved on the night of 20th/21st by the 8th West Yorkshire Regiment; their company commander was no more than a boy whose survival was due to his being out of the line. All the remaining officers had been wiped out. Following the hand over, the Cheshire battalion marched by companies and platoons independently to the west of Talus Bois.

At about this time rumours began to circulate that a corporal in the 16th Battalion Cheshires was to face a court martial for eating his iron rations which comprised a tin of bully beef, six biscuits, a tin of sugar and tea, and two tubes of meat extract. The emergency rations could only be consumed by permission of an officer; any soldier who disobeyed this regulation faced the full wrath of the military hierarchy.

Throughout the war no member of the Cheshire Bantams ever faced the firing squad. However, Bantams were 'shot at dawn'. The second man to be executed, namely Corporal J. Wilton of the 15th Battalion Sherwood Foresters appears to have cracked under the strain while occupying an isolated heavily shelled strategic position between Trones Wood and Guillemont. His orders were to hold the position for 48 hours, however several hours before this time elapsed he withdrew his men; his actions almost precipitated a panic stricken withdrawal. During the First World War a total of 312 personnel of the British Army were executed as a result of military courts martial. Included in that number were seven men from the 35th Division. Three men from the 19th Battalion Durham Light Infantry were executed in January 1917 as a result of one incident. Seven men had fled from their posts when attacked by a German patrol. The three NCOs, two corporals and a sergeant, were shot. They were the last in the Division to face this tragic form of death.

At the crack of dawn on 15th July a company of the 5th Cameron Highlanders, later reinforced by two companies of the 4th South African Regiment, launched an attack on Waterlot Farm. Ferocious fighting ensued and the Hun was driven back, an intense barrage then rained down on the new occupants of the farm ruins forcing the defenders to withdraw.

The defence of Waterlot Farm appears to be overshadowed in history by the South Africans' desperate fighting for the nearby Delville Wood. Both of these features existed within the confines of a sharp salient with its apex at Delville Wood. During the night of 16th/17th July the 105 Brigade relieved segments of 53 and 54 Brigades occupying the front line, reaching from the north of Bernafay Wood to south of Trones Wood. The Bantam battalions were now under the directive of the commanders of these two brigades.

Various adjustments and reliefs were now made to the Fourth Army on Bazentin Ridge; the 16th Battalion Cheshires was attached to 54 Brigade and were ordered to take over the line at Trones Wood on the 17 July. The rifle companies dug themselves into shell holes in front of the wood before connecting these up with the supports in deep former German trenches in the wood. Each company had its two Lewis guns and four Vickers machine guns positioned along their frontage.

On the 17 July one company of the 15th Battalion Sherwood Foresters took over Maltz Horn Trench from the 7th Battalion East Kent Regiment (Buffs) on the same morning the Cheshire Bantams received orders from 54 Brigade to take over from the Camerons, two Lewis gun nests in front of Waterlot Farm that lay to the southeast of

Second Lieutenant Richard Powell Scholefield

The son of Mr. and Mrs. Henry E. Scholefield of Poulton Hey, Bromborough. He was an old boy of the Liverpool College, as well as of King William's College in the I.O.M. Specialising in chemistry, he entered his father's firm, Messrs Powell & Scholefield's of Liverpool. He enjoyed tennis and was also a member of Bromborough Golf Club.

Within a month of the outbreak of war he enlisted in the 19th Battalion King's (Liverpool Regiment), Third Liverpool Pals. He gained a commission in the 17th Battalion Cheshire Regiment 11 July 1915 prior to being drafted overseas on 29 January 1916 with the 16th Battalion. In mid July the thirty-one year old officer was mortally wounded during the stubborn defence of Waterlot Farm, a position that was held for two days and nights against overwhelming superiority mainly due to the robust pluck of this officer and his platoon. He succumbed to his wounds on 25 July 1916 without gaining consciousness.

Longueval. The farm was in reality a sugar refinery, simply called a farm to distinguish it from the drab buildings on the Guillemont – Longueval road. Successive artillery bombardments had reduced the structure of the buildings into heaps of rubble that the Germans had transformed into a defensive strongpoint of their main second position.

Lieutenant H.D. Ryalls, whose W Company was to occupy the position and intervening ground, made a reconnaissance to see if the Camerons' relief could be made during daylight. He was accompanied by Lieutenant Royal MacLaren who had served in the South African war; MacLaren was wounded and later died. The bombardment intensified drowning out the sounds of German rifle and machine gun fire, so it was decided to relieve the isolated Cameron posts at night. The company had no other option than to sit tight in their trenches under heavy shellfire until night time. They remained in contact with battalion H.Q. due to the sterling efforts of Private Hoare and other runners and signallers, who continually braved the shells and bullets, as they crossed open ground carrying messages.

Under the cover of darkness W Company prepared to set off, when at about 9-30 p.m. a heavy German attack began on Delville Wood. Any movement now became impossible. The sound of shells going overhead was reputed to be like the mass flight of birds migrating, and the noise of the crashing and rending was terrible. The storm of steel gradually quietened down and W Company, under the command of Lieutenant Ryalls, carefully advanced in the direction of the farm completing the relief by 12-30 a.m. Two platoons were detailed for the northwest, and two for the south. From the farm, light railways ran to Guillemont, and the defensive outposts some 300 metres apart were connected by the railway cuttings.

The platoons at the south post worked throughout the night improving these German trenches and making a block on the right, the flank of the British Army. The French left was about half a mile away. The Pioneer Battalion began work on a communication trench and a section of the Machine Gun Corps also arrived. On the morning of the 18th, the garrison of Waterlot Farm did some excellent work in strengthening its position. Lieutenant R.P. Scholefield, who was in command of the north post, had the military foresight to have a fresh trench dug which was to be a surprise for the advancing German infantry.

At 2 p.m. the ever present bombardment increased in intensity, an hour later things began to take a turn for the worse when strong detachments of the enemy began to infiltrate along the light railway cutting leading from Guillemont. Lieutenant Harry Douglas Ryalls sent off Private Hoare to Battalion H.Q. with an urgent request to Lieutenant Colonel Johnston for reinforcements.

The request was reluctantly declined, in his post war memoirs Lieutenant Colonel Johnstone explained why.

> We got a request from our brother battalion [the 16th] to send them two companies as reinforcements, but as they were in one Brigade and we were in another this was impossible.[3] Furthermore, we were each holding a wood, they run parallel, with instructions to hold it to the last man. If we sent two companies, we could not be sure of doing our job – in fact we could not risk it. The wires were all cut and we could not get Brigade except by messages carried along a heavily shelled road by runner. Requests came from the same source for ammunition and bombs. The large dump had been cleared during the afternoon and we had few to spare, but we fished around and sent them all we could – about 20,000 small arms' ammunition and some bombs.

Ryalls sent forward a party with bombs and a Lewis gun to a brick wall 250 yards south-east of the farm, (Point D on the map) which ran parallel to the line of the enemy's advance; the Hun got close under the wall where a hand to hand fight ensued before they were bombed out and he turned his Lewis gun on the enemy as they retired down the railway embankment. This repulsed attack proved to be the advance guard of a 300 strong enemy attack that advanced armed with two Maxim machine guns along the railway embankment. A Vickers gun was placed by Ryalls in the angle of the trench (Point C); this gun successfully halted the advance. Colonel Browne-Clayton despatched a machine gun commanded by Lieutenant Frazer of the M.G.C. and the gun team established a position in a shell hole north east of Trones Wood (Point G), and a platoon of 15th Battalion Cheshires also arrived. Despite the Germans' repeated attempts to sweep round the south end of Waterlot Farm the cross fire of both machine guns and rapid fire from the Lee Enfield rifles halted any advance. The machine gunners' prompt intervention and somewhat late artillery support halted the German advance and they made no more advances from the south. At

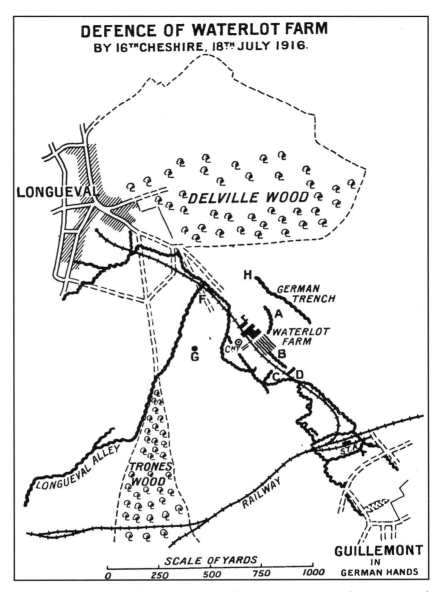

DEFENCE OF WATERLOT FARM
BY 16TH CHESHIRE, 18TH JULY 1916.

LONGUEVAL

DELVILLE WOOD

H

GERMAN TRENCH

F

A

E

WATERLOT FARM

CH?

B

G

C D

TRONES WOOD

LONGUEVAL ALLEY

ST.

RAILWAY

GUILLEMONT
IN
GERMAN HANDS

SCALE OF YARDS

0   250   500   750   1000

this stage in the battle enemy casualties were estimated in excess of forty. The enemy retired leaving behind snipers who took cover in the shell holes who caused considerable losses, the Cheshires sharpshooters were ordered to eradicate the problem. There then ensued a deadly game of cat and mouse between opposing snipers, until our garrison marksmen finally eliminated the enemy.

At precisely 9 a.m. on the 18th, the Germans began an intensive bombardment on the farm and railway cuttings. The new posts, dug well forward of the farm, got no shells at all, except our own 'shorts'. Less fortunate were the defenders of Bernafay Wood, the remainder of

Reserves resting during the fighting south of Delville Wood.

the 16th Battalion and 15th Battalion also suffered badly. To the north east of the farm a company of the enemy emerged from the south-east corner of Delville Wood, entered the German trench (Point H) and set off in the direction of Guillemont. At the same time directly in front of the farm an entire battalion of Germans sprung up from a German trench, they advanced on the farm in lines six deep. The wave of attackers had a nine-to-one superiority over the Cheshires, but the Cheshires had an ace in the hole.

Unknown to the Germans a wrecked trench forward of the farm (Point A) had been secretly occupied by two platoons of Bantams who lay in wait. Both platoons led by Lieutenant Scholefield held their fire until the Germans were almost on top of them, and then let fly. The Lewis guns at 300 yards' range were devastating – the Germans in tight formation did not stand this fire for long. The two platoons were also supported by the fire of the Camerons and X Company, who engaged Germans coming out of Delville Wood on the left. The attack broke down, an officer was seen trying to rally his men but they fled leaving behind many casualties. During his moment of glory thirty-one year old Lieutenant Scholefield was wounded; he was evacuated to the 21st C.C.S. where he later died. Sergeant Cook who took over command of two platoons estimated the enemy's casualties to be at least 500.

On the night of 18 July the depleted 18th Division, after three bloody weeks of conflict were relieved from their positions on the Eastern side of Trones Wood and Maltz Horn trench by the 35th (Bantam) Division, who already had a company of the 16th Battalion Cheshires at Waterlot Farm.

The next day the enemy made no infantry attack on Waterlot Farm, but the entire line held by the battalion was heavily bombarded throughout the day; and the trench (Position A) held by Sergeant Cook was obliterated, so intense was the bombardment that shell explosions buried the Lewis gun three times but each time it was recovered and remained in action. The remnants of the garrison with the recovered Lewis gun relocated to the trench southeast of the farm (Point B). The evacuation of this trench left Lieutenant Ryalls left flank vulnerable but this weakness was remedied by the Vickers and Lewis guns positioned in the strong point to the west of Waterlot Farm (Point F), this manoeuvre protected Lieutenant Ryalls's exposed flank allowing

Lieutenant A.C. Styles.

him to maintain his position. Up to this time the Cheshire losses at the Farm were about eighty. The German losses can only be estimated at between 600 and 700, mostly caused by Lieutenant Scholefield's half company.

The heavy German shelling caused as many casualties as the Cheshire Bantams had lost on the previous day. A shell scored a direct hit on the Battalion H.Q. killing the occupants; R.S.M. Giles, a 26 year old Londoner, Lieutenant A.C. Styles, an Orderly Room Sergeant, and also severely wounding the Adjutant, Captain Charles Johnston. Amongst those killed was Lieutenant Alfred Cornwall Styles, the battalion signalling officer who had a great love for felines and who was lying on his back asleep with a cat curled up on his chest. The shell-burst riddled Styles with shrapnel killing him instantly, miraculously the cat escaped unhurt and was adopted as a regimental mascot. The farm was handed over to the 14th Battalion Gloucestershire Regiment on the night of 19 July.

The book *History of the Cheshire Regiment in the Great War* states:

> *This small operation was extremely well conducted. The tactical dispositions and the bravery of the men defeated all German attacks. The Battalion worked together as one man. Every message was anticipated, and reinforcements allowed nothing to stop them getting forward. Food, water, small arms' ammunition and the bombs arrived at the right time, though a water cart was blown up on its way forward.*

Before the survivors were allowed a brief respite, numerous rewards were given for gallantry; among them the C.O. Colonel Browne-Clayton and Lieutenant Ryalls won the D.S.O. Private Brace/Bruce, the undaunted ubiquitous C.O.'s runner, who 'took over' Battalion H.Q. when it was hit, received a well earned D.C.M. Another runner, who did fearless work, was Private Saballa. Sergeant Cook, Privates Campbell and Lowe each received a D.C.M. were wounded.

The Company, well backed by the rest of the Battalion had held a position of vital importance at a critical moment. The action proved costly to the Bantams: Lieutenant A.C. Stiles was killed outright, Second Lieutenant R.P. Scholefield, and Second Lieutenant A.M. MacLaren later died of wounds. Second Lieutenant W.H. Findley, Captain and Adjutant C. Johnson, Lieutenant Colonel R. Browne-Clayton, Major R. Worthington, Lieutenant H.D. Ryalls, Second Lieutenant J.A. Blake were wounded.

Lieutenant Colonel Browne-Clayton, Major Worthington were slightly wounded and remained on duty. Casualties in the ranks consisted of Battalion Sergeant Major Giles and thirty-one N.C.O.s and men killed. A further 175 were wounded, another four were wounded but remained at duty. Seven were posted as missing; shell shock claimed a further five victims; one was accidentally wounded and one was sick. This made a total of 244 men of all ranks killed or wounded in the two-day action. The defence of this vital position was mentioned in Sir Douglas Haig's despatch of 23 December 1916.

Sergeant James C. Speight. KIA July 1916.

The 16th Battalion headquarters were located at the Briquetrie, the remnants of the gallant defenders of the farm now joined their fellow Bantams who were holding the shelled trenches within Bernafay Wood. The Battalion was relieved that night and marched to bivouac at Talus Boise; the camp was strafed by artillery resulting in the wounding of five 16th Battalion Cheshire men, Sergeant Walshe subsequently died.

The 15th Battalion had suffered high casualties during a bombardment on the 18th. The following day they were in Chimpanzee trench, situated to the south of Bernafay Wood, along with two Brigades of the 35th Division, including 105 Brigade who also occupied Arrow Head Copse. The 15th Battalion remained there until the 21st when they reunited with their fellow Cheshires at Talus Boise.

After being separated for two days the brigade reassembled under the command of General Marindin. The 20 July saw the re-grouped Bantams of 105 Brigade in action to cover the advance of the French who were expected to make a major effort this day, astride both banks of the Somme. In fact there was no discernible French movement on the Bantams' right, but the Bantams nevertheless stuck to their task, which was the capture of German trenches between Maltz Horn Farm and Arrow Head Copse, the latter lay a little to the east of Trones Wood, south of the Guillemont road. The purpose behind this extremely hastily prepared attack ordered upon the 15th Battalion Sherwood Foresters was to create a more advantageous position from which the general attack on Guillemont and the German second

Casualty report in the Birkenhead News.

position could be launched. The Sherwoods were in no condition for an attack as they had been under shellfire for two days, while wearing gas masks all day, confined in trenches soaked with phosgene. Consequently, only two companies were available; they were brought up to strength by the arrival of two companies of the 23rd Battalion Manchesters. The ill-advised attack commenced at dawn. The Manchester Bantams advanced into a hail of bullets, briefly entering the German trenches before being driven out into the shell swept battlefield. A later attack by the Manchesters and Sherwood Foresters advanced into the sights of the waiting German machine gunners; the attack melted away. The survivors withdrew and despite all their efforts the Bantams' attack resulted in no progress.

The 23rd Manchesters lost nine officers, including the commanding officer and 162 other ranks, while the 15th Sherwood Foresters suffered ten officers killed, nine wounded, thirty-nine other ranks killed, 146 wounded with a further thirty-six missing. They had suffered 450 casualties from concentrated machine-gun, rifle, shellfire, and gas. With the rising tide of casualties it was proving increasingly difficult to replace them with fit Bantam reinforcements to the high quality of the original volunteers. But at least the French were happy, for the next day General Pinney received a letter from the commander of the French 153rd praising the courage of the 23rd Manchesters. The French commander's observers on the flank had observed the Bantams advancing 'as if on parade' against heavy fire, but with the position being on the forward slope of an incline, it gave the troops no chance of holding the ground. Perhaps under the circumstances it was the best he could do. At least the French attack further south had advanced about 2,500 yards.

Despite being the height of summer the 23 July was a cold overcast day which offered little cheer to the men sheltering in the trenches. Anyone foolish enough to look over the parapet would have seen the village of Maricourt set on fire by the British heavy guns. That evening 125 men from each company under Major Shaw and eight officers set off on yet another working party under the 35th Division pioneers. The battalion relocated that night to a new camp North of Carnoy.

In the early hours of the morning the Bantams who were now in support filed into Silesia trench and support area that had until fairly recently been a part of the German front line, the section was heavily shelled with pinpoint accuracy as the former occupants knew the precise coordinates of their old position.

At 3 a.m., 26 July, the company commanders of the 15th Battalion were detailed to carry out a reconnaissance of the Maltz Horn trenches, lying south of Arrow Head Copse and south-east of Trones Wood, prior to the battalion's relief of the Bantams of the 18th Battalion Lancashire Fusiliers. The Cheshires' entry into the line was hampered by a very badly maintained communication trench lined with men, and a steady procession of stretcher-bearers who muttered and cursed as troops from both directions struggled to get past each other in the narrow passageways. After a delayed exchange, the four companies fanned out into the front line, and immediately began to create new trenches and improve the existing ones. The battalion slogged away all night and were no doubt spurred on by the harrowing sight of the wounded in the communication trench. They dug for all they were worth, for dawn would bring considerable danger. At daybreak, when the artillery spotters could see where their shells erupted, the deadly artillery duel recommenced and continued until evening. As the allied artillery shelled Ginchy and Guillemont, the Germans retaliated by bombarding Trones and Delville Wood, Longueval and Waterlot Farm. During the storm of steel a German

German dead litter the battlefield.

shell ignited a box of Stokes mortar bombs with catastrophic results, as the blast was confined within the trench the explosion killed and buried several of the Cheshires and severely shook up two of the officers.

The following morning the relentless shelling continued. About midday a shell landed in one of the company officer's dugout, killing outright Second Lieutenant Colin Dickenson and wounding Second Lieutenants S. Scholefield and J.N. Watson. The chance landing of the shell had left the company of men without any officer leadership, so arrangements were hastily made for Second Lieutenant Cunningham to take charge of the company. That night, under cover of darkness, the 16th Battalion Cheshires began filing into the line to replace their brother battalion, however before they could get into position the German artillery opened up. The trenches were congested with men from both battalions when salvoes rained down on the left and central trenches. The company on the left were well entrenched in their new positions and suffered few casualties as the enemy was concentrating his efforts on Trones Wood. Unfortunately their luck never lasted as in the dying moments of the firestorm one shell annihilated an entire Lewis gun team and buried several men. The guns ceased at 11-30 p.m. the battalion completed their relief a few minutes after midnight on 29 July and returned to dugouts at Talus Bois. According to the Official History the farm fell to the allies on the 30 July.

The 16th Battalion, now only 604 men strong, held the frequently bombarded line at Maltz Horn Trench for a couple of days. During this period two men were killed, twelve wounded and one gassed. On the 26 August the Fifth Army relieved the 35th (Bantam) Division on Maltz Horn Ridge and their position extended along the entire eastern slope. On 30 July the line was handed over to the 30th Division. The battalion then marched by companies to a bivouac South of Carnoy; the first two miles of this journey was carried out under heavy shell fire, a considerable amount of soldiers suffered the effects of gas poisoning but remained at duty.

After two days' rest the 15th Battalion moved up the gradient to North of Carnoy, south west of Montauban where they were held in reserve. On the final day of July the 15th Battalion moved to Sandbag Alley near the much derided village of Meaulte. The strain of almost constant trench warfare interspersed with backbreaking work was beginning to have a noticeable effect on the little men; officers and men were reported as being over tired and morale was in decline. The first week in August offered little to improve the situation for the infantry of the Division. This period was scheduled to be a rest period but the days were now spent carrying out physical drill, bayonet fighting and practice in trench attack. The overworked men were also required to carry out night-time exercises, practising trench attacks, carried out in front of the Brigadier. This disappointing course of events came about due to the arrival of fresh drafts of men, the vast majority of whom were poorly trained and physically underdeveloped. Converting these men into troops fit to enter the line demanded considerable attention from the officers and left little time for more relaxing pastimes.

The battalion now under command of Major H.P.G. Cochrane set off on a five mile march to the railhead at Mericourt where they boarded cattle trucks for the train journey to Saleux. After a five hour delay a series of jolts heralded the train's departure. Upon arriving at their destination they detrained and set off through a cold dark night for a twelve-mile march to Oissy. The journey was particularly difficult for the recently arrived draft as unaccustomed to their weighty backpacks they struggled to keep up with the veterans. The weary men needed frequent halts and, although these were of only ten minutes' duration, officers and men frequently required awakening. The battalion arrived at Oissy at approximately 7 a.m. on Sunday 6 August. During their stay in this location the Bantams were put through yet another series of company parades, physical drill, lectures and building a rifle range.

Although the 35th Division was scheduled to remain in this area for at least a week they were soon on the move. On 10 August 105 Brigade received its marching orders for a move this time to The Citadel near Happy Valley.

On a blistering hot day the Bantams arrived at Mericourt. Shortly after lunchtime they set off under the blazing sun on the dusty eight-mile march to the Citadel (now the site of Citadel New Military Cemetery). The conditions were taking their toll and the men's spirit was described as very bad and disappointing. Unusually, three men fell out of the column while others had to be continually spurred on. It took all the efforts of the officers to keep the men going; even the N.C.O.s were full of apathy. Eventually they arrived at their destination for the now routine succession of inspection and training exercises. On the evening of 12 August a five hundred strong working party was loaned to the Royal Engineers, the details are vague but the workers seemed to have been caught out by heavy shelling. One officer was wounded, two men were killed, eight wounded while another was missing believed wounded.

The Citadel camp was inspected by the G.O.C. and during the visit General Pinney took the opportunity to lecture the officers, pointing out that work with the shovel was just as important as that with the bayonet. This was no doubt to soften the blow, for a couple of days later the entire battalion was to be used as a working party digging two long communication trenches to be used in the coming operations against Guillemont. The importance in carrying out this task successfully was explained by the Brigadier to all the N.C.O.s before the battalion left. It had rained heavily all afternoon. The ground and

Lance Corporal Spencer is kneeling on a piece of paper.

tracks were very slippery underfoot as the 15th Battalion set off into the night guided by a Royal Engineers' officer. The officer attempted to find a track with a good surface and in doing so lost his way; struggling along in his footsteps were 800 Bantams. Some idea of the complexity of the trench system and surrounding areas is imaginable when it is reported that the guide took the working party three miles further than was necessary. Once the correct position was reached the Bantams worked well, successfully completing their labours within four hours, during this episode seven of the Cheshires were wounded.

Two drafts of men arrived on the 16 August from the Cheshire Regiment, 103 of the men from 11th Battalion and sixty-one from the 10th Battalion. The fresh draft was to be divided between the two Cheshire Bantam battalions in billets at the Citadel, however the 15th Battalion wisely accepted only a handful of men.

On the evening of the 20 August men of the 16th Battalion slithered their way through greasy mud-lined trenches before taking up positions at Arrow Head Copse. The 24th and 35th Divisions were now garrisoning XIV Corps front, and received orders to prepare for an assault upon Guillemont. The task charged to the 35th Division consisted of the capture of a double line of trenches approximately ninety yards east of Arrow Head Copse to an orchard in the southwest perimeter of Guillemont. The distance between the two points was approximately 400 yards and was to be attacked by the 16th Cheshires. Any tactical strongpoint between the two opposing forces was to be captured. As it was anticipated the enemy redoubt would prove a severe stumbling block to the advance. It was arranged for heavy artillery to bombard this target, and the lighter calibre field artillery would form a box barrage around it when the heavy artillery terminated.

As a precautionary measure, to avoid unnecessary loss of life, the forward trenches were to be evacuated during the heavy bombardment and reoccupied when the heavies ceased fire. The Cheshires were scheduled to advance at 9 p.m. but a few minutes prior to zero hour the commanding officer, Lieutenant Colonel R. Browne-Clayton, reported to his superiors that the heavy artillery still rained down and was firing short. Beneath this maelstrom of friendly fire it was impossible to prepare for going over the top, as sections of trench were blown in and most of the Stokes ammunition was buried. The Brigade Major informed the 16th Cheshires' commander that the attack must still proceed. Zero hour would now be one hour later than originally planned, should the Cheshire Battalion fail the 14th Battalion Gloucestershires were to carry out a raid on the strongpoint. In reply to this order Browne-Clayton advised against any further attack that night as he considered his men to be demoralised. This advice fell on deaf ears as the Brigade Major visited Browne-Clayton's headquarters. It would seem that he settled for a compromise, whereby a small raiding party would reconnoitre the strongpoint; if they found it was unguarded, they were to capture and consolidate the position. A raiding party patrol led by Lieutenant Milne with eight volunteers, mainly skilled in bombing, set out into No Man's Land. Lieutenant Colonel Browne-Clayton, Captain Ryalls and the Brigade Major, Captain Glover, accompanied the raiders as far as the front line, possibly to investigate the reason for the failure of the previous attack. They discovered the front line was practically obliterated apart from a short section of trench north of the Guillemont road. Lieutenant Milne's patrol reached a barrier close to the strongpoint and they remained there waiting for reinforcements. A patrol from the 14th Battalion Gloucestershire Regiment approached the strongpoint but was checked by wide belts of barbed wire. The German machine guns now burst into life wounding the patrol's leader. As both raiding parties were facing such impregnable defensive measures they returned to their own lines.

During the two days in the line they sustained three deaths. The twenty wounded were chiefly suffering from shell shock. The Brigade Commander accepted that the artillery had contributed to the failure of the assault, both in preparation and in shattering morale but he raised grave concerns over the poor standard of recent drafts joining his brigade. Before going into the line the 16th Battalion had taken into their ranks 150 men from the new draft, these were found to be much below the standard of the veterans both in physique and military prowess. They were to prove a constant source of anxiety to the experienced Bantams during their stay in the line. The retention of these men and other men was considered likely to undermine the morale of the entire 35th Division.

The 15th Battalion Cheshires who were now in Brigade reserve at Silesia Trench supplied working parties carrying assorted projectiles forward to the 16th Cheshires during the night of 20/21st. To maintain the supply of ammunition to the forward areas was an essential task that was much hated by the infantry, this particular evening the casualties sustained were one man killed and a further three wounded. The battalion was relieved by the 18th Battalion Highland Light Infantry; afterwards the men marched back to north of Bernafay Wood.

The 35th Division had incurred severe losses on the Somme and fresh drafts of men were posted to all the depleted battalions. Amid increasing concerns over the standard of casualty replacements the draft recently received on 18th were inspected by A.D.M.S.[4] on 25 August. Fifty of these men were rejected as unfit for general service and marked for service in Pioneer Battalions. On the 29 August the G.O.C. inspected all drafts that had joined the 15th and 16th Battalions since 16 July. On the 31st while the 15th Battalion moved to billets at Milly and Bout des Pres the new drafts marched separately under an officer to Lucheux where they were inspected by none other than the Adjutant General to the armed forces. The G.O.C. 35th Division, Major General H.J.S. Landon was of the opinion that the men were simply undersized and not real Bantams. He considered they were physically underdeveloped and unfit men of low moral standard who lowered the standard of the Division. A determined effort was now made to remove the undesirables, many of whom were weaklings or degenerates, lacking the strength and stamina of the original Bantams, and a very large proportion of these men were marked for Pioneer Battalions.

The simple fact was that burly Bantam recruits were a thing of the past for the prime specimens, who had rushed to enlist in such preponderance that they formed one and a half divisions, had been selected from the pick of the crop. In a war of attrition it proved impossible to replace the casualties to the same high standards as their predecessors, men who had originally been rejected for fighting had been retained at the depots and infantry camps, these men of a medical low grade were, unfortunately, now arriving at the battlefront. Despite the huge question mark hanging over the division its brigades were continually involved in minor but costly attacks in the vicinity of Falfemont Farm Ridge; in several instances representation at command level was made pointing out the small odds of success, as any advance would be dispersed by artillery fire. Despite the dire warnings during the latter part of August, components of the division repeatedly attacked objectives leaving in their wake a trail of dead and dying wee men.

August had proven to be a terrible month for the 35th Division, the reader might dismiss the infantry division as a failure but prior to doing this it would only be fair to reflect upon the circumstances that had conspired to prevent the division from winning perpetual fame and glory upon the Somme. During the 35th Division's acclimatisation period serious losses occurred while units were employed trench digging or fought attached to other infantry divisions. When the division arrived on the Somme, the situation was extremely critical. The salient at Longueval and Delville Wood simply had to be held at all costs by XIII Corps. The lifeblood of 105 and 106 Brigade Bantams flowed freely on these battlefields, and the cream of the proud Bantams faded away as they held their ground. Consequently, when the division was offered the opportunity to show its worth, the men who could have carried the day were no longer there, and their replacements had proven to be woefully inadequate.

Notes

(1) A salient is an indent into the enemy front line, into which hostile fire will be received from the front and two sides.

(2) George Fredrick Austin joined the Inns of Court O.T.C. in July 1915, receiving his commission five months later when he proceeded to France. He has no known grave.

(3) On the night of 16th/17th July the 105th Brigade had relieved part of the 53 and 54 Brigades in the line,to the north of Benafay Wood and to the south of Trones Wood. The battalions were now under the orders of commanders of these two brigades.

(4) A.D.M.S. is an army abbreviation for Assistant Director of Medical Services.

CHAPTER EIGHT

The Thin Edge of the Wedge

A S THE MONTH OF AUGUST 1916 concluded the division was transferred to VI Corps, Third Army. Over the next few days the men of the 15th Battalion made their way to the Arras sector. The ancient town was traditionally a centre of trade, beneath the town were two major cave systems reputed to date back to the seventeenth century. Specialist New Zealand tunnelling companies set about excavating a series of tunnels that eventually interlinked

Bandimont Gate, Arras.

twenty-five large caverns. These underground shelters carved out of the chalky substrata could accommodate 11,000 soldiers and even had the benefit of running water, ventilation and electric lighting and, far more importantly, were safe from shell-fire.

The 15th Cheshires arrived at Arras shortly before midnight where they spent the remainder of the night at billets in a Girls' College. The Bantams' only complaint was that the girls had left. The next day they headed for the trenches. 105 Brigade relieved 110 Brigade in J sector, whose northern boundaries were three mine craters named Clarence, Cuthbert and Claude. The territory extended from the banks of the Scarpe to north of the Douai road.

On 5 September, under cover of darkness, a patrol consisting of a sergeant and two men from W Company, set off to investigate at close quarters the German wire. As they neared the German front line an alert sentry shouted out a challenge, hearing no reply he threw caution to the wind and hurled a clutch of bombs and wounded the trio. As the game was now well and truly up the lesser wounded pair set off for their own lines, dragging between them their critically wounded comrade Jimmy Smith. As they drew near to their own wire, at a position close to Claude Crater, the two wounded men decided to leave behind the mortally wounded twenty year old Birkenhead man. Later two search parties scoured the area attempting to find Private Smith but to no avail. A search party led by the C.O. successfully located and recovered 19083 Private Smith, but he died later at the Dressing Station.

As autumn approached the Arras sector appeared to be relatively quiet and an attitude of live and let live appeared to have settled on the area, as the opposition were reluctant to engage the British. The opposing sides were both recovering from fighting on the Somme. The German army preferred to strafe the forward lines with trench mortars that caused considerable damage to the trench system, and generally unsettled the troops.

The 16th Battalion also marched to Arras as the Brigade continued its relief of 110 Brigade, they completed their relief early in the evening of 2 September and spent their first night in the underground caves. The next day they marched to the front line trenches to the east and northeast of Arras and relieved the 9th Battalion Leicestershire Regiment. They now found themselves occupying dilapidated trenches and appear to have worked continually reinstating their lines. As the line was quiet, each night they sent out wiring parties and patrols. The enemy showed very little activity. The war diaries of the 16th Battalion are, to put it mildly, extremely vague; this is best summed up in the fact that the diarist, Major Worthington, summed up the entire month of September in just nine lines.

During a conference at Brigade H.Q. the decision to liven up the

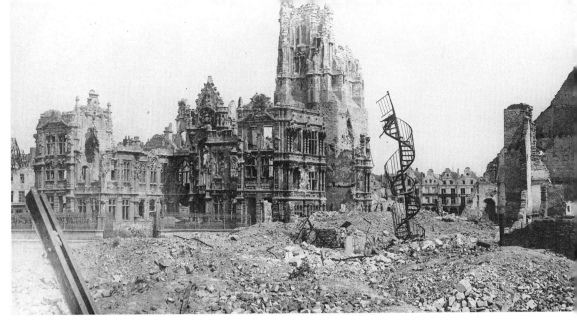

Ruins of the Hôtel de Ville, Arras.

sector was taken, this would be carried out in the form of a major raid on the enemy frontage on the 14th instant. The preparation for the raid coincided with the relief of the 21st Divisional artillery by the Bantams' own artillery. With the advantage of hindsight, the decision to change the guns at this particular time was questionable; for the replacement gunners required time to register their weapons accurately on the enemy lines. The precision marksmanship of gunners familiar with the terrain was vital if infantry attacks were to succeed. The change over would only benefit the entrenched Germans.

In the early hours of the morning several wagons arrived to collect the 15th Cheshires selected for the forthcoming raid. Inside the wagons were men of the New Zealand Tunnelling Company who greeted the men with friendly banter concerning their height as they hauled them aboard. The wagons roared out of Arras at 5 a.m. then trundled along the roads in the direction of Duissens, where a replica of the German line was taped out to scale. Here the raiders were drilled on the plan of the attack, before simulating the raid. As the object of the exercise was primarily to gather intelligence, the duration of the intrusion into the hostile lines was intended to be brief, therefore a planned orderly withdrawal was also practised.

At 8 p.m. on 14 September the plan was set in motion when the artillery opened the attack by pounding the zone, between Claude and Kate craters. At 8-15 and 8-18 p.m. respectively the New Zealand Engineers set off four large camouflets (subterranean mines) which erupted with a deafening roar, their shock waves were felt in Arras. But the newly arrived gun crews were firing wide of the mark and dropping short, causing a dozen Bantam casualties. As the light faded the advancing raiders discovered the Hun resistance was far greater than expected; although the wire had been cut, the front line and support trenches had hardly been touched by the bombardment. A further setback was the designated point of entry into the line which was destroyed and now hindered the raiders' access to the German trench. The enemy had now mounted their parapet and commenced rapid fire. About thirty-five determined Bantams, mainly aggressive bombers, succeeded in entering the line, whereas the remainder, including a party of New Zealand miners, were stalled at the point of entry. The bombers were generally hand picked athletic men with a reputation for daring, although any soldier had access to the use of grenades/bombs. For attack or raiding purposes the British formed official nine-man teams of bombers, consisting of one N.C.O., two throwers, two carriers, two bayonet men and two spare men. The party would progress along a trench, lob grenades into the next bay, and after the explosion the bay would be entered by the bayonet men who would see off any survivors still capable of resistance before signalling the throwers to advance to the next bay.

Although the bombing parties kept up a brisk exchange of bombs they were unable to open enough room for their comrades to rush in. The raiders held on gamely for approximately forty minutes but they never established themselves sufficiently to search for documents or mine entrances. In the face of stiffening German resistance and dwindling supplies of bombs at 9 p.m. the signal was given to retire.

Shortly after returning to their own lines a roll call established the 15th Cheshire casualties; two were killed and another was missing, a further 27 were wounded, of these half were scattered around No Man's Land. Several search parties went out; the bodies of two dead men were recovered and also fifteen wounded men including Second Lieutenant Jones who had a bullet wound in the leg. An unnamed Kiwi officer and one sergeant were reported as missing and one man severely wounded. The Commonwealth War Graves Commission database gives the following 15th Cheshire casualties for this day:

Dunning. F.   Private 23100 KIA.
Simpson. J.R.   Private 19572 KIA.
Mooney. H.A.   Sergeant 198600 DOW.
Walker. J.   Private 19827 KIA.
Worden. H.   Lance Corporal 19205 KIA.

Forty-three minutes after the withdrawal a large crimson flame similar to an ignition of ammonal shot up from the German line. Perhaps the missing New Zealand officer had ignited the mine – we will never know.

The earlier mentioned camouflets ignited by the New Zealanders were underground explosions used as a counter-attack on enemy miners. In an attempt to break the stalemate of trench warfare the protagonists went underground. The object of the mining was to position a large quantity of explosive beneath the enemy front line. The mines were ignited at a predetermined time usually to coincide with an attack and in the mayhem the attackers could hopefully capitalise on the shock tactic and occupy the remnants of the enemy front line. Both sides employed tunnellers, normally ex-miners to excavate the tunnels, in most instances the shafts were barely large enough to permit a man to stand upright within this claustrophobic world. The sons of a couple of Bantams have confirmed that former Cheshire Bantams were employed in this work. After reaching a position beneath the enemy, a chamber at the head of the tunnel would be packed with charges positioned in such a manner that the blast of the explosion would be directed upwards. From the charge electric cables trailed back towards the front line where the mine could be safely detonated. If this type of warfare was not dangerous enough the enemy also employed the same tactics, both sides listened intensely using the unaided ear or with geophones (a form of stethoscope) for the slightest sound of enemy mining operations. If the enemy was detected a counter mine would be dug with the intention of breaking unnoticed into the enemy tunnel and then destroying it with an explosive charge. If the invaders were rumbled, fierce fighting would take place as each side fought to gain possession of a tunnel. A less risky method was to use a device known as a camouflet; this involved extruding a long tube towards the mine, when it reached the enemy tunnel an explosive charge on the head of the camouflet was ignited thus destroying the enemy's tunnel. Throughout the summer, while the fighting raged on the surface of the western front, the allied sappers won total ascendancy over the Germans in the underground war.

The men of the 15th Cheshires entered the line on 24 September when the sector was relatively quiet, except for sporadic activity from hostile trench mortars. Two companies held the line while the remaining two occupied nearby billets. The nightly patrols into No Man's Land continued unabated and work continued both day and night on maintaining their section of the line.

The month of October brought with it continuous rain which caused a great deal of discomfort along with some consternation as the trenches proceeded to dissolve and slip inwards. Also at that period trench mortar fire claimed the lives of Second Lieutenant Chamberlain and two other ranks. A new draft of men arrived; they were immediately inspected by the C.O. and a Medical Officer, the men were familiar faces as they were all old hands returning after wounds or illness. The enemy spent the third day of the month strafing a section of the 15th Cheshires' line with trench mortars. As each shell blasted the trenches the resulting explosion threw copious amounts of debris into the air, which when it descended could block a section of trench, or bury a man alive. A series of these shell explosions succeeded in isolating a platoon of the Cheshire Bantams for some three hours. The entire line stood to ready to repulse an attack but it failed to materialise. The Bantams considered themselves extremely fortunate to get off so lightly given the ferocity of the bombardment. As their section of the line was now almost destroyed the entire night was spent repairing the line and removing tons of debris.

At 8-45 p.m on the 8 October the Brigades to the right and left of the 15th Cheshires released poison gas. The wind gently carried the toxic cloud across the German lines. The Cheshires contribution was a two-hour enfilade of rifle grenades, Lewis guns and rifle fire. The enemy put up slight resistance and claimed the life of one man and wounded two others. The C.W.G.C. records state that 23413 Private Devitt was killed on 9 October 1916 but this is most likely the man killed a day earlier.

After all the mayhem a period of quiet now descended on the sector; the tranquillity was only disturbed by the occasional explosion or gun shot, probably taken to relieve the monotony than for any other purpose. One isolated bomb did find a target when it wounded Second Lieutenant Kidd. There was a constant rotation of officers as they plied back and forth to various schools of instruction, went off to hospital or returned to Blighty on leave. The posting of Captain Spencer Fleming Morgan to the 10th Cheshires appears to be the straw that broke the camel's back. Due to the continued drain on officers the Commanding Officer and Second-in-Command had to take watches in the front line. Concerns were expressed that the battalion's fighting ability would be critically weakened in the likelihood of an attack, for the majority of officers were second lieutenants with only a few months' front line experience.

On the night of 28 October the 15th Cheshires were employed carrying poison gas cylinders to the 104 Brigade frontage. The first day of November found the 15th Battalion still in the line near Arras where the weather was described as bad. The incessant rain set off small landslides in the trenches, which were beginning to accumulate a build up of water and mud. The German trench mortars continued to cause severe

Captain Spencer Fleming Morgan.

problems when, one evening, a direct hit on a trench resulted in one officer and four men being buried alive. Frantic efforts from their comrades succeeded in rescuing all the men. The following day the trench mortars systematically strafed our front lines doing considerable damage. A total of 22 Cheshires were buried alive; of these seven were killed and three men suffered from the effects of gas poisoning. Once again, consulting the C.W.G.C. data-base, I believe the men to be:

20013. Private W. Brown.

30738. Private J. Moult.

20426. Private H. Harrop.

19978. Private S. Oxley.

19558. Private W. Jackson.

19774. Private C.G. Watson.

The seventh man was most likely 23345 Private A. Davies, who according to the same records died of wounds on 4 November 1917.

When darkness descended on the night of November 3/4 a 15th Cheshire raiding party successfully crossed the neutral zone and despite resistance managed to enter the German line. After withdrawing four men failed to return, bombs wounded two other men, and several others were cut by enemy wire. The C.W.G.C. records show the deaths of:

20084. Lance Corporal. W.C. Sproul.

23007. Corporal. J.J. Foster.

23345. Private A. Davies (who died of wounds).

23084. Private J. Wroe.

The inclement weather deteriorated. The rain now fell in torrents for days on end, damaged parapets collapsed and the men in the line began to succumb to the effects of exposure and trench foot, for the men in many parts of the front line were standing in knee deep stagnant pools of water. The artillery carried on regardless of the weather, continually smashing gaps in the barbed wire defences; each side strove to repair the gaps before the enemy attacked through the breach in the wire.

On the 25 November Lieutenant Fitzgerald led a twenty-man patrol from the 15th Battalion on a raiding party against the hostile line to the south of Chantecler. They discovered that the enemy wire had been insufficiently cut by the trench mortars, and according to orders did not press home the raid. Three days later it was a quiet and frosty day and the battlefield was enveloped in a thick blanket of fog, reducing visibility to less than thirty yards, prompting the Cheshires to examine their wire and to carry out work in No Man's Land. Unfortunately, that decision cost them two casualties, namely Captain Wolstenholme and an Artillery officer who had gone out to see the lie of the trenches. The body of the Bantam captain was brought back to the lines, that night an attempt was made to find the missing R.A. officer's body. Unfortunately, in the process Lieutenant Fitzgerald was wounded. For the next couple of nights patrols scoured the shell craters searching for the missing artillery officer without success. On 24 November the 2nd Birkenhead Battalion bid farewell to Lieutenant Colonel Browne-Clayton who was promoted to the command of a brigade. Lieutenant

Colonel E.T. Saint replaced him as commander of the 16th Cheshire Battalion.

On 1 December the 35th Division received orders advising of the relief by the 9th Division. After having endured thirty-five days continually in the front line and support trenches the 1st Battalion South African Infantry relieved the Cheshires on the evening of 3rd December.

George Moffatt was a strong and tough former Cammell Laird shipyard worker who served with the 15th Battalion. After one tour of the line he told his family how they were cold, soaking wet, tired, hungry and extremely thirsty. They arrived at a French farm, which had a drinking well sited in the centre of the courtyard; the top of the well had a stout timber cover and was firmly padlocked. 23032 Lance Corporal George Moffatt asked the farmer for the key who promptly refused. Reporting this to his officer he was told to 'Shoot off the lock, and if the frog gets in the way shoot him too'. The farmer took the hint and the small soldier promptly shot off the lock, and the men quenched their thirst. Lance Corporal Moffatt survived the war; he returned home with a great respect for the Germans and a passionate hatred of the French. After his demob he was reunited with his wife who died soon afterwards of consumption (T.B.). Two decades later both his sons were killed with 4th Cheshires following the fall of Dunkirk in the Second World War.

Sergeant George Eames.

Prior to serving with the colours Sergeant George Eames was a long serving employee of Lever Brothers of Port Sunlight, Wirral. He was renowned for his fine baritone voice which was well known on concert and music hall platforms. He originally joined the 13th Battalion Cheshire Regiment, Wirral Pals and went with them to France in September 1915. While serving in the first battle of the Somme with the 15th Battalion Sergeant Major Eames was severely wounded. He permanently lost his sight, had a finger shot off and sustained severe shrapnel wounds to the left arm. He spent a lengthy period in the care of St. Dunstan's Hospital for Blind Servicemen where, as part of his rehabilitation, he was taught poultry farming. In 1921 the highly impressive Port Sunlight war memorial was

Artillery spotters using bonoculars, periscope and field telephone.

completed. Lord Leverhulme suggested the honour of unveiling the memorial should not be carried out by himself, but should be invested in an ex serviceman, chosen by a ballot of his former comrades in arms at Port Sunlight. Lever Brothers in-house magazine *The Progress* reported,

> *So it came about that the choice fell upon an old servant of the company (Sgt Eames) that he should also have been the one man in all that vast concourse for whom the beauty of the memorial must always remain a matter of report, was a circumstance that gave the occasion a vivid poignancy. The sightless figure of Sgt Eames stood as a symbol of the blind cruelty of war and as the symbol of the dauntless soul of man triumphing over tribulation. George Eames died suddenly at his Tranmere home on 21 April 1935; he was survived by a widow, three sons and two daughters.*

The entire 15th Battalion proceeded to Arras from where they travelled by bus to Wanquentin later marching to billets at Izel-Les-Hameau. As the men marched they gave a rendition of a popular 35th Division marching song:

Now see the poor Bantams their feet are so sore.
Splashing in mud and in water galore.
When in the trenches they all do their best.
They'd sooner stay in than come out for a rest.

Now some say its Etaples and some say Boulogne
But we don't give a cuss if we go to Hong Kong
Any old place in this wide world we'll roam
So long as they don't take us back on the Somme.

The following days were spent in route marches, cleaning equipment, and inspections. A big effort had been made to get the equipment and

The streets of Arras.

uniforms clean especially as the battalion was to be inspected by the G.O.C. The man was extremely disappointed with the turn out of the Bantams; this came as a big disappointment to both officers and men, as the effects of exposure and neglect during their thirty-five days in the trenches, made it impossible to get the smartness and cleanliness aimed at. Immediately after the inspection the A.D.M.S. inspected the battalion, this time he appears to have been satisfied with the physical condition of the men.

On the 12 December there was snow and sleet all day but despite the poor weather the men were detailed to commence a new rifle range, the more fortunate ones were involved in training inside the billets. The working parties, training and lectures continued throughout December, the majority of the time the men were either working or training.

On the 6 December a circular letter was distributed amongst the Officers of the 35th Division advising that henceforth they would no longer be referred to as a 'Bantam Division'. In future replacements would be of men of average height as due to the shortage of manpower all battalions were now accepting small men. Eleven days later a new draft arrived of twenty other ranks from the Gloucester Regiment, closely followed by an additional eleven men from an undisclosed battalion. Their arrival prompted yet another inspection from the Corps Commander Major General H.J.S. Landon, a man who appears to have been determined to finish off the Bantams. He immediately prowled up and down the line weeding out men. By the time he was finished 141 men had been ignominiously rejected, these were all small men and were to be replaced by drafts of average height men; the Bantam battalions were to be no more. Lieutenant General Haldane in his memoir *A Soldier's Tale* recounts how faced with such devastating pruning of the Division he sought higher authority to strip the Division of so many men. The Army Commander personally decided to carry out the inspection unaware of the fact it was stage managed to a certain extent by Haldane. The men to be rejected were lined up in Companys on open ground that sloped away from the path the C.O. would take. Thus a man who was not lacking in height assessed the assembled lines of men who due to the lay of the land now looked even smaller than usual with the result that the ensuing cull was devastating. According to Haldane, by the end of December, the 35th Division strength was reduced by a quarter as 2,800 men were rejected as unsuitable. There is some dispute in the numbers involved here as some battalions do not quote figures – the *History of the 35th Division* quotes a very similar amount. Regimental pride may account for the much lesser figure of 1,439 men being rejected as unsuitable. Unfortunately amongst those to be dismissed were men who performed admirably and it was with regret that their officers lost the services of men whose physical disability had not affected them in any way. These rejected men remained with their units waiting for the army to determine their fate. In defence of the rejected Bantams it appears that no one had considered the average age of these volunteers – for that's exactly what they were, volunteers. While I have not mathematically calculated the average age of the men[6], It does appear the average declared age of many of these men was just over nineteen years of age. This proportionate cross section of the Bantam's age could well reflect the reasons for the slight build of the majority of rejected volunteers, for they were no more than lads who had yet to develop into maturity, many never did!

On Christmas Day the battalion dined in estaminets; a welcome break from the daily grind was a football competition and also rapid-fire competitions. On the 28th December the battalion minus W company marched to Arras and relieved the 18th Lancashire Fusiliers. Meanwhile W company marched to Buneville and relieved the 1st company of the 18th Lancs. Fusiliers. As the old year drew to a close 350 men from the battalion found themselves in working parties for the 3rd Army Signals.

Notes

(1) Towards the end of June the *Birkenhead Advertiser* reported the wounding of a twenty-five year old Rock Ferry officer who lay wounded in a London hospital. During the start of the new offensive on 7 June 1917 Captain Spencer Fleming Morgan was one of the first to go over the top and sustained a gunshot wound in the right thigh after going about 600 yards with his regiment, (10th Cheshires) who performed prodigies of valour on the Messines Ridge. Though the wound bled freely Captain Morgan went on another 500 yards with his men before he dropped and had to be removed from the battlefield. The next day he was admitted to base hospital and on 12 June his parents received a wire from him which stated, 'Just arrived Dover. Cheerio'.

(2) The Commonwealth War Graves Commission database reveals the age of a high proportion of casualties; this is the only set of statistics available to me to access the average age.

CHAPTER 9

1917 – The End of the Bantams

Alas the Bantams' battalions cease to exist.
For just one year after leaving Albion's shore.
The Bantam Brigade will be no more.
Too many little men have now gone west.
While hundreds more failed Landon's physical test.
He forgot we volunteered and were not fetched.
For we did not slack, we followed the rest.

Not enough of the small uns now remain.
To maintain our Birkenhead founder's name.
Taller men now join our ranks in battle.
Fighting a foe we were not scared to tackle.
So join in the old Bantams' glorious fight.
We will still prove that small is right.
To send the Kaiser packing is still our aim.

The fat sausage eaters will rue the day.
When the Cheshire Bantams passed their way.
Through thick and thin we will soldier on.
And one day soon our great day will come.
For the last Bantams will fight to the end.
Across Flanders fields and bloody Somme.
For old England's glory we shall defend.

Anon

AS THE NEW YEAR DAWNED the 35th Division marked time waiting for reorganisation, the 15th battalion said farewell to sixty-one of their chums who had earlier been rejected by the A.D.M.S. The remainder of the battalion were given daily practice in musketry or supplied working parties.

The 35th Division now moved to the rear area and was out of the front line until the middle of February. This withdrawal provided an opportunity to reorganise the Division and carry out training. As the reinforcements were from disbanded yeomanry regiments and the cavalry depot the new arrivals had to be schooled in infantry tactics. The training was constantly interrupted due to the demands for large working parties in connection with the preparations for the forthcoming spring offensive; amongst the workers were the men of

A Cheshire Bantam with two regular height members of his regiment.

the 16th Battalion. In mid January the battalions were under strength due to the combing out of rejects. A fresh draft of 114 men arrived and were immediately sent to the recently established 35th Divisional Depot Battalion at Averdoinet for training. Here they honed their musketry skills and received fresh instruction in infantry tactics whether they were new recruits or an old hand. Two days later an additional eighteen N.C.O.s and 286 other ranks arrived at Buneville and remained there for the purpose of training. It is not recorded what happened to the majority of rejected Bantams; they would still have remained in the military in one capacity or another, and for some it might have been a blessing in disguise. The fate of former 16th Battalion men is disclosed for 211 of those rejected found themselves at the Base involved in employment of various capacities. An additional thirty-two men, possibly former miners, were sent to the 23rd and 24th Tunnelling Companies, where they would continue their war underground. As January drew to a close the Battalion's strength stood at thirty-three Officers and 946 O.R.s and were once again back to their fighting strength, even if they were no longer considered to be a Bantam battalion.

Not all the deaths in military service are attributed to enemy action abroad, for the accidental death of Corporal W.H. Suckley of the 17th Battalion occurred at Prees Heath on 9 January 1917. The twenty year old had joined the Bantams on their formation. He sustained very serious bodily injuries whilst instructing some men in the use of high explosive bombs. Corporal Crew, a comrade of the deceased, made a gallant attempt to resuscitate him until he himself was overcome by fumes and was afterwards found unconscious. Lever's Brothers formerly employed Private Suckley; where he worked in No. 2 frame room.

During the first week of February the 15th Battalion vacated Arras and in a series of daily marches headed for their destination of Fienvillers, where they underwent intensive training in all available infantry weapons. Later, while in camp at Flesselles, the Cheshires celebrated the anniversary of Meanee Day with an impromptu concert by the Na Poos, a firm favourite with the battalion.

The Commanding Officer of the 15th Battalion Lieutenant Colonel H.P.G. Cochran had recently returned from leave and was taken ill, on the 10th instant. He was taken to the New Zealand Hospital at Amiens. With no one at the helm Major H. Johnston assumed temporary command and Captain W. Hodson M.C. was appointed second in command. This arrangement stood until the arrival of Major P.S. Hall D.S.O. who took command of the battalion on 18 February. Earlier that morning the battalion had entrained at Flesselles station and crowded into the railway wagons to be conveyed to Wiencourt. Upon arrival a group of officers visited the section of the line near Rosières; they were to take over from the French 154th Division. To their horror they found the trenches were in parts three foot deep in thick mud as a rapid thaw had led to large sections of the parapet falling in. The deep mud created a problem that was all the more severe due to the still strong presence of five foot tall soldiers in their battalion. The winter had been an extremely cold one and the thaw had begun swamping the battlefield in flood water, which drained into the maze of trenches, producing a muddy quagmire in sections of the line. Before leaving the ruined village of Rosières for the trenches on 20 February the entire battalion had their feet massaged with whale oil as a preventive measure against the condition known as trench foot, a painful ailment producing symptoms of bloated feet, infected with ulcers, blisters, diseased toe nails and, in severe cases, gangrene.

A French guide steered the battalion through the trenches but eventually the entire battalion found themselves bogged down in a river of stinking mud that partly filled the Lunette II communication trench. The powerful suction of the thick soup of mud sucked the boots and socks off scores of men in the struggle to move forward, rifles and equipment slid beneath the surface of the mud and became lost. All the exertions combined with a gas alert due to two gas shells, were sapping the men's energy and after eight hours of these atrocious conditions the decision was taken to climb out of the quagmire. Before midnight the battalion climbed out of the cover of the trenches and set off over the top where eventually they relieved a battalion of the French 413th Regiment at Piaine, in the Caix sector. It proved impossible to bring forward any food or supplies to the marooned troops who were now living on their iron rations. Any visiting officers could only reach the position if they went over the top under cover of darkness.

Fortunately, the new section was relatively quiet. A weak February sun slowly began to dry up the trenches and the men set about the difficult and tiring task of clearing the mud. This tour of the trenches was concluded on 1 March when the battalion, now caked in mud from head to toe, was relieved by the 16th Cheshires. The casualties sustained during their stay in the line were two killed, five wounded and three gassed. A medical officer in the village of Rosières weighed the uniform of one of the casualties brought in; the clothes were clogged with mud and turned the scale at 90 pounds (40 kilos).

The 16th Battalion was based in camp one mile South of Caix. They marched to Vrely on 21 February acting as reserve to 105 Brigade in the left sub sector of Chilly Sector[1]. On 1 March they relieved their fellow Birkenhead battalion in the line; the quiet interlude was abruptly halted on the following very cold evening when the enemy launched a raid on two sections of the Cheshires' front line. At 6-45 p.m. an artillery bombardment descended on the front and support trenches occupied by the 16th Cheshires. The shells formed a barrage around the sap situated approximately 1,000 yards north-east of Chilly to about 400 yards either side. Simultaneously the allied artillery in the vicinity was shelled with explosive and gas shells severing communications. The German infantry launched a raid on W Company's frontage which was successfully repulsed, although one officer was gassed. The attackers failed to enter this part of the British front lines. The attack on the Y Company front was however a different story, for with the assistance of poison gas the invaders managed to enter the line and desperate hand to hand fighting ensued. One of the enemy was killed and the remainder retreated.

As all communications were severed Lieutenant Baxter and his servant braved the bombardment and went forward to access the situation. He encountered two Germans and fired his revolver at them, before being wounded by a bomb. His batman was knocked out cold by a blow from a spade. The following Cheshire casualties

Unidentified short, but wide, Bantam.

were recorded: three officers wounded, one officer gassed, six O.R.s killed, fifteen O.R.s wounded and gassed, and nineteen O.R.s missing. The enemy also suffered heavy casualties during both of the raids. When they withdrew, they took with them a trophy in the form of a captured Lewis gun. Several days later the wounded men from this action Second Lieutenant H.E. Marrow, W. Pickford, H.S. Baxter and the gassed Second Lieutenant Horsfall and R.A. McKnight were all evacuated to England. At 5-30 a.m. on 3 March a repeat of the previous hostile bombardment commenced, this time it concentrated on the previously mentioned Lunette II, held by the right platoon of the 19th D.L.I. and the left sub section of the 16th Cheshires. During the onslaught a forty-five strong enemy infiltrated the British line through a sap at the end of Lunette, their bombers blasted their way through the north and south section of the frontage.

As the hand to hand fighting raged in the trench enemy artillery engaged our batteries simultaneously shelling the rear areas to prevent the arrival of reinforcements. The defenders' Lewis guns were in continuous action throughout the raid to prevent the build up of the enemy attack; as the Cheshires fought for all their worth a sentry post north of the Boyau de Rennes successfully halted the advance of the southern arm of the raiding party, whilst the northern limit was stemmed in the area near Boyaux Tomalsi. Twenty-one men from the Cheshires were originally posted as missing; they were probably buried during the bombardment. The Germans considered to be from the 175th Infantry Regiment retired under the cover from smoke bombs. Three dead raiders and one fatally wounded man were left behind; later patrols discovered the German raiders had suffered severe casualties. The majority of the missing men survived the onslaught as only five of the 16th Cheshires are listed as killed on the day of the attack.

The 23rd Battalion of the Manchester Regiment relieved the 16th Battalion on 6 March. After a couple of days' rest at Rosières they spent the rest of their time in training, until the 14th day when they marched back to the Chilly Sector support line.

The first week of March found the 15th Cheshires at Decauville Camp undergoing intensive training for a planned attack, the men were weary and a request for shorter hours was declined and the preparations for the forthcoming raid continued. Due to the continual combing out of the ranks, spiralling casualties, wounds and trench feet the battalion was now greatly under strength; a further eighty-three rejects departed, a further twenty-two had been seconded to railway work. On the 12 March the battalion's strength was down to 400 men, yet the depleted battalion was still expected to fulfil the manpower demands of an entire battalion.

After raining all night the 14 March brought a nice spring morning to brighten up the spirits of the saturated soldiers. They set off for Lihons, Chilly sector, to relieve the 17th Royal Scots at dusk but the terrible mud and continual rain made the conditions in the line so atrocious that the relief was severely delayed. Some idea of the conditions is given by one of the officers who wrote, 'Very difficult to visit companies in the line, three hundred yards of trench taking an hour to struggle through'. Less than 400 men were now expected to hold a 1,600 yards' frontage.

On 9 April 1917 the British and the Colonial armies entered into what they hoped would be the final campaign of the war – the Arras offensive. This was a plan known as the Blaireville project that was conceived as early as June of the previous year, it was envisaged as a supplement to the Somme offensive but never went ahead as the appalling Somme casualties had absorbed all the available manpower. The slow but

Private T.E. Johns (left) and 22130 Private John Owen Williams, 16th Battalion.

steady British advance eastwards on the Somme had left a German held salient between the Rivers Scarpe and Ancre. This bulge in the line presented an opportunity for a pincer blow converging towards Cambrai. If all went well the German forces within the bulge would be cut off, offering the advancing forces an opportunity to carve a gap through the German defences too wide for the German Reserves to plug. Once this was achieved Haig could focus his attention on the Ypres Salient where he truly believed the war would be won.

The hard fought allied gains on the Somme resulted in the Germans' loss of the high ground and produced an irregular profile front line. As the Somme battles had depleted German manpower it made military logic to withdraw to higher ground and in doing so to straighten their frontage, producing a shorter front that required less manpower to guard. Towards the end of February the Germans began to pull back to a new line of defence referred to by the British as the Hindenburg Line or the *Siegfried Stellung* to the defenders. The British witnessed the fortifications being built but were virtually powerless to prevent its construction. In April 1917 Nivelle launched his French Army into an attack along a fifty mile front, early success rapidly turned to disaster when the troops were dashed against the new German fortifications. The life-blood of 50,000 Frenchmen ebbed away into the earth, and a further 60,000 were maimed and wounded. With the French Army in open mutiny, Nivelle was swiftly replaced by General Petain. For a month he toured the front visiting nearly every Division, listening to their grievances and acted upon them. The French army required easing back into the war with new tactics and training, for the remainder of the year the British Empire's 64 divisions would bear the brunt of the Flanders campaign.

Between their original front line and their new fortification the Germans created a barren wasteland. To make the abandoned area as uninhabitable as possible all drinking wells were poisoned, any man-made structure, road or natural cover was systematically destroyed and the entire area was littered with booby traps, and delayed action bombs. On the 16 March the 15th Cheshires' observers watched the Hun setting fire to the villages behind the German lines. The much practised raid by W Company on the enemy front and support lines was also ordered to go ahead that night. At 5 p.m. the Cheshire patrols entered the old German line and found it unoccupied, the battalion advanced cautiously, two platoons per company advanced until all four companies found themselves safely in the abandoned German line. A foothold of 200 yards was consolidated before pushing forward patrols down his communication trench; at every twist and turn they expected to encounter the enemy. By 8-30 p.m. our patrols reported that they had reached their second objective, two miles behind the old enemy front line and had met with no opposition.

Early on the 18th day, as part of a general advance, the 15th Cheshires moved forward and reinforced the patrols guarding the second objective, before taking the third objective lying four miles to the rear of the old Hun front line. In mid afternoon the 16th Cheshires leapfrogged their brother battalion, the 35th Division was now crammed between the 32nd and 61st Divisions and were effectively squeezed out of the line. On the morning of 19 March the entire Division was ordered to move back to Lihons. This had been a relatively successful tour of the line as they had only incurred three wounded including Captain W. Hodson. The 15th Battalion arrived at their billets in old trenches near Lihons, here they had a few hours respite that allowed an opportunity to examine their bulging coat pockets of souvenirs acquired during their exploration of the Hun lines.

Although the British army had abandoned the use of Bantam battalions their Italian ally began to recruit their own Bantams. The *Liverpool Daily Post* 19 April 1917 reported: 'A decree is issued reducing the height of the Italian army to 4 feet 11 inches' (one inch less than the British standard). It was anticipated the reduction would permit the enlisting of many more recruits.

The retiring German Army had wrecked the entire infrastructure of a 900 square mile area; legions of men were assigned to reconstruction, including the 15th Battalion and 14th Gloucesters who were employed for a couple of days along the snow covered Lihons – Chaulnes road. For the remainder of March the 35th Division toiled away in bitterly cold conditions on the wrecked Chaulnes – Nesle railway. After completion of their task the 15th battalion moved to Voyennes.

The 16th Cheshires reinstated the wrecked railway from Chaulnes station, and the succeeding days were spent on the railway work east of Nesle. The first four days of April the 15th Cheshires were working away bridging a large crater in the railway embankment close to the River Ignon east of Nesle, they in filled and levelled the track bed in readiness for the plate laying French repair crews. The French and Royal Engineers were so pleased with the speed the task was completed they issued the following-

Congratulatory C.R.O., 1080:

The Corps Commander wishes to thank the troops for the excellent work they have done in repair of damaged roads in the area regained from the Germans. The 105 Infantry Brigade has done most useful work on the railway and has greatly contributed to the completion of the line to Nesle in so short a time.

Work carried on upon a succession of destroyed roads and railway tracks in the vicinity of Voyennes, occasionally the labouring was interrupted while the men engaged in training attacks on a village. By the beginning of April all the 35th Division's battalions were employed in the forward area of the Somme battlefield. On 9 April the division received orders to relieve the 61st Division in the left sector of the Corps frontage to the north east of St. Quentin. The 105 Brigade replaced 184 Brigade in Divisional Reserve. At sunrise on the 14th a brigade from 32nd Division attacked and captured Fayet village, this prompted the 17th Lancashire Fusiliers to advance on Gricourt, where despite stiff resistance, they captured the churchyard then the village itself. This momentum was carried forward by the 17th, 18th, and 20th battalions of the Lancashire Fusiliers who resolutely pressed home the attacks and gained ground. The 23rd Manchesters cautiously entered Pontruet to find the Germans had withdrawn. Meanwhile the 17th West Yorks rushed an enemy held crater north of Pontruet; the startled enemy took to their heels and fled.

The conditions of battle had altered during the Division's period in reserve soldiers who had grown accustomed to static trench warfare now found themselves engaged in semi open warfare. The weather on the night of 16 April was abysmal; the wind lashed the rain against the infantrymen of 105 Brigade as they groped their way in the dark along the cluttered communication trenches. The outgoing 104 Brigade had sustained approximately 400 casualties during the previous 48 hours. The 15th Cheshires were still a depleted force who found they were

Engineers resting from their labours in a large crater. The 15th and 16th Cheshires were involved in assisting the Engineers during April 1917.

now garrisoning a sector of the line east of Maissemy abandoned by the Germans who ensured no shelter or rudimentary comfort remained. The general condition of the trench left a lot to be desired; it was in a filthy condition, and extremely shallow in parts even for Bantams. The line was so devoid of cover that battalion headquarters could only be established under a flimsy tarpaulin. The battalion suffered badly from exposure due to a lack of cover, rain and biting cold making a mockery of anti-frost bite precautions. Three companies established themselves in an abandoned German trench; a hundred yards forward, the men of X Company established themselves along the sunken Pontruet to Gricourt road. The sunken road afforded a degree of natural protection to the defenders, however, enemy artillery rapidly found the range of these wide natural trenches and they invariably became death traps. The Germans knew every inch of this terrain and wasted no time in persecuting the newcomers with salvoes from their 4.5 field howitzers, the freshly set up H.Q. received their unwanted attentions. For three long hours a slow but steady strafe of shells straddled the flimsy H.Q. accounting for three N.C.O.s and one O. R. casualty. Also a front line bombardment shrapnel burst wounded another five men.

For the next couple of days the Cheshires endured the sporadic bombardments, on the 18th the murderous shells swept down upon the old Bosche trench and claimed the lives of three members of W

Company and wounded three others. The deceased soldiers were Privates Ryan and Welbourn. The third man killed is not listed in Soldiers Died. One of those killed in action was Private Joseph Welbourn, a 41 year old married Stockport man. He was a South African war veteran with eighteen years' military service, before leaving and taking up employment as a painter. He re-enlisted for service in the Great War on 1 January 1915 and must originally have gone overseas with a battalion other than the 15th Cheshires as he was awarded the 1914-15 Star. As a result of his death by shellfire he left behind a widow and four children. The four day stint in the line concluded on the evening of the 20th when the 16th Cheshires relieved their brothers in arms who then proceeded to bivouacs in a valley south west of Maissemy.

Lieutenant Colonel Saint, commander of the 16th Cheshires, was appointed to command the recently formed Divisional School at Boves, Lieutenant Colonel Dent returned from the Depot and took over command. Until now the men of the 16th Battalion had been employed improving the destroyed roads and railways and they now filed back into the line keen for a fight. On the 20th instant the 105th Brigade relieved the 96th Brigade in the Twin Copses area south of Gricourt. Within hours of taking over the line the Lieut. and Adjutant C.E.E. Heywood with Second Lieutenant Jones and No 9725 Corporal Leech explored the area and carried out a skilful reconnaissance of the sunken road between Pontruet and Les Trois Sauvages where they came across an advance German post.

The 22 April witnessed two platoons from Z Company advancing along the sunken road south of Pontruet, the enemy were alert and a small skirmish ensued upon the roadway, during which several Germans were seen to fall. The Cheshires' party realised they were facing stouter opposition than was anticipated and made a tactical withdrawal, bringing with them one prisoner (wounded) from the 452nd Infantry Regiment. The raid was costly for the Cheshires. Captain Sturla was wounded, Second Lieutenant R.J. Morris was killed, three other ranks were missing believed killed and a fourth man was killed outright. The post-war records for this battalion only record the deaths of two private's on this date.

The following night W company attacked another position further north along the sunken road, finding the position unoccupied they captured and held the post, until the next day when they were relieved by the 15th Cheshires, and returned into support at Maissemy.

Opposite is a charge sheet issued by Lance Corporal G. Moffat while on 35th Division Traffic Control mid way between Tierry and Marie Court on 25 April. Overleaf is the following hand written badly faded statement-

26-4-17. Statement of evidence against 081064 Private Jeffrey.
Sir.
On the 25th inst at 3-15pm I was on duty at Caulaincourt when I saw the above named soldier driving ambulance No 15038 against the Traffic Circuit, I took his no and name for report.

G. Moffatt. L/Cpl.   Traffic Controller. 35th Division.

The morning of 27th was quiet but during the afternoon Battalion Head Quarters were lightly shelled killing two O.R.s and wounding two others. That night three patrols crept towards positions occupied by a jumpy and alert foe, the left patrol drew fire, the centre patrol was fired on from bushes to the west of a copse, while the third patrol commanded by Second Lieutenant G.K. Mowle encountered a hostile three man patrol. The latter patrol was no match for the Cheshires; two of them were killed outright and the third was taken prisoner and provided valuable information to his captors.

The next day was quiet until the enemy fiercely shelled the outpost line for almost an hour, after a two hour interlude a more intense bombardment strafed the front line. The machine gun emplacement received a direct hit instantly killing four of its crew and wounding another, the Battalion Head Quarters was lightly shelled resulting in the deaths of two O.R.s. At dusk a patrol crept out in the direction of the distant copse and found it occupied by the enemy, the information was reported to the Commanders who prepared a plan of action. The war diaries do not explain why the location of the troublesome artillery pieces to the east of Bellenglise could not be located; the man who located them was twenty-three year old 19423 Private Johnson, an original Bantam who was detailed as an observer, although his official trade was that of a sniper. Major Keith from the Royal Artillery A/157 Battery joined the small Bantam in his tiny outpost and from there calculated the range and direction and called for aid from the howitzers of D battery; acting as an artillery spotter he successfully eliminated three guns and blew up an ammunition store. This transpired to be the battery that had caused so much damage to the Cheshires' lines. The intelligence provided by Private Robert Johnson prompted the Lieutenant Colonel of the R.F.A. to report the matter to the officer commanding the 15th Cheshires.

Later that evening a Cheshire patrol set off to capture a post to the west of the copse, they successfully worked their way round the back of the post and bombed it to good effect. But the Teutonic defenders seemed to have anticipated this patrol and large numbers of Germans appeared on either flank of the group. The outnumbered Cheshires put up a strong fight and inflicted considerable damage on the enemy before retiring; one other rank was wounded, while another was posted as missing.

The 15th Battalion missed their chance to storm the copse they had reported as being occupied, for the task was given to the 16th Cheshires who advanced and passed through the 15th Battalion's position as their fellow Cheshires looked on enviously. The 16th Cheshires were ordered to attack two copses approximately 600 yards west of the St. Quentin to Le Catelet road. On 28 April W, X and Y Companies of the 16th Battalion assembled in a sunken road close to the windmill some 1,200 yards north of Gricourt. From there they moved to a designated point of departure where Captain G. Playfair organised X and Y Company to line out as assaulting companies, W Company was held in reserve. At 1 a.m. next morning both assaulting companies advanced from the sanctuary of the sunken road, they faced sporadic rifle fire, and a short burst of machine gun fire, which ceased when the prearranged standing barrage rained down upon the enemy front line. A creeping barrage swept before the advancing

No 19423 Pte Johnson
X. A Coy 15 Cheshires

O.C. 15 Cheshires
Owing to the intelligence of the
above man, he was able to
point out to Major Keith A/157
a Battery in action in G.36.C.
in which we had much pleasure in
doing in this afternoon —
I told Pte Johnson I should have
much pleasure in reporting this to
his Colonel, as he was the man
who originally spotted the Battery —
D B Stewart L/Col
157 Bde R.F.A.

28/4/17.

19423 Private Johnson

attackers, every four minutes the barrage lifted and the shells exploded a further 100 yards forward. The assaulting companies surged into the northern copse sweeping all before them, anyone offering resistance was killed, six were captured, those who failed to surrender were sent to their maker. The Cheshires formed up about 50 yards to the North East of the copse, each company then sent out a patrol towards the German wire. Shortly before two in the morning in reply to our barrage the enemy shells descended to the rear of our assaulting companies and the North East edge of the sunken road to prevent any consolidating advances taking place. When our guns ceased at the prearranged time the enemy guns also fell silent, allowing our assaulting companies to withdraw unmolested while covered by patrols, and reached their point of departure at 3-30 a.m. The casualties for the raid were Second Lieutenant Wood wounded, 1 O.R. killed, 26 wounded (2 later died of wounds) and 2 O.R.s were reported as missing. A day later the battalion was relieved by the 17th Royal Scots and marched to camp at Trepcon on the afternoon of the 30 April.

Private Norman Thomas King, 15th Cheshires.

All and sundry from the 15th Cheshires felt they had been 'done out of a good show'; their final day in the line was a very quiet day. The usual patrols went out and found the copse still held by the enemy, during one of the night patrols one O.R. was wounded and another was posted as missing. Both men must have been on a patrol prior to the 10-30 p.m. relief by the 17th Battalion Highland Light Infantry. There is only one known death for this date to this battalion and I feel safe to assume it was the missing man namely 45754 Private Norman Thomas King. By anyone's description he would be described as a baby faced twenty year old man. He lived with his parents in Liscard, Wirral.

On the 30 April the 105 Brigade was relieved by the 106. The month of May proved to be uneventful for the 15th battalion who spent the entire month training, and working. They vacated Soyecourt to act in support in the Fresnoy Section. On the night of the 10th under cover of darkness X, Y and Z companies carried out wiring forward of the 16th Battalion's front. While working they were attacked by an enemy patrol who were easily driven off, during this incident the C.O. of Z Company Captain H.F.A. Le Measurier was wounded. On the night of the 13th they relieved the 16th Cheshires in the Fresnoy section of the line near Maissemy, some six miles distant from St. Quentin. A few nights later three companies were ordered to transfer the German wire from west to east side of the old German trench; on their way forward nine other ranks were wounded, one of these men died later. The transferring of the wire proved to be easier said than done, as due to

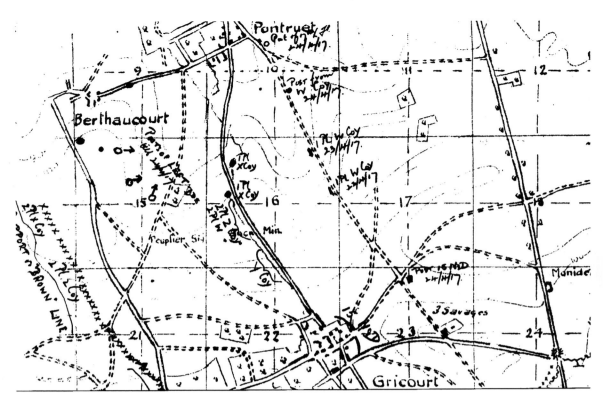

The position of the 16th Battalion late April 1917.

the appalling nature of the terrain the wire became badly tangled and was abandoned. On the 25 May 105 Brigade, including this battalion, moved to bivouacs near Peronne.

The first half of May was also uneventful for the 16th Cheshires until they relieved the 15th battalion Cheshires in Fresnoy section of the front line. On the 17th Major R. Worthington was killed while doing the rounds of posts at Pontruet.

Thirty year old Major Ralph Worthington had been second in command of the battalion since July 1915. A former soldier of the Rhodesia Volunteers, he returned to England on the outbreak of war. He was a married man who resided in Glasgow, before enlisting into the Northumberland Fusiliers in Oct 1914, where he obtained a commission and was gazetted Second Lieutenant in the same regiment. He was promoted Lieutenant, followed by promotion to Captain in December 1914, and Major in the following year. A transfer to the 16th Cheshire Regiment resulted in him serving on the Somme where he was wounded prior to being killed in action near St. Quentin. The Brigadier General Commanding 105 Brigade wrote, 'Major Worthington was a most zealous, painstaking and conscientious officer, always looking after the good of his battalion and to the service'. He was succeeded by Captain W. Hodson, a 15th Battalion

Captain W. Hodson, took over the 15th Battalion.

officer; at about this time Lieutenant Colonel Newell who had recovered from wounds received on the Somme resumed command of the 15th Battalion.

The 35th Division now handed over the command of the area north of the River Omignon to the 5th Cavalry Division. As the divisional sector was to be ceded to the French, on the 19 May 105 Brigade was relieved by the 87th French Division. Later that night the 91st French Infantry Regiment arrived to relieve the 16th Cheshires, but as it was a bright moon lit night the relief of Post 34 was delayed. When they had gone a short distance they were bombed by a 30-40 strong enemy in occupation of the outpost. This surprise attack resulted in six casualties to the Cheshires who retired to their piquet lines, shortly after midnight the post was occupied by its garrison without opposition, as the Germans had retired. The relief by the French was completed without further incident. The following day 35th Divisional Head Quarters relocated to Peronne, where they came under the orders of XV Corps.

The 16th Battalion proceeded to Soyecourt were they were given a two day break, after their rest the entire 105th Brigade set off for Peronne, for a brief stay before moving to a camp near Templeux-La-Fosse. As a component of the Brigade in Divisional Reserve they spent the remainder of the month in training exercises. The remainder of the Division held a quiet section of the line whose geography consisted of open grassland interspersed with woods and valleys, where the November battles of Cambrai later occurred.

On the 2nd of the month the 35th Division came under the command of III Corps, due to the withdrawal of XV Corps from the line. On the same day the 105 Brigade relieved the 106 in the right sector. Throughout June the 35th Division were not involved in any operations of significance. Meanwhile on the 7 June the Second Army carried out a successful limited attack on the Messines Ridge, with the surprise element of nineteen huge mines simultaneously igniting below the German lines. During the first ten days of June the 15th Cheshires' tour of the trenches proved to be totally uneventful; the time was spent patrolling, deepening trenches and improving the barbed wire defences; they were relieved by the 16th Cheshires. Towards the middle of the month the entire battalion were involved in 'Trench Jumping' creating a new length of trench each night. This was a task fraught with danger for the diggers had to work as quick and as quiet as possible so as not to draw attention from the enemy. On the 18 June the battalion was relieved by the 23rd Manchesters, they then set off for camp at Aizecourt-Le-Bus.

At the camp five hours of each morning were dedicated to training, the afternoons were spent bathing, entertainment was provided by the Divisional Band and the Cheshires' concert party the 'Na Poos'. The entertainers christened their troupe after a term in familiar trench use, Napoo being the British Tommies' version of the French phrase *n'y en a plus*, this roughly translates as there is no more, finished, dead or gone. On the 26th the all too brief respite ended and the battalion moved off to relieve the 17th West Yorkshire regiment, located in the right frontage of the Gauche Wood Section. The first two days in the line were quiet but on the anniversary of the Big Push on the Somme the enemy artillery opened a furious two-hour bombardment of Turner Quarry, the front lines and supply roads to the rear. The remainder of the day was quiet and shortly before midnight the battalion was relieved, they then left for the Divisional rest camp at Villers Faucon.

On 1 June the 16th Cheshires had a fighting strength of 38 officers and 712 O.R.s and were in training at Templeux-La-Fosse. A few days later 100 O.R.s and 3 officers were detached for special duty to the 178th Tunneling Company Royal Engineers. The nature of this special duty is not disclosed, their role may have been the carrying of 50 pound sacks of ammonal explosives through the line to the head of an underground mine. The risks involved in this task were considerable; each man carried his burden maintaining a space of 50 yards from the nearest man, for in the event of an explosion this spacing would prevent a chain reaction. After this, three companies rested by day and worked throughout the night, this continued until the relief of the 15th Cheshires on the night of the 10th.

Shortly before noon on 3 June members of the battalion heard a gun shot ring out from the confines of the trench, and were shocked to find that Second Lieutenant Ronald Millie Hamilton was dead; the 27 year old formerly of the 5th Battalion had accidentally killed himself with his revolver.

105 Brigade were relieved on the night of the 18th; the 16th Cheshire battalion was relieved in the trenches near Villers Guislain. They then headed for the camp at Templeux-La-Fosse where exercises were held on musketry skills and bayonet fighting. On the 23rd a draft of three officers and seventy-two other ranks arrived and the Brigadier General immediately assessed their quality. Four days later the battalion relocated to Revelon, the remainder of the month was spent digging a new front line trench and dug outs. The 35th division infantry in the line were relieved by the 40th Division on the 2 July and marched to reserve billets.

The Division now shifted to the south to relieve the cavalry corps who held the Epehy sector. Their new frontage consisted of a group of

French and British troops during a hand-over.

unconnected posts reaching out from south of Hargicourt on the south flank to Targelle Ravine in the north. The posts stood on the high ground west of the canal, excluding the Guillemont Farm area and the Knoll. Both of these features dominated the landscape having a 35 to 40 foot higher elevation than the scattered posts. Both armies held the Guillemont Farm area; the Knoll was firmly in the grip of the enemy.

The 16th Battalion were again involved in training until the night of 6 July when platoons of X and Z companies relieved the cavalry garrisoning Ossus Post. The following week the entire Brigade were involved in nightly working parties.

On the night of 7 July the 15th Cheshires relieved the 5th Lancers, in support east of Epehy. The battalion was now employed on jumping a trench from Ossus No. 1 post to Bird Post; four isolated posts were gradually connected up with each other. Soon after midnight on the 12/13th, the enemy opened up an intense bombardment on the Northumberland Fusiliers' section and 15th Sherwoods' trench at Bird Post position. For fifty minutes a hail of steel flew in all directions, caught out by the salvoes was the 15th Battalion who were working in the newly constructed trench. Above them on the exposed ground was a covering party from Y Company 16th Cheshires commanded by Captain Burnett. One of the original Bantams, Sergeant Bourner, and Private J. Clarke were killed and four men were wounded[2].

The Northumberland Fusiliers and the Sherwoods suffered somewhat heavier casualties. The enemy failed to enter the new trench and the Bird Cage; an outpost of three trenches in bird cage design whose base consisted of a small escarpment.

On the night of 12/13 July 1917, a reconnoitring patrol in No Man's Land was trapped by a sudden hostile barrage; amongst the casualties was Lieutenant Irving Gledsdale. The circumstances of his death were described by Major Harrison Johnston who wrote as follows to the parents of the deceased officer.

Lieutenant Irving was commanding Z Company who were due to raid the German trenches on the night of the 13th instant. On the night of the 12th your son, Lieutenants Vincent and Chuck, and two N.C.O.s started out on patrol at 12 midnight to examine the ground. At 12-12 the Germans put a barrage along our frontage, which was severe. The patrol was caught in this. A heavy trench mortar shell landed very close to them, killing your boy instantly, and burying Lieut. Vincent. Vincent although very badly shaken, insisted on returning to try and find your son, but had no success. Chuck made repeated efforts without success until nearly daylight. Last night Chuck and the Company Sergeant Major again went out, and this time succeeded in finding his body, and bringing same in safely. Our Commanding Officer and several other brother officers (as many as we can spare from the line) are away now at the funeral. He is being buried in a little cemetery well behind the line here .... Although your boy had not been with the Battalion very long he has proved himself a capable and a splendid officer. We are all very upset at the sad loss, and our hearts go out to you in your great trial. The boy was a hero, and died a soldier's death doing his duty.

Lieutenant Irving Gledsdale was twenty-four years of age when he met his death. The cemetery referred to is Villers-Faucon Communal Cemetery. His parents resided in Brompton Avenue, Sefton Park, Liverpool. A former pupil of the Liverpool Institute, he was a member of the O.T.C. and attained the rank of Sergeant. Upon completing his education he joined Gledsdale and Jennings employed as an apprentice printer. In 1912 he joined the Territorials of the 10th (Scottish) King's Liverpool Regiment, being a Lance Corporal when war was declared. He immediately volunteered for active service and was granted a commission in 3rd Cheshires. He arrived in France in May 1916 and was attached to 1st Cheshires. He was wounded in the Somme fighting 3 September after a short time in hospital, he took a course in signalling, passed his examinations, and was appointed instructing officer, attaining the rank of Lieutenant in February 1917. In May he returned to France and was attached to the 15th Cheshires. Eighteen days after his death his parents were notified that

Lieutenant Irving Gledsdale

another son, Second Lieutenant Arnold Gledsdale, of the Liverpool Scottish was killed in action at Ypres.

On the 15 July 105 Brigade was relieved by 106. The 15th battalion was relieved in support by the 18th Lancashire Fusiliers shortly before midnight. They now spent almost nine days in training at Aizecourt-le-Bas, at this stage in the conflict the British Army had evolved into a highly trained and proficient army whose personnel were required to be highly proficient in formerly specialist skills.

At about this time the 15th battalion was joined by R.S.M. Lyons; a professional soldier who originally hailed from Kelsall near Chester. In 1896 he enlisted into the 1st Cheshire battalion subsequently serving six years in India, prior to being stationed at Londonderry. At the outbreak of war the 1st battalion hastily left Ireland and raced to France to stem the German advance. The heroic action at Mons produced many casualties and it is possible that Lyons was amongst them for in late September 1914 he was hospitalised in Sheffield while recuperating the 'Old Contemptible' took up duties at the depot Chester Castle, where amongst his other tasks he trained the Chester Civilian Association, a unit of Home Defence Volunteers. He returned to his battalion in France for an eight month period, during which he was promoted to Regimental Sergeant Major in succession to the late R.S.M. T. Francis. R.S.M. Lyons was acknowledged as one of the army's finest drill instructors and seems to have been in demand. He returned briefly to the U.K. and on his third crossing to the war torn continent served for sixteen months. This was interrupted by a return to Birkenhead where he was posted as an instructor to the 3rd battalion employed in defensive port operations. Following this he returned to France for service with the 15th Battalion where his bravery in the field was recognised by the award of the Military Medal. He returned to England again in April 1918 and after another spell of duty at the Depot was invalided out on 8-12-19. Extensive military service had taken its toll on his health and following a lengthy illness he died in March 1921; he was fittingly accorded a full military funeral.

On the 24th 105 Brigade relieved 10 Brigade near Lempire, the 15th Cheshires relocated and relieved the 17th Royal Scots. Early the following morning a group of the 15th Cheshires were occupying a forward post (south-east of Fleeceall Post) when an alert Cheshire shouted out a challenge into the dark, immediately two ten strong hostile raiding parties arose from amongst the long thistles and hurled their stick grenades in the garrison's direction. One of the projectiles landed in the post causing two casualties, a fierce skirmish ensued and the Germans were driven off. The garrison of this post consisted of: 15/19599 Corporal J.W. Rose; 3/26943 Corporal Windsor (wounded); 15/19698 Lance Corporal Charlton; 3/45740 Private Roberts;

3/44095 Private Shone (wounded); 3/45381 Private Holland; 3/45397 Private Hayes; 17/13202 Private Marchington.

An official commendation for the defence of the post was received on the 28 July.

The undermentioned officer and other ranks were included in the report by the Divisional Commander for good work in the 35th Divisional Special Order No 3: On patrol 25 July, Second Lieutenant S.J. Flinn, and 13 O.R.s for repulsing an enemy raid on 25 July against F.1 Post. 15/19590 Corporal Rose and eight O.R.s.

Throughout the month various battalions of the 35th repelled determined German raiding parties, the remainder of the month passed relatively quietly for the 15th battalion. Shortly before midnight on the 29th soldiers of the 15th Notts and Derby regiment relieved the battalion, a couple of hours later they were all settled down in the safety of the cellars in Lempire. They remained here briefly as the left support battalion; unfortunately for X Company they were attached to the 180th Tunnelling Company as a working party.

The 16th Cheshires provided a covering party for their brother battalion on the night of 13 July. While they were out in No Man's Land the enemy raided the Birdcage, which was held by the 15th Sherwood Foresters. A heavy artillery bombardment accompanied the raiders. The enemy were seen by the British wire entanglements and were repelled by rifle and artillery fire. The fierce shelling succeeded in

The above photograph has the words 'TL Wood 3rd Cheshire Regt with Robin. Died of wounds Rouen 26th June 1917'. Wood was originally a Cheshire Volunteer and a resident of Eccleston near Chester. On 29 April he was wounded north of Gricourt during the 16th Cheshires' attack. He sustained a seriously wounded right knee, ankle and right arm. His left leg was so badly mutilated that it had to be amputated. As his health deteriorated his mother and his wife Edith travelled to France and were at his bedside when the 32 year old succumbed to his wounds.

trapping in the neutral zone the group of 16th Cheshires; their leader Captain Burnett kept his head, and formed a flank guard, they stayed out until the situation returned to normal. As a result of the bombardment two of the Cheshires were killed; another four were wounded. The Northumberland Fusiliers and Sherwood Foresters who took the full force of the attack suffered heavy casualties. The 23rd Manchesters relieved the battalion shortly before midnight on 15 July.

Following training at Aizecourt le Bas, three companies of the 16th Cheshires returned to the trenches, while W Company stayed on at the Army Musketry camp at Pont Remy. Late on the night of the 23rd three quarters of the battalion relieved the 17th West Yorkshires near Lempire. The next day the three companies filed through the trenches and were employed on working parties. That night there was another revolver incident when Second Lieutenant G.E. Waltho accidentally shot himself through the left shoulder. There are no other details recorded but if a lowly Private had wounded himself in such a manner there would have been severe repercussions. Blighty wounds were the one sure way to get away from the western front for a brief while or hopefully forever. The M.O.s were aware of this fact and any wound that medics considered suspect was closely scrutinised for any indication that the wound had been received at close range.

Preparations were now well in hand for planned operations against the enemy's commanding positions at Guillemont Farm and the Knoll, the attack on the latter was allocated to 105 Brigade. 105 Brigade was relieved by 106 Brigade on the first night of August, once this was safely completed the 16th Cheshires then marched to camp at Templeux-La-Fosse where 105 Brigade had concentrated. A week of training now commenced for the Brigade attack on The Knoll; to simulate the geography of the attack area X and Y Companies were detailed to prepare a full size mock up of their primary objective the Knoll trenches and the jumping off trench. The 15th Cheshires and the 15th Sherwoods practised continually from the 6th until the day of the attack. Companies of 16th Cheshire also took part in some of the simulated attacks, watched by legions of soldiers.

On the evening of 10 August the

Two standing and one seated Cheshire Bantams.

16th battalion climbed aboard a convoy of lorries and were ferried to St. Emilie, from here they marched to positions in the vicinity of Lempire. The battalion spent this period in the line preparing jumping off places, laying out dummy wire and any improvements beneficial to the impending attack.

The preparations for the coming attack were meticulous for the army of 1917 was a better trained army than the one that fought on the Somme. On 16 August Battalion Attack Order No 118/2 was issued, and in three days time the troops would go over the top. The 15th (Service) Battalion the Cheshire Regiment in conjunction with the Sherwood Foresters on their left flank were given the task of capturing and consolidating the German trenches on the Knoll.

Scouting patrols had reported the Germans were expecting an attack as the wire on The Knoll had been extensively reinforced; there was also increased activity in the German saps and artillery activity. On the 17th the heavy artillery launched counter battery operations. Aircraft observers assisted in directing the fire onto observation posts, wire entanglements and embedded gun pits.

16th Cheshires' patrols established a route through the wire and shell holes to the Knoll. As darkness enveloped the trenches, wooden bridges and ladders were erected. At 10 p.m. both attacking battalions worked their way forward to the assembly positions. Zero hour was set for precisely 4-00 a.m., forty minutes before Zero all the companies were in position and waited, pondering on whether or not they would survive to see the following sunrise. At zero minus fifteen minutes, two assaulting companies moved out of the assembly trench and pensively inched forward to the previously laid out directing tapes.

The allied artillery shattered the silence at four a.m., when projectiles of all calibres blasted key enemy positions. At zero hour the whistles blew, on their shrill command ranks of Tommies rose from their prone positions on the ground and for six minutes advanced into their destiny. The battalions advanced in two waves in a two company front, the 15th Cheshires had the 15th Sherwoods on their left flank. Complying with the plan the attacking waves halted within fifty yards of the creeping barrage; seven minutes after zero they rushed forward, passing through the covering parties of W Company 16th Cheshires. W Company led by Captain G.E. Schultz were the right assaulting company and were the first to make contact with the foe, several of the enemy were trapped in No Man's Land by the barrage, and these were swiftly disposed of. The value of the good patrol work was acknowledged in Special Divisional Order No. 6 when Second Lieutenant R.D. Howells and 11 O.R.s from W Company were mentioned.

Throughout the attack frontage the enemy was concealed in shell holes and the remnants of the opposing front trench. Both of our

Cheshire Bantams are conspicuous amongst their taller comrades.

attacking companies were involved in fierce fights methodically crushing the scattered enemy. Lightly wounded men returning to their lines brought with them the heartening news; the wire was cut for 500 yards either side of the Knoll and the assault was running like clockwork. The enemy trenches had fallen just as the barrage lifted allowing the support companies to mop up and consolidate. On receipt of this information X and Z companies of the 16th Cheshires were ordered forward carrying boxes of ammunition. As Z Company were preparing to move off a shell erupted hurtling red hot shards of shrapnel, 11 O.R.s were wounded along with their Commanding Officer Captain Bacon, and C.S.M. Hughes. The remaining men stoically advanced, as the carrying parties neared the Knoll they noticed the first of the Hun prisoners being shepherded to the rear.

Meanwhile the two assaulting companies pumped with adrenaline swept over the front line trench and followed hard on the heels of the barrage, reached the line they were to take up, while the consolidating company (Y company led by Captain H.M. Turner, M.C.) dug for all they were worth along the new line taped out by the Royal Engineers. Red flares were lit in the old German Line at 4-15 a.m. to indicate that the consolidating companies were in positions. Thirty minutes after zero hour the attackers were mopping up small parties of men, Lewis guns were set up in forward positions and gains were consolidated. Almost as soon as the objective was gained an enemy counter attack emerged from the direction of Lone Tree, the newly positioned Lewis guns spat a steady stream of bullets; under this rain of rifle and Lewis gunfire the grey clad advance abruptly ended.

The Reserve Company (Z Company led by Captain H.F.A. Le Measurier) had followed up behind the Support Company and established two ammunition dumps. Bombers led by Second Lieutenant C.F. Tissington successfully blasted their way down Knoll trench before setting up the right hand bombing block, and the Stokes gun crews quickly set up their guns in readiness to lay barrages on Willow and Lone Tree trenches.

One hour after zero the victorious assaulting companies passed through the reserve and consolidating companies and returned to their shelters in Sart Lane and Lempire. As daylight broke upon the battlefield 39945 Lance Corporal Morgan and 28794 Private W. Winstanley saw a group of ten Germans close to a dug out in front of our new

A German trench mortar position.

line. The Cheshires' blood was up and they immediately rushed the party, three of the enemy were killed, five ran off, two were wounded and taken prisoner. The party had abandoned three 77mm. trench mortars and these prized trophies were gleefully taken back to the rear area, for this form of booty never failed to impress the Staff officers. At 6 a.m. the enemy launched a counter attack from the direction of Lone Tree Trench, they faced a withering fire from a combination of rifle and Lewis guns, the attack melted away. Meanwhile the 15th Sherwoods had progressed a fair distance along Tino trench and established a bombing block.

The enemy retaliated by intermittently shelling the captured ground. Both company commanders holding the Knoll decided to defend the new position with three posts. These were established in the old German line in conjunction with the Sherwood Foresters; another was set up in the new line and the last was set up on the South side of the Knoll Communication trench.

About 4 p.m. a German bomb was thrown over the right hand bombing block, also about 15 men were seen filing into Lone Tree Trench; an hour later an enemy patrol was spotted crawling up under cover of the trees in the vicinity of the earlier mentioned dug out. In

160

broad daylight they were attempting to locate the abandoned trench mortars, while doing so a score of .303 rifle barrels lined up on their targets. A rattle of musketry resulted in three of the searchers being killed outright, while four of them dived for cover in the dug out.

At 7-30 p.m. a heavy enemy bombardment rained down upon the Knoll and the Sunken Road running through Fleeceall and Ego Posts, also the track leading to the Knoll. The intensity of the bombardment staggered the defenders, jagged fragments of red hot metal seared into the positions slicing into the khaki clad infantry. Here and there the blast of the explosions hurtled men into the air, their crushed bodies cart wheeling through the air like rag dolls before descending back to earth. Within minutes of the opening salvoes bursting upon them S.O.S. flares burst into the sky; in response pre-ordained artillery strikes rained down upon the German positions, temporarily stalling the Hun counter attack.

An hour later 500 grey clad figures advanced from the direction of Macquincourt Valley, also bombers attempted to storm the Eastern end of the Knoll communication trench. Once again the S.O.S. flares shot up into the sky and the British barrage, which had decreased in tempo, quickened up immediately. The survivors of the barrage pressed on towards Y company's forward position, they calmly held their fire until the Hun were within sixty yards of their trench. Short sharp bursts of Lee Enfield and Lewis gunfire halted the counter attack, forcing the enemy to retreat leaving behind many dead. Simultaneously to the frontal attack a determined bombing attack was launched against the right bombing block, this manoeuvre had been anticipated and was successfully repulsed by our bombers and Stokes mortars. Amongst the casualties was Second Lieutenant Tissington who later received the Military Cross, the citation for which must surely relate to this action. 'When in command of a party told off to construct a bombing block during an attack, he attacked single handed four of the enemy, killing two and wounding another. When wounded himself he refused to leave the captured trench, until ordered to do so. He set a fine example of courage, dash and promptitude to his men.' (In 1918 he was also awarded the D.S.O.)

After 9 p.m. a lull in the fighting afforded a chance for the reserve companies W and X to relieve the front line companies.

The 15th Battalion's attack on the Knoll had cost the lives of Second Lieutenant J. Grace and 27 O.R.s killed. Captain G.B. Schultz from Birkenhead, the leader of one of the assaulting companies, later died of his wounds, Second Lieutenant C.F. Tissington commanding the reserve company and 96 O.R.s wounded and 7 others were reported as missing. The Cheshires also captured 9 unwounded prisoners and 5 wounded. Trophies consisted of telephone equipment, Zeiss periscope, and 4 trench mortars.

Several times during the night 19th/20th hostile barrages rained down on Ego and Fleeceall Posts and the Knoll. During breaks in the bombardment the 14th Gloucester Regiment erected a concertina wire and apron fence around the Brigade frontage, for the intensity of artillery fire indicated that the Germans were preparing to retake their lost ground. The following day The Knoll was heavily shelled, our artillery's counter battery work effectively silenced the hostile guns. Sections of the enemy had been observed gathering in Willow Trench and Grub Lane, this shelling dispelled the build up of a counter attacking force.

Shortly before the eleventh hour on August 20th the Hun commenced a fresh bombardment upon the Knoll. As the enemy were massing in Macquincourt Valley, all available guns were brought to bear on this area, preventing the attack from materialising. There was sporadic hostile shelling throughout the day, at 7-45 p.m. an intense bombardment opened on the Knoll. Later that night two companies from the 14th Gloucester Regiment relieved the exhausted men of the 15th battalion.

Private E. Finnigan K.I.A. 2(August. A married man he wa\: the first in Birkenhead to joi\: the Bantams.

Amongst the wounded was Private Ernest Hopley who had sustained severe frostbite and returned to Blighty for recuperation, upon his recovery he returned to the battalion; while going over the top on the 19th he received gunshot wounds to the head, hip and back. The mortally wounded soldier died a month after being admitted to hospital, his mother was at his side when he passed away.

The depleted 15th Cheshires arrived at St. Emilie camp in the early hours of the next morning, although the men were tired they were said to have been in exceedingly good and cheerful spirits. Their fellow attackers the 15th Sherwood Foresters suffered 27 killed, 51 wounded and 5 missing.

The 14th Gloucesters later repulsed a German flame-thrower counter attack against the Knoll. As the result of this action Second Lieutenant H.F. Parsons was posthumously awarded the V.C. for conspicuous gallantry. He was in command of the southern bombing post. The bombers holding the post were forced back by the liquid fire, but the second lieutenant remained at his post, although single handed, and severely scorched by the flame throwers, he continued to hold up the Germans with bombs until he was fatally wounded. His gallantry delayed the enemy long enough to allow the organisation of a bombing party which succeeded in repelling the enemy before they could enter any section of the trenches.

After a very short break the 15th battalion returned to the Knoll on the night of the 22nd, by this time a good communication trench had

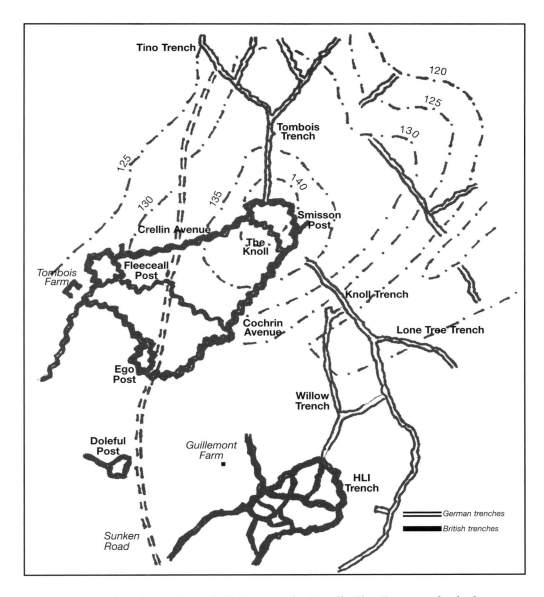

been dug from Fleecehall Post to the Knoll. The Pioneers had also excavated a communication trench back to the sunken road, later constructing another; these were named Cochran and Crellin Avenues after the two battalion commanders, these trenches linked The Knoll with Fleecehall and Ego Posts. Two posts on the right and left flanks of The Knoll were named Dolan and Smisson, in honour of the two chaplains attached to the 15th Cheshires and 15th Sherwoods who had advanced with their units during the attack.

In mid afternoon and evening the enemy bombarded Lempire and the Knoll and again the following day the Knoll was again pounded with artillery shells. On the night of 24 August the battalion was relieved by the 15th Sherwood Foresters, they then headed for camp east of Lempire. The following night the majority of the battalion wired the new trench on the north of the Knoll, also a score of men assisted the 205th Field Company Royal Engineers to clean and deepen Cheshire Trench. A further 100 men made one journey to the Knoll each carrying two wooden crates of Stokes mortar ammunition, containing 3 eleven inch shells plus the necessary fuses, each full box weighed at least 40 pounds. A further 20 men were provided with five stretchers and detailed to carry out the grisly task of removing the dead from the Knoll. Next day the battalion relieved the 14th Glosters in shelters at Lempire. They were then briefly attached to the 106th infantry Brigade carrying barbed wire to the front line.

The 18th H.L.I. relieved the worn out 15th Cheshires late on 29 August, at Aizecourt-Le-Bas camp the men had a couple of days to relax, clean equipment and clothing, and no doubt reflect on the passing of many of their old friends. Their self-sacrifice had however been in vain for on the night of 30/31st after days of severe hostile bombardments from guns of all calibre, the enemy under cover of a mist and a smoke barrage infiltrated the Knoll. Two companies of the 17th West Yorkshires valiantly attempted in vain to hold the position. Despite their stoic defence The Knoll was wrested back into German hands, days earlier the recently gained Guillemont Farm was captured by the enemy. This was a severe setback but the 35th Division's ten day occupation had allowed an insight into the layout of German positions along the canal. Prior to the attack one enemy battalion from the 195th Division held the line between the Knoll and Guillemont Farm, due to the 35th Divisional attack Germanic reinforcements from the 6th, 8th, and 24th Jager Regiments, 16th Bavarian, 20th Bavarian Pioneers and the 5th Battery Field Regiment of Artillery and other units were hastily brought forward. Their losses were severe and were claimed to be greater than ours which approximately amounted to 60 officers and 1,200 men killed, wounded and missing.

The 16th Cheshires had played a small but vital role in the capture and subsequent defence of the Knoll commencing with their gathering of intelligence prior to the attack by members of X and Y companies. When the attack was launched W company provided covering patrols for the advancing troops, while doing so the battle zone was heavily shelled; on the first day four men died, another fourteen were wounded, one fatally. Amongst the wounded were Captain Bacon, and 2nd Lieutenants Johnston and Miller. The 22 August was a comparatively quiet day allowing 16th Cheshires to be relieved by the 14th Glosters.

At St. Emilie camp the 16th Battalion was granted a day's rest, permitting The Acorns an opportunity to stage one of their impromptu concerts. After the show the C.O. read out congratulatory messages from the Staff of Second Army, III Corps, 35th Division and 105 Infantry Brigade. A holiday atmosphere prevailed but it was all too good to last for the following day they were out wiring the south side of Cochran Avenue.

On 25 August the 16th Cheshires relieved the heavily shelled 15th Sherwoods on The Knoll which at this time was still in our hands. The following day Sergeant Wilson led a party of bombers and attacked the block erected by the enemy to the south of Dolan post, 5 casualties are recorded. Next day the 16th Battalion were relieved and proceeded to camp at Templeux-La-Fosse, here they took part in shooting competitions, followed by inspection and congratulatory address by the Corps Commander.

The first day in September the 16th Cheshires relocated to camp at St. Emilie as Brigade Reserve, this was the usual euphemism for make yourself available for working parties. Two companies then spent several days erecting barbed wire between Guillemont Farm and Island Traverse. On the 7th day the battalion occupied the posts near Ken Lane. Two days later the Guillemont Farm area was bombarded by heavy trench mortars causing considerable devastation and

Exhausted German infantry grab a rest whilst a comrade keeps guard.

German prisoners.

obliterating the trench, until all that remained was a series of shell holes. One of the shells erupted in a sap burying alive an unspecified amount of men, the onslaught snuffed out the lives of eight O.R.s of the 16th Cheshires three more were wounded including Second Lieutenant Barber as he made a valiant attempt to recover one of the bodies.

Next day the gallantry of members of the 16th battalion was recognised by the advance notification of the following awards. Second Lieutenant Barber was to be awarded the Military Cross. Sergeants Brown and Day along with Privates Clarke, Nurser, Walters, and Lance Corporal Peake were each to receive the Military Medal for bravery in the field.

On the 11 September the 104 Brigade took over the Lempire front from the 105th Division, as a result the 16th Battalion went to Aizecourt camp. On the 18th the 105 Brigade returned to the line, the 16th Cheshires relieved the 17th Royal Scots in the Adelphi section, four positions known as Ossus Posts 1-4 were garrisoned by the men from X and Z company. The remaining riflemen worked with the Tunnelling Company on Pigeon Quarry wiring and revetting.

On the evening of the first of September the 15th battalion left the camp at Lempire and returned to the line. The next day two companies of the Cheshires were detailed to wire the assembly trench previously dug for the attack on the 19th instance; this became necessary due to the loss of The Knoll. For the remainder of the week the Cheshires worked on their defences while the enemy continued fortifying the captured Knoll.

A Brigade relief occurred 11 days later, the 15th Cheshires were relieved and proceeded to camp at Aizecourt-le-Bas. On the 18th the entire 105 Brigade was inspected by Lieutenant General Sir W.P. Pulteney, the Commander of III Army Corps, who presented the following officers and men with gallantry decorations.

Captain C.B. Kidd (Y Coy) Military Cross.
Lance Corporal Lees. (Z Coy) Distinguished Conduct Medal.
Military Medals were awarded to:
Sergeant Johnston. (Y Coy)   Sergeant Waring. (W Coy)
45953 Private Kemp. (W Coy)   18282 Private Pugh. (X Coy)

In the afternoon the 15th Cheshires set off for the ruins of Epehy where they relieved the 19th Durham L.I. as support battalion Ossus Sector. A system of rotation existed where tours of the front line generally lasted for several days, after which there was a period in reserve or

Dead Germans collected and awaiting burial.

support trenches, followed by a period at the rear for training or recuperation, followed by a return to front line duties; this was the standard routine of the infantry battalions. The continual shuffling back and forth was necessary to limit the rigours of trench life's detrimental effect on mind and body and to a lesser degree combat boredom. The exchanges occurred at night to lessen casualties, but enemy artillery frequently strafed the communication trenches during relief when twice the complement of men briefly occupied the line.

22130 Private J.O. Williams.

After a few days of working parties in the line the battalion relieved the 16th Cheshires in the front line of the Ossus Sector. Z and Y Companies garrisoned four of the Ossus Posts, while X and W Companies remained in support at the location of Holt and Cox's Banks. It has often been said that it is a dangerous honour to be in support, for it is here that the enemy's counter barrage is likely to fall. There could not have been much enjoyment in lying under shellfire hour after hour, perhaps for two days, without seeing the enemy or having an opportunity to exact revenge. The ground becomes strewn with dead and wounded; it is then that to 'hold on' means the highest heroism. The next day 23 September, the enemy had a severe case of the jitters and for no apparent reason bombed his own wire and laid down a bombardment. Machine guns opened up pouring bursts of lead on to the outposts, killing Private Millward of Y Company.

At the commencement of October the 35th Division infantry and artillery moved to the west of Arras, for twelve days of refitting and training in preparation for the conditions prevailing in the Passchendaele Ridge sector to which the Division would soon proceed, but no training on earth could have prepared the infantry for the horrors they were due to face.

Notes

(1) Although the war diaries record both of these battalions being in the same trench on the same day, the diarist records them as being in different sectors. I can only assume the trench was on the border-line of the two sectors, hence the confusion.

(2) Although the war diary records this incident as occurring on the 13th it actually happened on the 14th. This is corroborated by the two deaths in Soldiers Died and the 15th battalion's war diary entry; a very easy error in the fog of war.

CHAPTER TEN

1917 – Ypres Salient – Third Ypres

HAIG'S REACTION to the dilemma of keeping the Germans occupied while the French recovered, took the form of the Passchendaele offensive, officially known as Third Ypres. The medieval cloth town lay on a plain dominated by the German held Passchendaele Ridge, from where they could observe all the comings and goings within the Ypres Salient. War was no stranger to this town for it was of vital strategic importance and had resisted numerous German attempts to occupy a town that they had marched through and vacated during their initial invasion in the first days of the war. Should the enemy break through here they could sweep through to the channel ports severing the allies' supply routes and also be able to turn the entire line, and drive the allies back to the sea. Centuries earlier the Flanders plain around Ypres had lain on the bottom of a shallow sea, generations of agricultural workers had gradually reclaimed the land from the salt water. The heavy earth proved to be very fertile, but prone to flooding even in the slightest rain. A vast system of drainage ditches and dykes helped solve the problem, and providing they were

Coming towards the Menin Gate, Ypres with the ruins of the Cloth Hall in the background.

Bantams on parade.

maintained on a regular basis the problem of the high water table in an area almost at sea level was manageable.

The onset of war and continual artillery barrage and counter barrages annihilated the drainage systems; an extremely wet August simply made matters worse, as streams became blocked and over-flowed, water logged shell holes developed into lakes, and solid earth was transformed into liquid mud. The Ypres offensive gradually became bogged down in a quagmire of mud, although the military brass had confidently expected the ridge to be captured within four days, its capture would take four tortuous months.

Approximately four miles south of the city of Ypres, at the northern extreme of the Wytschaete-Messines ridge the elevated ground spreads north-easterly for ten miles to Passchendaele, and then two miles further northwards to Westroosbeke from where it blends into the Flanders Plain. A less pronounced outcrop of this range reached out from the old British line at Hooge, and carried on for a further four miles to the vicinity of Pilkem. The south-eastern part of this had been in British possession since 1914, however the north-western section the Pilkem Ridge had been in enemy hands since spring 1915. Four miles north of Pilkem lay the 1,500 acres of deciduous woodland known as Houlthulst Forest, this magnificent woodland was once considered by Napoleon to be the key to the Low Countries and would become infamous to the men of the 35th Division. The June battle of Messines had resulted in the capture of the Wytschaete-Messines Ridge; British attention now focussed on capturing the remainder of the high ground overlooking Ypres. The offensive to capture the Passchendaele ridge was set for 25 July; prior to this date a preliminary bombardment of over 3,000 artillery pieces pulverised the battlefield for almost ten days. On 31 July the main offensive began, and resulted in the capture of Pilkem Ridge; from here the line steadily advanced to a point in front of Passchendaele, Poelcapelle and Bixschoote.

In mid October the 35th Division's infantry brigades were entrained to the Proven area, approximately four miles north-west of Poperinghe. Over the next five days the 15th Cheshires travelled by rail and foot to 15 Wood in the support area north-west of Elverdinghe, where they relieved the 2nd Irish Guards, 2 Brigade of Guards. On the left flank of the Divisional front stood the revitalised French army; to the right was the 34th Division. The Cheshires found themselves in an area of saturated ground bisected with sandbagged defences. On the 17 October the first of four evenings' work was commenced, 400 men were employed carrying wooden duck boards up to the front. These boards were laid across the sea of mud, meandering their way around the water filled shell craters, in a hopeless attempt to make travel easier across the saturated muddy bogs. Also one officer and fifty men were detailed with the unenviable task of clearing the roads of destroyed wagons and scores of dead horses in various states of decomposition. The preparations were now in full swing for a forthcoming diversionary attack east of Poelcapelle and the ground south of Houlthulst Forest.

The minor operation launched by the 5th Army utilised XIV Corps and the 34th and 35th Divisions, yet is not mentioned in the official battle list. The intention of the two operations was to mislead the Germans over the direction of the main Passchendaele offensive. This side thrust involving XIV Corps in conjunction with the French 2nd Division would advance northwards into Houlthulst Forest and in doing so provide a strong left flank to the main advance. The 35th Division determined that 104 and 105 Brigades would launch the

A working party carrying duckboards to the trenches pause for the camera.

Views of Houlthulst Forest, the killing ground for the Cheshires in 1917.

initial attack as 106 Brigade was significantly weakened; the strength of the 17th West Yorkshires now stood at only 450 riflemen.

Wiser counsel would have realised that the imminent attack stood little chance of success, for the rain had conspired with the defenders of the 600 acres of mangled tree stumps known as Houlthulst Forest, where the surface was nearly pure clay. In fair weather it would have posed a hard nut to crack, yet men were now expected to flounder through the mud hampering all rapid movement as they advanced towards pill boxes spitting flame; the advancing infantry never knew if they were about to step into a muddy puddle or a several foot deep flooded shell hole, considering the shortage of fighting material this action was virtually guaranteed to deplete human resources further for no great military gain. In his classic account of the Flanders' campaign Leon Wolff *In Flanders Fields* sums up this diversionary feint thus: 'On the 22nd there followed a curious, half hearted attack by the French and elements of the Fifth Army, in which almost 1,000 allied troops were lost. A few yards were gained, some of which were retaken later in the day by enemy counter attacks. It is a rare mention of this forgotten or overlooked engagement.'

On the eve of the attack 21/22 October the weather was extremely cold, practically everyone was sniffling and sneezing due to the common cold and instances of influenza were extremely prevalent. After midnight heavy showers saturated the miserable legion of men heading towards the assembly points. As the 16th Cheshires moved forward Y Company went via Vee Bend, past the collection of small pill boxes named Egypt House and Les 5 Chemins. W and Z Companies moved up along the duckboards of Clarges Street and north of Suez Farm. During this movement the following casualties were suffered:

Y Company, one officer and twelve O.R.s.

Battalion H.Q., six O.R.s.

Z and W company each had one casualty.

The Poilus of the 1st French Division were on the extreme right of their frontage, alongside them were 105 Infantry Brigade with 104 Brigade on their right flank, facing the attacking force was a landscape that looked like an alien world. Fading away into the distance was a sea of mud liberally pockmarked with a mass of putrid water-filled shell holes. For the attack the 16th Cheshires were positioned on the right front, 14th Glosters were on the left front, the 15th Sherwood Foresters were in support on the line Strong Point, while the 15th Cheshires were held in reserve in the locality of Wijdendrift.

The enemy guns laid down a barrage of varying intensity throughout the night along the line of Les 5 Chemins to Louvois Farm, shortly before dawn the barrage spread northwards and rained down on the 16th Cheshires' front line position and assembly point incurring casualties. At 5-30 a.m. on the 22 October our barrage began, components of the Division including the 16th Cheshires advanced. The poor state of the boggy ground can be imagined when it is learnt that the pace of the barrage was timed to allow the infantry eight minutes to advance 100 yards. Despite the slow creeping barrage the thick mud made it extremely difficult for the attackers to keep pace with the barrage. The high water table made the terrain unsuitable for trenches, the Teutonic defenders' solution was a system of concrete pill boxes arranged in a chess board pattern, each affording covering fire to its neighbour; they dominated the boggy landscape. These redoubts were fashioned in reinforced concrete with sides up to ten feet thick, capable of surviving all but a direct hit by a heavy shell.

Shortly before 7 a.m. Captain Burnett proudly reported at Battalion H.Q. that Z Company had taken Marechal Farm, to their left the 14th Gloucesters had gained ground and now occupied Panama House. Less welcome news was that the centre and left attacking force's were held up by fire from block-houses in the wood approximately 500 yards north-west of Colombo House. Most of the attacking forces rifles were useless as they were clogged with mud, and casualties were heavy. Upon hearing this Lieutenant Colonel Dent (Commander of the 16th Cheshires) arranged with Major Morton the Commander of the 15th Sherwoods for Y Company to advance further forward, their vacant position to be occupied by W Company of the Sherwoods. As the situation was becoming critical Lieutenant Colonel Dent went forward to assess the situation accompanied by Captain Burnett, en route they collected some stragglers near the south edge of a wood. These men were ordered to outflank one of the numerous pill boxes; despite the low odds they succeeded in forcing the enemy to abandon the pill box. Any further advance was delayed owing to rifle fire and harassing fire from another pill box. Throughout this attack enemy aircraft flew a couple of hundred feet over the British positions with their machine guns blazing. Artillery shells rained down everywhere; one shell landed in the midst of a group of H.Q. signallers and runners, six of them were badly wounded including Private Austin. The twenty-eight year old runner was severely wounded in both legs, he was carried by stretcher to a dressing station where he succumbed to his wounds.

Lieutenant Colonel Dent then headed for the concrete pill box at the ruined Colombo House Farm, where Captain Millington M.C. and his Z Company men had captured the pillbox complete with its machine gun, its crew lay dead on the ground. 57865 Private W.A. Johnson, a former Bedford Territorial, had on his own initiative dashed forward, shot the machine gunner and captured the weapon. For this he was awarded the D.C.M. He was killed in action 23 March while serving with the 15th Cheshires. Fifty yards forward of this position the remnants of X Company were also consolidating their position, due to the heavy casualties sustained X and Z companies were at half their fighting strength and were now merged into one company. At 2-15 p.m. a company of the 15th Sherwoods moved up to Colombo House and occupied the original front line. Y Company of the 15th Cheshires acting under orders of Lieutenant Colonel Dent (16th Ches.) moved up in artillery formation attracting heavy shell fire from the Vee Bend area, the survivors relieved 15th Sherwoods in the old British line.

With the situation under control and the imminent arrival of reinforcements from Y Company 15th Cheshires who formed a defensive flank to Colombo House, Lieutenant Colonel Dent returned to Battalion H.Q. Meanwhile the advance of W, X and Y Companies of the 16th Cheshires was held up until around 4-30 p.m. when a strong enemy counter attack accompanied by an intense barrage was launched against the left frontage. The enemy broke through the line and was then able to fire on the wood held by the remnants of W, X, Y Companies 16th Cheshires and Y Company 15th Sherwoods with an enfilade of fire, before withdrawing 100 yards to another position but were forced back to our original front line. The withdrawal of this flank allowed the enemy to bring reverse machine gun fire on the left of Captain Millington's position at Marechal Farm; to prevent even heavier casualties his left withdrew to Colombo House – Marechal Farm road and faced west. The 17th Lancashire Fusiliers on the right of Captain Millington's force then withdrew to the line of the road, this manoeuvre left Millington's company isolated so they in turn

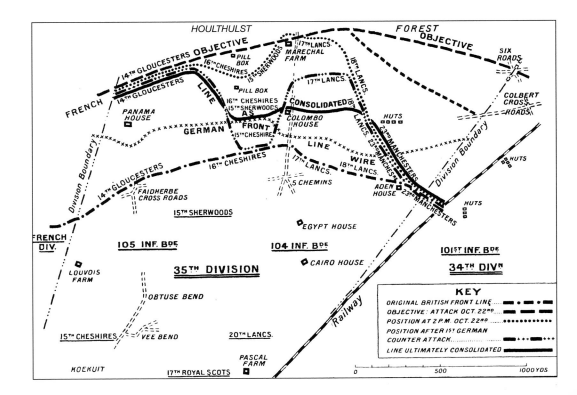

withdrew to Colombo House Farm. The 18th Lancashire Fusiliers continued the line on the right flank while the 14th Gloster's retained their original objective. While these events were occurring the 17th and 18th Lancashire Fusiliers had repulsed an enemy counter attack with heavy losses. This was the general situation by 7-30 p.m. that evening; no further action occurred on the 22nd.

The casualty returns give an indication of the toll taken by this engagement, but little insight into the individual soldiers who paid the ultimate price. Amongst those lying dead on the battlefield were Private Ernest Bradley, an 18 year old who appears to have enlisted under an alias, as his mother was a Mrs. Hazeldene. Private Albert Hale had fought on the Somme until his mother requested he be returned home, as he was only eighteen years and four months old. When attaining the required age of 19 he returned to France; he never saw his twentieth birthday. Another young soldier was Private F. Moran who enlisted at the age of 16, when he was 17 his true age was discovered and he was sent home. He was called up and posted to France in late 1916; he was 18 years old when killed. Another deceased was Private Fred Ramscar who died aged 17, Private A. Halsall was bayoneted and died instantly. Another casualty Private Edwin A. Roberts was a former member of the Shaftsbury Boys Club for disadvantaged young men. In 1909 the club organised a holiday in Wales it would prove to be his first and last vacation. Amongst the deceased's effects was his membership card for the Club, a cherished memento of halcyon days.

The conditions endured by the infantry in this action were appalling; scores of men were sheltering in shell holes waist deep in cold festering water, shelled throughout. The rainfall drained into the craters; as the water level increased the wounded who had crawled for safety into the craters discovered they were in a watery grave, too weak to climb above the rising water they often drowned. The many wounded fared no better for in the height of battle it was impossible to evacuate the wounded further than the Regimental First Aid post and Vee Bend. On the night of 22/23 October there were over thirty seriously wounded stretcher cases stranded at Vee Bend Aid post, many of whom were left out all night through pouring rain and intermittent shell fire as there was no other option available. The 15th battalion sustained its heaviest loss of life in this engagement; the vast majority of the fallen have no known grave, their final resting place being known only to God.

Another casualty of the day's fighting was Lance Corporal Harwood. In January 2000, Mr Percy Harwood a ninety-seven year old gentleman recounted the tale of his twenty year old brother (who probably added two years onto his age in order to enlist) who died serving his country almost three generations earlier. According to Mr.

Harwood his brother died of wounds on 29 September 1917, a date of which he was absolutely certain. The official records give his death as precisely five months earlier on 29-4-17.

Mathew Harwood was a resident of Liverpool who travelled to Birkenhead to enlist into the recently raised 16th battalion. He was a keen sportsman, while the battalion was at the Meols camp he established Harwood's Boxing Team. While serving in France 21832 Lance Corporal Mathew Harwood was severely wounded in action resulting in the loss of a leg. He was evacuated upon a hospital train but bled to death during the journey. His mother received a letter from Harwood's close friend Jack Mathews (years later he became famous as an actor in television's 'Coronation Street' playing the role of Albert Tatlock, Ken Barlow's Uncle) saying her son was wounded. Some time later Captain Stirla (a Liverpool man whose family owned clothing stores, a Stirla's cheque provided clothes on credit) visited the bereaved mother and presented her with a German helmet, which was in the family for many years. There might be a little confusion in this account as during the period specified the battalion was not on the Somme, although Lance Corporal Harwood was interred on the Somme at Nesle Communal Cemetery this may be due to the 21st Casualty Clearing Station being based here, or perhaps the deceased were removed from trains here. For decades the Harwood family proudly displayed the helmet, medals and photograph upon the walls of their Huyton home in remembrance of the brave soldier who gave

A typical Ypres Salient enemy strongpoint with concrete pillboxes.

his life for freedom, a fact that would not have occurred to the burglar who stole them.

Early 23 October reorganisation of the line occurred involving both assaulting battalions, the 15th Cheshires now relieved their brother battalion. Colombo House was taken over by X Company, Y Company were in close proximity. Meanwhile W Company of the 15th Cheshires dispersed to the west on our original front line and linked up with the Glosters. Shortly before dawn the niggling enemy barrage increased in intensity, a challenge that was matched by our own artillery. The enemy pinpointed their guns on our front line, support lines and the road running from Les 5 Chemins, pounding the area in a preliminary to a strong counter attack. One citation for the Distiguished Conduct Medal read: 'During the bombardment Lance Corporal Crosby, after all his senior N.C.O.s were either killed or wounded, took charge and by his coolness and indifference to danger maintained the morale of the groups of his platoon. Later in the day he and his group were twice blown out of position and when the position was most critical he established communication on each flank and held the line together.'

All available men were ordered to stand to; at 5-30 a.m. a platoon of the 15th Cheshires holding the left flank noticed two of the Kaiser's men moving down the road linking the sites of Renard Farm and Panama House, this was the boundary line of the two allied armies. The Cheshires opened fire, simultaneously half an enemy company attempted to pass the Cheshires' left flank; the Hun counter attack melted away beneath rapid small arms' fire. The enemy continued probing the defences, this time with a full company; S.O.S. rockets were sent up from our lines and in response our barrage roared down on the attackers. They found themselves in the hopeless position of

Troops crossing the Yser Canal and entering the Ypres Salient.

35th Division badge.

being boxed in by our guns to their rear, while to their front they faced a hail of bullets. The Hun counter attack failed; 40 dead were spread-eagled before the Cheshires' defences, 20 others wisely surrendered.

In the midst of battle confusion reigned over which Companies were in the line and where, Colonel Cochran (15th Cheshires) arrived and having clarified the dispositions of various units accepted the hand over of the line from Lieutenant Colonel Dent. At approximately 10 a.m. the 16th Cheshires began to file out of their positions, their numbers were seriously depleted as within less than 30 hours the 16th Cheshires had sustained casualties of 9 officers and 327 other ranks.

After the failure of the dawn attack, the enemy relied upon their artillery to harass the 15th Cheshires and other forces along the Divisional frontage. However, at 9 p.m. the 15th Cheshires advanced unopposed, before acting as covering parties while other companies moved forward and set up new positions along the Colombo House-Panama House Road. This resulted in an advance of 200 yards to the original first objective, and straightened out the British front line. The quagmire hampered all attempts to replenish the front line troops with materials, small arms ammunition and drinking water. Two soldiers making their first appearance in the line witnessed their company commander being buried by a falling spout of mud thrown up by an exploding shell, and had struggled since 10 a.m. to extricate the trapped man. Throughout heavy shellfire the men tried in vain to dig him out, in an attempt to make his movement easier Private Cadden stripped off and immersed himself in the bog but all the attempts to recover the trapped man failed. Both Privates accompanied him until Private Cadden was wounded on the night of the 24th Private Adshead remained until the N.C.O. died of hypothermia shortly before the next sunrise. During the night the 18th H.L.I. successfully arrived with much needed supplies, and the opportunity was taken to bury the dead. The 106 Brigade relieved the 105, however the 15th Cheshire battalion remained in the line.

On the 24th an air of fearful retribution prevailed over the battle-field, at 3 p.m. this materialised as a severe hostile bombardment upon the British front line and the road from Les 5 Chemins. Although the main thrust of the attack focussed on the 19th Durhams the Cheshires were also bombarded causing considerable damage and countless casualties, but they held the line and repulsed all attempts to dislodge them. The right Company H.Q. sited at Colombo House received a direct hit and a section of Machine Gun Corps were lost. Corporal H. Hobson, a former Barnsley miner, was returning to report on the situation when a shell exploded next to him killing him instantly, he was buried where he fell. The survivors grimly held the line, and after two hours all the companies in the line had used up their supports. Runners were sent out at half hour intervals in the hope that at least one would survive the maelstrom and reach the 17th West Yorkshires with a request for immediate assistance. This proved to be unnecessary as at 8-30 p.m. the relief by the 18th Highland Light Infantry was confirmed, it had previously been impossible to get relief orders through due to the ferocity of the bombardments. Shortly before midnight the relief of the 15th Cheshires was completed with only a few casualties. Their total casualties for this all too brief tour of the line were 22 killed and 75 wounded.

Although this large scale attack of the 35th Division earned the praise of the military brass, it was not a complete success as the tenacious attacking battalions were hampered by several unexpected factors. A prime factor was the inability to connect with the 34th Division on the right flank, allowing the enemy to escape before returning fire on the flanks and rear. The 23rd Manchesters attack had been scythed down by unexpected fire from an unnoticed position, severely hampering the initial advance. Enemy aircraft activity and snipers within the protection of the forest continually harassed the front line troops who also had to cope with the appalling weather. Despite the meticulous planning of the covering barrage conditions on the ground dictated the progress, consequently the barrage was rolling forward either too fast or slow. The units attempting to advance through a woodland choked with thick undergrowth and fallen trees were left behind by the fire storm, those advancing across open country found the barrage moved too slowly. In the first instance those who kept up with the barrage arrived in such a state of exhaustion their fighting ability was affected. Despite these factors between 18 and 25 October the 35th Division captured 85 prisoners from three separate German divisions, whose losses were known to have been extremely severe. The 35th Division's infantry losses between the 18th and 29th consisted of 368 killed, 1,734 wounded, and 462 missing.

Lance Corporal Antrobus is certainly a man of mystery. Along with the above photograph his death was announced in the Birkenhead Advertiser. After a month of speculation on his fate his wife received official notification of his death the date given was 7 July 1916. This date is at odds with the CWGC and the Soldiers Died. His name appears on the Tyne Cot Memorial with the date 22 October 1917. His age was given 19, yet he was a married man with six children.

The 15th Cheshires were rested at St. Emilie Camp near Elverdinghe, until the evening of the 29th when they relieved the 10th Sherwood Foresters in the front line near Koekuit. After two days in the line they left for De Wippe camp.

On 30 October the 35th Division transferred from XIV Corps to XIX Corps, a fortnight later the Division's infantry transferred to II Corps. On 5 November the 15th Cheshires moved to Putney Camp near Proven, for ten days of training. The 105 Brigade went into Divisional Reserve near Poperinghe, where specialist weapon training was carried out. On the 24th the battalion struck camp travelling via the light railway to the north east of Ypres. They later set off for the line

A boyish looking Private Joseph Flowers killed by shellfire 24 November 1917. The twenty-two year old Londoner was one of the original members of the 16th Battalion when he enlisted at Birkenhead.

south west of Poelcapelle, and while passing through an area known as the Triangle, they were shelled resulting in the deaths of 5 men, including Private Joseph Flowers; a further 14 were wounded. In biting cold weather two companies now took up positions in slimy craters, strafed by artillery. The battalion was relieved on the 28 November and set off to Siege Camp south of Elverdinghe.

Before daybreak on 23 October the remnants of the 16th battalion passed into Brigade Reserve upon relief by 15th Cheshires. After a week of working parties the 16th Cheshires relocated to De Wippe where they absorbed a draft of five second lieutenants and 236 O.R.s as battle replacements for the casualties sustained near Houlthulst Forest. Within a week the battalion shifted to Piccadilly Camp, near Proven, where at noon on 6 November the Brigade was inspected by the Divisional Commander. Two days later the 16th Cheshires marched to Wellington Camp via Elverdinghe, from here they provided labour for maintenance of tramways under C.E. II Corps until 24 November. The tramways were essentially a fifteen inch minimum gauge rail track used for the transportation of hardware, munitions and troops. The battalion left Elverdinghe to relieve the 20th Lancashire Fusiliers in the line near Poelcapelle.

The battalion war Diary entry for 25 November as vague as ever reports that 'The line was moderately quiet. Second Lieutenant Joice and several other ranks became casualties'. The casualties transpired to be Privates P. Birdsall, J. Carey, G. Riley, T.W. Shipp, Lance Corporal W. Wright and Sergeant Mowbray all killed in action. While at least three others died of wounds, Private E.N. Craven and Private H. Wallbank passed away 26 November. The wounded Second Lieutenant P.S. Joice lingered on until the first of December before succumbing to his wounds.

On the 26th the Sherwoods relieved the Cheshire battalion who passed into support based at Kempton Park, they later rejoined their Brigade in support at Siege Camp south of Elverdinghe. After ten days of training the 16th Cheshires set off to relieve the 20th Lancashire Fusiliers in the Poelcapelle area. The rain had now given way to fine but frosty days tempting the enemy to commence raiding, during the night of the 6/7 December a sentry spotted a small German patrol infiltrating their frontage, consequently W Company opened fire killing several Germans and captured a prisoner, two days later a similar raid was repulsed. At dusk 9 December the Cheshires were relieved, it appears that during the relief the battalion may have been caught in a barrage as they sustained five casualties. The 16th Battalion entrained for Le Noveau Monde, near Herzeele where they spent a few days resting, prior to rejoining 105 Infantry Brigade at School Camp near Poperinghe, where the training continued. As the Christmas festivities began to appear on the horizon other activities were to be organised, the latter part of December the brigade was involved in assault at Arms competitions. The 16th Battalion excelled for they won the Officers revolver shooting competition, number 9 platoon won the brigade platoon rapid fire contest and Z Company won the Brigade bombing contest. In the Finals of the boxing competition five events out of a possible six were won by this battalion, we can but wonder how many of the late Private Harwood's 1915 boxing team had survived to enter this competition.

The Brigade Sports were postponed for Christmas day when church parades were held, followed by Christmas dinner inside decorated huts. The competitions resumed on Boxing Day, the battalion was victorious in the rapid fire competition, the laurels were also won by W Company the victors of the brigade Lewis gun competition.Two days after Christmas, Lieutenant Colonel Dent the battalion's former C.O. relinquished the temporary command of 105 Infantry Brigade and proceeded to England for duty with a machine gun battalion. The battalion's loss would be the Machine Gun Corps gain but this move may have been pre-empted by the rumours appertaining to the battalion's demise.

Harrison Johnston was one of the battalion's early officers. He resided at 46 Queens Avenue, Hoylake, Wirral. He was promoted from Temporary Captain to Temporary Major while employed at Head Quarters 7-10-16. He took command of the battalion 8-3-17 and was later awarded the Distinguished Service Order, which was recorded in the *London Gazette* 4 July. While on a brief leave he attended Buckingham Palace for the Saturday investiture on 30-6-17 when King George V presented the Cheshire officer with the DSO. He rose to the rank of Lieutenant Colonel. His gallantry throughout the conflict was also recognised by three mentions in despatches.

This officer recorded his war in a diary, which was published in the post war years. His often lengthy notes provide a valuable insight into the personal thoughts and exploits of a popular front line officer, today they remain the definitive personal account of a 15th battalion soldier.

Harrison Johnston, finished the war as a lieutenant colonel.

CHAPTER ELEVEN

1918 – The Beginning of the End

THE WINTER OF 1918 was said to have been the coldest weather experienced by the troops living a troglodyte existence in the labyrinth of trenches. Subzero temperatures caused the River Seine near Paris to freeze over for the first time in living memory. The soldiers guarding the frozen tundra wore as many layers of clothes as possible in an attempt to keep body heat, they also tied sandbags around their boots to maintain their footing as they slithered along frozen duck boards. Men cursed and stamped their feet in an attempt to keep warm while despairing of the futility of occupying the line when both sides had effectively ceased operations for the winter as both sides patiently bided their time for the weather to improve.

Through heavy snow 105 Brigade moved forward to relieve 173 Brigade, 58th London Division east of Poelcapelle on 8 January, 1918. The 35th Division was distributed along a line extending from the Lekkerboterbeek in the south to the banks of the Brombeek and north to the Ypres-Staden railway, holding the left frontage of II Corps.

In the growing daylight of 9 January the 16th Cheshires marched to Proven Station entraining there for Elverdinghe in the Salient. After alighting they marched to Bridge Camp, where they were reunited with 105 Brigade in Divisional Reserve. In mid January the snow gave way to 48 hours of heavy rain, this coincided with the 16th Cheshires route march to Kempton Park where the saturated soldiers relieved the 20th Lancashire Fusiliers as the right support battalion. Two companies occupied the Pheasant Farm trench for 48 hour stints, rotating with X and Y Companies. During their period the Cheshires maintained and improved the Corps barbed wire lines near Poelcapelle.

In mid January the 15th Cheshires relocated, this time they found themselves in a quiet water logged muddy sub sector of the Brigade frontage near Poperinghe. They were relieved by their brother battalion on 20 January and moved into left support. Three nights later a 5.9 shell scored a direct hit on a flimsy shelter in Pheasant Farm trench killing outright 20077 Sergeant D.C. Jennings and two men of whom I can only trace one, 25580 Private G. Williams. It was impossible to recover their remains so the Chaplain conducted a service over the site of the explosion; their grave was later marked by three wooden crosses. On 20 January the 16th Battalion relieved the 15th Cheshires in the line, the dispositions remaining fairly similar to that previously mentioned.

A radical shake up of British army divisions now commenced, with the reduction of infantry divisions from a thirteen battalion basis to ten battalion strong units. All divisions on the Western Front were to be reduced but we are only concerned with the pruning of the 35th Division's strength, which eventually resulted in the disbanding of the 16th Cheshires, 20th Lancashire Fusiliers, 23rd Manchesters and the 14th Gloucesters. These losses were offset a little by the absorption of the 12th Highland Infantry from the 15th Division, which joined 106 Brigade the 35th Division. As a result of the reorganisation the fighting strength of the units was affected, compounded by an unfamiliar grouping of units, new methods of tactical handling now required to be implemented and the discarding of tried and tested methods which commanders had become accustomed to.

On 1 February preparatory measures began for the disbanding of the 16th Cheshire Battalion, it was to be carried out in true military fashion, efficiently and swiftly. Captain Sturla [wounded 22/4/17] returned to the battalion just as it was facing extinction, on 3 February the Cheshires were relieved as right Support battalion by the North Staffordshires. After arriving at Bridge Camp the battalion was inspected by the Brigadier General, who then spoke to a group of five officers and 100 other ranks announcing they were to merge with the 1/6th Cheshires. The following day the surplus men boarded the train at Poperinghe and were trundled off to their new battalion. Other men were more fortunate as a hand picked group of fifteen officers and 310 other ranks were transferred to the 15th Cheshires. On 8 February the remaining surplus details left Woeston by train; their destination was II Corps Reinforcements [Surplus Wing] at Bollezeele, from here they marched to Merckegham and were officially handed over to Major W. Hancock DSO, the officer in charge of Surplus Wing.

The following letter was received by the 16th Battalion's Commanding Officer, Major (Acting Lieutenant Colonel) W. Hodson M.C.

From Brigadier General Pollard C.M.G.
[Acting Divisional Commander].

I am sure I am voicing General Frank's feelings in writing to you to say how sorry I am that your gallant battalion is being broken up, and to sympathise with all those keen people of all ranks who must be very fond of the old battalion. But I hope everyone will be able to carry on the old spirit in their new homes.

From Brigadier General Mandarin D.S.O. 105th Infantry Brigade Commander.

It is hardly necessary for me to say with what very great regret I view the breaking up of your battalion. During the 21 months I have commanded *this Brigade, your battalion has done consistently well and has gone on getting better and keener and more efficient, till finally by its gallant conduct in the attack at Houlthulst, it gained a very high reputation as a fighting battalion.*

The Brigade and the battalion are at the very top of their form and a strong 'esprit de corps' exists throughout the Brigade. The loss of your Battalion will be felt keenly throughout the Brigade and by none more so than myself. I can only wish you and all ranks of your battalion the best of luck wherever you go and am absolutely confident that wherever individuals go, they will remember the traditions of their old Battalion and the old Brigade.

A secret army order dated 10 February 1918 revealed the fate of the men held at the surplus wing. Under instructions issued by G.H.Q. 3rd Echelon, the surplus personnel of disbanded battalions not immediately required for reinforcements were to be formed into Entrenching Battalions. These battalions numbered from 1 to 25 existed for only a short period, yet would prove vital at a crucial period. The 12th Entrenching Battalion formed from the remnants of the 16th Cheshire, 23rd Manchester, 20th Lancashire Fusiliers and 14th Gloucestershire regiments would later be heavily involved on 21 February 1918 defending against the German advance in the vicinity of Tergnier-Quessy, while in support to the 58th division.

The first day of February the 15th Cheshires vacated Huddlestone Camp to relieve the 18th Lancashire Fusiliers in the right sub sector of the brigade front, around Poelcapelle. The following morning was cold and a thick fog had gradually enveloped the water logged No Man's Land shortly after two in the morning out of the mist emerged a twelve strong patrol from the 94th Battalion, 103rd R.I. Regiment. The Germans rushed the isolated post, rendering a sentry unconscious. A comrade alerted the rest of the squad, before being assaulted by two of the enemy. In the ensuing fight the fist flaying Cheshire dragged two of the raiders into a water filled shell hole and kicked himself free. Despite the post's resistance the Germans succeeded in capturing two other ranks and a Lewis gun. As the Hun retired they were fired on from a neighbouring post and one man was killed. Patrols were immediately sent out all along the battalion frontage, but no trace of the retiring Germans could be found. The raiders were said to have been exceptionally large men, armed only with revolvers and were evidently a hand picked raiding party. Allied raiding parties were greatly reduced during the first few months of the year yet 125 raids were still carried out, 77 of these recovered information in the form of prisoners or identification; the enemy was more active carrying out a total of 225 raids upon the allied lines.

Group of NCOs of the 15th Cheshires and the 15th Notts and Derbys. Sitting on the bench second from left is Sergeant Fay D.C.M., 15th Cheshires. He earned his D.C.M. while attached to a trench mortar battery, 'For conspicuous gallantry and devotion to duty. He worked a machine gun with only one man for three days and three nights in the front line. He set a splendid example throughout the operations.'

The Cheshires spent the next couple of days extensively wiring forward of their outposts, and mounting regular patrols. The 5th was reported as a quiet day, yet one Cheshire was killed and four were wounded. In the early evening the battalion was relieved without incident by the 4th North Staffs, and the battalion marched off eventually joining the Brigade in reserve. By the ninth day they were at St. Emilie Camp near Elverdinghe, progressing through Cambridge and Bridge camps from which they provided working parties primarily for the 289th Army Tunnelling Company Royal Engineers.

On 22 February, six months to the day since their action at Houlthulst Forest the battalion returned as relief troops, two days later they went into support. They appear to have immediately been ordered to carry duckboards up to the front line and to establish stores dumps of wiring materials for work to be carried out the following day. The rifle companies were allocated separate tasks, reinforcing positions, wiring parties and carrying forward more duckboards. Early on the evening of the 26th the battalion relieved the 15th Sherwood Foresters in the right sub sector. The Cheshires immediately began work fortifying their new positions, while patrols reconnoitred the terrain and enemy dispositions directly in front of Gravel and Memling Farm, in preparation for a forthcoming raid.

The next day the enemy bombarded the Cheshire frontage, the remainder of the day passed quietly allowing the men of W and Y companies to carry out the preparations for the impending raid. Shortly before 8-00 p.m. the 32nd Division occupying the Cheshires' left flank launched a massive raid in conjunction with a severe artillery bombardment. This prompted the Hun to retaliate; as a consequence of this the neighbouring Cheshire frontage received numerous salvoes, these claimed the lives of three of the Cheshires and wounded four more. The tempo of the guns gradually subsided, and what passed for normality returned to the sector. They recommenced patrolling waste land dividing the two armies, attempting to gather any information, which may affect the forthcoming raid.

The 28 February was a quiet day in the line; the soldiers occupied themselves as best as they could, many of them would have been writing what may have been their final letter home as that night 105 Brigade was scheduled to launch four simultaneous raids on facing enemy posts. The other half of the two-pronged attack involved the 4th North Staffords who would attack posts to the east of Colombo House. When darkness descended on the battlefield the final preparations were in hand, zero hour was to be 8 p.m. As our guns roared into life four separate raiding parties from the 4th North Stafford's and the 15th Cheshires climbed over the parapet and advanced under cover of the barrage towards the two southern-most objectives.

The forty strong Cheshires raid on Memling Farm was to be commanded by Second Lieutenant G.D. Howells. The officer accompanied by his servant and another soldier were standing approximately forty yards behind the assembly point, were killed instantly by one of the first shells of our barrage which fell short of its target. Undaunted by the tragedy, Second Lieutenant Heape took command of the raiding party which reached its objective only to find it abandoned. Bivouacs were located and searched for documentation, then destroyed. The party returned unharmed.

Meanwhile the second party of Cheshire raiders pressed home their attack on Gravel Farm; the attack extended along a line from Taube house to the Watervlietbeek. The raiding party commanded by Second Lieutenant G.K. Mowle M.C. advanced under an accurate artillery barrage, until a belt of uncut wire blocked them 300 yards from the farm. An explosive device was positioned under the wire and detonated, clearing a path through it; the Cheshires advanced only to be halted by more barbed wire. The raiders were now vulnerable to any form of retaliation, but instead they withdrew under the Cheshires' rapid fire. Once they had by passed the wire they discovered a machine gun post whose gun had become buried in the bombardment. The Cheshires killed the detachment of gunners before unsuccessfully attempting to recover the weapon. With their adrenaline surging the raiders pressed on destroying enemy shelters, six occupants who refused to surrender were killed; two others survived and were taken prisoner, the shelters were torched. Their mission was now accomplished and Lieutenant Mowle gave the order to withdraw, as a heavy barrage was now falling on the vicinity of their setting-out point near Taube House the party remained out until the firing had stopped. At 8-50 p.m. the raiders complete with their two prisoners from the 22nd I.R. [11th Reserve Division] returned to Taube House; surprisingly only three of this raiding party had received wounds.

The known casualties for these two raids consist of Second Lieutenant G.D. Howells, Privates R.D. Marshall and C.R. Newton, who were killed in the Memling Farm raid. The latter raid produced three wounded, amongst them was the fatally wounded Private J. Sabala, an original Bantam. When Colonel Cochran submitted his report he singled out the capacity for command exhibited by Second Lieutenant Mowle in the recent action.

On the first of March 105 Brigade was relieved by 104 and passed into a support role. The 17th Lancashire Fusiliers relieved the Cheshires who then remained at Kempton Park camp for seven days of refitting and working parties. Nine days later the 35th Division was relieved by battalions from the 1st and 32nd Divisions and moved into G.H.Q. Reserve where they were to be held in a state of readiness to advance within twelve hours' notice.

The Cheshire battalion set off by route march and train for Noyon Camp near Crombeke. A spell of good weather now set in, for almost a fortnight the Cheshires were put through their paces within the camp, training

An unknown Cheshire Bantam in leather equipment issued to Pals-type battalions.

in the latest development in infantry tactics. For entertainment a Divisional sports competition was held; the battalion's footballers carried an unbeaten record through to the semi final of the football competition, the sharpshooters from 9 platoon Y Company won the rapid firing competition. The officers of the 15th Cheshires spent the evening of 21 March indulging themselves in a fancy dress party, their costumes owed more to the ingenuity of the wearer than to a theatrical costumier. There was an abundance of pirates garbed in assorted shades of khaki with charcoal drawn beards. As all ranks enjoyed their break from the nightmare of the Front the war seemed so distant, yet a turn of events would bring the pleasantries to an abrupt halt when a signal from the Divisional Headquarters arrived. The 35th Division was brought from the Ypres Salient to the Somme front where they came under the command of the Fifth Army. The 35th Division was ordered to relieve the exhausted riflemen of the 21st Division who had spent almost three days stubbornly resisting the Germanic advance.

The primary cause of the sudden British change from the offensive to the defensive lay in the fact that the German fighting strength on the western front was increased by almost a third between November 1917 and 21 March 1918. As Russia had descended into revolution their involvement in the European war withered. In three and a half months twenty-eight German infantry divisions had been transferred from the eastern [Russian] front and an additional six infantry divisions arrived from the Italian theatre. German artillery had also been increased dramatically. On the other hand the British army strength had been reduced by twenty-five per cent compared with the previous summer; the prolonged waste of lives in the quagmire beyond Ypres had led the wily Lloyd George and his cabinet to withhold reinforcements for fear of encouraging the further squandering of lives. Lloyd George, who constantly thwarted Haig's attempt to procure more recruits for slaughter at the continental charnel house attempted to manoeuvre Haig into accepting a less autocratic role, this took the form of a Supreme War Council in control of a general inter-allied reserve. Haig considered this to be nothing more than fighting a war by committee and wanted no part of it, he refused to contribute his moderate quota of nine divisions. In doing so he scuppered the War Council, and thereby excluded the army from calling on a proposed reserve of thirty divisions. Although Haig was expecting a spring attack he preferred to rely upon an agreement with Petain for mutual support, if the worse case scenario transpired he was confident he would be reinforced by up to eight French divisions. He conjectured that if he could not mastermind a major break through after years of offensives, then it was logical that any German attack could be contained for at least eighteen days. The closest Britain had come to a breakthrough had been in late November when a massed attack by tanks briefly gained new territory near Cambrai, as Germany had very few of these wonder weapons Haig confidently expected the line to be held. Aerial reconnaissances had confirmed the build up of ammunition and supply dumps and the improvement of German road and rail routes, by the end of February it was apparent the attack would strike on the frontage of the British Third and Fifth Armies.

The three year old Royal Naval blockade of German ports was exerting an ever tightening stranglehold on German imports, leading to growing civil unrest amongst the malnourished population. American troop ships were now arriving at French ports disembarking fresh-faced Dough Boys albeit at a slow rate, but the rising numbers would eventually tip the balance of power back in the allies' favour. If Germany were to emerge victorious from this war they had to act soon, the timing of the attack was more or less determined by the improving weather; as the dry ground would then be more favourable for an infantry assault. A wealth of preordained plans had been lying around in German Head Quarters gathering dust for quite some time, one such plan code named Operation Michael was adapted for the forthcoming Spring Offensive. The main thrust of the attack was to originate near the German held town of St. Quentin and extended to the north almost to Arras. The main blow would strike at the boundary of the French and British armies thus creating maximum confusion. In January 1918 the British took over two sections of the French line extending to five miles south of the River Oise, they were now unknowingly occupying the area targeted for the whole of the German attack. The Germans' intention was to punch through the British line on a fifty-mile wide front, then turn north and systematically destroy the British force sweeping it back to the sea. If all went to plan a decisive victory would have produced a similar result to the fall of France in 1940.

Douglas Haig records that on the eve of the Kaiser's battle at least sixty-four German divisions prepared to go over the top. Facing this imminent onslaught stood the Third Army fielding eight divisions on the front of the enemy's original attack, with seven divisions in reserve. The Fifth Army defence consisted of fourteen infantry divisions and three cavalry divisions in reserve. The entire British force disposed along the original battle front on 21 March stood at twenty-nine infantry divisions and three cavalry divisions, of which nineteen were in the line.

German offensive

At 4-40 p.m. on 21 March the deafening sound of almost 6,500 German guns announced the launch of the German offensive upon a fifty-four mile wide frontage, even by Western Front standards this barrage eclipsed all previous others. The assorted calibre artillery pieces were

The **Leviathan,** *formerly the German passenger liner* **Vaterland,** *packed with troops is nudged out of an American harbour bound for France. The round trip took about a month and transported 12,000 soldiers each trip.*

approximately half of the Hun weapons available on the entire Western Front; during a ferocious five hour bombardment they would fire approximately 1,160,000 shells. Amongst the high explosive shells there were a high proportion of poisonous phosgene gas shells that also delivered an eye irritant for which the British gas masks offered no resistance. The bombardment blanketed the entire sector from the Oise to the Scarpe river; while roads and rail links as far back as St. Pol were targeted by high velocity guns, wiping out assembly areas, artillery positions, crossroads, all forms of communication and shattered morale and resistance.

Enemy infantry had also developed innovative infantry tactics using more fluid movement of men, a new breed of soldier the 'storm trooper' was used to spearhead the advance and surge forward to capitalise on the breakthrough. Positions offering fierce resistance were to be bypassed, as nothing was to halt the breakthrough, their orders were to penetrate as deep as possible, assisted by a rolling barrage. In due course standard infantry would follow on, encircle the exposed defences and wipe out the isolated defenders. When the whirlwind of destruction had done its worst, through swathes of fog that made it impossible to see more than fifty yards in any direction

A 1918 photograph of men of the 15th Cheshires. The kneeling soldier is Private R. Johnston; visible on his left sleeve are two wound stripes. On his right sleeve can be seen overseas service stripes.

the grey clad infantry emerged and overwhelmed the lightly held forward positions; by nightfall German troops had infiltrated across forty miles of the British front. Amid scenes of utter chaos battalion commanders attempted in vain to contact H.Q. for intelligence reports or operational orders, the mist prevented visual signalling, some units fell back; while others held their ground unaware they risked becoming encircled. Frequently fierce engagements were fought, and where the Hun attempted a frontal attack upon the entrenched positions he was generally repulsed with great loss.

As the enemy had committed all his troops to this one battle Haig hastily withdrew eight divisions of valuable reinforcements from across the Western Front, the earlier agreement made with the French was now called on resulting in the French taking over a portion of the battle front. Amongst those rushed to the battle zone was the 35th Division which arrived amongst scenes of unprecedented chaos. The Spring Offensive is covered in detail in a host of publications specifically dedicated to the series of battles, for a full account these should be consulted, as we are only concerned with the events concerning the 15th Cheshire battalion and the 35th Division.

On the 22nd after marching eight miles to the railhead at Ypres, the 15th Cheshires commenced a twelve hours' rail journey of jolting and stopping and starting, guaranteed to prevent even the weariest of passengers from snatching some sleep. The tired troops who had been packed forty to a cattle truck now detrained and marched seventeen miles through a frosty night from Mericourt l' Abbe on the Somme to the village of Suzanne near Bray. The roads were congested with transport of every description, retiring troops and despondent civilian refugees filled the roads, all heading in the opposite direction to the fresh reinforcements. Against this tide of humanity the 35th Division struggled, at every halt the troops fell asleep at the roadside.

A general retirement had been ordered to the line of the Somme, yielding precious ground steeped in the allied blood of the Somme battles. The Brigade pushed on three miles more to a rendezvous, where it was hoped to snatch some rest and food before going into action. They finally reached their billets at 4 a.m. but at the moment of their arrival, demoralised troops from the 9th and 21st Divisions came streaming back to the rear reporting that the Hun was hard on their heels. So there was nothing for it but to move against the enemy, these events were meticulously recorded in the diary of Lieutenant Colonel Harrison Johnson (at this time he was a Major) and remain the finest account of the battalion's involvement in this battle, passages from the diary are included in the subsequent account.

Before midday on Palm Sunday 24 March the 15th Battalion was ordered to attack and regain two lines of trenches yielded after much carnage by the embattled 21st Division. The Cheshires now launched a spirited counter-attack against Clery Ridge, south of Marrieres Wood. They advanced for more than a mile in splendid order advancing as if involved on an exercise, successfully retaking both of their objectives, as a result the enemy had to withdraw 150 yards. They captured the

Field artillery lay down fire on British positions at the opening of the German spring offensive, 1918

Clery-Bouchavesnes Ridge, suffering serious casualties in the process; after a morning of sharp and fluctuating fighting, they established themselves and prepared for an imminent counter attack. The 15th Sherwoods were deployed north of Hem Wood thereby attacking on the left of the 15th Battalion, with a big gap between, and share the glory of this admirable action. Each battalion consisted of only three companies, the fourth having been kept behind to unload the train. The Germans regrouped and both battalions were desperately counter attacked by a force of superior numbers, who attacked in waves supported by high explosive gas shell, rifle and machine gun fire, and grenades. Above their heads enemy aircraft continually buzzed the allied line and sunken road dropping bombs from an altitude of only fifty feet. The two forward companies of the 15th Battalion Z and X though completely surrounded by the enemy, owing to the wide gap between them and the Sherwoods, held up the German advance all day. Our boys' casualties steadily rose and the sunken road west of Hem Wood became lined with approximately 45 stretcher cases awaiting evacuation, all requests for ambulances dispatched through cyclist, telephone, and runner met with no response. A steady stream of demoralised men from assorted regiments and corps were now rushing past the Cheshire officer, who ordered the Regimental Sergeant Major supported by military police to round up the stray men and order them back into the line. The Cheshires were now joined by a group from 13th Sussex Regiment and a Canadian Motor Machine Gun Company who assisted on the right flank mowing down swathes of field grey clad infantry. When their ammunition ran out the vehicles drove off for fresh supplies, taking with them as many of the wounded men they could manage. This company carried out invaluable work until early afternoon; by this time all their officers were killed or wounded and insufficient men remained to man the few surviving guns.

The Cheshire regiment's left flank began to falter, prior to falling back slightly, two tanks now rumbled forward and restored the situation. The continual onslaught produced a similar effect on the right flank that also began to waver until reinforcements arrived. The numerically stronger enemy continued to advance steadily; both forces were now in such close proximity they were able to shout at each other. At such a short range the enemy snipers rarely failed to hit; 60 yards forward of X company's line a deadly marksman was steadily whittling down the company. Twenty-one year old Captain Kidd M.C. the commander of X company was sniped, swiftly followed by the No.1 and No. 2 of three Lewis gun teams of X company, Lieutenant [Tp] Edward H. Hodson was also killed about this time. An unnamed volunteer resolved to eradicate

Captain Kidd M.C.

194

the sniper; the Cheshire soldier broke cover and set off alone across the intervening ground, zig-zagging his way towards the sniper. He bravely got within ten paces of the sniper before spinning around with a bullet through his throat; he stumbled forward a few steps and fell down dead.

Meanwhile Z Company led by the Battalion C.O., Lieutenant Colonel H.P.G. Cochran, found itself in an increasingly untenable position. The withdrawal of Brigade H.Q. prompted Johnston to despatch Doran, the C.O.'s servant, forward with a message and the officer's revolver. Doran located Z Company but failed to find the officer commanding. Doran reported back and, accompanied by another man, they set off laden down with bandoliers of ammunition and water for the location of Z Company. Returning to the trench they discovered two Germans; Private Doran shot both men with the revolver, before scrambling into the next trench occupied by members of Z Company. While dispensing the ammunition he spotted a German who had advanced to within fifty yards of the trench, Doran borrowed a rifle, took careful aim and gently squeezed the trigger; a shot rang out and the Hun fell dead. With his mission now completed Doran reported back to Lieutenant Colonel Johnston advising him that Z Company were almost surrounded. By the time he imparted this information Lieutenant Colonel Cochran, the Adjutant Captain, V.G. Barnett and Major H.F.A. Le Measurier and approximately thirty men were themselves completely encircled by the Germans. Fighting with determination isolated Cheshires were either killed or captured. The Sherwoods found themselves in a similar position and towards 3-30 p.m. both companies were outflanked by the enemy and wiped out.

At approximately 5 p.m. the order came to retire to the line reaching from Curlu to the village of Hardecourt, north east of Maricourt; the 17th Royal Scots who had been in support provided covering fire, assisted by as many slackers from other units Johnston could find. Many men succeeded in fighting their way out, carrying their wounded with them, they fell back to the sunken road to the west of Hem Wood, where they remained until receiving the order to withdraw. The unevacuated wounded were not abandoned for when the majority of the battalion had safely pulled back, the covering party were ordered that no one could leave without the corner of a stretcher upon his shoulder. Due to a lack of stretchers they were improvised from rifles and tree branches, other wounded were carried piggy-back style. The weary troops wound their way along the sunken road with shells exploding to their left and right. Men lay dead all around this escape route, including two groups of five corpses formerly four stretcher bearers and their patient, all victims of the shelling. Further along the road Johnston encountered a youth of 19 lying in a roadside ditch and another soldier attempting to persuade him to get up. The teenager had been shot through the mouth, and the wound had swollen terribly, Johnston advised the youth of the consequences of falling into enemy hands but his spirit was broken and he had no fight left in him. Eventually they coaxed the youth to his feet and with arms around him both men practically carried him for almost a half mile to the next position. One of the divisional cookers was set up here and the famished men seized the opportunity for a scalding hot brew of tea. The General now gave Johnston a roasting for allowing his men to stand around drinking tea! He ordered the Cheshires to line the road from the junction to the river.

By 6 p.m. the dispositions of the battalions were: the 13th Sussex upon the north bank of the River Somme, the 17th Royal Scots extended this line to a point 100 yards to the north of the Clery-Maricourt road. The 15th Cheshires, who were now severly reduced in numbers, carried on the line for an additional 1,500 yards. The 15th Sherwood Foresters covered their left flank towards Maurepas, the North Staffords remained in support at Maricourt. The orderly retirement continued while the 17th Royal Scots provided cover for the retirement to the line Curlu-Hardecourt. Immediately on arrival there the German army launched another attack, this was repulsed with withering rifle and machine gun fire. Once the new line was firmly established and all the wounded recovered, the 13th Sussex and 17th Royal Scots withdrew to the right flank.

Major Johnston was all too aware his section of the line was undermanned and began to remedy the situation by rounding up South African stragglers, and a Lewis gun team. By 8 p.m. all was in order, the Cheshire battalion established forward patrols and prepared themselves for a hostile night attack.

As the hellish day drew to a close a layer of hoar frost appeared adding to the discomfort of the exhausted soldiers. Johnston had to continually move up and down his section of line to keep his men awake. No further action took place that night; as so heavily had the enemy been punished, the new line was not attacked. The battalion remained on outpost much strengthened and encouraged by the arrival from the railhead of W Company at 11 p.m. During the night the remainder of the 35th Division was united with their scattered battalions and dispositions were adjusted accordingly. An outpost line was also established in the vicinity of Trones Wood, the line snaking through Faviere Wood was garrisoned by composite battalions from the VII Corps Reinforcement Camp under command of Colonel Hunt. Amongst these entrenching battalions were former members of the recently disbanded 16th Cheshire now serving with the 12th Cheshire entrenching battalion that had been in action two days earlier.

The 15th Cheshire casualties were heavy and the opportunity was taken to reorganise its hierarchy as the battalion had lost its colonel,

German troops employ a flame-thrower during their attack on British positions.

Herbert Philip G. Cochran, D.S.O.; despite his high rank his surname is often misspelt as Cockrane or Cockran. He was an experienced officer, a veteran of the South African war who was later employed with the West African Frontier Force from 1906-11 Also missing were the Adjutant-Captain V.G. Barnett, and Major H.F. Le Measurier, M.C. the command of the battalion was now temporarily transferred to Major H. Johnston D.S.O.. A wounded Cheshire had recently arrived in hospital where he revealed the death in action of Cochran, the other two missing officers had survived, Barnet and Le Measurier were captured when their position was encircled. The wounded man was taken prisoner with them; seeing he was wounded in the shoulder his guard pushed him to one side. The Cheshire soldier took the opportunity to escape and in doing so was fired at receiving an additional two bullets in his other shoulder. During the day's fighting the three Cheshire companies had lost 14 officers and over three hundred men, although the losses were considerable they were said to have been small in proportion to those inflicted upon their opponents. The heroic endeavours of the battalion were recognised by the immediate awards of a D.S.O. to Captain Stewart of the Royal Army Medical Corps [attached to the 15th battalion] for the devotion he displayed in superintending the evacuation of the wounded. Three D.C.M.s and 18 M.M.s were also awarded.

From dawn of the 25th the Cheshires were heavily shelled, originally it was thought to have been our own artillery shells firing short, however the shells were emanating from the right flank, a location that had previously been thought to be in allied hands. As the morning progressed the shelling became deadly accurate, fountains of earth laced with searing shrapnel were erupting all around, consuming the trench defenders at an ever-increasing rate. The position was becoming untenable, to remain any longer in the sunken road would have been suicidal; Johnston consulted with Colonel Crellin and the decision was taken to withdraw. Nearby two companies of the North Staffords, assisted by artillery, almost regained the original line, but rising casualties forced a withdrawal. Captain Milne commanding the relatively fresh W Company was ordered to set up a position on a lofty ridge and cover the retirement of all the troops within their range. Once again this manoeuvre was carried out in an orderly fashion, the men including the Cheshires regrouped outside the village of Maricourt north of the Somme where they occupied a strong defensive position with an extensive field of fire. From here Johnston sadly observed the enemy moving up to occupy the position they had vacated earlier.

At 1 p.m. a demoralised mob of retiring troops from assorted army Divisions were stopped in their tracks by the Commander of 105 Brigade, Brigadier General Marindin. Amongst those called upon to halt the rout was Major Johnston who stated 'I was roped in to assist some staff officers in stopping the rot and making men return and

A British position is overrun by the advancing Germans resulting in a number of prisoners.

reinforce our new positions'. Revolvers had to be produced, and it was extremely difficult to hold the mob that was then ordered to take up new defensive positions to the north and north east of the village.

Towards midday, the enemy broke into Maricourt, and were only ejected after heavy fighting, but the 15th battalion with the Sherwoods and Royal Scots to their left maintained their ground. At approximately 9 p.m. a German patrol consisting of two officers and sixteen other ranks clashed with a Cheshire patrol. Despite being outnumbered by two to one the Cheshires killed nine Germans, and captured two others. Around 10 p.m. the battalion was relieved by the 17th Lancashire Fusiliers and proceeded to billets at Suzanne, where the men had their first decent meal for some time; the meal was interrupted by orders to march immediately to a defensive line on the Bray-Meaulte road.

The Brigade withdrew under fire, and marched five miles to the new line. Upon arrival it was impossible to catch up on some sleep, as it was a cold miserable night too cold to rest, and the men had to walk about to keep warm. The heaps of debris transpired to be the village of Bray now a strategic outpost line; its defences were now occupied in the early hours of the 26th. Forward outposts were established along the railway about 2,000 yards to the north east of the road; the actual front line now ran through Maricourt station. That night the troops caught up on their sleep followed by an early morning breakfast. A tank battalion had abandoned a nearby camp; and contrary to orders their well-stocked stores had not been destroyed. The Cheshires took this opportunity to replenish their stores and clothing, men undressed in the open and exchanged old tunics and trousers for new, any other useful items were also liberated. Harrison Johnston ordered the men to restock their ammunition from the dump and an additional forty boxes were taken as reserve. No sooner had he returned to his section than a runner arrived from Brigade with a message that an enemy advance had been sighted on the ridges east of the Bray-Albert road.

Initially cautious probing attacks tested the allied line before a determined attack began on the 9th Division and the left of the 105 Brigade; this fresh assault was repulsed by rifle and machine gun fire. Meanwhile at approximately 10 a.m. 26 March the enemy confidently advanced on the 15th Sherwoods' and 15th Cheshires' frontage. A vast tide of enemy troops boldly advanced in extended lines, to their rear German cavalry trotted forward ready to capitalise on the impending breakthrough. Both battalions however stood their ground; the overwhelming numbers were whittled down by small arms fire aimed with deadly effect into the advancing hoards. For several hours the battle raged but the field grey clad soldiers determinedly pressed home their attack eventually they reached a position within 300 yards of the Cheshires outposts and were halted. Despite the defenders' success their position was enfiladed by troublesome machine gun and sniper fire that severely hampered any movement thus preventing the reinforcing of weakened posts. Johnston sent a runner with a request for assistance, in response a tank appeared on the left flank and lumbered around eliminating German opposition. The enfilade fire ceased and all attacks were repulsed at the cost of only a handful of wounded Cheshires and two men missing. The enemy forces piled on the pressure and by 1 p.m. the entire frontage was engaged with the enemy.

Orders had previously been issued to the effect that units should not be too heavily involved with the enemy and any withdrawal should be in echelon from the right. In accordance with this order the 21st Division composite force began to retire other units also moved to the rear. The retirement rankled Major Johnston who preferred to stand his ground for he considered the position to be one of strategic value affording a good range of fire, but he had to comply with the order. At 2-45 p.m. 104 Brigade began to withdraw, thirty minutes later 105 Brigade also retired. The 15th Battalion then marched off along a route straddled by an artillery barrage; they headed for the River Ancre, east of Morlancourt. The ruined village presented the now familiar spectacle of hopeless congestion, civilian carts, guns, transport, wounded soldiers, civilians and leaderless men, all struggling westward. Here it was found that the battalion transport with food, blankets, and great coats, had been sent across the river. The only rations procurable were some biscuits found by the wayside, the last remnants of a dump made for the retiring troops, which naturally had been eaten by those who had first passed that way. However, by some means or other, the officers succeeded in getting the men some hot food, this was the first hot meal they had since leaving Ypres, three nightmarish days earlier.

All officers of 105 and 106 Brigades were summoned to a conference where the brigadier generals informed them of a change of orders. In direct contradiction of the morning's order not to become too involved with the enemy, they were informed 'That every effort must be made to check the enemy advance by disputing ground. It is to be distinctly understood that no retirement is to take place unless the tactical situation imperatively demands it'. Major General Franks sought the opinion of the commanders on the viability of retaking their

Major General Mack Franks C.B.

Field Marshal Sir Douglas Haig, Marshal Foch and General Pershing.

recently abandoned line. All concerned expressed grave doubts on the success of a counterattack by exhausted, if willing, troops; to say nothing of the shortage of food and ammunition.

Despite having received explicit orders from his superiors General Franks decided that a counter-attack was out of the question and the retirement should continue. As a consequence of his decision General Franks was relieved of his command. It was considered that he had misinterpreted his verbal instructions and no retirement should have been made from the Bray-Albert line. The 15th Cheshire war diary reflects favourably on the compassionate leader thus: 'We can have nothing but praise for the tenacity and equanimity of the Brigade Commander, whose skill and judgement had contributed so much to this brilliant episode'. Also Johnston refers in his personal diary to, 'a fine soldier and a splendid fellow who was willing to sacrifice his career for his men, and we are still going strong. If he had not had the pluck to break himself and ruin his future, none of us would be here now – I am certain of that'. The successor to Franks was Major General Marindin.

Elsewhere there was also a change in the command structure for the disaster had prompted the allies to implement a reorganisation at the very highest level. Following Haig's appeal and Lord Milner's intervention the French Marshal Foch was appointed on 26 March 1918 to co-ordinate the operations of the allied armies and also prevent the separation of both armies.

During the afternoon of the 26th VII Corps incorporating the 35th Division was transferred from the Fifth to the Third Army, as the Third Army had now assumed control of all troops north of the Somme. As the Third Army was continuing its withdrawal of its centre to the line of the River Ancre, the 35th Division crossed the River Ancre, units of 105 Brigade were now located along the roadside between the Ancre and the railway track forward of Buire. Shortly after 6 p.m. a telegram arrived cancelling the retirement and demanded that the line Bray – Albert was to be held at all costs. Reluctantly Marindin ordered a counter-attack on the ridge east of Morlancourt by the 4th North Staffords and 15th Sherwoods, supported by two companies of the 15th Cheshire Battalion. General Marindin protested, to the Corps commander, whose order would be obeyed, but had little chance of success when carried out by tired men with little ammunition.

Common sense seems to have won the day for the order was cancelled by Corps H.Q.

105 Brigade now established itself in a defensive line extending from near the station at Buire to the communal graveyard in the village of Dernacourt. Although their orders were to hold the river line at all costs, as a precautionary measure the Engineers ensured that all the bridges across the river were wired in readiness for demolition. The 15th Cheshires and an Entrenching battalion were held in reserve the 15th Battalion was commanded to hold a quarry on the right of the Brigade, less one company detailed to garrison the road. The area was rife with bursting shells prompting the Cheshires within the quarry to dig in as fast as they could. The salvoes targeted the road in an effort to prevent troop movement; the company of Cheshires took cover in large roadside sump holes, these were further extended to form good defensive positions. The battalion spent the remainder of a cold night digging in. At 10 a.m. on the 27th a massed German attack was launched from the Bray-Corbie road against the Division on the right flank, this assault was broken up by artillery but the Division wavered and began to retire. Various units were pushed forward to support the front line, the 26th South African Brigade mounted a counter-attack, for a while the situation remained anxious but the danger subsided.

At approximately midday the 12th H.L.I. relieved the 15th Battalion, who now relocated to a sunken road where they dug themselves in. Within the confines of the road the exhausted men erected groundsheets crawled underneath and slept, yet despite all they had been through the morale and humour of the men was reported as 'buoyant'.

The 28 March was a cold and miserable day that witnessed several attacks upon the 35th Division's front; all these attacks were repulsed by artillery, Lewis gun and small arms fire. Later that rain soaked night 104 Brigade was relieved by 105 Brigade. The 17th Lancashire Fusiliers vacated their position within the fifty acres of Marett Wood; W Company of the 15th Cheshires took over the defence. Two other companies established positions along the railway embankment from the village of Buire to the railway station at Maricourt, the remaining company was held in reserve.

The Germans now applied pressure on the right flank of the 35th Division frontage. On the 29th and 30th the 3rd Australian Division was heavily attacked. On each occasion the Diggers waited until the attackers were at close range before they opened fired scything down their attackers in waves. At the end of the month two Australian Battalions encroached on the 35th Division's section, thereby carrying out a Divisional relief.

During the whole of this period, the enemy never forced the 35th Division out of any position; all the withdrawals were effected in consequence of orders received from superior authority. There was no panic or stampeding, and no men left their posts without receiving orders to do so. The soldiers of the Division were justifiably proud of the fact that since the night of the 26th in compliance with fresh orders they had not yielded any ground. Indeed at battalion level the entire affair was acknowledged as a very fine performance, in keeping with the honourable traditions of the Cheshire regiment. The events of the last few days had drained the 15th Battalion of 3 officers and 52 other ranks killed, a further 15 officers and 385 rankers were wounded or missing due to the fighting. The Division casualties were approximately 90 officers and 1,450 men.

The fate of thousands of allied soldiers was unknown; these men were listed as missing or possibly taken prisoner. The following officers of the 15th Cheshire Regiment were originally reported as missing, they were later confirmed as Prisoners of War.

	Missing	Repatriated
Major H.F.A. Le Measurier.	24-03-18	01-01-19
Capt. E.W. Bigland.	24-03-18	25-12-18
Capt. V.G. Barnett.	24-03-18	13-12-18
Lieut. D.W. Mills.	24-03-18	11-12-18
2/Lieut. E.H. Bann.	24-03-18	11-12-18
2/Lieut. A. Chuck.	24-03-18	25-12-18
2/Lieut. T. Young.	24-03-18	25-12-18
2/Lieut. A.J.C. Walters (att from S. Lancs)	10-04-18	29-11-18

By the 27th German soldiers had penetrated almost forty miles behind the British front line, but Germanic euphoria was dashed the following day when nine divisions attacking Arras were repulsed. The lunge towards the deserted cathedral town of Amiens began to grind to a halt, due to exhausted troops and the logistical difficulties of supplying an army over such an extended area. British air attacks harassed any forward movement, and resistance stiffened aided by French reserves now deployed to help stem the breach. The tired and ill-nourished German troops were demoralised to find well filled supply depots that belied German propaganda claims of severe allied shortages brought about by the U Boat campaign. At a critical period in the advance the attack faltered near Albert as troops ransacked buildings for loot. The first stage of the enemy's offensive weakened and eventually ended on 5 April when the last gasp actions were fought at Villers Bretonneux approximately ten miles away from the rich prize of Amiens. With the failure of his latest attacks on 4 and 5 April the enemy offensive on the Somme front ceased for a while and normal trench warfare resumed. The Spring offensive had failed to split the British and French armies or attain the primary objective of sweeping the British back to the Channel ports, the allies had emerged badly shaken but united in their resolve to go on to victory.

The 15th Battalion was relieved by the 37th Battalion Australian Infantry and went into billets in La Houssoye about five miles west of Buerre. The majority of the Division was located here; on 2 April they were visited by the Corps Commander who thanked them for the work they had carried out under very trying circumstances. After their exertions the entire Division was allocated a period of rest but subject to working parties. For the first few days of April the decimated 15th Cheshire battalion was held in Corps Reserve. The recent fighting had stripped the battalion of seventeen officers, seven of whom occupied the position of company commander or above.

A captured German prisoner revealed an imminent attack would be launched south of the Somme in the early hours of 4 April, this attack forced a withdrawal of a section of the line to the west of Hamel. The 35th Division was put on standby with orders to be ready to move off upon thirty minutes' notice. 105 Brigade were not involved in this fresh onslaught but received orders for a daily stand-to at dawn

Two days later the battalion arrived at Hedauville where they relieved the 17th London Regiment in the front line north of Albert.

On 9 April the enemy launched a ferocious bombardment upon the Cheshires frontage, the deafening frenzy of savagery continued for a duration of about ninety minutes [meanwhile further north the Lys Offensive commenced]. Throughout the day sporadic shelling confined the men to the confines of their dug outs, during the onslaughts the battalion was fortunate in receiving only two slight casualties. The Hun artillery strafed various targets including the village of Bouzincourt where the battalion Aid Post was established; a direct hit upon the post killed instantly the battalion's Medical Officer Captain L.A.H. Bulkeley of the R.A.M.C. and his counterpart Captain Gardiner of the 4th North Staffordshire's. The next couple of days in the line were quieter with only occasional shelling; shortly before midnight on 11 April the decimated battalion was relieved in the line by the 15th Sherwoods.

General Ludendorff's diversionary attack on 9 April proved more successful than was originally expected; each small victory was used as a stepping-stone from where a more powerful assault was to be launched. The attacks are many and are beyond the remit of this book, an extremely brief synopsis of the battle follows. After managing to penetrate almost ten miles into the allied territory the British halted the German tide near the important railway junction of Hazebrouck, a vital supply artery. The invader attempted to expand the front towards the direction of Ypres but Haig had foreseen this manoeuvre and acted accordingly, also French reinforcements began to arrive. Faced with an overwhelming crisis on 11 April Haig issued a special order of the day containing the following excerpt.

> *There is no other course open to us but to fight it out. Every position must be held to the last man, there must be no retirement. With our backs to the wall and believing in the justice of our cause each one of us must fight to the end.*

Ludendorff had gained extensive ground producing a bulge in the German front, however he was reluctant to further extend this area in depth. The opportunity should have been seized for the British army was in a perilous state having suffered over 300,000 casualties; almost half of this number were replaced with drafts from Britain and Divisions brought back from Italy, Salonika and Palestine. Despite the reinforcements the advantage still lay in favour of Germany and a knockout blow would have ended the contest. Fortunately despite being on their knees the allied spirits never wavered; they beat the count and fought on, but it would take vital months before they fully recovered. Although initially extremely reluctant to become engaged in a European war, the American Divisions commanded by Black Jack Pershing, were, by the end of April, at a strength of 325,000 men and rising; their intervention now ensured the balance was shifting in favour of the allies.

The Cheshires proceeded into reserve in the sunken road by Hedauville; on the night of the 14th the battalion was relieved by the 12th H.L.I. and proceeded to billets in the village, where a large draft of 250 men had moved forward up from the transport lines. The fresh

A captured British position.

draft was conspicuous by their youth for the average age of these men was approximately 19 years old. Technically servicemen below the age of 19 should not have served overseas but thousands of these under aged lads manned the British army. In their fervour to enlist [prior to conscription] the underage lads gave false names and exaggerated their age by a year or two. An army desperate for manpower gratefully accepted these callow youths; although questions were asked in the Houses of Parliament concerning the boy soldiers the military simply turned a blind eye to the matter.

The new draft received their first experience of artillery the following evening when the village was so heavily shelled the troops were forced out; although casualties were sustained none of them appear to have been fatal. As the German guns had now zeroed in on the village it became expedient to withdraw from the shelter of the village, to the open country. The battalion relocated to the shelter offered by a grassy bank where they dug themselves in. The next morning the Cheshires provided a working party; a few slight casualties were caused by enemy shellfire. During the evening of 17 April the battalion relieved the 18th Lancashire Fusiliers east of Martinsaart village.

A couple of miles to the north of Albert the marshy River Ancre slowly meanders past Aveluy Wood, a mature densely planted woodland covering a breadth of 1,500 metres. Beneath the leafy boughs thick impenetrable undergrowth carpeted the woodland floor, effectively forming nature's own version of barbed wire defences. In late March the enemy captured a small segment of the wood, the 35th Division took over the sector; this included a front line running diagonally through the wood from the north-east corner to approximately 500 yards north of the south-west corner. For a refreshing change the British were occupying the high ground from where the German-held village of Aveluy nestling in the river valley was visible, further a field stood the village of Martinsaart, while a mile further to the south-west stood Bouzincourt.

At dawn on the 19th the battalion to the left of the Cheshires attempted to advance around the left perimeter of Aveluy Wood; this manoeuvre looked like failing prior to the assistance rendered by Y company under the command of Second Lieutenant Gallagher who succeeded in establishing a flank. Amongst the morning casualties was Second Lieutenant Bishop who was hit in the ankle by a machine gun bullet.

The Cheshires frontage was dominated by a series of enemy machine gun posts, one in particular known simply as Lone Tree was particularly troublesome, and had to be eradicated. Shortly before dawn, on the 20 April a party of 25 men led by a Birkenhead officer Second Lieutenant W.N.D. Tyson assembled in the forward line; after a two minute Stokes mortar and rifle grenade bombardment the raiding party leapt from the trench and advanced towards the hornet's nest. They were met with a heavy enfilade of machine gun fire in the course of which Second Lieutenant Tyson was wounded in the head, 4 other ranks were killed and 10 others wounded. Despite the casualties the small force succeeded in capturing one post, killing its garrison but the situation was untenable for as the daylight grew the enemy machine guns and snipers caused heavy casualties, consequently the post had to be evacuated. Although the enemy fired on the stretcher bearers all the Cheshire wounded were eventually brought back to their lines and evacuated. The work of stretcher bearer 57906 Private Crosby received the attention of his superiors when he dashed out for sixty to seventy yards in broad daylight and brought in a wounded man, on another occasion he was responsible for saving two of his comrades.

The artillery salvoes ceased; during this lull the Cheshires conveyed wire and ammunition to the forward positions in readiness for the impending attack on Aveluy Wood and the nearby valley. This attack was to be made by the 35th and 38th Divisions with the intention of seizing the remaining elevated ground inside the woodland. The assault on the fortified wood was to be carried out by the Cheshires on 22 April in conjunction with the 15th Sherwood Foresters under the protective cover of a creeping artillery barrage. Zero hour was scheduled for 7-30 p.m. when W company led by Lieutenant Harford would lead the attack. Two platoons of Z Company were to provide

Germans operating a captured British Vickers machine gun.

support, while the other two platoons were to carry forward the picks, wire and materials required to consolidate any gains.

Preceding the infantry advance the artillery pounded the edges of Aveluy Wood for precisely three minutes, before sweeping forward on a creeping barrage. At 7-20 p.m. the predetermined range of the guns would then provide a protective barrage in front of the battalion's objective. At zero hour as the officers' whistles blew the patrols set off across No Man's Land to their objective. The barrage had failed to eliminate the German resistance; their machine gun bullets were soon zipping across the intervening ground, ripping into the khaki clad figures with deadly results. The 19th D.L.I. while in the support trenches had been caught out by a hostile barrage, their bad luck continued for as they advanced they were silhouetted against the setting sun and paid the ultimate price. Despite fierce fighting on the Cheshires left flank the 15th Sherwoods' attack on a strong point failed to eliminate the garrison, the defenders' stubborn resistance also prevented the Cheshires from advancing. Lieutenant Harford rallied his diminishing band of men, then moved off across the bullet swept fields to assist the hard pressed Sherwoods capture the strong point, while doing so the gallant Lieutenant Harford was wounded, but while being carried to the rear by stretcher bearers he was killed.

As the advance had stalled Captain Miln M.C. came forward and seeing the enemy strong point on the perimeter of the wood had halted the advance and ordered in additional patrols from Z Company. When Captain R. E. Warner commanding Z Company was wounded, Sergeant Read then displayed fine qualities of leadership and took control of his men, despite being wounded he refused any treatment until his wounded men had been attended to. Further to the right heavy machine gun and rifle fire was emanating from the direction of Lone Tree position. Despite repeated attacks against the German garrison equipped with three machine guns the position remained invincible. Reluctantly the Cheshires began to withdraw to their original positions, by 9-30 p.m. the centre of the Brigade attack had achieved a gain of 200 yards but little headway was made on the flanks of the attack. To prevent any further build up of troops the enemy guns laid a sixty-minute barrage on the Cheshires frontage. 105 Brigade was relieved on the night of 24 April.

The battalion casualty report for the action launched on the evening of 22nd concluding 23 April records the deaths of Captain G.G. Miln M.C. from Chester who was killed by two machine gun bullets to the head [his parents received notification of his M.C. three days prior to notification of his death] and also Lieutenant A.W. Hanford. Captain A.E. Wenner and Second Lieutenant T. Heap M.C. were wounded. The other ranks sustained six men killed, thirty-seven wounded three missing.[1]

In the small hours of the morning the weary battalion arrived at their dug outs near Hedauville, the remainder of the month passed without any noticeable incidents, carrying parties and a brief tour of the line at Bouzincourt occurred. The battalion's casualty rate for April consisted of three officers killed, five wounded. The other ranks had thirteen killed, ninety-four wounded, a further five were wounded but remained on duty, finally seven men were simply listed as missing, their fate being unknown.

During six weeks of almost constant combat from the 21 March to the end of April, a total of fifty-five British infantry divisions and three cavalry divisions were engaged against a hostile force of 109 German divisions. Throughout this period a total of 141 enemy divisions were engaged against the combined forces of Britain and France. Although the German advance had been successfully halted the cost had been considerable, as May approached eight British divisions had been weakened to such an extent they were no more than cadres and were effectively written off as fighting units.

Within the tranquil Cotswold village of Great Rissington a farm labourer's cottage was the humble home of Julia Ann Souls [Annie] and her husband William; their union had produced three daughters and six sons. The boys received rudimentary education within the village school, before leaving at the age of 11 to work as agricultural workers in the sleepy Gloucestershire countryside. As the storm clouds of war gathered five of the farm hands enlisted, Percy was ineligible; as he was under military age he remained behind only to die of meningitis. The five brothers never returned to the leafy Cotswold

Albert Souls
aged 20
Killed in action
1916

Arthur Souls
aged 30
Killed in action
1918

The five Souls brothers who lost their lives in the Great War.

Frederick Souls
aged 30
Missing in action
1916

Walter Souls
aged 24
Died of wounds
1916

Alfred Souls
aged 30
Killed in action
1918

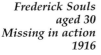

Dales, their self sacrifice is confirmed by the C.W.G.C. who know of no other British family who made a greater sacrifice than the Souls family, three of whom were originally Cheshire Bantams. Eight decades after their passing a lost cyclist named Michael Walsh visited the village pub where he noticed a faded newspaper cutting relating to the death of the Souls brothers. With his curiosity aroused he visited the village war memorial within Great Rissington's Church; the memorial is unusual for it includes faded photographs of the proud fallen soldiers. Intrigued by the predominance of the Souls brothers, Michael Walsh in conjunction with the Souls' octogenarian nephew Victor Walkeley revived the tale leading to its publication in the November 2001 issue of the *Saga* magazine.

The first brother to enlist was Albert, standing directly behind him in the queue was Walter; they became Privates 17208 and 17207 serving with the 2nd Worcester Regiment through the purgatory of the battle of Loos. Both were transferred to the Machine Gun Corps in January 1916, Albert the youngest of the lads was killed on 14-3-18. During the Somme offensive on 20 July Walter was wounded in the left leg resulting in his evacuation to 25th Stationary Hospital at Rouen. From here he wrote a cheery postcard to his mother, by the time she received it he was dead. The hospital matron forwarded a letter informing Annie Souls of the death of Walter, who was recovering well until he collapsed and died of an embolism.

As Fred, Alf and Arthur were a little on the short side the Stow on the Wold recruiting centre directed the men to the 16th Cheshire Battalion. By midsummer 1916 Frederick was in the line in the vicinity of Trones Wood and Waterlot Farm where the enemy heavily bombarded the line on 19th July 1916; Fred was killed on this day but his body was never recovered.

Alf and Arthur were identical twins; they appear to have been transferred upon the disbandment of the 16th Battalion, unfortunately the inseparable twins were assigned to different battalions. Alf went to the 11th Cheshires where he was engaged countering the Spring offensive, before being killed on 20th April 1918. Upon hearing of his sibling's death 21683 Lance Corporal Arthur Souls was said to have lost the will to live. He was now serving with the 7th Royal West Kents holding the Bretonneaux Plateau during which six officers were killed wounded or missing the other ranks suffered fourteen killed, eighty-six wounded and 128 missing amongst the dead was Arthur, who before he died performed an undisclosed act of valour for which he was awarded the Military Medal. The two twins born an hour apart had died within five days of each other.

According to the war diary the beginning of May was an uneventful period for the 15th Battalion[2], following the relocation of the Brigade; the 15th Cheshire marched to the village of Mirauaux, where they were joined by a fresh draft of 20 men. On the afternoon of the 8 May the Corps commander held a ceremonial parade and presented medal ribbons to fourteen of the Cheshires for their heroism in the recent operations. The next day they struck camp and relocated between Rubempire and Contay a village on the main road from Amiens to Arras.

After a respite of almost three weeks the battalion boosted by a further draft of three officers and thirty-one other ranks left camp early 20 May and marched to a wood near Bouzincourt. That evening during a lengthy gas bombardment they relieved the 17th R. W. Fusiliers in the Aveluy right sector. Throughout the bombardment the infantrymen in their claustrophobic gas masks with misted up lenses struggled to complete the change over, however the task was eventually completed around about 1 a.m. Then a steady trickle of gas casualties began to arrive at the aid posts, and by midday the number had risen to twenty men suffering from the effects of gas

British prisoners of war taken during the German Spring offensive in 1918.

While there were considerable reconstruction being carried on behind the allied lines the fighting troops were not idle especially on the frontage occupied by the Fourth and Second armies, infantry and artillery alike con-tinually harassed enemy positions in an attempt to prevent the build up of the anti-cipated assault. A series of raids un-successfully aimed at capturing a German prisoner for identification purpose were launched. On the 25th a platoon from Y Company attempt-ed a raid on a trench facing the town of Bouzincourt, they were met by heavy bouts of grenade throwing and fierce machine-gun fire, forcing the Cheshires to withdraw.

Trench raids were particularly hazardous operations especially for the short Bantams who frequently came upon an adversary who towered above them. Although he was only five foot two and a half inches tall 23032 Lance Corporal George Moffat boasted of being the tallest man in his battalion excluding the officers. He occasionally regaled his grandson Trevor with tales of his wartime adventures; during one patrol into No Man's Land he recalled how the Germans spotted the two privates and officer. This prompted the Germans to launch a customary bracket of shells upon their location; the trio cowered in a shell hole expecting the worst. For in such instances the German's always fired in the same pattern, one long, one short and one in the middle, the latter shell slammed into the earth next to the three men and fortunately failed to explode!

On another unknown raid into the German trenches Lance Corporal Moffatt was confronted by a very large German. During their training the Bantams were instructed to spit in the face of the Hun, invoking a reflex action when anybody would momentarily close his eyes, during this split second the small man would have the advantage. Instantly he spat at the German to distract him simultaneously both adversaries lunged forward with their bayonets – they both missed. In such instances the usual practice was to swing the butt of the rifle round and try to strike the opponent but the German side stepped before smashing his rifle butt into the small soldier's face smashing his nose. Lance Corporal Moffatt was rendered unconscious slumping onto the trench floor. When he regained consciousness he found himself back in his own lines. One of his chums had witnessed the duel and, after killing the German, he carried George Moffatt back to their position.

As it was considered imperative to maintain the ascendancy on their Germanic foe the raids were ordered to press ahead. The enemy were also active for it is recorded within a twelve hour period the 17th Lancashire Fusiliers repulsed five raids. The next day, despite heavy rain, preparations continued for the nocturnal raid on the notorious Lone Tree position and trench system, close to the Albert-Bouzincourt road, which was softened up by artillery. Zero hour was before midnight on the 24th. At the appointed hour the infantry dashed forward beneath the barrage. The Cheshires swept into the enemy post and trench only to find them unoccupied. Within fifteen minutes the raid was over, as were the lives of two of the Cheshire raiders; a further six were wounded chiefly attributable to our Stokes mortar barrage. The enemy retaliation was swift and protracted lasting until 2 a.m. but fortunately caused little damage. After another couple of days of sporadic shelling the battalion was relieved on the night of the 26th, they then proceeded to trenches to the north and south of Bouzincourt as part of the Brigade reserve.

Unknown Cheshire Bantam. 1918.

While in reserve the Cheshire companies carried out night digging and wiring parties, in the process Z Company sustained two casualties in the early hours of 27 May. Two days later the battalion was relieved without incident by the 15th Sherwood Foresters. The final day in May was scheduled for a gas bombardment on Aveluy Wood, but the prevailing wind was blowing onto the allied frontage, consequently a normal barrage was launched. This as predicted prompted a retaliatory bombardment, resulting in slight casualties to the Cheshire battalion.

The 104 Brigade on the Cheshires left launched an attack on the south-west part of the fortified woodland; they fought valiantly seizing their objectives at great loss of life. At midday the enemy brought up substantial reinforcements and mounted a determined counter attack, forcing them to withdraw from the wood. The casualties on both sides were said to be very severe due to the close fighting and artillery barrages. The enemy now anticipated a fresh attack on the wood, the following day [2nd June] the Divisional frontage was pounded by artillery. Throughout the day gas and high explosive shells exploded around the front and support lines, during the onslaught the Battalion's C.O. Major H.J. Dresser visited the front line and was killed by a shell. Later that evening a familiar face returned to the battalion, Lieutenant Colonel Harrison Johnston D.S.O. arrived to reassume command of the battalion. As the week progressed the front became much quieter, a brigade relief occurred on the 5th.

At Hedauville three days were spent in working parties. Lieutenant Colonel Johnston succumbed to illness and was evacuated on the 9th; consequently the temporary command of the battalion was handed over to Major Trestrail. On 16 June the 35th Division was relieved by the 12th Division and went into G.H.Q. Reserve. As Lieutenant Colonel H. Johnston had fallen ill the battalion was now under the command of Lieutenant Colonel W. Hodson, D.S.O. M.C. on completion of relief they headed for billets in Acheux. They remained here for almost a week deepening a line of trench in the vicinity of Mailly-Maillet five miles north of Albert; the remainder of the Brigade were located near Puchevillers.

The battalion rejoined the brigade on 21 June; for the remainder of the month the 35th Division carried out training exercises. Late on the night of the 30th the 15th Cheshire Battalion left camp for the railway station at Candas. After detraining at Wizernes, the battalion was granted a day's rest before carrying on the route march to the north, through countryside they had last passed through an eternity ago when they first arrived in war torn France. Over four days they journeyed on, mainly by foot, eventually arriving near Abeele. Late on the evening of the 5th the battalion began a long tiring march into the Locre sector where they relieved the French 358th Regiment of 71st Division. They now found themselves in a sector that was practically guarding the coast; their stint in the line proved uneventful, the battalion was relieved shortly before midnight on 9 July, they then marched to Roykens Akker where they acted as brigade reserve. Three days later the battalion were in support at Mont Rouge, one of a series of isolated hills forming a two-mile chain across the plain. Since the beginning of the war this region had been a reserve billeting area, but the fighting of 9 and 10 April 1918 had changed all that. The Cheshires now provided nocturnal working parties on the heavily shelled southern slopes of Mont Rouge.

On 16 July a heavy thunderstorm heralded the start of the new day, the rumble of thunder was emulated throughout the day by hostile artillery. During the evening the artillery altered its sights and now pumped a series of poison gas and shrapnel shells at the network of roads behind the Cheshires' position. The majority of the four Cheshire companies were busily assembling for a working party; as they were due to set off the enemy laid down a salvo of 150mm shells on the road near Brigade H.Q. The flying shards of scorching hot shrapnel killed Lieutenant H.A. Wainwright and four other ranks. Other casualties were Second Lieutenant H.D. Gallagher M.C. and twelve other ranks wounded. The accuracy of the enemy artillery was attributed to an enemy observation aircraft that had flown at a low altitude across the area the previous evening. The following evening, during a bombardment, the battalion relieved the 15th Sherwoods in the line during the relief the Cheshires suffered three casualties. The tour of the trenches at Locre was uneventful; 21 July the battalion was relieved by the 4th North Staffords, during the relief a Cheshire infantryman became a casualty. Within a few days the Cheshires were back in support on Mont Rouge; each night they provided carrying, wiring and digging parties. On the night of the 28th while the working parties were out a brief salvo of steel descended upon the working party killing two of the men. The next day the battalion relieved the 15th Sherwoods in the line at Locre without incident, remaining here until they in turn were relieved hours before the month ended. The 15th Cheshires were duly relieved shortly after midnight on the final night of July.

From the opening overtures of the March offensive to the end of July the German casualties amounted to 227,000 killed in action or missing, 765,000 wounded with a further 1,960,000 troops ill, chiefly through the pneumonia epidemic so prevalent upon the western front.

Advance to victory
The army now commanded by Sir Douglas Haig had beeen expanded; for the drafts from home and abroad had largely been incorporated. The number of effective fighting divisions had risen from forty-five to fifty-two. This improved situation prompted Haig to launch a combined tank and infantry counter offensive. East of Nieppe Forest a surprise attack on a 6,000 yard front resulted in the capture of the line along with 450 prisoners. Early July saw the Australian Corps, aided

by four companies of Americans and sixty tanks capture our old positions east of Hamel and cleared the Villers Bretonneux plateau. Additional gains followed elsewhere, after the collapse of the enemy counter stroke in mid July and the brilliant success of the allied counter-offensive south of the Aisne the military situation now looked very different.

The German army offensive had been launched at great risk essentially in the hope of producing an overall victory or provoking a crisis so severe the allies would have no other option than to sue for peace. The calculated gamble had failed on both counts furthermore the German army was now left in an immensely weakened state for its period of maximum strength had now passed and the majority of the reserves accumulated during the winter had also been expended. The rejuvenated British army with its rapidly growing allegiance of American troops was ready to take the offensive to the Hun. The battle of Amiens commenced on 8 August within five days the town and its vital railway centre had been delivered from the threat of attack, during the action Anglo-American units supported by almost 400 tanks, heavily defeated twenty-two German divisions. Almost 22,000 German prisoners were captured together with 400 guns permitting our line to advance to a depth of some twelve miles in this vital area. This stunning victory remorselessly driven home by Canadian and Australian troops was a devastating blow for the German high command. General Erich von Luddendorff famously referred to the 8 August as 'The blackest day of the German army in the history of this war', enemy losses were estimated as being in the region of 30,000. The effect of this victory following hard on the heels of the allied victory on the Marne boosted British morale and had the exact opposite result upon the Germans. The victory that had appeared so tantalisingly close was denied them and they in turn were conceding ground as they began to straighten out vulnerable salients in his front line, their policy had now shifted from one of offensive to that of a defensive nature.

Away from the fighting the month of August was an exceptionally mundane month for the Cheshire Battalion who were primarily involved in Brigade training, interrupted by periods in Corps Reserve.

On the 18th the battalion was briefly billeted in the pleasant village of Ste. Marie Cappel, where Lieutenant Colonel H. Johnston resumed command of the battalion. On the 29th 105 Brigade moved forward, the Cheshire Battalion relieved the 1st Royal Irish Fusiliers in the support position in the St. Jan Cappel sector. From their positions the soldiers looked on as the enemy torched buildings, as the flames leapt into the night it became evident the enemy was retiring in the direction of Bailleul. Daylight patrols later confirmed the village had been abandoned. For this reason within 24 hours the relief had been reversed as the 35th Divisional relief was cancelled. The battalion returned to its familiar billets in the vicinity of Eecke. Throughout the Western Front the indications of an impending victory were becoming apparent, as British troops had captured Merville, Albert and Bray the 30th Division captured Dranoutre ridge. The German army now began a gradual retirement from the Lys salient where they were constantly under fire from our artillery. Their defensive line now began to shrink backwards in the direction of Lille.

On 31 August the 35th Division was notified of a transfer to II Corps, where the 35th Division was to relieve the 30th American Division by 4 September. While preparations were carried out throughout the Division, 105 Brigade relocated to Tunnelling Camp, near Poperinghe in the Ypres salient. Once there the training continued, and the football final of the Brigade Cup was held. After leading for most of the game the footballers from X Company were defeated 4 goals to 3 by the Sherwood Foresters.

During the night of 2/3 September the enemy fell back quickly along the entire frontage of the Third Army and the right of the First Army. Twenty-four hours later the 15th Cheshires entrained on the light railway for the Canal sector where they entered the line and relieved 1/120th American Battalion. Throughout September the 15th Battalion rotated in and out of the trenches between the Canal at the intersection of the Ypres-Lille road and the western edge of Zillebeke lake.

Sporadic salvoes rained down on their new position a situation that prompted the Cheshires to engage in a series of patrols to keep up the men's morale and to harass their counterparts. On the 7th a strong mist enshrouded No Man's Land providing an ideal cover for a W Company raiding party led by Second Lieutenant Shaw. They discovered two unoccupied posts, before valiantly rushing a third, capturing six prisoners. The patrol returned unscathed and was congratulated for its fine performance. Also two patrol leaders,

British artillery put down fire on the retreating Germans.

Sergeant Mace and Corporal Richards, were especially praised. The prisoners revealed they had been forewarned of the arrival of the 35th Division in their sector, by German intelligence who had an unerring ability to anticipate divisional relief. Later that day the battalion was relieved by the 18th Lancashire Fusiliers and went into reserve near Eerie Camp.

Three days later they returned to the reserve position in the right sub sector of the canal sector. The days passed without incident until the night of the 17th when a patrol was sent out. Second Lieutenant H.C. Mann was in command of the men from Z Company. They penetrated the German advanced posts and came upon a substantial working party on what was called the Mound. As they withdrew the Cheshires captured an enemy corporal and killed a sergeant returning unscathed with their prisoner along with the deceased sergeant's paperwork for intelligence appraisal. Considerable skill was shown in this small operation the company commander being admirably assisted by Sergeant Robinson, both of whom were singled out for praise within the war diary. While this scenario was occurring Y Company carried out a similar raid and located the enemy, upon receipt of the intelligence the artillery brought their guns to bear on the Mound and craters with unknown effect.

The Germans were now alerted to the 15th Battalion's aggressive nature and took defensive measures. The following night Y Company put out a patrol led by Lieutenant W.G. Stott which approached the enemy's advanced listening posts only to discover the observers had withdrawn. Suddenly, a hail of enemy machine-gun bullets converged on the patrol, followed by artillery salvoes which resulted in the death of Lieutenant Stott and one other (believed to be 19547 Private H. Clarke, one of the original Bantams). A further five battalion members were wounded.

The Battalion runners namely 52283 Private Olley, 40403 Private McKay and 16631 Private Houghton received high praise for their good work during this and the previous tour of the front line. As the telephone lines were constantly being severed the runners were required to make daylight journeys over open ground under direct observation by the enemy and subject to heavy shellfire.

During the night of the 19th the battalion was relieved by the 14th Argyles prior to a move to billets near Belgian Battery Corner, a mile outside of Ypres. The men were reported as being in fine spirits, their morale was further raised by the Divisional and Brigade commanders congratulatory message to the battalion for their recent fine work in a series of well conducted, daringly executed patrols. For the next couple of days the battalion rested by day and provided carrying parties throughout the night. They returned to the line occupying trenches in Les Trois Sector, early on the 25th a stray shell hit one of X

Company's trenches wounding Second Lieutenant J.C. Slater and two other ranks; 8473 Lance Corporal W. Talbot was killed. Next night the battalion was relieved and proceeded to their billets at Assam Farm.

Now it was their turn to join in an attack, following a day of preparations the battalion bolstered by other members of the Brigade returned to Les Trois Rois sector. Away to their left the artillery supporting the Belgium army was about to end its three-hour bombardment to coincide with the Divisional attack to be launched at 5-30 a.m. on the 28th. The first objective extended from the canal, south east of Battle Wood, through Klein Zillebeke onwards along the ridge to a position to the south east of Sanctuary Wood. Five minutes before zero our artillery launched their barrage, accurately directed onto their targets by the increasingly effective use of observers in contact aircraft. Heavy rainfall pelted down upon the Brigade assaulting battalions as they advanced across the pitted ground, they and the remainder of the Division gained their objectives without much difficulty. The 15th Battalion was not involved in the first day of this attack as it was held in brigade reserve near Bedford House. Although, despite this, four of the Cheshires are recorded as dying on this day. The battalion's contribution consisted of providing escorts for ten German officers and over 300 other ranks, prisoners of war, who were taken to the Divisional prisoner compound. At approximately midday the 41st Division passed through the 35th Division amid favourable reports on the success of the attack. Throughout the day the components of the Division pressed home their advance with great tenacity, one by one enemy positions were overwhelmed; each gain was consolidated every small gain spurred the attack on further. As darkness descended no further progress was possible, however the days fighting had resulted in an advance of almost four miles, a considerable achievement that eclipsed any gains the Division had previously attained. A single day's fighting had produced a previously undreamt of victory at the modest cost of less than 600 casualties to the 35th Division, in addition almost 800 prisoners were taken plus field guns, trench mortars and machine guns, it was a remarkable day's work by anyone's standards.

During the night the following day's orders were issued: 105 Brigade was to move up through Zanvoorde with the intention of capturing the line extending from Tenbrielen village to Blagnaert Farm and their environs. If progress was good the attacking troops were instructed to press on to Wervicq. 104 Brigade relieved 105 in readiness for the forthcoming attack. In the early hours of 29 September the 15th Cheshire battalion set off from their billets to join with the two other battalions ordered to attack and capture the previously mentioned line. The battalions concentrated at Klein Zillebeke where they halted while the officers attended a conference with the Brigadier General,

Temporary Lieutenant William Noel Tyson. Age 21.
In March [it was in fact 20 April] Lieutenant Tyson was wounded in the head during a night attack in Aveluy Wood, but returned to France in August. Shortly after his return he was killed in action on 29-9-18 while leading his men in an attack. His C.O. wrote 'Our battalion was advance guard to the brigade; he was in command of the vanguard when they struck a strong enemy position with many machine gun nests. He extended his men and boldly attacked the position, being killed instantly by machine gun fire, but doing his duty by locating and finding the strength of the enemy position, probably thereby saving many lives, as we were enabled to make a strong circling movement and capture the village within a few hours. He died a noble death and by giving his life without hesitation undoubtedly saved heavy losses amongst his comrades'.

who informed them of their objective also giving an assurance that Zandvoorde was safely in allied hands, upon arrival at the village their orders were to break into artillery formation before attacking down the ridge were little opposition if any would be met.

At 8 a.m. on a chilly September morning the 15th Cheshires, due to spearhead the attack set off through a blanket of mist for Tenbrielen via Zanvoorde, and soon became disorientated in the swirling mist. After regaining their bearings the decision was taken to press on but instead of approaching Zandvoorde from the north-west, the battalions came at the village from a westerly direction. Arriving at the western inclines of the Zanvoorde Ridge the battalions dispersed as ordered into artillery formation. The 15th Cheshires confidently advanced in the direction of the heaps of rubble, formerly the village of Zandvoorde, and reputedly safe in allied hands. At the outskirts of the village very heavy hostile machine gun fire from the extreme point of Zandvoorde Spur opened up on the Cheshires. The totally unexpected bursts of lead sliced into the Cheshires killing Lieut. W.N.D. Tyson and several men, many more were wounded. A brave attempt to storm the machine gun emplacement failed, adding to the death toll of the battalion. Sustained shellfire and enfilading machine -gun fire resisted all efforts to eliminate the machine-gun nests; the ground was soon littered with heroic fallen attackers. A small artillery salvo was then put down upon the village; simultaneously three companies of Cheshires unsuccessfully attacked the emplaced machine guns, sustaining seven casualties. The field guns also failed to eradicate the heavily protected machine gun posts, at 12-30 p.m. Colonel Harrison Johnston received orders stating no further attack was to be made, and ordered a return to behind the ridge from where the attack had commenced. At 3 p.m. the 4th North Staffords and 15th Sherwoods enveloped the village and cleared the opposition away. The Divisional artillery brought a murderous fire to bear, following a fierce skirmish the entire Zandevoorde ridge was captured.

The wartime experiences of Private J. Nelson Spencer an original Bantam who originally served with the 17th Reserve Battalion prior to serving with the 15th Battalion, have survived in a typewritten letter. In one paragraph he refers to the Hun making a stand somewhere near Menin, which would place the incident about here within this narrative. As a group of 15th Cheshires moved forward across open ground they drew artillery fire, some of the men gained shelter behind a low earth bank but the remainder including Private Spencer had gone beyond this. They sought the only available shelter and dropped into old shell craters of insufficient depth to shelter them from the blasts of hurtling shrapnel; soon the screams of the wounded rent the air. Private Spencer attended to them as best he could, and after dressing the wounded with their field dressings he braved the shower of shrapnel and piggy backed the wounded to the rear of the earthworks where two officers were taking cover. It is assumed the officers recommended Private Spencer for the Military Medal for his citation read 'For rescuing wounded under fire'.

The 15th Cheshires then pushed W and Y Companies down the slopes of the ridge in the direction of Tenbrielen, and although the Germans were withdrawing they did not concede ground lightly. As darkness drew a curtain on the infantry activity, the enemy artillery pounded the neighbourhood until midnight. Throughout the night heavy rainfall poured down upon the soaking wet infantry huddled within their hard won positions.

Throughout the day across the Divisional front the German machine guns had stoutly resisted the infantry whose advances were also carried out through intense barrages of explosive and gas shells, the latter hampered the advance by compelling the effected units to wear gas masks as they advanced. Inevitably the Hun withdrew conceding ground to the 35th Division; the captured positions enlightened the new arrivals to the extensive trench system developed by the German's for the western slopes of the ridge were intersected by a warren of deep trenches affording excellent cover for the enemy troops held in reserve here during the fighting for supremacy within the Ypres salient. The static war was now a thing of the past for the hate filled trench systems of the Western Front were now to their rear, the conflict would be waged in open country upon virgin soil.

During the early hours of the 30th orders were received advising that a mixed force from 105 and 106 Brigades would attack and recapture Tenbrielen together with the northern outskirts of Wervicq. Heavy rain spurred on by a strong wind continued to sweep across the countryside, at 6-15 a.m. the advance commenced, acting in support of the leading battalions were the 17th Royal Scots and 15th Cheshires, the latter was to provide close support to the 18th Highland L.I..

Initially the advance progressed successfully until three quarters of a mile from the railway north of Wervicq where hostile heavy machine guns were emplaced. The leading battalions were caught in the open by sustained machine gun fire from their front and flanks, under their murderous fire the attack stalled, a company of the supporting Cheshires were now ordered forward upon the right flank to eradicate the machine gun position. Shortly afterwards two companies of the 12th H.L.I. briefly encroached into the periphery of Wervicq before being driven back by enfilading machine gun fire. A further company of Cheshires was now brought into the fight to compensate for the severe casualties sustained by the Highlanders. More reinforcements were called up and one of the companies's encircled the enemy machine gun dispensing death from within a farm on the Wervicq-Gheluvelt road, the position was rushed and the weapon fell silent. All attempts to make headway were continually hampered by machine gun fire yet two companies of 17th Royal Scots managed to advance within 400 yards of the outskirts of the village. They negotiated a thick belt of barbed wire and were swiftly greeted with bullets from a nest of pill boxes located on the left flank, undaunted they rushed the nearest position and captured the garrison, all attempts to eliminate the other emplacements proved unsuccessful. The rifle companies were by now severely depleted, their positions were rapidly becoming untenable, and no contact could be established with the 29th Division

In this photograph of captured German troops passing through a Canadian held sector Bantams can be seen among the onlookers.

on their left flank.

The enemy now launched a counter attack against the flank of the supporting companies, including W Company of the Cheshires. As the situation continued to deteriorate the order to retire was received, all the leading units were successfully withdrawn apart from the survivors of two platoons who were so far advanced they became isolated and were left to the mercy of their captors. The commanders of the 104 and 105 Brigades arrived from the advanced H.Q. to investigate at first hand the situation, rapidly concluding that further progress was impossible without extensive heavy calibre artillery preparation.

The remnants of the brigades did their best to consolidate their new positions. Rain had persisted throughout the action and scores of men began to show indications of suffering from the effects of exposure. Throughout the night the enemy artillery shelled the allied line and the Cheshires' Battalion H.Q., sited in a captured pill box, received a direct hit from a shell. Possibly the reinforced concrete structure saved the occupants for no casualties were reported. Two days earlier the trench strength of the 105 and 106 Brigades stood at 2,280 and 2,050 men respectively. On 30 September these figures were 900 and 500 and, due to their low strength, these brigades were spared any further immediate action.

The next afternoon a dozen Germans approached under cover and commenced throwing bombs at W Company. The raiders were swiftly driven off by machine-gun and rifle fire. That night the battalion was relieved by the 7th Royal Irish Regiment and relocated to bivouac in a wet crater strewn field devoid of any accommodation somewhere between Kruiseecke and Gheluvelt crossroads. Captain H.E. Vincent recorded in the war diary 'The battalion maintained its good reputation throughout the operations and the men, although subjected to heavy fighting and great fatigue, were magnificent'. The total casualties from all causes from 29 September to 1 October inclusive were approximately five officers and 150 other ranks. During the earlier series of engagement the 35th Division had succeeded in capturing almost 1,100 prisoners along with assorted weapons and gained eight miles of enemy territory, even the most pessimistic Tommy must have realised that the tide was finally beginning to turn in their favour.

In late September the allies launched a battle of nine days duration during which the First, Third and Fourth armies successfully stormed the line of the Canal du Nord and broke through the Hindenburg Line. With the entire Hindenburg Line in allied hands the advance posed a new threat to the German positions on the River Lys.

The first day out of the line provided an opportunity for the Cheshire Battalion to rest and dry out their saturated uniforms. Next day they left camp at 3-15 a.m. bursting into song as they marched along the Menin to Ypres road before passing through the notorious Shrapnel Corner before arriving early evening at Swan Château. Their respite was interrupted at noon on the 5th when sudden orders were received to despatch two rifle companies to the line forward of Terhand to relieve the 2nd Irish Rifles; acting in support, Y and Z Companies remained there for approximately twenty-four hours.

A planned attack involving the 15th Cheshires was postponed, consequently, on 11 October, the battalion left the training grounds at Swan Château and marched along the Menin Road to Molenhoek where, shortly before midnight, they relieved the 18th Highland Light Infantry in the front line.

Shortly after 3 p.m. the next day orders were received for both front line Cheshire companies to send out daylight patrols, to check if the foe had withdrawn. Lieutenant Walker and Second Lieutenant R.F. Drummond set off with their patrols. Immediately a series of enemy S.O.S. rocket signals shot skywards. As a result a heavy artillery barrage of all calibres was put down on the Cheshires front line, Battalion H.Q. and rear positions. As a further precautionary measure machine guns systematically poured a torrent of bullets in the direction of the British positions.

Both patrols were trapped in the shell blasted wasteland while the 45 minute fire storm rained down all around them; miraculously, only one other rank was wounded. The men of Z Company were holding the position known as Turnbull Farm, which sustained a direct hit claiming sixty casualties; it is assumed most of this figure consisted of injuries as only one killed in action death, and two deaths as a result of wounds are recorded for the 12 October.

It is most likely that amongst their number was Private J. Nelson Spencer in a surviving type written letter he recounts how the retreating German artillery compelled them to take shelter in a farm outbuilding where they decided to remain until after sunset. When a shell detonated upon the farm shed most of those taking cover were killed or wounded by shrapnel. After midnight stretcher bearers loaded Private Spencer onto a stretcher and headed through the inky night towards a waiting ambulance. Unseen in the darkness the stretcher bearers stumbled over a dead mule, and inadvertently pitched the wounded Bantam onto the floor, his landing was harder than expected for he landed on the two Mills bombs in his pockets. At Poperinghe Casualty Clearing Station his wounds were cleaned and dressed by a nurse who was terrified to discover the contents of his pockets. The next day he was transferred to Number 5[2] Canadian Hospital at Rouen to await repatriation to England. He recuperated at Bournemouth Hospital from where he was discharged from the army as no longer medically fit. For him the war was over.

The 35th Division's remorseless pressure against the enemy recommenced; the objective of their attack extended from a position on the Terhand to Courtrai road almost a mile to the south of Gullegham, on the left flank to a small incline almost one mile to the south of Moorseele. Once this line was captured the Division would be in reach of the banks of the River Lys. The 13th October was an uneventful day for the 15th battalion until mid evening when the Division on their left attempted to capture Gold Flake Farm. While repulsing this attack the enemy laid a counter barrage upon the allied front line, resulting in stray shells sweeping down upon the Cheshire battalion killing one officer and 13 O.R.s including 39930 Private Joseph Clarke [pictured below] whose death was recorded on the bookmark I had discovered at the car boot sale over half a century later.

While the fighting continued in the south the allied forces in Flanders worked diligently in repairing adequate communications in the area of the old Ypres battles. Seven divisions inclusive of the 35th garrisoned the British sector; their frontage extended approximately ten miles from Comines to the tiny village of St. Pieter, along the Menin-Roulers road. An allied force of French, British and Belgian troops prepared to attack at 5-35 p.m. on 14 October the entire front between the River Lys at Commines and Dixmude.

In advance of zero hour the 15th Cheshires vacated Cavender Farm earlier than scheduled thereby missing the full force of a barrage that unexpectedly rained down upon the vicinity of Cavender House.

At daybreak the troops advanced through a heavy ground mist, tackling with heroic endeavour numerous machine gun positions, although the Cheshires were worn out and suffering from exposure they rose magnificently to the occasion, they were recorded as putting on the best show ever displayed by the battalion, and subsequently reflected by several gallantry awards. Sergeant Finnigan, one of the original Bantams lead the first assault on the machine gun nests, totally indifferent to self preservation his leadership and gallantry inspired his men to storm the posts whose defenders were eliminated or taken prisoner. As our troops advanced the thick mist concealed an enemy pill box whose occupants duly came out firing into the backs of the advancing troops. Corporal Walker and four other ranks turned the Lewis gun on them; under the withering fire the enemy took cover within their pill box. Corporal Wilson seized the initiative by bravely racing forward to the pill box then commenced firing through the loophole killing and

Private J. Clarke. (see page 229)

wounding several men; an additional 11 surrendered to the heroic Cheshire. Further on the Cheshires were again pinned down by a pill box from which a steady stream of machine gun fire emanated, C.S.M. Coulter accompanied by an N.C.O. under covering Lewis gunfire rushed the position before hurtling a mills bomb through the pillbox aperture silencing the weapon. His bravery citation records his capturing of five machine guns and the killing and wounding of fifteen of the enemy. After two hours of hard fighting they captured their objective Dukes Farm also six field guns, two anti tank guns, two light mortars and over thirty machine guns plus over 120 prisoners including eight officers. The battalion sustained over a hundred casualties Lieutenant J. Miller was killed, Lieutenants A. Walker, O.R. Sidebottom and Second Lieutenant Wych were wounded, also Second Lieutenant Hope required evacuation due to shell shock. A total of twenty-four recorded deaths occurred on this day a further seven wounded men died the following day. The low casualties were directly attributed to the quality of leadership by the battalion officers.

Elsewhere the 17th Lancashire Fusiliers had a particularly torrid time as they had encountered numerous machine-gun posts. By approximately 7-15 a.m. they and the Cheshires the two leading companies had attained their objectives and halted to allow the 15th Sherwoods, 18th Lancashire Fusiliers and the 19th Durham L.I. to pass through their positions and successfully hammer home the attack. On their flanks after experiencing difficulties the 41st and 36th Divisions gained ground and 105 Brigade linked up with 104 Brigade and established a line in advance of the one originally ordered.

The following day the attacks were renewed against stiff pockets of resistance sited in assorted farm buildings; the isolated garrisons were tackled at leisure or offered an opportunity to surrender. It became imperative to remain in contact with the retiring forces as a result patrols set off to probe the enemy positions'; upon finding the area deserted 104 Brigade and the 41st Division established posts in advance of the previously mentioned line. During a murky rainy night a patrol passed through the village of Welveghem now devoid of Germans and advanced as far as the River Lys at Lauwe. From sunrise the previous day the soldiers had advanced nearly five miles capturing over 500 prisoners and practically an arsenal of weaponry from an enemy taken by surprise by the rapid pace of the advance. To the north great progress was made, Ostend fell on 17 October, and three days later the northern flank of the allied line rested on the Dutch border. As the allied tide swept along it left in its wake thousands of prisoners, captured weaponry and ammunition that Germany could ill afford to lose.

The ailing Ottoman empire of Turkey faced up to the inevitable and capitulated, prompting Germany's other ally Bulgaria to follow suit while Austrian cooperation began to waver. The only real military operation now available to the German generals was a withdrawal to the shortest possible frontage requiring a minimum defensive force. The deteriorating weather might also hamper the allied advance, allowing Germany an opportunity to regroup throughout the winter.

After much bloody fighting the advance moved on. Throughout the 17th the troops occupied the following positions 106 Brigade along the River Lys, 104 in support south west of Moorseele and 105 in reserve. As the enemy had destroyed the bridges the 204th Field Company moved forward with pontoon equipment and as darkness fell attempted to construct three bridges. Despite a covering artillery barrage from all three brigades the bridge builders were faced with strong hostile opposition. Heavy machine-gun fire raked the structures and gas shelling hampered the engineers in their work. Eventually two half submerged barges connected by a foot bridge breached the divide permitting parties to establish posts on the far bank of the Lys. Others raided the enemy north of Marke.

Right is a transcript of the now very faded original pencil written letter penned by Sergeant Noonan as he prepared for the forthcoming attack. Upon completion he appears to have folded it in four most likely placing it in his tunic pocket awaiting an opportunity to forward the letter. Within 48 hours the soldier was killed in action, his now blood stained letter was forwarded along with his effects to his bereaved mother.

As instructions had been received not to force the river in face of strong opposition the Lys was not crossed until the night of the 18th/19th, the troops waited ready for the dawn attack, their task would be simplified as during the night the engineers completed constructing seven bridges. On the 19th the village of Marke was captured from a demoralised enemy, meanwhile battalions of the 104 Brigade, supported by artillery, reached the Aelbeke-Coutrai road. The field artillery units advanced across the bridges taking up positions in readiness for the next stage of the advance to ultimate victory.

105 Brigade, which had remained in support, moved forward to

France 18 October 1918

Dear Mother,

...I have just heard from the sergeant major that all leave has been stopped again, but I do not know how long for, it might be only for two days, a week or a month, so all we will have to do is wait and hope for the best. I suppose you will have seen the papers that we have been very busy again helping Fritz on his way home, and I was lucky enough to pull through it all again, although it was not all pie while it lasted. But there was one thing that helped us a lot, and that was the mist, although it was the cause of our lads losing their way, we could not see ten yards in front of oneself. There are very few fellows who can say that they went over the top and found breakfast waiting for them, we quite surprised Fritz, and he could not see us coming through the mist and there were a couple of farms and houses which we went in after we found him just going to have breakfast, so all we did was send him down to the cage and then sat down and ate his breakfast for him, which was composed of a few eggs, bread and butter, and coffee, so I think that we did quite well considering, what do you say? One of our corporals has just come in and told me that there are some of our men going on leave tomorrow, so I am thinking I will be home in a month as I told you in my last letter. I think this will be all for now, so I will close, Hoping to hear from you soon. From Jim.

rejoin the fighting. Shortly before midnight on the 19th the Cheshire Battalion crossed the Lys before halting briefly near the tile works in Marckbeeke. Several hours later they moved to Pottleberg, a village to the south of Courtrai, where they were greeted enthusiastically by hundreds of civilians. Then at 2-30 p.m. a patrol from X Company encountered machine-gun fire to the east of Courtrai and, in accordance with orders, duly noted the positions and withdrew. A Brigade attack was imminent upon objectives sited three to four miles to the south-east of Courtrai.

The 35th Divisional front was manned by 104 Brigade on the right, with 105 Brigade on the left with 106 Brigade in support. Both of the attacking brigades employed all three battalions in the line. To the Division's right was the 34th Division, while the 29th Division occupied the left flank.

The launching of the attack was not heralded by the customary barrage; possibly due to this fact some of the attacking waves appear to have caught the enemy off guard. The 17th and 18th Lancashire Fusiliers made good progress, on the left of the Brigade the 19th Durham L.I. met resistance as they stormed two ridges shelled by the enemy, before reaching their objective.

At 7 in the morning 105 Brigade advanced with the 15th Battalion Cheshires fulfilling its role by easily capturing the village of Berkstraat and the neighbouring ridge. The enemy were still on familiar territory and as resourceful as ever had withdrawn to a naturally defended position. Beyond the village the ridge decreased by almost 100 feet, at its base meandered the uninviting Keibeek, whose original purpose was to drain the surrounding fields. All approaches to the Keibeek were covered by machine guns sited in farm buildings to its rear, 1,000 yards behind this formidable barrier additional machine guns poked out menacingly from the high ground. As the artillery was still advancing the infantry advance now ground to an abrupt halt. Lieutenant Mann, accompanied by two men, attacked the flank of a farm; their heroism in the face of heavy machine gun fire, allowed the unit on their right the chance to advance and capture the farm. Meanwhile the 15th Sherwoods had fought their way through Swevegham.

All the Cheshire battalion's attempts to advance were prevented by the machine gunners and shelling until 1500 hours when a slackening of the machine gun fire became noticeable, the Cheshire battalion tentatively pushed out patrols and successfully crossed the Keibeek. Once on the far bank posts were established and despite the machine-gun fire continued to make progress pressing on in the dark until they reached their first objective. The day's fighting cost the battalion fifty casualties Second Lieutenant J.S. Brown was killed along with six men from the ranks. 106 Infantry Brigade had also attained its objectives and the front line was adjusted accordingly.

On 21 October units of the 41st Division passed through the 35th Division's sector and occupied the line. The 35th Division had been fighting for six days culminating in an arduous twenty-three hour long battle fought through liquid mud and continual rain. The outgoing infantry were soaked to the skin and physically exhausted. The bedraggled Cheshire Battalion then marched to billets at Courtrai. The majority of 105 Brigade was allocated accommodation in the barracks and monastery at Pottelberg, where the Division remained resting and re-equipping within the vicinity of Courtrai until 26 October.

The rejuvenated 35th Division relieved the 41st Division late on the night of 26 October; 104 and 106 Brigades occupied the line, while the 105 remained in support to the east of Sweveghem. On the 26th instant the 15th Cheshires marched to billets at the shell damaged village of St. Louis. Numerous dead horses were strewn along the main road and the Cheshires spent the day burying them. Further days were spent here carrying out practise attacks until noon on the 30th when the battalion marched to billets at Kattetestraat where they were held in reserve at the tactical disposal of 104 infantry brigade.

France 24 October 1918

Dear Mrs Noonan,
It is with deep regret that I write to tell you that your son 50390 Sergeant J.H. Noonan was killed in action on the 20th instant, while the battalion was pushing back the Germans in this neighbourhood. Your son was acting very gallantly at the time he was killed pushing forward with his platoon officer to see whether it was possible to advance further and outflank one of the enemy machine guns, which was causing a great deal of trouble. Death was instantaneous and occurred within a few minutes of his platoon officer being killed, your son's loss is a great loss to me and his company commander and to most of his platoon to say nothing od the battalion. Also we can ill afford to lose good NCOs such as your boy was in these strenuous days. In conclusion please accept my sincere sympathy on my behalf and that of his platoon and the company in general. The funeral took place yesterday in a village cemetery near here and was conducted by Father Dolan, the senior Roman Catholic chaplain of the Division.
Yours sincerely,
P. Light. Lieutenant

Meanwhile the advance continued at dawn on the 27th, two battalions of Lancashire Fusiliers advanced to meet with stout opposition from the elevated ground near Tiegham, artillery fire from across the river Scheldt impeded the advance forcing the infantry to retire. Orders now arrived for an attack along the left bank of the Scheldt, the first objective was the line extending from Waermaerde to south of Tieghem, a second reached from Kerkhove to Haelendries. The attack commenced at 5-25 a.m. on the final day in October and, despite resistance, an hour later the line of the first objectives had been reached. This released a further dozen villages from German occupation. After a planned two hour tactical pause the advance continued, the opposition was more severe but this did not deter the troops. Shortly before 10-00 a.m. the final objective was captured, amidst reports of the enemy retreating towards Audenarde.

After midday orders were received to exploit the advance by capturing the village of Eeuwhoek, resulting in the gain of a further 1,000 yards, the German withdrawal greatly benefited our French ally who was able to make a long advance towards Audenarde. The attacking British had suffered 428 casualties of all ranks; a high percentage of these belonged to the 18th Lancashire Fusiliers.

The 35th Division was relieved on the first day of November when the 15th Cheshire battalion marched via Courtrai to billets in Maarke. Several days later the Division was ordered to take over the line from a point east of Rugge across the northern arm of the river to Tenhove, requiring a forced crossing of the river. The attack was scheduled for 11 November, but during the night of the 8th reports were received of an enemy withdrawal from the riverbank, and patrols of the 41st Division and the French had crossed the watery divide. 105 Brigade was ordered to cross the river by any available method; simultaneously 104 Brigade was despatched to Tiegham. Early next morning the 18th Highlanders crossed the river by a rickety canvas boat, ninety minutes later the 15th Sherwoods crossed the Scheldt by ferry and a floating foot-bridge constructed by the Royal Engineers. Components of the Cheshire Battalion initially made the crossing by canvas boats, but later a trench shelter bridge was used to span the water. By noon the battalion was on the opposite bank without having a shot fired in its direction. The 15th Sherwoods and 18th Highland 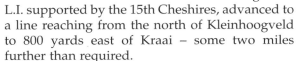 L.I. supported by the 15th Cheshires, advanced to a line reaching from the north of Kleinhoogveld to 800 yards east of Kraai – some two miles further than required.

104 Brigade was then ordered to pass through the 105th Division and continue the pursuit. The infantry began the chase at 7 a.m. on the 10th and within two hours the Renaix-Nukerke road was reached without meeting any resistance. As they advanced the troops received enthusiastic welcomes from the inhabitants of all the Belgian villages along their route. On 9 November the enemy was in general retreat on the entire front of the British army, and although opposition hardly existed the advancing troops had difficulty in keeping up with the pace. The artillery especially were hampered by blocked roads pock marked with shell craters, working parties hurriedly toiled away reinstating the roads to a standard suitable for wheeled traffic. Amongst the working parties were the 15th Cheshires who were detailed to repair the main Renaix road. As they worked away the main topic of conversation centred on a rumoured armistice.

Since the beginning of November the allies had

Elements of the German army in full retreat passing through a Belgian town in November 1918.

destroyed German resistance beyond the possibility of recovery. The enemy had been vanquished, his best divisions had been fought to a standstill and rendered incapable of organised opposition by 59 British divisions, which, in the final three months of the war, had engaged and defeated 99 separate German divisions.

At 8-30 p.m. on 10 November news was received that the armistice terms had been accepted, but 105 Brigade was to advance early next morning for billets at Audenhove. Simultaneously the remainder of the Division would attempt to reach the river Dendre before hostilities ceased.

At 8-30 a. m. on 11 November a wire arrived at divisional headquarters advising that hostilities would cease at 11 a. m. that day. The Cheshire Battalion received the news while marching to their billets at Audenhove. Upon arrival the men settled down quietly incredulous that the curtain had finally been brought down on the Great War for civilisation.

Because the Division was in advance of the general line it was earnestly hoped they would advance into Germany, or at least remain in their current pleasant surroundings for a while. Unfortunately, the 35th Division was denied both of these favoured options as they were ordered to march back to billets in the St. Omer vicinity. The decision

230

was certainly an anticlimax. The general advance into Germany was to begin on 1 December as the armies headed eastwards the front would decrease, while the supply lines would grow steadily longer. Due to these factors a redistribution of troops became necessary; it was simply unfortunate that the 35th Division was not required. However, it mattered little to the troops who had stubbornly pressed onwards against determined resistance. To make the matter worse the Division was expected to travel by foot to the rear area as all available transport appeared to be required for the advance towards the Rhine.

Notes

[1] Post war figures for 15th Cheshire casualties on this day are given as 14 by the C.W.G.C.

[2] Although there is no reference to the incident in the war diary, a summary of the battalion's casualties for the week ending 5-5-18 reveal the following other ranks casualties. 1 killed, 11 wounded, 1 missing and one man wounded self inflicted.

The covert of a 35th Division Christmas 1918 greeting card.

CHAPTER TWELVE

Post Armistice

WITH THE WAR EFFECTIVELY OVER the 35th Division commenced a series of moves towards the Channel coast. Four weeks after the armistice the Division commenced demobilisation. The first men to be returned were former miners, tradesmen or professionals whose skills were urgently needed for the regeneration of the nation's commerce. This rankled with the longer serving servicemen who thought they merited repatriation priority and their indignation turned to open resentment against military authority. Parades of all kinds were now detested, as they seemed irrelevant to men who just wanted to go home. Over night notices appeared on billet doors demanding an ending to the constant drilling and training. In response, the 35th Division officers adopted a more relaxed attitude. A more varied diet was introduced and Christmas 1918 was celebrated in grand style with ample quantities of continental beer.

Elsewhere disaffection spread to Calais where impatient troops mutinied. They refused to accept orders and the exasperated camp officers were rounded up then securely locked-up in a large hut. On 28 January 1919 the 15 Cheshire were ordered to head for Calais at the utmost speed to contain and control the rebellious troops. The fully armed Cheshires marched through the town then took up key defensive positions. By the time the 35th Division arrived in strength, the less militant mutineers had melted away; once the camp was encircled, the remainder saw the futility of their actions. By the afternoon of the 31st the bloodless mutiny was over, officers entered the camp and the mutineers grievances were listened to; they received promises of an improvement to their circumstances, although their ringleaders were arrested.

105 Brigade remained at Calais where it was made available for possible use by the Base Commandant until 2 February, when the 15th Battalion entrained for Audruicq where demobilisation began in earnest. Every day the Battalion shed about fifty men and by 10 February, the Battalion was approximately at company strength. A notable event occurred on 3 March when Lieutenant Colonel H. Johnston D.S.O. relinquished command of the unit he had commanded for the past year. Major Trestrail D.S.O. succeeded him as Commander.

The final overseas ceremony occurred on the 14th when the King's

Colour was presented by Major General Marindin D.S.O. he later went on to take up a command on the Rhine. A group of five officers and 190 other ranks chose to remain in the army; they bid farewell to their old battalion and departed for new careers with the 26th Royal Welsh Fusiliers. They would be spared the indignities suffered by some of those who returned to civilian life, to a society changed out of all recognition.

On Tuesday, 22 April 1919 a cadre of the 15th Cheshire and a contingent from the remainder of the Division boarded the 600-ton Russian steamer S.S. *Viagaitch* homeward bound. Equipment was loaded on the S.S. *Cluna* a tramp steamer of the Donaldson line. The *Viagaitch* cruised leisurely across a mirror smooth Channel before reaching Southampton water at 7 p.m. where the ship's anchor and cable clattered over the side. She then waited for the incoming tide before entering harbour. After remaining onboard overnight, the cadre finally disembarked in their homeland. By 4-30p.m. on Friday 25 April they were travelling by train for Ripon camp in North Yorkshire.

The men were demobilised that Monday, with the exception of the colour party, and by the end of the month, the 35th Division ceased to exist except in the memory of those who had served. Arrangements had been made to present the colour to the Mayor of Birkenhead by the officers of the cadre, Acting Lieutenant Colonel Trestrail D.S.O., Captain Henry Turner, M.C. and the Quartermaster, Captain Halsall. The colour party comprising Second Lieutenant Sage, [an original Bantam], C.Q.M.S. Menzies, Sergeant's Gough and Dean would travel to Birkenhead by train on 1 May.

On a fine morning the Colour party alighted at Woodside station,

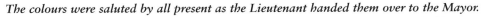

The colours were saluted by all present as the Lieutenant handed them over to the Mayor.

the band of the Sherwood Forresters played the party up the hill to the Town Hall, where gathered outside was the Mayor (Mr. Rowlands), Alfred Bigland, Lieutenant Colonel Ellis and notable dignitaries. Several ex-officers of the 15th Cheshires and officers who were incorporated upon the breaking up of the 16th Battalion attended. The Mayor welcomed the colour party with a speech recalling with pride the origins of the first Birkenhead Bantams. He declared the record of the Battalion as 'second to none' citing the awards gained by the unit as: D.S.O.s four, M.C.s twenty-one, bars to M.C. three, D.C.M.s sixteen, M.M.s seventy-four, bars to M.M. three, M.S.M.s four, French Croix de Guerre nine, Mentions in Despatches twelve. He considered it a great honour to be asked to receive the colours of such a fine battalion for safe custody. Alfred Bigland then made a speech in which he mourned the fate of many of the brave men who crowded into the Town Hall in 1914. Lieutenant Colonel Trestrail acknowledged that his battalion and the 16th owed their origin to Birkenhead and the energy of Mr. Bigland. He went on to say 'We have had some sticky times, but we were in on the death, and it may interest you to know that our division, the 35th got the furthest east of all units in the advance'. The colours were saluted by all present as the Lieutenant handed them over to the Mayor.

A land fit for heroes
Life for the former soldiers had altered irretrievably; their loved ones and relatives noticed dramatic changes in the character of men whose experiences were unimaginable to those who had remained at home. The men missed the comradeship so peculiar to the warrior bonded as they had been in adversity. Some men failed to adapt to civilian life and rejoined the army; the majority struggled on in a world disinterested in the ordeal they had experienced. Employers who had promised in 1914 to keep open the jobs of the servicemen had employed others who were now established within the positions. To add insult to injury their stand-ins were often men who had been spared military service. Men who had given their all to King and Country discovered they had not returned to a land fit for heroes but an almost bankrupt nation offering them unemployment and hardship. The final humiliation for the less fortunate was a means tested benefit system dispensed with curmudgeon at the discretion of a pen pusher who had never seen a bayonet-brandishing German. The wounded and maimed received a miserly pension and continued to eke out an existence by whatever casual employment they could get.

Throughout the austere 1920s, the invalided men struggled on with their injuries or tortured lungs until gradually succumbing to lingering deaths. The 15th and 16th Battalions had incurred over 900 deaths. The British Empire's battle deaths were estimated at 888,000

A kneeling Captain C. Johnston receives the 16th Battalion Colour.

approximately fifty per cent greater than the Second World War, and in Britain's case 230 per cent greater. The figures for the wounded surpassed the dead by between two and four to one.

On a fine 17 February [Meeanee Day] 1921 the consecration and presentation of the Colours to the 8th, 9th, 10th,11th, 12th, 13th, 16th, [Service] battalions, and the 23rd and 52nd also the 1st and 2nd Garrison battalions was held at the Castle Square, Chester. The square was lined with spectator's old officers, soldiers and friends. Placed around the muzzle of a huge German gun, captured by the 1st Battalion Cheshire Regiment, was an arrangement of drums upon which were eleven silken colours. At 11.00 a.m., a short ceremony commenced followed by a service of consecration for the colours. His Majesty's representative, the Lord Lieutenant of the County presented each colour to an officer representing the battalion who received the emblem on the knee. Captain C. Johnston received the colour on behalf of the former 16th Battalion. After awarding the colours, a speech on the significance of the Colours to a regiment was made, stating that the Colours represent the soul of the regiment – the regimental spirit that was immortal. To a soldier the regimental spirit was sacred.

The New Army battalions received a plain King's Colour (Union flag only); the Regiment at its own expense had the centre medallion embroidered on each. The 15th Battalion colour bore the honours 'Somme 1916-18', 'Ypres 1917-18', 'Bapaume 1918', 'Courtrai' [no date]. The 16th Battalion received 'Ypres 1917' and 'Somme 1918'.

In accordance with Army tradition battalion colours are generally displayed in a local church in the region where the battalion was raised. Alfred Bigland presented both the Bantam colours to St Mary's Church on the day of the Birkenhead churches centenary celebrations. They remained there until the church was demolished in the late sixties. Somewhat the worse for wear, the Colours were then placed for safekeeping in the Williamson Art Gallery and Museum, Slatey Road, Birkenhead. They have been restored for posterity inside a protective glazed frame but unfortunately, due to lack of space in the gallery they are seldom on display.

On Saturday 6 August 1921 the altar, reredos and shrine in the Regimental Chapel of St. George in Chester was dedicated to the 8,417 fallen Cheshire soldiers whose lives were recorded on vellum on the *Book of Honour* kept in the Shrine.

This event draws to a close the account of the Cheshire battalions we have followed from the cradle to the grave. Was the Bantam initiative a success or a failure well that is up to you to decide. From the outset, the Bantam soldiers had a point to prove, they rose magnificently to the challenge and silenced their critics. It is however ironic that the relaxation of the 1914 army height standard proved to be their Achilles Heel. For in a war of attrition it was no more viable to maintain battalions of small men than it was to raise lofty Guardsmen or legions of Pals. What was important was the ability to field men in the defence of the King and Empire; the initial volunteers filled this role admirably. Yes, it is true there were one or two shaky periods but as we sit in our comfortable armchairs nestled in our centrally heated homes, who are we the majority of whom have never fired a shot in anger, to look without compassion on men from a distant generation who were continually pitched into the fray. Time after time, both the Birkenhead battalion's proved their critics wrong, and maintained the illustrious honours of the old 22nd Foot, the Cheshire Regiment. Throughout the war, there was hardly a medal ceremony where at least one of the tough resilient fighters was not present. Although they will never be with us again, they have lived long in the loving memory of their descendents. To this end I earnestly hope the tale of the Bantam's continues to live long in the memory of those who were privileged to call them Father or Grandfather.

'To live in hearts we leave behind is not to die'.   Anon

Roll of Honour: 15th and 16th (Service) Battalions Cheshire Regiment

Name	Rank	Number	Place of birth	Cause of death	Date of Death	Burial/ Memorial Place
Hannan R.W.	Pte	20114	?	Died	28-12-14	Flaybrick Cem Birkenhead
Ballard T.W.	Pte	19492	Bury, Lancs	Died	02-02-15	Flaybrick Cem Birkenhead
Johnstone J	Pte	19168	?	Died	05-03-15	Flaybrick Cem Birkenhead
Cunnah B	L/Cpl	19618	Mold, Flints	Died	28-06-15	Masham, Church yard, York
Weightman. J.	Pte	23045	Liverpool.	K.I.A.	27-02-16	Guards Cem. Windy Corner.
Abela C	Pte	19605	Cospicua, Malta	K.I.A.	02-03-16	Guards Cem. Windy Corner
Harrison W	Pte	19918	Longton, Preston	K.I.A.	02-03-16	Guards Cem. Windy Corner
Shenton. F.	Pte	19656	Oldham, Lancs.	K.I.A.	02-03-16	Guards Cem. Windy Corner
Smith. F.	Pte	23089	Ashton-U-Lyne, Lancs.	K.I.A.	05-04-16	Rue-Du-Bacquerot London Cem.
McClinchie. M.	L/Sgt.	20237	Gilford, Co. Down.	K.I.A.	21-04-16	Rue-Des-Berceaux Mil. Cem.
Thompson. J.	Pte	19519	Blackburn, Lancs.	K.I.A.	21-04-16	Rue-Des-Berceaux Mil. Cem.
Thomas. W.	Pte	22118	Liverpool.	K.I.A.	30-04-16	Rue-Des-Berceaux Mil. Cem.
Taylor. J.W.	Pte	19608	Ryhope, Durham.	K.I.A.	01-05-16	Rue-Des-Berceaux Mil. Cem.
Relph. R.	Pte	19364	Leeds.	D.O.W.	03-05-16	Merville Comm. Cem.
Martin. J.E.	Pte	19935	Suffolk.	D.O.W.	06-05-16	Merville Comm. Cem.
Lowther. W.	Sgt.	19877	Castlefield, Yorks.	K.I.A.	18-05-16	Pont-Du-Hem Mil. Cem.
Davis S.W	Sgt	19038	Everton, Lancs	K.I.A.	29-05-16	Pont-Du-Hem-Mil. Cem.
Churcher H.L	Pte	19863	Brandon, Canada	K.I.A.	30-05-16	St Vaast Post Mil Cem
Parr. H.	Pte	39989	Crumpsall, Lancs.	D.O.W.	01-06-16	Merville Comm. Cem.
Oakes. E.	Pte	26349	Warburton Green, Ches.	K.I.A.	07-07-16	Thiepval Memorial.
Cox J	Pte	19251	Liverpool.	K.I.A.	17-07-16	Bernafay, Wood, Brit Cem
Greenlees J	Pte	20331	Loanhead, Scotland	K.I.A.	17-07-16	Thiepval Memorial
Gregory W	Pte	19748	Sheffield, Yorks.	K.I.A.	17-07-16	Thiepval Memorial
Leslie. W.	Pte	20321	Dysart, Fife.	K.I.A.	17-07-16	Bernafay Wood Brit. Cem.
Ord. R.	Pte	20307	Banff, Scotland.	K.I.A.	17-07-16	Bernafay Wood Brit. Cem.
Richardson. W.	Pte	19616	Sunderland, Durham.	K.I.A.	17-07-16	Thiepval Memorial
Harrison J	Pte	19273	Great Harwood, Lancs	K.I.A.	18-07-16	Thiepval Memorial
Holmes W	Pte	20004	Leeds, Yorks.	K.I.A.	18-07-16	Thiepval Memorial
Riggans. H.	Pte	19448	Airdrie, Lanark.	D.O.W.	18-07-16	Peronne Road Cem.
Saven. J.C.	Pte	29625	Liverpool.	K.I.A.	18-07-16	Thiepval Memorial
Anderson V.A	Pte	20690	Haggerston, London	K.I.A.	19-07-16	Thiepval Memorial
Austin G.F	2/Lieut	?	?	K.I.A.	19-07-16	Thiepval Memorial
Benson M.V.F	Pte	19043	Carlow, Co, Kildare	K.I.A.	19-07-16	Thiepval Memorial
Burns. T.	Pte	19027	Liverpool	K.I.A.	19-07-16	Pozieres Memorial
Gormley. J	Pte	19769	Ashton in Makerfield, Lancs.	K.I.A.	19-07-16	Thiepval Memorial
Kyne. A.W.	Sgt.	19874	Hackney, Middx.	K.I.A.	19-07-16	Thiepval Memorial.
Welsh. J.	Pte	19059	Liverpool.	K.I.A.	19-07-16	Thiepval Memorial.
Carr. W	Pte	19728	Blackburn, Lancs	D.O.W.	20-07-16	Dive Copse Brit Cem.
Edmunds A	Pte	19452	Creaton, Northants	D.O.W.	20-07-16	Corbie, Com, Cem, Ext.
Hough T	Pte	20339	Bolton, Lancs.	K.I.A.	22-07-16	Danzig Alley Brit Cem.
Atkinson F	Pte	22029	Everton, Liverpool	D.O.W.	23-07-16	La Neuville Brit. Cem. Corbie
Gilroy A	Pte	19015	Liverpool.	D.O.W.	23-07-16	Peronne Road Cem.
Allan W.M	Pte	20318	Edinburgh	D.O.W.	25-07-16	Corbie Comm. Cem Ext.
Wilkinson. J.	L/Cpl	23254	Liverpool.	K.I.A.	25-07-16	Peronne Road Cem.
Taylor. W.	Pte	20267	Pittingdon, Durham.	D.O.W.	26-07-16	Corbie Comm. Cem. Ext.
Bate A.V	Pte	19121	Burslem, Staffs	K.I.A.	27-07-16	Thiepval Memorial
Branscombe H.B	Pte	19039	Birkenhead, Ches.	K.I.A.	27-07-16	Thiepval Memorial
Carter G	A/Cpl	19641	Sunderland, Durham.	K.I.A.	27-07-16	Thiepval Memorial
Green W.J.	Pte	19966	Chatburn, Lancs	D.O.W.	27-07-16	La Neuville Brit. Cem.
Crowe W	Pte	23236	Castletown, Isle of Man	K.I.A.	27-07-16	Thiepval Memorial
Rushton. H.	Pte	19113		K.I.A.	27-07-16	Thiepval Memorial
Dickinson. C.J.H.	2/Lieut			K.I.A.	28-07-16	Flat Iron Cem.
Hughes. B	Pte	19806	Ellesmere, Salop.	K.I.A.	28-07-16	Thiepval Memorial
Taylor. W.E.	Pte	39920	Wellingboro, Northants.	K.I.A.	28-07-16	Thiepval Memorial
Clark. J	Driver	20328	Arbroath, Scotland.	K.I.A.	29-07-16	Thiepval Memorial
Cole. G.	Pte	29685	Liverpool.	K.I.A.	29-07-16	Thiepval Memorial
Forster. J.	Pte.	20201	Sunderland, Durham.	K.I.A.	29-07-16	Thiepval Memorial
Hegerty. J.	Pte.	19576	Everton, Lancs.	K.I.A.	29-07-16	Thiepval Memorial
Simon. C.	Pte	20020	Leeds.	K.I.A.	29-07-16	Thiepval Memorial
Wallace. J.	Pte	19535	Hull.	K.I.A.	29-07-16	Thiepval Memorial.
Wilding. J.	L/Cpl	19524	Blackburn, Lancs.	K.I.A.	29-07-16	Thiepval Memorial.
Glasstone. A.	Cpl	19036	Edinburgh	D.O.W.	11-08-16	Liverpool [Anfield] Cem.
Harper. D.	Pte	19101	Darlaston, Staffs.	K.I.A.	13-08-16	Thiepval Memorial
Makinson. A.	Pte	20039	Warrington, Lancs.	D.O.W.	13-08-16	
Barnes. W.	Pte	39970	Patricot, Lancs.	K.I.A.	15-08-16	Thiepval Memorial
Wilson. F.	Pte	19327	Threlkeld, Cumberland.	D.O.W.	16-08-16	Bronfay Farm Mil. Cem.
Millar. W.	Pte	20215	Shankhill, Co. Dublin.	K.I.A.	20-08-16	Thiepval Memorial.
Capon. O.B.	Pte	20070	Battersea, Middx.	D.O.W.	21-08-16	Carnoy Mil. Cem.
Cotton. R.	Pte	20117	Camberwell, London.	K.I.A.	21-08-16	Flatiron Copse Cem
Fielding. J.	Pte.	33244	Glossop, Derbyshire.	K.I.A.	21-08-16	Flatiron Copse Cem.

Name	Rank	Number	Place	Cause	Date	Memorial
Heal. R.	Pte	33220	Liverpool.	K.I.A.	21-08-16	Flatiron Copse Cem.
Thomson. J.	Pte	20317	Kikcaldy, Fife.	K.I.A.	21-08-16	Quarry Cem.
Hickman. T.	Pte	23287	North Kensington, Middx.	D.O.W.	25-08-16	La Neuville Brit. Cem.
Billington. R.	Pte	36329	Birkenhead, Ches.	K.I.A.	02-09-16	Spec. Mem. 9 Blighty Valley Cem.
Smith. J.	Pte	19083	New Ferry. Ches.	D.O.W.	06-09-16	Faubourg D' Amiens Cem.
Dunning. F.	Pte	23100	Nantwich, Ches.	K.I.A.	14-09-16	Faubourg D' Amiens Cem.
Simpson. J.R.	Pte	19572	Harrowgate, Yorks.	K.I.A.	14-09-16	Faubourg D' Amiens Cem.
Mooney. H.A.	Sgt.	19860	Greenwich, Kent.	D.O.W.	14-09-16	Arras Memorial.
Walker. J.	Pte	19827	Manchester.	K.I.A.	14-09-16	Arras Memorial.
Worden. H.	L/Cpl	19205	Preston. Lancs.	K.I.A.	14-09-16	Arras Memorial.
Beech. J.	A/CSM.	19323	Penk Hull, Staffs.	K.I.A.	04-10-16	Faubourg D' Amiens Cem.
Gill. J.	Pte	22210	Stalybridge, Ches.	K.I.A.	04-10-16	Faubourg D' Amiens Cem.
Devitt. T.	Pte	23413	Liverpool.	K.I.A.	09-10-16	Faubourg D' Amiens Cem.
Hesketh. R.	Pte	19742	Ashton- U- Lyne, Lancs.	D.O.W.	13-10-16	Faubourg D' Amiens Cem.
Prydderch. J.T.	Pte	21374	Wigan, Lancs.	D.O.W.	14-10-16	Avesnes-Le-Comte Com. Cem. Ext.
Dale. H.J.	L/Cpl	20090	Brighton, Sussex.	D.O.W.	20-10-16	Habarcq Com. Cem. Ext.
Simm. W.	Pte	23379	Wooler, Northumberland.	D.O.W.	21-10-16	Warloy-Baillon Comm. Cem. Ext.
Brown. W.	Pte	20013	South Shields, Durham.	K.I.A.	02-11-16	Faubourg D' Amiens Cem.
Harrop. H.	Pte.	20426	Ashton-U-Lyne	K.I.A.	02-11-16	Faubourg D' Amiens Cem.
Jackson. W.	Pte	19558	Middlesborough.	K.I.A.	02-11-16	Faubourg D' Amiens Cem.
Moult. J.	Pte	30738	Stockport, Ches.	K.I.A.	02-11-16	Faubourg D'Amiens Cem.
Oxley. S.	Pte	19978	Leeds.	K.I.A.	02-11-16	Faubourg D' Amiens Cem.
Watson. C.G.	Pte	19774	London.	K.I.A.	02-11-16	Faubourg D,Amiens Cem.
Davies. A.	Pte	23345	Bootle, Lancs.	D.O.W.	04-11-16	Regina Trench Cem.
Foster. J.J.	Cpl	23007	Byker, Northumberland.	K.I.A.	04-11-16	Arras Memorial
Sproul. W.C.	L/Cpl	20084	Rotherhithe, Kent.	K.I.A.	04-11-16	Arras Memorial
Wroe. J.	Pte	23084	Hollingworth. Lancs.	K.I.A.	04-11-16	Arras Memorial.
Timperley. J.T.	Pte	23285	Glasgow.	Died	10-11-16	Accrington Cem. Lancs.
Leatherbarrow. J.	Pte	28827	Liverpool.	D.O.W.	16-11-16	no trace
Wolstenholme R.F	Capt.			K.I.A.	28-11-16	Faubourg D' Amiens Cem.
Lee. J.	Pte	52997	Bradford, Yorks.	K.I.A.	29-11-16	Faubourg D' Amiens Cem.
Aspin. J.	L/Sgt	19521	Blackburn, Lancs.	D.O.W.	04-12-16	Tockholes Churchyard, Lancs.
Holden. J.	Pte.	23205	Haslinden, Lancs.	K.I.A.	25-02-17	Fouquescourt Brit. Cem.
Alcock. H.	L/Cpl.	241105	Stockport, Ches.	D.O.W.	26-02-17	Cerisy-Gailly Mil. Cem.
Bath. J.	Pte.	45652	Stockport, Ches.	D.O.W.	26-02-17	Cerisy-Gailly Mil. Cem.
Jones. J.	Pte.	28808	Toxteth, Lancs.	K.I.A.	28-02-17	Thiepval Memorial.
Rusk. J.	Pte	33610	Liverpool.	Died.	19-03-17	Liverpool [Anfield] Cem.
Baines. B.	Pte.	23018	Morley, Yorks.	Died	11-04-17	St. Sever Cem. Ext.
Ryan. J.	Pte	58094	Hadfield, Derby.	K.I.A.	18-04-17	Roisel Comm. Cem. Ext.
Welbourn. J.	Pte	25268	Stockpor. Ches.	K.I.A.	18-04-17	Roisel Comm. Cem. Ext.
Tefft. J.	Pte	13046	Manchester.	K.I.A.	26-04-17	Chapelle Brit. Cem.
King. N.T.	Pte.	45754	Seacombe, Ches.	K.I.A.	30-04-17	Grand-Seraucourt Brit. Cem.
Barton. G.R.	Pte.	23427	Paddington, London.	K.I.A.	05-05-17	Chapelle Brit. Cem.
Cooke. J.S.	Pte.	243966	?	Died	05-05-17	Duisans Brit. Cem.
Barton. F.	Pte.	58114	Hyde, Ches.	K.I.A.	11-05-17	Vadencourt Brit. Cem.
Hough. A.	Pte.	17825	Winsford, Ches.	D.O.W.	18-05-17	Marteville Comm. Cem.
Burke. J.	Cpl.	19876	Leeds.	D.O.W.	06-06-17	La Chapellette Brit. & Ind. Cem.
Gledsdale	Lt.				13-07-17	Villers-Faucon Comm. Cem.
Hansbury. E.	Pte.	20041	Marylebone, London.	K.I.A.	13-07-17	Villers-Faucon Comm. Cem.
Horan. J.H.	Pte	23429	Clerkenwell, London.	K.I.A.	17-07-17	Quarry Cem.
Walton. F.W.	Pte	23098	Altringham, Ches.	D.O.W.	29-07-17	Poperinghe New Mil. Cem
Schultz. G.E.	Capt.			D.O.W.	12-08-17	Villers-Faucon Comm. Cem.
Bibby. W.H.	Pte.	41653	Liverpool.	D.O.W.	19-08-17	Villers-Faucon Comm. Cem.
Eddings. T.	Pte.	30663	Reddish, Lancs.	K.I.A.	19-08-17	Templeux-Le-Guerard Brit. Cem.
Ellison. A.	Pte.	202115	Over, Ches.	K.I.A.	19-08-17	Thiepval Memorial.
Gilson. T.	Pte.	31107	Denton, Lancs.	K.I.A.	19-08-17	Thiepval Memorial.
Grace. J.	2/Lieut.			K.I.A.	19-08-17	Villers-Faucon Comm. Cem.
Hawker. T.R.	Pte.	37850	Birmingham.	K.I.A.	19-08-17	Thiepval Memorial.
McGann. J.W.	Pte	14064	Wilmslow, Ches.	D.O.W.	19-08-17	Tincourt New Brit. Cem.
Nash. J.	Pte	14774	Birkenhead, Ches.	K.I.A.	19-08-17	Thiepval Memorial.
Rushby. W.	Pte	52376		D.O.W.	19-08-17	Tincourt New Brit. Cem.
Smith. W.	Pte	49570	Furness Vale. Ches.	K.I.A.	19-08-17	Thiepval Memorial.
Taylor. T.	Pte	12388	Willaston, Ches.	K.I.A.	19-08-17	Thiepval Memorial.
Turner. J.	Pte	14734	Great Budworth, Ches.	K.I.A.	19-08-17	Thiepval Memorial.
Turner. T.C.	Pte	45819	Dublin, Ireland.	K.I.A.	19-08-17	Thiepval Memorial.
Whyte. C.	Sgt	7623	Oxford.	D.O.W.	19-08-17	Villers-Faucon Comm. Cem.
Winterbottom. B.	Pte	52682	Stalybridge. Ches.	K.I.A.	19-08-17	Thiepval Memorial.
Cook. J.	Pte	24226	Knutsford, Ches.	K.I.A.	20-08-17	Templeux-Le-Guerard Brit. Cem.
Edwards. W.T.	Pte	49198	Whittington, Salop.	K.I.A.	20-08-17	Thiepval Memorial.
Finnegan. E.F.	Pte	19004	Birkenhead.	K.I.A.	20-08-17	Thiepval Memorial.
Hall. W.	Pte	9252	Stanton Lacey, Salop.	K.I.A.	20-08-17	Thiepval Memorial.
Hattesley. G.	Pte	37085	Withington, Lancs.	K.I.A.	20-08-17	Thiepval Memorial.
Holme. F.	Pte	48693	Liverpool.	K.I.A.	20-08-17	Villers-Faucon Comm. Cem.
Hope. E.	Pte	26934	Stockport, Ches.	K.I.A.	20-08-17	Thiepval Memorial.
Hopkins. G.	Pte	10378	Wandsworth, London.	K.I.A.	20-08-17	Thiepval Memorial.
Hunt. A.E.	Pte	8925	Fullwood, Preston.	K.I.A.	20-08-17	Thiepval Memorial.
Hurst. W.	A/Sgt	60264	Hollingwood, Lancs.	K.I.A.	20-08-17	Thiepval Memorial.
Jepson. A.	Pte	45045	Cheadle Hulme, Ches.	K.I.A.	20-08-17	Thiepval Memorial.
Johnstone. S.	Pte	15926	Wallasey, Ches.	D.O.W.	20-08-17	Tincourt New Brit. Cem.
Langstaff. J.	Pte	19658	Oldham, Lancs.	K.I.A.	20-08-17	Thiepval Memorial.

Name	Rank	Number	Place	Cause	Date	Memorial/Cemetery
Lloydd. D.	Pte	52058	Lampeter, Cardigan.	K.I.A.	20-08-17	Thiepval Memorial.
Prendergast. A.	A/Csm	9571	Birmingham.	K.I.A.	20-08-17	Unicorn Cem.
Horsfield. W.	Pte	30353	Hyde, Ches.	D.O.W.	21-08-17	Tincourt New Brit. Cem.
Smith. J.	Pte.	11347	Birkenhead, Ches.	D.O.W.	21-08-17	Villers-Faucon Comm. Cem.
Smith. J.	Pte	11347	Birkenhead. Ches.	D.O.W.	21-08-17	Villers-Faucon Comm. Cem.
Tomkinson. R.S.	Pte	32918	Preston, Lancs.	D.O.W.	21-08-17	Tincourt New Brit. Cem.
Brown. W.H.	Pte	58517	North Kensington, London	K.I.A.	24-08-17	Thiepval Memorial.
Delderfield. A.	Pte.	14135	Hadfield, Derby.	K.I.A.	24-08-17	Villers-Faucon Comm. Cem.
Hunt. J.	Pte.	47708	Liverpool.	K.I.A.	24-08-17	Thiepval Memorial.
Jones. G.	Sgt.	19136	Liverpool.	D.O.W.	24-08-17	Tincourt Brit. Cem.
Hopley. E.	Pte.	50453	Winsford, Ches.	D.O.W.	17-09-17	Etretat Churrchyard Ext.
Millward. J.	Pte	20463	Bilston, Ches.	K.I.A.	23-09-17	Villers-Faucon Comm. Cem.
Middlebrough. J.H.	Pte	19080	Walton, Lancs.	Died.	05-10-17	Bruay Comm. Cem. Ext.
Leahy. W.	Pte	23314	Liverpool.	D.O.W.	19-10-17	Dozinghem Mil. Cem.
Leah. E.	Pte	62401	Stockport, Ches.	K.I.A.	20-10-17	Tyne Cot Memorial.
Pearson. A.E.	Pte	20579	Stepney, London.	K.I.A.	20-10-17	Tyne Cot Memorial.
Barton. T.	Pte.	44153	Tabley, Ches.	K.I.A.	22-10-17	Tyne Cot Memorial.
Price. C.	Pte	62061	Stockport, Ches.	D.O.W.	22-10-17	Dozinghem Mil. Cem.
Tomlinson. J.	L/Cpl.	18117	Stockport, Ches.	K.I.A.	22-10-17	Bleuet Farm Cem.
Whitaker. E.A.	Pte	40466		K.I.A.	23-10-17	Poelcapelle Brit. Cem.
Alty. J.	Pte.	292321	Boothstown, Lancs.	D.O.W.	24-10-17	Dozinghem Mil. Cem.
Astles. C.	Pte.	50286	Winsford, Ches.	K.I.A.	24-10-17	Tyne Cot Memorial.
Atkinson. J.	L/Sgt.	39922	Sale, Ches.	K.I.A.	24-10-17	Tyne Cot Memorial.
Beddows. B.	Pte.	33523	Ironbridge, Salop.	K.I.A.	24-10-17	Tyne Cot Memorial.
Berry. F.	Pte.	62068	Liverpool.	K.I.A.	24-10-17	Tyne Cot Memorial.
Christie. J.M.	Pte.	292259	Bolton, Lancs.	K.I.A.	24-10-17	Tyne Cot Memorial.
Davies. A.	Sgt.	51021	Knutton, Lancs.	K.I.A.	24-10-17	Tyne Cot Memorial.
Davies. H.	Pte.	40433	Oldham, Lancs.	K.I.A.	24-10-17	Tyne Cot Memorial.
Evans. W.	Pte.	40447	Adbaston, Staffs.	Died	24-10-17	Artillery Wood Cem.
Fitzpatrick. J.	Cpl.	19552	Wigan, Lancs.	K.I.A.	24-10-17	Tyne Cot Memorial.
Hague. R.	Pte.	45673	Glossop, Derby	D.O.W.	24-10-17	Dozinghem Mil. Cem.
Hindley. J.	Pte.	W/272	Widnes, Ches.	K.I.A.	24-10-17	Tyne Cot Memorial.
Hobson. H.	Cpl.	39980	Barnsley, Yorks.	K.I.A.	24-10-17	Tyne Cot Memorial.
Hughes. R.	Cpl.	7071	Thornton Hough, Ches.	K.I.A.	24-10-17	Tyne Cot Memorial.
Hutchison. H.	Pte.	20319	Dysart, Fifeshire.	K.I.A.	24-10-17	Tyne Cot Memorial.
Judson. F.	Sgt.	15714	Nantwich,Ches.	K.I.A.	24-10-17	Tyne Cot Memorial.
McHale. J.W.	Pte	40404	Dukinfield, Ches.	K.I.A.	24-10-17	Tyne Cot Memorial.
Parker. C.	Pte	10777	Shocklach, Ches.	K.I.A.	24-10-17	Tyne Cot Memorial.
Quinn. J.	Cpl	19882	Leeds, Yorks..	K.I.A.	24-10-17	Tyne Cot Memorial.
Rendall. W.	Pte	52298	Newcastle On Tyne.	K.I.A.	24-10-17	Tyne Cot Memorial.
Riley. J.	Pte	9939	Warrington, Lancs.	K.I.A.	24-10-17	Tyne Cot Memorial.
Roberts. P.	Pte	18108	Stockport, Ches.	K.I.A.	24-10-17	Tyne Cot Memorial.
Whittle. J.	Pte	16543	Liscard, Ches.	K.I.A.	24-10-17	Tyne Cot Memorial.
Williams. M.	Pte	19772	Accrington, Lancs.	K.I.A.	24-10-17	Artillery Wood Cem.
Bellis. R.	Pte.	52453	Handbridge, Ches.	D.O.W.	25-10-17	Dozinghem Mil. Cem.
Pedley. F.C.	Pte	49636	Nantwich, Ches.	D.O.W.	27-10-17	Dozinghem Mil. Cem.
Ingham. H.	Pte.	49063	?	K.I.A.	30-10-17	Artillery Wood Cem.
Bailey. A.	Pte.	13896	Northwich, Ches.	K.I.A.	01-11-17	Tyne Cot Memorial.
Dodd. W. M.M.	Pte.	45029	Hoylake, Ches.	K.I.A.	01-11-17	Tyne Cot Memorial.
Halliwell. J.H.	Pte	292266	Middleton, Lancs.	K.I.A.	01-11-17	Tyne Cot Memorial.
Livesley. H.	Pte	19076	Salford, Lancs.	K.I.A.	01-11-17	Tyne Cot Memorial.
Newnes. T.H.	Pte	45512	Tarporley, Ches.	K.I.A.	01-11-17	Tyne Cot Memorial.
Newsome. F.	Pte	19900	Leeds.	K.I.A.	01-11-17	no trace
Marshall. A. M.M.	Pte	29674	Ashton-U-Lynne, Lancs.	D.O.W.	02-11-17	Dozinghem Mil. Cem.
Schofield. G.	Pte	40484	Oldham, Lancs.	D.O.W.	04-11-17	Dozinghem Mil. Cem.
Clarke. G.	Pte	26718	Stockport, Ches.	D.O.W.	05-11-17	Dozinghem Mil. Cem.
McDonald. S.	Pte	W/769	Birkenhead.	D.O.W.	05-11-17	Dozinghem Mil. Cem.
Slack. T.W.	Pte	7942	Nantwich, Ches.	D.O.W.	05-11-17	Dozinghem Mil. Cem.
Evans. J.	Pte	292380	Manchester.	D.O.W.	08-11-17	Pendlebury church yard, Lancs.
Lee. A.	Pte	40482	Radcliffe, Lancs.	D.O.W.	11-11-17	Dozinghem Mil. Cem.
Worthington. J.W.	Pte	49291	Wilmslow. Ches.	D.O.W.	13-11-17	Abbeville Comm. Cem. Ext.
Adams. M.H.A.	Pte	241105	Ashford, Derby.	D.O.W.	14-11-17	Boulogne Eastern Cem.
Edwards. A.	Pte	W/687	Ellesmere Port, Ches.	D.O.W.	19-11-17	Dozinghem Mil. Cem.
Keough. J.	Pte.	22064	Birkenhead.	D.O.W.	21-11-17	Mendinghem Mil. Cem.
Flowers. J.	Pte	20056	Marylebone, London.	K.I.A.	24-11-17	Cement House Cem.
Hopkins. G.	Pte	15268	Stockport, Ches.	K.I.A.	24-11-17	Cement House Cem.
Hunt. E.	Pte	29562	Liverpool.	K.I.A.	24-11-17	Tyne Cot Memorial.
Jackson. J.	Pte	64154	Hale, Ches.	K.I.A.	24-11-17	Cement House Cem.
McNulty. W.	Pte	51404	Burnley, Lancs.	D.O.W.	24-11-17	Tyne Cot Memorial.
Preece. G.W.	Pte	25869	Davenham, Ches.	D.O.W.	24-11-17	Duhallow A.D.S. Cem.
Reed. S.	Pte	57051	Bristol.	K.I.A.	24-11-17	Tyne Cot Memorial.
Turtle. J.H.D.	Pte	40463	Leeds.	D.O.W.	25-11-17	Dozinghem Mil. Cem.
Astles. H.	A/Cpl.	16909	Winsford, Ches.	K.I.A.	27-11-17	St. Julian Dressing Station Cem.
Gandy. H.	Cpl.	50376	Stockport, Ches.	K.I.A.	28-11-17	Tyne Cot Memorial.

Waring. W.	Pte	24112	Childer, Ches.	K.I.A.	28-11-17	Tyne Cot Memorial.
Thorpe. P.	Pte	40427	Huddersfield, Yorks.	D.O.W.	30-11-17	Dozingham Mil. Cem.
Williams. S.	L/Cpl	17679	Brecon.	K.I.A.	20-01-18	Minty Farm Cem.
Jennings. D.C.	Sgt	20077	Peckham, London.	K.I.A.	23-01-18	Cement House Cem.
Williams. G.	Pte	25580	Chester, Ches.	K.I.A.	23-01-18	Cement House Cem.
White. A. M.M.	Pte	24159	Bebington, Ches.	D.O.W.	04-02-18	Duhallow A.D.S. Cem.
Newbegin. A.W.	Pte	50810	Hoxton, London.	K.I.A.	05-02-18	Tyne Cot Memorial.
Greenaway. F.	Pte	15767	Helsby, Ches.	K.I.A.	27-02-18	Cement House Cem.
Harrison. J. M.M.	Pte	19137	Liverpool.	K.I.A.	27-02-18	Cement House Cem.
Worthington. S.	Pte	40351	Kearsley. Lancs.	K.I.A.	27-02-18	Cement House Cem.
Marshall. R.D.	Pte	57882	Tobermore, Co. Derry.	K.I.A.	28-02-18	Cement House Cem.
Newton. C.R.	Pte	268546	Southport, Lancs.	K.I.A.	28-02-18	Cement House Cemetery.
Sabala. J.	Pte	22125	Liverpool.	D.O.W.	28-02-18	Cement House Cem.
Watts. J.	Pte	38977	Manchester.	K.I.A.	02-03-18	Tyne Cot Memorial.
Weaver. A.	Pte	244641	Helsby, Ches.	K.I.A.	03-02-18	Minty Farm Cem.
Haslam. T.	Pte	12446	Wallasey, Ches.	Died	11-03-18	Mendingham Mil. Cem.
Beet. J.	Pte	267928	Middleton, Lancs.	K.I.A.	21-03-18	Pozieres Memorial.
Acland. E.	L/Sgt	21866	Birmingham.	K.I.A.	24-03-18	Pozieres Memorial.
Ballantyne. J.	Pte	51373	Larkhall, Lanarkshire.	K.I.A.	24-03-18	Pozieres Memorial.
Bamford. F.	Pte	242829	Leek, Staffs.	K.I.A.	24-03-18	Pozieres Memorial.
Band. H. M.M.	Pte	558216	Disley, Ches.	K.I.A.	24-03-18	Pozieres Memorial.
Bladon. J.	Pte	13757	Sale, Ches.	K.I.A.	24-03-18	Pozieres Memorial.
Bleackley. J.	Pte	24467	Stockport, Ches.	K.I.A.	24-03-18	Pozieres Memorial.
Butler. H.	Pte	39923	Nottingham.	K.I.A.	24-03-18	Pozieres Memorial.
Carroll. J.	Pte	292997	Flint, Wales.	K.I.A.	24-03-18	Grand-Seraucourt Brit. Cem.
Charlton. J.	Pte	23093	Little Hulton, Lancs.	K.I.A.	24-03-18	Pozieres Memorial.
Clough. G.	Pte	16829	Waterloo, Lancs.	K.I.A.	24-03-18	Pozieres Memorial.
Coates. J.	Pte	45846	Birkenhead.	K.I.A.	24-03-18	Pozieres Memorial.
Cochran. H.P.G.	Lt. Col			K.I.A.	24-03-18	Delville Wood Cem.
Court. J.A.	Pte	21631	Weston-Sub-Edge, Worcs.	K.I.A.	24-03-18	Pozieres Memorial.
Dexter. J.R.	Pte	50635	Rothley, Leicester.	K.I.A.	24-03-18	Pozieres Memorial.
Duckworth. R.E.	Pte	267031	Blackburn, Lancs.	K.I.A.	24-03-18	Pozieres Memorial.
Edwardson. R.	Pte	51620	?	K.I.A.	24-03-18	Pozieres Memorial.
Evans. J.V.	Pte	36652	Denbigh, Wales.	K.I.A.	24-03-18	Pozieres Memorial.
Eyre. T.J.	Pte	27581	Chelsea, Middlesex.	K.I.A.	24-03-18	Pozieres Memorial.
Farmer. J.A.	Pte	30824	Nantwich, Ches.	D.O.W.	24-03-18	Bronfay Farm Mil. Cem.
Fender. H.	Sgt.	19797	Blackburn, Lancs.	K.I.A.	24-03-18	Pozieres Memorial.
Fitzpatrick. C.	Pte	W/959	Liverpool.	K.I.A.	24-03-18	Pozieres Memorial.
Foster. R.	Sgt.	23316	Liverpool.	K.I.A.	24-03-18	Pozieres Memorial.
Foster. W.E.	Pte	315816	Manchester.	K.I.A.	24-03-18	Pozieres Memorial.
Geary. H.A.	Pte	57849	?	K.I.A.	24-03-18	Bray Hill Cem.
Gomm. F. M.M.	Pte	29572	London.	K.I.A.	24-03-18	Pozieres Memorial.
Harper. W.A.	Pte	61954	Newmarket, London.	K.I.A.	24-03-18	Pozieres Memorial.
Hogg. A.	Pte	33546	Burnley, Lancs.	K.I.A.	24-03-18	Pozieres Memorial.
Holmes. J.W.	Pte	51753	Stanton-in-Peak. Derby.	K.I.A.	24-03-18	Pozieres Memorial.
Johnson W.A. D.C.M.	L/Cpl.	57865	Bedford	K.I.A.	24-03-18	Pozieres Memorial.
Jones. B.	Pte	51682	Trefiw, Carnarvon.	D.O.W.	24-03-18	Hem Farm Mil. Cem.
Jones. J.	Pte.	23262	Liverpool.	K.I.A.	24-03-18	Pozieres Memorial.
Kidd. C.B. M.C.	Capt. Tp			K.I.A.	24-03-18	Pozieres Memorial.
Marley. G.	Pte.	W/724	Aigburth, Lancs.	K.I.A.	24-03-18	Pozieres Memorial.
Marsden. J.	Pte	19829	Blackburn, Lancs.	K.I.A.	24-03-18	Pozieres Memorial.
Marshall. A.	Pte	244770	Salford, Lancs.	K.I.A.	24-03-18	Pozieres Memorial.
Mills. T.L.	Pte	240763	Northwich, Ches.	K.I.A.	24-03-18	Pozieres Memorial.
Nettleton. W.	Pte	51795	Thorner, Yorks.	K.I.A.	24-03-18	Pozieres Memorial.
Norman. W.	Pte	51631	Liverpool.	K.I.A.	24-03-18	Serre Road Cem. No 2
Patrick. F.	Pte	51778	Kingston Upon Hull, Yorks.	K.I.A.	24-03-18	Hem Farm Mil. Cem.
Pearson. R.A.	Pte	201919	St. Annes, Lancs.	K.I.A.	24-03-18	Pozieres Memorial.
Richardson. J.	Pte	26708	Leicester.	K.I.A.	24-03-18	Pozieres Memorial.
Roberts. W.E.	Pte	40405	Accrington, Lancs.	K.I.A.	24-03-18	Pozieres Memorial.
Sharples. J.	Pte	45333	Darwen, Lancs.	K.I.A.	24-03-18	Pozieres Memorial.
Sykes. J. M.M.	Cpl	52994	Bolton, Lancs.	K.I.A.	24-03-18	Pozieres Memorial.
Tate. H.O.	Cpl	200046	Stepney, London.	K.I.A.	24-03-18	Pozieres Memorial.
Thomas. E.D.	Pte	66742	Cwmavon, Glam.	K.I.A.	24-03-18	Pozieres Memorial.
Toole. H.	Pte	36471	Birkenhead.	K.I.A.	24-03-18	Pozieres Memorial.
Westray. C.	Sgt	29568	Preston, Lancs.	K.I.A.	24-03-18	no trace
Williams. J. M.M.	C.S.M.	10728	Neston, Ches.	K.I.A.	24-03-18	Delville Wood Cem.
Williams. J.A.	Pte	40437	Wallasey, Ches.	K.I.A.	24-03-18	Pozieres Memorial.
Wright. E.E.	Pte	51715	Newbridge-on-Wye. Radnor	K.I.A.	24-03-18	Pozieres Memorial.
Wright. J.	Pte	33536	Waterloo. Lancs.	K.I.A.	24-03-18	Pozieres Memorial.
Bulger. P.	Pte	37006	Rock Ferry, Birkenhead.	K.I.A.	25-03-18	Pozieres Memorial.
Breeze. E.	Pte	41614	Aberhosan, Mont.	K.I.A.	25-03-18	Pozieres Memorial.
Mottram. A.	Pte	13840	Nantwich, Ches.	K.I.A.	25-03-18	Pozieres Mmorial.
Hargrove. A.E.	L/Cpl.	52439	Alvanley, Ches.	K.I.A.	26-03-18	Beacon Cem.
Hill. J.	Pte	49441	?	D.O.W.	26-03-18	Pozieres Memorial.
Sykes. E.	Sgt	51379	Stalybridge, Ches.	D.O.W.	26-03-18	St. Sever Cem. Ext.
Banks. J.	Pte	292248	Atherton, Lancs.	K.I.A.	27-03-18	Pozieres Memorial.
Blackburn. H.	Pte	19723	Clayton-le-woods. Lancs.	K.I.A.	27-03-18	Pozieres Memorial.
Blanchard. W.	Pte	267612	Battersea, London.	K.I.A.	27-03-18	Pozieres Memorial.
Bradley. J.	Pte	48567	Blackburn, Lancs.	K.I.A.	27-03-18	Pozieres Memorial.
Brake. G.	Pte	22123	Liverpool.	K.I.A.	27-03-18	Tyne Cot Memorial.

Bryan. A.	Pte	292256	Salford, Lancs.	K.I.A.	27-03-18	Dadizeele New Brit. Cem.
Buckley. C.	Pte	49455	Birkenhead.	K.I.A.	27-03-18	Pozieres Memorial.
Bufton. A.D.	Pte	51657	Penybont, Radnor.	K.I.A.	27-03-18	Pozieres Memorial.
Cartwright. J.T.	Pte	60541	Waters Upton, Salop.	K.I.A.	27-03-18	Pozieres Memorial.
Cash. H.	Pte	21669	Dudley, Worcs.	K.I.A.	27-03-18	Pozieres Memorial.
Clarey. J.	Pte	260189	St. Helens, Lancs.	K.I.A.	27-03-18	Pozieres Memorial.
Collier. W.H.	Pte	51611	Haydock, Lancs.	K.I.A.	27-03-18	Pozieres Memorial.
Deakin. A.	Pte	240932	Chester.	K.I.A.	27-03-18	Pozieres Memorial.
Derbyshire. J.	Pte	51737	Chester	K.I.A.	27-03-18	Pozieres Memorial.
Evans. P.	Pte	51669	Wem, Salop.	K.I.A.	27-03-18	Pozieres Memorial.
Finn. M.	Pte	268083	Liverpool.	K.I.A.	27-03-18	Pozieres Memorial.
Garratt. T.	Pte	292818	Countesthorpe, Leics.	K.I.A.	27-03-18	Pozieres Memorial.
Haworth. R.	L/Cpl.	62369	Darwen, Lancs.	K.I.A.	27-03-18	Pozieres Memorial.
Hoare. R.	Pte	315764	Manchester.	K.I.A.	27-03-18	Pozieres Memorial.
Hollies. O.	Sgt.	21676	Dudley, Worcs.	K.I.A.	27-03-18	Pozieres Memorial.
Jordan. S.A.	Pte.	51351	Southrepps, Norfolk.	K.I.A.	27-03-18	Pozieres Memorial.
Kershaw. H.	Pte.	63818	Oldham, Lancs.	K.I.A.	27-03-18	Pozieres Memorial.
Lamb. W.H.	Pte	51384	East Malling, Kent.	K.I.A.	27-03-18	Pozieres Memorial.
Lane. A.	Pte	57871	St. Albans. Herts.	K.I.A.	27-03-18	Pozieres Memorial.
Light. J.S.	Pte	51402	Horsforth, Yorks.	K.I.A.	27-03-18	Pozieres Memorial.
Loveday. B.C.	Pte	57980		K.I.A.	27-03-18	Pozieres Memorial.
Madeley. W.	Sgt.	7685	Wybunbury, Ches.	K.I.A.	27-03-18	Pozieres Memorial.
Mallen. J.	Pte	52380	Jarrow, Durham.	K.I.A.	27-03-18	Pozieres Memorial.
Matthews. F.N.	Pte	15267	Stockport, Ches.	K.I.A.	27-03-18	Pozieres Memorial.
Maycock. J.	Pte	315167	Glossop, Derby.	D.O.W.	27-03-18	Roisel Comm. Cem.
O'Dea. P.	Pte	51726	Warrington, Lancs.	K.I.A.	27-03-18	Pozieres Memorial.
Parfit. P.C.	Pte	40299	Canton, Cardiff.	K.I.A.	27-03-18	Pozieres Memorial.
Rasburn. W.	L/Sgt	19550	Upholland, Lancs.	K.I.A.	27-03-18	Pozieres Memorial.
Trueman. H.	Pte	51723	Macclesfield, Ches.	K.I.A.	27-03-18	Pozieres Memorial.
Atkinson. G.	Pte	23139	Liverpool.	K.I.A.	28-03-18	Pozieres Memorial.
Ballagher. R.	Cpl.	23057	Ashton-U- Lyne.	K.I.A.	28-03-18	Pozieres Memorial.
Benson G.H.	Pte	19005	Liverpool.	D.O.W.	28-03-18	Roisel Com Cem Ext.
Beswick. V.	Pte	49675	Altringham, Ches.	Died	28-03-18	Pozieres Memorial.
Bruckshaw. W.H.	Pte	315006	Stockport, Ches.	K.I.A.	28-03-18	Pozieres Memorial.
Carr. H.	Pte	41506	Chorley, Lancs.	K.I.A.	28-03-18	Pozieres Memorial.
Clarke. B. M.M.	Cpl	57824	Clapham, Bedford.	K.I.A.	28-03-18	Aizecourt-Le-Haut church ext.
Haig. J.W.	Pte	50247	?	K.I.A.	28-03-18	Pozieres Memorial.
Howell. H.W.	Pte	51677	Hinstock, Salop.	K.I.A.	28-03-18	Pozieres Memorial.
Jones. B.	L/Cpl	51692	Wellington, Salop.	K.I.A.	28-03-18	Pozieres Memorial.
Lomax. J.T.	Pte	265787	Levenshulme, Lancs.	K.I.A.	28-03-18	Pozieres Memorial.
McCarthy. G.A.	Pte	58050	Liverpool.	K.I.A.	28-03-18	Pozieres Memorial.
Muir. W.	Pte	50925	Glasgow.	K.I.A.	28-03-18	Pozieres Memorial.
Owen. P.	Pte	51375	Llanfyllin, Mont.	K.I.A.	28-03-18	Pozieres Memorial.
Pickles. J.S.	Pte	291946	Blackburn, Lancs.	K.I.A.	28-03-18	Pozieres Memorial.
Ramshaw. T.	Pte	20207	Gilesgate Moor, Durham.	K.I.A.	28-03-18	Pozieres Memorial.
Richards. D.	Pte	51725	Newtown, Mont.	K.I.A.	28-03-18	Pozieres Memorial.
Rivers. O.	?	60296	Denton, Lancs.	D.O.W.	28-03-18	St. Sever Cem. Ext.
Roberts. D.	Pte	240602		K.I.A.	28-03-18	Pozieres Memorial.
Rudd. W.E	Pte	201806	Birkenhead, Ches.	K.I.A.	28-03-18	Pozieres Memorial.
Russell. E.J.	Pte	241297	Saltney, Ches.	K.I.A.	28-03-18	Pozieres Memorial.
Stead. C.	Pte	52096	Dawley, Salop.	K.I.A.	28-03-18	Pozieres Memorial.
Stevens. H.G.	Pte	51700	Plumstead, Kent.	K.I.A.	28-03-18	Pozieres Memorial.
Stevens. J.	Pte	20604	Bethnal Green, London	K.I.A.	28-03-18	Pozieres Memorial.
Taylor. S.	Pte	51703	Wolverhampton.	K.I.A.	28-03-18	Pozieres Memorial.
Taylor. T.	Pte	242436	Blackpool, Lancs.	K.I.A.	28-03-18	Pozieres Memorial.
Thomas. F.	Pte	35168	Alford, Ches.	K.I.A.	28-03-18	Pozieres Memorial.
Thomas. W.E.	Pte	40358	Felinfoel, Carm.	K.I.A.	28-03-18	Pozieres Memorial.
Tittle. E.	Pte	59224	Helsby, Ches.	K.I.A.	28-03-18	Pozieres Memorial.
Walsh. J.T.	L/Cpl.	19897	Stockport, Ches.	K.I.A.	28-03-18	Pozieres Memorial.
Watson. E.	Pte	63831	Liverpool.	K.I.A.	28-03-18	Pozieres Memorial.
Wright. P.E.	Pte	23348	Narther, Norfolk.	K.I.A.	28-03-18	Pozieres Memorial.
Parkes. S.	Pte	30006	Blackburn, Lancs.	K.I.A.	29-03-18	Pozieres Memorial.
Goodwin. S.	Pte	201996	Dukinfield, Ches.	D.O.W.	02-04-18	Etaples Mil. Cem.
Jackson. H. M.M.	Pte	242141	Britannia, Lancs.	D.O.W.	07-04-18	Mont Huon Mil. Cem.
Bulkeley. L.A.H.	Cpt		Lamercost Priory. Cumbld.	K.I.A.	10-04-18	Verennes Mil Cem.
Hitchen. W.	Pte	36581	Winsford, Ches.	K.I.A.	16-04-18	Varennes Mil. Cem.
Britten. G.S.	Pte	60302	Fordinghambridge, Hants.	D.O.W.	19-04-18	Bagneux Brit. Cem.
Hughes. T.	Cpl.	19636	Hanley, Staffs.	D.O.W.	19-04-18	Varennes Mil. Cem.
Bishop. S.T.	Pte	49735	Eccleston, Ches.	K.I.A.	20-04-18	Martinsart Brit. Cem.
Davenport. C. M.M.	Pte	45598	Macclesfield, Ches.	K.I.A.	20-04-18	Martinsart Brit. Cem.
Herrity. A.	Pte	40317	Salford, Manchester.	K.I.A.	20-04-18	Martinsart Brit. Cem.
Parker. H.	Cpl	45382	Stockport, Ches.	K.I.A.	20-04-18	Martinsart Brit. Cem.
Retford. A.	Pte	292471	Swinton, Lancs.	K.I.A.	20-04-18	Pozieres Memorial.
Hodkinson. B.	Pte	53379	?	D.O.W.	21-04-18	Serre Road Cem.
Richmond. F.	Cpl	53536	Salford, Lancs.	K.I.A.	21-04-18	Martinsart Brit. Cem.

Name	Rank	Number	Place	Cause	Date	Cemetery/Memorial
Scholfield. H.	Pte	291907	Burnley, Lancs.	D.O.W.	21-04-18	Bagneux Brit. Cem.
Smith. A.	Pte	51415	Leicester.	K.I.A.	21-04-18	Pozieres Memorial.
Miln. G.G. M.C.	Capt.			K.I.A.	22-04-18	Varennes Mil. Cem.
Oldfield. F.	Pte	33629	Seaforth, Lancs.	D.O.W.	22-04-18	Bagneux Brit. Cem.
Burke. T.	A/Cpl.	265896	?	K.I.A.	23-04-18	Pozieres Memorial.
Fairclough. J.A.	Pte	67363	Southport, Lancs.	K.I.A.	23-04-18	Martinsart Brit. Cem.
Green. J.	Pte	260207	Warrington, Ches.	K.I.A.	23-04-18	Martinsart Brit. Cem.
Gullis. F.W.	Pte	53552	?	K.I.A.	23-04-18	Martinsart Brit. Cem.
Hanford. A.W.	Lieut.			K.I.A.	23-04-18	Varennes Mil. Cem.
Jones. C.	Pte.	244483	Little Neston, Ches.	D.O.W.	23-04-18	Doullens Comm. Cem. Ext. No. 1
Huson. W.A.	Pte	67583	Wrexham.	K.I.A.	23-04-18	Pozieres Memorial.
Jordan. F.	Pte.	23066	Hooley Hill, Lancs.	K.I.A.	23-04-18	Pozieres Memorial.
Lightfoot. J.	Pte	53574	Warrington, Lancs.	K.I.A.	23-04-18	Bouzincourt Ridge Cem.
Long. J.	Pte	53558	Whitehaven, Cumberland.	K.I.A.	23-04-18	Pozieres Memorial.
Smith. R.W.	Cpl	20834		K.I.A.	23-04-18	Martinsart Brit. Cem.
Worrall. A.	Pte	65486	Frodsham. Ches.	K.I.A.	23-04-18	Martinsart Brit. Cem.
Hodson. E.H.	Lieut.			K.I.A.	24-04-18	Pozieres Memorial.
Eckersley. H.	Pte	292588	Leigh, Lancs.	D.O.W.	25-04-18	Hautmont Comm. Cem.
Doran. A.P.	Pte	10476	Chester.	D.O.W.	27-04-18	Doullens Comm. Cem. Ext. No. 1
Coventry. A.	L/Cpl.	67553	St. Helens, Lancs.	K.I.A.	29-04-18	Pozieres Memorial.
Jones. J.M.	Pte.	19599	Ruabon, Denbigh.	Died	30-04-18	Crossen P.O.W. Cem. Mem. No. 2
Eaves. J.	Pte	26162	Preston, Lancs.	D.O.W.	01-05-18	Doullens Comm. Cem. Ext. No. 2
Leather. F.	Cpl	19557	Rastrick, Yorks.	D.O.W.	01-05-18	Bagneux Brit. Cem.
Kay. J.	Pte.	30636	Bolton, Lancs.	D.O.W.	05-05-18	Niederzwehren Cem. Germany.
Ridley. G.	Pte	50292	Chester.	Died.	12-05-18	Berlin South West Cem.
Carr. F.G.	Pte	64176	Hanley Castle, Worcs.	K.I.A.	17-05-18	Pozieres Memorial.
Clay. J.	Pte	315386	Leighton, Salop.	K.I.A.	17-05-18	Pozieres Memorial.
Evers. J.	Pte	51411	Hanley, Staffs.	K.I.A.	17-05-18	Pozieres Memorial.
Hassall. E.	Pte	53028	Manchester.	K.I.A.	17-05-18	Pozieres Memorial.
McGowan. W.	Pte	65259	Liverpool.	K.I.A.	17-05-18	Pozieres Memorial.
Pridmore. T.C.	Pte	51346	Glinton, Northants.	K.I.A.	17-05-18	Pozieres Memorial.
Rimmer. W.	Pte.	51708	Upper Brighton, Ches.	K.I.A.	17-05-18	Pozieres Memorial.
Standing. R.	Pte	26164	Preston, Lancs.	K.I.A.	17-05-18	Pozieres Memorial.
Walton. N.	Pte	63623	Birmingham.	K.I.A.	17-05-18	Pozieres Memorial.
Davies. W.A.	L/Cpl	33207	Over, Ches.	K.I.A.	25-05-18	Varennes Mil. Cem.
Murphy. W.	Pte	32603	Mobberley, Ches.	K.I.A.	25-05-18	Varennes Mil. Cem.
Morgan. S.T.	Pte	67627	Barry, Glam.	K.I.A.	26-05-18	Varennes Mil. Cem.
Boothman. W.	Pte	267454	Barrowford, Lancs.	K.I.A.	27-05-18	Varennes Mil. Cem.
Woodruff. E.	Pte	51488	Margate. Kent.	D.O.W.	27-05-18	Varennes Mil. Cem.
Jarvis. H.	Pte	260185	?	D.O.W.	30-05-18	St. Sever Cem. Ext.
Dresser. H. J.	Mjr				02-06-18	Harponville Comm. Cem.
Davies. E.T.	Pte	51663	Llanea, Radnor.	D.O.W.	05-06-18	Mont Huon Mil. Cem.
Hill. H.	Pte	50825	Earl Shilton, Leic.	D.O.W.	16-06-18	Bagneux Brit. Cem.
Pemberton. W.T.	Pte	45971	Bidston, Ches.	K.I.A.	21-06-18	Englebelmer Comm. Cem. Ext.
Walsh. J.	Pte	48730	Manchester.	D.O.W.	21-06-18	Hedauville Comm. Cem. Ext.
Cockerton. S.J.	Pte	52071	Bow,London.	Died.	22-06-18	Bagneux Brit. Cem.
Pettifor. W.H.E.	Pte	67638	Gateshead, Durham.	D.O.W.	28-06-18	Bagneux Brit. Cem.
Worrall. J.	Pte	34780	Birkenhead.	D.O.W.	29-06-18	Hamburg Cem. Germany.
Gibby. P.	Cpl.	40724	Dinass Cross, Pembroke.	K.I.A.	04-07-18	Westoutre Brit. Cem.
Formby. R.	Pte	260190	St. Helens, Lancs.	Died.	12-07-18	Valenciennes Comm. Cem.
Cotterell. J.T.	Pte	40320	Birkenhead.	K.I.A.	16-07-18	Abeele Aerodrome Mil. Cem.
Wainwright. H.A.	2/Lieut.			K.I.A.	16-07-18	Abeele Aerodrome Mil. Cem.
Keane. A.	A/Cpl.	19655	Oldham, Lancs.	K.I.A.	16-07-18	Abeele Aerodrome Mil. Cem.
Littlewood. F.	Pte	25697	Stockport, Ches.	K.I.A.	16-07-18	Ypres Reservoir Cem.
Lively. F.	Pte	27968	Romiley, Ches.	K.I.A.	16-07-18	Abeele Aerodrome Mil. Cem.
Whalley. H.	Pte	243448	Macclesfield, Ches.	K.I.A.	16-07-18	Abeele Aerodrome Mil. Cem.
Booth. T.H.	Pte	3/10009	Hyde, Ches.	D.O.W.	17-07-18	Cabaret-Rouge Brit. Cem.
Morley. T.	Pte	23056	Liverpool.	D.O.W.	17-07-18	Esquelbecq Mil. Cem.
Barlow. H.	Pte	63475	Rusholme, Manchester.	Died.	18-07-18	Valenciennes Comm. Cem.
Irwin. J.F.	Pte	65482	Manchester.	D.O.W.	18-07-18	Esquelbecq Mil. Cem.
Evans. R.D.	Pte	67570	Talyllyn, Merioneth.	K.I.A.	19-07-18	Abeele Aerodrome Mil. Cem.
Jefferson. J.	Pte	67396	Southampton.	K.I.A.	19-07-18	Abeele Aerodrome Mil. Cem.
Cole. F.	Pte	67551	Plymouth.	K.I.A.	29-07-18	Bailleul Comm. Cem. Ext.
Smith. F.	Pte	45670	Dunham Massey, Ches.	K.I.A.	29-07-18	Bailleul Comm. Cem. Ext.
Byrne. T.	Pte.	244388		K.I.A.	8-8-18	Quent Rd. Cem. Buissy.
Bernstein. H.	Pte	35697	Stockport, Ches.	D.O.W.	12-08-18	Terlincthun Brit. Cem.
Morgan. H.E.	Pte	316061	Swansea.	Died.	12-09-18	Terlincthun Brit. Cem.
Harper. H.	Pte	40311	Workington, Cumberland.	Died.	13-09-18	Valenciennes Comm. Cem.
Clarke. H.	Pte	19547	Wakefield, Yorks.	K.I.A.	19-09-18	Voormezeele Encl. No. 3
Newton. J.	Pte	51630	Warrington, Lancs.	Died.	24-09-18	Cologne Southern Cem.
Talbot. W.	L/Cpl	8473	Greenwich, Kent.	K.I.A.	25-09-18	Hagle Dump Cem.
Edmonds. R.	Pte	27137	Loughborough, Leics.	K.I.A.	28-09-18	Hagle Dump Cem.
Goldman. D	Pte	315819	Manchester.	K.I.A.	28-09-18	Hagle Dump Cem.
McDonald. T.	Pte	8266	Stockport, Ches.	D.O.W.	28-09-18	Lijssenthoek Mil. Cem.
O'Neill. P.	Pte	241014	Runcorn, Ches.	D.O.W.	28-09-18	Lijssenthoek Mil. Cem.
Bingley. T.	Pte	40220	Hayle, Cornwall.	K.I.A.	29-09-18	Tyne Cot Memorial.
Courage. G.	Pte	51420	Sutton, Kent.	K.I.A.	29-09-18	Menin Road South Mil. Cem.
Hall. A.	Pte	67586	Garston, Lancs.	D.O.W.	29-09-18	Lijssenthoek Mil. Cem.
Hudson. A. M.M.	Pte	45772	Gatley, Ches.	K.I.A.	29-09-18	Tyne Cot Memorial.
Tyson. W.N.	Lieut.		New Brighton, Ches.	K.I.A.	29-09-18	Zantvoorde Brit. Cem.

242

Name	Rank	Number	Place	Cause	Date	Cemetery
Lewis. I.	Pte	67618	Ton-Petre, Glam.	K.I.A.	29-09-18	Oxford Road Cem.
Stafford. T.	Pte	51385	Liverpool.	K.I.A.	29-09-18	Oxford Road Cem.
Thorne. R.P.	L/Cpl	58007		K.I.A.	29-09-18	Menin Road South Mil. Cem.
Bramwell. P.	Pte	13314	Chapel-en-frith, Derby.	K.I.A.	30-09-18	Tyne Cot Memorial.
Lewis. G.J.	Pte	53934	Clydach, Glam.	K.I.A.	30-09-18	Zantvoorde Brit. Cem.
Rose. I.	Pte	26361	Whitby, Ches.	D.O.W.	30-09-18	Lijssenhoek Mil Cem.
Smith. W.	L/Cpl	45965	Chester. Ches.	K.I.A.	30-09-18	Zantvoorde Brit. Cem.
Taylor. J.H.	L/Cpl	19318	Warrington, Ches.	K.I.A.	30-09-18	Tyne Cot Memorial.
Muggeridge. W.C.	Pte	51410	Sutton, Surrey.	K.I.A.	01-10-18	Tyne Cot Memorial.
Reynolds. H.H.	Pte	37633	Llandenny, Mon.	D.O.W.	01-10-18	Zantvoorde Brit. Cem.
Jones. L.	Pte.	260194		D.O.W.	02-10-18	Lijssenthoek Mil. Cem.
Fernihough NT M.M.	Pte	67300	Bolton, Lancs.	D.O.W.	04-10-18	Lijssenhoek Mil. Cem.
Skeen. A.	Pte	21099	Tynemouth, North'bld	D.O.W.	04-10-18	Lijssenhoek Mil. Cem.
Oates. J.	Pte	64088	Heywood, Lancs.	Died.	05-10-18	Heywood Cem. Lancashire.
Lucas. R.	Pte	67408	Trowbridge, Wilts.	D.O.W.	09-10-18	Terlincthun Brit. Cem.
Parker. A.	Pte	61960	Belgrave, Leics.	Died.	11-10-18	Landrecies Comm. Cem.
Atherton. W.	Pte	260227	St. Helens, Lancs.	K.I.A.	12-10-18	Ypres Reservoir Cem.
Kay. T.	Pte	67402	Hollins, Lancs.	D.O.W.	12-10-18	Ypres Reservoir Cem.
Stagles. W.R.	Pte	53566	Liverpool.	D.O.W.	12-10-18	Lijssenthoek Mil. Cem.
Atkinson. J. M.M.	Pte	45655	Hyde, Ches.	K.I.A.	13-10-18	Dadizeele New Brit. Cem.
Boyle. C.	Pte	260228	Manchester.	K.I.A.	13-10-18	Dadizeele New Brit. Cem.
Clarke. J.	Pte	39930	Macclesfield, Ches.	D.O.W.	13-10-18	Ypres Reservoir Cem.
Davies. W.J.	Pte	67561	Llansanuan, Denbigh.	K.I.A.	13-10-18	Dadizeele New Brit. Cem.
Done. R.	Lieut.			D.O.W.	13-10-18	Tyne Cot Memorial.
Downs. W.H.	Pte	292702	Woolwich, Kent.	K.I.A.	13-10-18	Dadizeele New Brit. Cem.
Gore. J.	Sgt.	20458	Preston, Lancs.	K.I.A.	13-10-18	Ypres Reservoir Cem.
Griffiths. G.	Pte	67581	Abererch, Caernarvon.	K.I.A.	13-10-18	Dadizeele New Brit. Cem.
Hall. J.	Pte	23053	Dukinfield, Ches.	K.I.A.	13-10-18	Dadizeele New Brit. Cem.
Shaw. T.B.	Sgt	44080	Birkenhead, Ches.	K.I.A.	13-10-18	Dadizeele New Brit. Cem.
Talbot. W.	Pte	53923	Blackburn, Lancs.	K.I.A.	13-10-18	Dadizeele New Brit. Cem.
Tomkinson. J.	Pte	50139		K.I.A.	13-10-18	Dadizeele New Brit. Cem.
Williams. F.	Pte	39959	Nottingham.	K.I.A.	13-10-18	Dadizeele New Brit. Cem.
Williams. S.	Pte	27571	Fenton, Staffs.	D.O.W.	13-10-18	Ypres Reservoir Cem.
Anderson. E.L.	Pte	51371	Tunniff, Aberdeen.	Died.	14-10-18	Maubeuge-Centre Cem.
Bellyon. G. D.C.M.	Sgt.	20127	Bethnal Green, London.	K.I.A.	14-10-18	Tyne Cot Memorial.
Brocklehurst. W.	Pte	76822	?	Died.	14-10-18	Dadizeele New Brit. Cem.
Dowbekin. H.	Sgt.	19502	Burnley, Lancs.	K.I.A.	14-10-18	Tyne Cot Memorial.
Evans. W.	Pte	76769	Birkenhead.	K.I.A.	14-10-18	Dadizeele New Brit. Cem.
Foley. B.	Sgt.	20290	Ryhope, Co. Durham.	K.I.A.	14-10-18	Dadizeele New Brit. Cem.
Friend. J.	Pte	64149	Manchester.	K.I.A.	14-10-18	Tyne Cot Memorial.
Hargraves. G.W.	Pte	23076	Ashton-U-Lyne, Lancs.	K.I.A.	14-10-18	no trace
Hargraves. F.	Pte	67391	Burnley, Lancs.	K.I.A.	14-10-18	Dadizeele New Brit. Cem.
Haworth. W.	Pte.	21545	Blackburn, Lancs.	K.I.A.	14-10-18	Tyne Cot Memorial.
Hewitt. J.	Pte	19241	Shockridge, Ches.	K.I.A.	14-10-18	Dadizeele New Brit. Cem.
Leather. J.A.	Pte	35248	Liscard. Ches.	D.O.W.	14-10-18	Lijssenhoek Mil. Cem.
Miller. J.	Lt			K.I.A.	14-10-18	Dadizeele New Brit. Cem.
Morrey. R.	Pte	20952	Madeley, Staffs.	K.I.A.	14-10-18	Dadizeele New Brit. Cem.
Mungeham. E.G.	Pte	51644	Faversham, Kent.	K.I.A.	14-10-18	Tyne Cot Memorial.
Parkinson. R.	Pte	52734	Frodsham, Ches.	K.I.A.	14-10-18	Tyne Cot Memorial.
Rees. T.	Pte	67982	Cwmbwria, Swansea.	K.I.A.	14-10-18	Dadizeele New Brit. Cem. Mem 2
Richards. H.	Pte	65540	Ketley, Salop.	K.I.A.	14-10-18	Dadizeele New Brit. Cem.
Roberts. S.	Pte	32519	St. Helens, Lancs.	K.I.A.	14-10-18	Dadizeele New Brit. Cem.
Taylor. H.E.	Pte	76840		K.I.A.	14-10-18	Tyne Cot Memorial.
Towler. A.H.	Pte	242598	Manchester.	K.I.A.	14-10-18	Dadizeele New Brit. Cem.
Turner. T.J.	Pte	53508	London.	K.I.A.	14-10-18	Dadizeele New Brit. Cem.
Wachter. E.	Pte	76842	London.	K.I.A.	14-10-18	Dadizeele New Brit. Cem.
Wilson. T.	Pte	32629	Bootle, Lancs.	K.I.A.	14-10-18	Dadizeele New Brit. Cem.
Aspinall. G.	Pte	W/435	Rock Ferry, Ches.	D.O.W.	15-10-18	Lijssenthoek Mil. Cem.
Crellin. W.H.	Pte	60490	Maryport, Cumberland.	Died.	15-10-18	Hautmont Comm. Cem.
Elward. A.V.	Pte	67563	Cardiff.	D.O.W.	15-10-18	Lijssenthoek Mil. Cem.
Jones. G.A.	Pte.	67600	Welshpool, Mont.	D.O.W.	15-10-18	Lijssenthoek Mil. Cem.
Holmes. H.H.	Pte	51347	Holme-on-Spalding Moor.	D.O.W.	15-10-18	Lijssenthoek Mil. Cem.
Longstaff. J.J.	Pte	52270	Blyth, Northumberland.	D.O.W.	15-10-18	Lijssenthoek Mil. Cem.
Robertson. D.	Pte	21049	Glasgow.	D.O.W.	15-10-18	Lissenthoek Mil. Cem.
Bates. T.	Pte	67320	Liverpool.	K.I.A.	20-10-18	Harlebeke New Brit. Cem.
Brown. J. S.	2/Lt			K.I.A.	20-10-18	Bissegem Comm. Cem.
Green. T.	Pte	67373	Liverpool.	K.I.A.	20-10-18	Bissegem Comm. Cem.
Noonan. J.H.	Sgt	50390	Liverpool.	K.I.A.	20-10-18	Bissegem Comm. Cem.
Owen. R.E.	Pte	67632	Abergele, Denbigh.	K.I.A.	20-10-18	Bissegem Comm. Cem.
Porter. H.	Pte	40352	Bury, Lancs.	K.I.A.	20-10-18	Bissegem Comm. Cem.
Smart. H.	Pte	58002		K.I.A.	20-10-18	Harlebeke New Brit. Cem.
Woollams. H.	Pte	28065	Castle Church. Staffs.	K.I.A.	20-10-18	no trace
Phillipson. R.	Sgt	19206	Preston, Lancs.	D.O.W.	21-10-18	Lissenthoek Mil. Cem.
Ecclestone. J.	Pte	31096	Middlewich, Ches.	Died.	23-10-18	Rocquigny-Equancourt Rd. Brit. Cem
Roberts. W.H.	Pte	67643	St. Asaph, Flints.	D.O.W.	24-10-18	Terlincthun Brit. Cem.
Thorley. W.	Pte	23075	Stalybridge, Ches.	D.O.W.	28-10-18	Terlincthun Brit. Cem.
Nethercote. F.	Pte	20086	Nunhead, Kent.	D.O.W.	02-11-18	Kezelberg Mil. Cem.
Pye. H.	Pte	51632	Huyton Quarry, Lancs.	D.O.W.	04-11-18	Whiston Churchyard, Lancs.
Ingham. A.G.	Pte	32920	Tranmere, Ches.	D.O.W.	18-11-18	Terlincthun Brit. Cem.

A total of 535 casualties.

Roll of Honour of the 16th [Service] Battalion [2nd Birkenhead].

Name	Rank.	Number	Place of birth	Cause of death	Date of death	Burial/Memorial Place.
Brown. J.H.	A/Sgt	20547	Leigh, Lancs.	Died.	26-12-14	Flaybrick Cem. Birkenhead.
Tindall. J.S.	Pte	20828	Flimby, Cumberland.	Died	05-01-15	Whickham Ch/yd. Durham.
Philips. I.J.D.	Capt.			Died.	08-03-15	Interred at Edinburgh.
Marsh. J	Pte	21777	Bryn, Lancs.	K.I.A.	10-03-16	Guards Cem. Windy Corner.
Wile. G.R.	Pte	20635	Tynemouth, North'bland	K.I.A.	10-03-16	Guards Cem. Windy Corner.
McCue. J.J.	Pte	21984	Rishton, Lancs.	K.I.A.	12-03-16	Guards Cem. Windy Corner.
Adams. J.	Cpl.	21456		K.I.A.	13-03-16	Guards Cem. Windy Corner.
Morrison. W.R.	Pte	29511	Glasgow.	D.O.W.	14-03-16	Bethune Town Cem.
Reeder. C.	Pte	21363	Barnsley, Yorks.	D.O.W.	21-03-16	Bethune Town Cem.
Easwood. A.	Pte	20677	Leeds, Yorks.	K.I.A.	31-03-16	Royal Irish Rifles Graveyard.
Todd. R.G.P.	L/Cpl	21348	Maryhill, Lanark.	K.I.A.	03-04-16	Royal Irish Rifles Graveyard.
Hallsworth. A.	Pte	23277	Denton, Lancs.	K.I.A.	11-04-16	Royal Irish Rifles Graveyard.
Mann. G.	Pte	20928	Southwick-on-Wear. Sundl.	K.I.A.	11-04-16	Royal Irish Rifles Graveyard.
Marsh. J. T.	Pte	21672	Sedgley, Staffs.	K.I.A.	11-04-16	Royal Irish Rifles Graveyard.
Duckworth. H.	Pte	29641	Hyde, Ches.	K.I.A.	25-04-16	Rue-Des-Berceaux Mil. Cem.
Asher. J.H.	Pte	20525	Nottingham.	K.I.A.	27-04-16	Rue-Des-Berceaux Mil. Cem.
Hickman. J.	L/Cpl	21845		K.I.A.	27-04-16	Rue-Des- Berceaux Mil. Cem.
Tull. J.W.	Cpl	21145	Deptford, London.	K.I.A.	27-04-16	Rue-Des- Berceaux Mil. Cem.
Dacy. J	Pte	19798	Burnley, Lancs.	D.O.W.	28-04-16	Merville Comm. Cem.
Malpas. H.	Pte	21821	Horsley, Glos.	D.O.W.	28-04-16	Merville Comm. Cem.
Lea. J.	Pte	29634	Bootle, Lancs.	K.I.A.	03-05-16	Rue-Des-Berceaux Mil Cem.
Farnworth. J.	Pte	21445	Darwen, Lancs.	D.O.W.	05-05-16	Merville Comm. Cem.
Bowen. T.	L/Cpl	21668	Tipton, Staffs.	D.O.W.	19-05-16	Merville Comm. Cem.
Brown. J.	Pte	23250	Birmingham.	K.I.A.	26-05-16	St. Vaast Post Mil. Cem.
Corcoran. M.	Pte	20920	Sunderland.	D.O.W.	27-05-16	Merville Comm. Cem.
Corrigan. W.	Pte	21329	Manchester.	D.O.W.	05-06-16	Vieille-Chapelle New Mil. Cem.
Brown. F.	Pte	21981	Liverpool.	D.O.W.	14-06-16	Ford Cem. Liverpool.
Stocks. H.	Pte	20805	Leeds, Yorks.	D.O.W.	17-07-16	Thiepval Memorial.
Hughes. A.	Pte	29864	Liverpool.	Died.	30-06-16	Bethune Town Cem.
Powell. P	Pte	22035		D.O.W.	18-07-16	La Neuville Brit.Cem.
Saunders. C.	Pte	29877	Wycombe Marsh, Bucks.	K.I.A.	18-07-16	Peronne Road Cem.
Ayre. T.	Pte	30136	Liverpool.	K.I.A.	19-07-16	Thiepval Memorial.
Bosson. F.	Pte	23218	Hanley, Staffs.	K.I.A.	19-07-16	Thiepval Memorial.
Brazil. F.C.	Pte	21549	Cheltenham, Glos.	K.I.A.	19-07-16	Thiepval Memorial.
Buck. J.L.	Pte	20523	Nottingham	K.I.A.	19-07-16	Thiepval Memorial.
Calvert. W.	Pte	21050	Leeds, Yorks.	K.I.A.	19-07-16	Thiepval Memorial.
Chadwick. E.	Pte	21758	Accrington, Lancs.	K.I.A.	19-07-16	Thiepval Memorial.
Cooke. A.J.	Pte	22165	Liverpool.	K.I.A.	19-07-16	Thiepval Memorial.
Davies. A.	Pte	21972	Vauxhall, Lancs.	K.I.A.	19-07-16	Thiepval Memorial.
Dolan. J.	Pte	29665	Stockport, Ches.	K.I.A.	19-07-16	Thiepval Memorial.
Duncombe. H.	L/Cpl	29563	Islington, London.	K.I.A.	19-07-16	Thiepval Memorial.
Garner. G.	Pte	21961	Liverpool	K.I.A.	19-07-16	Thiepval Memorial.
Gibbons. H.	A/Cpl	23347	Shrewsbury, Salop.	K.I.A.	19-07-16	Delville Wood Cem.
Hogg. J.	L/Cpl	20620	Preston, Lancs.	K.I.A.	19-07-16	Thiepval Memorial.
Holt. P.	Pte	21217	Haswell, Durham.	K.I.A.	19-07-16	Thiepval Memorial.
Honeyball. A. W	Pte	20608	Rotherhithe, London.	K.I.A.	19-07-16	Thiepval Memorial.
Hurley. W.	Pte	20669	Notting Hil, London.	K.I.A.	19-07-16	Thiepval Memorial.
Lake. P.	L/Sgt	21405	Warrington, Lancs.	K.I.A.	19-07-16	Thiepval Memorial.
Lee. M.	Pte	20634	Worksop, Notts.	K.I.A.	19-07-16	Thiepval Memorial.
Lincoln. J.B.	Pte	20717	S. Shields, Durham.	K.I.A.	19-07-16	Thiepval Memorial.
Lowe. D.	Pte	23412	Bolton, Lancs.	D.O.W.	19-07-16	La Neuville Brit. Cem.
Lowe. G.	Pte	20544	Longton, Staffs.	K.I.A.	19-07-16	Thiepval Memorial.
McDonald. W.	L/Cpl	23426	Liverpool, Lancs.	K.I.A.	19-07-16	Thiepval Memorial.
McEwan. D.	Pte	20554	Glasgow.	K.I.A.	19-07-16	Thiepval Memorial.
Mitchell. C.W.	Cpl.	21169	Newcastle, Ireland.	K.I.A.	19-07-16	Thiepval Memorial.
Niblock. J.	Cpl	21361	Shankhill, Antrim, Ireland.	K.I.A.	19-07-16	Thiepval Memorial.
O'Grady. W.	Pte	29606	Cork, Ireland.	K.I.A.	19-07-16	Thiepval Memorial.
Rowley. J.	Pte	20639	Tynemouth, Northumberland.	K.I.A.	19-07-16	Thiepval Memorial
Sibbert. F.W.	L/Cpl	20623	Preston, Lancs.	K.I.A.	19-07-16	Thiepval Memorial.
Slingsby. H.	Sgt	20590	St. Pancras, London.	K.I.A.	19-07-16	Thiepval Memorial
Smith. L.	A/L/Cpl	22181	Newton, Ches.	K.I.A.	19-07-16	Thiepval Memorial
Smith. R.	Pte	21635	Ashton-Under-Lyne, Lancs.	K.I.A.	19-07-16	Thiepval Memorial
Soper. H.	Pte	21806	Bolton, Lancs.	K.I.A.	19-07-16	Thiepval Memorial
Souls. F.G.	Pte	21686	Great Rissington, Glos.	K.I.A.	19-07-16	Thiepval Memorial
Speight. J.C.	Sgt	19096	Barnsley, Yorks.	K.I.A.	19-07-16	Thiepval Memorial
Speight. T.	Pte	20775	Leeds, Yorks.	K.I.A.	19-07-16	Thiepval Memorial
Styles. A. C.	Lt			K.I.A.	19-07-16	Peronne Road Cem.
Wandless. A.	Pte	21238	Blyth, North'd.	K.I.A.	19-07-16	Thiepval Memorial
Wilden. H.	L/Cpl	21220	Washington, Co Durham.	K.I.A.	19-07-16	Tyne Cot Memorial.
Winfrey. C.H.	Pte	21188	Scunthorpe, Lincs.	K.I.A.	19-07-16	Tyne Cot Memorial.
Woods. G.	Pte	21902		K.I.A.	19-07-16	Thiepval Memorial
Wrigglesworth. E.	Pte	20560	Wakefield, Yorks.	K.I.A.	19-07-16	Thiepval Memorial

Name	Rank	Number	Place	Cause	Date	Cemetery
Appleby. G.	Pte	20726	Leeds, Yorks.	D.O.W.	20-07-16	Corbie Comm. Cem. Ext.
Bird. J.	Pte	20891	Somers Town, Middx.	D.O.W.	20-07-16	Peronne Road Cem.
Troughton. T.W.	L/Cpl	21110	Manchester.	D.O.W.	20-07-16	Corbie Comm. Cem. Ext.
Allen. J.	Pte	21665	Accrington, Lancs.	D.O.W.	21-07-16	La Neuville Brit. Cem.
Smith. W.	Pte	21689	Oldbury, Worcs.	D.O.W.	23-07-16	St. Pierre Cem.
Maclaren. R.	2/Lt			D.O.W.	24-07-16	Dive Copse Brit. Cem.
Scholefield. R.P.	2/Lt			D.O.W.	25-07-16	La Neuville Brit. Cem.
Randles. W.	Pte	23155	Liverpool, Lancs.	K.I.A.	25-07-16	Peronne Road Cem.
Walsh. D.P.	Sgt	20500	Liverpool.	D.O.W.	25-07-16	Abbeville Com. Cem.
Mather. J.	Pte	23123	Stockport, Ches.	D.O.W.	26-07-16	La Neuville Brit Cem.
Dalton. D.	Pte	21933	Liverpool.	D.O.W.	28-07-16	St. Sever Cem.
Kay. E.	Pte	23184	Stalybridge, Ches.	D.O.W.	28-07-16	Corbie Comm. Cem. Ext.
Spence. J.W.	Pte	20738	Southwick, Sunderland.	D.O.W.	28-07-16	Boulogne Eastern Cem.
Dawson. J.	Pte	21835	Everton, Lancs.	K.I.A.	29-07-16	Caterpillar Valley Cem.
Jackson. F.	Pte	23201		K.I.A.	29-07-16	Thiepval Memorial.
Pentland. C.A.	Pte	21955	Everton, Lancs.	D.O.W.	29-07-16	St. Sever Cem.
Wootton. H.	Pte	21524	Norwood, Surrey.	K.I.A.	29-07-16	Thiepval Memorial.
Salmon. E.	L/Cpl	20406	Wolstanton, Staffs.	D.O.W.	06-08-16	Hanley Cem. Stoke-on-Trent.
Worthy. L.W.	A/L/Cpl	21351	Birkenhead, Ches.	K.I.A.	15-08-16	Thiepval Memorial.
Catton. W.	Pte	20809	Gainsborough, Lincs.	D.O.W.	19-08-16	Etaples Mil. Cem.
Dutton. E.G.	Pte	30785	Crewe, Ches.	K.I.A.	20-08-16	Thiepval Memorial.
Hartley. H.W.	Pte	29861	Liverpool.	K.I.A.	20-08-16	Thiepval Memorial.
Mitchell. G.	Pte	21135	South Shields, Durham.	K.I.A.	20-08-16	Thiepval Memorial.
Holt. J.	Pte	21502	Blackburn, Lancs.	D.O.W.	21-08-16	Netley Mil. Cem. Hamps. U.K
Wakeman. F.T.	Pte	29564	Birmingham.	D.O.W.	21-08-16	Carnoy Mil. Cem.
Chambers. J.G.	Pte	20858	Osmaston, Derby.	D.O.W.	26-08-16	Londonthorpe Ch/yard, Lincs
Gilligan. J.	Pte	20443	Darlington, Durham.	D.O.W.	26-08-16	Abbeville Comm. Cem.
McNichol. M.	Pte	21604	Stockton on Tees.	K.I.A.	06-09-16	Faubourg 'D' Amiens Cem.
Stokes. R.B.	Pte	21720	West Bromwich, Staffs.	K.I.A.	06-09-16	Faubourg 'D' Amiens Cem.
Legg. G.	Pte	20793	Old Machar, Aberdeen.	K.I.A.	07-09-16	Faubourg D' Amiens Cem.
Nuttall. W.	Pte	21788	Church, Lancs.	Died	07-09-16	St. Pol Comm. Cem. Ext.
Bowers. J.E.	Pte	29603	Stockport, Ches.	D.O.W.	08-09-16	Harbarq Comm. Cem. Ext.
Jones. J.	Pte	21732	Prescot, Lancs.	D.O.W.	08-09-16	Aubigny Comm. Cem. Ext.
Keen. W.	Pte	21790	Bristol.	D.O.W.	08-09-16	Habarcq Comm. Cem. Ext.
Morris. E.	Pte	22036	Liverpool, Lancs.	K.I.A.	12-09-16	Faubourg 'D' Amiens.
Haywood. J.	Pte	21677	Dudley, Worcs.	Died	21-09-16	Dudley Borough Cem. U.K.
Myers. G.W.	Pte	20754	Newcastle-on- Tyne	K.I.A.	01-10-16	Faubourg ' D' Amiens Cem.
Bootherstone. J.T.	Pte	20411	Longton, Staffs.	D.O.W.	06-10-16	Faubourg D'Amiens Cem.
Johnstone. T.	L/Sgt	21371	Liverpool, Lancs.	K.I.A.	09-10-16	Faubourg D'Amiens Cem.
Richardson. J.	Pte	21383	Calverton, Lancs.	K.I.A.	21-10-16	Faubourg D'Amiens Cem.
Robinson. T.	Pte	21093	Gateshead, Durham.	K.I.A.	26-10-16	Arras Memorial.
Smith. J.	Pte	21867	Liverpool, Lancs.	K.I.A.	05-11-16	Faubourg D'Amiens Cem.
Flint. J.	Pte	29703	Stalybridge, Ches.	D.O.W.	13-11-16	Habarcq Comm. Cem. Ext.
Baskett. R. M.	2/Lt		14th batt att 16th	D.O.W.	14-11-16	Faubourg D'Amiens Cem.
Dackombe. R.	Pte	20583	Strand, London.	D.O.W.	22-11-16	Faubourg D'Amiens Cem.
Welsh. W.		29750	Birkenhead, Ches.	K.I.A.	25-11-16	Faubourg D'Amiens Cem.
Hodgson. S.	Pte	20504	Ardsley, Yorks.	D.O.W.	26-11-16	Faubourg D'Amiens Cem.
Moore. S.	Pte	30115	Stockport, Ches.	D.O.W.	03-12-16	Habarcq Comm. Cem. Ext.
Mayfield. E.	L/Cpl	21023	Nottingham.	D.O.W.	09-12-16	Carrington Ch/yd, Notts. U.K.
Boyle. W.J.	Pte	22134	Liverpool.	Died.	01-01-17	Habarcq Comm. Cem. Ext.
Walker. J.H.	Pte	28170	Bishop Middleham. Co Durham	Died	06-02-17	St. Hilaire Cem.
Bird. H.	Pte	57811	Scottow, Norfolk.	K.I.A.	03-03-17	Fouqescourt Brit. Cem.
Clutton. E.H.	Pte	50297	Cuddington, Ches.	K.I.A.	03-03-17	Fouqescourt Brit. Cem.
James. W.H.	Pte	25841	Crewe, Ches.	K.I.A.	03-03-17	Fouqescourt Brit. Cem.
Southern. S.	Pte	26921	Northwich, Ches.	K.I.A.	03-03-17	Fouqescourt Brit. Cem.
Whipp. M.	Pte	30762	Manchester.	K.I.A.	03-03-17	Fouqescourt Brit. Cem.
Stanton. A.	Pte	30677	Glossop, Derby.	Died	05-03-17	Fouqescourt Brit. Cem.
Pearce. H	Pte	57994		Died	07-03-17	Cerisy-Gailly Mil. Cem.
Norton. A.	Pte	50314	Stockport, Ches.	D.O.W.	12-03-17	Boisguillaume Comm. Cem.
Hagger. F.	Pte	57855	Southhoe, Hunts.	Died.	29-03-17	Mesnil-St. Nicaise Churchyard.
Marshall. J.	A/Cpl	20939	Darlington, Durham.	K.I.A.	17-04-17	Vadencourt Brit. Cem.
Oakley. W.	Pte	58170	Broseley, Salop.	K.I.A.	18-04-17	Vadencourt Brit. Cem.
Venables. J.	Pte	45531	Marston, Ches.	D.O.W.	18-04-17	Nesle Comm. Cem.
Allan. G.W.	A/Cpl	21610	Doncaster, Yorks.	K.I.A.	22-04-17	Chapelle Brit. Cem.
McKeon. J.	Sgt	W/405	Waterford, Ireland.	K.I.A.	22-04-17	Chapelle Brit. Cem.
Kent. A.	Pte	50445	Eastham, Ches.	K.I.A.	22-04-17	Thiepval Memorial.
James. F.W.	A/Cpl	21818	Princes Risborough, Bucks.	K.I.A.	24-04-17	Chapelle Brit. Cem.
Harvey. G.	Pte	57854	Billingstone, Suffolk.	K.I.A.	28-04-17	Thiepval Memorial.
Kelly. R.C.E.	Pte	61977	Douglas, I.O.M.	K.I.A.	28-04-17	Thiepval Memorial.
Adshead. R.	Pte	50293	Altringham, Ches.	K.I.A.	29-04-17	Thiepval Memorial.
Harwood. M.	L/Cpl	21832	Bootle, Lancs.	D.O.W.	29-04-17	Nesle Comm. Cem.
Rhodes. G.	Pte	50438	Stalybridge, Ches.	Died	29-04-17	Grand-Seraucourt Brit. Cem.
Rix. R.J.	A/L/Cpl.	20742	Newcastle-on-Tyne.	K.I.A.	29-04-17	Chapelle Brit Cem.
Clarke. J.	Pte	60271	Chadderton, Lancs.	D.O.W.	03-05-17	Nesle Comm. Cem.
McKay. C.	Sgt.	7155	Chester, Ches.	D.O.W.	11-05-17	Nesle Comm. Cem.
Ford. G.	Pte	57844	Cranfield, Beds.	D.O.W.	14-05-17	Nesle Comm. Cem.
Worthington. R.	Mjr.			K.I.A.	17-05-17	Chapelle Brit. Cem.
Collier. W.H.	Pte	58223	Willaston, Ches.	K.I.A.	19-05-17	Thiepval Memorial.
Davenport. H.	Pte	60275	Oldham, Lancs.	D.O.W.	18-06-17	St. Sever Cem. Ext.
Trasler. W.J.	Pte	58008		D.O.W.	19-06-17	Berlin South West Cem.

Name	Rank	Number	Place	Cause	Date	Cemetery/Memorial
Wood. T.L.	2/Lt			D.O.W.	26-06-17	St. Sever Cem.
Bourner. G.W.	Sgt	19809	Hull, Yorks.	K.I.A.	13-07-17	Villers-Faucon Comm. Cem.
Clark. J.	Pte	60273	Ashton-U-Lyne, Lancs.	K.I.A.	13-07-17	Villers-Faucon Comm. Cem.
Mellor. L.	Pte	20273	Stalybridge, Ches.	D.O.W.	17-07-17	Boisciullaume Comm. Cem. Ext.
Baker. L.	Pte	50295	Winsford, Ches.	Died.	08-08-17	Tincourt New Brit. Cem.
Earle. C.E.	Lt. Col.				11-08-17	Highgate Cem. London.
Silcock. P.B.	2/Lt. Tp.			D.O.W.	11-08-17	Brandhoek New Mil. Cem.
Christie. A.	L/Cpl	21379	Kirkcaldy, Fifeshire.	K.I.A.	19-08-17	Templeux-Le-Guerard Brit Cem
Daniels. S.	Pte	202180	Hazelgrove, Ches.	D.O.W.	19-08-17	Villers-Faucon Comm. Cem.
Dwyer. A.J.	Pte	28340	Portland, Dorset.	K.I.A.	19-08-17	Villers-Faucon Comm. Cem.
Grimshaw. C.	Pte	26086	Stockport, Ches.	K.I.A.	19-08-17	Villers-Faucon Comm. Cem.
					19-08-17	Templeux-Le-Guerard Brit Cem
Banks. M.	Pte	26636	Bury, Lancs.	K.I.A.	20-08-17	Villers-Faucon Comm. Cem.
Corr. J.	Cpl	20930	Sunderland.	K.I.A.	21-08-17	Thiepval Memorial.
Lawrenson. R. F.	Lt.			D.O.W.	05-09-17	Tincourt Brit. Cem.
Pope. A.S.	Pte	49214	Brocton, Salop.	D.O.W.	07-09-17	Tincourt Brit. Cem.
Beckett. E.W.	Pte	50347	Leicester.	K.I.A.	09-09-17	Villers-Faucon Com. Cem. Ex.
Bonner. E.H.	Pte	50325	Quorn, Leics.	K.I.A.	09-09-17	Villers-Faucon Com. Cem. Ex.
Day. O.S. M.M.	Sgt.	7953	Newton Abbot, Devon.	K.I.A.	09-09-17	Thiepval Memorial.
Downey. T.E.	Pte	202235	Little Neston, Ches.	K.I.A.	09-09-17	Villers-FauconCom. Cem. Ex.
Lea. N.W.	Pte	50309	Holmes Chapel, Ches.	K.I.A.	09-09-17	Villers-Faucon Com. Cem. Ex.
Richardson. P.	Pte	26685	Halton, Ches.	K.I.A.	09-09-17	Thiepval Memorial.
Robinson. W.F.	Cpl	51026	Blackburn, Lancs.	K.I.A.	09-09-17	Thiepval Memorial.
Smith. R.	Pte	58286	Northwich, Ches.	K.I.A.	09-09-17	Villers-FauconCom. Cem. Ex.
Wynn. A.	Pte	61979	Everton, Lancs.	D.O.W.	09-09-17	Calais Southern Cem.
Armstrong. A.	Pte	57787	Clapham, Beds.	D.O.W.	10-09-17	Tincourt New Brit. Cem.
Street. A.	Pte	23307	Birmingham.	K.I.A.	10-09-17	Villers-Faucon Com. Cem. Ex.
Youde. T.	Pte	202147	Birkenhead, Ches.	D.O.W.	11-09-17	Villers-Faucon Com. Cem. Ex.
Bishop. W.C.	Pte	21741		K.I.A.>	19-10-17	Buttes New Brit. Cem.
Evans. W.E.	Pte	52872	Welshpool, Mont.	K.I.A.	20-10-17	Artillery Wood Cem.
Clarke. J.	Pte	15/23436	Leeds, Yorks.	Died>	21-10-17	Tyne Cot Memorial.
Albiston. L.	Pte	242800	Stockport, Ches.	K.I.A.	22-10-17	Tyne Cot Memorial.
Alderson. A.	Pte	27122	Waterfoot, Lancs.	K.I.A.	22-10-17	Tyne Cot Memorial.
Aitken. A.	Pte	59767	Kirkdale, Liverpool.	K.I.A.	22-10-17	Tyne Cot Memorial.
Ambrose. P.J.	Pte	57793	Chatteris, Camb.	K.I.A.	22-10-17	Tyne Cot Memorial.
Antrobus. S.	Pte	58260	Dunham Hill, Ches.	K.I.A.	22-10-17	Tyne Cot Memorial.
Atherton. W.H.	Pte	58261	Kings Wood, Ches.	K.I.A.	22-10-17	Tyne Cot Memorial.
Austin. G.	Pte	57947		K.I.A.	22-10-17	Tyne Cot Memorial.
Austin. W.	Pte	50425	Marple, Ches.	K.I.A.	22-10-17	Tyne Cot Memorial.
Ball. J.	Pte	40385	Blackpool, Lancs.	K.I.A.	22-10-17	Tyne Cot Memorial.
Beckett. J.	Pte	29763	Stockport, Ches.	K.I.A.	22-10-17	Tyne Cot Memorial.
Bennett. T.	Pte	40382		K.I.A.	22-10-17	Poelcapelle Brit. Cem.
Bibbings. R.	Cpl	40297	Cardiff.	K.I.A.	22-10-17	Tyne Cot Memorial.
Birch. H.J.	Pte	61964	Waterloo, Lancs.	K.I.A.	22-10-17	Tyne Cot Memorial.
Bird. S.	L/Cpl	21003	Ardsley, Yorks.	K.I.A.	22-10-17	Tyne Cot Memorial.
Booth. W.	Pte	241572	Hyde, Ches.	K.I.A.	22-10-17	Tyne Cot Memorial.
Bradley. E.	Pte	58230	Rainow, Ches.	K.I.A.	22-10-17	Tyne Cot Memorial.
Bradshaw. G.H.	Pte	61973	Formby, Lancs.	K.I.A.	22-10-17	Artillery Wood Cem.
Brayzier. B.	Pte	40309	Clayton, Manchester	K.I.A.	22-10-17	Tyne Cot Memorial.
Brockwell. F.	L/Cpl	57952		K.I.A.	22-10-17	Tyne Cot Memorial.
Bryant. E.	Sgt	21474	Derby.	K.I.A.	22-10-17	Poelcapelle Brit. Cem.
Canovan. A.	Pte	26374	Stockport, Ches.	K.I.A.	22-10-17	Tyne Cot Memorial.
Chambers. A.	Pte	23458	Liverpool.	K.I.A.	22-10-17	Tyne Cot Memorial.
Chorlton. W.	Pte	40364	Manchester.	K.I.A.	22-10-17	Tyne Cot Memorial.
Clynch. J.E.	Pte	45845	Birkenhead, Ches.	K.I.A.	22-10-17	Tyne Cot Memorial.
Coan. H.	Pte	242952	Manchester.	K.I.A.	22-10-17	Tyne Cot Memorial.
Collins. G.W.	Pte	57829	Hallow, Worcs.	K.I.A.	22-10-17	Tyne Cot Memorial.
Connor. J.	L/Cpl	20749	Leeds, Yorks.	K.I.A.	22-10-17	Tyne Cot Memorial.
Cooke. H.	Pte	12134	Hyde, Ches.	K.I.A.	22-10-17	Tyne Cot Memorial.
Cooper. A.R.	Pte	49249	Chester, Ches.	K.I.A.	22-10-17	Tyne Cot Memorial.
Cosgrove. J.F.	L/Cpl	40361	Colwyn Bay, Denbigh.	K.I.A.	22-10-17	Tyne Cot Memorial.
Cottam. J.	Pte	266707	Stockport, Ches.	K.I.A.	22-10-17	Tyne Cot Memorial.
Cox. A.	Pte	60314	Wigan, Lancs.	K.I.A.	22-10-17	Poelcapelle Brit. Cem.
Cox. A.	Pte	290364		K.I.A.	22-10-17	Tyne Cot Memorial.
Culkin. J.	Pte	40325	Wigan, Lancs.	K.I.A.	22-10-17	Tyne Cot Memorial.
Davies. H.	Pte	316108	Llanelly, Carm.	K.I.A.	22-10-17	Tyne Cot Memorial.
Davies. T.	Pte	266339	Wrexham, Wales.	K.I.A.	22-10-17	Tyne Cot Memorial.
Dodd. R.	Pte	40335	Bolton, Lancs.	K.I.A.	22-10-17	Tyne Cot Memorial.
Dunkerley. S.	Pte	60274	Failsworth, Lancs.	K.I.A.	22-10-17	Tyne Cot Memorial.
Elliot. J.D.	2/Lt			K.I.A.	22-10-17	Tyne Cot Memorial.
Evans. R.S.	Pte	61951	Pendleton, Lancs.	K.I.A.	22-10-17	Tyne Cot Memorial.
Freeland. P.M.	Pte	60276	Ashton-U-Lyne, Lancs.	K.I.A.	22-10-17	Tyne Cot Memorial.
Furay. T.	Pte	242479	Harpurhev, Manchester.	K.I.A.	22-10-17	Tyne Cot Memorial.
Gardner. J.	Pte	61970	Southport, Lancs.	K.I.A.	22-10-17	Tyne Cot Memorial.
Garley. C.	Pte	57963		K.I.A.	22-10-17	Tyne Cot Memorial.
Gater. F.	Pte	12970	Crewe, Ches.	K.I.A.	22-10-17	Tyne Cot Memorial.
Greenhalgh. E.	Pte	50044	Marple, Ches.	K.I.A.	22-10-17	Tyne Cot Memorial.
Greenwood. F.	Sgt	8697	Bathomley,Crewe Ches.	K.I.A.	22-10-17	Tyne Cot Memorial.
Hale. A.	Pte	26796	Birkenhead, Ches.	K.I.A.	22-10-17	Tyne Cot Memorial.
Hall. E.	Pte	45124	Farnworth, Lancs.	K.I.A.	22-10-17	Tyne Cot Memorial.

Halsall. A.E.	Pte	18824	Birkenhead, Ches.	K.I.A.	22-10-17	Poelcapelle Brit. Cem.
Haw. H.	Pte	50354	Redcar, Yorks.	K.I.A.	22-10-17	Tyne Cot Memorial.
Hefferman. C.	Pte	202213	Birkenhead.	K.I.A.	22-10-17	Tyne Cot Memorial.
Herity. A.	Cpl	8523	Hurdsfield, Ches.	K.I.A.	22-10-17	Tyne Cot Memorial.
Hill. A.	Pte	40334	St. Helens, Lancs.	K.I.A.	22-10-17	Tyne Cot Memorial.
Hill. H.	Pte	58164	Hyde, Ches.	K.I.A.	22-10-17	Tyne Cot Memorial.
Holden. J.	Pte	21925		K.I.A.	22-10-17	Tyne Cot Memorial.
Howard. C.W.	A/Cpl	51339	Gillingham, Kent.	K.I.A.	22-10-17	Tyne Cot Memorial.
Huerdine. J.F.	Pte	40316	Drogheda, Co. Louth.	K.I.A.	22-10-17	Tyne Cot Memorial.
McCullough. R.J.	2/Lt			K.I.A.	22-10-17	Tyne Cot Memorial.
James. W.	Pte	40368	Gt. Harwood, Lancs.	K.I.A.	22-10-17	Tyne Cot Memorial.
Jones. A.V.D.	Pte	45592	Wrexham.	K.I.A.	22-10-17	Tyne Cot Memorial.
Kearton. R.B.	L/Cpl	51354	Richmond, Yorks.	K.I.A.	22-10-17	Tyne Cot Memorial.
Kellett. G.	Pte	40314	Woodley, Derby.	K.I.A.	22-10-17	Tyne Cot Memorial.
Kirkham. W.	Pte	50355	St. Helens, Lancs.	K.I.A.	22-10-17	Tyne Cot Memorial.
Knight. R.A.	Pte	202209	Birkenhead, Ches.	K.I.A.	22-10-17	Tyne Cot Memorial.
Lambert. W.	Pte	40360	Bowes, Yorks.	K.I.A.	22-10-17	Tyne Cot Memorial.
Leigh. W.	L/Cpl	32681		K.I.A.	22-10-17	Tyne Cot Memorial.
Lewis. T.	Pte	241584	Neston, Ches.	K.I.A.	22-10-17	Tyne Cot Memorial.
Lowe. A.	Pte	57876	Kempston, Beds.	K.I.A.	22-10-17	Tyne Cot Memorial.
Mannion. W.	Pte	292994	Flint, Flints.	K.I.A.	22-10-17	Tyne Cot Memorial.
McCullough. R. J.	2/Lt			K.I.A.	22-10-17	Tyne Cot Memorial.
McCullough. W.	Pte	40356	Gt. Clifton, Cumberland.	K.I.A.	22-10-17	Tyne Cot Memorial.
McGregor. P.	Pte	40310	Horwick, Lancs.	K.I.A.	22-10-17	Tyne Cot Memorial.
McHugh. T.	Pte	29842	Liverpool. Lancs.	K.I.A.	22-10-17	Tyne Cot Memorial.
McKinnon. H.	Pte	50308	Glenco, Canada.	K.I.A.	22-10-17	Tyne Cot Memorial.
McVey. H.	Cpl	51025	Liverpool. Lancs.	K.I.A.	22-10-17	Tyne Cot Memorial.
Moores, H.	Pte	45858	Hyde, Ches.	K.I.A.	22-10-17	Tyne Cot Memorial.
Moran. F.	Pte	202234	Birkenhead, Ches.	K.I.A.	22-10-17	Tyne Cot Memorial.
Morris. F.	Pte	60286	Wigan, Lancs.	K.I.A.	22-10-17	Tyne Cot Memorial.
Nicholls. W.V.	Pte	58283	Winsford, Ches.	K.I.A.	22-10-17	Tyne Cot Memorial
Ogden. W.	Pte	60288	Oldham, Lancs.	K.I.A.	22-10-17	Poelcapelle Brit. Cem.
Parkington. H.	Pte	291904	Gt. Harwood, Lancs.	K.I.A.	22-10-17	Tyne Cot Memorial.
Peacock. J.A.	Pte	50315	Didsbury, Lancs.	K.I.A.	22-10-17	Tyne Cot Memorial.
Pimlott. G.	Pte	201920	Hale, Ches.	K.I.A.	22-10-17	Tyne Cot Memorial.
Poole. G.	Pte	291906	Accrington, Lancs.	K.I.A.	22-10-17	Tyne Cot Memorial.
Poynton. T.	Pte	58199	Macclesfield, Ches.	K.I.A.	22-10-17	Poelcapelle Brit. Cem.
Priestley. G.E.	Pte	57997		K.I.A.	22-10-17	Tyne Cot Memorial.
Purtill. N.	Pte	40357	Stockport, Ches.	K.I.A.	22-10-17	Tyne Cot Memorial.
Puzey. H.	Pte	19000	Tonbridge, Kent.	K.I.A.	22-10-17	Tyne Cot Memorial.
Ramscar. F.	Pte	40304	Heaton Norris, Ches.	K.I.A.	22-10-17	Tyne Cot Memorial.
Richardson. C.	Pte	57999		K.I.A.	22-10-17	Tyne Cot Memorial.
Rigby. J.	Pte	292610	Leigh, Lancs.	K.I.A.	22-10-17	Tyne Cot Memorial.
Roberts. E.A.	Pte	45571	Birkenhead, Ches.	K.I.A.	22-10-17	Bedford House Cem.
Robertson. W.	Pte	40393	Bolton, Lancs.	K.I.A.	22-10-17	Tyne Cot Memorial.
Rose. J.	Pte	290591		K.I.A.	22-10-17	Tyne Cot Memorial.
Rourke. A.	Pte	40354	Warrington, Lancs.	K.I.A.	22-10-17	Tyne Cot Memorial.
Royle. J.	Pte	40353	Warrington, Lancs.	K.I.A.	22-10-17	Poelcapelle Brit Cem.
Salts. F.	Pte	292824	Burnley, Lancs.	K.I.A.	22-10-17	Tyne Cot Memorial.
Shaw. E.A.	Pte	58001		K.I.A.	22-10-17	Tyne Cot Memorial.
Shaw. W.	Pte	45564	Altringham, Ches.	K.I.A.	22-10-17	Tyne Cot Memorial.
Singleton. G.	Pte	40346	Blackburn, Lancs.	K.I.A.	22-10-17	Tyne Cot Memorial.
Smallman. T.C.	Pte	21562	Bridgnorth, Salop.	K.I.A.	22-10-17	Tyne Cot Memorial.
Smith. E.W.	Pte	200768	Risca, Mon.	K.I.A.	22-10-17	Tyne Cot Memorial.
Smith. R.	Pte	40348	Hull, Yorks.	K.I.A.	22-10-17	Tyne Cot Memorial.
Springate. P.	L/Cpl	30306	Stockport, Ches.	K.I.A.	22-10-17	Tyne Cot Memorial.
Steele. W.	Pte	19202	Preston, Lancs.	K.I.A.	22-10-17	Artillery Wood Cem.
Stewart. J.L.	Pte	50935		K.I.A.	22-10-17	Tyne Cot Memorial.
Stott. M.	Pte	40398	Hindley, Lancs.	K.I.A.	22-10-17	Tyne Cot Memorial.
Sumner. A.	Cpl	36110	Crewe, Ches.	K.I.A.	22-10-17	Tyne Cot Memorial.
Tate. H.O.	Pte	292566	Castleford, Yorks.	K.I.A.	22-10-17	Tyne Cot Memorial.
Tattersall. M.W.	Pte	40321		K.I.A.	22-10-17	Poelcapelle Brit. Cem.
Thomas. E.	Pte	292999	Welshpool, Mont.	K.I.A.	22-10-17	Tyne Cot Memorial.
Thompson. J.	Pte	25946	Ashton-U-Lyne, Lancs.	K.I.A.	22-10-17	Tyne Cot Memorial.
Turner. F.	Pte	50340	Stockport, Lancs.	K.I.A.	22-10-17	Tyne Cot Memorial.
Underwood. F.	Pte	58009		K.I.A.	22-10-17	Tyne Cot Memorial.
Ward. W.	Pte	50423	Sheffield.	K.I.A.	22-10-17	Bedford House Cem.
Warhurst. J.	Pte	45433	Hadfield, Derby.	K.I.A.	22-10-17	Tyne Cot Memorial.
Whitfield. S.	Sgt	20389	Halton, Yorks.	K.I.A.	22-10-17	Tyne Cot Memorial.
Wilde. H.	Pte	58248	Millbrook, Ches.	K.I.A.	22-10-17	Tyne Cot Memorial.
Willetts. H.	Sgt	28697	Bury, Lancs.	K.I.A.	22-10-17	Tyne Cot Memorial.
Wooley. J.S.	Pte	44059	Chinley, Derby.	K.I.A.	22-10-17	Tyne Cot Memorial.
Wooley. J.	Pte	40331	Ashton-U-Lyne, Lancs.	K.I.A.	22-10-17	Tyne Cot Memorial.
Worthington. G.	Pte	58174	Hyde, Ches.	K.I.A.	22-10-17	Tyne Cot Memorial.
Jenkinson. N.	Pte	21600	Brierfield, Lancs.	D.O.W.	23-10-17	Artillery Wood Cem.
Nolan. J.	Pte	241493	Weston, Ches.	D.O.W.	23-10-17	Dozinghem Mil. Cem.
Barrett. A. E	Pte	22046	Everton, Liverpool.	K.I.A.	26-10-17	Tyne Cot Memorial.
Dailey. W.	Pte	58256	Stockport, Ches.	K.I.A.	26-10-17	Tyne Cot Memorial.
Harris. D.	L/Cpl	50352	Chester, Ches.	D.O.W.	26-10-17	Wimereux Comm Cem.
Barton. H.	Pte	29231	St. Helens, Lancs.	D.O.W.	27-10-17	Dozinghem Mil. Cem.

Name	Rank	Number	Place	Cause	Date	Cemetery
Hardwick. W.	Pte	36185	Dukinfield, Ches.	D.O.W.	27-10-17	Dozinghem Mil. Cem.
Taylor. J.	Pte	21656	Sheffield.	D.O.W.	28-10-17	Dozinghem Mil. Cem.
Jackson. W.	Pte	W/1087	Rock Ferry, Ches.	D.O.W.	29-10-17	Mendinghem Mil. Cem.
Masterson. E.	L/Cpl	20903	Dipton, Co. Durham.	D.O.W.	29-10-17	Etaples Mil. Cem.
Pawley. A.R.	Pte	40322		D.O.W.	31-10-17	Ghent City Cem.
Connor. H.	Pte	22032	Kirkdale, Liverpool.	D.O.W.	12-11-17	Etaples Mil. Cem.
Wellings. T.	Pte	290498	Macclesfield, Ches.	D.O.W.	13-11-17	Larch Wood Cem.
Birdsall. P.	Pte	51659	Shrewsbury, Shrops.	K.I.A.	25-11-17	Tyne Cot Memorial.
Carey. J.	Pte	51614	Warrington, Lancs.	K.I.A.	25-11-17	Tyne Cot Memorial.
Mowbray. J.	Sgt	13076	Brightside, Yorks.	K.I.A.	25-11-17	Tyne Cot Memorial.
Riley. G.	Pte	27379	Daresbury, Ches.	D.O.W.	25-11-17	Ghent City Cem.
Shipp. T.W.	Pte	52621	St. Pancreas, London.	K.I.A.	25-11-17	Tyne Cot Memorial.
Wright. W.	L/Cpl	202144		K.I.A.	25-11-17	Poelcapelle Cem.
Craven. E.N.	Pte	51728	Flint, Wales.	D.O.W.	26-11-17	Minty Farm Cem.
Wallbank. H.	Pte	50421	Buxton, Lancs.	D.O.W.	26-11-17	Dozinghem Mil. Cem.
Joice. P.S.	2/Lt			D.O.W.	01-12-17	Dozinghem Mil. Cem.
Thomas. T.	Pte	51721	Alderbury, Salop.	D.O.W.	19-12-17	Etaples Mil. Cem.
Nicholas. H.	Pte	51645	Shrewsbury	Died	12-01-18	Wimereux Com. Cem.
Hart. T.	Pte	17812	Golborne, Lancs.	K.I.A.	22-01-18	Tyne Cot Memorial.
Horton. C.B.	Pte	51608	St. Helens, Lancs.	K.I.A.	22-01-18	Tyne Cot Memorial.
Hulmes. J.	Pte	260184	Warrington, Lancs.	K.I.A.	22-01-18	Tyne Cot Memorial.
Morris. H.C.	Pte	51702	Hull, Yorks.	K.I.A.	22-01-18	Tyne Cot Memorial.
Padgett. W.	Pte	19793	Worsborough, Yorks.	K.I.A.	22-01-18	Tyne Cot Memorial.
Rogers. H.	Pte	202249	Wallasey, Ches.	K.I.A.	02-02-18	Minty Farm Cem.
Barlow. J.	Pte	50405	Northwich, Ches.	K.I.A.	22-03-18	Pozieres Memorial.
Griffiths. W.	Pte	64294	Salford, Lancs.	K.I.A.#	22-03-18	Pozieres Memorial.
Maney. J.	Pte	51714	Stalybridge, Ches.	K.I.A.#	22-03-18	Pozieres Memorial.
Redman. F.S.	A/Cpl	51358	Danbury, Essex.	K.I.A.#	22-03-18	Pozieres Memorial.
Goostrey. H.	Pte	51675	Stockport, Ches.	K.I.A.#	23-03-18	Pozieres Memorial.
Hill. G.E.	Pte	21529	Cippenham, Bucks.	K.I.A.#	23-03-18	Pozieres Memorial.
Judge. W.G.	A/Cpl	51350	Goudhurst, Kent.	K.I.A.#	23-03-18	Pozieres Memorial.
Maloney. J.	Pte	51739	Prescot, Lancs.	K.I.A.#	23-03-18	Pozieres Memorial.
Ollier. C.	L/Cpl	58263	Middlewich, Ches.	K.I.A.#	23-03-18	Pozieres Memorial.
Palmer. L.	Pte	51801	Nottingham.	K.I.A.*	23-03-18	Pozieres Memorial.
Parker. R.	Pte	51777	Hull, Yorks.	K.I.A.#	23-03-18	Pozieres Memorial.
Pryce. P.L.	Pte	45833	Stockport, Ches.	K.I.A.#	23-03-18	Pozieres Memorial.
Redford. R.	Pte	316012	Northwich, Ches.	K.I.A.#	23-03-18	Pozieres Memorial.
Rowe. J.	Pte	34363	Swansea.	K.I.A.#	23-03-18	Pozieres Memorial.
Williams. R.	L/Cpl	63367	Birr, Kings Co. Ireland.	K.I.A~	23-03-18	Pozieres Memorial.
Grubb. G.	Pte	51674	Alton Cross, Hereford.	K.I.A.	24-03-18	Pozieres Memorial.
Smalley. F.	Pte	315678		K.I.A.#	24-03-18	Pozieres Memorial.
Smith. H.	Pte	63562	Sale, Ches.	K.I.A.#	24-03-18	Pozieres Memorial.
Kissach. A.A.	Pte	51688	Onchan, Isle of Mann	D.O.W.	27-03-18	St. Sever Cem. Ext.
Hawthorne. R.	Pte	61971	Bootle, Lancs.	D.O.W ^	28-03-18	St. Sever Cem. Ext.
Dryden. W.E.	Pte	51361	Selkirk, Scotland.	K.I.A.*	02-04-18	Pozieres Memorial.
Bell. R.	Pte	260202	Leicester.	K.I.A.	04-04-18	Pozieres Memorial.
Davies. J.J.	L/Cp	50246	Runcorn, Ches.	K.I.A. *	04-04-18	Pozieres Memorial.
Houghton. P.	Pte	260191	St. Helens, Lancs.	K.I.A. *	04-04-18	Adelaide Cem. Somme
Ingham. J.	Pte	49668	Stalybridge, Ches.	K.I.A. *	04-04-18	Pozieres Memorial.
Kinsey. C.	Pte	316066	Elton, Hereford.	K.I.A. *	04-04-18	Pozieres Memorial.
Oldham. J.	L/Sgt	9627	Rochdale, Lancs.	K.I.A.	04-04-18	Pozieres Memorial.
Randall. C.H.	Pte	64200	Sheffield.	K.I.A.*	04-04-18	Pozieres Memorial.
Wiswall. H.	Pte	59764	Cheadle, Ches.	K.I.A.*	04-04-18	Pozieres Memorial.
Wood. H.	Pte	51710	Hale, Ches.	K.I.A.	04-04-18	Caix Brit. Cem.
Ellis. P.	A/Cpl	51356	Upton Pyne, Devon.	D.O.W.	06-04-18	Namps-Au-Val Brit. Cem.
Foster. J.G.	Pte	260182	Toxteth, Liverpool.	D.O.W.	09-04-18	Namps-Au-Val Brit. Cem.
Jones. O.H.	Pte	44236	Liverpool, Lancs.	K.I.A. *	09-04-18	Gentelles Com. Cem.
Binyon. S.	Pte	30796	Hyde, Ches.	D.O.W.	10-04-18	St. Pierre Cem.
Hatton. J.	Pte	316049	Winsford, Ches.	D.O.W.	10-04-18	Namps-Au-Val Brit. Cem.
Jones. S.	Pte	40305	Barton, Lancs.	D.O.W.	21-04-18	St. Sever Cem. Ext.
Davies. J.E.	Pte	51729		Died *	24-04-18	Pozieres Memorial.
Jones. J.	Pte	23432	Liverpool, Lancs.	D.O.W.	24-04-18	Pozieres Memorial.
Morrison. F.C.	Sgt	7655	Rangoon, Burmah, India.	K.I.A.	24-04-18	Hangard Comm. Cem. Ext.
Eagle. R.	Pte	51746	Liverpool. Lancs.	K.I.A.	25-04-18	Hangard Comm. Cem. Ext.
Garner. H.	Pte	57848	Wavendon, Beds.	K.I.A.	25-04-18	Hangard Comm Cem Ext mem 4
Souls. A.W. M.M.	L/Cpl	21683	Great Rissington, Glos.	K.I.A.	25-04-18	Hangard Comm. Cem. Ext.
Westby. T.	Pte	26116	Higher Walton, Lancs.	K.I.A.	25-04-18	Pozieres Memorial.
Price. E.J.	Pte	267684	Bethnal Green, London.	D.O.W.	03-05-18	St. Sever Cem. Ext.
Gibson. F.	A/Cpl	51348	Tranton, Durham.	D.O.W.	04-05-18	Nottingham General Cem. U.K.
Thurgood. E.F.	Capt			K.I.A.	31-05-18	Chambrecy Brit. Cem.
Thomas. J.W.	Pte	51610	Glasgow.	Died	12-07-18	Berlin South Western Cem.
Ainsworth. H. H.	Pte	63493	Whitley, Ches.	Died	25-07-18	Berlin South Western Cem.
Bennett. D.	Pte	57796		Died.	17-10-18	Bedford Cem. Beds.
Galliers. P.	Pte	51672	Felton, Hereford.	Died	13-11-18	Berlin South Western Cem.
Page.C.	Pte	16/2209		Died~	31-10-18	Rake Lane Cem. Wallasey U K.

386 Casualties

* Denotes attached to 7/Queens Own (Royal West Kent Regiment).

Notes

# Denotes attached to 12th Entrenching battalion, Cheshire regiment.
^ Denotes attached to 16th Entrenching battalion, Cheshire regiment.
~Transferred to 232 Division Employment Co Labour Corp- Private 224823
>Transferred to 8/Yorks.

17[Reserve] battalion Cheshire Regiment.[

Whitter. E.	Pte	23136	Leek, Staffs.	Died	26-09-15	Congleton Ch/yd. Ches.
Clover. W.	A/Sgt	23234	Waterhead, Lancs.	Died	10-03-16	Greenacre Cem. Oldham. U.K.
Fleetwood. T.E.	Pte	21343	Dudley, Worcs.	Died	24-04-16	Dudley Cem. Worcs.
Lewis. S.	A/Sgt	8766	Lymm, Ches.	Died	07-06-16	Lymm Ch/yd. Ches.
Chandler. J.C.	Lt	Attached to	11/Cheshires	K.I.A.	12-07-16	Bouzencourt Comm. Cem. Ext.
Lackabane. H.	Pte	41264	Preston, Lancs.	Died	02-08-16	Preston Cem. Lancs.
Howarth. A.	Pte	46955	Rochdale, Lancs.	Died	05-08-16	Rochdale Cem. Lancs.
Collins. J.	Pte	39520	Clifton, Lancs.	Died	08-08-16	Bronington Ch/yd. Flints.
Dutton. H.	Pte	46726	Alpraham, Ches.	Died	20-08-16	Ste. Marie Cem. Le Havre.
Statham. E.	Pte	A/21767		Died	16-09-16	Puchevillers Brit. Cem.
Edge. D.	Sgt	23318		Died	23-10-16	Bebington Cem. Ches.
Hennessey. W.	Pte	46251	Manchester.	Died	05-11-16	Ste. Marie Cem. Le Havre.
Suckley. W.H.	Cpl	22003		Killed	09-01-17	St. Andrews Cem. Bebington.

Known Post war Deaths.

Murphy. P	Pte	26873	15th batt.	Died	19-11-18	Crewe Cem. Ches.
Nuttall. J.	Pte	41883	15th batt.	Died	01-03-19	Rawenstall Cem. Lancs.
Elliott. W.P.	L/Cpl	23353	16th batt.	Died	25-04-20	West Derby Cem. Liverpool.
Pilsbury. J.	Pte	18561	15th batt.	Died	28-04-20	Norbury Ch/yd. Ches.
Wild. H.	L/Cpl	23055	15th batt.	Died	04-07-21	Nantwich General Cem. Ches.

a family in mourning, the black second button down on the soldiers uniform denotes the loss of a brother in service.

The following pages contain an extensive listing of gallantry awards presented to both of the former Bantam battalions. The information has been collated through my research in documents, medal catalogues, newspapers and the World Wide Web and does not claim to list every award made, simply those that the author is aware of.

Honours and Awards

15th [Service] Battalion, Cheshire Regiment
1st Birkenhead Battalion

ALBERT MEDAL

Shooter. W. 19556 A/CSM. Albert Medal.
On 8-4-1916 while bombing instruction was being given in a trench occupied by two officers, Sergt. – Major Shooter and a private, the private who was about to throw a bomb from which he had withdrawn the safety pin, dropped it. Without giving any warning of what had occurred, he ran away. After about two seconds had elapsed Sergt. – Major Shooter saw the bomb. He could easily have escaped round the traverse, but in order to save the others he seized the bomb and threw it away. It exploded in the air before Sergt. – Major Shooter could take cover, wounding him [in the thigh]. By risking his life he undoubtedly saved the two officers who were with him in the trench from serious or fatal injury. He was one of only three men from the regiment awarded the Albert Medal in WW1. Two of which were awarded for incidents in the U.K, the third was recognized for an event in France. Only two are recorded in the Crookenden regimental history.

DISTINGUISHED SERVICE ORDER.

Cochran. H.P.G. Lt. Col. att 15/Ches. D.S.O. [L.G. 1-1-18] M.I.D. 6-1-17 Croix De Guerre 30-11-17. Believed to be awarded for Houlthulst Forest. [see Sgt. Westray citation]
Johnston. H. T/Major. Mention [3] D.S.O. [L.G. 4-6-17].
Newell. F.W.M. T/Lt. Col. Mention [3] D.S.O. [L.G 3-6-19] O.B.E. M.C. Orde de la Couronne [Bel] Croix de Guerre [Bel] M.I.D. 6-1-17. He was awarded the French Croix de Guerre with star. The citation read To Lieut Col. F. Newell in command of Railways who has exhibited the most brilliant military qualities and rendered exceptional services throughout the heavy fighting in Flanders with the French and British armies.

Tissington. C.F. T/Capt. D.S.O. and M.C.   M. C. citation: When in command of a party told off to construct a bombing block during an attack, he attacked, single handed, four of the enemy, killing two and wounding another. When wounded himself he refused to leave the captured trench until ordered to do so. He set a fine example of courage, dash and promptitude to his men.   D.S.O. citation: During the operations before Zandvooide on 29-9-18, after securing the high ground in front as a jumping off point for other troops, he pushed forward his Lewis guns so as to neutralize enemy machine-guns when the attack was launched. Thanks to his pluck and initiative the attack made progress.

Tresrail. A.E.Y. T/Mjr. att 15 Ches. Mention [2] D.S.O. [L.G. 8-3-19]
During the operations East of Terhand on 14-10-18, he led his men to the attack in the most determined way, and when heavy hostile machine-gun fire was encountered from numerous strong points, he got his men to surround them and either killed or captured the occupants. His marked gallantry, cheeriness and initiative were largely responsible for the objective being carried promptly.

Woodyer.H.M. Lieut. Special reserve att 15/Ches. D.S.O.

For conspicuous gallantry and devotion to duty during the operations before Wervicq on 30-9-18. He pushed forward with his company, seizing the railway embankment and being unable to find the unit on his right, immediately formed a defensive flank and he held on until the troops on his right came up. His courage and example inspired his men,

MILITARY CROSS

Allen. T.W. T/Lt. Mention. M.C.
As Battalion Intelligence Officer, he did fine work before and during the attack on the 14-10-18, East of Terhand. He laid a tape marking the assembly position under heavy fire. He collected much valuable information about enemy strong points before the attack. His example of pluck and endurance was invaluable and his good organization of observers and runners greatly assisted in the success of the operations. L.G. 4-10-1919 p54

Billington. E. T/Lt. M.C.

Chatterton. W. T/LT. M.C.
On the 23 Oct 1917 this officer was in charge of the left section of the captured position at the South of Houlthust Forest adjoining the French lines. This point was strongly counter-attacked by the enemy after heavy artillery preparation. With the utmost coolness this officer allowed them to get within 50 yards of the position and then by skilful use of a Lewis and a Vickers gun, drove them back, killing from 40 to 50 and capturing 20. This officer had also done magnificent work on two separate occasions in the reconnaissance's rendered necessary by the mobile nature of the operations and had brought back most valuable information under heavy shellfire. He shewed [sic] throughout the utmost courage, coolness and resource.

Davies. H.C.E. Lt. att 15/Ches. M.C.

Dolan J.F. Reverand. Army Chaplain Department. att 15/Ches. M.C.

Heap. T. 2/Lt. [Temp]. M.C.
He took command of a raiding party after the officer in command had been killed early in the operation. He led his men to the final objective with great dash and determination, under heavy fire and carried out the withdrawal in a most skilful manner. He showed splendid leadership and courage.

Hodson. Capt. M.C. Notified of award of Military Cross 14-9-16

Jones. J.O. R.S.M. 19347. M.C. L.G. 1-1-18. His initials are R.T. in History of 35th Div.

Kidd. C.B. Capt. M.C.
He did remarkably fine work when his company was holding a position for many hours, from early morning until late at night, while heavily shelled. It was entirely due to his efforts that the men were kept together. He encouraged his men throughout the day, continually going up and down the trench. His conduct was splendid and he set a fine example. Awarded at Vendeuile during August 1917.

Kirkbride. Thomas Coulthard. 2/Lieut. Ches Regt Special Reserve att 15th btn. M.C.

During the operations east of Terhand on 14-10-1918, he led his platoon to the attack with great gallantry and determination, and dealt with numerous strong machine gun nests with success. His skilful handling of his command enabled the operations to be carried through with very few casualties. On arriving at his objective he promptly set several captured enemy machine guns in order and placed them in position for use against the enemy.   L.G. 4-10-1919 p96

Le Mesurier. H.F.A. Mjr. M.C.   Awarded M.C. January 1918. L.G. 1-1-18.

Mann. Henry Cecil. T/2Lt. att 15 Ches. M.C.
He showed marked gallantry in the operation east of Courtrai on 20th October 1918. He attacked a farm with two men from a flank in face of heavy machine – gunfire and enabled the troops on the right to get forward and capture the farm. Later in the day he crossed the Kleibeek and pushed forward with two sections from farm to farm and made ground at a time when it was much required. L.G. 4-10-1919 p102.

Miln. G.G. Capt. 16/Ches att 15th batt. Mention. M.C.
He organized a piquet line and commanding outposts during a heavy attack by the enemy. He never spared himself in his duties and by his brilliant powers of leadership and example of courage inspired the greatest confidence in all his men.[Capt Miln was killed in action almost immediately after winning his M.C.]

Partington. W. M.C. Mention. Italian silver medal for valour.

Shaw. H.V. T/2Lt. att 15 Ches. M.C.
Whilst in command of a day-light patrol he visited three hostile posts and finding the first two unoccupied, he pushed on to the third, which he rushed, capturing six prisoners, gaining valuable information and bringing back his patrol without casualties. His determined leadership and personal courage were deserving of high praise.

Turner. H.M. Lieut. M.C. Croix de Guerre [French].

Vincent. Henry Edward. 2/ Lieut. Mentioned in despatch by Field Marshall Douglas Haig.   M.C.
During the operations east of Terhand on 14-10-18, without any staff to assist, he got orders out promptly, his instructions being always clear and short. During the attack he collected stragglers belonging to various units and put them to their own areas, thereby greatly assisting in the success and rapidity with which final objectives were reached. L.G. 4-10-19.

Waide. Ernest Frederick. T/Lieut.   M.C.
During the attack east of Terhand on the morning of 14th October1918, he set a fine example of gallant and determined leadership in pushing on to his objective, maintaining excellent direction despite the heavy mist. With but few men he overcame resistance at several enemy strong points, and although greatly outnumbered by the enemy, caused them to surrender. He and his party were responsible for about 35 prisoners.   L.G. 4-10-1919 p132.

Woodyer. H.M. Lieut. Ribband presented 19-11-18.
During the operations before Wervicq, on 30th September, 1918 he pushed forward with his company, seizing the railway embankment, and being unable to find the company on his right, immediately formed a defensive flank and held on until the troops on his right came up, his courage and example inspired his men.

BAR TO MILITARY CROSS
Coulter. P. 11056 C.S.M.   M.C. D.C.M. Citation for bar:
For most conspicuous gallantry and devotion to duty. On the 14-10-18, during the operations east of Terhand, he by his bold initiative affected the capture of 25 enemy and five machine – guns and killed or wounded some 15 of the enemy. Accompanied by a N.C.O., under cover of his Lewis gun, he rushed a pillbox, from which machine – guns were firing and flung a bomb in. He accounted for 40 enemy and five machine – guns as above stated. He shewed [sic] fine courage and leadership.
The M.C. appeared in the *Oak Tree* of July 1918, but with no citation. During the South African war as 5497 Pte. P. Coulter, South Lancs. Regt. he was awarded the D.C.M. 'Relief of Ladysmith'   L.G. 27-9-1901: AO 15/02

Tissington. C. F. 2/Lieut. M.C. Bar ribband awarded 17-11-18.
No record of his M.C. award. In the *History of the 35th Division* the surname is Tissingham.

MERITORIOUS SERVICE MEDAL
Howard. 19489. Sgt. M.S.M. Ribband presented 17-11-18.
Potter. H. 50437 Pte. M.M. M.S.M. Ribband presented 17-11-18.
In recognition of valuable services rendered with the forces in France during the present war. L.G. 17-6-18

Scott. R. 23378 A/Qms.   M.S.M.
In recognition of valuable services rendered with the Armies in France and Flanders. L.G. 18-1-1919

DISTINGUISHED CONDUCT MEDAL
Bellyou. G. 20127 L/Sgt. D.C.M.
During the period 23rd March 1918 to 16th September 1918, he has rendered exceptional service in the front line. Of a fearless nature, he has at the same time a cheerful disposition, and is of the greatest value in inspiring the men under his command with confidence, and getting the most out of them. Whenever patrol work had to be done he always volunteered, and has done most useful work in this respect. He is at his best when danger is greatest.
L.G. 3-9-19. p7

Burns. Pte.   D.C.M Notified 14-7-16

Bush. Sgt. 39926. D.C.M. ribband 17-11-18.

Crosby. W. 50284. L/Cpl. Awarded 20-11-17.
On the morning of 23 Oct 1917 when his Company was holding a position in the captured position South of Houlthulst Forest all his senior N.C.O.s were killed or wounded in an intense bombardment which preceded an enemy counter attack. This N.C.O. who had no officer to assist him immediately took charge and by his coolness and indifference to danger maintained the morale of the groups of his platoon the enemy were successfully repulsed. Later in the day when in a new position he and his group were twice blown out of position and when the position was most critical he established communication on each flank and held the line together.

Emmens. W. Pte. 19901

Finnigan. E. Sgt. 19297   D.C.M. L.G. 2-12-19
He did excellent work during the attack east of Terhand on the 14th October 1918. showing the greatest gallantry and initiative he was the first to attack the numerous enemy

machine gun posts encountered by his platoon and his indifference to personal danger, coupled with his leadership, was so inspiring to his men that the posts were mopped up and their occupants killed or captured. Resided Leigh, Lancashire.

Fay. H. Cpl. 19234.   D.C.M. Ribband 17-11-18.
D.C.M. earned while attached to Trench Mortar Battery- For conspicuous gallantry and devotion to duty. He worked a machine gun with only one man for three days and nights in the front line. He set a splendid example throughout the operations.

Harvey. S. 7389 Sgt.   D.C.M.   6-1-17

Johnson. W.A. Pte [L/Cpl]. D.C.M. L.G. 4-3-18

Kenyon. W.J. 19864. C.Q.M.   D.C.M.
Ribband awarded 17-11-18.
This warrant officer, who has served in France with the battalion for over two years, has displayed great gallantry in action and conspicuous devotion to duty. Exceptionally cool under fire, his example has been of the greatest assistance to his company commander, to who he has proved a reliable support, no matter how bad the conditions.

Lees. L/Cpl. Z Coy.   D.C.M. Awarded 18-9-17

Walker. T. Cpl. D.C.M. L.G. 29-11-19. p75
For marked gallantry and initiative during the attack east of Terhand on the 14th October 1918. He with 4 O.R's. came on a pillbox from behind which the enemy machine guns were firing into the backs of our troops, who had passed without seeing it in the thick mist. On fire being opened with a Lewis Gun the enemy ran into the pill box and he dashed forward, fired through the loophole, killing and wounding several men and forcing the remaining 11 men to surrender. This splendid action and dash in face of greatly superior numbers was the means of saving heavy casualties to our troops. Resided Eastham, Cheshire.

Williams. Sgt. 21583.   D.C.M. 6-1-17

MILITARY MEDAL

Adamson. E. 20225. Pte. Awarded 13-11-17.
During the German counter attacks South of the Houlthulst Forest on the 23 Oct. 1917 this man shewed [sic] magnificent courage and disregard for personal danger and himself killed several of the enemy. At a critical period he acted as a runner and guide and took men up to most difficult positions at a time when their presence was urgently required by the tactical situation.
Adshead. T. 45761. Pte. Awarded 9-11-17. [Shares the citatation with Pte. B. Cadden]
During operations South of Houthulst Forest at 10 a.m. 23-10-17 the section commander of these men was buried by a shell and stuck fast in the mud. These two men endeavoured to dig him out and notwithstanding heavy shellfire remained with him and were unremitting in their efforts. Pte. Cadden removed his clothes to get into the marshy ground, and did not leave until wounded on the night of 24 Oct. whilst Pte. Adshead remained until the N.C.O. died of exposure at 3 a.m. 25 Oct. This was six hours after the relief of his Company. Both men were in the line for the first time.
Aspinall. H. 13802 Pte.
Atkinson. J. 45655 Pte.
Baird. R. 39943 Sgt. [A/Csm] Ribband awarded 17-11-18.

[Resided Nelson].
Band. H. 558216 Pte.
Brooks. J. 52117 Pte. [A/Cqms] L.G. 20-8-1919. [From Hereford].
Brown. W. 67532 Pte. Ribband awarded 17-7-18. [From Portishead].
Byrne. M. 16601 Sgt. Resided Birkenhead.
Cadden. B. 201802. Pte. [See the citation for Pte. Adshead.]
Clarke. B. 57824 Cpl.
Clark. E. 67547 Pte.
Coates. G. 50163 Pte. [L/Cpl] From Prestwick].
Davenport. C. 45598 Pte. For gallantry KIA. whilst carrying in wounded 20-4-18.
Dodd. W. 45029 Pte. Awarded 13-11-17. [Shares the citation with Pte. A. Marshall]
On the 23 Oct. 1917 during operations South of Houlthulst Forest these men held on to a post under a heavy bombardment at a most critical time. Not withstanding that the shell holes they were occupying were blown in they promptly moved forward and occupied another shell hole and behaving with great courage were largely instrumental in preventing the flanks from being broken.
Elliot. F. 23024 Sgt. Ribband awarded 17-11-18. [From Rock Ferry].
Emmens. 24420 Pte. For the Somme.
Fernihough. N.T. 67360 Pte.
Gomm. F. 29572 Pte.
Hardman. A.R. 67593 Pte [L/Cpl]   Ribband awarded 17-11-18. [From Bury].
Harrison. J. 19137 Sgt. M.M awarded November 1917.
Hoddinott. T.I. 67389 Pte. Ribband awarded 17-11-18. [From Pontypridd]
Hudson. A. 45772 Pte.
Jackson. H. 242141 Pte.
Johnson. W.H. 53550 Pte. [From Royston].
Johnson. Pte.
Johnston. J. 19137 Sgt. Awarded 9/11/17.
During the operations South of Houlthulst Forest on 24/10/17 this N.C.O. established touch with his left flank Company at a time when the flank appeared likely to become exposed and during heavy shellfire. Throughout the whole day he was constantly cheering his men by his presence and his work in re-organising the line when it had been weakened by casualties, together with his utter disregard for personal danger did much to maintain our position at a critical period.
Jones. Pte. This may be 19347 J.O. Jones awarded the M.M.
Kemp. 45953. Pte.
Lands. 19901. L/Cpl.
Leach. J.H. 34214 Pte. L.G. 20-8-1919. [From Walkden].
Llewellyn. T.R. 67621 Pte.   Ribband awarded 17-11-18. [From St. Fagans].
Lowes. W. 51774 Pte. [From Murton Colliery].
Lyon. R. 5357 R.S.M. Ribband awarded 17-11-18.
Mace. H. 39963 L/Sgt.
Madeley. F.J. 45737 Pte. Ribband 17-11-18.
Mansell. W.H. 29542. Pte. Awarded 13-11-17. [Shares the citation with Pte. J. Kay.]
These men acted as Battalion H.Q. runners during operations South of Houlthulst Forest on Oct 21/24th 1917. They were continually on duty as owing to shellfire no other means of communication was available. They never failed to carry out their duties and invariably delivered their messages and returned with answers in very quick time. The conditions were very adverse and the going was heavy whilst the difficulty in finding routes by night were very great but they

surmounted this not withstanding that they were continually under shell fire. Both men showed conspicuous courage, resource and devotion to duty.

Marshall. A. 29674 Pte. [see Pte. W.H. Dodd citation.]

Marshall. Robert Douglas. 57882. Formerly 1674. R. E.

Moores. A. 45751 Pte.

Munnings. F.L. 20173 CQMS. L.G. 20-8-19.

Newton. G. 51405 Pte. [L/Cpl] Ribband awarded 17-11-18. From Knutsford].

Nightingale. B. 51027 Cpl [A. Sgt.] Ribband awarded 17-11-18. [From Hyde].

O'Connor. Sgt. 20767. D.C.M. Ribband awarded 17-11-18.

Potter. H. 50437 Pte. Valuable services rendered in France during the present war. L.G. 17-7-18 His ribband was awarded at a ceremony on 17-11-18. [Lived Moreton].

Pratt. J.J. 242740 Pte. Ribband awarded 17-11-18. [Lived Woking].

Pugh. Pte. 18282. Awarded 18-9-17.

Reynolds. H. 45372 Pte. Ribband awarded 17-11-18. [Lived Bromborough].

Robinson. R. 19794 Sgt.

Rose. J.W. 19590. Cpl. Of Y Company. On 3/8/17 he was presented with the M.M. in recognition of his gallant and soldierly conduct on the occasion of an enemy raid on the 26-7-17 on F1 Post.

Sands. J. 19479. L/Cpl.

Scholes. A.H. 40930 Pte. Ribband presented 17-11-18. [lived Werneth].

Siddall. J.W. 12485 Pte. [Lived Middlewich].

Smith. 24420. L/Sgt [Attached for the Somme].

Smith. W. 244734 Pte. [L/Cpl] Ribband presented 17-11-18.

Smith. W. 20501 Pte. Ribband presented 17-11-18.

Spencer. J.Nelson. 51022 Pte. For rescuing wounded under fire.

Topliss. J.H. 52995. L/Cpl. Awarded 9/11/17.
On the 23 Oct. 1917 during operations South of Houlthulst Forest this young N.C.O. when all his senior N.C.O.s were casualties took charge and showed great initiative during an enemy counter attack, and by his great coolness and disregard of danger did much to maintain the morale of his men to beat off the enemy with heavy losses.

Walker. E.19047. Sgt. Awarded 9/11/17.
During the operations South of Houlthulst Forest on the 24 Oct 1917, this N.C.O. was indefatigable in his efforts to maintain touch with his right flank Company when the intervening posts had been obliterated by shell fire. On four successive occasions he walked through intense barrages carrying messages of vital importance. His devotion to duty and cheerfulness even when exhausted did much to keep up the spirits of his men at a most trying time and to maintain the line intact.

Waring. Sgt. Awarded 18/9/17.

White. A. 24159 Pte.

Williams. J. 10728 C.S.M. For the Somme.

BAR TO MILITARY MEDAL

Aspinall. H. Pte. 13802.
Awarded with M.M. ribband on 17-11-18.

MENTION IN DISPATCHES BY FIELD MARSHAL SIR DOUGLAS HAIG

Burnham. W. 20937 Sgt.

Collinson. V. 19070 L/Sgt.

Crompton. C.H. 290098 Sgt.

Edwards. R.A. 22218 L/Cpl. [A/QMS] att H.Q. 105 Inf. Brigade.

Gwinett. W.E. 40339 Pte

Hackney. G. 3/64003 Pte. [A/Cpl]

Halsall. H. Q.M. and T/Capt.

Hassell. F.P. T/Capt.

Johnston. H. T/Lt. Col. D.S.O.

McNight. E. L/Cpl. [A/Cpl]

Trestrail. A.E.Y. T/Mjr. D.S.O.

Vincent. H.E. T/Capt. M.C.

Brigge. R. 15/19778 Mention also Italian Bronze Medal.

Foden. J. Pte. 29661 Mention 6-1-17

Rose. J.W. Cpl. 19590 Mention 6-1-17 [see also Rose in 16th Battalion]

Whitelock. N. 15/19646

FRENCH CROIX DE GUERRE

Donovan. Pte. 29730. Att. to 105th T.M.B. Awarded 6-12-18.

Donovan. J. Pte. 65480. Awarded 6-12-18.

Gibson. P. Sgt. 291639. Awarded 6-12-18.

Munnings. F.L. C.Q.M.S. Awarded 6-12-18.

Newell. Fred W. M. Lieut Col. See D.S.O.

Turner. H.M. Capt. M.C. Awarded 6-12-18.

Watson. A.E. Pte. 61441. Awarded 6-12-18.

Westray. C.V. Sgt. 29568.

A.K.A. Thomas Haworth. [Shares a citation with Lt. Col H.P.G. Cochran]
Ordre General N0 67. Le General Nollet commandant le 36 Corps d' Armee cite a l'ordre du Corps d' Armee les militaries [dout les moins suivent] qui an fait preuve des blus brilliants qualities militaries et render d'exceptiouels servoces au cours des combats liures in Flandre in Octobre 1917 per les troupes France Britanniques.
(Loosely translated the awards were granted for- Brilliant military qualities rendered in exceptional circumstances during the fighting in Flanders in October 1917, by the armies of France and Britain.)

Walkey. C. 9719 Sgt.

BELGIUM CROIX DE GUERRE

Kirkness. J.W. 15/23015

ITALIAN BRONZE MEDAL

Bridge. R. Pte. 15/19778 M.I.D.

16th (Service) Battalion Cheshire Regiment, 2nd Birkenhead Battalion

DISTINGUISHED SERVICE ORDER

Browne – Clayton. R.C. Mention [2] D.S.O.
During five days of operations , he commanded his battalion with great coolness, and inspired his men with a fine fighting spirit. Promoted Brevet – Lieut- Colonel. Order of the White Eagle.

Ryalls. H.D. Mention. D.S.O. Awarded September 1917, for gallantry at Waterlot Farm. [L.G. 20-10-16] M.I.D. January 1917.
He held on to his position during a very heavy bombardment. Though he had suffered heavy casualties, and was attacked by strong forces of the enemy on both flanks, he handled his company and machine gun with such skill that the attacks were repulsed with great loss.

Trestrail. Mjr. D.S.O. See 15th battalion.

See 15th battalion.

MILITARY CROSS

Barber. 2/Lt. M.C. Awarded for an incident during October 1917. This award is possibly for attempting to recover the body of one of his men from No Man's Land. During the attempt he was wounded.

Burnett Donovan. T/Capt. M.C. 21-11-17
For conspicuous gallantry and devotion to duty. Very early in the attack he found himself the only officer left in his company, and fifteen minutes later, hearing that the companies on both flanks had lost their commanders, he visited each flank and took charge of the remnants of the three companies. His personal example and exertions inspired all those under him with confidence. L.G. 23-4-18

Findlay. W.H. M.C.
He was of great assistance to his C.O. repeatedly volunteering to undertake any difficult or dangerous work. On one occasion he guided a party of stretcher-bearers to some wounded under heavy shell fire.

Gallagher. Hamilton Dick 2/Lt. M.C. [Attached to Cheshire Regt.] 21-11-17
For conspicuous gallantry and devotion to duty in leading his platoon against a position strongly held by the enemy. Under cover of a bombardment of rifle grenades he successfully led his men to the assault. During the whole day's operation he deployed exceptional powers of leadership and resource and his example was largely responsible for the success of the attack in this part of the line.

Millington. L. 2/Lt. [Temp.] M.C.
He showed the greatest determination when holding an advanced post during one night and the whole day, although heavily attacked by the enemy.
Stewart. F.N. Captain. R.A.M.C. M.C. For the devotion he displayed in superintending the evacuation of the wounded. 21-11-17

DISTINGUISHED CONDUCT MEDAL

Brace. W.H. 22053. Pte. D.C.M.
For conspicuous gallantry during operations. A Commanding Officers runner he carried messages to all parts of the line. When the adjutant signalling officer, and assistant adjutant became casualties he did splendid work, and though only a boy, knew exactly what was going on all along the line. He was twice blown off his legs close to the C.O. L.G. 20-10-16

Burns. T.H. 19365 Pte. D.C.M.
For conspicuous gallantry. As a water cart driver he kept the battalion supplied with water under circumstances of great difficulty. When his companion was wounded, he drove both carts alternatively without interruption and refused to be relieved. L.G. 20-10-16

Bruce. Pte. [CO's runner] D.C.M. Waterlot Farm.

Campbell. Pte. 23156 D.C.M.
For conspicuous gallantry of operations. As company runners to the officer holding an advanced post, Private's Campbell and Lowe repeatedly went backwards and forwards carrying messages over open ground under artillery, machine – gun

and rifle fire at 300 yards range. Their devotion to duty was very fine. L.G. 20-10-16 (His brother was awarded the V.C.)

Cook. Sgt. 21139 D.C.M.
For two days he held an isolated post, after his officer was wounded, until the trenches were obliterated. He then saved his machine – gun, and with the remains of his garrison, fell back to the main trench. His sticking so long to his post aided much in the general defence of the position. L.G. 20-10-16

Ingram. W. Pte. 16/20482 M.M. D.C.M.
During an attack his fearlessness and resolute conduct did much to inspire his section. Though wounded at the start, he carried on, capturing an enemy machine – gun and its team. L.G. 25-8-17

Johnson. W.A. Pte. 57860 D.C.M. 21-11-17
For conspicuous gallantry and devotion to duty. He was on the flank of the battalion which was held up by an enemy machine gun during an attack. On his own initiative he dashed forward shot the gunner, captured the gun and enabled the advance to continue. He showed splendid courage and disregard of danger throughout the operations. L.G. 4-3-18. He was killed in action 24-3-18 with 15 Ches.

Lowe. V. Pte. 21772. D.C.M for Waterlot Farm, he shared a citation with 23156 Pte. Campbell. L.G. 20-10-16

MILITARY MEDAL
Ames. Corporal. 18-11-17
Band. Pte. 18-11-17
Browne. Sgt. Notified 10-10-17.
Clarke. Pte. Notified 10-10-17.
Cropper. R.H. 61958
Day. O.S. Sgt. 7953. Notified 10-10-17.
Hudson. Pte. 18-11-17
Humphries. E. 316043 Pte [L/Cpl]. In March 1918 he served as G/21433 7th R.W. Kent Regt.
Marshall. Pte. 18-11-17
Moat. Cpl. 18-11-17
Peake. L/Cpl. Notified 10-10-17
Rose. Cpl.
Souls. A.W. 16/21683
Titterton. Pte. 18-11-17
Walker. Sgt. 18-11-17
Walters. Pte. Notified 10-10-17.
Hurser or Mercer. Pte. Notified 10-10-17.
Waring. G. Pte. 19172

MENTION IN DISPATCHES
Elliot. J.D. 16/20909 Mention
Freestone. W.E. Cpl. [W Coy] M.I.D. L G 14-12-17
Hodson. W.T. 28121 Mention.
Rose. J.W. 290591 Mention
Thomas J.H. 16/20741 Mention
Grace. J. Promoted 2/Lt as an honour.

CROIX DE GUERRE
Coulter. P. C.S.M. 11056. 1-12-17. See also 15th battalion awards.

See also 15th battalion awards.

17th[Reserve] Battalion Cheshire Regiment

Whiteley W. 17/30666 M.S.M.

Index

SILENT
HIGHWAYS

THE FORGOTTEN HERITAGE
OF THE MIDLANDS CANALS

RAY SHILL

Frontispiece: Galton Bridge, Birmingham Canal Navigation (New Main Line). This bridge was constructed to the design of Thomas Telford and ironwork was supplied by the Horseley Iron Company, Tipton. (Author)

First published 2011

The History Press
The Mill, Brimscombe Port
Stroud, Gloucestershire, GL5 2QG
www.thehistorypress.co.uk

British Library Cataloguing in Publication Data.
A catalogue record for this book is available from the British Library.

ISBN 978 0 7524 5842 7

Typesetting and origination by The History Press
Printed in Great Britain
Manufacturing managed by Jellyfish Print Solutions Ltd

SILENT HIGHWAYS

CONTENTS

ACKNOWLEDGEMENTS

Material has been drawn from a variety of sources. Part of the text and some of the illustrations have been drawn from visits to the waterways, organising guided tours and preparing talks, lectures, seminars and Waterways History Workshops and Conferences. Photographic surveys have also been compiled during canal boat trips along the Midland Waterways: 1978, 1979, 1995–1998, 2001, 2002, 2004, 2008 & 2010.

In compiling this book the author has drawn on the help and knowledge of the following people:

Alan Baker
Joseph Boughey
Grahame Boyes
David Brown
Peter Brown
Philip Brown
E.H. (Ted) Cheers
Neil Clarke
Mike Constable
Steve Crook
Peter Cross-Rudkin
Alan Faulkener
Tom Foxon
Henry Gunston
Roger Hetherington
Laurence Hogg
Caroline Jones
Christopher Jones
Pat Jones
John Miller
Martin O'Keefe
Max Sinclair

Peter Stevenson
Rhodes Thomas
Patrick Thorn
Brenda Ward
Also the staff at:
Birmingham Library Archives and Local Studies
Coventry Library
Derby History Centre
Leamington Public Library
Leicester Public Library
Leicester Record Office, Wigston
Public Records Office, Kew
Nottingham Library
Nottingham Records Office
Smethwick Local History Centre
Staffordshire Records Office at Lichfield, Stafford
   and Stoke
Warwick Records Office
Waterways Archives at Gloucester
William Salt Library, Stafford
Worcester Records Office
Worcester History Centre

Compilation of the image portfolio was assisted through boat hire from the following hire-boat centres (past and present):

Alvechurch Boats, Anderton
Andersen Boats, Middlewich
Bijou Line, Penkridge
Silsden Boats

Viking Afloat, Rugby and Worcester
Water Travel, Autherley Junction
Willow Wren, Rugby

INTRODUCTION

Midlands canals and river navigations lie at the crossroads of once-important waterway highways. They provide a wealthy legacy of architectural and transport history, yet many of the reasons for their making are forgotten. We now live in an age where speed matters. Goods are moved by aeroplanes, fast trains and heavy goods vehicles across the country. Computers track every load.

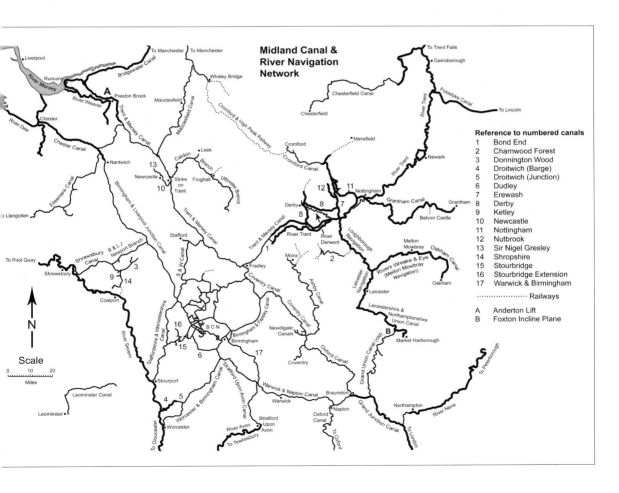

Midland Canal & River Navigation Network

Reference to numbered canals

1	Bond End
2	Charnwood Forest
3	Donnington Wood
4	Droitwich (Barge)
5	Droitwich (Junction)
6	Dudley
7	Erewash
8	Derby
9	Ketley
10	Newcastle
11	Nottingham
12	Nutbrook
13	Sir Nigel Gresley
14	Shropshire
15	Stourbridge
16	Stourbridge Extension
17	Warwick & Birmingham

···················· Railways

A   Anderton Lift
B   Foxton Incline Plane

Whilst trade and transport patterns continue to change, the canals and rivers remain. They are a silent monument to past engineering prowess. This was a hard-won skill that grew out of mistakes and experiments. Through sweat, toil and the most basic of tools, artificial navigations, or cuts, were made across the face of our country. Communication was improved and a competitive transport system first came into being.

Navigations were borne out of the need to transport goods. They competed against or were in partnership with the turnpikes, but navigation infrastructure came at a cost. Financing such ventures encountered many obstacles; not all proposed navigations were ever started, and some never finished. What was built is the heritage legacy of today. It is something to be appreciated and to be understood, for learning from the past can be of assistance to the present.

Within the British waterways network are many structures, comprising aqueducts, cuttings, embankments, reservoirs and tunnels, that are in effect a lost heritage and there is a tremendous variation in these structures from navigation to navigation. Midlands navigations, be they canals or rivers, were a significant testing ground for the development of construction skills that led especially to improved methods in canal building and these skills were translated into railway building and, subsequently, modern roads. Within this region there is also tremendous variety in construction of these navigations.

The author has previously dealt with many aspects of building the Birmingham Canal Navigations and the connecting waterways in *Birmingham and the Black Country's Canalside Industries*, Tempus Publishing, 2005. This work expands on those comments and references made there to discuss the many, and varied, navigations in the East and West Midlands.

It is a discussion that extends beyond mention of how these waterways were made, but also mentions how they developed or were changed to compete with railways and then with road competition. A strong element of this subject has been told in the many waterways histories written and published in the last fifty years.

No one book can condense properly what has been previously published. In this study, emphasis is placed on how a select number of waterways were constructed with particular reference to the surviving structures. This study then follows the changes and modifications as new methods were incorporated into navigation construction and leads into modern times when British waterways tried to emulate developments in Europe.

The need to improve and widen certain waterways came about through a determination to carry more goods. Looking to the example provided by waterways in Belgium, France, Germany and Holland, hopes for similar improvements were entertained in this country. Yet lacking suitable finance, many schemes failed to progress beyond the drawing board.

Amongst those that decided to invest in improvement was the Grand Union Canal Company. They rebuilt locks and widened the canal between Braunston and Birmingham. Their chairman W.H. Curtis was an active publicist for the scheme and he coined the term 'silent highway'. Curtis noted that motor-lorries and cars were a noisy mode of transport and his vision of transport along the canals by 'modern' motor barge was a better option. When it is considered that canals and river navigations were generally silent modes of transit, the author has considered it a suitable title for this book.

CHAPTER 1

MILLS AND RIVER CHANNELS

Two major river systems were to have a considerable effect on Midlands trade. These were the rivers Severn and Trent. Each of them was a lengthy waterway that served as a transport route from the coast inland. The Severn rises in the hills of Wales and flows through Shropshire, Worcestershire and Gloucestershire and into the Bristol Channel on the West Coast. The Trent originated in North Staffordshire, near Biddulph, and made its way through to the Humber estuary on the East Coast.

The Severn and Trent were naturally navigable for a considerable distance inland. The Severn was tidal as far as Tewkesbury and supplied with enough water for craft to regularly reach Worcester. North of Worcester navigation relied on the 'Springs', where flows of water enabled vessels to pass upstream through to Bewdley, Bridgnorth and Shrewsbury. The upper limit of navigation for small craft was Pool Quay, near Welshpool.

Craft using the Severn were flat-bottomed sailing vessels known as trows. Their masters were called 'Owners' and these people benefited from the trade on the river. Bewdley, Bridgnorth and Shrewsbury had riverside warehouses for the trade that came up from Bristol or by road from the Midlands and North West.

The Trent was a navigation whose upper limit changed with time. Boats travelled upstream as far as Nottingham where the Trent Bridge limited onward navigation. But eventually craft continued onto Wilden Ferry where goods could be exchanged with wagons on the road from Derby to London. North of Wilne the route was lined with watermills that tapped the power of the river.

Other rivers were harnessed for the needs of mill owners, where waterwheels drove machinery to grind corn, work metals and treat cloth. Sometimes the flow was strong enough to act directly on the waterwheel, whilst at other times artificial channels had to be made to bring the water to act on the wheel. The techniques developed for making the leats, mill streams, mill pools and floodgates provided a useful basis for the making of other artificial waterways, or canals.

Passing each mill weir required a mechanism that enabled the boat to change levels. Early means involved a type of single barrier lock built into the structure of the weir. Such locks were used to pen back water for mill use, navigation or both. The single barrier lock is a general term that encompasses different types that include the flash lock, the staunch, and the water gate. Whatever the type, enabling boats to pass the weir meant loss of water to the mill owner and passage of boats was therefore restricted to times of the day or week that suited the mill owners.

Pound locks, or sluices, were a more suitable alternative for navigation. Yet the making of pound locks, that is locks with upper and lower gates enclosing a pound of water to hold a boat, involved a certain expense. The entrance channel, exit channel and chamber needed to be excavated through soil, gravel or rock. The chamber itself was often lined with bricks, stone or wood. Others had turf sides. The gates were made of timber and a mechanism fitted to these gates admitted water to the chamber or released water from it to enable the craft to pass between the different levels. Such a rise or fall varied with the height of the weir. A balance beam was fitted to each gate to assist opening and closing.

Providing single barrier locks involved less engineering. Navigations with the single barrier are generally considered older and more primitive than those with pound locks. Nevertheless this system continued long into the pound lock era and persisted long enough on parts of the River Thames to be recorded and photographed.

The essential principle of a single barrier lock was to have a gate or gates with a system that enabled the selective release of water from the level above the gate until the level below and above were equal. The gate was then opened to allow passage of the craft. With craft going upstream it was necessary for a capstan or a similar haulage device to be installed upstream so that craft could be drawn through the opening against the current. Once the boat had passed through, the opening was closed and the water would rise again to the former levels. The craft was then allowed to pass onto the next lock or barrier. Haling the boat on navigations with this type of lock was frequently conducted by men, who apart from using their strength to get the craft along the river, were also needed at the lock working the paddles and capstan.

Flash locks were often part of the structure of the weir and were only drawn when required for navigation. The mechanism comprised a beam fitted with removable lashers (paddles) and rimers. It was a structure that was made of masonry and wood, with an iron pivot for the beam. Drawing the lashers released water from above the weir. As it gushed through the openings a 'flash' of water was created, hence the term 'flash lock'. When the water was level on both sides, lashers and rimers removed, the beam was swung through 90 degrees to allow the boat to pass.

Staunches and water gates were at a separate location to the mill weir and provided a temporary means of raising water in the river. It is difficult to distinguish between the meanings of these terms within West Midlands waterways, as the use tends to blur and both names appears in contemporary documents. The structures also vary. The gates might be single or paired. Gates were opened with either a balance beam or with the assistance of a winch and chain. The term staunch was particularly favoured in East Anglia. The Ouse Navigation had both staunches and sluices; elsewhere in this part of England there was a different structure. The gate assembly was of the guillotine type, and such gates were raised or lowered by turning a wheel.

There were several challenges for the people making a river navigable, which included masons' and carpenters' skills at the locks, whichever type was used. Labourers were also required to improve the haling path, scour out the channel or make a lock cut for a pound lock.

The River Severn was nominally a free waterway, although in the thirteenth century 'murage' was charged for vessels reaching Shrewsbury. Murage was a levy generally for road traffic to supply funds for the repair of town walls. Worcester and Gloucester also made charges for river vessels. Passage was made possible by sail or bank haling.

Several tributaries of the Severn were particularly favoured for watermills. The Bristol Avon, Frome, Salwarpe, Teme, Warwickshire Avon, Worcestershire Stour and Wye all flowed into the River Severn or the Severn estuary. The Worcestershire Stour had a particularly useful role in driving watermills dedicated to the early metal trades of rolling and slitting iron. Mill owners provided dams to raise levels and provide a head of water to drive the wheel. Such acts also provided the possibility of navigation where depths were sufficient. All these rivers became targets for navigation schemes where the promoters were often in conflict with the mill owners over water.

Rivers including the Soar and Warwickshire Avon were considered for navigation schemes during the reign of King Charles I at a time when granting improvements was made by letters patent. It was an effective means of raising money for the Crown. William Sandys of Fladbury was one such entrepreneur who in 1636 obtained letters patent for making the Warwickshire Avon navigable. Sandys himself owned Fladbury Mill and he was clearly interested in improving transport in this region and on a wider scale. Sandys also entered into partnership with Thomas Sandys of Miserden, Gloucester, and Joseph Atkinson of London following a patent granted to them in 1638 for a duty on coal exported to Ireland, Guernsey, Jersey and the Isle of Man on paying a rent to the Crown of £10,000.

Sandys' patent for river improvement granted the making of the River Avon and drains navigable and passable for boats of carriage through the counties of Worcester, Gloucester and Warwick, and a distance of about 50 miles within these counties. Provisions were made for men to 'drag' the boats with the granting of rights of passage along the river bank.

William Sandys, the promoter, was born at Ombersley, and was the son of Sir William Sandys of Miserden, Gloucestershire. Sandys, the son, was also a person of influence; he was bailiff of the hundred of Oswaldslow, a Justice of the Peace for Worcestershire and elected member of both the Short and Long Parliaments for Evesham.

The navigation was to be carried unto or near Coventry. It was William Sandys' intention to make the river more passable for trade. It is possible that with the river navigable towards Coventry the transport of coal from mines north of Coventry would be included. During the sixteenth century coal was mined on land between Stockingford and Nuneaton and also at Bedworth and Griff. Those around Bedworth and Griff were enlarged and improved by the Newdigate family during the early part of the seventeenth century, whilst Coventry Corporation owned land at Hawkesbury that also came to be mined for coal in Sandys' time.

Sandys initially started the work himself but evidently found the task too difficult to arrange privately with the riparian landowners. He sought the aid of King Charles I, and as result an order was made in Council, 9 March 1635, which established a Royal Commission to assist the making of the work. Such commissioners were to be employed to value the land so that recompense made by William Sandys was just, but this commission was also empowered to hire workmen and carry out any necessary work for reasonable wages to be paid by Sandys. The commission comprised thirty names and included Lord Windsor and Sir William Russell, treasurer of the navy.

The Binton Bridges near Welford present a timeless scene. (Author)

Some three months later, on 1 June 1636 (the calendar year, at this time, changed in March), the Lords meeting at the Star Chamber heard from the Attorney General that a dispute had risen between William Sandys and Sir William Russell, who then also held the post of Sheriff of Worcester. Sandys had sent a boat to view the river, but this boat had been seized by Russell's servants and Sandys' men assaulted. Russell, in support of his actions, claimed Sandys' men had entered his lands and dug turf. The dispute between them became a major threat to the works and Russell continued to challenge Sandys.

The commissioners met on 30 August 1636 at Evesham and determined that the length of stream to be navigated was to be 40 miles and that sluices (pound locks) and cuts were to be made at the thirteen mills on the river north from Tewkesbury towards Stratford. This has been interpreted by some researchers to be locks at Tewkesbury, Strensham, Nafford, Pershore, Wyre, Fladbury, Chadbury, Evesham, Harvington, Cleeve, Bidford, Welford and Stratford. A rent of 40s an acre was fixed for land either for locks or landway (towing or haling path). For making the locks it was stipulated that not more than one acre should be taken at each place, whilst for the landway, the maximum width was to be 1ft 6in. Payments were also made for taking down obstructions such as trees and willows.

Russell's dispute with Sandys concerned the placing of the lock of Strensham Mill. The lock cut, when made, separated the mill from the bank and the roadway to Eckington. The commissioners had hoped to meet Russell at the mill in August 1636 to discuss the prospect of making a bridge over the lock cut. Russell never attended this meeting. Leaving Strensham the commissioners went on to Tewkesbury to meet attorney Richard Dowdeswell, who also happened to be Russell's agent. Dowdewell objected to the location of the lock linking the Avon with the Severn. Dowdeswell believed his meadow would be more liable to floods if the work went ahead. The commissioners disagreed. They were convinced that making the lock would have the opposite effect. Two other objectors, Thomas Copley and Thomas Saunders, did not want the landway to cross their land and finally there was Edward Pratt. Mr Pratt seemingly worked for Russell and had tried to secure further opposition to the navigation.

In September Russell wrote to the Council that he could not get warrants executed at Oswaldslow and Pershore, where Sandys was bailiff. He followed up this complaint in November 1636 by imprisoning two of Sandys' men (Richard Hollington and Peter Noxon). The King's Council determined to settle such disputes by calling Russell and Dowdeswell to attend a meeting. Russell asked for time to attend to other issues, such as the matter of ship money and their commitment to navy matters. Thus Sandys was also caused delay at Strensham and Tewkesbury.

Russell petitioned the Council three months later in January 1636, when Sandys sent a stock boat to Strensham. They were denied passage by 'an old milner' and he was assaulted by Sandys' men. Sandys' version was that ten of Russell's men beat up three of Sandys' who were going for 'sea coales'. Such disputes continued yet, despite the delays, improvements went on until 1639, when some £40,000 is said to have been spent.

William Sandys made a powerful enemy in the person of Russell. How much of the navigation from Tewkesbury was completed by him remains uncertain because of the dispute. Sandys is credited with providing pound locks, flash locks and water gates on the River Avon between Tewkesbury and Stratford. He also made some attempt to improve a section of the Arrow. The diamond-shaped lock chambers that existed at Wyre, Pershore, Chadbury and Cleeve have been credited as being original Sandys locks. Water gates are believed to have been erected by him at Cropthorne and Pershore.

The growing unrest that led to the civil war curtailed Sandys' business developments and work on the Avon. Ownership of the Avon passed to a supporter of the parliamentary cause, William Say. Like Sandys before him, Say is said to have made sluices and built embankments on the Avon in the years of their rule. The work actually done has equally been never determined. With the

Top: Bidford Bridge in was existence when the Avon was first made navigable by William Sandys (1636–39) and remained a major crossing point throughout the life of the navigation. With the restoration of the Avon (1969–74), workers engaged in dredging the river selected a specific arch where the river course was deepened to permit passage of boats. (Author)

Above: The Warwickshire Avon joined the Severn at Tewkesbury through a group of channels, some adapted for watermill use. Boats entered the navigation through the barge lock (centre-left of picture). (Author)

restoration of Charles II to the throne, ownership of the Avon Navigation changed again and was acquired by Lord Windsor, who effectively divided the river into two separate organisations. That above Evesham, known as the Upper Navigation, was leased to a syndicate of people including Andrew Yarranton. They too are said to have made further modifications. Lord Windsor retained the Lower Avon and improved it as required.

Improving the Warwickshire Avon was accomplished over a period of two centuries; specific elements being done as the need arose. Andrew Yarranton contributed to the work, particularly on the river above Evesham; his vision for improvement included flax-weaving mills and new communities along the river at and near Stratford. Such developments did not happen although flax weaving was conducted in this area.

The Worcestershire Stour was also improved by Andrew Yarranton and his family. It was authorised by Act of Parliament and comprised a series of pound locks that bypassed the mill weirs. There is evidence to suggest that the navigation was completed between Stourbridge and Mitton, now Stourport, although floods damaged the work from time to time. In addition to the pound locks there is also documentary evidence for the making of 'turnpikes', which in this case is believed to have been a type of single barrier lock. The name turnpike could apply to a type of pound lock (as found on the River Thames) and was more commonly applied to a road that collected tolls for all traffic that passed along it. With roads and perhaps navigations the term turnpike was derived from the gate where the tolls were collected.

Navigation along the Worcestershire Stour lasted for perhaps a dozen years. Some traffic has been recorded as passing from Stourbridge to Worcester, but was principally confined to the section between Kidderminster and Amblecote, where such trade included coal. Periodic floods led to high repair costs. The cost of maintenance is believed to have finally caused through navigation to cease. This had happened by, or during, 1680.

A fundamental reason for making new river navigations was trade. The Worcestershire Stour Navigation arose through the need to transport coal and ironstone. Sandys' improvement of the Warwickshire Avon had the transport of coal first in mind, whilst at Droitwich proposals for navigation along the Salwarpe were made to improve transport of both coal and salt.

Salt was found in various parts of the country and primarily in the counties of Cheshire, Lincolnshire, Sussex and Worcestershire. At Droitwich, salt was extracted from brine. The brine collected was heated in pans using wood as a fuel. The Domesday Book refers to the pans producing quantities in mitts (8 bushels) or summa (a horse load). Once concentrated, the salt was sent by packhorse along the various saltways that radiated from the town. An important saltway ran south-eastward to Lechlade on the River Thames, for transfer to boat. Others went on to Worcester and Gloucester, whilst the shortest route to the Severn was to Holt.

Navigation of the Salwarpe was clearly possible by the fourteenth century, when in 1378 King Richard gave letters patent to the bailiffs of Droitwich to levy tolls which included three pence on every ship by water with goods for sale. This patent was renewed in 1399 and 1427. The construction of mills on the river may have hindered navigation thereafter.

A new factor came to influence navigation improvements of the Salwarpe in the seventeenth century. The dependence on wood as a fuel meant that local supplies were depleted and carriage of wood was made at greater and greater distances. Coal was seen as a suitable substitute, but this too involved carriage from the nearest pits in Worcestershire or Shropshire. In the latter case coal from Shropshire was brought down the Severn.

The burgesses resisted a plan of William Sandys to make an artificial canal to the Severn as part of his general plan to improve transport in the region. Lord Windsor succeeded, however, in getting an Act to deepen the river and improve the navigation in 1662 and the burgesses thanked Lord Windsor for completing the works in 1664. The original proposed number of six locks was reduced to five, leading to many published accounts since stating that the navigation was never finished. Even with improvements to the Salwarpe, navigation was restricted and coal was also transported by road, as was salt. Another century would pass before James Brindley surveyed a new navigation, which became the Droitwich Canal.

South of Mitton, a navigation was created along the Dick Brook to Astley Forge. Published accounts have connected the modifications with Andrew Yarranton, although more recent research by Dr Peter King has indicated the navigation of two known locks was made later. One of the locks has a date stone showing 1717. Dr King suggests that these locks were of the single barrier type, whose role was to pound water above them and facilitate the passage of boats up to the forge when required to do so.

The River Wye permitted navigation to Hereford for small craft carrying up to 4 tons. Improvements were considered during the seventeenth century and some work was done from 1662 by William Sandys and his family that involved the making of pound locks at the weirs. This work was carried out under an Act of Parliament made in 1662 and thereafter further work was done progressively. Further improvement Acts followed in 1695 and 1727. Navigation was made possible through both single barrier and pound locks. Locks for the Lugg from the Wye to Leominster were also approved in 1662 as part of the Wye Navigation Act, but little if any work was done by Sandys or his partners. It is believed that single barrier locks were installed on this section to enable navigation to Leominster.

Some of the tributaries of the Severn served as navigations for their lower reaches. The River Teme was naturally navigable as far as the Powick Bridge and weir and a haling path existed on the north bank. Beyond Powick evidence of navigation by boats has often been a subject of discussion by transport historians.

When William Sandys made the application to the Court of King Charles I for making the Warwickshire Avon navigable, there was the intention to make the Teme more passable for wood, iron and pitcoals from the Severn towards Ludlow. The commissioners who reported on the Avon investigated the landowners of the Teme, but unlike the Avon, found no cause for objection. Yet little seems to have been done as Sandys appears to have given priority to the Avon project.

Whilst there are paintings showing boats on the river at places such as Ludlow, these have been interpreted as artistic licence by some. Yet these paintings have given credence to the hope there might have been a form of navigation that used flash locks placed in the millers' weirs to pass up and downstream. Supporting evidence of a through navigation from Powick is, however, hard to find. It has been suggested that a partial navigation existed where sections of the river were used by craft, yet the present consensus of opinion is that this was a rare occurrence and there is little to support the suggestion that the river above Powick had a commercial role. That is, apart from the supply of water power. The ironworks at Bringewood, near Ludlow, was placed at a spot where the current was strongest and best adapted to driving waterwheels. Such locations were not best suited for navigation. Besides, records for the ironworks on the Teme show pig iron and finished goods being carried by road to the Severn and shipment by trow from places such as Bewdley.

The River Wye was the main waterway transport route to Hereford, until the canal was completed in 1845. Trows worked principally along this river to Bristol. During 1819 the five-arch iron bridge shown was constructed over the Wye at Chepstow to the design of John Urpeth Rastrick. (Author)

Powick was definitely served by boats. There was a watermill used for flour milling and a forge that was once owned by the Lloyd family. In 1803 the forge comprised three fineries, a chafery, a balling furnace and rolling and slitting mills, which were clustered about the mill stream opposite the flour mill. Navigation was possible up to wharves above Old Powick Bridge, but below the mills. By 1825 the flour mill had been rebuilt and enlarged and the forge was converted into a mill for grinding materials for the porcelain makers Granger of Worcester. There was also a coal yard and wharf. The flour mill was advertised for sale in August 1825 and prospective purchasers had the right to the free use of the towing path from the River Severn to the premises.

Further upriver the Tern was navigable for small barges that went up to Tern Forge and perhaps even to Upton Forge. The mouth of the River Perry is believed to have been used by craft serving Bromley Forge. The Vyrnwy was used by barges to carry pig iron upstream to Llanymynech, whilst lead ore and limestone was brought downstream.

A harder case to determine is what Charles Hadfield called the Eardington Forge Canal in his book *Canals of the West Midlands*. Further research has indicated that the tunnel between the upper and lower forge at Eardington was a navigable link from the Mor Brook. Eardington Ironworks in 1807 belonged to Samuel Twamley, ironmaster. The upper works, or top forge, comprised four puddling furnaces and a balling furnace. The lower forge and rolling mill were placed close to the banks of the Severn where river craft might load with the rolled iron.

Shoals and shallows on the Severn restricted the passage of craft from time to time. There were also the fish weirs that were erected to trap and catch fish in the river, which also limited navigation.

The Staffordshire & Worcestershire Canal proprietors were particularly keen to improve this situation so as to benefit their trade from Stourport. Proposals were drawn up by William Jessop, in 1784, for narrowing the river in places and for locks above Worcester. A subsequent enquiry revealed that much opposition to Jessop's proposals existed. Important landowners such as the Earl of Coventry were particularly concerned about flooding if jetties were made to restrict the flow. Such was the opposition that this scheme failed. A revised scheme was produced by Jessop in January 1786.

His printed paper to the noblemen, gentlemen and owners of land on the banks of the River Severn put forward his plan to build locks between Meadows Wharf, Coalbrookdale, and the deep water at Diglis, Worcester, and to erect weirs to maintain a depth of 4ft in the driest season. Jessop was concerned that the landowners would object to flooding of their fields and designed the weirs in such a way that the effects of flooding would be reduced. He considered lengthening weirs; placing each at an angle and fitting removable boards would assist his plan. At Diglis, for example, the weir was to be 4ft 8in high but only comprised of 4ft of solid weir and the remainder was comprised of removal boards.

G. Young's plan (1786) shows the location of proposed locks at Diglis, then: north of Worcester; near Holt; south and north of Stourport; at Bewdley; near Arley; at Highley; north of Eardington Forge; south and north of Bridgnorth; south of the wooden bridge at Coalport; near Jackfield; and finally south of the Iron Bridge – fourteen locks in total. Despite the benefits of a deeper navigation the Bill failed.

An important factor was the free trade aspect, as craft were not charged tolls for the goods they carried along the river. A toll per mile and per commodity as on other navigations proved a powerful argument to resist, whatever the present handicaps. Water supply was actually declining. Thomas Telford attributed this fact to land improvement. River improvements along the Upper Severn had included the raising of banks to protect fields. In previous times of flood, water covered these fields, and acted as a temporary reservoir that slowly released water back into the river and aided navigation. With banking the water kept to the channel and flowed quickly away. Such water was now lost to aid boats after the floods subsided.

Free trade also led to hostility against making a towing path along the banks. A towing path was sanctioned from Bewdley to Meadows Wharf after an Act of 1772, but little was done. Towpath construction powers for the Bewdley towpath were modified and strengthened by an Act of 1799 that enabled the path to be finished from Coalbrookdale to Bewdley (c.1800). A second path from Bewdley to Stourport and Diglis was authorised in 1803 and completed about 1804. These paths were later continued under new Acts to Shrewsbury (1809) and to Gloucester (1812) and together formed a communication between Shrewsbury and the partings at Gloucester. They were built for and maintained by the four towing path companies. They collected tolls for horse traction and made it possible for narrowboats to work through to Severn ports such as Bewdley, Bridgnorth, Coalbrookdale, Worcester, Tewkesbury and Gloucester. The towpaths were not confined to one bank or the other, but changed sides from west to east, partly to avoid bridging rivers and brooks and partly to bypass industrial premises such as wharves and quarries.

The Shrewsbury Towpath Company looked after the path north of Meadows Wharf. The Severn Horse Towing Path operated between Meadows Wharf and Bewdley. From Bewdley to Diglis a third company, the Severn Towing Path Extension Company, maintained the way between Bewdley and Worcester, whilst the Gloucester & Worcester controlled the river bank between Diglis and Gloucester. They all acted like turnpikes with toll houses. The Severn Towing Path, like some of the road contemporaries, let the toll for three separate sections of the towing path:

1 Bewdley Bridge–Bridgnorth Bridge
2 Bridgnorth Bridge and Wood Bridge, near Coalport
3 Wood Bridge and Meadows Wharf

Their path followed the west bank from Bewdley through to Jackfield, north of Coalport. From here the path crossed over and continued along the 'north' bank to Meadows Wharf. Infrastructure included bridges, some made of iron, where the towing path passed over a stream or river. Some structures still remain. There is an iron bridge built by J. Onion of Broseley (1824) over the Mor Brook and another iron bridge built by the Coalbrookdale Company (1828) across the Borle Brook. Towpath bridges were also provided by the other towing path companies, including a stone bridge over the Leighton Brook (Shrewsbury Company) and the Stour (Severn Extension Company).

River bridges were used by the horse owners to cross the Severn at convenient places. Stourport Bridge served as a cross-over point for the Severn Extension Company when their path changed from west to east bank, whilst the Gloucester & Worcestershire used Upton Bridge to change sides from east to west bank. The Shrewsbury Company used Cressage Bridge to cross from the east to west bank.

Ferries were provided to carry the horses from one side to another when the path changed sides. The Shrewsbury Company employed a horse ferry near Underdale, Shrewsbury. The Severn Company provided a ferry at Jackfield, whilst the Severn Extension Company had a ferry at Grimley, near Hawford. The Gloucester & Worcestershire Company path crossed near Ashleworth, Gloucestershire.

Another horse towing path company controlled towage along the River Wye between Lydbrook and Hereford. The Act authorising the path received Royal Assent in 1809 and the towing path was opened during 1811. It was 37 miles long and had five horse ferries at the places where the path changed sides.

There were times when politics rather than trade influenced the development of navigations. The town of Burton upon Trent lay within the manor owned by Lord Paget. It was a town that was benefiting from increased prosperity, but relied on the roads of the time for the movement of goods and merchandise.

William, the sixth Lord Paget, was a member of the House of Lords at one of the crucial points of British history, when the Prince of Orange took his place on the British throne as William III. Lord Paget was a supporter of the protestant cause and gained royal favour through his support. In September 1689 William Paget was appointed British Ambassador at Vienna and subsequently served as Ambassador Extraordinary to Turkey. The appointment in Turkey proved to be a successful one and Paget earned respect for his role in the negotiations for various peace treaties with the Turks. These achievements would have helped Paget with affairs at home. A few months before the Treaty of Carlowitz was signed, the Act to improve the Trent Navigation was presented to Parliament:

> An act for making and keeping the River Trent in the Counties of Leicester, Derby and Stafford navigable

> Be enacted that the right honourable William Lord Paget, Baron of Beaudesert, Lord of the Manor of Burton in the counties of Stafford and Derby, his agents, workmen etc are hereby empowered to make said River Trent navigable for boats, barges, lighters and other vessels from a certain place called Wilden Ferry up the said river to the town of Burton-on-Trent. Erecting all such dams, locks, turnpikes and other things necessary and convenient for the making thereof. And also to make, set out and appoint towing and haling paths and ways convenient for towing, hauling and drawing of boats, barges and other vessels passing on said river.

Navigation of the Trent to Burton became possible after an Act of Parliament sanctioned the work in December 1698. Making the river navigable took time, but eventually two locks were built at Burton and Kings Mill. Ownership of the navigation to Burton was controlled by the Paget family and the later Earls of Stafford and Marquis of Anglesey.

An important landowner in the district, at this time, was the Coke family who owned the Manor of Castle Donington and the Wilden Ferry, which had become a vital river crossing on road from Derby to Loughborough and London. John Coke was active in the revolution that brought William and Mary to the throne, whilst his son Thomas Coke (1674–1727) was Member of Parliament for Derbyshire.

Traffic on the Trent was in the hands of a select group of carriers, most notably the Fosbrookes. The Fosbrookes were descended from a family of mercers and river traders based at Trent Bridge, Nottingham, who in 1609 signed an agreement to carry coals down the River Trent to Gainsborough for Sir Percival Willoughby of Wollaton. Their headquarters was subsequently transferred to Wilden Ferry when the ferry and adjacent land were leased from the Cokes. From here they built up a lucrative navigation trade.

Men named Leonard headed several generations of the Fosbrooke family. The first Leonard Fosbrooke died in 1670, and his son Leonard was in charge of the navigation trade along the Trent from Wilden Ferry to Gainsborough. Wilden became a transhipping place for goods between river and road, especially for traffic bound for Derby and parts of Staffordshire. It was here that the Fosbrookes built a warehouse and such were the profits of this trade that Leonard Fosbrooke II

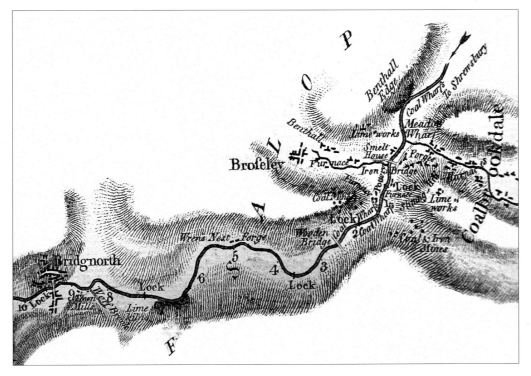

G. Young's Map of 1786: Locks for Severn Navigation – plans to build locks between Diglis and Coalbrookdale were put forward in 1786. In this 10-mile section of Young's map for the part from Bridgnorth–Meadows Wharf, there are five locks. Coal wharves, limeworks, forges and furnaces are identified, as are the Iron Bridge at Coalbrookdale and the wooden bridge at Coalport.

Above left: Mythe Bridge spans the River Severn at Tewkesbury in a single iron span. Completed during 1825, Mythe was one of three single-span bridges constructed for new roads across the Severn in the 1820s; the others were at Holt Fleet and Haw. The foundation stone for the Mythe Bridge was laid in October 1823 for a three-span bridge on stone piers to the design of George Moneypenny. This design was changed in 1824, when a new proposal by Thomas Telford was agreed for the single 175ft span. (Author)

Above right: Mythe Bridge was built as a river crossing from Mythe Hill for the Tewkesbury Roads. The toll house at the bridge remains. (Author)

Above left: Atcham Bridge was a masonry bridge that spanned the Severn south of Shrewsbury. Provision was made for the Horse Towing Path Company to pass under the bridge. (Author)

Above right: The limit of the Trent Navigation in 1699 was near Shardlow, shown here. (Author)

Above left: The bridge house at Cavendish Bridge on the Leicestershire bank. (Author)

Above right: Tolls were taken at Cavendish Bridge. (Author)

was able to purchase land at Shardlow and between 1680 and 1684 built Shardlow Hall, its grounds stretching down to the River Trent.

Wilden's crucial role was about to change as schemes to make navigable both the Upper Trent to Burton and the River Derwent to Derby were proposed. Paget's Bill was presented before Parliament in the session August to December 1698. Parliament sanctioned this Act and gave rights to the right honourable William Lord Paget and his men to make the River Trent navigable for vessels from Wilden Ferry up to the town of Burton-on-Trent. He was to erect dams, locks, turnpikes and whatever else was necessary for the making of the navigation, and also to make towing and haling paths for towing, hauling and drawing of all vessels passing along that section of river.

Some crucial wording gave William Paget the exclusive right to make warehouses and wharves. Only those wharves and warehouses already made were out of William Paget's control and thus any future developments would benefit Paget's agents through charging wharf dues.

Boatmen or halers were prohibited from the lands of the Earl of Huntingdon, on the south side of the River Trent, which effectively restricted the haling path to the northern, or Derbyshire bank of the river. Duties, rates or prices exceeded not three pence by the 'tun', and so were proportionate to that rate for any greater or lesser quantity. Permission was given to make a lock or locks between the four floodgates then placed in the weir of the said Earl and the end of Weston Pasture.

Arrangement for making the navigation was left in the hands of Paget's son Henry, who was MP for Stafford. Initial improvements to the Trent between Burton and Wilden appear somewhat minimal.

Some twelve years would elapse since the passing of the Upper Trent Navigation Act before any significant improvement would be made. William Paget was now dead and Henry Paget was in control of Paget family affairs. Fosbrooke had handled trade on the river up to Burton, but by 1711 the service provided by Fosbrooke was considered unsatisfactory and arrangements were made with George Hayne to lease the Upper Trent Navigation. Hayne saw profit particularly in the rights for warehouses and wharves on the river and spent some £5,000 making improvements to the Upper Trent. This work was conducted over a number of years and included the building of the lock at Kings Mills, a haling path, horse bridges and wharves at Burton and Willington.

Two pound locks were maintained on the Upper Trent; the other was at Burton Mill, east of Burton Bridge. When George Hayne died, Henry Hayne (brother to George) took over the lease and finally John Hayne had it when Henry died (1757–62). The lease was due for renewal in 1762 and control of the navigation passed to the Burton Boat Company with effect from 10 October 1762.

Those that navigated the Upper Trent also had legal rights for transport through to Gainsborough. The real power, however, lay with the Corporation of Nottingham who controlled the wharves at Trent Bridge. Though wide and sometimes fast-flowing, the Trent had its share of shoals and shallows. There were bends where the river course sometimes meandered into loop. All such obstacles limited navigation to a group of flat-bottomed barges that became commonly known as 'Trent Boats'. Those who navigated this part of the river were well aware of its limitations and worked with them. They gave names to geographical features that later surveyors and engineers would use as landmarks for any improvements they cared to suggest.

The part from Nottingham eastward comprised ancient river navigations. According to Charles Deering in his *History of Nottingham* (1751), the Trent was one of the four great rivers of England, then navigable to Burton upon Trent:

> But has been frequented by vessels of burthen as far as Nottingham, time immemorial, and that it was so before the conquest appears clearly by the doomsday [sic] book, where it is said that waters of the Trent, the ditch and the road to York, was kept by Nottingham, in as much, that if any one should hinder the passage of vessels, plough, or dig a hole within two perches of the king's highway, he should pay a fine of 8 pounds.

For the Trent, tributaries included the Tame, Dove, Derwent, Erewash, Soar and Leen. In 1634 Thomas Skipwith obtained a grant of letters patent to make the Soar navigable from the Trent to Leicester, influenced principally by the prospect of moving coal by water. This work was carried out for some 5 or 6 miles and then abandoned for lack of funds.

Derby lay beside the River Derwent and various attempts to make this river navigable at least as far as Derby were made with applications to Parliament at various times from 1664–98, but objections from landowners and businessmen had halted the progress at the House of Commons stage. In 1702 a more determined effort was produced, supported by a survey conducted by George Sorocold. The improvement included four cuts, three designed to avoid bends in the river and a channel to avoid the weir at Wilne. The first channel and lock was at the junction with the Trent. A lock at Wilne Cut was then followed by another cut with two locks that rejoined the Derwent near Borrowash Mill. There was a lock at Borrowash Mill and then another new cut with three locks that avoided bends of the river near Alverston. There was a final lock on the mill stream at the Holmes and close to this a wharf for Derby, near the Morledge, was planned. The rise was stated as 50ft from the Trent to Derby Wharf. The 1702 scheme passed the Commons and went before the House of Lords, where again the Bill was defeated. At some point the long cuts were omitted from the application. Fresh attempts were again made from 1717 and the Derwent Navigation Bill finally passed the Lords on 17 March 1720 and received Royal Assent on 7 April. The navigation was 16 miles long.

It should be remembered that at this time the calendar year was from April to March and authority to make the navigation was made in 1721. Work was quickly carried out when locks were provided at Wilne, Borrowash, and near the terminus of the navigation at Derby near the Morledge.

When in 1789 an enquiry was held into water being diverted from the Derwent to supply the proposed Cromford Canal, John and William Holmes were called to give evidence as to the levels of water in the river. John noted the shortages in the summer and the limitation to navigation that resulted in the use of lighters. William Holmes, bookkeeper at the Wharf, confirmed summer loadings were reduced to one third or less, but with a lighter might carry 4 tons more. The principal trade was to Gainsborough but traffic on the Derby Navigation comprised six boats a week travelling up to Derby. The weekly volume of traffic is an indication that locks on this navigation were of the single barrier type.

Navigation works on the Soar, conducted by Skipwith, had been allowed to decay when a century later interest in the navigation of the Soar was rekindled. Plans to build a navigation through to the Rushes and Hermitage pool at Loughborough had been granted in an Act of 1766, but frequent floods along the Soar had made the task difficult. James Brindley surveyed the navigation after the Act had been obtained. He provided costs for different options but was principally in favour of making a canal for much of the route. The navigation proprietors did not have the powers to do as Brindley had suggested and chose to do nothing. Another nine years would pass before a group of Derbyshire coal owners and Loughborough businessmen led to a revival of the Soar Navigation. They promoted a second scheme in 1775. The Bill was one of a group that King George III was pleased to give Royal Assent on 2 April 1776 at the House of Peers. It was a mixed bag of Acts that included the better regulation of pilots conducting vessels into and out of the port of Boston in Lincolnshire, the Dudley Canal Act and the Stourbridge Canal Act. The Loughborough Bill enabled the River Soar to be made navigable from the Trent to Bishop's Meadow at Garenton and the making of a short canal 1½ miles long constructed to the Rushes at Loughborough.

John Smith was appointed engineer in charge of the work and he was granted a contract to first make the river navigable to Bishop's Meadow. Smith had worked on navigations such as the River Ure Navigation and the Market Weighton Canal. He presented the estimate (£3,418) at a proprietors' meeting held at the home of Michael Ella in May 1776. A contract was drawn up where Smith was answerable for all risks either by floods or other accidents that may happen in forming the navigation.

Meanwhile the company set about land valuation for cuts, towing paths and locks. The first lock to be made was to be done at Kegworth. In June, Smith produced plans for this lock and a swivel bridge. A piece of ground in Kegworth pasture was also dug for clay and it was here that a kiln was later erected. During October 1776 Smith presented an estimate (£1,999) for the cut from Bishop's Meadow to the Rushes. He also decided to use Donnington stone for the Kegworth lock.

North of Kegworth and near the Trent, a single barrier lock, or staunch, was erected. The site chosen was at Redhill. Here the work comprised making a weir, lining the banks of the river with stone and erecting a windlass to haul the boats through the staunch. A toll house was also to be built. The committee were keen to have the navigation open to Kegworth lock by 1 August 1777.

By May 1777 Smith was completing the Redhill Dam. He had made the cut across Kegworth Pasture, scoured and deepened the river there, built Kegworth Mill Lock and also made the cut back into the Soar. The cut to Zouch Mill lock was finished and he then made the lock pit at Zouch Mill as well as preparing the lock at Bishop's Meadow for the canal to the Rushes.

During the summer of 1777 Smith started to encounter several problems. The committee criticised the cement and mortar used in the locks and he was told to replace them. As soon as the staunch was used the difficulties of navigating through it became clear to the committee and they told Smith to build a replacement pound lock there. They also decided to make an arch bridge instead of a swivel bridge for the turnpike at Zouch. This was all unplanned and extra work for Smith, who fell behind with his other tasks. Summer floods on the Soar also caused havoc.

William Jessop was asked to report on the work done. He made various recommendations that would cost the proprietors in excess of £2,000. Jessop complimented Smith's work but indicated the cutting of the locks and lock cuts should be deeper. Much of the expense was directed towards the uncompleted canal section to Loughborough and the replacement of the staunch at Redhill

The weir and mill at Burton as seen from the end of the old lock cut. (Author)

with a lock and new weir to the south, nearer Radcliffe. During April 1778 the order was given for building a lock at Redhill to the same dimensions as the lock then being built in Thorpe Field.

John Smith left the contract, and much of the new work and alterations was conducted under the supervision of John May. He was responsible for building swing bridges and making the towing path from Thorpe Field to Loughborough. A temporary bridge at Zouch Mill built by Smith had given way and May was requested to replace it with a brick bridge. Certain turns in the Soar at Lockington and Kegworth were also cut straighter for the convenience of the boats.

Improvements carried on after the nominal opening of the waterway in 1778. A summary of May's 'overlooking' of the works since John Smith had left made in April 1779 included the following:

1   Thorpe Field Lock and Redhill Lock
2   Taken up staunch and had deepened and widened the river
3   Made assigned places in cuts, which were made by Mr Smith the same not sufficient before the passage of the boats
4   Rebuilt Radclife Dam that was blown up some time before Mr Smith left the works
5   Repaired several embankments
6   Made three swing bridges in Thorpe Field, Bishop's Meadow and Kegworth Mill
7   Made several haling bridges and towpath gates
8   Additional stone work at Zouch Lock to prevent overflowing
9   Taken down temporary bridge and built one with a brick arch over canal near Zouch Mill
10 Walled and paved the proprietors wharf and secured the banks of bason with piles and planks, put down at Proprietors Wharf, erecting a weighing machine
11 Made several cloughs and dams for taking water from the malt mill and Thorpe Brook
12 Cutting of River Speight in Lockington and Kegworth

Like other river navigations, the Soar to Loughborough was subject to alteration and improvement. With the rising of weirs and deepening and straightening of the river course, the arrangement of locks came to total seven. There were five on the river section and two on the canal. Starting from the Trent these were Redhill, Ratcliffe, Kegworth Shallow, Kegworth Top, Zouch, Bishop's Meadow and Loughborough.

Until 1783, the Trent remained essentially an unaltered waterway where halers walked along the side of the river as they did on the Severn. The perils of haling are aptly demonstrated by the following published report of May 1778:

> Yesterday se'nnight an uncommon tho' fatal accident beset one William Smith, a net maker of Sawley in this country- He was requested in what is called hailing a down boat off a gravel bed a little above Thrumpton and being the last of seventeen and nearest the boat , the rope unfortunately broke between his an the next man before him, by the elasticity or spring of which, he was suddenly cast three or four yards in the air and fell down upon a gravel bed and tho' no bones were broke yet so great was the concussion that a whole mass of blood was coagulated, his body soon appeared black and he died early the next morning . He has left a disconsolate widow and children who are real objects of charity to opulent benevolence.

Derby Mercury, 8 May 1778

The River Trent and the entrance to the Erewash Canal. (Author)

The River Trent Navigation route to Nottingham was changed with the completion of the Beeston to Lenton cut (1796) and the making of an L-shaped weir to raise levels of the Trent between Cranfleet and Beeston. (Author)

Sawley Lock – the double lock on the Trent Navigation. (Author)

Improvement of the River Trent had been made at Newark in 1773, with the provision of a weir at Averham and the making of a canal from the top of the weir through land to join up with the River Devon. Two locks at Newark and Newark Nether then lowered the navigation enough to rejoin the western course of the Trent north of the town.

Further improvements were now sought, yet ten years were to pass before any work would be done. A meeting was held at the White Lion, Nottingham, on Thursday 23 August 1783 to consider application to Parliament to improve the River Trent. Further meetings followed at public houses at Newark and Nottingham where plans and estimates were produced. The Trent, although a long-established navigation, had no proper towing path and the various shallows and bends hampered navigation. During 1783 the Trent Navigation Company was established to improve river navigation and build haling paths for the canal carriers. William Jessop was appointed engineer for the Trent Navigation. He came to this region with a lengthy list of canal engineering successes on waterways such as the Aire & Calder and Calder & Hebble.

Work began on obtaining land for the towing path from Cavendish Bridge through to Gainsborough and then laying out the path. Such work included the provision of suitable bridges where streams and tributaries were crossed. Certain bends in the river were also eliminated. Yet essentially it remained the same navigation as before.

Once revenue from tolls started to accrue, further improvements were done. The first was the straight cut through marshland at Hemmington Pasture near Sawley, which was started during 1790. The cut was made through the land of Henry Harpur, who gave permission for the making of a single lock, but no flood lock or gates. Then came the important survey conducted by Robert Whitworth and William Jessop that looked at the shallows and winding course of the river.

The two engineers made their report to the Navigation Board in 1793. Their suggestions involved major reconstruction, including the building of weirs at Sawley, Soars Mouth, Beeston and Holme. The weir across the Trent east of the meeting of the Soar benefited both the Trent and Soar navigations and led to the making of the Cranfleet Cut and Lock on the Trent and the new Redhill Lock on the Soar. Deepening, further straightening and the making of additional towing paths were also needed.

At Beeston the weir raised levels on the section through from Cranfleet to Beeston, and with the making of the Nottingham Canal underway, Whitworth and Jessop suggested a union between river navigation and canal to bypass the difficult and shallow approach by river to Trent Bridge. A new cut from Beeston to Lenton to join the Nottingham Canal was proposed, accepted and ratified by Act of Parliament in 1794.

In order to preserve trade to Wilford a second lock was provided at Beeston for Trent Boats to pass onto the Trent again. Any boat choosing to avoid the tolls on the Nottingham Canal could also pass this way and face the troubles of the shallows to Trent Bridge. Making the cut and weir at Holme, north of Trent Bridge, raised water in the river there, creating a pool for boats entering or leaving both the Grantham and Nottingham canals.

CHAPTER 2

CANAL INFRASTRUCTURE:
EARLY CANAL CONSTRUCTION

The fabric of our waterways is one of the most enduring features that has survived down to the present day. It is a varied heritage that includes aqueducts, bridges, cuttings, embankments and locks. The contribution of scores of engineers has left a unique legacy throughout Britain. Many different styles are preserved in brick, iron or stone, each a continuing testament to the skills of the designer and those that built it.

West Midlands canals were constructed over a lengthy time period. More than ninety years would pass between the first and the last. In calendar years this effectively amounted to 1766 through to 1863. For the East Midlands the period of canal making was shorter, starting with the Erewash Canal (1777) and finishing with the completion of the (Old) Grand Union Canal in 1814.

Canal making began in the Midlands with two major waterways and both were conceived as part of a greater scheme. They were the Grand Trunk, or the canal from the Trent to the Mersey, and the Wolverhampton Canal that became better known as the Staffordshire & Worcestershire Canal. The complete scheme was known as the Grand Cross and the main objective was intended to unite the rivers Severn, Mersey and Trent through inland navigation.

Both canals followed closely river valleys and were somewhat direct. The engineer in charge of the work was James Brindley (1716–72). Brindley seems to have chosen river valleys as convenient paths for his waterways, and such routes were an improvement to the former practice of making the rivers navigable. Historians have often dubbed Brindley as the constructor of winding navigations lacking major engineering works and adhering to the contours of the land. Yet whilst this was true for a select group of waterways, it cannot be said to specifically apply to Brindley and the canals that he was directly responsible for. The more circuitous navigations can be attributed to those projects where his assistants came to have control. The Oxford Canal is a particular example where the surveyor-cum-engineer Samuel Simcox chose to tackle the terrain by crossing streams and rivers at the head of the valley and curving the navigation around the hillside, thereby reducing expensive cutting, embanking and tunnelling.

Work started almost at the same time on both waterways. Construction methods were similar, although the understanding of how this was done is better documented for the Staffordshire & Worcestershire Canal. Here James Brindley exercised direct control over construction. Brindley's official status was Surveyor, as the role of canal engineer was then not properly defined. His name appears in company records in matters of surveys and construction. Yet here too were his lieutenants Robert Whitworth and Samuel Simcox, who acted as assistant surveyors. Cutting began around and below the agreed summit level at Compton during September 1766 and continued onto the Severn at Mitton where the original barge basins and locks formed the means of communications between the canal and river. The hamlet that grew up around the basins became known as Stourport.

Part of the challenge presented to Brindley was the design of suitable locks, the placing of these locks and setting the amount of fall. Cutting and embanking to fit in with the locks at the correct level was a key element to the making of the waterway. James Brindley seemed keen to set the fall of each lock as near to 10ft as possible.

A steady descent took the canal from the summit level down to Wombourne and the Bratch locks, which were originally built as a staircase with three chambers, each with an approximate fall of 10ft. Here there was a steep slope and Brindley and his team decided to build a staircase arrangement of locks instead of spreading the locks apart. There would have been a saving in construction costs using this method. Brindley used a similar arrangement at Meaford, Etruria and Lawton on the Trent & Mersey Canal main line. With the staircase type the bottom gates of the top chamber became the top gates of the next chamber and the same applied to the gates between the middle and bottom chamber. John Fennyhouse Green carried out an accurate survey of this canal complete with compass bearings in 1772. He shows the locks as a staircase and a circular weir. South of the Bratch, Brindley built a two-chamber staircase at Botterham complete again with a circular weir.

Making lock gates required a special skill with carpentry, and in this respect the Staffordshire & Worcestershire Canal was lucky to find a local man. Thomas Dadford was married to Frances Brown in Wolverhampton during 1759. His skill originally lay with carpentry and he was appointed carpenter to the canal company. A minute book entry records the appointment:

17 March 1767 at Red Lyon Inn, Wolverhampton

That a contract be made by our clerk with Thomas Dadford a carpenter and joiner to serve us in a way of said trades in prosecuting and carrying on the navigation for the space of five years if

The Bratch Locks as seen in 1979 – these locks were altered on at least two different occasions. The additional gates were installed when Thomas Dadford was asked to improve the locks. He provided side pounds, one to supply water to the middle lock and the other for the bottom lock. Later the side pound arrangement was further changed so that water cascaded down through the pounds from the upper level. (Author)

the said navigation shall not be sooner completed at salary of twenty pounds per annum payable monthly, but if from sickness or any other cause the said Thomas Dadford should not be able to attend upon his said office or employment or should fail so to do, a proportional abatement to be made in his said salary. The said Dadford to provide the persons necessary to work under his direction but to have no profit whatsoever from them.

Dadford was evidently employed from an earlier time than the minute records. John Baker's cash accounts record the first payment to Thomas Dadford on 6 December 1766.

The job of clerk of works had been given to John Baker and this was confirmed at the company meeting held on 24 June 1766. His salary was £200 per year. Baker's assistant was John Fennyhouse Green who surveyed and measured up the completed work. His appointment was confirmed at the same meeting as Dadford's, but Green's salary was a lowly £50 per year. Green also started measuring up contractors' work from October 1766, previous to his recorded appointment.

Many of Green's detailed notebooks and sketches for the construction of the canal have survived and these provide a window into the long-forgotten age of early canal building. They included levelling details and the setting of the stakes that determined the route of the canal. At this period the route could be varied depending on water supply, possession of land and opposition from landowners.

Work on building the canal was allocated in sections with the canal company exercising strict and direct control on the appointment of canal cutters, bricklayers, brickmakers, stone cutters and stone getters. The cutters worked with shovels, barrows and planks. It was a hard manual job working across a varied terrain, and in all weathers. Green was the man on the spot, checking their work on a regular basis. He most likely did this on horseback, in view of the distances covered between inspections. Allowances were made for the material moved and apart from earth, rock and sods of grass, there was gravel, 'running' gravel and quicksand. Trees had to be felled, bushes cut down and all the roots dug out. Green's records mention all this in the contractor's expenses. Every-day use of barrows and planks for wheeling was recorded and charged. Every different type of strata encountered had a different rate. Such a complicated pay structure was not the best formula and, with subsequent canal making, was simplified. Water courses were altered and new drainage channels put in. Aqueducts, brick-arch bridges, locks and wooden swivel bridges constructed. Cuttings were dug, embankments made and tunnels excavated, all done with the most basic of tools.

The design and making of locks for narrow waterways are often said to have originated on the Staffordshire & Worcestershire Canal. The credit for the design is laid firmly with James Brindley. L.T.C. Rolt mentioned this fact in his book *Navigable Waterways* (1969), where he noted that Brindley developed an experimental lock in the grounds of his home at Turnhurst, near the summit of the Trent & Mersey Canal. The standard became a chamber with a single upper gate closing against a cill (sill) at right angles to the lock walls and double mitre gates at the opposite end. These lower gates had to extend to the bottom of the chamber and the weight of timber required was considered too heavy for a single gate. Sluices or paddles were raised by rack and pinion gear to admit water into the chamber or drain it out. Paddles had become a standard feature on river navigation locks, but these were restricted to the gates. With Brindley's design, ground paddles were provided to prevent water discharging from the upper gate over the bows of the boat.

Such is the flow of water on the canal that bypass weirs and channels were installed. Brindley no doubt appreciated that the diversion of the flow made opening the top gates an easier task and prevented water flooding over the gates.

It is quite possible that Brindley's experiments with lock design extended to the first-made locks on the Staffordshire & Worcestershire Canal. The steady fall presented several possible test sites. It is also possible that side weirs were not considered necessary at first, but were incorporated after trials with the first locks. With construction stretching out along the length towards

Wombourne, there was opportunity for experiment as cutters made the channel. Where streams were encountered it was possible to run water to the lock chamber and test the method.

Published histories have recorded that the first lock was made at Compton. The reasoning being that this connected with the summit level and had access to water from the Penford Feeder. The design of the circular weir adopted at Compton is also seen as a key reason for the claim that the first lock was there. Circular weirs became a standard feature along the canal as it was constructed towards Kinver and Debdale. Yet the existence of simple bypass channels at Wightwick Lock and Dimmingsdale Lock give credence to an alternative course of progress. The basic weir and open channel was a simpler device than the circular weir and such a device might be considered to pre-date the more carefully engineered circular weir. For this reason Wightwick Lock with its basic weir may well have been put into use before Compton using water from a stream that was culverted under the canal above the lock. Dimmingsdale has an even more basic bypass channel that starts some distance from the lock on the opposite side to the towpath. The arrangement there now is similar to Green's drawings of the channel in 1772, and so this lock can also be considered a candidate for the title of the first trial lock.

Green's notebooks reveal that by October 1766 contractors were working on different parts of the route that stretched out from Penford on the summit through Compton and Wightwick to Wombourne. The first mention of the location of locks appears in the December 1766 measuring for John Beswick reaching up to the head of Compton Lock. He was also cutting at Mopps Farm to the south of Wightwick, whilst John Embries was cutting south of Compton.

The main contractors, as listed in Baker's accounts for 1766, were John Beswick, William Bowker, John Embries, James Hogg and Thomas Trannter; they all signed with their names and therefore they had certain literacy. Beswick, an experienced contractor who had worked on building the Bridgewater Canal, had a team that included John Clegg; both Beswick and Clegg would sign for moneys received for the Staffordshire & Worcestershire contracts. Beswick's wife Ann also collected money, but she signed with a mark.

Construction work was also done by a Ralph Shephard, who signed with his mark. Bowker, Embries and Shephard continued on with cutting, embanking and digging throughout the building of the canal; Beswick went onto other projects, such as the Birmingham Canal. James Hogg was sacked from his contract, in 1768, and replaced by his foreman Harry Hurst.

Some bricklayers also signed their name, whilst brickmakers signed by a mark. Thomas Pratt received several payments for bricklaying; he signed his name. The making of bricks was rarely done in the kiln at this time but in a temporary structure known as the clamp. This was a hit-and-miss process that sometimes led to a considerable waste of burnt bricks. In June 1768, Edward Bedall (who signed with his mark) was paid £7 12s 3d for 14,500 bricks burnt in a clamp of 25,500. The other 11,000 were unsuitable as they were burnt 'too soft' the previous year.

Wightwick Lock on the Staffordshire & Worcestershire has a fall of 8ft 8in and, unlike Compton and Wightwick Mill Lock, lacks a circular weir, but has a simpler arrangement of overflow weir and channel. (Author)

Circular weir, Compton – the circular weir was installed at many of the earliest locks on the Staffordshire & Worcestershire Canal. It is a design linked to James Brindley. (Author)

Samuel Brawn, a mason, signed with his name, as did his sons James and John. As the contract to build the canal neared its completion, John Brawn, mason, was engaged with increasingly varied works to do with the making of this canal. This no doubt provided suitable experience for the time when he would take on the task of building a complete canal.

An essential part of the work was the cutting of the canal, erecting bridges and making the towpath. When the site of a lock was decided, contractors would first dig out the 'lock pitt'. There are references to William Fewster and Robert Perry cutting out the 'pitt' at Wightwick in March 1767. They went on to excavate others including Greens Forge and the bottom lock chamber at the Bratch.

These were early days for the 'canal contractor'. John Baker's accounts show the relationship between company and contractor as essentially one of employer and employee. The company had the right to dismiss when the work did not reach the required standard. Different people were employed for different skills and whilst those who agreed to do the job may have a number of men under their control, they worked to the instructions of the canal company, their staff and appointed engineers.

Those responsible for cutting the canal, essentially the navigators (or 'navvies'), were a specific breed of men. They endured often harsh conditions to dig out the channel. Such people are often depicted as itinerant workers moving from job to job, following the work as they found it. Some were loyal and stayed with the contractor as he arranged the jobs. This of course was not simply canals, but might be drainage or mill work, or possibly making turnpikes or tramroads. Such contractors might have work in different parts of the country and deployed men accordingly.

Following the lives of the navigators is often difficult as spelling of their names varied. John Beswick, who worked for Brindley on the Bridgewater Canal, was referred to as 'Busick' in Brindley's notebooks. He undertook a number of canal-building projects at the same time as working on the cutting of the summit level of the Staffordshire & Worcestershire Canal through Aldersley, and had also a contract to make Kymer's Canal in South Wales. James Hogg, whilst building the canal in the Kidderminster district, was also engaged in work on the Coventry Canal.

A key element was money. Canal construction had become the biggest spender in Britain. Considerable finance was required to complete such extensive and complicated engineering projects. Men were drawn to the work to get a wage and perhaps escape alternative occupations such as agricultural labouring. Yet at the same time new groups of workers were created. Most important were the professional contractors who went from job to job and canal to canal. In this way a nucleus of skilled workers came into being that enabled canal building to evolve and techniques improved with

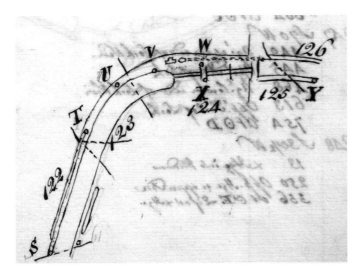

A sketch from John Green's notebook for Bratch, dating from 1772. (The original is at Staffordshire Records Office, MS 3186)

Left: Staffordshire & Worcestershire Canal, Dunstall Water Bridge. (Author)

Below: Dunstall Water Bridge was built to convey the Smestow Brook over the canal. James Brindley took particular interest to ensure that this 'aqueduct' was completed to his specific instructions. (Author)

experience. Credit for this development must be placed at the door of the canal proprietors and their legacy was skilled contractors moving from canal to railway construction in later times.

The making of artificial waterways, such as the first canals or the eighteenth-century Fens drainage schemes, may be said to have created civil engineering. Men were drawn into this discipline as more became known about the methods of cutting, bridge building, aqueducts and tunnels. Pioneers like James Brindley and John Smeaton laid the foundations for this new discipline, followed by such worthies as Robert Whitworth, William Jessop, John Rennie and Thomas Telford. Of these men, Telford is best recognised, at least in historical texts, for furthering the cause of civil engineering and when the institution for this discipline was set up, Telford became the first president.

John Smeaton also left his mark in civil engineering, and some accounts credit him with the invention of the term. Smeaton engaged in diverse projects including the Eddystone Lighthouse, various bridges and windmills. His canal works were just as diverse. From 1758 until 1764 he was surveyor to the Calder & Hebble Canal in Yorkshire, which established the barge navigation from Wakefield to Sowerby Bridge. Smeaton's design of the locks formed a model for others to follow, no doubt being useful for James Brindley, his replacement, in 1765. Brindley's association with the Calder & Hebble, though brief, must have been invaluable when considering the different engineering challenges narrow canal locks would present.

The frequent references to James Brindley in Green's notebooks indicate that he made regular visits to the works and was particular in his instructions, expecting them to be carried out.

During September 1767, James Brindley visited Ralph Shephard's work at Gothersley and observed the bad slipping there. He stopped the work and arranged for Green to measure up what was done and then ordered Green to survey a new route around the slip. A month later, Brindley was at the summit inspecting Beswick's work. Here there were problems of slipping, quicksand and cutting through rock. Extra allowances were agreed for the work.

There was a piece of work known as the 'Water Bridge'. This structure was constructed to carry the Smestow Brook over the route of the canal, in John Beswick's work. The Smestow was an important water supply to drive the various mills along its route, which included Grange Furnace.

James Brindley inspected the construction in 1769 when it began and was clearly unhappy about the progress. He told Green that the 'battering' on the outside piers should begin at the bottom water level. Edward Guest, contractor for the bridge, had not done this. Green received a reprimand in letter form from the canal committee as a result:

To John Green

We are informed that the workmen employed at the water bridge are pursuing methods very contrary to Mr Brindley's directions and doubt will provide injurious to the proprietors, who have already suffered greatly from mismanagement therefore we insist your strict observance of Brindley's orders and hereby empower you to discharge any workman, that attempts to deviate from the same – and if you find any alterations requisite in what is already done wrong desire you'll give order therein, and take account of same.

Wolverhampton, 5 July 1769

Signed
J. Weston Smith
James Perry
P. Hinkes
Wm Wenman
Henry Wood junior

For Thomas Dadford the building work encountered on this canal was particularly helpful for it enabled him to learn the basis of map drawing and surveying. Green mentions Dadford's assistance in this matter on several occasions. Dadford visited Tewkesbury in January 1769 to view the arrangement of the Avon River Lock there, then Green and Dadford worked together in setting out the locks into the River Severn during March 1769. Ralph Sheppard excavated the basins and 'lock pitts' in August 1769.

Part of the work involved diversion, at places, of the River Stour. At Falling Sands near Kidderminster, Harry Hurst and his men had to move the bed of the Stour before making the waterway. Green also mentions in his notebooks evidence of the former River Stour Navigation, which had been made a century earlier.

Construction of the Staffordshire & Worcestershire Canal may have started in the direction of Stourport, but the gradual opening to trade and traffic happened in reverse with sections of the canal opening to Kidderminster, Stewponey and then Compton and Tettenhall. Construction then continued northward through Penkridge to the outskirts of Stafford finally crossing the Trent by an aqueduct near Great Hayward Junction.

Making the sections north of Aldersley was under way by 1769 and during the next three years continued gradually northwards until Great Hayward was reached. Problems continued to arise and one concerned the route the canal took through Calf Heath. Brindley and Simcox clearly differed on the deviation needed there. Meanwhile contractors continued to be allotted different sections, but the terrain was different to the southern section. The work lay across fields and pasture where temporary roads were laid to assist the work.

Harry Hurst altered the water course at Shut Hill Lock, whilst other contractors moved the course of the Sow to make the aqueduct. The canal near Haywood was made along a raised embankment, where soil and turf from the adjacent fields was gathered up for 'ramparting' and 'sodding'. By February 1772, Hurst was digging out the basin at Great Hayward and the bed of the canal, ready to form a junction with the Trent & Mersey Canal.

Following Brindley's death Thomas Dadford was appointed engineer to the Staffordshire & Worcestershire Canal. It became his task to make the waterway fit for trade. This included the

The original and main basin at Stourport, on the Staffordshire & Worcestershire, was a rough square excavation that was dug out to form a haven for river barges and trows that came up the two barge locks into the basin to exchange cargoes with narrowboats. Early traffic included pig iron from Shropshire and china clay destined for the Potteries. Merchandise was also important traffic and large warehouses were constructed around the perimeter of the basin. Many were erected between 1780 and 1810, including the 'Long Room' beside Mart Lane. This long, narrow structure, seen here before demolition, had various openings for fly boats and barges to moor alongside to load and unload goods. (Roger Hetherington Collection)

Right: The Long Room extended as far as Mart Lane Bridge, which was made just wide enough for barges to pass underneath to Mart Lane Basin. (Roger Hetherington Collection)

Left: Botterham Locks in 2010 – this staircase pair has altered little since the canal opened to trade. They are arguably the last surviving example of a Brindley staircase lock in the West Midlands. All the staircase locks on the Trent & Mersey have been replaced and the Bratch locks have been altered. Other Brindley staircase locks exist on the restored and unrestored parts of the Chesterfield Canal. (Author)

building of watch houses, warehouses and wharves. He was given a house at Compton, which became his base and home through to 1776, when much of the duties required of him had been done.

Making a canal from the Trent to the River Mersey was a scheme that came to be surveyed first in 1755 and then in 1759. James Brindley was associated with the 1759 survey at a time when he was also engaged in planning the canal from the coal mines at Worsley into Manchester.

James Brindley had settled in Leek and was employed as a millwright, a job connected with the construction and repair of windmills and watermills. He is known to have worked on various flint mills that crushed flints used in pottery manufacture. The digging of channels and diversions of streams to bring water to drive the waterwheel was just as important as the making of the wheel and associated machinery. It was knowledge such as this that must have aided Brindley with his navigation making.

A prime mover in getting the Trent & Mersey Canal built was Josiah Wedgwood, a Burslem potter. Wedgwood, together with friends Thomas Bentley and Dr Erasmus Darwin, collected facts and evidence to support the making of the canal and enlisted the help of the Duke of Bridgewater and Earl Gower. The Act passed the Lords and received Royal Assent on 14 May 1766. James Brindley was appointed surveyor-general with a salary of £200, whilst Hugh Henshall was appointed Clerk of Works with a salary of £150. Work began on this waterway from 26 July 1766.

The Trent & Mersey Canal also employed contractors and workmen directly, like the Staffordshire & Worcestershire Canal, and commenced at various points, such as at Harecastle (for the tunnel) and through the valley of the Trent from Haywood through Rugeley, Armitage, Fradley and Alrewas. The section from Haywood was a part that required the construction of locks at Haywood and Colwich and it is possible that locks built here were contemporary with those at Compton and Wightwick on the Staffordshire & Worcestershire Canal. Engineering features on this part included the aqueduct over the Trent near Rugeley and Armitage Tunnel. Lock construction was sufficiently advanced by the summer of 1768 for Brindley to send John Bushell from the Droitwich Canal for instruction on the techniques of making locks.

Construction then continued through Fradley to Alrewas, where the canal joined the River Trent for a short navigable section. Here Brindley's skills as a millwright would have been used. The navigation descended from Alrewas Lock into the Trent below Alrewas Mill, following the main channel of the Trent and then the channel to Wichnor Mill. Here a lock was made for the canal to descend towards Barton and water from the Trent was used to supply the navigation as it dropped towards Burton and beyond.

As the contractors approached Shobnall during 1768, work on the private Bond End Canal was in progress. The owners of the Bond End Canal, the Burton Boat Company, were keen to form a junction between the two waterways, but the Trent & Mersey proprietors prevented this from taking place and made a wharf and warehouse at Horninglow to cater for the brewery trade. The Burton Boat Company, lessees of the Bond End Canal and Upper Trent Navigation, were able to exchange traffic with boats moored on the Trent & Mersey at Shobnall where they had a wharf and warehouse.

From Horninglow the Trent & Mersey Canal and locks were made to barge width and the wide canal crossed over the mill stream for Clay Mills by a short brick aqueduct and then the River Dove by a long, twelve-arch brick aqueduct. Work on the Dove Aqueduct had started by 1769 as Brindley is recorded as sending William Cole, carpenter on the Oxford Canal, for training to the Dove in July 1769. The route then continued on by Willington and Swarkestone to Weston. Here there was a temporary terminus where goods were exchanged with Trent Boats on the

LONGPORT.

1	*Tunstall Bridge Wharf.*									
$1\frac{1}{6}$	$\frac{1}{6}$	*Tunstall Brick-kiln.*								
$1\frac{4}{6}$	$\frac{4}{6}$	$\frac{3}{6}$	*South-end of Harecastle.*							
$2\frac{1}{6}$	$1\frac{1}{6}$	1	$\frac{3}{6}$	*Turnrail Coal.*						
$2\frac{4}{6}$	$1\frac{4}{6}$	$1\frac{3}{6}$	1	$\frac{3}{6}$	*Birchenwood Coal.*					
$3\frac{1}{6}$	$2\frac{1}{6}$	2	$1\frac{3}{6}$	1	$\frac{3}{6}$	*North-end of Harecastle.*				
$3\frac{2}{6}$	$2\frac{2}{6}$	$2\frac{1}{6}$	$1\frac{4}{6}$	$1\frac{1}{6}$	$\frac{4}{6}$	$\frac{1}{6}$	*Gilbert's Crane.*			
$3\frac{3}{6}$	$2\frac{3}{6}$	$2\frac{2}{6}$	$1\frac{5}{6}$	$1\frac{2}{6}$	$\frac{5}{6}$	$\frac{2}{6}$	$\frac{1}{6}$	*Heathcote's Wharf.*		
$3\frac{5}{6}$	$2\frac{5}{6}$	$2\frac{4}{6}$	$2\frac{1}{6}$	$1\frac{4}{6}$	$1\frac{1}{6}$	$\frac{4}{6}$	$\frac{3}{6}$	$\frac{2}{6}$	*Pool Colliery.*	
$4\frac{1}{6}$	$3\frac{1}{6}$	3	$2\frac{3}{6}$	2	$1\frac{3}{6}$	1	$\frac{5}{6}$	$\frac{4}{6}$	$\frac{2}{6}$	RED BULL.

Above left: The Trent & Mersey Canal at Shardlow – Shardlow became an inland port about the same time as Stourport. Merchandise was exchanged at the warehouses, either belonging to the canal company or other carriers, with Trent Boats that journeyed along the River Trent to Gainsborough. (Author)

Above right: The Trent & Mersey Canal, Colwich Lock – this shared a common structure with some Staffordshire & Worcestershire locks where a bridge was placed over the tail of the lock. (Author)

Above: Colwich Lock and House is a heritage survival from the earliest time of the Trent & Mersey Canal. The lock is one of the oldest on the canal. The lock, cottage, cottage privy and lock bridge are all Grade II listed structures. (Author)

Opposite: The Trent & Mersey Canal distance table, dated 1795, included a mention of side tunnels and loading wharves in the old Harecastle Tunnel. (Public Records Office)

Above left: The long towpath across the River Trent at Alrewas. (Author)

Above right: Preston Brook Tunnel, north portal. The physical boundary between the Trent & Mersey and the Bridgewater canals lay north of here. Both waterways were constructed under James Brindley, after whose death in 1772, Hugh Henshall (Trent & Mersey clerk of works), took over, his work including the Cheshire tunnels. Barges and flats worked up to Preston Brook, but the tunnel was only wide enough for narrowboats. (Author)

Upper Trent Navigation. It is believed that the interchange was across a wharf, although in later times there was a lock made here.

The first part to open therefore was from Haywood through to Weston and shortly after this the canal was finished to Derwent Mouth. Shardlow became an inland port devoted to the interchange of goods between narrowboats and Trent Boats travelling along the Trent to Nottingham, Newark and Gainsborough. Goods were also transferred between boats and road vehicles that travelled along the important turnpike that linked Derby and Loughborough. The navigation then was finished northwards to Stone and then Stoke. The main obstacle was the cutting of the tunnel through Harecastle Hill to Kidsgrove.

Land purchase and acquisition, as with other waterways, was an important issue that affected the construction and route of this canal. Sometimes a jury, and otherwise commissioners appointed by the Act, was required to determine the value. The appointed commissioners were required to decide the value of land at Findern Common:

TRENT AND MERSEY CANAL NAVIGATION

We whose names are hereto subscribed being commissioners named and appointed by Act of Parliament passed in the sixth year of the reign of his present majesty intituled 'An Act for making a navigable cut or canal from the River Trent at or near Wilden Ferry in the County of Derby to the River Mersey at, or near Runcorn Gap and acting for the county of Derby, do hereby, in pursuance of an application made to us in that behalf by BENJAMIN WARD of Willington, in county of Derby esq, JOHN COOKE in Findern in said county of Derby, Gent, and the reverend JOHN ORRELL of Findern, aforesaid, Clerk on behalf of themselves and the rest of the freeholders at Findern aforesaid, appoint a general meeting of commissioners, in and by the said act named and authorised to be holden at the George Inn in Derby on Saturday the Seventeenth day of December next by ten o'clock in the forenoon on the same day, to settle, determine and adjust or by a jury to be then returned for that purpose to enquire of assess and ascertain the recompense to be made to the said freeholders, for the damages by them sustained, in and by the company of the proprietors of the aid navigation, their agents, workmen or servants, by taking away and converting to the use of the said proprietors of the said company of proprietors, several acres of land, parts of a certain common or waste called Findern Common, lying within the liberty of Findern aforesaid for the purpose of making the said navigable cut or canal; and for digging and taking clay and making bricks and getting turf on said common; And also to expedite, transact and do all other articles, matters and things necessary or authorised to be done by said commissioners, or and seven or more of them, in, about or concerning the premises by virtue and authority of the Act of Parliament aforementioned, given under our hands this seventeenth day of October, One Thousand, Seven Hundred and Seventy Four.

Samuel Crompton, George Mellor, Francis Ashby. Gilbert Fox, John Heath, Joseph Greaves, Leonard Fosbrooke, Ralph Burgin.

Derby Mercury, 11 November 1774

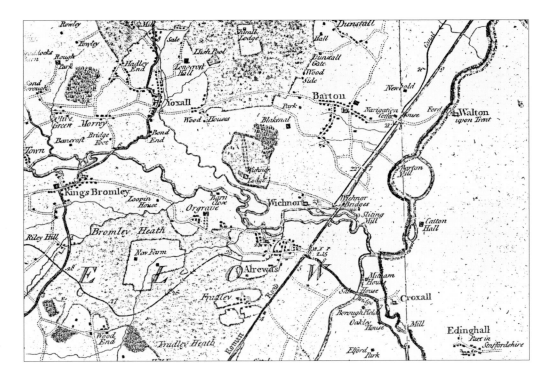

Above: Snape's Staffordshire Map shows the section of the Trent & Mersey Canal that used a short length of the Trent between Alrewas and Wichnor Mills.

Left: Trent & Mersey Canal, Woodend Lock. (Author)

Constructing Harecastle Tunnel proved to be a long process. The challenges were very different to the short rock tunnels on the Staffordshire & Worcestershire Canal. In addition to the main tunnel, side tunnels were driven to mine workings under Harecastle Hill and two of these are mentioned in distance tables published in 1795. Meanwhile cutters and lock makers pressed on northwards. The long descent from Kidsgrove summit included locks to Wheelock and then through to Middlewich. Three more tunnels were needed to take the canal along the side of the Weaver Valley and ultimately join the Bridgewater Canal at Preston Brook.

Preston Brook Tunnel marked the dividing point between the Bridgewater and the Trent & Mersey canals. A stop lock at Dutton was made near the south portal of this tunnel. The slight rise in level preserved the water of the Bridgewater Canal and ensured a continued supply from the Trent & Mersey. Preston Brook Tunnel is reasonably straight, but the intermediate tunnels at Saltisford and Barnton are not. The curves and bends in Saltisford Tunnel are an indication of the lack of a method for accurate surveying and the rough and ready skills of the professional miner.

In addition to locks, bridges and tunnels, aqueducts and culverts were constructed. These included Croxton Aqueduct over the River Dane near Middlewich, Chell's Aqueduct and Snapes Aqueduct. In these last two cases the canal crossed over roads.

Making this final part and finishing Harecastle Tunnel was not fully achieved until 1775, some nine years after starting work. James Brindley had died in 1772, but supervision and surveying was conducted by Hugh Henshall. Once the main line was completed traffic started to pass between the Midlands, Potteries, the Mersey and Manchester.

During 1769 John and Thomas Gilbert took a lease of the Caldon Limestone Quarries and this provided an incentive to build a canal to serve these quarries. James Brindley went out to survey this canal in 1772. He is said to have caught a cold when engaged in this duty and the virus is believed to have contributed to his death later that year. Applications to Parliament finally led to the Caldon Act (May 1776). Construction of the Caldon Canal started during June 1776 on the line from Etruria to Froghall and on a connecting railway from Froghall to the quarries at Caldon Low.

Building the Caldon provided the link with the first Knypersley Reservoir. A feeder from this reservoir entered the canal at Norton Green. This reservoir, in turn, derived water supply from the River Trent. When sections were completed, they were opened to trade and this process went on until the original terminus at Froghall was reached (1778). The railway then climbed through an incline to the level of the quarry.

Another canal made to follow a river valley was the Droitwich. The Salwarpe had been made navigable, but the extent of this navigation has never been fully determined. Coal for the salt pans was generally brought from the coal mines near Dudley by road, yet the location of some of the brine pits near the Salwarpe has led to suggestions that some salt might have been carried by water to the Severn for onward transport. James Brindley surveyed improvements to the River Salwarpe but recommended a canal route. A company was formed and Act obtained. James Brindley was appointed inspector of works for the Droitwich Canal and John Priddey was made resident engineer. Work started in June 1768 starting at Hawford. Eight barge locks, 64ft by 14ft 6in, were constructed. No towpath was provided and part of the Salwarpe was diverted as the canal took over the former river bed. The canal was completed to Droitwich in 1771.

John Priddey was given the responsibility of setting on the contractors and the supervision of the construction of the waterway:

To contract with such persons as he shall find proper to build the locks and that he go into Yorkshire with Mr Brindleys instructions for that purpose. That he also go to such navigations as are making in order to improve himself and be allowed ten guineas to dispose of in such manner as he sees proper to procure such improvement.

PRO Rail 821/1, 1st meeting Droitwich Canal Company, George Inn, Droitwich, 4 March 1768

Construction started at the Hawford end. A boat of 40-ton burthen was authorised to be purchased to carry stone and other material. The road between Hawford and Ladywood was to also be improved to assist transport of goods for the works. Timber and stone were brought along the Severn. The stone was quarried at a nearby riverside quarry and a triangle ('A'-frame) was erected at the quarry and another at Hawford for lifting the stone. A shed was erected at Hawford for the use of the stone mason and carpenter.

During November an order was made for clay to be thrown up along the line to Ladywood. The amount of clay required had to be sufficient for making 200,000 bricks. John Priddey also had an assistant appointed. His name was John Southall and he was allowed 8s a week wages.

By March 1769, brick making had commenced and 1,000 tons of limestone was purchased and delivered to Hawford. The task of building the locks and cutting the channel through to Droitwich was accomplished in two years. In March 1771 the waterway was nearing completion and staff were appointed to look after barges on the canal:

A person appointed to attend locks near Ladywood and it be his employment to conduct vessels navigating on canal down to lock at Papist Mill, here a second person be stationed through other locks to Severn, a third person stationed near junction to conduct vessels coming up canal and deliver same to person at Papist Mill such persons to have watch house built.

Rail 822/1, General Meeting, George Inn, 1 March 1771

Proposals for a branch to the Salwarpe at Droitwich were made in 1773 and contracts advertised for making this branch. The committee subsequently decided that this link was considered too difficult to make and the work was cancelled. £850 was paid in compensation to Richard Norris for the failure to make this branch.

The Birmingham Canal Navigations are at the heart of the Midlands canal network, a synthesis of a number of different canals made principally for coal traffic and the needs of the local iron trade. The original Birmingham Canal was first united with the separately promoted Birmingham & Fazeley Canal and together they forged new additional waterways such as the Walsall Canal.

With some canal projects, change and modification was part of the development. The Birmingham Canal began simply as a waterway to link the mines at Bilston and Wednesbury with Birmingham, providing cheaper transport than by the existing turnpike. The policy changed after James Brindley became involved. A canal that joined the Staffordshire & Worcestershire Canal became the preferred option.

Construction started first on the Birmingham to West Bromwich section. The route followed the contours of the land crossing from valley to valley. A major engineering feature was the intended Smethwick Tunnel, but on starting the tunnel quicksand was found and it was decided to make a flight of locks over the summit instead. In effect there were six locks up and six locks down in the line between the collieries near West Bromwich and the Birmingham terminus. This part was opened first (November 1769) and then contractors went on to make the main line through Oldbury, Tipton, Bradley, Coseley and Wolverhampton until a junction was finished with the Staffordshire & Worcestershire Canal and the canal opened throughout in 1772.

Little remains of the early period when the Birmingham Canal construction was supervised by Samuel Simcox. The route was frequently changed to meet the needs of the local coal masters and it was principally down to Simcox to survey and make the alterations. Thus when the long flight of seventeen locks from Wolverhampton down to Aldersley became twenty, the man who planned the changes was probably Simcox. The Wolverhampton Flight of narrow locks passed from the town quickly into the countryside. Below the top lock is Little's Lane Bridge, which is distorted with age and appears to be original. The remnant of a wooden post is a reminder of the times when a gate across the towpath prevented access to the top lock, when the company chose to stop boat movements.

Sections of the Brindley Canal are best preserved in the loops known as Winson Green, Icknield Port and Oozells. Any major or minor bridges or accommodation swivel bridges have long been lost with road improvements and changes to the waterway. The few aqueducts over streams are difficult to find but the sharp-eyed might find the course of the brook under the canal at Bloomfield, Tipton or the stream near Whimsey Bridge in Oldbury that also flows under the old line of the canal.

The Coventry Canal Company also started to make their canal in 1768. At their first General Assembly on 19 February 1768, James Brindley of New Chapel, Staffordshire, was elected engineer and surveyor of works at a salary of £150 per year. He undertook to 'give at least two months attendance in whole in every year upon the design'. Joseph Parker was elected clerk of works, also with a salary of £150, 'for himself and assistant to be appointed to satisfaction of committee'.

Contracts for making wheelbarrows, brickmakers and carpenters were amongst the early commitments made by the Coventry Canal Committee. The wheelbarrows were delivered to Bedworth. John Roberts was the first to sign a contract for supplying wheelbarrows. Twenty a month were delivered to Bedworth, carriage free. Roberts charged 7s for each barrow.

Building the waterway involved making a level canal from the existing coal mines at Bedworth and past the Hawkesbury estate of the Parrot family. Such mines had been in operation for generations and were targeted by William Sandys in his Avon navigation scheme. The Parrots had made a canal through their estate, and now the Coventry Canal was to incorporate this private waterway into their main line.

In March 1768, contracts were arranged with Richard Holmes for further barrows. James Oakley of Foleshill agreed to take the post of carpenter at 11s a week and Thomas Bates of Bedworth agreed to make bricks at kilns provided at the expense of the company. He agreed to make 800,000 bricks; 500,000 were to be delivered to Mr Parrot's canal and the remaining 300,000 to Longford.

A tunnel was planned to be cut through Bedworth Hill, and the colliers from Bedworth Colliery were employed to assist with the excavation of the canal there. Work on this project was stopped in 1769 and the colliers discharged. Bedworth Tunnel was opened out as a cutting.

The committee decided to keep tight control on spending. Cutting the canal could be expensive, particularly if payments were made according to material cut through. They made the following order:

Ordered that all works beyond Bedworth Hill shall be surveyed and the number of cubic yards in each division ascertained and that no future contracts for cutting be made until the quantity is first set out and surveyed in the several proportions of work proposed to be executed nor until such survey and admeasurement has been produced to the committee and submitted for their consideration.

Committee Minutes, 9 May 1769
Rail 818/1

Supervision of the construction was conducted under clerk of works. One was Samuel Bull. Brindley suggested 'he go for his improvement to the Staffordshire and other navigations now forming for a time not exceeding three weeks'. John Parish, recently employed as a carpenter, was also sent for improvement. In his case it was 'to the Birmingham Navigation and there remain during the building of one of the locks to inform himself fully of the nature and construction thereof'.

Construction proceeded south to Coventry incorporating a private canal at Hawkesbury in the route. The route was made through Longford to the Bishops Gate terminus beside the turnpike

Left: Coventry Canal Basin has a fine example of a canalside warehouse. Some parts were constructed during 1790 when Thomas Sheasby enlarged the wharf, ready to receive commercial traffic, once the Coventry was linked to the rest of the canal network. (Author)

Below: The Coventry Canal at Atherstone. This canal terminated at the pound above the top lock (1771) before the route was opened to Fazeley (1790). (Author)

in Coventry. In June 1769 Thomas Newman agreed to do the stone work at Bishops Gate Basin at 3s 6d per yard.

As the contractors finished the canal to Coventry, Brindley made some final improvement suggestions. He then ceased to be the engineer. His other responsibilities left little time to fulfil his commitment to the Coventry Canal. James Brindley was dismissed from the company's service.

It was perhaps the worst outcome for the Coventry, for despite Brindley's taciturn nature canal construction progressed: whether through him, or his lieutenants, the routes were completed. For the Coventry, years of limbo would ensue. Construction of the Coventry Canal proceeded for a while, through Nuneaton to Atherstone where the canal finished at a wharf at the top of a slope where the land fell away. John Parish would have little opportunity to practice lock gate-making skills.

15 December 1769 was an important date in the canal builders' calendar for this was the day when representatives from the Trent & Mersey, Staffordshire & Worcestershire, the Oxford, Coventry and Birmingham Canals met at The George at Lichfield to decide on a general policy common to all. Amongst the decisions made was a regulation specifying the size of locks and minimal depth of navigation.

> It was proposed that a standing order be made at the General Assembly of all Navigations that all locks hereafter to be made of a size not less than the dimensions following viz 74ft 9in in length and 7ft in width, that the depth o each canal in water shall not be less than 4ft 4in and that Mr Brindley do take it upon him the charge of inspecting the several locks and canals already made, to see that they in no material instance vary from such dimensions, and make his report to see that they in no material instance vary from such dimensions, and make his report there at each next succeeding General Assembly.

Building the Coventry Canal ceased at Atherstone, but recommenced under the superintendence of Thomas Sheasby. The route followed the valley of the River Anker through to Fazeley.

The Oxford Canal was planned to meet the Coventry at Longford, but work on construction principally commenced from Hawkesbury towards Wyken tapping the mines of the Hawkesbury Colliery. The Oxford and Coventry remained unconnected for a period whilst a decision was

made as to where the junction should be made. Finally the junction was set at Longford with the result that a length of parallel canal was made from Hawkesbury to Longford with all boats making the detour until another junction was made (1803) at Hawkesbury to enable craft bound for Fazeley to avoid the Longford detour.

Contractors building the Oxford Canal followed the contours of the land winding and turning through Stretton, Brinklow and Newbold. Lengthy deviations were made northwards to cross the River Swift and then the River Avon by stone and brick aqueducts as the canal skirted Rugby to pass onto Hillmorton and then Braunston. Another deviation took the Oxford Canal through Wolfhampcote to cross the Leam and then on to Napton where the

The original (Old) Newbold Tunnel on the Oxford Canal was placed alongside the churchyard. Only the south portal remains. (Author)

waterway was raised through locks to the summit near Fenny Compton. Farm accommodation bridges were frequently wooden swing bridges.

The summit level from Napton to Banbury included inlets for reservoirs and a 1,138yd tunnel at Fenny Compton. This tunnel was 12ft high and 9ft wide. A passing point 16ft wide was provided within to reduce the wait at either portal. There were also iron rings fastened into the brickwork by wooden blocks placed at 12ft interval on both sides. By this device boatmen could pull themselves along unlike other narrow canals where poling and legging were the only options. Reservoirs were made at Byfield (Boddington) and Clattercote. Later a third reservoir was constructed at Wormleighton whose feeder joined the canal east of Fenny Compton Tunnel.

Work on cutting the Oxford was continued initially as far as Banbury when boats finally reached this long-sought object in March 1778. With finances drained they kept Banbury as a terminus until finance was available and making the final section to Oxford did not commence until 1787. At this time James Barnes was resident engineer and Samuel Simcox one of the contractors to build this waterway.

Such deviations considerably increased journey times and delayed carriage of goods to Banbury and Oxford. This being also an early inland route to London proved to be a considerable handicap for the carriage of merchandise. Carriers such as Pickfords chose to transfer cargoes to road and use the turnpike network at the earliest opportunities.

New canal construction gained momentum once the initial network of the Trent & Mersey, Staffordshire & Worcester and Birmingham canals had been completed. Their monopoly of trade was initially jealously safeguarded, opposing every new scheme that was proposed. Thus when Lord Dudley and Ward, one of the most powerful landowners in the Black Country, commis-

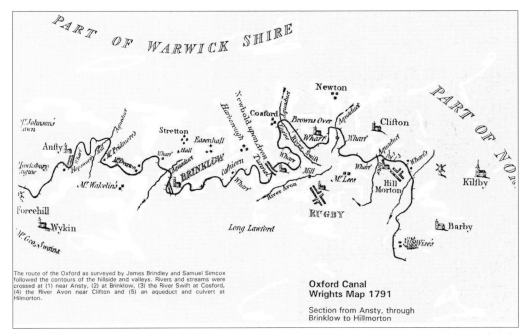

The route of the Oxford Canal followed the contours of the land and had aqueducts over streams and rivers at the heads of each valley. (William Wright's survey, 1791)

sioned Robert Whitworth to survey a route to Stourbridge and his mines near Pensnett Chase, opposition developed from both the Staffordshire & Worcestershire and Birmingham canals and proved a severe obstacle for this Act passing through Parliament. They stated that coals mined at Bilston and sent by boat to Stourport would be at a commercial disadvantage to the new supply of coal from the Dudley area. The arguments were sufficient for the proposals to be delayed, but not stopped. The promoters of the new canal decided to reconsider their scheme and present it as two separate Acts. One canal was to join the Staffordshire & Worcestershire Canal at Stewponey to Stourbridge and Black Delph and the other from Black Delph towards Dudley. Their titles became respectively the Stourbridge and Dudley canals.

For the Stourbridge this was a vast improvement on an earlier survey made by James Brindley to reach the glass-making town of Stourbridge, for it carried on through Amblecote to the mines of coal, ironstone and fireclay that existed around Brettell Lane, Brierley Hill and Netherton.

The battle to build the Stourbridge Canal was finally won after a detailed enquiry investigated the reasons and arguments for and against making the canal during November 1775. Robert

Left: The view from Lock 8 up to Lock 10 and the Lock Cottage at Buckpool. The two paired locks 9 and 10 were probably the first of the type to be built for Dadford. (Author)

Below: There were sixteen locks in flight on the Stourbridge Canal between Stourbridge and the Leys. The view from Lock 10 looks down on the warehouse (known as Dadford's) and the Redhouse Glass Cone. It is an area known as Buckpool and Thomas Dadford lived here with his family whilst making the Stourbridge and Dudley canals. (Author)

Whitworth produced his plan for the navigation where the key supply of water was arranged partly by the making of a new storage reservoir that collected rain water, supplemented by water pumped from the existing coal mines at Brettell Lane.

Steam engine power was then confined to the use of Newcomen engines and the volume of water raised was measured by Whitworth in units of hogsheads and translated into the equivalent of a lock, based on a 10ft fall. Mathematical skills such as this were essential to the job of a canal engineer.

The enquiry also revealed that Lord Dudley had lost revenue from his mines at the Level. Production had suffered from competition from mines at Tipton and Bilston which were able to send coal by canal to Kidderminster and Droitwich, whilst the Level mines had to rely on the more expensive system of land carriage. Such was Lord Dudley's political standing that his views were listened to and a helpful influence for the Bill. Sufficient guarantees were also made to appease the mill owners along the Stour and the Bill passed through Parliament.

Principal engineering challenges were the crossing of the Stour and the steady climb to the summit level at the Lays. It was also here that three reservoirs were located to supply water to the canal. The group of pools were filled by feeders from the watershed at Pensnett Chase as well as by mine-pumping engines. Thomas Dadford senior was employed by the Stourbridge Canal as their surveyor and it was his task to supervise the contractors as well as survey the various parts of the waterway and produce the plans for the committee to authorise. Dadford left his mark in the form of the Stour Aqueduct and the two lock flights on the Stourbridge Canal. The main rise of sixteen locks was constructed near his home at Buckpool. They included the two locks, Nos 9 and 10, where one lock chamber came close to the other. It is an arrangement that came to be associated with Thomas Dadford.

Dadford was also appointed engineer to the Dudley Canal when that waterway was conceived as an independent company. The original plan as surveyed by Robert Whitworth provided for a rise at the Delph of some 53ft and a level section towards the Ox Leasowes where another rise of 21ft was suggested to reach a terminus east of the Knowl Brook.

Alternatives to the route were subsequently considered and the shareholders were given the task of deciding on a route with a lock at the Ox Leasowes and one that had no lock there. The choice apparently was for the former and the contractors were given the task of constructing a lock near the terminus, and this may have been constructed. There then seems to have been a change of policy when work went ahead with the making of nine locks at the Delph. These locks were constructed under Dadford's supervision and included a grouping of three and a grouping of two locks in the fashion adopted at locks 9 and 10 on the Stourbridge Canal.

This was a period when independent canal contractors had begun to tender for and gain contracts to complete large sections of canal. Whereas previously shorter sections were let with cutting, bridge building and tunnelling conducted separately, there now were contractors that would undertake a specific length for a set contract price and to be completed within a set time. In a sense they were to follow Pinkerton's lead on the Erewash Canal.

The Birmingham Canal was the first part of a much greater network of waterways. Before 1790 it simply had one connection, the Staffordshire & Worcestershire Canal. The Birmingham & Fazeley Canal has more major structures to consider. This was a canal made through political compromise. Promoted as an independent waterway, the line would have been entirely separate. But construction started after the merger with the Birmingham Canal and involved a main canal from Birmingham through Minworth and Curdworth to Fazeley and a detached section from Ryders Green to Broadwaters near Wednesbury.

The canal from Ryders Green to Broadwaters was constructed by the contractor John Pinkerton, who was much criticised for his subsequent work on the Dudley Canal Tunnel and the Birmingham & Fazeley from Minworth to Fazeley. With the Broadwaters Canal, it seems his work was satisfactory and this included the construction of the eight locks at Ryders Green and a stone and brick aqueduct over the Tame at the bottom of the locks.

This was an industrial heartland with several mills and mill pools on the Tame and associated tributaries. The main river was crossed by an aqueduct below the eighth lock at Ryders Green, but there were also crossings of streams and mill leats at Butlers Forge and near Willingsworth. The route passed close to the long pool that provided water for Wiggins Mill and this pool was effectively drained following the canal construction and the subsequent making of the Monway Branch.

Thomas Sheasby had the contract to build Farmers Bridge Locks and Aston Locks, whose flights of thirteen and eleven locks respectively provide an impressive, if time-consuming, ascent to the Birmingham Canal main line. Another of Sheasby's works was the aqueduct over the Tame at Salford Bridge. Pinkerton was responsible for Curdworth Tunnel and the Curdworth Locks, but claims of shoddy workmanship led to him and his men being thrown off the works, with Birmingham Canal men completing the task. Pinkerton also made the canal from Fazeley through to Whittington Brook; again apparently without mishap.

From Salford Bridge to Fazeley the Birmingham & Fazeley followed the valley of the River Tame, descending from the Erdington Level at Minworth Locks, and which included a substantial embankment over the Plants Brook to a level that passed through Curdworth and a short tunnel to the top of eleven locks that lowered the waterway to Fazeley.

Above left: John Pinkerton was awarded the contract to build the detached section of the Birmingham & Fazeley Canal from Ryders Green to Broadwaters. This work included the making of an aqueduct over the River Tame at the bottom of Ryders Green Locks. The west face of this aqueduct was subsequently rebuilt and refaced by Birmingham Canal Navigation labourers and bears a 1901 date plate. (Author)

Above right: The Birmingham & Fazeley Canal crossed the River Tame at Salford Bridge on a low but compact aqueduct. It is a structure that has been rebuilt and repaired from time to time. The large 'cut water' pillars were necessary as the flow on the river could be strong. (Author)

The Birmingham & Fazeley Canal was one that was let in long sections. There were essentially four lots. The first covered the part from Pudding Green to Broadwaters and included the eight locks at Ryders Green and the aqueduct over the Tame close to the bottom lock. The second was from Farmers Bridge (Newhall Branch) to Minworth and the third was from Minworth to Fazeley to join the Coventry Canal. A fourth part was from Aston Junction through a short tunnel at Ashted and down six locks to a terminus near Digbeth, which became known as the Digbeth Branch.

John Pinkerton was given the contract to make the canal to Broadwaters and also later had the task of making the canal from Minworth to Fazeley. Thomas Sheasby had the task of making the canal from Farmers Bridge to Minworth and the Digbeth Branch.

These contractors were also at work on the Coventry Canal, which was under construction from Fradley to Atherstone. The complex arrangement between the various interested parties had led the Trent & Mersey Canal Company to let the work from Fradley to Whittington Brook; the Birmingham Canal Navigations (then trading under the lengthy title of the Birmingham and Birmingham & Fazeley Canal Company) let the work from Whittington Brook to Fazeley; and the Coventry Canal Company arranged for the remainder from Fazeley to Atherstone.

Sheasby constructed the part from Fazeley through Glascote to Atherstone that involved an aqueduct over the Tame at Fazeley, two locks at Glascote and eleven at Atherstone. Pinkerton had the contract to make the line from Fazeley towards Fradley. The Trent & Mersey part was set out by Thomas Dadford, who was then their engineer. Mr Bough set out the line for the Birmingham Canal section. John Pinkerton also had the contract to build Dudley Tunnel.

Pinkerton was a major contractor of his day. The Pinkerton name is common in certain parts of Scotland. Comparing known dates of birth for John and his brother James, the most likely place of birth was in Lanarkshire, where Robert Pinkerton and his wife Rae lived.

John Pinkerton's construction career had begun in Yorkshire working with his brother James. Projects included work on the Driffield Navigation, Market Weighton Canal, Selby Canal, Calder & Hebble and Erewash Canal. Following his Midlands contracts, his reputation was later tarnished through claims of shoddy work. He also has the dubious distinction of probably being sacked from more contracts than any other contractor. Yet all the time he and his family were given contracts and payments were regularly made to them as the work progressed.

John Pinkerton left the Dudley contract following concerns about the way the work had been done. Pinkerton later said that he had been given bad advice when he tendered and had quoted a low price. He was released from the work on payment of £2,000, and was evidently glad of it. The Dudley Canal Company decided to take on the task on cutting the tunnel themselves, but fared little better and consequently construction was delayed and this canal link did not open until 1792.

Pinkerton completed the Coventry Canal contracts and the Broadwaters without any serious issues. Yet there was an element of ill-feeling that developed. This was due in part to Pinkerton himself, who seems to have had an abrasive and argumentative character. John Pinkerton and Bough, engineer to the Birmingham Canal, had many disagreements and this ill-feeling did not help the working relationship. This dissent began on the Broadwaters and carried over onto the Minworth section. Pinkerton had advised the Birmingham Committee of the decision to leave the Dudley Canal and gave assurances for completion of his other work. The Birmingham committee responded by having a supplemental clause inserted into the Minworth Contract.

Instructions were frequently given to contractors through the 'Orders of Committee'. BCN orders were usually handwritten by the clerk. Two orders dated 19 and 26 January 1787 reported first a draft of Mr Pinkerton's contract be prepared and then, in the second, directed Mr Meredith that a covenant be inserted enabling the committee, in case he should neglect to proceed in the execution, agreeable to their expectations, to take the work into their own hands and get the same executed by workmen and agents of their own appointment and charge expense to his account.

It was a crucial document that was later to have serious consequences for Pinkerton and without the giving up of the Dudley contract may never have happened. Whilst Sheasby carried on his work, evidently in an untroubled fashion, Pinkerton had clear difficulties with Bough getting work set out. Looking at the different perspectives of Pinkerton or the company, how serious this handicap became has become a matter of historical conjecture.

From Pinkerton's point of view he claimed that he was disadvantaged by the actions of the Birmingham Canal Company and their engineer. From the viewpoint of the company he was not disadvantaged and should have done more to complete the work, on time, and in a satisfactory manner.

Here on the Minworth–Fazeley contract, the Birmingham Canal Company did find fault. There was an issue regarding the quality of the work done and this gave the Birmingham Canal Company the authority to take over the remainder of the unfinished work, repair some of the defects and complete the canal using their own workmen.

Later the canal company sought to reclaim money from Pinkerton and a court case was pursued. Pinkerton also claimed money owed and the result of that case was a ruling made in favour of Pinkerton. His printed account of the proceedings in 1801 provides useful information about canal contracting at this time. Part of this account was seen as a libel on Houghton, the Birmingham Canal Company clerk and the subsequent civil action led to Pinkerton being placed in prison for three months.

Pinkerton's main issue with the Birmingham Canal Navigations (BCN) was that he was tied up with the Trent & Mersey line from Fradley to Whittington and the connecting BCN line from Whittington to Fazeley. He had men that could be released to work on the Minworth Contract but he had to wait for setting out and land purchase. Much of this did not happen until 1788, leaving little time to make Curdworth Tunnel, the eleven locks from Dunston and the aqueducts at Fazeley.

John Pinkerton's account, and that of nephew Francis, indicates a certain commitment by contractors that included going over the route and making a survey to base the quote on. He looked for springs and other water courses to fill the waterway to a level suitable for moving such items as spoil and bricks. There was also a need to find sources of sand and good clay to make bricks.

It was Pinkerton's intention to make bricks in 1786 at Curdworth Field, Curdworth Hill, near Coleshill Road and at Fazeley. The clay with sand would make good bricks without having been previously prepared by a winter's exposure. He also meant to cut in Marston Field; if clay was dug in 1786, and had been turned over in time, it would have been sufficiently tempered to make bricks in early 1787.

His subsequent start was delayed until the summer of 1787. An essential part of canal construction was the making of bridges, locks and tunnels that required strong and well-burnt bricks. Clay was collected in the winter months and piled up to enable the winter frosts to break down the clay so that it can be ground and moulded into bricks ready for firing. It was turned over in the spring to complete the weathering process. The 1786/1787 season was good for brick making, and had Pinkerton been granted the possession of the works in 1786 then he could have made good bricks for the contract in 1787. 1788 was a wet year and a bad time for brick making, yet this was the year brick making commenced and this is reflected on the quality of bricks made.

The supply of men was also an issue at that time. In June 1787 Pinkerton noticed Dunton Field was fallow and began to dig, but was soon stopped as the possession for cutting had not been agreed with the landowners. His men, believing that there was no certainty of constant work there, went off to work on the harvest and were lost to the contract. Pinkerton did everything he could to replace the lost workforce. He wrote to nephew Francis Pinkerton, then superintending a contract at Rye Harbour, Suffolk, to bring what men he could. They arrived in November 1787, but there were still areas where cutting could not begin.

Whilst waiting for the land to start the cutting, John Pinkerton did what he could and this included the much-needed preparation of material, such as getting stone and making agreements with stone masons and bricklayers. Benjamin Simcox was employed to do all the bricklaying on the line. Stone was obtained from a quarry near Fazeley belonging to a Mr Bretton. Pinkerton set up a gin, railways and stone drugs at this quarry to get the stone. Agreements were made with a Mr Shesher of Over Whitaker for stone for locks and Mr Emery for timber for locks. Other arrangements were made with road carriers and suppliers of coal to stock for burning bricks.

The timber was by agreement free from sap, shake and black knots. Pinkerton arranged for timber for swivel bridges, and for plating and land ties for brick bridges, and with the same people for post and rails. Thomas Wells was employed as a carpenter. He had worked for Pinkerton before.

Another issue was the quality of cement used, which Pinkerton insisted was to a tried-and-tested formula used by William Jessop. The mix of lime and sand had been used on building locks on the Erewash Canal and this had been satisfactory.

These various issues provided the basic reasons for Pinkerton's dismissal. It was perhaps not such a major problem to John, as he was also engaged on making the Basingstoke Canal. This was a contract which he began during 1788 and worked on until this canal was completed from the River Wey to Basingstoke in 1794. He worked on the Gloucester & Berkeley Canal and also started work on building part of the Lancaster Canal with John Murray. The Lancaster Canal Committee and their clerk Samuel Gregson were initially pleased with the progress of their contract, but gradually found fault with the progress. There were issues with the way stone was quarried in particular and the works in general.

It was on the Lancaster Canal that a fault of the contracting system was found. Pinkerton's method was to contract for the work and then undertake all aspects of the work. They employed the brickmakers, bricklayers, masons, cutters, carriers and general labourers and many were local men. Profit was then derived from the difference between the contract price and the cost of materials, carriage dues and men's wages. It was a system that worked only if there was adequate supervision to ensure standards were maintained. With Pinkerton and Murray's work on the Lancaster, supervision was lacking. The Lancaster committee decided to dismiss the contractors, but keep the men under direct control and set up new contracts with them, thus re-establishing direct control of the construction work.

Pinkerton then went on to make the Barnsley Canal, but again fell foul of the committee, and again left the works. The Barnsley was his last canal project. He continued, however, with several new drainage projects and worked on construction and cutting until his death in 1813.

Thomas Sheasby completed the Coventry Canal contract, although he had a few problems with the Tame Aqueduct. Sheasby also built several lock cottages and wharf houses and was responsible for the enlargement at Coventry Basin which included the extensive carriers' warehouses erected there. Bricks were made at Bedworth and boated from there. Thomas Gadsby was frequently employed on this job.

The BCN employed workmen on a most crucial canal improvement. This was the lowering of the summit at Smethwick. Canal workers were employed to dig out the canal bed between the third and ninth lock, remove six locks, rebuild bridges and duplicate the three locks at Smethwick with three new locks along a parallel canal. Some 18ft was taken off the level and the summit level now extended from Smethwick through to the top lock of Wolverhampton. In any single act of canal improvement, the lowering of the Birmingham Canal summit must rate as one of the most important steps ever taken.

Supply of water was no longer restricted to a narrow section that relied on that drawn from Smethwick Reservoir or by back pumping. The much longer section could now draw on other sources that included a feeder from Titford Pools and the mine pumping engines' proprietors who were paid to deliver water into the canal. The movement of canal boats was less handicapped through the reduction of the number of locks and trade in general benefited with the improvements.

These improvements, coupled with the completion of the Fazeley Canal, coincided with the growth of the South Staffordshire iron industry and no doubt contributed to the success the ironmasters enjoyed.

CHAPTER 3

CANAL MANIA:
EXPANDING THE NETWORK

The success of canals such as the Trent & Mersey and Staffordshire & Worcestershire led to a number of other, more ambitious schemes. Engineers now developed a confidence for cutting waterways across terrain to achieve shorter, more competitive routes. These ideas gave rise to the Leominster & Kington Canal, Stratford-upon-Avon Canal, Warwick & Birmingham Canal, Warwick & Napton Canal, the Worcester & Birmingham Canal and the Wyrley & Essington Canal.

Many of the new West Midlands schemes were planned as narrow canals to supplement the existing narrowboat network. But there were two significant new projects that were the Worcester & Birmingham and Stratford-upon-Avon canals, which promised new links between the West Midlands and the River Severn and Avon, respectively. Both were planned as barge canals enabling craft up to 14ft beam to reach Gas Street in Birmingham. Most waterways in the East Midlands were made to take barges up to 14ft wide, the typical dimensions of a Trent Boat.

Whilst each scheme was promoted during the last decade of the eighteenth century, the impact on commerce and credit which came about through the outbreak of war with France curbed many schemes and handicapped others.

With canal construction certain trends came to the forefront. Contractors took on a wider and greater role. They would bid for larger amounts of work and employ more men. They may, and did, subcontract work and quality sometimes suffered. The nature of the work became harder with cut and fill techniques being adopted to make canals to cross hills and valleys.

For the canal companies there remained the financial hurdles to overcome, such as raising capital for construction, land purchase and parliamentary expenses. Canals already built had a distinct financial advantage for they could claim revenue from tolls and rents.

Canals such as the Coventry and the Birmingham & Fazeley heralded an age of canal construction across the country. Yet not all projected waterways were built; they failed for a variety of reasons. Sometimes it was rejection at the time the Bill was presented to Parliament, at other times it was through lack of finance.

An important factor for success was the lack of opposition from existing canal companies, which might support or oppose a new canal Bill. The Birmingham Canal Navigations became adept at opposing other projects. They continued to oppose rival schemes, yet some new schemes had a better reception than others. The Warwick & Birmingham Canal received support from the Birmingham Canal Navigations committee and the junction at Digbeth went ahead unopposed. By contrast, a junction between the Worcester & Birmingham Canal and the BCN was not welcomed by the Birmingham committee. The solid 'Bar', 7ft wide, that separated the two canals near Broad Street remained until 1815 with corresponding disruption to trade.

The construction of the Digbeth Branch, in Birmingham, made possible another transport route from Birmingham through to the Oxford Canal. Two canals – the Warwick & Birmingham and the Warwick and Braunston – came into being during the 1790s. When Thomas Sheasby made the branch to the terminus in Bordesley Street a section of embankment was needed across the low-lying land that formed the slope of the River Rea Valley and a stream that fed it. The first task for the Warwick & Birmingham Canal Company was to solve the problems of building up the bed of the canal from the level of the Rea Valley to the level of the Birmingham Canal. Their waterway was made on an embankment from the Digbeth Branch across the Rea and the mill stream that served Cooper's Mill.

William Felkin was appointed engineer to the Warwick & Birmingham Canal and he carried out the instructions of a canal company committee with a strict authoritarian policy. They started with an order made during August 1793 for John Horton to build the foundations of the aqueduct over Cooper's Mill Stream.

A brick kiln was constructed in Cooper's field to burn local clays for the general, or common, bricks. The value of harder, or engineering, bricks was evidently appreciated even at this time as Felkin was sent to Oldbury and adjacent districts for bricks. Hard bricks were purchased from J. & J. Aston of Tipton Green for the aqueducts over Cooper's Mill Stream and the River Rea. They were delivered by boat from the Tipton brickyard.

The canal from Birmingham to Warwick was surveyed and built with a summit level from Camp Hill through to Knowle. The canal crossed the Rea Valley and ascended Camp Hill through six narrow locks. Halfway along the lock flight a bridge was made to carry the Coventry turnpike over the waterway. In order to reduce water loss to the Birmingham Canal, an engine house was erected in Bowyer Street where a Boulton & Watt pumping engine was installed to return water to the top of the locks.

From Camp Hill the line of the waterway passed through the Warwickshire countryside and the villages and hamlets of Yardley, Olton, Solihull and Catherine-de-Barnes. It crossed the River Cole and Hay Mill Stream on a tall embankment with aqueduct channels provided for both the river and mill stream.

A view looking from the top cill of the bottom lock at Camp Hill, on the Warwick & Birmingham Canal, into the chamber. The brick lining, stone quoins, metal rubbing strips and ground paddle chambers are part of the lock structure. (Author)

From the start plans were made for making of tunnels at Rowington, Shrewley and Yardley as well as the more difficult engineering tasks such as deep cutting. During 1793 it was decided that these tunnels should be 16ft wide, perhaps with a view that the canal might be widened at some time. By July 1794 a contract was arranged between the engineer and Robert Pinkerton for cutting and embanking between Rowington and Shrewley. This decision was rescinded at a subsequent committee meeting, held at the company offices, Deritend, on 31 July:

> Whereas at a meeting of the committee at Knowle on Friday the 18th instant Mr Greenaway was ordered to prepare the draft of a contract between the engineer of the said company and Robert Pinkerton for taking the earth out of the hills at Rowington and Shrewley on the line of the said canal and embanking the valley between the said hills at Rowington and Shrewley and whereas it has been made to appear to this Committee that the said Robert Pinkerton endeavoured by undue means to injure this company by making improper offers to their engineer, it is therefore resolved that the said Robert Pinkerton shall not be employed by the said committee on the said line of canal and that Mr Greenaway need not prepare the said draft of the contract between the said company and the said Robert Pinkerton.
>
> Resolved that Mr Greenway prepare the draft of a contract between the engineers of the said company and messr William Bowler and Thomas Keeling for making the embankment between Rowington and Shrewley and to cut and complete the canal from the mouth of the tunnel at Rowington Hill to the mouth of the tunnel at Shrewley Hill and to take such further quantity of earth as may be wanted for making up the embankment from the Shrewley Hill at eleven pence per cubic yard for the embankment only without anything being paid for any other part of the cutting – but if such additional earth shall be taken from the Rowington Hill then the company shall pay ten pence half penny per yard for the embankment only, the additional earth for the embankment to be taken either from the Rowington Hill or Shrewley Hill as the committee shall direct – the puddling and all the other work to be executed to the satisfaction of the company and under the directions of the company's engineer.
>
> Public Records Office, Rail 887/7

The tunnel at Yardley was replaced by a cutting and a short tunnel under the road from Yardley to Acocks Green. This area was found to have springs and running sand and was an unsuitable place for a long tunnel. To the south of Yardley Tunnel, the Acocks Green Feeder brought water into the canal. There was a good supply of water in this area from streams and brooks that made their way in either the Cole or Blythe valleys.

Brick making was conducted at various places on the route. The produce of any kiln was variable and the canal committee were keen to ensure only the better bricks were used in making the canal. In May 1795 Mr Felkin was told to immediately employ a proper person to sort the bricks at the kilns as soon as they were drawn and inspect making of the same. During 1796 the company improved the process further when the engineer was requested to purchase a machine for grinding clay for making bricks intended for the canal. Such machines were known as pug mills and they became an essential tool for any brickyard, as they improved the way clays were broken down into the form required for moulding.

Construction of the canal at Yardley Cutting and across the Cole Valley was in the hands of William Fletcher, who later went on to build another section of canal at Kingswood. Work proceeded satisfactorily and in May 1796 it was decided to open the canal to Henwood, where a wharf was made to receive the traffic. Meanwhile contractors continued with the construction further south. This included the building of an embankment and aqueduct over the River Blythe and six locks at Knowle that lowered the canal for a level that continued through Kingswood and Rowington to Hatton. Another feeder was provided at Heronfield and there was an aqueduct over the Cuttle Brook. In June 1796 arrangements were made with William Fletcher for making Shrewley Tunnel for a sum not exceeding thirteen guineas a yard.

Ever since the Robert Pinkerton episode the relationship between the committee and the engineer had deteriorated. In December 1795 they decided to advertise for another engineer. Then the Blythe Aqueduct collapsed and had to be rebuilt. Felkin was retained a little longer in the post of engineer. During March 1796 he was ordered to sink shafts on the line of Shrewley Tunnel to establish the nature of the soil.

A major part of this construction was the work at Rowington and Shrewley conducted by Bowker and Keeling. Whilst excavation of Shrewley Tunnel went ahead, plans for a tunnel at Rowington were abandoned and a cutting made instead. Financial pressures led to an order for the contractors to reduce their workforce. The clerk was instructed to pay Bowker and Keeling only enough money to cover the weekly wages of twenty-five men.

Beyond Shrewley Tunnel and cutting was the start of a section that led to the top of Hatton Locks. At Hatton began another major work, which was the making of the locks that carried the waterway down to Budbrooke near Warwick. Bricks were made at Hatton brick kiln.

A bridge was made for the turnpike from Warwick to Hockley House and six locks already begun were to be finished, but the engineer was only to employ ten men for the task. By August 1796 Keeling was asked to produce 2 million bricks at the Hatton Hill brickyard. The section from Rowington to Hatton had been a detached piece of the construction work, but as the year 1796 drew to close, contractors were asked to complete the part from Kingswood to Turners Green.

The services of William Felkin, engineer, were again dispensed with, this time on a permanent basis. He was replaced by James Houghton, then of Shrewsbury, who had worked on the building of the Shrewsbury Canal. Several payments continued to be made to Felkin, who seemingly had some unfinished surveying commitments. Houghton's salary was set at £250 per year and his duties were to commence from 21 December 1796.

Construction was now carried out along the whole line between Henwood and Saltisford with cutters employed on the uncompleted sections. In February 1797 William Fletcher was ordered to finish the deep cutting at Shrewley, and by April 1797 was to sign a new agreement for the canal between Kingswood and Turners Green. Meanwhile the task of bricklaying was conducted by a team that included Blastus Hughes and James Cope. In July 1797 another agreement was signed with Jonathan Gee for cutting the section from Turners Green to Rowington Hill. Gee's previous work had included the northern part of the Staffordshire & Worcestershire Canal. At the end of August 1797, Francis Turner was allowed the use of the company kiln at Shrewley Common. Turner promised to throw up all the clay needed by December and make bricks next season at £1 2s per thousand.

With the route now taking shape, plans for a reservoir at Olton were proceeded with. Land was acquired from Charles Lloyd and this was linked to the canal by a feeder that delivered water into the Warwick Canal at a point nearly 5¼ miles from the start of the canal at Digbeth.

Hughes was dismissed as engineer as an economy measure; he was replaced by Phillip Witton, who added engineering to his other duties of clerk and accountant. For a second time Blythe Aqueduct had structural problems, with an arch failing. Mr Witton was instructed to ensure repair without delay.

In April 1798 advertisements were published requesting people to build the brickwork in the remaining 'fourteen' locks at Hatton (twenty-one were completed, in total), furnish timber for the locks, perform carpentry work for these locks and supply wrought ironwork.

The connecting link from the Warwick & Birmingham Canal to meet up with the Grand Junction Canal to London was initially called the Warwick & Braunston Canal. Separate surveys as to the most suitable route were conducted by William Felkin, James Sheriff and Charles Handley It was decided the best route was to meet the Oxford Canal at Braunston, west of the turnpike bridge. The Bill received Royal Assent on 29 January 1794. William Felkin became engineer to the company. Preparatory work started in January 1795 with the engineer marking out the line of canal from its junction with the Warwick & Birmingham Canal in the parish of Budbrooke on the intended line into the parish of Offchurch. He was also to examine where stone might be quarried in the parish of St Nichols or in the parish of Milverton.

A major alteration was made to the route when in August 1795 Charles Handley of Barford suggested a plan for diverting the intended canal from the Fosse Road leading through the parishes of Offchurch, Ufton, Stockton and Napton. Handley believed that by taking the canal to Napton there would be a saving to the company on the cost of construction of approximately £50,000. The committee chose to adopt the alteration and arranged to make their canal to Napton. Such a decision would have later benefits as the new route took the canal through areas where limestone could be quarried for cement making. Once the decision was agreed on, the company name also changed to become the Warwick & Napton Canal Company. The Act that authorised the changes passed through the House of Lords in May 1796.

This canal formed the essential link that united the Warwick & Birmingham Canal with the Grand Junction route to London. It started with a descent of two locks at the Cape, Warwick, to a level section that crossed the Avon Valley to Leamington. From here there was a steady climb through a series of narrow locks to the Oxford Canal at Napton.

Building the Napton Canal was undertaken by direct labour, with some contractors working on both the Warwick canals. During December 1795 men were employed to throw up sufficient quantity of clay in the parish of Offchurch on the line of canal to make bricks.

An important engineering feature on the Napton Canal was the aqueduct over the River Avon located between Warwick and Leamington Priors. In April 1796 Felkin was requested to arrange the excavation of the foundations for this aqueduct. It was also ordered that Benjamin Lloyd and Moses Wilson be employed in building the piers and in doing other mason work there and that they each be paid 4s per day for the time they work. Lloyd and Wilson were to deliver at the office from time to time an account of the number of men they employed under them, including the wages paid to each man.

With regards to completing the aqueduct, advertisements were placed in local newspapers for people to make centres for an aqueduct across the Avon 42ft wide and 13ft high and to find the necessary timber. The centres were to remain the property of the contractors. John Docker later delivered an estimate for making centres for the aqueduct over the River Avon, for fixing and

Avon Aqueduct. Whilst vegetation obscures part of the aqueduct, the structure comprises three arches with two central piers placed in the river. The concrete parapet was added in 1909. (Author)

removing at £200 with Thomas Welton as partner and William Land as surety. A penalty of £500 was included in the contract with Docker and Welton should the centres not be fixed on time.

The terms by which Moses Wilson and Benjamin Lloyd were employed subsequently changed. They consented to carry on with wages at 6s per day for either partner whichever was engaged in the work and if both were there they still received 6s per day. Bricklaying and masons work at the Avon Aqueduct was continued through 1797 until May 1798. Embankment work was carried on longer. During January 1799 John Plant was still engaged in finishing the embankment there. Meanwhile the task of canal cutting proceeded gradually from the Cape and along the north side of Warwick. Cutters on this part included Plant and Thomas Hawkins.

The Warwick & Napton committee noted that Willam Felkin spent more time with the Birmingham line than the Napton and decided to invite another engineer to take over his responsibilities. John Turpin of Wisbech St Peters in the Isle of Ely agreed to serve as engineer from 12 September, on a trial basis, for a term of three calendar months. One of his first duties was to take a level of part of the line of canal from the lock nearest the river up to the aqueduct, then under construction, in order that the piers of such aqueduct may be immediately finished.

Whether Turpin actually started this task is questionable for his resignation is noted at the committee meeting held on 6 October; meanwhile Charles Handley undertook a part of these duties. These included the supervision of a culvert built across the Birmingham Turnpike Road that conveyed water from the Stankbrook and to inspect and sort out works for embankments near the aqueduct. He was to make contracts for 'such on the concern as he shall think fit'.

The committee were still keen to find an engineer. Charles Handley proposed to superintend business of the canal as engineer for an annual sum of 350 guineas and to include every part of business and valuing land. The committee resolved 'unanimously' to appoint him engineer and pay him the salary of 350 guineas commencing from 1 November 1796.

Bricks were purchased from outside contractors and made along the route. Clay was dug in Leamington Priors to make bricks. Brick making was also carried on at Napton where agreements were made with John Burrows, Joseph Greenhill and John Mercer at Walkers Brickyard and with William Smith to make bricks in a brickyard near Saltisford Common.

During February 1797 a contract was let for a tunnel at Leamington Priors in the lands of Matthew Wise. Thomas Keeling, contractor, proposed to make a tunnel in close called Malins Hill for £6 per yard and to make a towpath in said tunnel. The committee agreed that this tunnel was to be 16ft wide by 19ft high with an inverted arch to the opening 1ft of brick in thickness; other parts of brickwork to be made 14½in thick. The canal company were to supply bricks from their brickyard at Leamington Priors and lime from quarries 9 miles distant. An alternative to the tunnel was proposed by Charles Handley that involved a diversion of the canal through a cutting. This proposal was not favoured by Wise as it had the potential to affect the supply of salt water to a brine bath. Keeling may have started the work, but then Wise agreed to the route change and the canal was made as an open cutting. Further deviations were made at Radford Semele, in May 1798, taking the bed of the River Leam and land belonging to Earl of Aylesford.

During the summer of 1798 contractors commenced work on the canal through Stockton and Long Itchington. Handley was instructed to agree with Benjamin Lloyd upon terms he thinks best for doing brickwork at locks to be built at Stockton and Itchington field and also with a proper person to do carpenters work. Charles Handley was also asked to meet Walter Watson on behalf of the Stockton Charity respecting purchase of limestone, which was to be dug out when the canal was cut through their estate in Stockton, and agree the price for such limestone.

The locks at Stockton and Itchington were made as straight as possible through the limestone rock that lay beside the surface of the land. Short branches from the main line were subsequently made to quarry the stone for cement. As the canal reached Napton further locks were constructed at Calcutt. Handley first suggested that the two locks at Calcutt near Napton should be built 7ft

9in deep instead of the initial plan of 7ft. The committee at first sanctioned the change but later this decision was rescinded. Three locks, each 5ft 4in deep, were to be made instead.

In December 1798 the Warwick and Birmingham Canal Company permitted the Napton company to make bricks in their brickyard near Saltisford Common, paying 1s 6d per thousand for bricks made.

The Wyrley & Essington Canal was promoted between 1791 and 1792 leading to Parliament granting permission for the venture in April 1792. The Act provided for a canal from Wyrley Bank to Wolverhampton where a junction was to be made with the Birmingham Canal at Horseley Fields. Branches were to be made to Ashmore Park, Birchills and Pool Hayes. A stop lock was to be provided at the junction and all boats passing from or to the Birmingham Canal would be subject to a payment of toll to the Birmingham Company.

William Pitt was appointed engineer, but his role is better described as surveyor. Pitt was already a very competent surveyor and it is in the planning of the route of the canal that he was chiefly involved. The task of building the waterway fell to the Wolverhampton engineer, John Brawn. It was John Brawn who engaged men and completed the various aspects of the work. Hence the responsibility of building of this canal was essentially with the contractor.

The task of acquiring land lay with Mr Pitt and the solicitors. Pitt had to set out the route and detail all the landowners. A price was then agreed for the land taken for the use of the canal company. If a price could not be agreed then commissioners would be appointed to decide the value. Normally two commissioners would decide the amount, but if they could not agree a third would be called to give a final judgement. The commissioners called upon for this service included John Bishton, who acted on behalf of the company.

Essington Canal Top Lock, 1971. The Essington Lock Flight was made to serve Essington New Colliery by John Brawn senior. The locks were disused when the Wyrley & Essington Canal became part of the BCN network and may not have served Essington Wood Colliery when that mine opened. Yet the locks seem to have been a water supply to the main canal and were repaired from time to time. At the top lock, hand-made bricks and a stone quoin were evident long after closure. (Jim Evans)

As work progressed, Brawn suggested alterations to the route at Pool Hayes. After consultation with William Pitt, a shorter, and straight, section was added to the plan book. The Act of Parliament had authorised two short canal branches to serve coalmines at Ashmore Park and Pool Hayes, but there is no evidence to suggest either were built. Tram roads were made instead to bring coal down to the canalside from the collieries which developed around Pool Hayes. By January 1793 water had been let into part of the canal to enable Brawn to move soil by boat.

The Act of Parliament specifically states that a navigable canal was to be made 'from, or from near, Wyrley Bank', where coal mines existed. Yet the canal never reached this place at this time, but terminated short near Essington Wood Old Colliery belonging to Henry Vernon. Vernon had begun a new mine on the west side of Essington Wood. During February 1793 plans were made to build a canal from Whitmore's Meadow to the intended new engine accommodating Vernon's mines. This is the first mention of the branch canal that became known as the Essington Canal. This branch was probably constructed between 1793 and 1794. It was a branch that came to comprise five locks that brought the navigation up to the highest point on any Midlands canal. The upper part was however a long basin to serve the colliery.

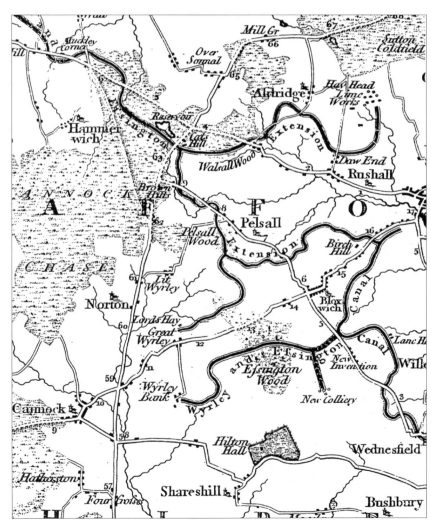

Wyrley & Essington Canal. Canal surveyors sometimes planned routes that were subsequently altered. This is frequently evident in the plans drawn by John Carey, who produced a range of maps based on the layout of authorised routes, rather than what was built. His plan here shows the intended canal to Wyrley Bank, which was only completed as far as Essington Wood and the intended course of the Hays Branch, that was made a short branch to Newtown. It is also clear to see how the nickname 'curly wurly' came about. This waterway comprised several bends and changes of direction as the canal was surveyed and constructed.

Work on the contract was meeting with delay especially in the Bloxwich area where the canal had to be taken around the hillside. There is little evidence now of a hill there, but subsequent mining operations have altered ground levels.

The number of men employed on the works now numbered between 100 and 120. In March 1793 Brawn had commenced to throw up clay for the Walsall Branch. Concern was felt amongst the members of the committee at this time that men were leaving the works for other canal contracts. The men were paid 3s a day by Brawn, but the committee suggested an inducement of a free dinner on Easter Monday plus 1s' worth of ale and that every man who did not leave the work should have another 1s' worth of ale on every first Monday of the month.

By May 1793, the Canal Committee had considered a new proposal for the extension of the route beyond Walsall to join the Coventry Canal, at or near Huddlesford. In order to raise money for the new scheme an additional share issue was proposed. William Pitt was entrusted with surveying the new route, which included branches to the limestone mines at Hay Head via Rushall and Lord Hayes Quarries. The new plans involved incorporating most of the Walsall Branch, from Sneyd to Birchills, then under construction, into the main line of the canal through to Huddlesford. From Birchills the canal turned northwards through Coalpool and Goscote to Pelsall, where there were collieries. The line was then continued to Brownhills, close to P. Hussey's coal works, and then by Catshill, Ogley, Muckley Corner and Lichfield. Excavation was required to take the waterway through the low hills at Catshill, but the most important engineering feature was the flight of locks that brought the canal down to the level of the Coventry Canal at Huddlesford.

An advertisement was inserted in *Aris's Gazette* for canal cutters on the Wyrley & Essington Extension to make the canal on Cannock Heath. The first to apply was a Mr Carne, who submitted quotes for the Catshill 'deep cutting'. Carne had developed a mechanical machine for cutting canals. This machine was used on the Hereford & Gloucester Canal, but seemingly his price was too high for the Catshill contract. Mr George Miles quoted a cheaper tender and his offer was adopted. Meanwhile John Brawn was given the contract to build the canal from Birchills to the far side of the Moat House, Pelsall.

Meanwhile preparations were being made to open the first part of the waterway from Essington and Bloxwich to Horseley Fields. Following arrangements made with the Birmingham Canal Navigations for a suitable stop lock, the communication with the Wyrley & Essington Canal and the Birmingham Canal was opened during November 1794. Coal traffic from the Essington coal mines was now free to pass through to the wharves and works on the canal network.

John Brawn was proceeding with the cutting towards Catshill. He proposed to complete all the brick and woodwork of the bridges (excepting the first bridge at Walsall), all weirs, drawbridges and stop gates by March 1795, so that water could be let in and navigation commenced. During June 1795 the committee went to Lichfield to view to the intended work from there to Huddlesford.

The line from Ogley to Huddlesford was roughly set out by Pitt, but the route was subject to change. Pitt was particularly concerned about water supply and he conceived a lock that would conserve water in segments of a semi-circular side pond. This trial for the conservation device was made at Lock 18 of the canal. Elsewhere the intermediate lock pounds were extended through side pounding, where space was available.

West of Lichfield, near Pipe Hill, there was a level section from Lock 12 to Lock 13. Here the canal crossed the valley of the stream from Hammerwich on a high embankment. The route then turned sharply and was followed by four locks (13–17) that lowered the canal to the bridge under the Fosse Way and then onto Lichfield.

John Brawn therefore completed the bulk of the main canal from Wolverhampton to Huddlesford. Construction work on this section was finished and the canal was opened to traffic throughout on 8 May 1797. William Pitt ceased to be surveyor for the canal company at Christmas 1796, but was paid an additional 50 guineas to complete the survey book including all settlements with the occupiers of land. Work was then concentrated on the two main branches to Hay Head and Lord Hays. That to Hay Head was constructed as it had been surveyed. The other line was altered to terminate at Newtown and never reached the quarries belonging to Lord Hays.

Henry Vernon was evidently not satisfied with the transport arrangements made for his coal and in 1798 commissioned Thomas Dadford to survey a railroad from his New Colliery, Essington, to the Staffordshire & Worcestershire Canal near Calf Heath. Vernon's application to Parliament to make the railway was opposed by the Wyrley & Essington Canal Company. The railway was not built, but considerable ill feeling persisted between Vernon and the Canal Company for a number of years. Part appeasement was made in the form of a railway, which was to link the New Colliery with the proposed Lord Hays Branch. In June 1799 Mr Bishton, surveyor, was requested to cost the railway and the same to be laid down under the direction of Mr Bishton and Mr Clare.

Despite being 'open', the main line was far from finished. In May 1799 John Brawn was instructed to finish up all his work and put the canal in a perfect state of repair. His son, John Brawn junior, who had no doubt helped him on his various projects, was also appointed engineer and surveyor to the Wyrley & Essington Canal Company.

Work had started on a new reservoir on Cannock Chase near Norton, where an earth dam was made across the valley of the Crane Brook that flowed down towards Pipe Hill. A feeder from this reservoir was to be cut through to the canal above the top lock at Ogley. The task of making this reservoir was given to John Brawn junior. Heavy rain fell in June 1799 that led to the earth dams at both Sneyd and Cannock Chase failing. The uncompleted Cannock Chase Reservoir had the more spectacular result when the flood rushed down the brook course to Shenstone, drowning livestock. The Brawns were ordered to repair Sneyd Dam, whilst Thomas Dadford was employed to redesign the Chasewater Dam.

The effects of these accidents were to delay work elsewhere as repairs to the reservoir and canal were carried out. In September 'Mr Brawn' (presumably the senior) was authorised to cut and puddle the Lord Hays Branch, whilst John Brawn junior was required to employ a sufficient number of men to throw up the ground for Mr Vernon's Railway on or before 5 October.

Work on the canal to Hay Head is rarely mentioned in the surviving minutes, but by November 1800 the committee were urging its completion. How much of this work was done by John Brawn senior is not certain, because by now the rigours of canal construction had begun to take their toll on him. John Brawn senior died in May 1801. Hay Head was the last section of waterway to be finished. This lengthy canal branch left the main line at Catshill and travelled through Walsall Wood, Rushall and Daw End before terminating at the limestone quarries at Hay Head. This section became known in later times as the Daw End Canal.

John Brawn junior carried out the outstanding work on the main line and the branches and the canal was finally announced as being complete on 30 November 1801. John Brawn junior was retained as engineer through to 1802, when the company advertised for a new engineer. Richard Stevens was appointed and retained this post through to 1840, when the Wyrley & Essington Canal was merged with the Birmingham Canal Navigations.

Elsewhere in the West Midlands, canal modification became important with increased traffic. On the Staffordshire & Worcestershire Canal, the Bratch Locks remain a heritage feature on the canal to this day, where modern boaters experience the same frustrations as their working boat predecessors whilst waiting their turn at the locks. This restriction to trade may well have been averted if a plan put forward in 1804 for three separate locks around the Bratch had been accepted.

A staircase lock has a disadvantage in that a boat must pass through all three before another boat passing in the opposite direction could have a turn to go through. The canal company evidently sought to improve the Bratch Locks by slightly enlarging the chamber arrangement, adding separate top gates for the middle and lower chamber and making the feed from newly constructed side ponds enter the space between the bottom gate and the newly installed top gate. Only a matter of a few feet separated the top lock gate of one lock with the bottom of another. The alteration made to the brick and stone work is clearly seen.

This type of lock construction came to be associated with Thomas Dadford who reproduced this style of lock on the Stourbridge and Dudley Canals and other waterways. According to company records this work was done long after he had moved on to other tasks. In March 1797 Thomas Dadford was asked to attend the committee and report on a way of improving the locks at the Bratch. This was clearly done as James Sherriff's map of 1804 for the diversion locks shows side ponds linked to the existing locks, a feature necessary for the revised type of lock arrangement. Subsequent to this the side ponds have been altered and enlarged and the road diverted to allow for the lower pond enlargement. With the Bratch Locks there was another alteration made, involving a change of lock chamber depths. As a staircase the locks would not have functioned properly if there was not an equal fall. Yet following the making of side ponds, and presumably with Dadford's modifications, the fall of each chamber was changed. The present situation is that the top chamber has a fall of about 10ft, the middle is 8ft and the bottom chamber is 13ft. Water to fill the bottom chamber is partly derived from the lower side pond.

Whereas the Birmingham & Fazeley Canal, in South Staffordshire, comprised the piece of waterway from Ryders Green to Broadwaters, various branches from this canal to mines and ironworks were completed subsequent to Pinkerton's contract that was completed in 1786. This new work was performed by men working directly for the Birmingham Canal Navigations Company. These were Dank's Branch (that involved an aqueduct over the western branch of the Tame); a branch to Ocker Hill (that conveyed water to the Ocker Hill pumping engines); the Gospel Oak Branch and the Monway Branch. An independent project was a private canal from Toll End to Horseley Heath which was built with initially three locks to the mines of Dixon, Amphlett and Bedford.

In 1794 a new Act authorised the extension of the canal at Broadwaters through the Walsall. The contract was let in two stages. Both lots were awarded to the contractors Jacob Twigg and Joseph Smith. The work included an embankment and aqueduct over the north branch of the Tame at James Bridge. The canal was completed to the terminus basin at Walsall in 1799. Branches from this waterway were made to Bilston and towards Willenhall. There was also the private Bradley Canal, which had four locks.

Canal accommodation provided by the Birmingham, Dudley and Stourbridge Canals was beneficial to industry alongside the banks. The iron trade especially benefited through the movement of minerals and finished products. The invention of the puddling process had proved of particular benefit to the canal-based ironworks, and which grew in number, in consequence. Increased trade

James Bridge Aqueduct, Birmingham Canal Navigations – the Walsall Canal crossed Bentley Mill Lane and the north branch of the River Tame. (Author)

led to the making of a number of private waterways that linked to the Birmingham, Dudley and Wyrley & Essington canals. Lengths varied from basins to branches complete with locks. Twenty-six private waterways of length can be identified:

Canals with Locks	No. of Locks	Location
Bradley Marr	Staircase pair	Old Main Line, Bradley
Bromford Ironworks	1	New Main Line, Oldbury
Dumaresq Branch	2	Gospel Oak Branch
Foxyards Canal	4	Main Line, Bloomfield
Gibsons Arm & Baskerville Basin	1	Newhall Branch
Robinsons Tarworks	1	Walsall Canal, Ryders Green

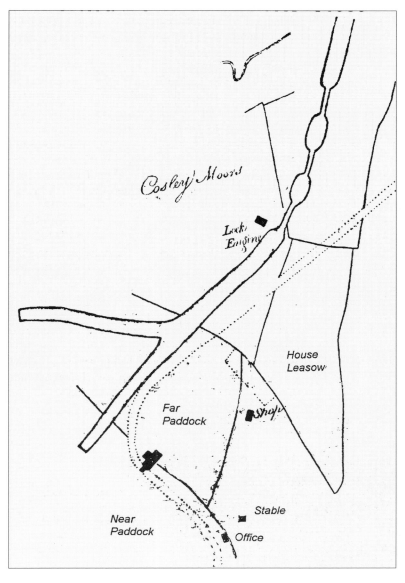

Private branches of the Birmingham Canal – the Foxyards Canal was built for the Lord Dudley and Ward to serve the mines at the Foxyards. Four locks were constructed, one at the junction with the Birmingham Canal at Bloomfield and three others. This map, which was part of a lease plan for Tipton Furnaces, shows three locks and the lock engine that raised water to the upper level. Later, water supply was obtained from a tunnel extension into limestone workings. (Original at Dudley Reference Office)

Roundshill Canal	1	Main Line, Bloomfield
Scott & Foley's *	4	Walsall Canal
Slough Arm	1	Wyrley & Essington, Brownhills

* Canal became part of Bradley Branch Canal and Locks, 1849

Canals without Locks — **Location**

Bickley's Arm	Main Line, Bilston
Gilpins	Wyrley & Essington, Pelsall
Grazebrook Furnaces	Dudley No. 1, Parkhead
Houghton Arm	Old Main Line, Oldbury
Ladymoor Colliery	Main Line, Bilston
Minerva Arm	Main Line, Wolverhampton
New Cut (Limeworks)	Old Main Line, Tipton Green
Pelsall Ironworks	Wyrely & Essington, Pelsall
Pensnett Canal	Dudley No. 1, Parkhead
Plume Street Arm	Birmingham & Fazeley
Sandhills	Wyrley & Essington, Brownhills
Tangyes	Main Line, Smethwick
Tipton Green Furnaces (old arm)	Toll End Communication
Wallis's Arm	Digbeth Branch
Whitmore's Arm	Birmingham & Fazeley Canal

Tunnel Branches — **Location**

Wrens Nest	Dudley No. 1 Canal

A rare survivor of the Dudley No. 2 Canal to Selly Oak is the accommodation bridge built for the road to Weoley Park Farm that is now part of the access to the Park. (Author)

The Dudley Canal Company followed an ambitious course with their No.2 line that united Parkhead with Selly Oak and the Worcester & Birmingham Canal. Unlike the protracted construction of both the Stratford and Worcester waterways, the Dudley No.2 was completed in a relatively short period of five years. This route followed the contours of the hill around Netherton then went by Windmill End and through to Old Hill. A tunnel was made through Sleck Hill (Gorsty Hill) and the canal continued along the Halesowen hillside towards Manor Lane and the cutting that led to the western end of Lapal Tunnel. At 3,795yds, Lapal Tunnel became the fourth longest canal tunnel in Britain.

Once the Bill was authorised by Parliament on 17 June 1793, the Dudley Canal Committee met and elected to appoint Josiah Clowes (1735–94) as consultant engineer and William Underhill as clerk of works. Underhill was instructed to arrange to purchase half a million bricks from the brick kilns at Moor Street, a hamlet south-east of Halesowen.

Excavating the tunnel encountered subterranean springs and faulted zones in the strata. It is believed that thirty shafts were sunk to aid construction of the tunnel and boats were purchased to convey spoil from the workings. The tunnel was made specifically for narrowboats with a width of 9ft 7in and the crown of the arch at 12ft 7in.

Water problems continued and navvies worked in frequently appalling conditions. The company-authorised capital was spent by mid-1796 and this needed another Act to raise another £40,000.

Pumping was aided through the use of a fire engine installed at Moor Street. This engine was offered for sale on 29 September 1797. As construction neared completion one shaft was retained for ventilation. The greater part of tunnel was lined with brick; only two sections of sounder rock were left unlined. The tunnel was finally opened in 1798, although failures in the tunnel continued to plague the canal company for years to come.

Water supply to the Trent & Mersey Canal was improved with the making of the branch to Leek and the feeder from there to a new reservoir at Rudyard Lake. Construction began after the Act received Royal Assent in 1797 and was completed in 1801. The work included the extension of the summit from Endon to Denton, which led to the abandonment of the old section and three locks and the building of a staircase of three locks at Hazelhurst that took the canal to Froghall down to the former level. The stone bridges on the Leek Branch contrasted with the brick on the older waterway. These were a feature preferred by John Rennie, then engineer for the Trent & Mersey Canal.

Froghall Wharf was altered after an Act of 1783 permitted an extension by 530yds to a more convenient wharf for the limestone tramway. Part of this extension was through a 76yd-long tunnel, whose headroom was at best 6ft.

The Uttoxeter Canal was authorised by Parliament in 1797, but building this waterway of 13 miles took thirteen years. Construction was conducted under the supervision of John Rennie, but was delayed. Oakamoor, on the canal, was not reached until 1808. Work was finished and the canal declared officially open on 3 September 1811. The junction lock was made with the Caldon at the new Froghall Basin. There were seventeen locks from Froghall to the basin at Uttoxeter. There was a short tunnel at Alton (40yds long), the River Churnet was crossed on the level with protecting locks either side and the River Tean was spanned by an iron aqueduct. Once open, trade quickly developed to the warehouses placed beside the terminus wharf.

Authority was also given for the Trent & Mersey to build a branch to Burslem (opened 1805) and three connecting tramroads (also built about 1805):

Details of distances

Burslem tramroad	Burslem Wharf– Burslem	2¾ furlongs, rise 85ft 9in
Hanley tramroad	Etruria Wharf– Hanley	6¾ furlongs, rise 115ft 5in
–	Shelton Branch	¾ furlong, 3ft 0in rise
Lane End tramroad	Stoke Lane End	2 miles, 5 furlongs, rise 151ft 8in
–	Side Branch to Green Dock	2½ furlong, rise 25ft 4in

The 1867 NSR Byelaws (at Gloucester) state that these tramways were 3ft 8in gauge. The maximum tare weight of wagons was 10cwt and maximum gross weight 2.5 tons. The distance between axles was restricted between a minimum of 3ft and a maximum of 4ft. The maximum dimensions of the carriage were 6ft long by 5ft 6in wide.

Some West Midlands waterways were constructed as unconnected canals, made for specific purpose, which usually was the movement of three types of minerals; coal, ironstone and limestone. An early canal was the private Parrot Canal that was made to move coal at Bedworth. This waterway had a short independency, as it was incorporated into the route of the Coventry Canal. Another early navigation was the Donnington Wood Canal in Shropshire. This has the distinction of being the first canal in the Midlands.

The Donnington Wood Canal was built on the estate of Lord Gower, brother-in-law to the Duke of Bridgewater. Inspiration for the canal is said to have come from the building of Worsley Canal, near Manchester, the Duke's first canal venture. Lord Gower's mines were at Donnington Wood and the canal is believed to have connected with different navigable levels in the mines. Gower formed a partnership for the development of the Lilleshall estate in 1764. The level canal was constructed between 1765 and 1767 and was 5½ miles long. It brought coal to Pave Lane Wharf on the Newport–Wolverhampton turnpike. The canal was built for 3-ton capacity boats. These 'boats' were effectively water-tight boxes and the type became popularly known as 'tub boats'. Such a term was already in use and applied to craft that transferred goods from sea-going vessels to the shore. Smugglers found the tub boat of particular use for their purposes.

Another canal was made from Hugh Bridge to limestone quarries near Lilleshall village and was at a lower level to the Donnington Wood Canal. The Lilleshall Canal terminated in a tunnel and all traffic between the two was raised up and down one of two shafts (42ft 8in deep). This canal was about 2 miles long and from Willmore Bridge descended by seven small locks toward Lilleshall, where there were five branches to the mines and quarries there and at nearby Pitchcroft. Hugh Bridge tunnel shaft was subsequently replaced, in about 1797, by an incline plane 123yds long. This plane used railway wagons for transfer, rather than transporting tub boats.

Donnington Wood remained an isolated waterway until William Reynolds, ironmaster, started to build new tub-boat canals. It is fair to say that Reynolds played a significant role in the improvement of transport links in East Shropshire. At Ketley he arranged for the construction of two tub-boat canals to serve the ironworks there in 1787–88. These were the Ketley and Wombridge. Some 200–300 labourers were employed on cutting the canals. Both waterways were also linked to the proposed Shropshire Canal, which Reynolds was also connected with. Ketley Ironworks were located near to the turnpike and close to Smiths Hill. The Ketley Canal was made east from there to the bottom of an incline plane, which carried the boats up to a higher level and on towards the Wombridge Canal. Ketley Incline Plane was completed in 1788. It was the first successful canal incline plane to be built in Britain. Tub boats were raised up and down on cradles fitted with wheels that ran along iron tracks made from L-shaped plates. Larger craft were used on the Ketley Canal. They were 20ft long by 6ft 4in wide and could carry up to 8 tons of coal. The principal was that the 'heavier' cradle descended and pulled up the 'lighter' cradle using ropes, pulleys and a drum. Boats were raised 75ft from the lower canal and deposited in a 'chamber' at the top before passing into the upper canal.

The Ketley Canal was 1½ miles long. In this length was the incline plane, four over-bridges, a short tunnel at Potters Hill and a stop lock. There was also a short branch at the top known as Smiths Hill Branch. At Wombridge the canal was also 1½ miles long and like the Ketley had a short tunnel.

The Shropshire Canal was a public waterway surveyed by William Reynolds (1787) and authorised by Act of Parliament in 1788. It formed a navigation and incline transport link from Coalport beside the River Severn to the Ketley, Wombridge and Donnington Wood Canals. Three inclines were constructed on this canal, but unlike the Ketley, they employed steam engines on the inclines for haulage. Tub boats were drawn up on cradles from the lower canal but at the top there was a reverse slope that lowered the craft into the upper waterway.

The Shropshire Canal was completed between 1788 and 1792. The distance between the Donnington Wood Canal and Coalport was 7¾ miles. Tunnels were excavated at Southall Bank, Hollingswood and Snedshill on the main line, or Eastern Branch. The Western Branch was made from Southall Bank towards Brierley Hill, 2¾ miles long. A principal feature of this short waterway was a stone aqueduct. A boat incline plane had been intended to be built at Brierley Hill, but shafts (each 120ft deep) and tunnels were built instead to serve the Coalbrookdale Ironworks. This section also had another intended boat plane at Lincoln Hill that would lower craft down to the River Severn at Styches Weir 210ft below. The tunnel and shaft method lasted until 1794 when after failures in the working of the system the Coalbrookdale Company decided to replace it with a railway incline plane and railway. They constructed this line and another incline near the Lower Forge to the banks of the Severn and later extended it along the banks of the Western Branch to Horsehay Wharf.

A year after the Shropshire Canal was completed, the Act for the Shrewsbury Canal passed through Parliament. William Reynolds was at the heart of this scheme also. Josiah Clowes was appointed engineer and work began during 1793. Part of the Wombridge Canal was absorbed by the Shrewsbury so as to form the link with the Shropshire. There was one incline, at Trench.

The Shrewsbury Canal was constructed over a time period of three years (1793–96). There were eleven locks, four aqueducts and a tunnel. Clowes planned all aqueducts to be made in brick and stone. There was a small single-arch aqueduct at Pimley near Shrewbury that spanned a small tributary of the Severn and another single-arch aqueduct was made on the approach embankment to the crossing of the River Roden at Roddington. The River Roden itself was crossed by a three-arch aqueduct.

A much longer aqueduct was intended to span the River Tern at Longden-on-Tern. Here Clowes designed a substantial masonry structure. But a section was washed away in a flood before the work was completed. The floods coincided with the death of Clowes and the appointment of Thomas Telford as his successor. Telford chose to use a cast-iron channel and aqueduct to replace the damaged section. Telford at this time had little experience with engineering in iron and was assisted by William Reynolds in making the new design. It was Reynolds who supplied the iron plates and other ironwork from his ironworks at Ketley. The masonry arches and approach embankments were repaired to Telford's instructions and only the central span, 62ft long, comprised the iron aqueduct. It was 7ft 6in wide and 4ft 6in deep. Longden-on-Tern Aqueduct was finished by March 1796. It was the second iron aqueduct to be made in this country. The honours for making the first go to Benjamin Outram, who was responsible for making the aqueduct over the mill stream at the Holmes in Derby on the Swarkestone Branch of the Derby Canal.

Near Preston a 970yd-long tunnel was excavated, which became known as Berwick Tunnel. Clowes had designed it during July 1794, but the agreement to build a cantilevered towing path through it was made at the request of William Reynolds. The eleven locks were designed to take up to four tub boats at time. Each was 81ft long and 6ft 7in wide. Counterbalanced guillotine gates were used at the lower end instead of more conventional mitre gates.

On the Shrewsbury Canal, Josiah Clowes started the construction of the Longden-on-Tern Aqueduct, a masonry aqueduct across the River Tern which was damaged by a flood on the river. Thomas Telford rebuilt the central part using cast-iron plates supplied by Reynolds & Co. Whilst the Holmes Aqueduct at Derby has the distinction of being the first iron aqueduct in Britain, Longden was the longest at this time. It comprised a trough for the boats and a side trough that served as a towing path. (Author)

An enduring legacy left by the tub-boat system was the engineering skills developed to make the incline planes. Others copied these designs. In Prussia the incline plane concept was adopted in 1806 for the canal at Gliwice as part of a navigation that connected ironworks with the River Oder.

SHROPSHIRE CANAL INCLINE PLANES

Location	Canal	Rise
Hay	Shropshire Canal	207ft
Ketley	Ketley Canal	75ft
Trench	Shrewsbury Canal	75ft
Windmill Farm	Shropshire Canal	126ft
Wrockwardine Wood	Shropshire Canal	120ft

Another type of tub-boat canal was constructed in North Staffordshire to link Newcastle-under-Lyme with mines at Apedale. Known as Sir Nigel Gresley's Canal, the route of 3 miles was constructed between 1775 and 1776. Engineering for this level waterway was minimal, although map evidence show five bridges and the crossing of streams by aqueducts or culverts in three places. This isolated waterway might have been absorbed into the main canal network had the Commercial Canal been built. Yet despite this failure, a sort of link was provided later.

The Newcastle-under-Lyme Canal was 4 miles long. It was constructed between 1795 and 1800 and formed a link between the Trent & Mersey Canal at Stoke and the lower part of Newcastle. This canal finished at a terminus wharf alongside the same road that passed the terminus of Sir Nigel Gresley's Canal. A 'junction canal' between the two waterways was also made. This was in effect a 1⅛ mile-long branch of Gresley's canal and terminated at Stubbs Walk at a higher level than the Newcastle Canal, but only some 200yds distant.

That there was never a formal link between Stubbs Walk and the Newcastle has been published in several canal histories and to the present time remains a matter of conjecture. Map evidence shows a path or road between the two, implying a system of cartage may have been used to transfer goods and minerals between the two levels. It is also possible that an incline railway may have existed there for a time. Sales notices for Apedale Ironworks published in 1809 and 1818 indicate that this was the case.

West Midlands Canal & River network, c.1805. By 1805 key elements of the canal and river navigations in the West Midlands were complete and open to serve the growing industrial needs of Birmingham, South Staffordshire and East Worcestershire. Both the Stratford upon Avon and the Worcester & Birmingham canals are shown as only partially completed. Their history is mentioned in Chapter 5.

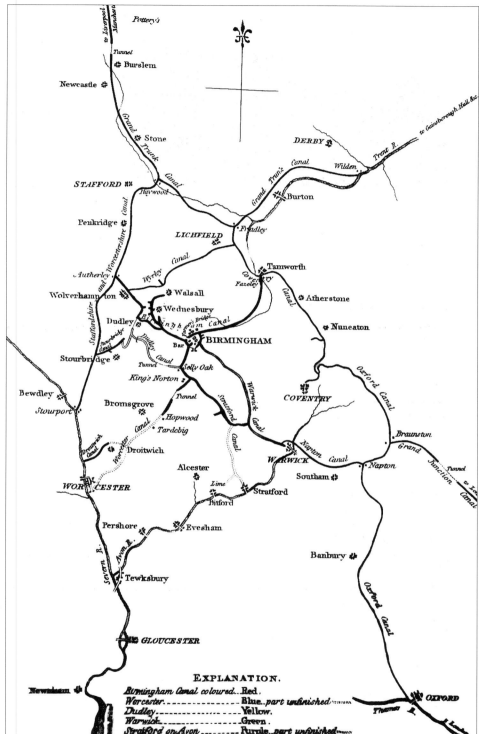

CANAL BUILDING IN THE EAST MIDLANDS

East Midlands waterway construction started with the Loughborough Canal and the Erewash Canal. Whilst John Smith progressed with making the Soar navigable to Loughborough, contracts were advertised for building the Erewash Canal to link the Derbyshire collieries with the Trent near the infall of the River Soar. Construction of the Erewash Canal was awarded to James and John Pinkerton, who quickly engaged in laying out the first 9 miles, which included locks, bridges and aqueducts. John Varley, who had previously been engineer to the Chesterfield Canal, was appointed as engineer to the Erewash.

The agreement with John Varley to overlook, manage and direct the work of said canal during the making and completing thereof was made in July 1777. His salary was set at £220 per year. The contract with James and John Pinkerton was not signed until September 1777. Yet they soon started and made rapid progress. In April 1778 Varley reported 9 miles of cutting and banking were finished and that one lock, three bridges, two aqueducts and six side tunnels were nearly built.

Both stone and brick were adopted as construction materials. Stone was in part obtained from a quarry at Castle Donington. The committee were keen that a stone bridge was built across the turnpike road leading from Nottingham to Derby and when the same was completed Mr Varley should settle the difference of expense between it and a brick bridge. They also decided that two arches were to be made at the aqueduct at Nutbrook instead of one as agreed with Mr Pinkerton 'for the greater convenience of conveying the water through'.

Bricks for locks and works were made by, or for, the company. Brick making had progressed from the temporary clamp to the more permanent 'kiln'. But quality varied and the selection of well-made bricks was realised by the Erewash Canal Committee. John Varley, or an assistant, had the duty to examine the several brick kilns where drawn and separate unfit bricks. Only those deemed fit were brought to the several locks and bridges. The contractors for bricks were to notify John Varley at what time their kiln was intended to be drawn.

By the end of May 1778 construction had reached the stage when water could be let into the canal from the Erewash. The committee were conscious of the effect the drain would have on Erewash mills. John Varley, or his agent, was to keep account of what damage might happen to the miller of Toton Mill on account of the Erewash water being let into the canal. Once water was let in, deficiencies in the making of the canal became evident through leaks in the banks.

Varley and Pinkerton clearly had different views on the type of cement that could be used and on lock construction. Varley sent a report to the committee that detailed the 'insufficiency' of several locks, bridges, cuttings and banking. The committee instructed the Pinkertons that such 'insufficiency', so far as related to banks, puddling and lock gates, should be rectified as soon as possible and the stone, brick and woodwork as soon as the season of the year allowed. In the case James and John Pinkerton neglected to set about stopping the leakage of banks, puddling and lock gates in such parts and locks as were mentioned in the report, then Mr Varley was instructed to set men to work in order to do so at the expense of Mr Pinkerton.

Above: The lock and lock house at Sandiacre on the Erewash Canal. North of the lock are the remains of the former junction with the Derby Canal. (Author)

Right: Sandiacre Lock House. (Author)

By April 1779 the canal was navigable from the Trent to Ilkeston and construction proceeded northward to Langley Mill. Construction was completed during 1779, but James and John Pinkerton were obliged to maintain the canal as part of their agreement with the canal company until 1783.

Proposals for a canal north of Langley Mill became fact with the passing of the Cromford Canal Act of 1789. The Bill was opposed by the Erewash, keen to preserve water supply. An enquiry held in 1788 examined in detail the claims from mill owners and others with reference to the River Derwent. Such were the resulting constraints on taking water from the Derwent that a supply was diverted from a lead mine leat into the canal near the terminus. This canal was constructed between 1789 and 1794 with William Jessop and Benjamin Outram devoting time as engineers to the project. Making this canal was to test the skills of both to the limit.

Fourteen locks were made to barge dimensions on the ascent from Langley Mill to Codnor. Major engineering works included Butterley Tunnel (2,996yds) and aqueducts over the River Amber and the River Derwent. Failures in these aqueducts during construction troubled Jessop who pledged recompense to the canal proprietors. From the east portal of Butterley Tunnel through to Cromford the canal was only made wide enough for narrowboats to pass. Trade on this

Cromford Canal, terminus of navigation – narrowboats loaded and unloaded cargoes beside this warehouse and wharf. (Author)

The aqueduct carrying the Cromford Canal over the River Derwent is known variously by the names of Wigpool or Leawood. Constructing the stone aqueduct over the River Derwent near Leawood proved to be a difficult task for engineer William Jessop; part of the aqueduct failed during the building work. (Author)

Left: Water supply for the canal was derived from a leat that ran from a lead mine and into the canal at the wharf. (Author)

Below: Buttress support for the Leawood Aqueduct. (Author)

section would be principally merchandise and limestone and perhaps the width was not critical. East of the tunnel 14ft-wide barges could load coal for the journey south.

From Whatstandwell the canal follows closely the north side of the Derwent Valley and at places runs alongside a steep slope and is embanked and walled. There are places where only a single boat might pass. At Leabrook the Cromford Canal crosses the Derwent by a long single span, although there are also two separate arches on each side of the river bank. Here is located the junction with the private Leawood Branch that turns north along the side of the valley and terminates at a wharf.

A third aqueduct was made over the Erewash north of Langley Mill and two reservoirs were constructed at Codnor Park and Butterley Park (Golden Valley). These reservoirs supplied water to the east side of Butterley Tunnel and provided the additional water needed for the barge navigation to Langley Mill.

The view of the aqueduct from below reveals a strong single arch, although there is evidence of buttress strengthening at the north end. (Author)

The Cromford had a strategic role in canal transport. Buckland Hollow became an interchange point between canal and road. Here goods were transferred to wagons to be hauled through the Peak District to Chesterfield, Sheffield, Leeds and York.

Butterley Tunnel passed directly under the Butterley Ironworks, originally operated by Benjamin Outram & Co. and later the Butterley Company. The tunnel was widened at this point into a space known as the wide hole. A pair of loading shafts linked the works above with the loading wharf in the wide hole. There were also headings to coal mines. One underground passageway went to the Carr Wood Colliery.

The Erewash Canal served an extensive coal and ironstone mining district. Iron smelting was conducted close to the canal at Dale Furnace. A branch canal from the Erewash in the direction of Dale was achieved with the making of the Nutbrook Canal that followed the valley of the Nut Brook, a tributary of the Erewash.

This waterway was built as a barge canal that climbed through thirteen locks towards Mapperley. Various tramways were built to mines on either side and there were two branches, Stanhope Arm and Hunloke's Arm.

Work started on building the Nutbrook Canal after the Act was obtained on 3 June 1793. This canal was built by labour under the supervision of Benjamin Outram. John Hodgkinson was Outram's assistant. Construction was finally completed during 1796 including a reservoir at Shipley. A second reservoir at Mapperley was completed during 1821.

Whilst the Dale Ironworks had a brief existence, coal and iron mining continued. Eventually two major ironworks were established at Stanton and West Hallam, which generated both railway and canal trade.

During the period known as Canal Mania, many new schemes were proposed throughout the East Midlands, making canals or adapting river navigations. Those built were the Ashby Canal, Derby Canal, Grantham Canal, Leicester Navigation, Leicestershire & Northamptonshire Union Canal, Melton Mowbray Navigation, Nottingham Canal, Oakham Canal and the Old (or Grand) Union.

East Midlands waterways were generally made to barge dimensions, unlike their West Midlands counterparts. Links with the Trent Navigation was an important factor in the decision for making locks 14ft wide so as to accommodate the Trent Boat that navigated those waters. The first was the section of the Trent & Mersey from Horninglow. This was followed by the making of the canal sections of the Soar to Loughborough and then the Erewash Canal. Further new barge waterway schemes followed that included the Ashby, Cromford, Derby and Nottingham canals.

Whilst work on making the Cromford Canal progressed, plans for a navigation along the Soar towards Leicester were considered. Loughborough merchants prospered at the expense of Leicester people, charging for goods as much as they dared. Eventually a scheme for continuing the Soar Navigation to Leicester was surveyed by William Jessop. Part and parcel of this survey was the inclusion of a transport link to reach the mines and limeworks located near Charnwood Forest. Navigation to Melton Mowbray was also investigated. Bills for the Leicester and Charnwood Forest Navigation and the Wreak and Eye Navigation passed through Parliament in 1791.

Work first started on the river line from Loughborough to the West Bridge at Leicester. Charles Staveley performed the job of resident engineer. The contract was let to Francis and George Pinkerton in September 1791 with work starting later that year. Robert Pinkerton also assisted. Bricks were purchased at first from local makers so that Pinkerton could 'expedite work'. Bricks were also made in company-owned brickyards.

The Forest Line comprised the unusual arrangement of a railway, a central canal section and a railway, which linked the Loughborough Canal Basin with the limestone quarries and coal mines at Charnwood. It was surveyed by Staveley in 1791 and contracts to build the railways were prepared for the Pinkertons to sign in February 1792. By March work on the railways was in progress. Yet progress was not to the board's satisfaction. They offered the Pinkertons a reward of £50 per week for every week they could save on the time allowed in their contract for completing the work. This bonus was to be paid on the navigation and railways being opened throughout.

Pinkerton's contracts still did not meet the standards required. They had one final chance in August 1792. William Jessop was ordered to inform them that he would survey their work within ten days. Jessop required their assurance to correct any faults, which he pointed out to them. Their failure to do so would result in a report to the committee that they were incompetent in the execution of their engagement and in that case the committee would take the work under their own management.

A key element to this investigation was Pinkerton's lack of security for items of value. Losses had occurred and the committee had applied to the magistrate, the Revd Burnaby, to apprehend persons who had stolen plant materials and other things belonging to the undertaking.

On 29 August 1792 Mr Jessop reported to the committee that he was not satisfied with the contractors and that workmen had now been employed directly under the direction of the surveyor. Mr Staveley was now in charge of construction and he had the task to employ as many men as he could upon the works. Instructions were also given during October 1792 to make as many bricks as possible at the brickyards belonging to the company as could be done. The company's agents were also directed to dig and get clay for making bricks for the works. Mr Staveley was to employ labourers for the task. The quality of bricks already made was questioned. The company petitioned the Board of Excise requesting drawback on excise duty for 254,000 bricks destroyed by rain.

Once bricks had been made for the summer of 1793, William Jessop was consulted as to the best mode of proceeding in erecting the several locks. He recommended that they proceed as fast as possible in building all the locks to a height of 4ft, so by that means they would be above the water from one end of the line to the other; the locks could then be completed afterwards at their convenience.

Much was still to be done and the committee were still concerned about the quality and progress of the making of the navigation. They asked Mr Staveley to answer the following questions:

1   How many bridges are to be built from Loughborough to Leicester and where?
2   How many parts of the river are to be scoured?
3   How many bricklayers?
4   Where will bricklayers find new work and where (sic)?
5   Why are the bricks so bad?

He was also told that in future none but good and well-burnt bricks would be received and he and Mr Elliot should take care that only such bricks were received from brickyards. Questions were also asked about the crucial brick-making process and the amounts of coal required. Mr Mansfield, the brickmaker, stated 9 tons of coal should burn 20,000 bricks. Mr Elliot stated 260,000 bricks had been burnt, but 300 tons of coal consumed!

By July 1793 work had progressed to a stage that Mr Allen was directed by the surveyor to proceed in preparing gates and other woodwork belonging to locks. In August orders were given to build North Bridge in Leicester and dig out the lock pit for North Lock. Work was so far advanced on the river line that in January 1794 the committee ordered that the navigation to be opened as soon as possible for the transport of coals. In February 1794 the town wharf was to be completed and a weighing machine house and shed erected there.

Making the navigation had required the cutting of lengthy lock channels from the Loughborough Canal, at Barrow upon Soar, Mountsorrell, Syston, Cossington, Thurmaston, Birstall and from Belgrave Mill to Leicester Town Wharf. This last cut then adapted the course of

Mountsorrell Lock, River Soar Navigation. (Author)

Barrow Deep Lock, Barrow upon Soar. (Author)

St Margaret's Ditch as the cut through to North Lock. From there the Soar was made navigable to the north side of the West Bridge. Locks were provided at Barrow Mill, Mountsorrell, Sileby Mill, Cossington Mill, Thurmaston Mill, Birstall, Belgrave and North Lock, Leicester.

Navigation to Melton Mowbray proceeded from the junction with the Leicester Navigation at Turnwater Meadow. When the river line of the Leicester Navigation was opened to traffic, contractors building the locks on the Melton Navigation had ensured that boats could travel as far as Rearsby. This navigation was essentially an improved river course utilising the Wreake and Eye. William Jessop surveyed the route and was assisted in this task by Christopher Staveley junior. Lock cuts and locks were situated at twelve places between the Soar and Melton, ten of which were at existing, or former, mill sites. Staveley was appointed engineer to this navigation when work began. Yet progress proceeded slowly, lock by lock, until Frisby was reached (in November 1794). Limited finance was the principle cause of the delay. Staveley was replaced by William Green in July 1795, and it was he who supervised the completion of the navigation. Leicester Navigation traffic tonnage receipts indicate that the route to Melton was open by, or during, 1797.

From Melton another canal was made to Oakham, which involved the construction of nineteen locks. From a junction with the Melton Mowbray canal basin the Oakham Canal followed the Eye Valley with locks near Bretingby and Wyfordby. After crossing a stream the canal turned south towards Market Overton and its end at Oakham. William Jessop surveyed the route and Christopher Staveley junior was engineer when work began. Staveley was later replaced by William Dunn of Sheffield, who completed the route. The Oakham Canal was reported finished in June 1802, although boats did not reach the terminus until the next year. Had Whitworth's survey of a canal from Oakham to Stamford (1809) been proceeded with, navigation from the Soar through to the Wash would have been accomplished.

Some canal schemes seemed fated to fail and others were completed against considerable odds. Making the canal known as the Ashby certainly faced many problems. It was also a canal that never reached its intended destination of Ashby-de-la-Zouch. This canal was made to barge width but generally had traffic in narrowboats, for the only connection to the national network was through the narrow Coventry Canal at Marston Junction. The only lock, a stop lock, was made to narrowboat dimensions. Elsewhere it was a wide waterway to Moira.

Ashby Woulds and neighbourhood was a mineral-rich district noted especially for Breedon Lime and various collieries. A survey for a canal that ran southwards from Ashby Woulds to the Coventry

The Ashby Canal was made to barge dimension. At Shakerstone the Ashby crosses the River Sense by a wide aqueduct. (Author)

Canal at Griff, through Market Bosworth and Hinckley, had been conducted by Robert Whitworth senior during 1781. This project was not proceeded with, as with another suggested by William Jessop in 1787, which sought an alternative route westward. Jessop's plan incorporated a tramway from Breedon Hill and 1½ miles of canal that descended through three locks to the Trent and another opposite that climbed through two locks to meet the Trent & Mersey Canal. Renewed attempts to make a canal to Ashby commenced in 1792, again with alternate schemes to join the Coventry or the Trent. Finally an Act was passed in May 1794 for the line to meet the Coventry Canal. The company had the choice of making their canal broad or narrow, and decided to build a barge canal, in the hope one day that the Coventry and Oxford might be widened as far as the Grand Junction Canal. Robert Whitworth was appointed joint engineer with son Robert, junior.

Notices to cut the canal appeared in local newspapers in October 1794. The *Derby Mercury* (23 October 1794) requested contractors to undertake seven sets of work:

1 the deep cutting upon Hills Farm, Snareston
2 the embankment at Hot Bridge between Measham Fields and Snareston
3 the deep cutting on the south of Measham
4 the embankment on the north of Measham
5 the embankment over Bramborough Brook, between Oakthorpe and Willesley
6 the deep cutting in Donisthorpe to the Woulds
7 and the embankment thence into the Woulds

Construction work was directed by Robert Whitworth junior, joint-engineer to the canal. Mr Whitworth directed the work from his base in Measham. Lots of level cutting was requested in April 1795 for Snareston, Okethorpe and Cotton near Bosworth, whilst in November 1795 more extensive engineering led to tenders being invited to build the aqueduct over the River Mease between Measham and Snarestone, for making embankment and deep cutting near Donisthorpe, for removing, carrying and conveying soil in boats to be found by the company from the deep cutting at Measham and Snarestone to the Islot Valley, and for getting stone at Marston Jabet.

During 1795 Robert Whitworth senior was involved in surveying the Commercial Canal. This was an extremely ambitious project that was intended to link the Ashby near Moira with the Trent, incorporate the Bond End Canal at Burton and Sir Nigel Gresley's Canal at Newcastle and pass through such towns as Uttoxeter, Cheadle and Burslem before finally joining up with the Chester Canal at Nantwich. This scheme was successfully opposed by the Trent & Mersey Canal and Grand Junction Canal Company who were keen to keep the established trading route from the North West and Potteries. Those who took part in the inquiry may also have been influenced by the suggested widening the Coventry and Oxford canals, a piece of engineering which was never carried out.

Robert Whitworth junior became ill in 1797 and was forced to relinquish his supervision of the canal. Thomas Newbold carried on these duties for a while until replaced by the experienced engineer William Crossley. Newbold still oversaw the day-to-day construction of the canal.

The canal was opened from Ashby Woulds to Market Bosworth in 1798, but there were few collieries then working along the route and the promise of supplying the country with coals was a far-off prospect. Meanwhile, and despite financial restrictions, the task of building the canal to join up with the Coventry at Marston Junction was carried on. The line was ready by April or May 1804. Major engineering structures included Snarestone Tunnel, the aqueduct over the River Sense near Shakerstone and Shenton Aqueduct (which crossed the road from Market Bosworth to Shenton). An extensive railway system was also constructed, that met the Ashby Canal at Willesley Basin, by Benjamin Outram. This railway, made to 4ft 2in gauge, passed through Ashby-de-la-Zouch and Ashby Tunnel (308yds long) to a junction at Ticknall (8 miles). From here one line continued north to limestone quarries at Ticknall and Dimsdale, whilst the other went onto Cloud Hill Quarry at Breedon. This line was completed during 1802. Construction was conducted under the supervision of John Hodgkinson.

The Derby Canal was a complex waterway system. The task of surveying and engineering this canal was entrusted to Benjamin Outram (1764–1804). A Bill was presented to Parliament in September 1792 for:

> … a navigable canal from the River Trent in the parish of Swarkestone, to and by the Town of Derby, to or near a place called Smithy Houses, the parish of Derby, and two branches or collateral cuts from the said canal, one of them from or near Coxbench, to or near Smalley Hill in the liberty of Smalley, and the other from or near the town of Derby to the Erewash Canal in the parish of Sandiacre.

> *London Gazette* notice, 18 September 1792

This notice was different from the canal as built. The section to Smithy Houses was made as a plateway. Yet following the successful application to Parliament, the Derby Canal Company held a meeting at the Bell Inn on 6 July 1793, where it was announced that work had already begun:

> Mr Outram and Mr Wootton having respectively caused land on the lines of the said intended canal to be broken up for the purpose of making bricks and likewise for cutting part of the canal, previous to the general meeting of the proprietors and which was done for the purpose of expediting the business.

George Wootton was appointed superintendent of the works with a salary of £150. His job as superintendent included seven principal roles:

1   To see that all surveyors are at their places
2   That materials were provided for each job of work where wanted
3   To purchase all small matters wanted
4   To see the ironwork, timber and other materials were sound and good
5   To view every part of the line at least twice a week
6   To see proper care is taken of fences and as little trespass is done as possible
7   To employ day men where he shall see necessary and to see their due attention and to attend all carriage work

George Wootton therefore had direct control of the construction. He had many close dealings with William White, the appointed book keeper at a salary of £105. It was White's task to admeasure all the cutting according to the bargains letter, the sawyers' work, the stone cutters, bricklayers, carpenters' work, to take from the surveyors accounts of all materials and implements delivered and to whom consigned to keep a debtors and creditors account with every workman and to attend the pay table to direct what the treasurer should pay to each workman and to be responsible for the accounts. There were five elements to the navigation:

1   Derby – Trent & Mersey Canal at Swarkestone
2   Swarkestone to River Trent
3   Derwent Navigation in Derby
4   Derby to Erewash Canal at Sandiacre
5   Derby to Little Eaton

There was also a tramway from Little Eaton to Denby and Smithy Houses that served coal mines and a pottery. It was generally known as the Little Eaton Gangroad.

Work started first on the Little Eaton and Sandiacre lines. Materials were purchased as required. During September 1793 a contract was entered into with Mr Evans to supply deal baulks for the locks near Derby and on the Little Eaton and Sandiacre line.

An advertisement for iron rails for the gangroad was published in the local papers:

DERBY CANAL
All persons to supply canal with 4000 cast rails of toughened metal one yard in length and weighing 28 lbs each of the form left at the Talbot Inn in Derby to be delivered to line of railway at Little Eaton, four miles from Derby in February 1794, to send proposals to Mr Upton in Derby on or before 23rd December 1793.

Derby Mercury, 12 December 1793

Metal rails for the tramway were supplied by Joseph Butler, of Chesterfield, at £10 10s 0d per ton to be delivered to Little Eaton in February 1794. Benjamin Outram was associated with iron making and foundry work in his own right, through partnership in the Butterley Company, and perhaps it is testament to his character that he did not arrange to supply the rails through his own business interests. Stone was quarried locally and was a popular building material for the canal:

DERBY CANAL

Any person inclined to contract for the carriage of 2,500 tons of stone, or any part thereof from the quarry at Stanton near the south end of Swarkestone Bridge to the locks and bridges on the line of the canal between the Grand Trunk and the Trent; and also 500 tons of stone from same place to be laid down between the Grand Trunk and Boston Moor are desired to send their proposal to the office of Mr Upton in Derby before 4th day of March next.

Mr Geo Wootton of Chellaston will show the places where the stone is to be delivered.

Derby Mercury, 20 February 1794

During December 1794 instructions were given to set out the line of the canal through the Holmes pasture. The route incorporated and altered the mill stream adapted for the Derwent Navigation. As a preparation arrangements were made to take over the wharfs and warehouses leased to Mr Hollingshead and belonging to the River Derwent Navigation Company until the following summer, at the same rent and terms that he held them.

The Derby Canal Company took over the river navigation and no doubt this was of assistance to the carriage of materials to the works. Certain parts of the Derwent were also incorporated into the Derby Canal. The southern route incorporated four locks from the Upper Trent Navigation to the Trent & Mersey Canal and further locks on the canal from Swarkestone to Derby. The route into Derby from the south came close to the Derwent and followed a parallel course close to Siddals Lane.

Contractors building the canal diverted Morledge Mill stream, which had formed part of the Derwent Navigation, and adapted the original river wharf into canal wharves and warehouses. Days Lock was constructed to enable craft to pass down to the former river bed level, whilst the mill stream was deepened and diverted onto a new route that passed under the canal. Here Outram was responsible for designing and having built the first cast-iron aqueduct in Britain. Beyond the Holmes Aqueduct was Peggs Flood Lock, which had an irregular-shaped chamber. There was then a masonry aqueduct that carried the canal over the tail race for Morledge Mill and into the Derwent. A weir on either side created a basin for the boats to cross to the opposite side where White Bear Lock was the entrance lock for the Sandiacre line.

Later improvements included the extension of the Sandiacre line north-west to join the Derwent near St Mary's Bridge above the Silk Mill Weir. This short length was known as the Phoenix Branch and craft had to pass Phoenix Flood Lock to reach a section of the Derwent which became navigable for about a mile northwards to serve other riverside mills.

The south bank of Markeaton Brook opposite Morledge Mill was developed by the Soresby family for carriers' warehouses. Access to their wharves was however limited by the weirs on the Derwent. There was a single barrier lock in the weir nearest Exeter Bridge and it is likely that craft used this lock to reach the Markeaton Brook.

Water supply for the Derby Canal was arranged through the careful placing of locks descending from the Derwent Pool at Derby to Sandiacre or Swarkestone. Only the Little Eaton Branch required a supply for the four locks that descended from the tramway terminus.

Water supply was a key factor to two other local waterways, the Grantham Canal and the Nottingham Canal. The Grantham Canal was a very different waterway to the Nottingham. It was principally a rural canal that served agricultural needs, whilst the Nottingham was essentially industrial in nature.

Earlier schemes for linking Grantham by a link using the Witham towards Lincoln changed in favour of one towards Nottingham. A meeting at the Guildhall in Grantham on 16 August 1791 set in motion the promotion of the Grantham Canal. The route originally was from Grantham following the Vale of Belvoir to the Trent at Ratcliffe. William Jessop was engaged as consultant engineer to survey the line. William King was appointed resident engineer in October 1791.

The choice of water supply was critical to the success of the venture. Potential supplies from the River Devon and Witham became a contentious issue. Jessop's suggestion was that the whole supply of the canal would depend on a reservoir located at Knipton to be filled only with flood water from the River Devon.

Whilst the Bill was presented to Parliament there was concern to protect also the water of the River Witham. Proceedings in this respect involved a well-known River Witham commissioner. He was Sir Joseph Banks, a landowner in the area and president of the Royal Society from 1778–1820.

The protecting clause had been there, but had been deleted by Lord Harrowby, a promoter of the canal, but who had chosen not to take shares in the venture. Banks visited Lord Harrowby to be told that Harrowby did not have a high opinion of Jessop's abilities as an engineer, and did not believe flood water alone could supply the canal and that tributaries to the Witham, that is the Denton Brook and the Maw Beck, were essential.

Sir Joseph Banks then informed the Witham Commissioners of these events and they decided to oppose the Bill. Meanwhile the Grantham Canal Committee met in London and sent Banks a copy of their resolution which confirmed their commitment not to take water from the Witham. Yet a commitment was not the same as specific wording in the Bill and Banks proceeded with the opposition case and persuaded the Commons Committee to postpone their deliberations until after Easter. Discussions between various parties eventually produced a compromise that the undertakers of the Grantham Canal would make reservoirs for floodwaters only from sources such as the Denton Stream.

A new factor was introduced with opposition from the town of Newark, fearing loss of water from the Devon and promoting the original suggestion of the route via the Witham to Lincoln. The Bill failed and the Grantham Committee were left to revise their Bill for the next session.

The science and mathematics of water supply became a crucial factor for the Bill to succeed. Measuring the river in times of flood was not considered the best indicator of flow. The times of low water and drought was also required to be evaluated. The Grantham Canal Committee arranged for new surveys of water from springs supplying the Denton in May, June and July, which provided accurate data for the water flowing into the Denton. These investigations were enough to satisfy the Witham Commissioners to withdraw their opposition and with this element gone the Grantham Bill passed through Parliament in 1793.

Water supply for the Nottingham Canal was an equally serious problem. William Jessop was surveyor and engineer to this waterway, which was made principally to serve various collieries north of Nottingham that had been disadvantaged by the Erewash Canal trade. The route comprised twenty locks; nineteen barge locks brought the canal up from the Trent to the summit level at Wollaton and Lock 'Twenty' was the stop lock where the Nottingham Canal joined the Cromford Canal at Langley Mill. There were three main branches (Greasley, Robinetts and Bilborough) that were made to serve mines. Other shorter branches were made at Nottingham. Water was provided by a reservoir near Greasley that was sometimes called Greasley and otherwise Moor Green. A long feeder brought water from this reservoir into the Cromford Canal near Langley Mill. A compensation reservoir was made at Butterley that fed water into the Cromford Canal near Butterley Tunnel.

Jessop produced the survey that gained a powerful ally in Nottingham Corporation. Jessop had many projects at this time and the day-to-day superintendence of the cutting and making the canal was assigned to James Green.

Green was to work under the directions of Mr Jessop, attend the purchasing of materials and the proper execution of the works and have for such superintendence, and for the expense of a clerk he could employ, an annual salary of 300 guineas. Advertisements were published for 'All persons who are desirous to be employed in making the canal and works or to provide materials for same will please apply to Mr Green at any time after 22 July'.

The task of computing the water supply was assigned to Benjamin Outram. He was appointed engineer to the Nottingham Canal Company for the express purpose of measuring the quantity of water flowing down to the Erewash Canal or mills on the Erewash such as Langley Mill. As with the Grantham Canal survey, summer 1792, the water flow of streams supplying the reservoir was to be calculated in the summer months of 1793 to establish the base level for the lowest flow and determine what might be taken for the use of the canal.

Construction commenced in Nottingham. The ceremony of cutting the first sod was held on 30 July 1792 and then contractors went to work on the section between Lenton and the Town (Leen) Bridge. By the end of 1792 contractors had altered the southern arm of the Leen and had worked westward towards Lenton and the Leen Valley.

Contractors then turned to making the River Leen navigable for Trent Boats from Sneiton Meadow towards the Town Bridge. The task effectively enlarged the river course, made a towing path and diverted the Leen into yet another man-made course through land to the east.

Near Town Bridge a channel was cut for the canal that made a sharp turn to the west and across the meadow land to join up the existing cutting on the southern Leen. Here a new bridge replaced the earlier 'flood arches' of Leen Bridge. The main course of the River Leen was allowed to flow in a covered channel north of the canal, whilst a branch from the Leen, known as the Tinker's Leen, was diverted onto a course to the south of the canal.

There was a certain urgency to make some sort of temporary navigation into Nottingham along the Leen as the works removed some of the warehouses and wharves used by river traders at Trent Bridge. Yet before this was done the location of Trent Lock had to be decided. Jessop had wanted to make the lock near the Trent; the Canal Committee thought otherwise. In May 1793, they asked Green to write to Jessop and suggest a basin be made for receiving boats from the Trent before passing the lock onto the canal. Jessop replied:

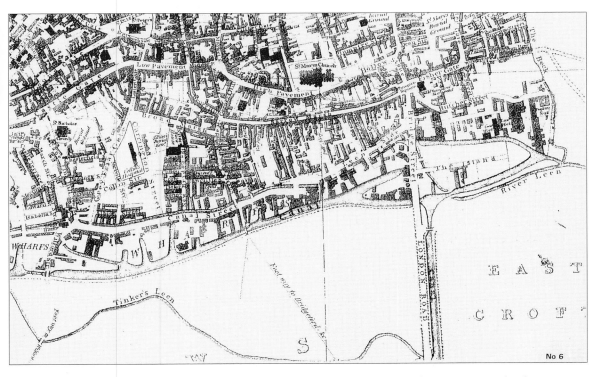

The canal as built incorporated parts of the Leen for the making of wharves for commerce and industry. (Staveley's Survey of Nottingham 1827–29)

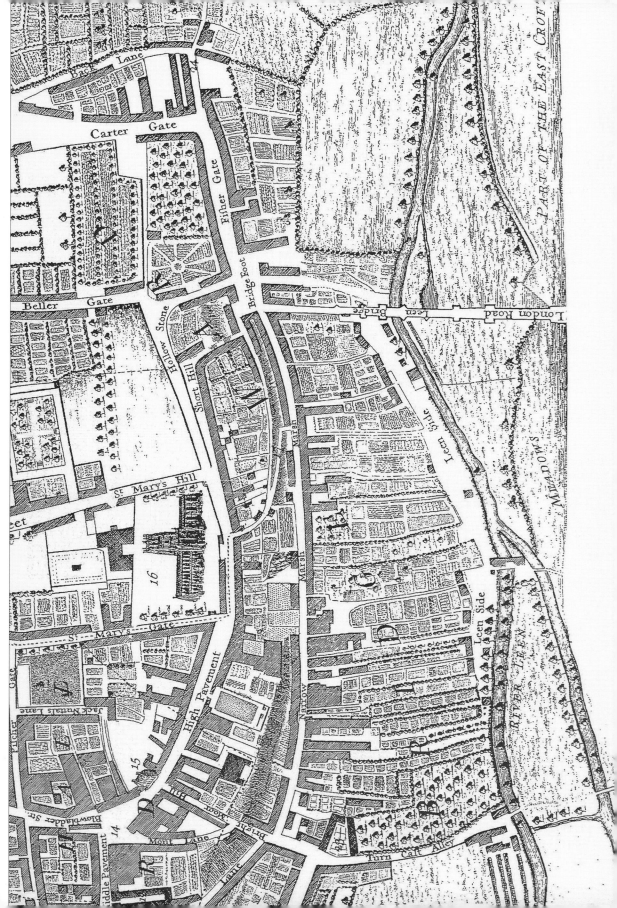

Opposite: Building the Nottingham Canal – Nottingham's river was called the Leen. The Leen rises in Sherwood Forest and flows through Hucknall and Lenton and at one time went onto Wilford and the Trent. The course was altered, perhaps in medieval times, to run near the rock cliff upon which Nottingham Castle stood. It flowed past and formed the southern boundary of the town. This was meadow land with two main channels and a watermill. They combined into a single channel that passed under Leen Bridge, into Eastcroft Meadow and then turned south through this meadow to empty into the Trent at Sneiton. An area west of Leen Bridge known as Leenside may have been a landing place for small craft navigating to, and from, the Trent along the Leen. The land to the south was essentially a flood meadow with small water channels that passed through flood arches under Loughborough Road into Eastcroft Meadow. (Badder and Peat's Plan of Nottingham)

This page:

Top: Lock 16 (Coach Road Bridge) as seen from the bridge. (Railway & Canal Historical Society)

Middle: Lock 18, top gate. (Railway & Canal Historical Society)

Bottom: Lock 3, Nether Mill, Bottom Gate. (Railway & Canal Historical Society)

There is some inconvenience always attending locks at the termination of canals which fall into rivers which is that the tail cut is liable to be obstructed by sand. If the lock is fixed very near to the river this sand may be may be blown away by the sluices of the tail gates, but if the tail cut is long one the velocity of the water will be insufficient to produce this effect. I therefore recommend that the lock should be placed no further from the river than was first proposed and do not at present see why it should be thought necessary.

W. Jessop
London, 6 May 1793

An 'official' opening for the Nottingham Canal as far as new wharves at the Town Bridge was made on 30 July 1793. Yet work here was far from complete. Jessop made use of the existing channel at Leen Bridge for the use of the navigation for wharves, with alterations done during the summer of 1794. Leen Bridge was retained for the main river course and east of this bridge was a weir followed by a section widened for the navigation that became known as the Brewery Arm. Beyond there the water flowed over a second weir and into the new Leen course to the River Trent. Another arm, the Poplar Arm, was created out of the water channels in Eastcroft Meadow. This branch joined up with the Brewery Arm and water from the Poplar Arm flowed over the second weir. William Jessop also arranged for surplus water flowing down the Leen to Leen Bridge to overflow at the first weir and pass into a culvert under the Poplar Arm and along a separate channel to meet up with the Leen beyond the second weir.

Making the canal to the Trent involved the reconstruction of the 'Flood Road' from Trent Bridge to the Leen Bridge. Part of the work included the making of new flood arches. Jessop wanted ten arches here; seven were constructed. Jessop also laid down specific instructions for the new Leen Course during November 1793. His plan shows an inverted arch river bed, 5ft wide, composed of rough stones.

Benjamin Outram (certified by John Smith of the Erewash Canal Company) presented a certificate for the water measurements that formed the basis for the calculations to make the reservoirs. In January 1794 Jessop recommended a reservoir not exceeding 53 acres on Lord Melbourne's estate at Greasby. Later, during June 1794, Mr Green was requested to arrange with the landowners for the intended reservoir at Butterley.

A scheme for a canal to link the Trent & Mersey Canal at Shardlow with the Nottingham Canal surveyed by John Varley was presented as a Bill to Parliament for the 1793 session but was not adopted. This failure opened the way for the Trent Navigation to apply for a new canal from Beeston to Lenton. The Act of 1794 authorised the link that would send most river craft navigating from Shardlow through to the Nottingham Canal and use this canal as the principal navigation from there to Gainsborough.

Meanwhile Green continued with the task of taking the canal through to Langley Mill, making locks at Castle Mill, Leather Mill and further along the line to the summit at Wollaton. Bricks were made on the land of Lord Middleton at Wollaton and also from clay dug on the line of the canal. A surplus of bricks had been accumulated by February 1795. The committee agreed to pay Lord Middleton £50 compensation for the excess made.

Making the Nottingham Canal carried on until 1798 when the whole route was declared open. There was some criticism of the work done and occasionally contractors were dismissed. Green faced some censure, part of which was due to his acceptance to build a section of the Grantham Canal.

The route adopted for the Grantham varied somewhat from the plan of 1791. It commenced at the Trent with the entrance lock nearly opposite Trent Lock on the Nottingham Canal. With the completion of the Holme weir, water levels were raised in the river at Trent Bridge and a pool of water was created for craft to pass between the Nottingham Canal and the Grantham Canal, or down the Trent to Newark via the Holme cut and locks.

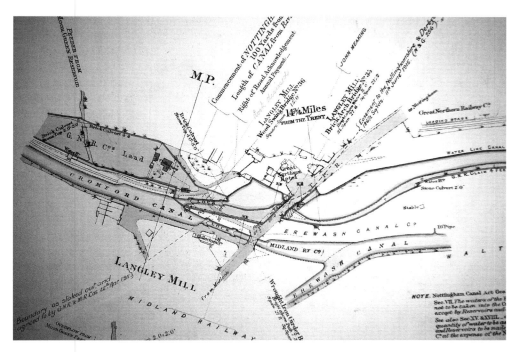

At Langley Mill, the Nottingham Canal formed a junction with the Cromford Canal, which then joined the Erewash. Together they form an intricate junction. (Great Northern Railway Plan, B.W. Archives, Gloucester)

Work started in the summer of 1793. William Hodgkinson was employed to mark out the line of the canal from Grantham to the lordship of Cropwell Butler and James Green was given the job of marking out the remainder of the line of the canal and also the line of the branch to Bingham. Samuel Wyatt of Burton-on-Trent and Thomas Fletcher of Whitwell were assigned to value the several lands to be used for the purpose of said navigation. Hodgkinson never finished his section and it was left to William King to complete the task.

William King, who had been associated with the planning and surveying of the Grantham as engineer, was now assisted by the Nottingham Canal engineer James Green. In July 1793 they were empowered to order such materials as they saw necessary to be provided for proceeding upon the works of the navigation. By September their separate roles had been clearly defined. At a committee meeting held at the George in Grantham, 30 September 1793, it was confirmed that William King would superintend the canal in Leicestershire and Lincolnshire, including two reservoirs (Knipton and Denton), and that James Green would superintend the remainder. Mr King was to proceed first with the deep cutting at Harlaxton Clays and reservoir at Knipton.

Building the canal would take nearly four years. Eighteen brick chamber locks were made and aqueducts were constructed over Thurbeck Dyke and the River Smite. There were twenty-three wooden swing bridges, forty-three brick bridges and the brick haling path bridge over the canal entrance at the River Trent, Nottingham. During February 1797 Mr King, superintendent of the Grantham District, stated that the canal was in a navigable state having at least 3ft of water. Mr Green was asked to report on the Nottingham section. The canal opened, quietly and evidently without ceremony, in April 1797. A projected branch to Bingham was not built.

The Belvoir Castle Tramway was constructed by the Butterley Iron Company to 4ft 4in gauge and was opened to traffic during 1815. The tramway ran from Muston Gorse Wharf on the Grantham Canal to the Belvoir Castle. The rails were cast iron of the fish belly type.

CHAPTER 5

WAR AND FINANCE:
INCREASING THE COST
OF CANAL CONSTRUCTION

Several canal schemes were to suffer through the spiralling cost of building waterways. Finance issues affected both the Worcester & Birmingham Canal and the Stratford-upon-Avon Canal. Other schemes simply were not finished.

The Worcester & Birmingham was constructed as a barge canal as far as Tardebigge. Gangs of navvies laboured to provide a direct waterway that unlike the earlier contour canals was made as straight as possible. The work was done at considerable expense as cuttings and embankments were made. Wide tunnels at Edgbaston, West Hill, Shortwood and Tardebigge were constructed. West Hill (now Wast Hill) was the longest. Hand-made bricks were fashioned at contractors' brick kilns, utilising a good supply of local clay that continued to be dug when commercial brick-making operations were commenced in the nineteenth century. Major embankments crossed valleys at Selly Oak, Bournville and Bittell.

Construction of the Worcester & Birmingham was accomplished in stages and limited by finance. Temporary termini moved from Selly Oak to Kings Norton and then Hopwood, where from 1798 a packet boat operated to Birmingham. Tardebigge Old Wharf was another terminus and, with the completion of the part-brick and part-rock tunnel through the hillside, finally reached the limit of the level from Birmingham. Here Tardebigge New Wharf was constructed overlooking the low-lying land beyond.

Supervision for the building of the canal from Birmingham through to Tardebigge Old Wharf was conducted principally by Thomas Cartwright, the resident engineer, who effectively had charge of the works after Josiah Clowes died.

Construction began at the Birmingham end of the canal with initially a grand scheme of building planned. An important part of the cutting was let to Morecroft & Co. They were to make the barge waterway from the Bournbrook Valley to the turnpike between Five Ways and Holloway Head. This work included the Edgbaston Tunnel and the embankments at Bournbrook and Gallows Brook with aqueducts over each brook.

To accommodate the needs of the navvies, two barracks were to be built at either end of the works. The one at the Birmingham end was first to be located near Edgbaston Hall, but Mr Wheeley may have objected and the site was moved further away. One hundred men were to be accommodated here in the barracks building and a separate structure was provided as a mess hall. A second barracks was constructed in the Bournbrook Valley for 120 navvies and again with a separate eating place. Morecroft & Co. were to provide the bedding and 'necessities'.

Clowes designed the tunnels and gave specific instructions for the sinking of the shafts. These had to go down 4ft below the invert so that a cess might be formed to collect water. Work on the canal began in the autumn of 1792 and within a few months concern for expenditure on navvies' wages led to an instruction being made for the weekly wage bill to be lowered to £800 per week as soon as it was practical.

Construction of both Edgbaston and West Hill tunnels was commenced during 1793. Edgbaston Tunnel was to be provided with a towing path from the start. The making of West Hill Tunnel was a long-term project involving millions of bricks to be burnt. This tunnel, like all others on the canal, was to be made without a towing path, meaning boats would have to be legged or poled through. Construction proceeded with the sinking of shafts and driving of headings. Brick linings for the tunnel walls, roof and invert gradually progressed in an environment of damp and gloom. Exploratory work was also carried on at the proposed site of Shortwood and Tardebigge tunnels.

Thomas Cartwright supervised the construction of the waterway to Hopwood and was also involved in the initial work of building reservoirs on the River Rea and Arrow for the canal company and the mill owners, although the making of these reservoirs slipped ever backward, hampered through finance. Company minutes often mention the intended work and the repetition of these references is evidence of the lack of progress.

Cartwright then began the work on extending the canal to Tardebigge Old Wharf, across the Bittell Valley, through Alvechurch and then Shortwood Tunnel. The Committee started to question Cartwright's estimates, checking his quotes. Tardebigge Old Wharf was reached in 1807 and arrangements were made to set the wharf out for the coal trade. A wharfinger was appointed and a machine house erected to check the weights of goods passing through the wharf. Frequent mention of a warehouse for the merchandise trade seemingly came to nought.

During 1808 Cartwright submitted extra expenses for the problems encountered in building Shortwood Tunnel, making the canal to Tardebigge and transporting puddling clay from Bittell. The committee decided to refer these charges to John Rennie, engineer of London, who had agreed to act on their behalf. In effect he became consulting engineer for the company.

Rennie had a number of canal projects in hand. Perhaps his most notable work at this time was the construction of the Kennet & Avon Canal. He was then actively working on this project. John Rennie also helped the Birmingham Canal Navigations with the Toll End Communication Canal that linked the Walsall Canal with the Upper Level at Tipton Green.

Plans were then made to extend the canal through Tardebigge Tunnel and the top of the locks. Rennie made various suggestions as to amending the route and tenders were invited for the various contracts. Contracts advertised comprised four projects:

1   North End of Tardebigge Tunnel
2   Tunnel
3   South End of Tardebigge Tunnel
4   Bittell Reservoir

Various contracts were arranged: John Mansfield and Thomas Ross were engaged to make 2 million bricks for the work. Mansfield gave as a reference that he had often made bricks for Thomas Dadford, of Wolverhampton. Mr Cartwright gave directions for clay for making the equivalent of 7 to 8 million bricks to be thrown up in proper places upon the line of the canal and for Mansfield and Ross to make bricks. By March 1809 the brickmakers were instructed to make as many bricks as they could in House Meadow next to the bye road. John Foster was also given a contract to make bricks in April 1809. The temporary yards were set up close to the intended route in the parishes of Tardebigge and Stoke Prior and arrangements made to build roads from the brickworks to the turnpike.

A start had already been made on Tardebigge tunnel, but some 500yds remained to be made. A contract was agreed with Joseph Smith of Ocker Hill, canal cutter, for completing the tunnel, whilst Thomas Wilkins of Burbage, Wiltshire, was given the task of making the deep cutting to the North End of Tardebigge Tunnel. Abraham Lees of Commonside, near Dudley, was awarded the South Deep cutting contract, but his price at 7¼d per cubic yard may have been too cheap. He evidently did not proceed with the work and later an agreement was made with Joseph Smith for 8¾d a cubic yard.

Two locks on the Worcester & Birmingham Canal were made to barge width so that trows could pass up to Diglis Basin and transfer merchandise with narrowboats. (Author)

In May 1809 John Henningsley of Cheslyn Hay, Cannock, and his sons Isaac, James and Henry offered to complete the reservoirs at Bittell for £540; their offer was accepted.

There seems to be some redefinition of the role Cartwright performed for the company when Rennie started to contribute to the engineering of the canal. Cartwright is recorded as applying for a post of 'engineer', which may have included much of his original job, but also incorporated more responsibility. His method of working and the pace he conducted these tasks was to face a strong test as the pressure to get plans drawn and work organised increased. The backlog of outstanding work was also now greater. The new role clearly taxed him and within a year he resigned that position through ill health. The Canal Committee decided he should relinquish all his duties. John Woodhouse was appointed in his place as engineer.

Woodhouse had been a resident engineer employed by the Grand Junction Canal. In 1806 he patented a design for a type of boat lift, where a pair of containers, known as conductors, was used to raise and lower boats between levels. The principal concept was that one conductor lay at the upper level and would receive a boat through a guillotine gate. The second conductor was placed at the lower level and again containing a boat that had been admitted through a similar gate. The concept was that the upper conductor was lowered and the lower conductor was raised enabling the craft to pass between the levels. The patent also detailed a concept for signalling between locks to inform lock keepers on the progress of boats.

Woodhouse brought his ideas of boat lifts to the Worcester & Birmingham Canal. Some company directors were taken with the idea of the building of a chain of these lifts through to Worcester. Indeed, Woodhouse was appointed because of his patent. The committee had already considered another lift that had been installed on the Dorset & Somerset Canal. The failure of that venture may have influenced the Worcester & Birmingham to seek out Woodhouse.

Meanwhile construction went ahead with the extension through Tardebigge Tunnel to the New Wharf and the Top Lock. Woodhouse accepted the backlog of work left by Cartwright and carried on the task of extending the canal. He was also frequently urged to complete his experimental perpendicular lift, however some people, including Rennie, were not convinced that this was the best option.

The experimental lift was constructed at Tardebigge at the point where the ground level changed. Work on construction of an enclosed lift was commenced in 1810 before the canal tunnel was finished. Some 30yds of canal was made either end and filled with water in order to conduct the trials. The design was radically different from the patent design, especially as only one conductor was provided. The rise and descent was assisted through a system of counter-balance weights. Illustrations of the devise produced in 1810 show the lift with the conductor connected to a series of eight ropes each passed over a large wheel arranged equidistantly along an upper beam. These ropes were tied to individual sets of weights whose combined tare matched closely the weight of the conductor, the water and boat with cargo. Experiments were conducted with craft passing through to a length of lower canal.

Those committee members who weren't in favour of the lift had a strong enough voice to influence the committee not to proceed with further lifts. The plan to finish the canal with narrow locks was decided. Meanwhile lift supporters pushed forward with further trials, once Tardebigge Tunnel was completed during January 1811. Extensive trials were conducted in February and March 1811, where lift journey times were frequently less than 10 minutes a boat. The lift was damaged by a lightning strike in June 1811, but was repaired and had a practical role transporting boats with construction material once work started again on building the locks.

Funds being limited, the narrow locks were the most economical option. Regrettably with the decision came the loss of the prospect of barges working to Birmingham. Thirty locks of the Tardebigge Flight were required to take the canal down the falling land to Stoke Works. Then further flights of locks were needed to carry the line through to Worcester. It is a route characterised by a number of surviving lock cottages.

Advertisements were published in local papers requesting tenders that came to include four contracts between Tardebigge and Offerton. John Woodhouse left the post of engineer to tender for one of the four contracts that took the canal from the lifting engine through to the village of Offerton. These were:

1 Tardebigge–Body Brook
2 Body Brook to Droitwich and Hanbury Road

The top lock on the Tardebigge Flight of the Worcester & Birmingham is made to the same depth as the boat lift that was installed at the time of construction. Woodhouse designed the lift, which was a single caisson lowered and raised vertically. The generous width of towpath between the replacement lock and the lock house lends certain credence to the possibility that the lock chamber was made to the side of the lift chamber. If this was the case the lift could continue to perform a duty whilst the lock was constructed. Another possibility is that the arrangement for the lift was wider. (Author)

3   Droitwich and Hanbury Road to Oddingly (including Dunhampstead Tunnel)
4   Oddingly–Offerton

Woodhouse took charge of the most difficult contract – that was the building of the locks that comprised the Tardebigge Flight, which remain a challenge to boaters through to the present day. The work involved was to continue through to 1815 with Woodhouse retaining the services of the lift until 1814.

John Woodhouse was replaced as engineer by William Crosley who was appointed at the suggestion of John Rennie. Crosley had been resident engineer to the Rochdale Canal (1802-04) and then worked as engineer to the Brecknock & Abergavenny Canal during the final years of that waterway's construction. He took up his duties on the Worcester & Birmingham Canal in August 1811 and contributed to the design, and probably the 'economies', of the lock section through to Worcester.

Published histories all agree that the lift was finally taken down and replaced by a conventional lock on the same site. It is difficult to find definite documentary support for this assumption except that the lift was dismantled at some point in either 1814 or 1815 and the metal parts offered for sale. An alternative option is that the lift and lock might have been adjacent to each other. Such a possibility would allow construction boat movement to continue whilst the deep lock was built. The wide towing path by the lock and the offset position of the chamber supports this possibility.

South of Tardebigge the economies made in some parts of the canal construction become evident. The side weirs were dispensed with and all water was channelled through the locks, with the boats. The engineering problems this caused are quite evident in the modern canal when boats follow each other. The water builds up in the pounds and overflows onto the towing path.

There is only one tunnel on the southern section of the Worcester & Birmingham Canal. This is located at Dunhampstead and like all others on the canal is wide enough to pass two narrowboats. Beyond Dumhampstead the route varied somewhat from what had been originally planned. It passed through Offerton and then Tibberton where the original village street was diverted to allow for the new waterway. The route into Worcester was via Lowesmere and then onto the Severn at Diglis.

The section from Offerton to the Severn was again let as four contracts. The last was to involve four barge locks, but this was reduced to two barge locks at Diglis.

Opening the canal was delayed for a few months in 1815 to allow the ground to settle and for the erection of wharves and warehouses. William Crosley left his post of engineer during the spring of 1815 and Samuel Hodgkinson, the Birmingham Canal Navigations engineer, was called in on occasions to report on the final work being done. Hodgkinson also supervised the building of seven lock houses.

Money worries were eased somewhat in June 1815 with the passing of a new Act granting the canal company to raise up to £90,000 from existing proprietors by the creation of new shares of £40 each, or by granting annuities or raising money by mortgages on tolls and rates.

With the opening of the canal further consideration was given to water supply. For with increased trade came greater boat movement and the need for more water. The Act of Parliament for the Worcester & Birmingham Canal had stated that when the canal was to be made over the River Rea, three reservoirs were to be made for the sole use of the mill owners.

The two barge locks used large quantities of water and it was decided, in 1817, to install a pumping engine to pump water back from the Severn into Diglis Basin. Work commenced on an engine house in November 1817 and the job was completed early the next year. Percival Jones of Bilston provided the engine for the work.

George Rew was an important canal employee. He was an experienced bricklayer who worked on various construction contracts that included the boat lift and Dunhampstead. He was eventually appointed clerk of works and was involved with various canal water supply issues.

A feeder from Wychall Reservoir, built for the mill owners on the Rea, was suggested in 1821, but not built until 1836. A new reservoir at Tardebigge on the site of an old claypit and brickworks at Dial House Farm was considered in 1822. A Mr McIntosh was given the contract to make

The arm of the Worcester & Birmingham from below Upper Bittell Reservoir was sometimes known as Jacob's Cut. It was navigable and was used to convey coal up to the pumping engine at Bittell. A wharf was provided at this bridge. (Author)

Upper Bittell Reservoir, Worcester & Birmingham Canal. (Author)

the reservoir and Jonathan Heaton was given the task of making the engine pit and headways. Tardebigge Engine House lay below the summit but pumped water back up the top lock. The steam engine was built by the Horseley Company and commenced pumping in 1823. The reservoir was deepened and increased in size to provide extra water and reduce the costly amount drawn from the BCN. The quality of McIntosh's work was questioned at times and he finally finished the job in 1826.

Tardebigge
Engine House.
(Author)

The Stratford Canal commenced at Kings Norton where the junction was made with the Worcester & Birmingham Canal.

The Stratford Canal has a number of interesting heritage features. The northern Stratford has the unique Lifford Stop with the two guillotine gates provided in 1814 when the original barge lock was reduced in size. Until this reconstruction was made, the lock had two pairs of mitre gates and could accommodate two narrowboats. It was a condition that the Stratford Canal kept their water at a higher level than the Worcester & Birmingham Canal. In order to minimise water loss, an instruction was issued in 1796 that when the difference in levels was 4in or more, the lock keeper was not to permit fewer than two boats at a time to pass through the stop lock.

Lifford Lane Bridge crosses over Lifford Stop. The span is undiminished following the narrowing of the lock. The guillotine gates were the same type as a gate used at Lapworth at a stop lock there. The iron gates and mechanism was assembled from castings made at William Whitmore's iron foundry in Lionel Street, Birmingham.

The Stratford, like the upper Worcester & Birmingham, was constructed as a barge canal as far as Hockley Heath, the original terminus. The route travelled through Worcestershire into Warwickshire, skirting various communities that lay to the south of Birmingham. The northern Stratford was completed first and such was the terrain that lift bridges were constructed for minor roads and farm access. One for Tunnel Lane, Lifford, received a certain historical significance when Tom Rolt tried to bring his boat *Cressy* along the Northern Stratford in May 1947. The canal at this time was owned by the Great Western Railway. Heavy wartime traffic over the bridge had damaged the structure and a fixed bridge was constructed that effectively prohibited through traffic. The bridge was thus permanently down and had to be jacked up by railway employees to enable the *Cressy* to pass. The act of getting the *Cressy* along the North Stratford became one of the beacons of waterways restoration. The lift bridge was replaced by a metal swing bridge, but even this has now disappeared.

Major engineering structures on the northern Stratford were:

1   Brandwood Tunnel
2   River Cole Aqueduct at Shirley
3   Countess Coppice Embankment, near Earlswood
4   Lapworth Locks

The Stratford-upon-Avon Canal crossed the valley of the River Cole at Shirley by an embankment and brick aqueduct. The aqueduct spanned both the river and a minor road. (Author)

Water supply was probably at first limited to the intersection of streams along the route.

Josiah Clowes was appointed engineer to the Stratford Canal. Clowes had assisted Robert Whitworth with the building of the Thames & Severn Canal and from 1789 had gone on to work on the completion of Dudley Canal (opened 1792) and had continued his association with the Dudley on the extension to Selly Oak and on the building of the Worcester & Birmingham Canal. He employed resident engineer Thomas Cartwright and his assistant James Jones to help with the construction of Brandwood Tunnel.

Clowes prepared the plans during the spring of 1794 for Brandwood Tunnel. The matter of making a barge or narrow canal was still to be decided and when contractors were requested, in December 1794, the length was to be 400yds, 14ft high and 9½ft wide. Subsequently this tunnel was made 16ft wide, which enabled two narrowboats to pass or a barge to travel through. Construction work went on for two years, sinking shafts and using horse gins in the same fashion any mine might be conducted. Work was conducted at both ends as the miners dug out rocks and earth and bricklayers lined the tunnel with hand-made bricks. Contractors finished their job at the tunnel around May 1796. Josiah Clowes had a very considerable workload with the Dudley, Stratford and Worcester & Birmingham canal constructions. In 1794 he also was engineer to the Shrewsbury Canal. He died in 1795.

Near Shirley the route crossed the valley of the Cole along an embankment. An aqueduct was constructed here for the river and a road alongside. The greatest work was the Countess Coppice Embankment. The route then followed a contour route towards Hockley Heath where a temporary terminus was made alongside the Birmingham to Stratford turnpike. The Stratford committee decided in June 1796 to make a wharf at Hockley Heath:

Committee Meeting, White Lion Inn, 25 June 1796

The proprietors to form and make the wharf at Hockley which is to be public for all carriers and no wharf paid for any goods or articles, whatsoever (except such goods that are particularly desired to be housed and the wharfage of same not exceed to the power given by the act) as the boat company have erected a weighing machine and engage to pay the annual rent for the wharf to the archer family they expect the profits of the said machine as a compensation but is understood that no person shall be compelled to weigh his goods before they are conveyed from the said wharf and price of weighing should not exceed 2d per ton, the proprietors to fix a crane on the said wharf if they should think it necessary but not otherwise.

The Stratford Canal was opened in sections. Hockley Heath terminus existed for six years before the canal was extended to Kingswood and the junction canal with the Warwick & Birmingham Canal. The route was altered to pass close to Kingswood and comprised a flight of twenty locks including the last at the start of the Junction Canal. Benjamin Outram, engineer of the Peak Forest Canal, had in 1799, reported on the line of the canal at Kingswood and suggested a tramroad option. During 1800 Samuel Porter, another assistant to Clowes, restarted the cutting of the canal from Hockley Heath, which was completed in May 1802. Here the work stopped, even though Samuel Porter had surveyed a route through Stratford and a junction with the River Avon.

Although work stopped with the junction with the Warwick & Birmingham Canal at Kingswood, a scheme for extending the canal further to the Avon finally got under way during 1811. The driving force behind this project was William James, one-time agent for the Earl of Warwick. James was a businessman with shares in coal-mining ventures at Wyken, Pelsall and Wednesbury and iron making at Birchills. He was keen to improve the navigation to Stratford and also leased the Upper Avon Navigation as part of a grander scheme. He was also a promoter of railways and was at the heart of an early railway project that would link London with the North West. A section of this railway was made between Stratford and Moreton-in-the-Marsh.

The legacy of James' association with the Stratford Canal was a number of engineering features. The altered junction at Kingswood is a remarkable historical record of these times. In order to prevent the loss of water from the Warwick & Birmingham Canal to the new southern Stratford Canal the last or bottom lock was altered from a conventional lock with top and bottom gates to a lock with bottom gates and a guillotine gate in place of the top gate. The junction at this lock thus formed was at right angles with the short junction canal, which also met the Warwick Canal at right angles.

The engineer responsible for constructing the southern Stratford was William Whitmore, iron founder of Birmingham. He produced weighing machines amongst his range of foundry goods, and some were canal boat weighing machines. Whitmore had a foundry in Little Charles Street and moved to premises in Lionel Street beside the Newhall Branch, leasing a strip of land from the Colmore family in 1790. Whitmore and his family subsequently enlarged this site with additional leases later.

William Whitmore had a long working relationship with William James, which included an ill-fated mining venture at Bexhill. The Stratford Canal construction involved some original infrastructure and the use of tramways to assist its construction.

There were three cast-iron aqueducts at Yarningale, Wootten Wawen and Edstone. Yarningale Aqueduct was placed between Locks 33 and 34 and carried the canal over a stream. That at Wootten Wawen was erected in October 1813 and crossed the Stratford-upon-Avon and Birmingham Turnpike Road, whilst near Bearley, the long iron aqueduct conveyed the canal over a valley, stream and road. Whitmore had the option of an earth embankment and short aqueduct, but chose to build the long aqueduct, which at 475ft 3in has the distinction of being the longest in England. The trough was equipped with an iron towpath on the east side.

Advertisements were published, in November 1811, for canal cutters to start the works on the 6 miles from the junction with the Warwick & Birmingham Canal. They were to apply to W. Whitmore of Newhall Street. In July 1812 a further advertisement asked for contractors and canal cutters to make the embankment at Edstone.

Whitmore made use of a contractor's railway made along the bank of the waterway that was used to bring bricks from the kilns, lime and contractor's spoil. This was an early use of a contractor's railway, but was to become a common tool on canal-building projects later. Building the southern Stratford involved the making of thirty-four locks to Bancroft Basin, where warehouses were constructed for the carrying trade. From Bancroft the canal passed through a final lock into the Avon. This section was opened to trade on 24 June 1816.

Other features of this waterway were the split iron foot bridges and barrel roof cottages. The cottages had curved roofs made in the same fashion as a bridge arch. Of the twelve original cottages on the Southern Section, six were of the barrel roof type and were constructed during the years 1812 and 1813:

Lock 22   Kingswood,
Lock 25   Dicks Lane
Lock 28   North of Lowsonford
Lock 31   Lowsonford
Lock 34   Yarningale
Lock 37   Preston Bagot

Yarningale Aqueduct as built by Whitmore was washed away in 1834 following a burst in the embankment of the nearby Warwick & Birmingham Canal that sent a torrent of water down the stream that flowed through Yarningale. The canal was closed whilst a replacement iron trough was provided by the Horseley Company.

William Whitmore also was involved with the making of a short length of canal in Birmingham that came to have his name. A basin was made in 1808 to serve a rolling mill in Newhall Street. About three years later, this basin was extended to form a branch that passed under Caroline Street and George Street through to Newhall Hill. The land was owned by the Colmore family and required no Act of Parliament to make the waterway. Built privately, the initial intention was to make a new inland port near Summer Hill as part of William James' greater vision for transport improvement in the district. James came to abandon the scheme, but the branch was briefly known as the James Level. On later maps such as the Ordnance Survey, this branch is called Whitmore's Arm. A towpath only existed as far as Caroline Street from the junction with the Birmingham Canal at Farmers Bridge Locks. Navigable for only narrowboats, craft were poled to the various wharves placed along the canal.

Traffic increases were a mixed blessing for several Midlands waterways. The needs for infrastructure improvement and for better water supply were two constant issues that were discussed in the various committee rooms. The Staffordshire & Worcestershire Canal Company had, from the start of operations, a limited supply of water and one that was restricted through rivers and streams being needed for the supply of watermills. In September 1799 application was made for an Act to build a waterway to Stafford from Radford Bridge. Whilst improving transport to Stafford, which then relied on road carriage from Radford Bridge Wharf, a source of water was also sought. The canal company intended to make a navigable canal to Stafford in the parishes of Berkswick and Castle Church with other collateral cuts and reservoirs.

Improved transport links to serve Stafford had been included in other schemes. A Bill of 1792 to join the Donnington Wood tub-boat canal in Shropshire with the Staffordshire & Worcestershire Canal, by a new waterway though Gnosall and Stafford to Radford Bridge, had failed. In 1798 a tramway from Stafford to Radford Bridge was proposed. The 1799 Stafford Canal Bill failed, and the decision was taken to build the tramway. A privately owned tramway was opened in November 1805 to move coal and lime to Stafford from Radford Bridge. This tramway had a working life of less than nine years, however. It was replaced during 1814 by a private navigation that used the River Sow to reach a wharf at Forebridge. Boats crossed an aqueduct and descended through a lock at St John's to enter the Sow. Unlike the previous canal company scheme, the river option did not affect the watermill at Stafford. There was, of course, a loss of water for boats passing onto and returning from the Stafford navigation, which the canal company made a charge for.

Those waterways on the Welsh border were particularly hard to finance. The canal from Stourport through Leominster to Kington suffered from limited capital, but required extensive engineering. Had the survey been more accurate as to cost, it is possible that the scheme would not have been proceeded with. Major engineering included the long lock flight up from the Severn towards Pensax, tunnels at Pensax, Southnet and Putnall Fields and aqueducts over the rivers Lugg, Rea and Teme. The route was surveyed by Thomas Dadford junior and it was with him as engineer that the canal was built.

The Act received Royal Assent in 1791. Construction began on the central section between Leominster and Southnet. It was on this section that much of the subscribed capital was spent and a debt of some £25,000 incurred. There were delays with land acquisition and the general construction, which was spread out across the route at different sites. The committee, concerned about progress, invited John Rennie, in 1794, to report on the works. Rennie was particularly critical of the building of the earthworks and aqueducts. He considered money wasted in land purchase and materials and believed the funds would have made the whole canal between Leominster and Pensax. With rising prices and funds nearing exhaustion, construction was concentrated on finishing Putnall Fields Tunnel and with this work the canal was opened from Southnet to a wharf beside the turnpike, 1 mile north of Leominster. The part open had sixteen locks, tunnels at Putnall (330yds) and Newnham (95yds) and aqueducts over the rivers Teme and Rea. Traffic was principally coal from Sir Walter Blount's collieries at Mamble to Leominster Wharf. Two streams fed a pool that acted as the canal head.

This pool was also the entrance point of the north portal for Southnet Tunnel, which was to be 1,250yds long by Dadford's survey. Some doubts have been expressed for the completion of this tunnel, despite many written accounts that verify the tunnel as being finished. Rennie, in his inspection, reported that 450yds of tunnel had been executed, but about 1,100yds remained to be done, whilst the length if completed would have been some 300yds longer than originally planned. It is a historical fact that when people have looked for the north portal, no evidence could be found of its existence on the ground, but the southern portal has been found, photographed and documented.

Canal House, Southnet, was built at the terminus of the Leominster Canal, where the tramway from Mamble brought coal down to the wharf to be loaded into boats. (Author)

As for the rest of the canal, work had started at Kingsland and a section was built towards the River Lugg that included two locks and a canal channel. Work on the stone-built Lugg Aqueduct was commenced but not finished. There was also excavation at Dumbleton Farm and at Pensax Tunnel. The Pensax Tunnel bore was made with 80yds of arched lining and 60yds of heading when Rennie viewed the works. Pensax Tunnel was to be 3,850yds long. In January 1793 a master brickmaker was advertised for to view the clay and make 1.5 million bricks at Pensax.

Had the Leominster Canal been finished it would have opened up a new canal route towards Herefordshire. Plans for another canal through Ludlow to the Montgomery Canal made a potential route for trade to Chester and the Mersey. The route was surveyed by James Dadford, son of Thomas, in 1793, and was planned to run from Garthmyl on the Montgomery via Bishops Castle and Ludlow to meet the Leominster near the Teme Aqueduct. It was to be 40⅓ miles in length with forty locks. Coupled with an improved Severn Navigation, these waterways would have provided a rival to existing canal navigation through to the Mersey. Estimated costs for the project may have been considered and under estimate, but nothing was done and there is little to indicate if a Bill was ever drafted.

The Staffordshire & Worcestershire Canal Company, keen to improve trade on their waterway, promoted schemes for towing paths on the Severn and also the final completion of the Leominster Canal. In 1801 a new Leominster Canal Act was sought to raise extra capital to from proprietors in order to liquidate the debts. With the passing years further attempts were made to link the existing canal with the Severn including a railway scheme. During 1811 a Bill was presented to Parliament for a tramroad to link the canal with mines at Cleobury Mortimer. This failed. Undeterred, the Leominster Canal Company continued to seek out ways that their canal might make money.

In 1833 Edward Powell, engineer, proposed a plan for making the unprofitable Leominster Canal into a money-making concern. Powell suggested a tramroad from the north-west side of Stourport Bridge that followed the Cannygreen Brook and went onto Newnham Bridge. A second tramroad was suggested from Leominster Wharf to Eardisley. A committee was appointed following a public meeting at the Swan Inn, 21 January 1834, which included Stourport carriers John Worthington and the veteran John Green Ames. Ames was appointed secretary. This scheme also failed and the future of Leominster Canal was destined to be the short length as made by Dadford.

A similar challenge was presented to promoters of a Leicestershire canal. The Leicestershire & Northamptonshire Union (LNU) was a scheme that linked with the Leicester Navigation starting at the West Bridge and used the River Soar towards Aylestone. The river section passed four mills and weirs before diverging from the Soar and starting the gradual ascent towards Foxton. This canal, as the name implied, was intended to be a navigation from the Soar that reached Northampton.

A junction was planned with the River Nene and the whole route was surveyed as a barge canal. The Grand Junction Canal was also promoted as a barge waterway from London to meet the Oxford Canal at Braunston. The Grand Junction also intended to build a barge canal through to the Nene. All these waterways, when linked together, created the possibility of through barge traffic from the East Midlands coalfields through to the Metropolis. As with many waterway schemes, such plans did not become reality. The Grand Junction failed to build the Northampton Branch Canal and made a tramway instead from Gayton to Northampton. The LNU found constructing the many locks a financial handicap and after many years of work only reached Market Harborough.

The LNU appointed two engineer-cum-surveyors, Christopher Staveley and John Varley, and decided to use direct labour rather than advertising for contractors to build sections of waterway. The chief materials needed were bricks and timber and advertisements were placed in the Leicester papers, during May 1793, inviting people to offer proposals for making bricks for the undertaking near the town of Leicester, whilst Mr Staveley dealt with Mr Oldham for quantity of timber.

By June surveyors were to 'deliver particular description of ground necessary for land and locks near Leicester'; meanwhile advertisements for bricklayers, brickmakers and diggers continued to be published. The committee also advised the appointed land valuer Mr Wyatt that 3–4 miles of the line were to be set out and measured in seven days. They requested he valued it.

The first obstacle to navigation was the old West Bridge. It was necessary to take this bridge down and rebuild it. But, in doing so, traffic along the Leicester & Hinckley Canal and Leicester to Narborough turnpike would be affected. A temporary bridge was constructed whilst the new bridge was built. As work proceeded to make the river navigable there were disputes concerning water supply with Alderman Fisher (North Mill) and the miller at Abbey Mill.

Bricks were supplied by makers such as Braithwaite, Stead and Stachel. The company also set up brickyards at Aylestone and Little Glenn and employed a brickmaker named Mansfield. They also advertised for carriers to move timber to the brickyards, no doubt to make shedding for drying the bricks. John Varley had the task of evaluating each proposal. Part of Staveley's role was to supervise brick making at the company yards. Varley's task was to visit Oldham's estate at Mary Leys and mark out trees for felling. By August 1793 he had selected forty-eight trees. During September 1793 Varley went to Mr Boultbee to purchase the timber needed for sixteen locks.

Mansfield was criticised for making poor bricks at Aylestone and Staveley was summoned to the committee to explain. He did not attend. Mansfield was dismissed and his place at the company brickyard taken by a Mr Nicholls.

Brick making became a prime concern. Clay had to be dug and contracts arranged for the next summer make. Contracts were made during November and December with four firms:

Brickmaker	Amount	Size specified
Goodman & Mitchell	1 million bricks	–
John Day	3 million bricks	10in long x 5in wide x 3in thick
William Dilkes	1 million bricks	10in long x 5in wide x 3in thick
Edward Jongsto	800,000 bricks	10in long x 5in wide x 3in thick

Staveley having left the company, supervision of brick making fell to John Varley who also decided the location of the kilns. Clay was dug on the lands of Lady Denbigh at Newton Darecourt.

The first four locks were river locks at Castle Mill, Swan Mill, St Mary's Mill and Aylestone Mill. From there the canal separated from the river and began the climb at Kings Lock. From here there were sixteen locks each with a 6ft rise to the River Sence Aqueduct and then another five of 6ft rise to the summit level. Here a feeder was to be made from a reservoir at Saddington.

In February 1794, contracts were let for lock making in groups of four to: (a) James Rouse of Leicester, (b) Ephraim Barlow of Blaby, and (c) John Allen of Blaby and Thomas Davis of Enderby, according to the proposals delivered by Mr Varley. Contracts were also sealed with: (d) John Insells, and (e) Smith and Bradley for building locks and bridges. Further brick-making agreements were made with James Dobson, Robert Glovers, Mr Dilks and Mr Day.

In May the company clerk had correspondence with Mr Carne regarding a quote for deep cutting, no doubt using his machine. Carne's quote does not appear to have been accepted.

By October 1794 a plan for a deviation of the canal to Market Harborough was suggested. The original proposal involved a tunnel at Foxton. Robert Whitworth was asked to report on the deviation scheme.

Market Harborough Basin on the Leicestershire & Northamptonshire Union Canal – this basin was the physical end of an unfinished barge navigation that was intended to connect Northampton with Leicester. (Author)

With the opening of the Leicester Navigation at the end of October 1794, the LNU decided to open their canal as far as Blaby. Orders were made to build a wharfinger's house at Blaby.

New contracts for brick making, in January 1795, were agreed for making 1 million bricks each with John Day, Goodman & Mitchell and James Dobson. By July two new yards were established near Smeeton where Stableford & Thomson were requested to get clay and make bricks.

By the summer of 1795 the canal was open to Kilby Bridge Wharf and a weighing machine was erected there, supplied by Hallam & Co. of Nottingham. Work was now proceeding on Saddington Tunnel. A large quantity of bricks was required to make the 880yd-long tunnel. Contracts for this tunnel were let to James Gladwell (west end) and Thomas Batchelor & Robert Biggs (east end). Batchelor & Biggs could not provide sufficient security for their work and were dismissed. Payment was made for the work done, and other contractors employed.

By the summer of 1795 the canal was open to Kilby Bridge Wharf and a weighing machine was erected there, supplied by Hallam & Co. of Nottingham.

John Varley was assisted by John Fletcher, the company clerk, on measuring the work done on the tunnel. They found that overpayments had been made to Thomas Hill, leading to Hill's dismissal and prosecution.

John Clark was employed in making deep cuttings on the approaches to Saddington Tunnel. He was told to concentrate his time on making the cutting at the west end portal, but also to build and 'back' bridges and 'back' the aqueduct at Saddington and the feeder from Saddington Reservoir to this aqueduct. In January 1796 the committee reported an inspection of the deep cutting done by John Clark; the greater part had fallen in. Varley recommended brick walls as a support, but the committee decided to reduce the angle of the slope.

A good supply of bricks was in hand and prospects for completing the tunnel looked favourable. Varley estimated that making the tunnel at a rate of 20yds a week, the remaining lengths to be done would be finished in twenty-one weeks. In April Varley and Fletcher reported 320yds of tunnel completed. Goodman & Mitchell were contracted to make another 400,000 bricks.

The method of checking that the tunnel was straight was done by ranging. In July 1796 Fletcher reported to the Board that the tunnel varied from the straight line. Mr Whitworth was consulted and then the committee asked John Barnes, the Grand Junction canal engineer. Mr Barnes reported that several parts of the tunnel were so much out of range that they must be taken down and rebuilt in order to render the tunnel navigable. Mr Varley was ordered to suspend all work until Mr Barnes finished his report.

Barnes noted that Varley had neglected to fix targets and proper objects for ranging. In his previous experience of passing boats on the Grand Junction and Thames where boats were built as broad at the bottom as at the top, tunnels needed to be built nearly straight so as to give free passage of boats.

He suggested altering a length of about 23yds and also found space to compliment. The brickwork in general terms stood extremely well and the state of earth through which the tunnel passed was calculated well to withstand pressure.

Building the canal was continued as far as Gumbley where a wharf was made. The final piece was not completed to Market Harborough until 1809. Thus the LNU never reached Northampton.

Promoters for a connecting canal formed a company called the Grand Union Canal, which like the LNU came to vary the route through various proposals. The final route was from the Grand Junction Canal at Norton, through Crick Tunnel and locks at Watford to reach the summit level. There was another tunnel at Husbands Bosworth before a 75ft descent by ten locks at Foxton. Part of the Watford Flight was set out as a staircase, whilst Foxton comprised two sets of a five-lock staircase. It was an arrangement both unique and time consuming.

The Grand Union Canal was opened on Tuesday 9 August 1814, with ceremony. The first boat was fitted up in style, with a band of music and with the flags of the different canal companies. She was followed by two other boats full with guests and then by two of Mr Pickford's fly-boats from London. All proceeded down the line to Welford, when another boat from the Welford Branch supplied with refreshments was brought up and moored alongside.

Husbands Bosworth Tunnel on the Old Union Canal – the first date over the tunnel portal is recognition of when the tunnel was completed. (Author)

Foxton Locks, the longest flight of staircase locks in Britain. There are two sets of five locks, with a central passing point. Boats entering either staircase must proceed from one end to the other, letting out or retrieving water from the side pounds. (Author)

The lower staircase connected with the Leicestershire & Northamptonshire and Union canals. (Author)

CHAPTER 6

NETWORK IMPROVEMENTS

With a substantial canal network established, some companies felt the need for improvement. The Birmingham and Oxford Canals had been handicapped with waterways tied to the contours of the land. The BCN chose Thomas Telford to assist them with canal improvements and from 1824 Telford embarked on a major program of new construction. Over the next ten years, until his death, Telford made important and beneficial improvements to the network and water supply. His new main line shortened the distance boats travelled between Birmingham and Wolverhampton and left a legacy of major engineering works that included the Smethwick Deep Cutting, the Engine Aqueduct, Galton Bridge, Dudley Road Turnpike skew bridge, Stewart's Aqueduct and the feeders to Edgbaston Reservoir.

The first major embankment to be constructed was from Farmer's Bridge Junction to Ladywood where the new line crossed the valley of Edgbaston Brook that was followed by a cutting through Ladywood and Winson Green, which led to the making of the Dudley Turnpike skew bridge and the parallel feeder from Edgbaston Reservoir.

Beyond the junction with the Winson Green Loop the canal followed sections of cuttings and crossings of redundant sections of the old route until reaching the junction with the Smethwick Lock Branch and the rise of 20ft to the Wolverhampton Level, where the route of the old main line was preserved, but the new route passed into a deep cutting that was maintained at the Birmingham Level through to Spon Lane and the junction with the locks there. This straight section of canal was wider than the original canal and possessed a towpath on either side to ease the passage of boats travelling in opposite directions and benefit trade in general. Compared to other canals, it was the motorway of its day!

Telford's improvement of the Birmingham Canal Main Line at Smethwick ranks as an important engineering achievement. The building of Galton Bridge that crossed the waterway in a single span was in itself a remarkable testament to the skill of the engineer Thomas Telford and the Horseley Iron Company that supplied the ironwork. (Author)

The Engine Arm Aqueduct was built to carry a navigable feeder from Rotten Park Reservoir over the New Main Line at Smethwick in 1829. Ironwork was supplied by the Horseley Iron Company to the designs of Thomas Telford. It remains one of the most ornate iron engineering structures belonging to British Waterways. (Author)

Left: The Engine Arm Branch joined the Old Main Line at Smethwick and then turned to follow both the New and Old Main Lines on a parallel course. The branch was made navigable up to the steam pumping engine plant at Bridge Street and beyond to Rabone Lane. (Author)

Below: Titford Top Lock marks the present highest navigable point on the Birmingham Canal. The waterway on the left is the feeder to Rotten Park Reservoir. (Author)

Completed in 1837, the Titford Canal provided a navigable route to collieries in the Titford Valley. The six locks were constructed with large side pound. Later at the halfway point along the lock flight a branch was constructed to Albright & Wilson's Phosphorus Works. (Author)

Three road bridges and two aqueducts were constructed on this part. At Smethwick the navigable feeder known as the Engine Arm was carried over the new waterway by the cast-iron aqueduct, built to Thomas Telford's specification by the Horseley Iron Company. Brasshouse Lane was carried over both the new and old lines by brick bridges, whilst Roebuck Lane spanned the new line and deep cutting by a single-arch cast-iron bridge, which became known as Galton Bridge. Spon Lane crossed the deep cutting by a brick bridge. Finally a brick and stone aqueduct was constructed to carry the Old Main Line over the new at Spon Lane.

The widened New Main Line then followed the course of the Walsall Canal to Pudding Green, where the Walsall continued as a separate canal and the New Main Line came to a temporary end at Albion and the junction with the Gower Branch.

It was a significant improvement that was to create a waterway backbone that sustained trade on the Birmingham Canal Navigations. This route was characterised by the use of cast-iron bridges supplied by the Horseley Iron Company, of Tipton, which were adapted as side and turnover bridges and erected between 1827 and 1829. The Horseley Iron Company also supplied the parts for Galton Bridge, and their bridges were also common along the shortened sections of the Oxford Canal.

Further improvements included the Titford Canal, opened in 1837. This canal climbed through six narrow locks to meet up with Telford's feeder above the top lock. The feeder was made navigable to Titford Pool and opened a communication with coal mines in the Titford Valley. Later this canal was to have another important role serving chemical and tar distillation plants.

Competition from other waterway routes and other projected waterway schemes influenced the Oxford Canal Company to reduce the convoluted mileage of their waterway from Hawkesbury to Napton to manageable distances. The rival promotion was aptly named the London Canal as its purpose was to unite the Stratford-upon-Avon and the Warwick & Birmingham with the Grand Junction Canal. The route was surveyed by Thomas Telford and promoted during the last years of his life. Many Birmingham and South Staffordshire industrialists favoured Telford's plan.

The Oxford responded first by employing Marc Brunel (father of Isambard) to survey improvements and shortenings of their line. They also employed Charles Vignoles to provide an alternative suggestion and the basis of Vignoles' survey was adopted in the Act of Parliament of 1829 that sanctioned the improvements.

These new works required some five years for completion and the result was a vastly improved North Oxford Canal. Much of the old winding route was replaced by a straighter and wider waterway. Redundant canal land was sold off, but some of the old route was retained to serve wharves and a group of limestone quarries near Rugby. The work included cuttings and embankments, whilst near Newbold a new tunnel wide enough for two narrowboats was constructed under the hillside rendering the first tunnel redundant. The short Wolfhamcote Tunnel near Braunston also ceased to be used once a new junction was made and the straighter route over the Leam Valley brought into use.

Where the junctions lay on the towpath side, cast-iron bridges were provided by the Horseley Iron Company. These were located at:

1   Bridge 32 Brinklow Arm
2   Bridge 39 Fennis Field Arm, Cathiron
3   Bridge 45 Newbold Arm
4   Bridge 53 Rugby Arm
5   Bridge 93 Triangular Junction Oxford New Main Line, Braunston
6   Bridge 94 Triangular Junction Oxford New Main Line, Braunston
7   Entrance to Old Oxford Canal Arm, Braunston

Some alterations of the Oxford Canal are of a less obvious nature. South of Hillmorton Wharf, there are a group of buildings whose alignment to the canal indicate an alternate course. This part of the canal was straightened during the 1831–34 improvements. (Author)

Hillmorton Bottom Lock – the Oxford Canal was level from Hawkesbury to Rugby. East of Rugby the canal climbed through three single locks. These were subsequently duplicated, to aid the passage of boats travelling towards and from the Grand Junction Canal at Braunston. (Author)

Left: The Loughborough Road Turnpike Aqueduct on the Oxford Canal was provided with a cast- and wrought-iron trough that was supplied by the Capponfield Ironworks (Parkes & Otway) at Bilston. (Author)

Below: The Horseley Iron Company towpath bridge over the entrance to the Newbold Arm – the original route passed under this bridge, whilst the new main line continued straight to Newbold Tunnel. (Author)

The increase in width is particularly noticeable at Brinklow where the original Brindley Aqueduct over a stream was widened for the improvements. Blue brick abutments face the north side, whilst red brick are a feature of the south side.

Construction work was conducted under the direct supervision of the Oxford Canal Company, with brickmakers, bricklayers, carpenters, hauliers, labourers and masons working to the instructions of the engineers Frederick Wood and James Potter. A start was made at the centre of the projected new line extending east and west as the canal was completed. Timber was purchased to make boats, wheelbarrows, plank runs, railway wagons and sleepers (for the contractor railways).

Canal maintenance was conducted through strategically placed workshops. The Oxford Canal established a workshop complex at Hillmorton that was located near the bottom lock. There was a short branch into the depot where there were carpenters and blacksmiths based. There was also a dry dock and boat-gauging dock. (Author)

The unaltered section of the Oxford commences at Napton, where the narrow locks ascend to the summit level. (Author)

Above: Hawkesbury Stop Lock has a minimal fall to preserve the difference of levels between the Oxford and Coventry canals and to prevent loss of water from the Coventry Canal to the Oxford. The junction between the two waterways was at first placed at Longford, and both canals ran parallel between Hawkesbury and Longford. During 1803 another junction was made at Hawkesbury for the benefit of craft travelling to and from Fazeley and Fradley. (Author)

Left: The junction bridge was replaced by a new iron structure in 1835 and bears the name of the Coventry Canal engineer John Sinclair. All craft have to turn almost through 180 degrees to pass from one canal to the other. (Author)

Above: Oxford Canal at Cathiron – looking east to Stretton. (Author)

Left: The Oxford Canal improvements (1829-34) included a brick and stone aqueduct over the, River Swift, at Rugby (left) and also over the Avon, near Clifton. (Author)

Contractors began work at different sites including Brinklow and the Brays Valley. Workshops were established at Stretton and brick kilns erected at Brinklow and Newbold. Those paid for making bricks included George Edwards, Benjamin Greenhill, Richard Greenhill, J. Greening and John Ward who were employed at Brinklow, whilst William Frost and John Whitmore made bricks at Newbold.

Bricklaying for bridges and locks was carried out under the teams headed by Joseph Calloway and John Leeson. Leeson was particularly active in building bridges and aqueducts. His work included the River Swift Aqueduct and the brickwork for the Iron Aqueduct, nearby (1830–31). Thomas Hough was paid for laying bricks in new Newbold Tunnel (1833).

Masons used local stone and imported stone for coping bridges and aqueducts. There was also an iron aqueduct at Rugby that carried the canal over the Loughborough turnpike. Castings and plates for the iron aqueduct were supplied by Parkes & Otway of Capponfield Ironworks, Bilston.

Parkes & Co. also supplied iron boats and rails for the construction tramways. Iron boats proved more durable and some were assembled on the Oxford Canal. C. Copson was paid, in 1831, for plating boats that comprised an order of six craft supplied by Parkes & Otway. The Horseley Iron Company also supplied iron boats.

The demanding job of cutting and embanking was given to a group of nine different contracting firms. The task of cutting began with nicking out and moving earth and spoil from hillside to valley with wheelbarrows and tramways. P. & E. Wallis began with the cutting of Walton Hill into the Easenhall Valley, went on to cut Perkins Hill and transport spoil to build up the embankment in the Swift Valley, then work on Nettle Hill, Holly Hill, Shilton Valley and Hopsford Valley. R. & C. Watson had one of the hardest contracts that involved the cutting of Brinklow Hill and the making of the embankments in the Brinklow Valley and the Smeaton Valley. This contract lasted for over four years and involved the largest payment by the canal company (£15,267 17s 1¼d). R. & C. Watson then went on to make good a slip in the Hopsford Valley (May–August 1834). Thomas Clarke cut from Brinklow Hill and worked into the Brays Valley.

George Watson started with cutting through Johnson's Hill and hauling spoil into the Smeaton Valley and then went on with earthwork and brickwork at Newbold Hill and the valley of the Avon. Charles Dutton had succeeded Watson on the Newbold Hill and Avon contract by January 1833. Charles Dutton also worked on several of the east-side contracts that included Barby Hill, 'Rowdyke Puddle', Sales Hill and the Hillmorton and Kilsby Cuts between 1830 and 1834, and as Upton & Dutton cut into Perkins Hill and moved spoil to the valley of Swift (1829–30).

John Harris engaged in banking, cutting and puddling on the west side at Sow Common, the Caters and the Ansty valleys (1832–34). M. Starling cut through Mawbeys Hill and hauled into the Smeaton Valley (1829–30). Samuel Reynolds & Son cut the canal at Cathiron Hill and then went on to work on cutting and embanking at Willoughby and Wolfhampcote hills, the Braunston Valley and 'Rowdyke Puddle' (1831–34). Finally, the ninth contractor, Thomas Lawrence, was employed on excavation assisting the removal of spoil from Nettle and Holly hills (1833–34).

The work at Braunston involved the embankment across the valley of the River Leam and a three-arch brick aqueduct that crossed this river at a height of 45ft. With the completion of this section the distance between Braunston and Napton Junction was reduced and the existing route through Wolfhamcote Tunnel (33yds long) closed.

Stone-walling and making towing paths (which included stone laying) were yet further aspects of the canal building. Goldstraw and Johnson were associated with stone-walling on the side of canals. Stone was brought from a variety of locations such as Hartshill and the Cherwell Valley and either boated or carted to the site. All the improvements were sufficiently completed by 1834 for the route to open throughout. The iron railways and tramway wagons were then offered for sale.

The stoppage between 4 and 13 May 1834 enabled the new route of some 11 miles of new waterway to come into use. Sections of the original canal were kept as either feeders or to serve existing wharves:

Wyken (Old Colliery)	0 miles 2¾ furlongs
Stretton	0 miles 2 furlongs
Fennis Field	0 miles 4 furlongs
Rugby	0 miles 1¾ furlongs *
Clifton Mill	0 miles 3½ furlongs
Newbold Lime works	1 mile 1 furlong
Cosford	1 mile 2¼ furlong

* shortened with the building of the Midland Counties Railway Aqueduct

The Dudley Canal had a winding, curving, contour canal between Parkhead and Windmill End that followed the side of Netherton Hill. At one point the route had two hairpin bends that was a handicap to boats navigating the waterway. Various improvements were made under Brewin, the engineer, in the 1830s. Most important was the making of Brewin's Tunnel, which cut through the hillside at Netherton and eliminated the two hairpin bends. The old bed was reclaimed and built up to form a new storage reservoir, which became known as Lodge Farm. Other short sections of canal were straightened at Primrose Hill and Netherton. The loop through Bumble Hole was left unaffected at this time.

Another Brewin improvement was the installation of steam engine and waterwheel at the east end of Lapal Tunnel. The engine created a current in the tunnel and assisted the passage of boats through the long tunnel.

From 1841 there was a request to link a new blast furnace at Withymore with the Dudley Canal at Netherton. The furnace proprietors, Messrs Best & Barrs, were keen for the canal company to build the short branch. John MacClean, engineer, surveyed the route and a contract was let in 1843 to build it.

Various improvements were also carried out to the Trent & Mersey Canal such as the replacement of staircase locks on the main line, lock duplication and the duplication of the tunnel at Harecastle. Much of this work was done to the designs of Thomas Telford, and is perhaps one of the less publicised aspects of his improvements made to the British Canal network.

The short Burslem Branch of the Trent & Mersey was constructed to a basin placed in the heart of the pottery trade. In this view taken in 1960, the arm was dewatered following a breach. (Ken Cheetham)

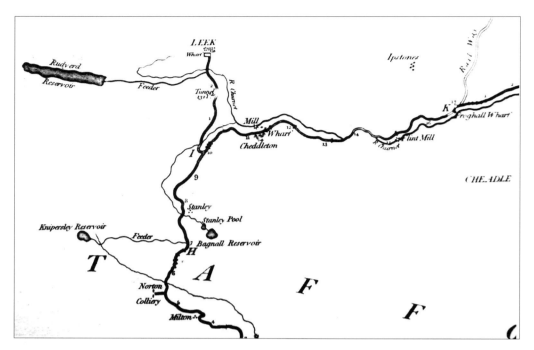

Carey produced a detailed survey of the Trent & Mersey, which shows tramways and the feeders to the Caldon Canal from Bagnall Reservoir, Knypersley Reservoir and Rudyard Lake. In Carey's plan a section of the Caldon Canal below Cheddleton was used to form part of the River Churnet to Consall Forge.

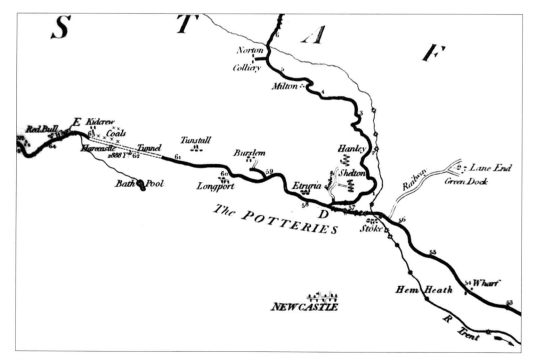

In another section of Carey's map, another water supply is identified; this is a feeder from Bath Pool to the north portal of Harecastle Tunnel. The high concentration of watermills on the Trent (marked by circles) is also worth noting.

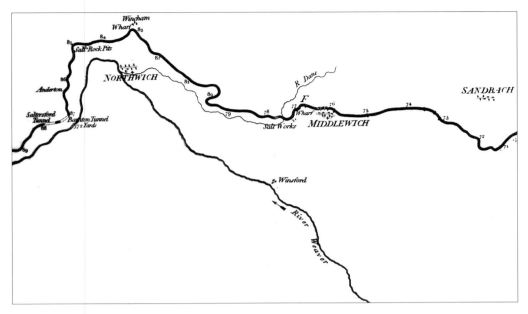

Carey's survey of the Trent & Mersey shows the Weaver Navigation, a number of salt works along the canal, the River Dane Aqueduct at Middlewich and the tunnels west of Anderton. No connection between the canal and the Weaver at Anderton is shown at this time

The decision to duplicate Harecastle Tunnel was a matter of long-standing debate caused through the needs to improve the navigation for the traders. But despite their needs and numbers, it was a voice muted by the cost of improvement at a time when Britain was at war with France. Plans had been made for improvement as early as 1807, and the need for a second tunnel was demonstrated by a survey made by John Rennie in 1820. Rennie also considered the option of rebuilding the existing tunnel and laying down a temporary railway to carry merchandise and goods over the hill whilst the work was done, as well as a third option of replacing the tunnel with locks. None of the options was chosen and especially the board did not consider the making of a second tunnel a 'matter of urgency'.

These views changed over a period of a single year. The canal committee were clearly conscious of competitive routes that were being suggested and the need for improvement did become urgent. The Navigation Office at Stone applied to Parliament, on 10 September 1821, for an Act to build the tunnel in 1822. This same application included the intention to make a new reservoir in the Knipersley Valley. The death of John Rennie, in 1821, led to the postponement of their application for another year.

Parliament sanctioned the making of the second Harecastle Tunnel in 1823 (4 Geo IV c 87). The new cut was to be parallel and onto the east side of the existing 2,880yd tunnel. The task of surveying the new tunnel was given to Thomas Telford, who chose to make the tunnel wide enough to provide a towing path along the east side wall. According the *Berrow's Worcester Journal*, work started on the tunnel in April 1824. The contractor was Daniel Pritchard, who was assisted by his son-in-law William Hoof.

Bricks were made at a yard south of the tunnel using local clays to mould bricks for the kilns, and a contractor's railway laid down to assist with the transport of materials and spoil. An estimate of 7 million had been quoted as the total make of bricks required for the Harecastle works. Initial expectations were that the construction would take five years. The tunnel was actually opened on

Left: Iron roving bridge at Hazelhurst Junction, Caldon Canal. (Author)

Below: The Caldon Canal was a busy waterway, particularly with regards to limestone traffic. This stone was a suitable fluxing agent for iron production and canal boats regularly travelled along this canal carrying stone to Staffordshire blast furnaces. A new junction was created at Hazelhurst (1841–42) with the construction of three locks. These locks eliminated the bottleneck for the limestone traffic created at the triple staircase. (Author)

16 March 1827, some three years and eleven months after commencing work. The new Harecastle Tunnel was 2,926yds long; that is 46yds longer than the original tunnel. Once open the two tunnels were adapted for one-way traffic. There was at least one side tunnel. This may have been part of the earlier Birchenwood Tunnel that joined with the Old Harecastle Canal Tunnel.

Pritchard was also contractor for the making of Knypersley Reservoir and the Trent & Mersey extension that connected the Trent & Mersey Canal with the Macclesfield Canal.

Further improvements included the doubling of most of the locks between Wheelock and Kidsgrove, during the 1830s; only two locks (Pierpoint) remained single and these provide a

The locks on the long descent from Hardings Wood Junction towards Wheelock were doubled as part of the general improvements made to the Trent & Mersey Canal under Thomas Telford. Lock 42, seen here, was the second lock in this descent. (Author)

reminder of how the flight looked before the doubling. The reconstruction work is generally attributed to Thomas Telford and was an important step towards the accommodation of the merchandise, pottery and salt trades using this canal.

At some time three bottlenecks to trade, which comprised the treble staircase locks at Meaford and Lawton and the double staircase on the main line at Etruria, were replaced by making a new canal around them and building separate locks. Those at Lawton were paired, yet it remains to be determined whether there was an intermediate period of three single separate locks there.

Another factor of influence was the carriage of potters' material, which increased with the provision of additional exchange facilities between the River Weaver and the Trent & Mersey Canal being made at Anderton and the setting up of the Anderton Carrying Company:

Staffordshire Advertiser December 23rd 1824
The Trustees of the River Weaver have resolved to apply to Parliament for repeal of the clauses of their act, which exclude potters material from coming up the river and being transhipped near Northwich to the Trent & Mersey Canal. Should these clauses be repealed this would open up another channel of communication between the Staffordshire Potteries and Liverpool.

The section from Endon to Hazelhurst on the Caldon Canal was altered for the second time in the years 1841–42. Congestion at the Hazelhurst triple staircase influenced the Trent & Mersey Committee to replace them with separate locks. A new flight of three locks with side ponds were constructed from a new junction east of Bridge 34. An iron roving bridge was erected to carry the towpath over the new locks for the craft using the Leek Branch. The Leek Branch was then carried over the Froghall Line by a masonry aqueduct.

Two important competing navigations were completed during this period. These were the Birmingham & Liverpool Junction Canal and the Macclesfield Canal.

Thomas Telford was appointed engineer to the Birmingham and Liverpool Junction Canal. His concept for a wide waterway from the Midlands to Nantwich cut as straight as possible with locks grouped together created a waterway comparable with a modern motorway.

Tenders for making the first 22 miles of canal from Nantwich to Norbury (contracts 1–3) were advertised in the local press. Telford reported the tenders received to the board meeting held at the Spring Gardens Hotel, London, on 2 December 1826. He recommended the best was £198,000 from John Wilson of Bangor for the whole works and that he had experience of Wilson's abilities. Wilson was the contractor for masonry for making the Menai and Conway Bridges.

During January 1827, the resident engineer, Mr Easton, carefully surveyed the line and marked it on the ground. Mr Wilson also lost no time and started in January with making the earthwork in several places along the whole of the route. He opened two quarries and prepared clay for making bricks. By the summer of 1827, the number of workmen on Wilson's contract amounted to 1,600.

Authority to build the Newport Branch from Norbury received Royal Assent on 21 March 1827, but tenders for the construction were not let until 1829, when the board resolved to accept the tender

Right: The Birmingham & Liverpool Junction Canal, Bridge 39 – W.A. Provis used local stone to make his bridges. High Bridge was made to carry the Newport–Eccleshall turnpike over the canal. (Author)

Below: A part of the Wilson Brothers' contract was to build the tall and wide bridge to carry the towpath of the Staffordshire & Worcestershire Canal over the Birmingham & Liverpool Junction Canal at Autherley Junction between both waterways. (Author)

Above left: The aqueduct at Nantwich was one of two similar iron aqueducts made across major roads. Both were built as part of contracts undertaken by the Wilson family. The Nantwich Aqueduct was constructed first under the contract awarded to John Wilson. The other at Stretton, across Watling Street (A5), was built as part of the Wilson Brothers' contract. (Author)

Above right: Woodseaves Cutting was part of John Wilson's first contract on the Birmingham & Liverpool Junction. The steep sides have provided a constant problem through slips. The width of the canal is narrow at this point with little space for narrowboats to pass. (Author)

of Mr William Alexander Provis for making this branch. Provis had been resident engineer for the Menai and Conway Bridges. William Provis was also awarded the 6¼-mile section (contract 4) from Norbury to Church Lane, which included the Shelmore Embankment. Provis's men started on the main line first during July 1829 and from 1830 on the Newport Branch. The remainder (11 miles) of the route to Autherley (contract 5) was given to John Wilson to build. He started work in July 1830.

Telford's report of October 1831 mentioned that some 1,230 workmen and 230 horses were employed on the works. John Wilson had died in January 1831, but contracts 1–3 and 5 had been carried on by his sons. With regard to the Nantwich–Norbury contract there were: twenty-seven locks; eleven aqueducts from 10–30ft span and 80–190ft in length; fifty-two bridges for public and private roads; fifty culverts; eleven let-offs and eleven waste weirs besides common earthwork. There were about 4 miles of embankment from 30–50ft high and 5 miles of cuttings from 20–60ft deep. With the exception of about 300yds next to the northern terminus, 21½ miles were now navigable. The rest was expected to be finished during October 1831. Only fifty men remained on this contract, employed extending wing walls and correcting slips.

Provis had made a start on the first Knighton Reservoir, with some thirty or forty workmen, tramway track and skips, making the reservoir head. Whilst on his 'main line' contract, works comprised some lengths over very uneven ground and almost the whole was in either deep cutting (Grub Street) or high embankment (Shelmore). It was a route principally determined to suit the needs of the local landowner, Lord Anson and 420 men and 97 horses were employed.

The story of the building of Shelmore Embankment has become a standard theme for inclusion in many canal histories. Lord Anson is frequently depicted in an unfavourable light in view of his opposition to Thomas Telford's plan to make the canal through his wood. The difficult alternative that became the route of the waterway required the making of the embankment, which followed a circular course to the west of the wood. For Provis the task proved immense. For Telford the problems of making it was carried with him to his grave!

Other issues developed on contract 4 during 1832. Problems were encountered with making the tunnel at Cowley that was intended to be 690yds long. It was found necessary to open out parts of the tunnel owing to rock showing signs of decomposition when exposed to the atmosphere. Only 81yds was made as a tunnel; the remainder was an open cutting.

At Watling Street, on contract 5, Telford had provided for a cast-iron aqueduct, which was supplied by William Hazeldine. There was considerable progress made here in 1832. The abutments and wing walls to carry the canal over Watling Street had been raised to the bottom level of the canal and the cast-iron arch was erected. The embankment each side was built nearly to the full height. At the junction with the Staffordshire & Worcestershire Canal, work on making both the entrance-bridge and stop lock had commenced.

Meanwhile Provis pressed on with the Shelmore Embankment. On the Newport Branch, making the embankment across the moors between Reston and the Buffery was underway. This section comprised twenty-three locks and thirty bridges. At Knighton Reservoir Provis made a new brook course along the north side of the reservoir and had completed the feeder to the canal.

Work started on making Belvide Reservoir after Telford's summer report of 1832. The Wilson Brothers made a start on building the dam head on 13 November 1832. Wheaton Aston lock was also finished by them during this period. Provis also finished Knighton Reservoir, which comprised 15 acres of water.

When Telford presented his report dated 18 July 1833, he was ill and commented chiefly on lot 5, the Wilson Brothers' contract, which was nearly finished. The whole of the earthwork, consisting of 7¼ miles of cutting from 10-44ft deep and 3¾ miles of embankment, with the exception of some levelling, was complete. The towpath was fenced. Of the twenty-six bridges, twenty-one were complete, three 'finished' and two in progress. Thirty-four culverts and three road aqueducts were completed. The task of making Belvide Reservoir was completed, 30 acres were contained there. The committee decided more storage water was needed and authorised a second reservoir at Knighton.

Telford asked William Cubbit to report on Shelmore Embankment and also problems with the deep cutting at Woodseaves (contract 1-3). Thomas Telford presented another report dated 31 March 1834 which included the prospect of Shelmore Embankment being finally completed. He died before it was.

Cubbit replaced Telford as principal engineer to the canal. His summer 1834 report included notes of slippages in contracts 4 and 5 and on the Newport Branch. By October 1834 the Wilson Brothers' last contract was completed and their section of canal filled with water. Thus the Birmingham & Liverpool had two navigable sections; one from Nantwich towards Norbury had been filled with water since 1831. Only Provis' work needed to be done so that the canal could be opened for trade. Finally, Cubbit presented a report dated 30 January 1835, where the works on Shelmore Embankment were discussed:

Shelmore embankment and the long delayed completion of canal.

I have now the satisfaction to report, is brought to such state as to enable me to speak with confidence as to its final and satisfactory completion and to venture to fix on a time for declaring the canal open to the public from end to end for all the purposes of trade and in order to give traders and others proper time for making their arrangements to enable the company officers, agents etc to be ready for the transaction of tonnage and also to allow a reasonable space for advertising the thing to the public. I propose that one clean month from this time be allowed and that on and from Monday 2nd March, the canal shall be opened to the public.

Fig 2_ Transverse Section

Fig 3_ Plan   Scale ⅜ of an Inch to a Foot

The Birmingham &
Liverpool Junction Canal
descended from the summit
level located between
Wheaton Aston and
Autherley to Nantwich.
The summit was about 6in
lower than the Staffordshire
& Worcestershire Canal
and boats passed through
a stop lock at Autherley
Junction in order to reach
the Birmingham & Liverpool
Junction. While loss of water
through the stop lock was
limited, other water was
taken from the Staffordshire
& Worcestershire through a
sluice. Charges were made for
the water that came through
the sluice. John Urpeth
Rastrick devised a system of
measuring the flow of this
water in 1837. (Staffordshire
Records Office)

At Adderley Locks on the Birmingham & Liverpool Junction, overflow weirs were carefully engineered into the main lock structure. (Author)

Much has been written about Shelmore, but Provis also had problems with Grub Street cutting where slippage occurred throughout the length. Provis was allowed to back cut the ground at Shelmore Farm, at the base of the embankment, for spoil to make the embankment. This spoil was to be taken to tips between the Grub Street Bridges (number 41) and High Bridge (39), and it was probably the intention to move this spoil with the cutting material to build up the embankment. By July 1830 spoil removed from the deep cutting at Grub Street amounted to about 230,000 cubic yards and the Eccleshall–Newport turnpike was rerouted across the High Bridge. Cutting at Grub Street took another three years until the work was judged finished, yet slips occurred for at least another ten years, when stability possibly assisted by nature was achieved.

Making Shelmore Aqueduct started in July 1829. Contractors were required to build two aqueducts over the Norbury to Gnosall Road and another over a stream coming down from Mill Haft. Stone for these aqueducts and bridges around Norbury were quarried in Windmill Field. A tramway was laid down to convey spoil for building up the embankment.

Authors such as Tom Rolt have squarely put the blame for the misfortunes at Shelmore with the decision to alter the course to skirt Lord Anson's land and the partridge-holding wood popular for game shooting. It has also been noted that Telford's 1825 survey for the route passed this wood to the east and that only the 1826 and 1827 modifications, caused through concessions to ease the passage of the Bill through Parliament, created a route through or by the wood. Lord Anson held shares in the Birmingham & Liverpool Junction Canal and was therefore not an opponent of the making of this waterway. Any objection raised by him as a man of influence was in due regard to his property. Making the embankment was the responsibility of W.A. Provis and his decision to back cut land at Shelmore Farm must also be considered. Shelmore Embankment rose to a height of 70ft above the fields of the farm. It is likely that when Provis surveyed the site he failed to notice the chance of instability of the embankment on marly soil. It is also probable that he or the resident engineer, Easton, did not fully understand the reasons for that instability. The end result was a protracted construction that delayed the opening of the canal. If any blame is to be given, that blame should rest on the shoulders of Provis rather than Lord Anson.

The Birmingham & Liverpool Canal, as built, was provided with a number of engineering features. Those worthy of mention include:

1   the aqueduct over the River Penk (1832) near Pendeford
2   the cutting south of Brewood and the ornamental balustraded bridge (Avenue Bridge)
3   Stretton Aqueduct (iron) over Watling Street (1832)
4   Wheaton Aston Lock
5   Shushions Embankment north of Wheaton Aston
6   Cowley Tunnel
7   Shelmore Embankment
8   Double Culvert Bridge
9   Grub Street Cutting
10   Shebdon Embankment
11   Woodseaves Cutting
12   Tyrley Locks
13   Berrisford Road Aqueduct, Market Drayton and culverts over the Tern
14   Adderley Locks
15   Audlem Locks
16   Hack Green Locks
17   Nantwich Aqueduct (iron) over Chester Road

Shushions Embankment was some 1,500yds long and crossed the fields here at an average height of 20ft. Two farm accommodation aqueducts were provided (12ft wide) and a culvert (8ft wide) for a brook. The north aqueduct comprised an iron trough. This is an example of a 'hidden' iron aqueduct, where the wing walls and facing is brick, but the central trough iron. Iron plates were provided at the time of construction (1834), but these were replaced in 1869 under the supervision of Shropshire Union Canal engineer, G.R. Jebb. Cochrane, Grove & Co. of Woodside Ironworks, Brierley Hill supplied the replacement trough.

Double Culvert Bridge was placed at the south end of Grub Street Cutting. It was built as a 'water bridge', or aqueduct, to carry a stream over the canal, 25ft above the waterway. This structure also carried a bridleway from the Eccleshall Road to Loynton over the canal.

Another important canal building project of this era was the making of the Macclesfield Canal. This route came directly out of a scheme proposed in September 1824 to link the Trent & Mersey Canal with the Peak Forest. A rival railway scheme was proposed at the same time.

Canals were subject to drought in summer and frost in winter. The canal scheme was made across high ground with water supply a problem. The canal was costed at £6,000 per mile, whilst a railway was cheaper. Thomas Telford reported in favour of a canal. His report suggested making a junction with the summit level of Peak Forest at Marple and continuing on that level through Macclesfield to the Dane-in-Shaw Valley and then locking down to summit level of the Trent & Mersey Canal. The canal route as suggested comprised a level waterway from the Peak Forest Canal to the single flight of locks at Bosley and from there another level section towards Kidsgrove.

The railway was not proceeded with and an Act was obtained to make the narrow canal that became known as the Macclesfield. William Crosley was appointed company engineer. He transferred from the Lancaster Canal, where he held a similar post. Thomas Telford was consulted for advice from time to time. Tenders were requested for the first 16 miles of canal. Plans were available at the Macclesfield Arms Hotel from 25 October until 13 November 1826.

Part of the agreement to build was an allowance for the Trent & Mersey Canal to build a mile of canal from their canal that passed over their main line by a brick aqueduct and continued on to join the Macclesfield Canal at Harding's Wood. Daniel Pritchard was awarded this work, and started it during 1827 after completing Harecastle Tunnel.

The ceremony of cutting the 'first sod' was conducted at Bollington on 4 December 1826. The committee decided to let the work as five lots from Marple to Bosley:

1 Peak Forest Canal to Lyme Hadley – let to Messrs Seed & Sons
2 3¼ miles with two embankments at Hagg Brook and between Pott Shrigley and Adlington
3 2¾ miles to Tytherington, including Bollington embankment – let to William Soars
4 3 miles to Sutton – let to Seed & Sons
5 To top of locks, Bosley – let to Jennings, Jenkinson and Otley

Construction proceeded quickly. Crosley reported in May 1828 that some 12¾ miles out of 16¼ miles were nearly ready to contain the full depth of water. The work included forty arched stone bridges, six swivel bridges and five aqueducts already completed, another four arch bridges, the arch of a road aqueduct at Bollington and eight more swivel bridges needed to be made on this part.

Plans for the remaining 10½ miles from the head of the locks in the township of Northrode to Hall Green were placed on show at the Bulls Head Inn, Congleton, from 19 November to 10 December. Tenders were received and three more contracts were let:

6 3 miles, Bosley locks (12) and from the bottom of the locks to Buglawton – Nowell & Sons
7 3 miles, with 4 embankments – William Soars
8 4 miles to Hardingswood – Pearce & Tredwell

Crosley in his report mentioned that Nowell & Sons had yet to start on the locks, but had opened a quarry at Bosley Cloud and had built a railway from this quarry to make the locks on the canal. The company then advertised for contractors to make the two reservoirs at Sutton and Bosley. Tenders were to be received by 23 September 1828.

Digging and puddling the bed proceeded less smoothly on the southern section. Telford made a tour of inspection in March 1829 along the works of the Trent & Mersey Canal and looked at the section of the Macclesfield, which Daniel Pritchard was making. Such duties were part of the job of principal engineer, which for Telford would keep him regularly touring the various projects he was engaged in. He noticed that the contractors were covering the clay puddle with a 'dense blue clunch'. Telford objected to the use of this substance as a covering material and ordered that it be replaced by gravel. Water was also penetrating below the clay puddle in places. The contractors intended to pave the bed of the canal in these places with flat stones and then line the canal with clay. Telford recommended that the water should be cut off by drains and brought into the canal at the proper level.

There were also issues concerning the building of the main canal. Crosley's report to the company in July 1829 mentioned his concerns regarding the making of the Bollington and Dane-in-Shaw embankments and the aqueduct over the Dane at Bosley.

With Bollington, the embankment had started to slip during heavy rains and a culvert had been damaged. Crosley stopped the works for six weeks, arranged for damage to be repaired and then allowed the work to proceed again. He had been worried about the reduction of the width of the

Left: Macclesfield Canal – the canal crosses a minor road near Adlington. (Author)

Below left: A long, tall embankment carries the Macclesfield Canal high above the roadway at Bollington Aqueduct. This tall aqueduct also spans a river that is hidden below the road. (Author)

Below right: At Grimshaw Lane, the Macclesfield Canal crosses by another stone aqueduct. Whilst from the top of Bollington Aqueduct pedestrians on the towpath can look down at the traffic far below, at Grimshaw Lane a building is erected alongside the towpath. People and boaters passing by are often oblivious to what lies below. (Author)

foundations for this embankment, which he undertook to save money, yet as the work suffered no further slips he decided to continue with his revised plan.

Making the Dane Aqueduct formed part of Nowell's contract. The foundations of this aqueduct were discovered to be 'unsound' and Thomas Telford was consulted for advice. Eventually a safe method was decided on to finish the aqueduct. Meanwhile construction proceeded with Bosley Locks, Bosley Reservoir and the reservoir feeder to the canal.

Thomas Telford inspected the works in the autumn of 1829. He was generally pleased with the workmanship. The forty-seven arched stone bridges and eleven swivel bridges were 'all judiciously' placed and 'well executed'. The material of which the aqueduct over the River Dane was composed was 'singularly good' and the workmanship 'equally so'. The issue that needed to be attended to included alterations to the river arch at Sutton for one of greater strength and curvature and placed on a better foundation. Bollington Culvert was to be abandoned and a new channel for the river made.

The Macclesfield Canal passes through Congleton and then turns to cross the Dane-in-Shaw Valley by an embankment, whilst the railway crosses by a tall brick viaduct. The stream meanders through the valley below and passes under the canal embankment by a circular stone culvert. (Author)

Dane Aqueduct was finally completed during October 1830. This stone aqueduct had an arch of 42ft that had the spring that started 24ft from the bed of the river below. The canal was finally opened throughout on 9 November 1831. Bosley Reservoir was not finished until 1834. Sutton Reservoir was completed during 1837.

The Macclefield is noted for the stone over-bridges and stone aqueducts, made of durable local stone. Stone aqueducts over roads were built at Red Acre, Bollington, Grimshaw Lane, Gurnett and Watery Lane. An iron aqueduct was erected at Dog Lane, Congleton. By contrast the short connecting Hall End Branch of the Trent & Mersey Canal has two brick built aqueducts. Poole Aqueduct was constructed to carry the branch over the main line of the Trent & Mersey Canal, whilst Red Bull Aqueduct spanned the nearby turnpike road. Another, perhaps unique, feature of the Macclesfield Canal are the Ramsdell Hall Railings. These line the towpath near the Hall. These comprise cast-iron railings set in stone and were erected at the request of the landowner.

Improvements to the Warwickshire Avon were continued through to the nineteenth century when William James leased the Upper Avon Navigation. James restored and repaired a navigation that clearly had fallen into disrepair. His aim was to improve movement of goods from the Stratford-upon-Avon Canal to the Severn, yet such repairs came at a cost to James, whose many other ventures in mining, railways and navigations brought him to the doors of the bankruptcy court.

Between 1827 and 1832 a syndicate that included Thomas Lucy, mill owner at Stratford, made yet further improvements to the Upper Avon. The work had begun at Stratford-upon-Avon, where during 1827 and 1828 the channel below Stratford Lock was deepened and a third set of gates fitted creating a staircase lock. Oldaker, a property owner beside the river there, brought an action for trespass against Lucy and other syndicate members in 1828. Oldaker's family had a ford in the river there where cattle were driven across and wagons taken across. The Avon proprietors, having dug out the bed to a depth of 3ft had destroyed the ford. The court ruled that Oldaker be paid £900 for the land taken and that he was to give up possession from 1 May 1828.

Locks then existed at Luddington, Welford, Grange, Cleeve, Harvington and Evesham. There was also a flash lock at Bideford Weir. The syndicate continued the improvements with the building of three additional locks at Luddington, Welford and Harvington. These were effectively the last to be made before ownership of the Upper Avon passed to the Oxford, Worcester & Wolverhampton Railway. They had little concern for river improvement, as did their successors the West Midlands Railway. After the West Midlands Railway, ownership passed to the Great Western Railway and they simply stopped maintenance from 1874 and allowed this part of the navigation to decay. The Lower Avon from Evesham to Tewkesbury was more fortunate and survived as a working waterway.

Any lock building provided a challenge for the contractors in times of fluctuating water levels and especially in periods of flood. The River Severn had been a regular target for improvement schemes. Mine owners and ironmasters in particular had long sought improvements to the River Severn for trade on this river was regularly handicapped by low water levels and shoals. The building of locks had long been resisted by the 'Owners'. Scheme after scheme fell prey to those that opposed everything but a 'free' navigation. Partial success was achieved with the making of the towing paths that were effectively riverside turnpikes where the towing path companies charged tolls for those crafts that were required to be haled or pulled by horses.

The year 1825 started with both railway and navigations schemes attracting speculators' capital. The Grand Junction Railroad company was formed and the Worcester & Gloucester Union Canal was suggested. With work proceeding on the Gloucester & Berkeley Canal, the continuing delays to navigation on the Severn through dry seasons and flood was seen as a suitable reason to promote the canal. Again this scheme failed. But the increased prospect of railway competition, especially to Gloucester and Bristol, led to renewed interest in Severn improvement. Another scheme was put forward in 1835 and initially was confined to the river between Gloucester and Worcester. The first lock was to be immediately below the ship basin lock. A new cut would then take the waterway to the west of Gloucester Bridge to rejoin the river. Cuts were also proposed to bypass the Haw, Mythe and Upton bridges. The proposals eventually underwent a metamorphosis into a wider improvement plan that extended from Gloucester to Stourport. A joint stock company was created to raise money by share subscription. This company was the Severn Navigation Company, and the money raised financed a survey of the river.

This survey was conducted by Thomas Rhodes, and assisted by a Worcester ironmonger, E. Leader Williams. They surveyed the river and produced the plan that would form the basis for the application to Parliament in 1837. The section to be improved was from Stone Bench, Gloucester, to the Gladders Brook at Areley Kings There were cuts to avoid bends and bridges, river deepening, weir building and lock making. Upton Bridge was also to be rebuilt. The Bill was defeated in the House of Commons by the majority of twenty-five in the 1837 session. Opposition from traders, Gloucester Corporation and the Worcester & Birmingham Canal Company had helped to defeat the Bill. With their remaining funds the Severn Navigation Company regrouped to present another application to Parliament for the 1838 session.

Two different proposals were now suggested. The Severn Navigation Company route was specified as from the Lower Parting at Gloucester through to Gladders Brook. Locks and cuts were proposed towards Stourport including Upton and Worcester. A navigable cut was to be made in Gloucester from the Severn and to join with the Gloucester & Berkeley Canal that drew the common water from the Frome, Stroudwater Canal and Cambridge Arm. A second proposal was made by the Birmingham Canal Navigations Company engineer, Francis Giles. He proposed two moveable dams across the river at Saxon's Lode and Wainlode Hill. The river was to be divided by strong piers into compartments from 60–80ft wide each, with a lock on the side of each dam structure.

Giles' scheme was quickly abandoned. Negotiations for the revised Severn Navigation Company went ahead, although they faced opposition from certain proprietors of the Gloucester & Berkeley Canal. A compromise between the Severn Company and the Gloucester & Berkeley Canal was finally reached in April 1838 when it was decided to place the improvement of the Severn entirely under the control of commissioners instead of a company of proprietors.

The sixth scheme was put forward under the title of the Severn Navigation Improvement Association, who appointed William Cubitt as engineer. In this final scheme proposals were put forward for deepening the Severn and the making of locks from Stourport southwards, which would be of benefit to the users of both the Staffordshire & Worcestershire and Worcester & Birmingham canals, but would not affect the river north of Stourport to Shrewsbury.

There were three major objections that caused the Severn Navigation Company Bill to fail in 1837. The first was that it was promoted by a joint stock company, who sought to profit from tolls raised. Scheme number six had a management controlled by commissioners chosen from all classes connected with, or contiguous to, the River Severn. They raised tolls to pay the interest on the capital raised and pay for repairs. It was the hope to reduce tolls with time. The second objection concerned land drainage, which would be affected by Rhodes' river improvement plans. It led many landowners to object. The commissioners' Bill hoped to reduce the complaints by tackling the drainage differently. The third major objection came from the Shropshire owners, who faced paying tolls for the passage of their vessels. Under the new Bill, Shropshire traders were exempt from the toll.

Despite the toll exemption Shropshire Owners still objected to the delays caused passing the locks after they had been built. It was an old argument that was as valid in 1841 as it was before. The trade could only be carried on during the period of the 'freshes' or 'springs'. The barges were kept ready-loaded, and when the water rose to a certain height, a whole fleet of them floated down the river and came from the coal districts of Shropshire to Gloucester in a relative short space of time. For those delivering coal or iron to Gloucester the object was to discharge and get back as quickly as possible before the 'fresh' was over. With locks constructed it was feared that in waiting turns for the locks along the way, that on return the 'fresh' would be missed and the owners would be compelled to wait for the next period of high water.

When the commissioners went to Parliament for their Act, it was proposed to obtain a level for a standard minimum navigable depth of water of 6ft at any time of the year. In order to assist this level six weirs were proposed. The first was at Upper Ham, then Upton and this was followed by Diglis at Worcester, one at Bevere Island, one at Holt Bridge and the last at Lincombe Hill 1¼ miles below Stourport. Whilst the Bill was in committee the weir at Upton was abandoned. Yet this was done despite the evidence of the commissioners' engineer that the required depth could not be obtained by dredging alone.

All forms of opposition and support for the Bill led to a lengthy committee session that started on 30 April 1841 and lasted until June 1841. One of the many items debated concerned the location of the lock at Worcester. Previously Thomas Rhodes had advocated a lock above the junction with the Worcester & Birmingham Canal, whilst Cubitt favoured a lock below. The BCN were concerned about the delay to their trade that passed along the Worcester & Birmingham Canal and argued to have the lock north of the junction. A powerful voice in their support was their chairman, ironmaster Phillip Williams. Richard Smith's agent for the Earl of Dudley was one of a group that supported Cubitt's plan. Richard Smith was a practical man and he was about to transform the Earl of Dudley's industrial empire arranging for the building of the Pensnett Canal, the Level Ironworks & Furnaces and the Pensnett Railway.

Smith wrote to Lord Hatherton with his concerns in a letter dated 15 May 1841. He had been told by his son that the lock at Worcester was to be placed above the junction with the Worcester & Birmingham Canal instead of below. Richard Smith noted that placing the lock below gave deep water and enabled vessels of burden at all time and seasons to take in and discharge cargo at the quays. Below Worcester the river was much more convenient for steamers and vessels in tow and Smith believed the port should have full benefit of the deepest water that can be given it. Again the deeper the water the less influence a flood would have on vessels at their moorings and they would experience less inconvenience in their arrival and departure. He saw numerous reasons why the lock should be below the Worcester Canal and no good one why it should be above.

There were two basic concepts for placing the proposed lock and weir below the entrance to Worcester & Birmingham Canal rather than above it as was advocated by the Birmingham Canal Company. Firstly, the land necessary for cut and works below was less by one third than if it were removed above. Secondly the proposed works would not interfere injuriously with any property adapted to the erection of mills, such as warehouses requiring water frontage, but on the contrary would render valuable for such purposes the land lying between the cathedral and the Birmingham & Worcester canal at Diglis. To place the weir above that canal would render almost valueless the only piece of building land which building the weir was calculated to improve, on a portion of which a steam power mill was already being built. The suggested alteration would place the weir opposite to these premises and thus render their Severn frontage useless, as it would be dangerous to have to load or discharge vessels immediately at the head or tail of the weir.

Other practical points noted included that the entrance of a weir above and so near the canal lock would tend to choke up the entrance of the canal. Also, with a lock above the canal, boats coming out of the canal for the Worcester quays would have to go a considerable distance down the stream before turning to enter the proposed river lock, whilst vessels coming up river for the Worcester & Birmingham Canal would have to be hauled against the wash of the weir to the entrance of the canal thus increasing the labour to that portion of the navigation. The site proposed by Mr Cubitt was free from all these objections. The only argument against it being the delay to the Birmingham trade in passing through the proposed lock, which would not be incurred if it was placed above the canal entrance.

In order to meet this last objection, it was suggested that two locks parallel to each other be made. Such a solution increased facility for the passage of boats and reduced delay to the trade. Smith considered it evident that boats could be delivered from the Severn Locks as rapidly as they could be supplied from the canal. With comments presented by Richard Smith and others the Diglis Lock arrangement of two locks side-by-side was approved and included in the Bill.

Unfortunately, with time exhausted for the 1841 session, further committee proceedings were held over until March 1842, when the contest for supporters and those that opposed the Bill resumed. Voices of opposition continued to be made by the Town Council of Tewkesbury and the Mayor of Tewkesbury. The Worcester & Birmingham Canal and the Town Council of Gloucester also opposed the Bill. The location of Diglis Locks remained uncertain until the end. Finally, agreement was reached once a clause was inserted that the first experimental lock be made above Worcester. The committee finished their deliberations on 28 April 1842. It was reported to the House of Lords, read for a third time and passed, then it went back to the Commons for them to approve the alteration and was passed. On Friday 13 May the Severn Navigation Bill received Royal Assent.

At the core of the 1842 Act was the general deepening of the navigation from Stourport to Gloucester to guarantee a minimum of 6ft depth at low water. At other times, such as at 'spring tides' or times of flood, the water could be much deeper. Dredging was the main method of maintaining depth, but there were a number of shoals comprised of sand, gravel or rock that had to be dug out. Blasting with gunpowder was employed to remove the harder rocks.

The new locks were constructed to the design of William Cubitt by the contractors Peto, Grissell and Betts and their sub-contractors. The whole proposal was put together under an Act of Parliament that created the Severn Commission. The plan involved dredging the river and making locks at Lincombe, Holt, Bevere and Diglis (Worcester). Work started first at Lincombe to meet the condition that a trial lock be made north of Worcester.

Above left: The paired lock at Diglis on the Severn came about through the need to balance the requirements of the Birmingham Canal, Staffordshire & Worcestershire and Worcester & Birmingham canal companies. (Author)

Above right: Diglis Lock with a pair of narrowboats ready to descend to the lower river. (Author)

Edward Leader Williams (1803-79) was residential engineer for the work. He lived at Diglis House, Worcester. His capable supervision was to be of great benefit to his son, also named Edward Leader Williams, who came to work as his assistant alongside his brother Benjamin. For his son Edward, valuable experience was gained for his own engineering projects such as the Weaver and Manchester Ship Canal.

Once the Act received Royal Assent the task of building the locks and dredging the river began. The contractors Samuel Moreton Peto and his cousin and partner Thomas Grissell were London building contractors, who already had some impressive building achievements, including Hungerford Market, the Reform Club and The Lyceum Theatre. They also executed parts of the Great Western Railway and the South Eastern Railway and in 1843 agreed to build the first part of the Eastern Counties Railway. The Severn Locks and the deepening of the river became part of their busy schedule.

Finance had been created through the granting of mortgages. Tolls were taken for all craft passing the locks. Despite the works and new locks, twelve major shoals existed between Diglis and Tewkesbury, where at low water only 4ft of water existed for navigation. The composition of these shoals was principally hard marl or gravel.

James Walker made a survey for the Admiralty in 1851. He found that in the 17 miles between Diglis and Tewkesbury, 7 miles were under the minimum recommended depth of 6ft. Between Tewkesbury and Haw Bridge, a distance of 5 miles, the greater part of the river was under the 6ft standard, but this depth was compensated by the additional depths of the springtides that rose 3 or 4ft in this part. From Haw Bridge to the Upper Parting, nearly 6 miles, there was only one shoal at Wainlode, and this no more than 12–18in under the standard depth.

Such reports contributed to thoughts of further improvements. A partial solution was the making of a lock at Upper Lode, near Tewkesbury. This had been considered as early as 1852 but the work did not commence until 1856 and was completed in 1858. The engineer had direct control of making the lock, whilst William Tredwell had the contract for the lock cuts.

Making Upper Lode Lock was a major undertaking. The site covered 17 acres and required the excavation of about 230,000 cubic yards of soil. A weir 500ft in length was constructed, whilst the length of the lock 'proper' was made 120ft long by 32ft wide and lay between end gates and intermediate gates to accommodate the river craft. Another length of 150ft by 80ft formed a basin between the intermediate and lower gates so that a steam tug and towed barges might pass.

Construction proceeded through 1857, and into 1858, digging out the foundations of the lock to a depth of 18ft through loam and clay. The clay was 15ft thick and was good-quality brick-making clay. With the completion of Upper Lode Lock, navigation on the Severn was better than previous, but more needed to be done on the length to Gloucester.

CHAPTER 7

CANAL BUILDING IN THE RAILWAY AGE

An important stage in the development of the public railway was the opening of the Liverpool & Manchester Railway in 1830. When this passenger and freight-carrying line commenced operating, the event was heralded as an important step forward. It was the first public passenger railway to use steam locomotives for haulage and with the opening of this important railway a renewed impetus was given to the promoters of other schemes. There had been a steady stream of suggestions for public railways throughout the preceding decade, and some had been built for the conveyance of freight using horses or steam locomotives, but now schemes reached a national perspective and, during the 1830s, the first steps to a British Railways network were made with the construction of the London & Birmingham and Grand Junction Railways.

Construction techniques for railways enforced the development of new skills to ensure the construction of the route, but also drew on the many common skills learnt on the making of the waterways. This included advances in bridge-building technology: waterway side bridges, roving bridges, road bridges and aqueducts now had elements of wrought iron incorporated into the structure. Such inclusion might be the whole structure or as composite bridges, where iron beams spanned the waterway with a superstructure of masonry.

Engineering, or blue, bricks became popular in railway construction schemes. Such types of bricks had been used on some of the later canal schemes, where the search for quality and consistency had led engineers to source brick making from outside firms. Clays from the ironstone mining districts were particularly suited to the making of engineering bricks and yards were common in parts of North and South Staffordshire, North Warwickshire and East Worcestershire. Kiln design was improved to produce greater quantities on regular demand and the trade ceased to be simply a summer occupation. Brick-making companies came to supply a wide range of demands from housing, factories and mills to public undertakings such as gasworks, waterworks and general transport infrastructure.

Public works contractors also came to work on both railway and canal construction. Thomas Townshend had work building parts of the Grand Junction Railway between Stafford and Birmingham as well as work for the Birmingham Canal.

Matthew Frost was another who gained contracts for both canal and railways. He built the Hatherton Branch Canal for the Staffordshire & Worcestershire Canal Company, built Churchbridge Reservoir, improved the Sow Navigation to Stafford and redeveloped Forebridge Wharf for the traders. He also constructed the Landywood Tramway from the Hatherton Canal to Great Wyrley Colliery, built various colliery tramways and later was employed by the Birmingham, Wolverhampton & Dudley Railway to build a section of their line. He was a staunch Methodist and was related by marriage to the Bloomer family who operated Pelsall Ironworks.

The Hatherton Branch joined the main canal at Calf Heath and ascended by locks to the Churchbridge terminus alongside Gilpin's steel works. It was made without Act of Parliament and arranged by land purchase from the riparian owners. This canal was open to traffic during 1841 and the connecting tramway finished in 1842.

James Frost, brother to Matthew, became associated with canal building when he was awarded the contract to make the Stourbridge Extension Canal (1837–40) from the Leys to Oak Farm.

The merger of the Birmingham Canal Navigations and the Wyrley & Essington Canal in 1839 led to new canal links being made between the two waterways. The Wyrley & Essington had considerable untapped industrial potential along its banks and the new union opened up greater trading opportunities, once the additional links had been made.

Walsall businessmen had long asked for better transport communication and in 1838 a scheme for the Walsall Junction Canal was proposed. James Frost and Peter Potter surveyed a scheme for the 860yd-long canal. Once the Birmingham Canal had agreed to merge their undertaking with the Wyrley & Essington Canal, in July 1839, the route of the Walsall Junction Canal was re-surveyed by William Fowler.

Under the terms of certain Birmingham Canal Navigations Acts there were powers to construct branches from existing waterways up to a certain distance. Soon after the merger agreement had been signed, the Birmingham Canal advertised for contractors to build a canal from the Birchills Branch of the Wyrley & Essington Canal to the Walsall Canal. Tenders were to be received by 8 August 1839. Thomas Townshend, contractor for work on the BCN New Main Line, was given the job. The work comprised cutting the canal, making eight locks and building three road bridges. The Birmingham Canal Navigations decided to purchase minerals near the junction at Birchills to reduce the risk of subsidence there.

Some major new canal lines were made to improve trade along the Birmingham Canal Navigations during this time. Increased traffic from and to South Staffordshire had led to congestion at the Farmer's Bridge Locks in Birmingham. The solution was a completely new line of canal along the valley of the River Tame from the Birmingham & Fazeley Canal at Salford Bridge to the heart of the South Staffordshire Iron Trade at Wednesbury, where the projected line was intended to join the Danks Branch.

Thomas Telford had died, but there remained some very capable engineers to take canal building into a new age. These included James Walker and William Fowler. The Tame Valley Canal, as originally surveyed, was to have locks evenly spaced along a winding and steady rising waterway. This plan was changed under the directions of the engineers James Walker and William Fowler, who wrote to John Freeth on 7 October 1839.

Both Fowler and Walker agreed that Telford's work with the New Main Line set new standards and principals. The proposed plan for the Tame Valley fell short of that and they argued for an amended and straighter line of waterway despite any additional expense that might be incurred:

> It cannot be required to prove that in making a new canal his great principal should be kept in view. They are also aware that to begin by doing the work in a second or third rate way, as by taking a curved and therefore a longer line in order to save the first expense of a straight one, leaves them open to reproaches, abuse, complaints and to claims for alterations by new cuts and otherwise, which after the sides of the canal become occupied by wharfs, docks, manufactories and other erections can be executed (if at all) only at great expense.
>
> It sometimes happens also that by consideration of the expenses contingent upon a work done in a cheap way, the saving is only apparent and that the bold measure of doing it well at first produces effects in the future working that would make it true economy to adopt it. The present subject illustrates this observation.

The list of suggestions for improvement included the reduction of the Parliamentary Line from 9½ miles to 8¹/₅ miles, changes to the location of the locks and the suggestion that only one engine be used to pump water instead of the intended three. All locks were concentrated on the section from Perry Barr to Salford and the route followed as straight as possible a route from Perry Barr cutting through a hillside and sandstone rock to Hamstead then high upon an embankment to pass Hamstead Hall. Another deep cutting took the canal under the Newton Road and then onto a long embankment across the Tame Valley to Wednesbury.

New factors had come into the route equation since the passing of the Act. With the merger of the Birmingham Canal Navigations and the Wyrley & Essington Canal, three new links were envisaged. One of them, the Rushall Canal, was to join the Tame Valley route. For Walker and Fowler the issue of how this was to be done led to the drawing up of two alternative plans for the BCN committee to consider. The first option suggested involved a canal crossroads with the four directions being to the Pleck at Walsall, Wednesbury, Salford Bridge and Rushall. The second, and simpler, option proved to be the one chosen. That is a single junction between the Rushall and Tame Valley with no separate branch through the Delves to Pleck.

Another decision made was the extension of the Tame Valley Canal from the terminus of the Danks Branch to join the Walsall Canal at nearby Ocker Hill. The Danks Branch served important ironworks at Goldshill. John Bagnall & Sons had ironworks that were served by the Danks Branch and the Balls Hill Branch. They imposed conditions on when the construction work could be conducted and asked for temporary basin accommodation whilst the works were in progress.

The contract for the Goldshill and Hateley Heath section of the Tame Valley was awarded to Thomas Townshend, who started work whilst still constructing the Walsall Locks. By August 1840 the foundations for the Goldshill Aqueduct over the East Branch of the River Tame were put down. In an earlier age the river had provided power for the watermills at Goldshill that assisted

Above left: Birmingham Canal Navigations, Tame Valley Canal, Spouthouse Lane Aqueduct. (Author)

Above right: Thomas Townshend's contract to build the Wednesbury–Walsall Canal section involved embankment and deep cutting. There were two aqueducts: one over a tramway, while the other was the three-arch brick Goldshill Aqueduct over the River Tame. (Author)

the eighteenth-century iron trade. Now steam engines gave the power needed for the mills and the waters of the Tame were of secondary importance.

Building the canal from the Walsall Canal through to the Danks Branch involved making an embankment almost throughout. In addition to the Tame Aqueduct at Goldshill, there was also an aqueduct over the single-track tramway that linked Bagnall's Goldshill Ironworks with coal and ironstone mines and Goldsgreen Furnaces. Part of the tramway aqueduct was made with iron castings. James Walker, in his report to the BCN in August 1841, noted that construction of this structure was delayed for want of castings from the foundry.

East of the Danks Branch Junction the canal passed into a long cutting that skirted the south perimeter of Wednesbury and cut through the hillside known as Holloway Bank. Provision had to be made here for a bridge for Telford's Holyhead Turnpike Road, which involved a diversion to turn the right of way onto a new bridge. From Holloway Bank the canal continued onto Balls

The Tame Valley Canal at Deykins Avenue descended through the final two locks to Salford Junction. Water was pumped back to the top of the locks using steam engines. These were located in the Engine House that is seen top right in this view. (Author)

Hill Cutting and another embankment to Hateley Heath. Townshend encountered considerable problems with both cutting and making it watertight. It consisted of shale, stone and other coal measures, part of which had been worked underground.

The second Tame Valley contract was awarded in February 1841 to Messrs Tredwell, Jackson & Bean. They began work on Monday 15 February at Newton, near Friar Park, and at Tower Hill. Within two days 120 men were at work. Their contract involved a number of iron aqueducts and bridges. The Horseley Co. of Tipton had agreed to provide the principal part of the ironwork.

Building the Tame Valley was conducted at a time when West Midlands iron making was steadily increasing. The local skill with wrought iron is evident to this day in the structures along the route of this canal. Iron aqueducts were provided at:

Old Walsall Road, Hamstead (Piercy)
New Walsall Road, Tame Bridge
Hateley Heath

There are also a number of iron side bridges and roving bridges across the waterway. Perhaps the most unusual is Goldshill Bridge, which is an iron humped-back bridge.

Brick aqueducts were made at:

Goldshill (over the Tame)
Grand Junction Railway
Newton (over the Tame)
Spouthouse Lane, Hamstead

The Goldshill Aqueduct carries the canal over the river by a three-arch brick structure with wing walls coped with stone. At the crossing of the Grand Junction Railway the canal was carried over the existing tracks by a tall brick aqueduct of three arches. The tall embankment was then carried around to span the Tame Valley close to the Bustleholme Watermill. A tall single-arch brick aqueduct was constructed to carry the canal over the river there. By contrast, Spouthouse Lane is a tall, narrow single-arch lined with stone and brick. The stone came from the nearby Tower Hill Cutting. The buttress near the top of the arch was added following subsidence caused by the nearby Hamstead Colliery.

Cutting and embanking provided constant employment and soon some 1,000 men were at work on the Tredwell, Jackson & Bean contract. From Hateley Heath to Perry Barr there were three deep cuttings. The first carried the canal through Bustleholme Hill where sand was found and later quarried commercially. The tall brick arch of Crankhall Lane Bridge spans the cutting at its deepest point. From here a long embankment carried the canal over the railway and the Tame Valley close to Bustleholme Mill. After this embankment the canal entered the deep cutting at Newton that involved constructing a bridge for the turnpike. Another embankment carried the canal over Spouthouse Lane and the Old Walsall Road before entering the final deep cutting at Tower Hill. Thereafter the canal passed under the turnpike road at Perry Barr and the started a long descent to Salford Bridge through thirteen locks: a flight of eleven, then another two placed close together at Deykins Avenue.

The Tame Valley Canal joined the Birmingham & Fazeley Canal at Salford Bridge and also formed a connection with the Birmingham & Warwick Junction Canal, which was a link in a chain of waterways that finally met up with the Grand Junction Canal and formed part of a direct navigation route to London.

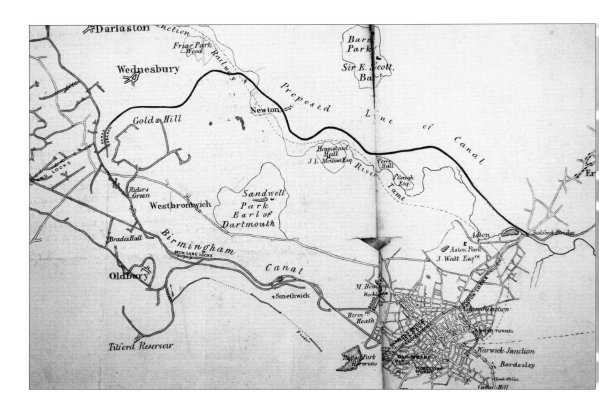

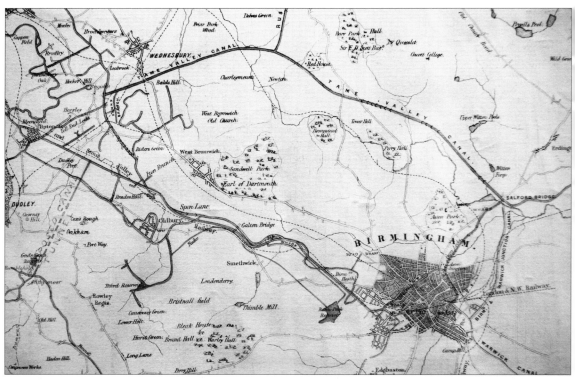

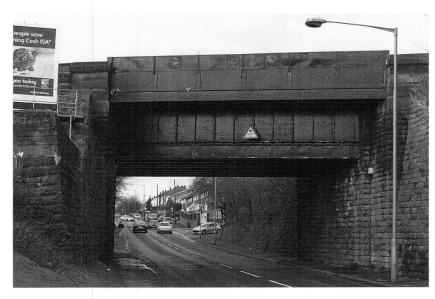

Iron Aqueducts on the Tame Valley Canal – Piercy Aqueduct, Old Walsall Road, Hamstead. (Author)

Opposite above: The route of the Bentley Canal, as built.

Opposite below: The original plan involved locks spaced out along the route of the waterway. The canal as built was constructed to changes suggested by James Walker and William Fowler.

James Potter was engineer to the Birmingham & Warwick Junction Canal. He was responsible for the making of this 2½ mile-long canal. Six locks were planned for this short waterway and Potter also planned a short tunnel under the London & Birmingham Railway. The number of locks was reduced to five and the tunnel became a tall railway bridge. During December 1841 three tenders were received for the construction work and that of Clarkson & Hall was accepted. Engineering features included cuttings, bridges, locks, a reservoir and an aqueduct over the River Tame near the junction with the Birmingham & Fazeley Canal at Salford Bridge. By October 1843 the work was well advanced. From the Tame Aqueduct to the bottom of Garrison Flight, the locks were almost finished apart from side walls. This canal was opened officially on 14 February 1844. The date corresponded with the opening of the Tame Valley Canal.

The second link between the Wyrley Canal and the Birmingham Canal was the Bentley whose construction was a compromise of different schemes, which started as separate branches and links. The first section from the Anson Branch was constructed by John Woodward towards the mines of the Thorneycroft brothers. Another proposed link was a canal from the Walsall Canal at Darlaston through the mining area to the west of Willenhall to join the Wyrley Canal at New Cross. The compromise chosen was to abandon the route from Darlaston, which would have involved another aqueduct over the Grand Junction Railway, and to divert the canal along a new course north of the railway to join up with Woodward's contract. This work was awarded to and built by local contractors Matthew Frost and John Bate. Another proposed branch to Wood Green was also never completed.

During 1852 an iron bridge was provided on the Walsall Canal to span the Ocker Hill feeder branch, which was made navigable to a coal wharf. (Author)

The surveying partnership of Walker and Burgess was responsible for several more important schemes on the BCN. These included the Rushall Canal, completed in 1847, and the Netherton Tunnel (1858).

In 1846 the BCN merged with the Dudley Canal Company, which hitherto had close ties with the Stourbridge Navigation. Local businessmen were soon keen to press for a new link between the Dudley and Birmingham. Initial proposals eventually developed into a concrete scheme that was let in 1855 to the contractor George Meakin. It was in fact a series of contracts that involved:

1   A new canal, the Netherton Branch, from the new main line to Netherton Tunnel
2   Groveland Aqueduct that carried the Old Main Line over the Netherton Branch
3   Netherton Tunnel
4   A new straight canal across the mines and furnace land at Windmill End
5   The removal and opening out of Brewin's Tunnel
6   The Two Lock line
7   New lock flight at the Delph Locks, Nos 2-7 in the Delph Flight

All the work was completed by August 1858.

The last canals made in the West Midlands were known as the Wyrley Bank and Cannock Extension, both of which were constructed by Chambers & Hilton of Birmingham. They were a firm of civil engineers that engaged in a variety of public works contracts. Their contracts for the Birmingham Canal were completed in 1858 when they transferred to a railway construction contract at Kirby Stephen. By this time the Wyrley Bank was completed to a terminus near Great Wyrley, whilst the Cannock Extension had reached Rumour Hill and formed a junction with the

Left: The alteration of route that made Brewin's Tunnel was further changed with the Netherton Tunnel works. The tunnel was opened out into a deep cutting and towing path. The wall on the right originally formed part of the tunnel side. (Author)

Below: From the top of Brewin's Tunnel and the road to the High Bridge, the junction of the Two Locks Line and the canal to Parkhead could be seen long after the Two Locks Line had ceased to carry traffic. (Author)

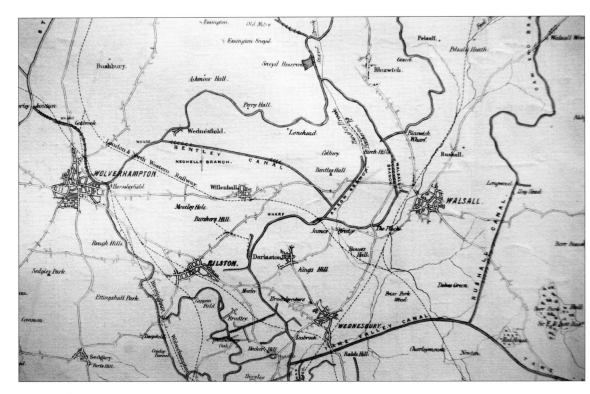

Above: The proposed line for the Tame Valley Canal.

Left: Dudley Canal improvements – the making of Netherton Tunnel was achieved over a two-year period and was opened in August 1858. Fifteen construction shafts were sunk as part of the work and seven were retained as air shafts. (Author)

Left: Birmingham building partnership Chambers & Hilton were given the contract to build the Cannock Extension Canal from Pelsall through to Rumour Hill, Cannock, which served several new mines established near Norton Canes. The route is characterised by sturdy brick bridges that crossed the canal for accommodation, footpath or road use. (Author)

Churchbridge Branch. The canal beyond was not completed until Francis Piggot, owner of the Hednesford Colliery, pressed for the completion to Hednesford. BCN canal workers completed this section, which included an embankment and aqueduct to carry the canal over Hawks Green Lane.

Two terminus basins were laid out at Hednesford, which formed an interchange between the canal and the standard-gauge Littleworth Tramway. This BCN-owned tramway was built with the assistance of the London & North Western Railway and provided the means for traffic from the Cannock Wood, Wimblebury, Hednesford and Cannock Chase collieries to be loaded into boats at Hednesford Basin.

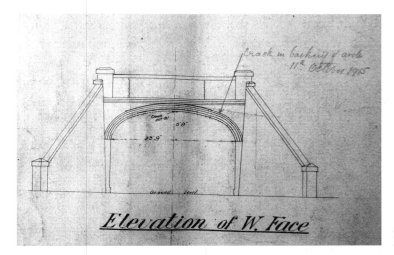

A rare line drawing of Hawks Green Aqueduct.

Delph Locks – the original route of the canal as built under the supervision of Thomas Dadford passed under the bridge on the left and descended through seven locks before rejoining the amended route above Lock 9. The straight and deeper new lock flight created six new locks, Nos 2–6, as well as the old No.9 becoming No.8 in the altered arrangement. (Author)

Canal building in Worcestershire was marked by the making of a link between the Droitwich Barge Canal and the Worcester & Birmingham at a time when the Oxford, Worcester & Wolverhampton Railway (OWWR) was constructing railways through Droitwich. Various junction canals had been suggested since 1792, and a railway was proposed in 1837. It was a well-publicised fact that 40,000 tons of coal and salt were annually hauled between Droitwich and Hanbury Wharf. Shares for the Droitwich and Hanbury Wharf Railway were made available on application to Mr Curtler, a solicitor of Droitwich.

The share issue was set at 400 shares of £20 each to raise a capital of £8,000 to pay for construction, land purchase, and so on. No details of any survey appear with the advertisements and the scheme appears to have failed.

Some fourteen years on it was the making of the OWWR that led the Worcester & Birmingham Canal Company to support a new canal scheme. The Bill was presented to Parliament in 1851. Powers were sought to incorporate the company, construct the canal to connect the Droitwich Canal with the Worcester & Birmingham Canal at Hanbury, to have powers to take water from the Worcester & Birmingham Canal, lease or sell the undertaking and to levy tolls.

Richard Boddington, Worcester & Birmingham Canal engineer, was engaged and paid to plan the route and later supervise the construction of the canal. The Bill went through the Parliament between February and May 1852. There was such considerable opposition to the scheme that a Select Committee was formed to examine the case.

Several complaints were made about the state of the Droitwich Barge Canal which charged high tolls, but limited navigation to the river vessels. The barge locks were 66ft long, effectively prohibiting a normal narrowboat of 70ft length from using them. The lack of a towing path was also considered a handicap. Despite these and other objections the Bill received Royal Assent on 28 May 1852.

Thus the Droitwich Junction Company was formed and at their first assembly meeting at Droitwich, 2 July 1852, the decision to lease their canal to the Worcester & Birmingham was taken. Letting tenders for the work was delayed until the end of the year. On 28 January 1853 they considered the tenders, which were as follows:

Charles Hodgkinson	£2551 7s 0d
John Harding & John Flintoff	£2162 10s 0d
Jennings & Yates	£1940 0s 0d
John Beck	£1875 1s 10d

John Beck's tender was accepted. Yet it seems that there was a problem with his quote and the contract was signed in February with Jennings and Yates. Work then started on making the navigation. The barge canal comprised five narrow locks that descended from Hanbury in a line parallel with the turnpike. The sixth lock enabled boats to descend to the River Salwarpe, which was made navigable for a short distance to join the Barge Canal. The connection was made through a new barge lock, fitted with four gates and a new canal section to join up with the present barge basin.

Cash payments to Jennings and Yates cease at December 1853, but later payments are made to W. & W.E. Wood on account for 'Droitwich Canal'. John Knight and William Brookes were paid for brick making, Thomas Chambers for lime and a William Chambers received a payment for lock making. One name missing from the contractor's list was the local firm of Tredwell, who were engaged in building the mixed-gauge Oxford, Worcester & Wolverhampton Railway from Worcester to Tipton at this time.

Seemingly contractors were retained and dismissed to Richard Boddington's instructions. There was also a considerable pressure to finish the waterway as early as possible. The Junction Canal Committee hoped their canal would be finished by September but the official opening was not made until 9 October 1854. Meanwhile work on improving the barge canal was carried out.

Birmingham Canal, Cannock Extension, Anglesey Branch Canal, Whitehorse Road – the feeder from Chasewater Reservoir to the Cannock Extension was made navigable by the contractor John Boys junior (1850–51). The work included widening and straightening and the building of four bridges. (Author)

The Worcester & Birmingham Canal Company had leased Droitwich Barge Canal for twenty-one years from 24 July 1853. Once this legal step had been taken, permission was then given to lengthen the eight barge locks from Hawford to Droitwich, which were completed by July 1854.

Some Droitwich salt makers were affected by the canal works and the construction had mixed benefits. The town of Droitwich was a very different place than the town of the present. A mini-industrial revolution had affected Droitwich. The rush to extract brine had led to unsightly pipes being laid across land and streets to the salt pans from the many wells placed across the town. There was a pall of steam and smoke above as pans were heated to concentrate and collect solid salt. Making the canal disrupted the operation of some works and land purchase lost potential supply from untapped sources. Most critical was the Droitwich Patent Salt Company. In March 1855 they sued the Droitwich Junction Canal Company for damages that amounted to £2,274 15s 6d. They argued that they had opposed the Bill, but at the subsequent enquiry had ensured a deed for the canal company to complete their canal by 1 July 1854.

Coal for the Patent Salt Works was carted by road from Hanbury Wharf. Some 60,000 tons of coal were delivered there each year. Following the delay in completing the Junction Canal, the

A short length of the Salwarpe was made navigable from Lock 7 to Lock 8 (top left) that formed the junction with the Droitwich Canal. In this early 1900s view some salt works buidings can be seen. (Author)

Patent Salt Company claimed for road cartage from July until October. Further claims accrued following a shortage of water flowing down the locks in November 1854 when boats had to reduce loads to get down to the Salwarpe Wharves of the Patent Salt Company.

Herefordshire was served principally by the Wye Navigation and the Hereford & Gloucester Canal. A scheme to unite Hereford and Gloucester was first suggested in 1774, which failed. A survey made by Richard Hall in 1789 formed the basis for the revised scheme and helped promoters apply to Parliament to make the canal. Josiah Clowes was appointed engineer. He re-surveyed the route and suggested a narrow canal from Hereford via Gloucester to Gloucester and a branch at Oxenhall for Newent to serve coal mines. The canal reached Over on the West Parting of the River Severn and was required to cross Alney Island to reach the quay at Gloucester, which lay south of the West Bridge.

Cutting began in 1793 on the line to Newent and across Alney Island to Gloucester. The cutting across Alney Island was performed by John Carne's men and a mechanical cutting machine. This task was nearly finished by October 1794.

When Josiah Clowes died, the post of engineer to the company was given to Robert Whitworth. Robert soon faced a problem with the Alney section becoming badly silted up. Whitworth suggested making a dam, but this prospect was opposed by the local fishermen. The company decided to abandon the Alney Island line and make the junction with the Severn at Over.

Construction continued northward. Oxenhall was reached by October 1795, but problems were encountered cutting Oxenhall Tunnel (2,192yds). Experienced miners and tunnellers were also needed for excavating and arching the mile-long Ashperton Tunnel, at Walsopthorne, in April 1796. They had to find their own tools, but materials were to be furnished by the company. Contractors finished the route as far as Ledbury, which was reached in March 1798, but went no further. Any work done on Ashperton Tunnel was abandoned. The route was 16 miles long with

The Skew Bridge on the Hereford extension of the Hereford & Gloucester Canal is a reminder of the engineering skill of Stephen Ballard, who was responsible for making this part of the waterway. (Author)

thirteen locks. The navigation failed to reach the important water source of the Frome, north of Ledbury, which left the canal badly short of water.

Stephen Ballard was appointed clerk to the canal company in August 1827. Later he was to become also their engineer. He was responsible for getting the canal completed to Hereford. The Act of 1839 raised funds for work to restart and by April 1840, 500 men were employed on the extension. Sections were opened one at a time. Canon Frome was reached in October 1842. Then Ashperton was complete. Ballard had the intended length reduced to 400yds with the remainder made in long cuttings. Withington Wharf was opened on 26 February 1844 and the canal was finally completed to Barrs Court, Hereford, on 21 May 1845.

Engineering works included a skew road bridge over the canal at Monkhide, an aqueduct over the River Lugg (Shelwick) and a tunnel through Aylestone Hill. In total, a further nine locks and 18 miles of waterway had been built.

Railway construction led to new aqueducts being made on canals where the railway crossed the route. A wide variety of aqueducts were completed, some entirely composed of masonry and others with iron troughs.

Perhaps the longest length of trough was constructed on the Bullbridge Aqueduct on the Cromford Canal. The building of the North Midland Railway (1836–40) was conducted under the supervision of the resident engineer Joseph Swanwick. George Stephenson was engineer in charge.

Bullbridge Aqueduct was completed in 1794. It spanned the valley of the River Amber, Bullbridge mill stream and the Ripley Turnpike. The railway route followed the narrow strip of land between the mill stream and turnpike. It was a challenge that was solved by Alexander Ross who suggested a pre-fabricated structure to reduce closure time for the canal. A wrought-iron tough 150ft long was fabricated by the Butterley Iron Company and delivered to Bull Bridge in sections. By arrangement the canal was stanked off and water pumped out. The iron trough was made to fit into the existing masonry aqueduct channel, but was still 9ft wide internally. The work was carried out over a 24-hour period from Saturday to Sunday. With the channel secured work could proceed with completing the railway passage underneath.

There is a certain irony in that at the time of making this aqueduct over the North Midland Railway, the Cromford Canal was a busy highway. Narrowboats traded back and forth to the turnpike interchange at Bull Bridge for road transport to Sheffield and the North East, or through to the Cromford & High Peak Railway and the tramway to Whalley Bridge. They were concerned to reduce disruption to their service, yet once the North Midland Railway was finished a new and quicker transport route became available to the North and the canal quickly suffered a decline in trade.

The Cromford Canal was also crossed by the Manchester, Buxton, Matlock & Midland Junction Railway that required two iron aqueducts at opposite ends of Leawood Tunnel. The contract to build these aqueducts was given to J. Lawton. That south of the tunnel carried the Cromford Canal over the railway. The second was installed to carry the private Leawood Branch by a trough placed close to the north portal of Leawood Tunnel.

Not all aqueducts were made with an iron trough. Brick and masonry aqueducts were constructed for the Grand Junction Railway at Darlaston, Wolverhampton and Walsall Railway at Birchills and the Midland Railway at Rushall.

AQUEDUCTS OVER RAILWAYS

(1) CONSTRUCTION COMPLETED WHEN RAILWAY MADE

Aqueduct Location	Canal Company	Railway Company	Dates Railway Constructed
Birchills (1)	BCN, Wyrley & Essington	South Staffordshire Railway	1856–58
Birchills (2)	BCN, Birchills Branch	Wolverhampton & Walsall Railway	1868–72
Brownhills	BCN, Anglesey Branch	South Staffordshire Railway	1847–49
Bull Bridge	Cromford	North Midland	1836–40
Congleton	Macclesfield Canal	North Staffordshire Railway, Biddulph–Congleton Line	1858–60
Darlaston	BCN, Walsall Canal	Grand Junction Railway	1835–37
Daw End	BCN, Daw End Branch	Midland Railway	1875–78
Dudley Port	BCN, New Main Line	South Staffordshire Railway	1848–50
Hazelhurst	Caldon Canal, Leek Branch	North Staffordshire Railway, Milton–Cheddleton Line	1864–67
High Peak	Cromford	Manchester, Buxton, Matlock and Midland Junction Railway	1846–49
Hill Top	BCN, Balls Hill	Birmingham, Wolverhampton & Dudley Railway	1852–54
Leawood	Lea Branch (Private Canal)	Manchester, Buxton, Matlock and Midland Junction Railway	1846–49
Middlewood	Macclesfield Canal	Stockport, Disley & Whaley Bridge Railway	1854–57
Warwick	Warwick & Napton	Birmingham & Oxford Junction Railway	1849–52

(2) CANALS MADE OVER EXISTING RAILWAYS

Aqueduct Location	Canal Company	Railway Company	Dates Canal Constructed
Grand Junction	BCN Tame Valley	Grand Junction Railway	1841–44

(3) CANALS MADE OVER EXISTING TRAMWAYS AND PLATEWAYS

Aqueduct Location	Canal Company	Tramway Owner	Dates Canal Constructed
Toll End	BCN Tame Valley	John Bagnall & Sons	1841–44
Groveland Colliery	BCN Netherton Branch	John Bagnall & Sons	1856–58

Sometimes railway construction avoided bridges or aqueducts and passed under the waterway by a tunnel. Examples of this in the West Midlands are in Birmingham where the Stour Valley Railway Tunnel north of New Street Station passed under the Newhall Branch and at Winson Green where the Birmingham, Wolverhampton & Dudley Railway went under the Birmingham

Cranfleet Cut was altered at the time of the construction of the Midland Counties Railway. The building of the railway from Leicester to Trent Junction provided for crossings over the cut and River Trent. (Author)

Heath Branch. At Wednesfield, near Woverhampton, the Grand Junction Railway was taken under the Wyrley & Essington Canal by a tunnel.

Canals were also diverted in places to accommodate railway building. Sometimes the alterations were minimal to accommodate bridges, but there were other cases where more substantial diversions were needed. In making the Birmingham, Wolverhampton & Stour Valley diversions of the Birmingham Canal main line were made at Bloomfield and Wolverhampton. With the South Staffordshire line between Walsall and Lichfield, it became necessary to divert the Wyrley & Essington Canal at Pipe Hill.

In the East Midlands the building of the Midland Counties Railway led to an alteration to the line of the Derby Canal at Borrowash Mill. A new, and straighter, channel was cut there to the north side of the railway line and a new lock constructed to replace the original canal lock, which lay across the route of the railway. Other alterations were needed near Redhill. The Midlands County Railway passed through the hill in a tunnel and then crossed the River Trent on the east side of the existing weir at Soars Mouth. The Trent Navigation Company, keen to protect navigation through Cranfleet Lock, had a clause inserted into the Railway Act that enforced the making of a new stone weir downstream of the railway bridge. The railway company subsequently argued against the construction of the new weir on the basis that it was not needed, as the existing one was adequate to the purpose. Whilst the Trent Navigation Company sought to force the Midlands Counties Railway to make the new weir, William Cubbit, engineer, presented a report in March 1841 that confirmed the new weir was not required. Cubbit suggested that an alternative option was to build stop gates in the entrance channel of Cranfleet Cut, which seems to have been done. The weir was moved, but this was done at a later date.

Railway ownership of canals and navigations was another aspect of this time. Purchases were sometimes made to acquire the trade and at other times the land. Canals such as the Oakham were adapted to make the railway between Melton Mowbray, Oakham, Stamford and Peterborough.

Each railway company had different policies towards canal ownership, which ranged from passive to active operation of the waterway. The North Staffordshire Railway Act included clauses for the takeover of the Trent & Mersey Canal. Whilst they arranged for the making of the railways, a carrying department was established to raise revenue for the company. This carrying arm was quickly

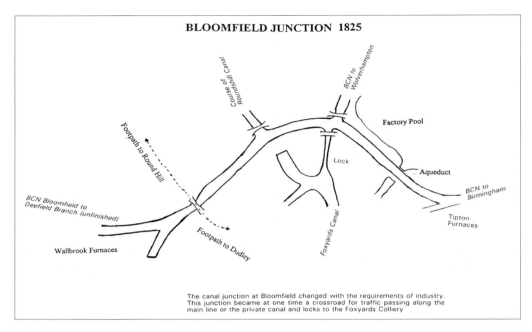

The original line of the Birmingham Canal at Bloomfield, Tipton, comprised the junction between the branch to Deepfields, the main canal to Bradley and Wolverhampton and the private Foxyards Canal.

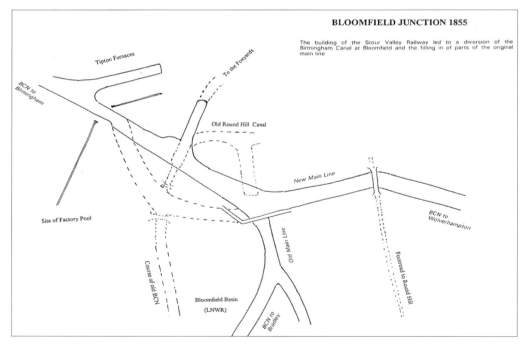

The Birmingham Canal was diverted to allow the making of the Birmingham Wolverhampton & Stour Valley Railway and utilised a section of the private Roundshill Canal for the altered line to Bradley. The Bradley route had ceased to be the main line with the completion of Coseley Tunnel and the main line was along the direct route to Deepfields.

disposed of once the railways were built, yet the wharves and warehouses generated important revenue from the local pottery trade. One special case was the Birmingham Canal where under the London & Birmingham Railway Arrangement Act, share dividends were guaranteed. In return the London & Birmingham Railway and their successors (the London & Western Railway and the London, Midland & Scottish Railway) had a say in the affairs of the canal company.

RAILWAY-LEASED NAVIGATIONS

Year	Navigation	Railway Company	Subsequent Ownership
1847	Shrewsbury	London & North Western Railway	London Midland & Scottish Railway
1847	Shropshire Union	London & North Western Railway	London Midland & Scottish Railway
1862	Hereford & Gloucester	West Midland	Great Western [*]
1863	Newcastle-under-Lyme	North Staffordshire	London Midland & Scottish Railway

[*] Purchased by Great Western Railway in 1870.

RAILWAY-OWNED NAVIGATIONS

Year	Navigation	Railway Company	Subsequent Ownership
1846	Ashby	Midland	London, Midland & Scottish Railway
1846	Oakham	Midland [Δ]	–
1846	Stourbridge Junction	Oxford, Worcester & Wolverhampton	West Midland; Great Western
1846	Trent & Mersey	North Staffordshire	London, Midland & Scottish Railway
1851	Newcastle-under-Lyme Junction (part)	North Staffordshire [‡]	–
1852	Cromford	Manchester, Buxton, Matlock & Midland Junction & Scottish Railway	Midland; London, Midland
1854	Grantham	Ambergate, Nottingham, Boston & Eastern Junction & North Eastern	Great Northern; London
1855	Nottingham	Ambergate, Nottingham, Boston & Eastern Junction & North Eastern	Great Northern; London
1856	Stratford-upon-Avon	Oxford, Worcester and Wolverhampton	West Midland; Great Western
1858	Leominster	Shrewsbury & Hereford	–
1859	Upper Avon	Oxford, Worcester & Wolverhampton	West Midland; Great Western
1870	Hereford & Gloucester	Great Western [†]	–

[Δ] Canal closed to commercial traffic and majority of route converted into a railway.

[‡] Section of canal converted into a railway.

[†] Canal closed to commercial traffic and majority of route converted into a railway 1881.

CHALLENGING TIMES

The last thirty years of the nineteenth century were difficult times for canal and river navigations. Some concerns remained profitable, successful and retained important trade. Then there were those that did not, and this was a list that got longer with time. Traffic dwindled on canals such as the Cromford, Derby, Droitwich and Grantham. The Hereford & Gloucester, after a period of expansion from Ledbury to Hereford, was converted into a railway and several other canals suffered a decline in fortunes. Yet there were attempts to increase competition with public railways. Innovation was part of the British way of life and talented engineering solutions have come to the forefront in many industries and communities. Such skills touched the waterways in different ways.

One such remarkable development was the Anderton Lift that connected the River Weaver with the Trent & Mersey Canal and had an important role in the movement of salt and pottery goods. The lift inauguration corresponded with improvements to the River Weaver and led to an application to Parliament for a corresponding widening of the Trent & Mersey Canal, including another range of wider locks through to the summit. The widening was partly done between Anderton and Middlewich, but plans to build the larger 'barge size' locks towards Kidsgrove were

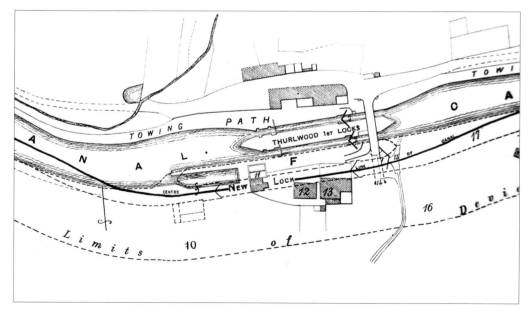

A proposed lock-widening scheme for large locks from Anderton towards Stoke on the Trent & Mersey Canal to serve the salt trade came to little, apart from widening a section of canal and the River Dane Aqueduct.

not implemented. These locks, improved in Telford's time, were left alone. Visible signs of the alterations still survive today in the form of the wider waterway and the reconstructed bridges.

Another dramatic innovation was the Foxton Incline Plane that enabled narrowboats to avoid the double staircase, each comprised of five locks, which was a considerable delay to narrowboats travelling between Leicester or Nottingham and London.

More basic alterations included drainage and flood work. In Nottingham, the Council Improvement Committee made a decision in 1882 to divert the River Leen into the Nottingham Canal near Lenton. The river was turned into the canal during 1884 and the river bed from Lenton filled in. These alterations meant that Castle Lock overflow weir was enlarged and certain parts of the Tinkers Leen modified. Subsequent to, or contemporary with, the making of the Nottingham Canal, the Tinkers Leen flowed under the London (Flood) Road and the canal in a siphon. With the 1884 improvements the siphon was considered too small and this was replaced by two 5ft 6in-diameter pipes.

The lowering of the River Soar at Leicester was essential to reduce flooding around the town. Eventually the Leicester Corporation took it on themselves to finance such an important work. The results were to benefit both navigation and the town, but the nine-year reconstruction was to draw in a number of contractors for the task.

The improvements concentrated on cutting new channels, embanking, lowering and straightening the bed of the Soar, which passed though the city and was the cause of frequent floods that affected canalside and riverside properties. An Act passed in 1868, entitled the Leicester Improvement, Drainage and Markets, was the first serious attempt to remedy the flood issue and authorised improvement from the stone weir in Beadhouse Meadows through to Swan's Nest Weir, at Belgrave, near the junction with the Leicester Navigation. This work included a new cut from Old Soar Corner to Braunstone Gate Bridge and also the replacement of the solid towpaths under Cow Lane Bridge and West Bridge with a towing path on piles. This part of the Bill was not proceeded with and another Act, the Leicester Improvement, was passed in 1874 that extended the improvement zone from the Old Stone Weir to Birstall Mill. This Act authorised the removal of Castle Mill Weir and Castle Mill Lock, the deepening of the bed of the Soar to Swan's Mill Lock and alteration of the levels of the Leicester Navigation and the Leicestershire & Northamptonshire Union Canal. The purchase of Castle Mill by the Corporation

The Soar Flood Relief program (1879–90) led to a new straight navigation from Freeman's Meadow to the West Bridge on the Leicestershire & Northamptonshire Union Canal. (Author)

in 1872 gave the means for the additional improvement. Excavation and river alterations began along the north part of Leicester near the abbey. Work first concentrated on the lower river section. Tenders were advertised in 1879 for improvement of the river between Hitchcock's, or North, Mill to Swan's Nest Weir, near Belgrave Mill. Benton & Woodiwiss of Derby and Stretford were awarded a contract. The contractors were to be supervised by the Corporation engineer, Mr Griffith. Samuel Crawshaw was appointed as his assistant for the flood works. Reconstruction would therefore affect both canal companies in Leicester.

Benton & Woodiwiss proceeded with the excavation of a new river channel and the work associated from Swan's Nest Weir to Belgrave from 1879–80. They erected the abutments and foundations for two river bridges, one at North Bridge and another at Abbey Gate Corner. The work also included making a diversion of the canal channel and construction of a lock at Swan's Nest Weir (Belgrave Lock). Work on this lock included excavation and the making of concrete walls and a floor to the chamber. Making this lock was conducted during the first months of 1880 and the new lock was finished and ready for use by June 1880.

The river channel through from Swan's Nest Weir to Abbey Corner Weir had been completed by July 1880 when a bad storm caused a flood to sweep down the river. Bridges were damaged as the flood waters raced downstream. From the West Bridge they passed over the weir at Evans Mill. A canal boat broke from her moorings and was taken over the weir, carrying away the footpath and hand railings for a length of 70ft.

The flood water washed into the new channel and carried the contractor's plant down to Belgrave, where it was recovered. Fortunately the contractor's work withstood the onslaught. Yet further construction was constantly harassed by more floods.

In August 1880 F. Griffith put forward a revised scheme for the flood works that included a new lock (of 7ft lift) near St Mary's Mill that would replace two existing locks (Swan's Mill Lock and Castle Mill Lock) on the Leicester & Northampton Union Canal, which each had a lift of 3ft. The remaining foot was to be a lowering of the navigation from St Mary's Wharf to the North Lock. The lock at St Mary's was placed according to Griffith's scheme between two weirs. One would channel water into the course of the Old Soar, the other into a new navigation channel to the West Bridge.

The changes were incorporated into a modified plan and application was made for a new Act of Parliament. This Act was passed in June 1881 and it authorised the council to widen and deepen the Soar, but confined the northern alterations as far as Belgrave. The authorised work commenced at a point about 100yds below the Midland Railway Viaduct at the Freemans Meadow northwards. A weir and lock was to be made near this viaduct. The lock was now to have a 7ft 6in lift. The Soar was then to be deepened and widened to a point near the North Lock at Frog Island where the Leicester Canal joined the Soar. The Soar was to be lowered in stages, the deepest excavation being from the new lock to Swan's Mill, which was to be 7ft 6in. From Swan's Mill to Castle Mill it was to be lowered to a depth of 4ft 9in and about 2ft at the Town Pond. All bridges, sluices and dams were included to ease the passing of the flood water.

West Bridge was also to be reconstructed. This part included the river navigations of the Leicester Canal and the Leicestershire & Northamptonshire Union Canal that met at the West Bridge.

Meanwhile work went on with the Lower Soar improvement and preparations were made for the lowering of the Leicester Navigation and diversion of St Margaret's Ditch and the Willow Brook, which had been part of the 1874 Act.

Benton & Woodiwiss assisted the canal improvement by making a temporary diversion for the navigation that included towpath bridges over the Pasture Channel at Tumbling Bay and the new river at Stone Weir. A temporary lock was also made at Abbey Corner Weir so that, in conjunction with the new lock at Swan's Nest Weir, craft might bypass the deepening work between Belgrave Mill and Lady Bridge (Belgrave Gate). They would then use an existing channel to rejoin the Leicester Navigation east of the North Lock.

This page: The Foxton Incline Plane (Grand Junction Canal). *Above:* The plane as built. *Left:* The plane in 2002 with the caissons and superstructure removed but the concrete base for the rails and caisons remaining. (Author)

The temporary bridges were completed by February 1881. With the diversion in place part of the Leicester Navigation could be closed for reconstruction. During February the contract for lowering the canal from Belgrave Gate to Swan's Nest Weir was awarded to the Whitaker Brothers of Horsforth near Leeds after their tender of £9234 7s 5d was accepted. The task included the alteration to the canal and towing path from the North Lock to the Public Wharf and excavation and deepening beyond to Belgrave Lock. A new canal lock was made east of the Public Wharf and basins. This lock was called Limekiln, after the nearby banks of kilns on the wharf. Whitaker Brothers also diverted the junctions of the canal with St Margaret's Ditch and the Willow Brook, whilst further work on widening and deepening the Willow Brook was awarded to Brian Ward.

Whitaker Brothers worked through 1881 building the new locks and diverting the canal at the Belgrave Mill, whilst Benton & Woodiwiss proceeded with the alteration to the Soar. The Whitakers' work was finished by October 1881, whilst Benton's work was completed during 1882.

During 1883 the main task of altering the Soar and Old Soar was let in two contracts. That north of Soar Lane Bridge was awarded to Kellett & Bentley during April, whilst the section south to Braunstone Lane Bridge and West Bridge was given to S. W. Pilling of Manchester.

The task of the reconstruction in Freemans Meadow was delayed by funding issues and another Act of Parliament in 1884 was needed to authorise additional finance. There was also still some indecision of how the river and the Leicestershire & Northamptonshire Union Canal lock cut from Castle Mill to Swan Mill would be made.

The contract to build the new lock and weir at Freemans Meadow was awarded to James Evans of Birmingham. But the contract details changed with yet another revision on how the work should progress. Town Council meetings frequently debated different proposals and letters published in the *Leicester Chronicle* reveal a public concern. The final plan chosen was similar to what had been suggested by Griffith in 1880 and essentially the construction was a straight navigation from the West Bridge through the Freemans Meadow with the single new lock replacing the original two.

Evans was awarded the contract in February 1887. He was to undertake the construction of the lock, weir and flood basin extending from a point near the viaduct of the Burton Branch of the Midland Railway towards the town for a length of about 285yds. The lock was constructed on the towpath, or west side, of the new cut. A long weir extended from the lock to the opposite, or eastern, bank of the flood basin.

The task of cutting the new straight channel to the West Bridge was awarded to Enoch Tempest. This task was completed in 1890 with the opening of the new navigation and the new West Bridge. Reconstruction had disrupted the navigation between 1881 and 1890 and had permanently affected the wharves and depots by the West Bridge.

Canal improvements to waterways in the Leicester area no doubt contributed to the takeover of the Leicester Canals by the Grand Junction Canal Company in 1894. Yet the biggest incentive was the control of water supply from reservoirs such as Naseby. The new owners made one further improvement. They arranged for the construction of the Foxton Incline Plane to speed up the passage of boats at Foxton Locks. Their decision was influenced, in part, by the canal carriers Fellows, Morton & Clayton who were keen to improve their trade in this region. Traders were particularly critical of the time needed to pass the staircase locks at Foxton and Watford. It was suggested that planes were needed at both Foxton and Watford and the caissons be designed to hold barges up to 14ft wide so that coal from Derbyshire and Nottinghamshire might be delivered to London at an economic rate.

Foxton Incline Plane was designed by Grand Junction engineer Gordon Thomas who was assisted by his cousin Barnabas James Thomas. Barnabas Thomas was resident engineer for the work.

Construction commenced in 1898. The work included two link canals. The upper canal link, complete with stop gates, diverged from offside and east bank of the main canal north of Gumley Road Bridge. It terminated at the upper docks at the top of the planes. There were two parallel inclined planes. Each plane had a large, barge-size caisson (called a movable dock by Gordon Thomas) that ascended and descended on parallel tracks. The lower basin joined the Market Harborough Branch east of the staircase lock entrance.

Access to and egress from the caissons was protected by large guillotine gates fitted to either end of each caisson and to the meeting point of each upper basin. With the upper basins the south plane met directly with the end of the upper canal. The north plane was reached by a steel aqueduct that carried the waterway across the top of the south plane to the north plane entrance.

The Worcestershire Stour was made navigable by Andrew Yarranton for a few years and parts retained a navigation of sorts thereafter. Once the Staffordshire & Worcestershire Canal was completed, a section of the Stour near Wilden Ironworks was used by craft passing between there and Pratt's Wharf on the canal. A lock was made at Pratt's Wharf for canal boats to navigate as far as Wilden in 1874. In order to pass a tight bend near the wharf a pulley was installed to aid boatmen. The towing rope was placed around the pulley wheel to assist with the turning of the craft around the bend. (Author)

Craft entering a caisson from the upper canal passed under paired guillotine gates and once inside both gates were lowered. One gate created the seal with the upper canal, while the other formed the south-end seal of the caisson. When this was done the caisson descended to the bottom.

The paired bottom basins were made deep enough to receive each caisson and allow it to submerge to the depth level of the lower canal. Once the levels were equal, the north-end guillotine gate on the caisson was raised to allow the craft to leave. Craft ascending the plane followed the reverse procedure.

Foxton boat-lift and canal channels took shape during 1899. Contractors cut the navigation and started to make the planes, winding engine house and boiler house. Work also included making a bridge over the lower basin to carry the footpath to Foxton village. A compound steam engine (of about 25hp) was installed to raise and lower the caissons. Steam was provided by two Lancashire boilers.

Work was finished by 25 June 1900, but the official opening was not recorded until 10 July 1900. Whilst this great work had the potential to improve transit of narrowboats along the canal, the important barge traffic was prohibited as widening the route through to the Grand Junction at Norton was never done.

Foxton Incline Plane was only used from 1900 until 1911 and then only in daylight hours. Plans for a lift at Watford were never proceeded with. During 1911 it was decided to discontinue the operation of the lift at Foxton, as the expected increase in trade had not occurred.

By contrast the completion of the Anderton Lift in 1875 had a marked impact on trade, changing the traffic flow for salt and pottery goods and eventually influencing the widening of the Trent & Mersey Canal between Anderton and Middlewich.

In November 1871 the Weaver Trustees announced their intention to apply to Parliament for construction of a boat lift at Anderton. Edward Leader Williams (1839–1910), engineer to the Trust between 1856–72, conceived the idea of a lift operated by hydraulic rams and after consultation with Edwin Clark (1814–94), civil engineer of London, settled on the concept of the vessel being lifted whilst floating in a tank of water. Clark and his London associates carried out the design. The contract was accepted, but at a price more than double Williams' original estimate. Williams had moved on to become engineer to the Bridgewater Canal and had been replaced by John Watt Sandeman as engineer to the Weaver Navigation Trust. He made changes to the specification that included strengthening the foundations. Cast- and wrought-iron parts of structure were fabricated by Emmerson Murgatroyd at Stockport and Liverpool.

The Anderton Lift was part of a greater scheme for river improvement through to the Mersey that was conducted initially under the supervision of Williams and then Sandeman. The lift structure was connected to the canal basin by aqueduct. It was an innovative design that Clarke went on to design for other navigations in Europe. They included the lift at La Fontinettes on the Neufosse Canal in Northern France.

During 1874 a connection was made at Pratt's Wharf near Wilden, between the Staffordshire & Worcestershire Canal and the River Stour, so that boats could navigate along the Stour as far as the Wilden Ironworks. These ironworks had a long connection with the iron trade and were at one time a water-powered forge and rolling mills. When the canal was constructed a transshipment wharf was made between river and canal, between boats based on the river and the narrowboats on the canal.

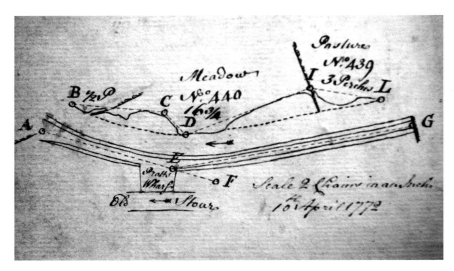

Pratt's Wharf, as reproduced from John Green's notebook. The original is at Staffordshire Records Office (MS 3186).

Owners of Wilden Forge included Benjamin Pratt and from 1848 members of the Baldwin family. In 1867 the Baldwins applied to the canal company to make a link with the river to avoid trans-shipment. Agreements were made in 1874 for the lock to be made.

Modification of the Severn Navigation was continued throughout the latter half of the nineteenth century. Navigation at Gloucester was improved through two new locks in 1870. Construction was carried out under the supervision of A. Williams to the designs of his father Edward Leader Williams. A narrow lock and weir was constructed at Maisemore near the Upper Parting, whilst a barge lock was made at Lanthony in the Eastern Channel.

Henry Marten was subsequently appointed engineer to the Severn Commissioners. Marten had been responsible for planning various waterworks schemes and also had been a long-term manager and partner in the Parkfield Ironworks, near Wolverhampton. Marten was responsible for further river deepening to Worcester and the building of a river trans-shipment dock at Diglis.

Wainlode Hill Rock Ford, approximately 5 miles north of Gloucester, had been a constant problem to maintaining navigation depth. With the Severn improvements (1842–57) a channel of 20ft was cut with the use of gunpowder, but the channel tended to fill with debris. Marten's solution was to use a dredger with steel claws placed between the buckets, by which method a channel 40-50ft wide was cut.

Henry Marten died in November 1892, yet later that month his son E.D. Marten attended a meeting at the Tontine Hotel, Ironbridge, regarding possible river improvement. Henry made a survey of the Severn between Stourport and Buildwas about the year 1886 when much, if not all, of the navigation had ceased above Bewdley. He found that the river was divided into a series of deep pools interrupted by shallows. The possible canalisation of the river there, providing locks of sufficient size to pass barges, was suggested. A committee was set up, but the cost of such work was evidently enough to prevent the scheme going ahead.

In the 1903 session of Parliament the Staffordshire & Worcestershire Canal Company applied for additional powers, which included authorisation for the canal company to pay the River Severn Horse Towing Path Extension Company towards maintenance of their path and other works. Other clauses provided for the constitution of the Hatherton Branch Canal, reservoir and locks as part of the undertaking of the company as well as the renewal of the lease for the Sow from Baron Stafford.

If the Soar periodically suffered problems from an excess of water, the River Trent had water shortage problems during the summer months. In December 1878 B.S. Blundell of Doncaster read a report at Newark Town Hall as to the state of the River Trent following a request by the Trent Navigation Company. They were keen to introduce steam towage on the river and generally to improve a declining carrying trade.

Blundell's investigation looked at the river from Nottingham to Gainsborough. With the Nottingham to Newark section, a distance of about 24 miles, there were eleven shallows, some of which had as little as 27in of water on them. The barges that traded between Nottingham and Gainsborough carried between 50 and 60 tons and when fully loaded had a depth of 3ft 6in.

There were then only four locks on the section north of Nottingham. Upper Holme Flood Lock, whose gates were only shut when the river was in flood, Lower Holme Lock, Newark Lock and Newark Lower (or Nether) Lock.

Amongst the suggestions made by Blundell was the system of wire cable steam towage adopted on certain rivers and canals in Germany. He noted that two steamers could work the 56 miles between Nottingham and Gainsborough. The improvements involved dredging shallows, lengthening Newark Lower Lock, altering the bridge at Newark Mill, cable laying and the purchase of two 20hp steamers.

This proposal was not carried out, but the Trent Navigation Company continued to pursue means of river improvement. Some members of the company decided to form a carrying company in 1883, which merged with the old Navigation Company to form a 'new' Trent Navigation Company authorised by Act of Parliament in May 1884.

A continuing matter of concern was a satisfactory depth for boats in the Trent. Additional capital was required to dredge the river to the correct depth and remove the shoals. During November another application was made to Parliament to raise more funds. This application changed the title of the company from Trent Navigation to the Trent (Burton-on-Trent and Humber) Navigation Company. Interchange of traffic was contemplated with the North Staffordshire Railway and widening of the Trent & Mersey Canal was suggested from Derwent Mouth as far as Branston Lock, west of Burton-on-Trent. Other interchange was considered with the Derby Canal, leading to a widening of the Derby Canal into Derby. A separate scheme promoted with the help of the Marquis of Anglesey was the Upper Trent Navigation Bill that intended to restore navigation to Burton-on-Trent.

A select committee was appointed to investigate the Trent Navigation Bill (1887). Henry Rofe, engineer to the navigation, gave evidence to support the need to raise money for dredging the river. A few modifications were made to the Bill including the protection of the riparian owners' right to gravel, and the Bill received Royal Assent (Victoria 50/51 c 115). The task of raising shares was announced in a prospectus published in July 1888. Lucas & Aird, contractors, had agreed to do the dredging work.

For the 1888 parliamentary session the Birmingham & Humber Navigation scheme was put forward. With the Birmingham & Humber Navigation was a proposed widening and deepening of the Tame from the junction of the Trent. This navigation was to form a junction with the Birmingham & Warwick Junction Canal at Salford Bridge and build a reservoir near Holford's Mill, Handsworth.

Both the Upper Trent and the Birmingham & Humber navigations failed. Yet groups remained keen for larger vessels to reach as far as Nottingham. The Corporation of Nottingham and various local businessmen along the route were keen to see larger craft on the river and looked for craft from 100–200 tons burthen on the river. R.P. Cafferta, plaster maker of Newark, was numbered amongst the group that supported river improvements. Such work would extend beyond the dredging; new locks to raise water levels were needed. The Trent Navigation Company was equally committed to improve matters and through their competent engineer, Frank Rayner, started to plan for the future.

CHAPTER 9

A NEW VISION

Despite railway competition certain improvements to river and canal navigations continued to be made. A strong influence was the improvements made to waterways in Belgium, France and Germany that led to calls from businessmen in Britain requesting similar alterations. The capacity of barge-carrying was increased on the Continent. In this country committees and commissions were set up to consider improvement with precise enquiry. The most comprehensive study was conducted in 1906 by the Royal Commission.

Their lengthy investigation looked at all waterways. Prominent carriers, engineers and canal owners were invited to contribute. The result was a recommendation of waterway improvement in the shape of a cross that benefited trade to London, Bristol, the Humber and the Mersey. One of the most fundamental observations made was the need to provide facilities for 100-ton barges. This aim was to influence waterways development in Britain for the next fifty years.

An ambassador for improvement of waterways was the Grand Junction canal engineer, Gordon Thomas. He gave evidence to the Royal Commission in 1906 and 1909. His suggestions included a vision of canals 45ft wide and 7ft deep and with a consequent increase in speed. Investment in modernisation of the Grand Junction Canal from the Erewash to London, a total of 157 locks from Langley Mill, could reduced the total of locks to seventy in number with the construction of twelve incline lifts. In reality the actual improvements made to the Grand Junction Canal were confined to maintenance and lock reconstruction during this period.

Colonel J.A. Saner, engineer to the Weaver Navigation Trust (1887–1934), also made a valuable contribution to the Royal Commission proceedings, which included canal widening from the Weaver to the Midlands. Saner was best known for his modifications to the Anderton Boat Lift. These were crucial to the continued operation of this important transport link. The principal of a balanced hydraulic lift was a good example of theory made into practice. An unfortunate drawback, however, was that the water used for the hydraulic support in the cast-iron columns was canal and river water that was contaminated by dissolved salt. With time the salt corroded the metal. In 1897 Saner substituted distilled water for the polluted water from the river and canal. This action might have slowed down the corrosion but did not stop the deterioration of the structure. Saner recommended the replacement of the hydraulic system and to substitute a lifting system powered by electricity.

The Trust sanctioned the changes in 1906, and the conversion was done between 1906 and 1908. The alterations included a massive steel superstructure above the original boat lift supported by 'A'-frame legs. Clarke's 1875 lift was dwarfed by the new encasing metalwork that held the many cogs and wheels required for the electrical operation of the lift.

G.R. Jebb provided information to the Commission about water supply and also was an advocate of improved navigation between the Weaver and the Midlands. Jebb was engineer both to the Shropshire Union Canal and to the Birmingham Canal Navigations. With the Birmingham Canal, he had the task of making the navigation fit for the twentieth century. His greatest achievement in that respect was an improvement to water supply. He designed two new back pumping plants at Smethwick and Parkhead that circulated water between the main levels of the waterway.

West Midlands waterways were particularly handicapped by narrow locks and shallow navigations that restricted barge dimensions to the hold of a 7ft by 70ft narrowboat. Suggestions for improving all canal routes to the industrial heartland located between Coventry, Walsall and Wolverhampton were frequently discussed in press articles, but without any practical work being done.

In the East Midlands, river navigations and canals were broader to admit craft up to 14ft wide, but there were hopes for larger craft to use the Trent as early as 1905. Such plans were initially put together by the Trent Navigation Company who obtained an Act that included the replacement of Holme Lock, Nottingham and Nether Lock at Newark, the construction of three new locks between Holme and Newark Town Lock and the making of another lock above Newark that was called Cromwell Lock. The river was also to be deepened.

The task of deepening the river was aided by a contract signed, in 1907, with Pearson & Sons, contractors for the new Joint Docks at Hull, to supply ballast. Ballast comprised essentially river gravel that was utilised in making concrete. A systematic dredging of the river was conducted. A fleet of twelve boats were provided to convey the ballast to Hull. Dredging commenced on 14 July 1908 and was later assisted through the purchase of a new dredger from Holland, which commenced work on 28 June 1909.

Work on making Cromwell Lock was authorised by the Trent Navigation Board in 1909 and carried out by navigation company staff under the directions of their engineer Frank Rayner. B. Woodger was appointed resident engineer at Cromwell Locks in May 1909. Steam cranes, steam powered piledrivers, pumps and a light railway were purchased and delivered to first Newark Town Lock where the lock was deepened.

Reconstruction took less than a month. The Town Lock was closed for traffic on 19 June and re-opened on 12 July 1909. The work comprised the lowering of the sills and deepening of the lock to give a minimum depth at all times of 6ft 6in. New tail gates were made and head gates rebuilt. The temporary light railway was laid through the lock for dealing with through traffic, although a portion of this trade was carted from Newark Town Wharf to the wharf on the basin beyond the lock.

The plant was then moved to the site chosen for the new Cromwell Lock and Weir. Twentieth-century lock construction was a very different practice to that conducted by eighteenth- and nineteenth-century navvies. The lock chamber was made from concrete with piling forming part of the approaches. The method adopted at Cromwell was first to dig trenches down to the bottom of the intended depth and gradually build the walls with concrete to the designated height. Once the walls were in place, the wing walls were made and then the spoil in between was dug out for the bottom to be made and covered with concrete. Gates then had to be fixed into place. It was a practice that was to be adopted in making all the other Trent locks.

A bungalow served as an office, a house was provided for the ganger and lodgings for twenty-eight workmen built. Construction took until May 1911 to complete. Work was dictated by the state of the river and delayed at times of flood. In the final stages dredgers were used on the approaches to link up lock with navigation. Only when the lock was operational did work start on the weir. The placing of coffer dams raised the level 2ft whilst the weir and sluices were constructed. Mr Rayner, in his report for September 1911, reported the weir and sluices complete.

No work was done on the making of the three new locks between Nottingham and Newark and with the onset of the First World War there was little chance for the work to begin. The challenge was then taken up by Nottingham Corporation who saw benefits for their city if larger barges were able to dock alongside wharves north of Trent Bridge. They obtained an Act in 1915 to take over the section north of Trent Bridge and the powers to rebuild Holme Lock and make the three new locks to Hazelford. The Trent Navigation Company still had the obligation to rebuild Newark Nether Lock.

A suggestion, made in 1917, that Nottingham Corporation use German prisoners of war to assist with the scheme was not taken up and any further construction left until the war was over. From 1919 the task of employing men returning from the war became an important issue. The Demobilisation (employment of sailors and soldiers) Committee circulated the following notice:

> That in view of the possible demobilisation of large numbers of men the several committees of the Corporation be desired to prepare schemes of work which would involve the employment of a considerable number of skilled and unskilled men and submit particulars thereof to this committee at an early date.

Nottingham Corporation considered ways servicemen may be employed that included road repair and the projected Trent improvement.

During 1919 the Corporation had discussions with the Canal Control Committee, which had come to operate the waterways during the latter period of the war. Captain Rayner, engineer to the Trent Navigation, and Edward Crutwell were asked to prepare a report and revised estimate for the Trent improvements to the Canal Control Committee. The nature of the discussions included funding for the project. These talks were transferred to the newly set up Ministry of Ways and Communications, which quickly became known as the Ministry of Transport. The Ministry first asked for a new survey to be made.

Sir George Beharrell, of the Financial and Statistical section of the Ministry of Transport, conveyed the Ministry viewpoint. He noted the minister regretted that proposed works were considered not to be of sufficient urgency to warrant a loan being made from exchequer funds. The application for funding was therefore refused. In an effort to diffuse such a blunt statement, Sir George then added that a general survey was about to be made into the question of the inland waterways in the United Kingdom.

Nottingham Corporation was forced to wait for the Committee on Waterways to be set up. Meanwhile Frank Rayner continued to engage further support for the Trent Locks scheme. During June Frank gained the help of Mr Impey, secretary to the Waterways Association. Joint deputations to the Ministry of Transport were arranged to take place on 11 August 1920. During November 1920 the Corporation was asked to make a presentation to the Committee on Waterways chaired by Neville Chamberlain.

By January 1921 the Trent Navigation Company were keen to start work on Newark Nether Lock and reminded the Corporation of their obligations for their section. Nottingham Corporation was financially handicapped in this respect, as they could not borrow money authorised under Act without consent of the Treasury. Fresh representations were made to the Ministry of Transport. A meeting was arranged with the Labour Government Ministry, who were sympathetic to the cause, but evidently not supportive enough to sanction a loan.

Support for the scheme continued to gather. The Ministry of Transport invited local Members of Parliament to discuss the interim reports of the Inland Waterways Committee, which specifically referred to the River Trent. Finally, when the second report issued by this committee was published, a way was opened for the work to commence. At the core of the proposal were employment for the unemployed and the setting up of a trust for the project.

The Trent Navigation continued to press for the Corporation to start on at least one of the works in connection with navigation of the Trent. Yet another Corporation deputation was formed and a meeting was arranged with Neville Chamberlain. The deputation had three key questions to ask:

1 Whether help would be forthcoming from the Government
2 To urge the early formation of the Trust
3 To promise the full support of the Corporation to the Trust when formed

Neville Chamberlain evidently gave the necessary assurances, for, at the Corporation Trent Navigation committee meeting held on 29 September 1921, authority was given to proceed with the work immediately. Men were engaged to start work on the new lock at Holme.

Both Sir John Jackson Ltd and Edward Crutwell offered to undertake the construction but the Corporation were tied to performing the work with the assistance of the Trent Navigation Company. Labour was recruited directly with the assistance of the Labour Exchange.

Frank Rayner became chief engineer for the project and P.B. Woodger was appointed resident engineer. Amongst the first tasks undertaken was to obtain a steam rail crane and standard gauge railway track for it to run along. Subsequently others were obtained; four were second-hand but two were purchased new from Smith of Rodley. 24in-gauge Decauville track with tip wagons were also purchased to assist with excavation work.

Improvement of the Trent had an important ally with the Departmental Committee on Inland Waterways and their chairman, Neville Chamberlain. Chamberlain summarised his views in a paper presented to the Institution of Civil Engineers in 1922. He was particularly concerned about the varied ownership of waterways that linked to the sea. About a third were owned by their principal competitors – the railway companies. Chamberlain wanted a new policy adapted to the time and one best suited for the businessman. Waterway improvement should proceed by steps and not all at once. Central management and control of the water communications was required throughout the district comprising the group. Properly equipped terminal facilities with adequate lay-by space, handling apparatus and warehouse accommodation were needed and above all regular and punctual services should be provided.

Such suggestions, if carried out, involved the transferring of railway-owned and controlled canals to the water groups to which they belonged. Expenditure of capital was also required. The absence of regular services had been, in Chamberlain's opinion, one of the principal causes of failure of canals and to offer satisfaction to the trader, the power at least of supplying them should be granted to those waterways. The Trent Navigation improvement was seen by the Departmental Committee on Inland Waterways as the first step. They fixed on the Trent Navigation as the most favourable field for experimental advance.

Nottingham Corporation had created a Waterways Committee in the 1880s, and with the 1915 Act gained a greater responsibility that not only involved the improvement of the River Trent from Trent Bridge to Averham Weir, but also lead them to build a new dock and wharf, be responsible for the maintenance and collect tolls on this section.

In addition to making locks, Nottingham Corporation were required to maintain a minimum channel width of 50ft and depth of 6ft. The Trent Navigation Company was required to have a minimum channel width of 30ft from Averham Weir to Newark Nether Lock and also ensure a depth of 6ft. A time limit was set for all lock building and dredging to be completed. It was a deadline that altered with the delays and legal arrangements needed for the agreements between the Corporation and the Navigation Company. Finally, when this was done, Nottingham Corporation assumed control of the Trent between Trent Bridge and Averham.

Frank Rayner's role as engineer for the Waterways Committee was one that ran parallel with the post he had with the Trent Navigation Company. Rayner was able to use his considerable skill to ensure the locks were completed to the required standard. Assistance for the work was also provided by the state under an Employment Relief Scheme.

Each new lock was made for craft up to 100 tons. Holme Lock was rebuilt first and was completed in September 1922 and Stoke Golding by October 1923. Gunthorpe was completed jointly with Hazelford in 1926.

Lock making, like others on the Trent, began with the excavation of parallel trenches where the concrete was poured to make the walls. A photographic survey of Stoke Golding Lock from October 1921 to September 1923 is particularly informative about the method of construction. Labourers

Above left: The new Nottingham Corporation Locks on the Trent were fitted with wooden gates. (Author)

Above right: River Trent, lock chamber. (Author)

started with the trenches and soon track was laid for the steam cranes to work along. There were three sets of track, one either side of the chamber and one in the middle. A siding from the track nearest the river led onto a jetty where goods could be unloaded from barges or narrowboats on the river. The jetty was placed near offices, cabins and a corrugated-iron engine house where the steam-powered pumping engine was placed. The task of digging out the earth and spoil in the middle commenced once the lock walls were made. Excavation of the two river cuts also began again with concrete walling being laid down. The 2ft-gauge track and skips were used to move the earth from the two lock channels and elsewhere on site. Each skip was propelled by hand; no locomotive or horses were used here. The steam crane compliment reached a maximum of five. These machines were essentially used for moving excavated earth from the chamber or entrance channels.

By the summer of 1922 the lock chamber was completed and the bottom concreted. Work then started on assembling the lock gates, which were assembled from timber at the lock. The frames were laid out at the bottom of the lock and then panelling was added and fittings for the paddle gear. The upper gates were completed first and fitted to the cill end. The larger lower gates were then constructed and fitted. When all gates were in place the paddle gear equipment was fitted to the gates. Each gate had two paddles that were raised and lowered by turning a large wheel fitted to the mechanism. Similar arrangements were installed for the ground paddles on either side of the gates. A lock house was constructed during this period. In order to expedite construction at Stoke double shifts had been commenced by April 1922.

Work was then concentrated on completing the two entrance channels, making outside walls along the river and building the weir. Dredging finally completed the task of clearing the links with the Trent at either end.

Men were then progressively transferred to the Hazelford Lock site. Work started in August 1922, when Holme Lock was nearly completed. Their distance from Nottingham led to the establishment of barracks for the men to sleep in, although most of the workforce travelled out to the work by train. A grievance developed at Hazelford when workmen objected to paying rail fares. Work was even stopped in January 1923. This dispute was not properly resolved, but the workers did restart on the lock building there. At the same time the number of men employed on dredging work was increased and perhaps some of the protestors were moved into this role.

By April 1923 a small number of men were at work at Gunthorpe Lock and by July that year the men employed on all works totalled 435:

Barges moored at Holme Lock, River Trent. (Author)

Nottingham Corporation arranged for the construction of cottages at all four locks under their control. Mr Evans' tender to build this cottage at Holme Lock for £550 was accepted in June 1922. (Author)

Stoke Bardolph	112 men
Gunthorpe	87 men
Hazelford	153 men
Dredging	83 men
Total	**435 men**

With Stoke Lock finished, the men were shared between dredging and construction at Gunthorpe and Hazelford. By January 1925 work had also started on Gunthorpe and Hazelford Weirs. Four dredgers

River Trent, Holme Lock. (Author)

were now at work on the channel and lock cuts. Plans for official opening of both Gunthorpe and Hazelford were delayed until June 1926 when Neville Chamberlain attended for the ceremony.

Dredging work now occupied the bulk of the workforce that fluctuated between tidying up duties at the locks and the river work. Numbers varied between 190 and 210 on dredging. When all locks were opened the decision to fill in the old Holme Lock chamber came before the committee. It was suggested that the lock might be deepened and adapted for pleasure craft use. This decision was accepted and the old lock modified.

Newark Nether Lock reconstruction scheme began in 1924 when W. Powell was appointed resident engineer. He commenced duties on 23 February, producing surveys and drawings. The work, in this instance, was let to tender and that provided by Logan & Hemingway (£25,923 12s 3d) was accepted. Excavation began in 1925 with the contractors cutting out a trench to build the north wall of the lock. Concrete was used as the construction material. As with other locks, trenches were dug, the walls were then made and then further spoil removed and so the construction proceeded. The contractors were hampered at times when the river was in flood. There was a particular difficulty in this case however as the north approach was restricted by the LMS Railway Viaduct. Finally a year later, with gates in place and ironwork complete, the time came to divert traffic through the new lock. The navigation was closed to traffic at 4p.m. on 24 March 1926 to allow the south wall of the old lock to be removed and a concrete dam built to permit traffic to recommence through the new lock on 31 March. Unfortunately a navigation wall collapsed and water swept through carrying the temporary dam, damaging navigation walls and undermining a pier of the LMS Viaduct. The railway was closed until single line working commenced on 11 April. Boat traffic started to use the new lock at 8a.m. on 12 April.

Trent Navigation, Stoke Golding – work at Stoke Golding began with excavating two trenches. An engine house complete with steam engine was provided to pump water from the trenches. A Clayton & Shuttleworth pump was purchased for the work. The standard-gauge track was used by the railway steam cranes used for excavation. (Author)

A jetty complete with steam crane was provided to transfer material delivered by barge to the works. (Author)

A small improvement to speed up traffic on the Trent & Mersey Canal was made at Harecastle Tunnel. The North Staffordshire Railway Company, as owners of the Trent & Mersey Canal, had introduced steam tugs on the short tunnels at Saltersford, Barnton and Preston Brook during 1864, but found it difficult to adapt the Harecastle Tunnel for this purpose. The one-way system of using the restrictive 8ft 6in-wide *old* 'Brindley' tunnel and the *new* 'Telford' tunnel with towpath remained a cause of delay. By 1909 the Telford tunnel was showing signs of subsidence and part of the towpath had sunk to a depth a foot below the waterline and empty boats came close to scraping the roof arch with their masts. In 1914 it was decided to close the old tunnel and use an electric tug powered by batteries in a boat attached to the tug. During 1931 this original haulage system was replaced by the London, Midland & Scottish Railway, who had taken over control of the canal with the railway groupings of 1923. They introduced tugs that drew power from an overhead wire similar to that employed on street tramways.

Railway companies came to adopt a policy of economy with their repair of waterways within their control. Three of the 'big four' (the Great Western; London, Midland & Scottish; and London & North Eastern railways) owned canal and river navigations in the Midlands. They chose to do as little as possible to improve and upgrade their respective navigations and in several cases promoted decay rather than growth.

Policies suggested by the Canal Commissioners were generally ignored by the railway companies. The independent waterways showed more commitment. On 2 March 1928 the energetic chairman of the Regent's Canal & Dock Company, W.H. Curtis, had a letter published in *The Times* that condemned railways for their meagre expenditure on canals as well as their strategic ownership of sections that prevented serious alternative competition.

Through ownership of the Shropshire Union and the Trent & Mersey and control of the Birmingham Canal, the LMS in particular had a tight control of trade that passed into and out of the Midlands.

Wilfrid Curtis was able to pursue his vision when the Regent's Canal merged with other canal navigations to form the Grand Union Canal Company. Plans were formulated to improve navigation between Birmingham and London. Curtis pursued many ways of increasing business and was an active ambassador for waterway improvement and the advantages of canal transport.

The Grand Union comprised the former Grand Junction, Regent's, Warwick & Birmingham, Birmingham & Warwick Junction and Warwick & Napton canals as well as the part of the Oxford Canal between Napton and Braunston. There was now a single owner on the route between Birmingham and London, the line via Crick and Foxton to Leicester, Loughborough and the Erewash Canal in their hands. These were a mixture of waterways comprising both barge and narrow canals.

Finance for the improvements to the Grand Union was put forward in a Bill presented to Parliament in 1931 and passed. Work began in May 1931 and was assisted by a grant from the Treasury that amounted to £500,000. The remainder of the costs was found by the company. As many as 1,000 men were employed on the construction, most being drawn from the ranks of the unemployed.

Following increased use of motorboat traction, the banks of the Grand Union Canal were suffering from erosion and this was particularly true for the former Warwick canals. The first object was to widen these narrow waterways through clearing the banks and dredging. The towpath was then to be lined with a type of concrete pile. These piles were mass produced at depots along the canal. The Warwick & Birmingham had depots at Saltisford and Tyseley.

The piles were topped with reinforced concrete coping that formed the surface adjacent to the towpath. Such work reduced the width of the towpath somewhat, but with reduction in horse haulage was perhaps of less importance. Now some of the coping concrete blocks have become eroded, some displaced and the thick steel rods protrude in places – testament to the method then used of wrapping concrete around metal.

More extensive engineering was conducted at the Knowle Locks, Hatton Locks and the locks on the Warwick & Napton Canal. Here the original narrow locks were superseded by new wide locks placed to the side of the old locks. Six narrow locks at Knowle were replaced by five new wide locks (of 12ft 6in beam) to the side. At Hatton the wide locks channel was sometimes cut through the narrow locks and otherwise was to the side. With the Napton Locks the old locks became side weirs and some are now listed structures. New road bridges and occupation bridges were built across the canal between Birmingham and Napton.

The contracts for the new work were carried out under the supervision of Sir Robert Elliott-Cooper & Son, the consulting engineer to the company. The contractors for these locks and bridges were L.J. Speight Ltd, and the walling and piling work was carried out by the company's own engineering department. The cost for the reconstruction on the Warwick section was put at about £500,000.

Construction at Knowle produced five new concrete locks on the west side of the original narrow locks, each complete with concrete-walled side ponds. Each side pond was split into two stepped economiser ponds, a higher and lower, where water from the ponds could assist with the filling of the locks. The locks themselves extended out into wide basins placed between each lock. All that was left of the old locks were lengths of towpath and lock wall on the east side. The construction work enclosed a wide strip of land.

Left: Hatton wide locks descend towards Warwick and the old narrow locks can be seen in this view on the right; these smaller locks were retained as weirs. (Author)

Below: A plan of new lock at Hatton Locks.

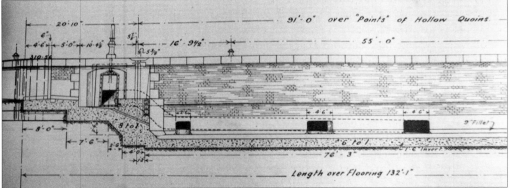

Grand Union Canal, Hatton Locks – the bottom lock and cottage at Budbrooke. (Author)

The lock design adopted was common to all. Gate paddles were dispensed with and only ground paddles were provided. The gate and paddle gear were supplied by Ham, Baker & Co. Ltd, Langley Green, to a patented design, and were operated by boatman's windlass. Water was drawn in from the upper pound through the raising of the paddle, which was placed in an inclined shaft. The underground channel made behind the wall of the lock divided into three separate openings along the length of the wall to admit water to the bottom of the lock chamber. Emptying the lock used a second channel that passed around the lower gates to the paddle gear. Once this paddle was raised water flowed out into the lower pound.

Certain elements of the construction were left out until later. This work included lock cottages and three public bridges. Contracts for seven new lock cottages were received in August 1932, but the cheapest quote was from William Moss, which amounted to £9,000. The Grand Union decided the maximum amount should be £800 per cottage and left Robert Elliot Cooper & Son to re-tender.

L.J. Speight tendered for the three bridges at Hatton Glebe, Ugly Road and Welsh Road and was awarded the work. With Ugly Road and Welsh Road a temporary bridge was erected whilst the new bridge was completed. With Hatton Glebe the new bridge was made alongside the old one.

In the original estimates of 1929, estimates for the parliamentary plan were based on reconstructing bridges on similar lines as the existing ones, but the protective clause for Warwickshire County Council in the Grand Union in 1931 materially altered the conditions. Speight produced a revised tender for the lock cottages. Their cost of £7,695 19s 7d was based on the use of reduced quantities.

An inspection made during the Knowle Lock construction found that the side ponds at Knowle were not working in a satisfactory manner 'through a technical error made in construction'. The matter was put right at extra cost to the company.

Hatton Locks were formerly declared open at a ceremony that took place at the top lock on Tuesday 30 October 1934. The Duke of Kent presided over the opening ceremony for the fifty-one new locks on the company's Warwickshire system when he inspected a length of 1 mile using the motor vessel *Progress*.

The Warwick & Napton Canal lacks a summit level and is a rare example of a canal that descends to a lower level and then climbs again. In this case the ascent is through a long series of locks to Napton Junction. The descent from the lowest level of the Warwick & Birmingham at Saltisford and Budbrooke occurs at the Cape, where two locks take craft down to the lowest level. The original narrow locks (right) were converted to weirs with the building of two barge locks as part of the Grand Union improvement scheme. (Author)

With the Hatton Locks some of the original narrow locks were adopted as overflow weirs. This technique was also adopted at the Cape and the locks through to Stockton and Calcutt. At Bascote the original locks were replaced by a staircase pair.

Work on improving continued along the section of the Oxford Canal between Napton and Braunston, control of which had been obtained at the same time as the establishment of the new Grand Union Company. Such work included towpath and bridge alteration, which was conducted in 1935 and 1936.

Wilfred Curtis, chairman of the Grand Union Company, gave a lecture to the Institute of Transport in March 1935 entitled 'canal betterment'. He recognised the recommendation of the Canal Commission that urged amalgamation of selected routes was a vital step before any development scheme could be considered. The Grand Union had spent over £1 million in bringing their waterways up do date. He believed as the trade of the country expanded there would be enough tonnage for every form of transport. Curtis also hoped that sooner or later the transport of the country would be more closely co-ordinated than in the past.

Another point made by Curtis was that traffic by canal was silent. About 750,000 tons of traffic passed along the Regent's Canal annually without noise or inconvenience to any members of the public. He wondered if the same could be accomplished by road or rail. Most canals in the country could then carry ten times the goods now passing over them without any congestion, and in the case of those waterways which had been kept in good working order by their managements, they offered a transport service, which had many attractions to the trader. But the betterment of canals could be initiated only by placing all canals receiving their trade from the same sources under one control.

Above left: The staircase pair which replaced the single locks in the Bascote Flight on the Warwick & Napton Canal. Parts of the original locks have been converted to weirs on the waterway. One weir is seen on the right-hand side of the image. (Author)

Above right: The ascent from Leamington on the Warwick & Napton can be segregated into various groups of locks. The longest is through Long Itchington where the Stockton Locks are to be found. This district is noted for limestone quarries that produced limestone for cement making. There were several points of interchange between quarry and canal. At Stockton the locks ascend in a straight line. The Grand Union improved the locks and the old narrow locks (far right) are seen in this view. (Author)

Thus Curtis was in favour of a nationalised waterway network. His observations about a silent highway came to be used in Grand Union adverts and it is his coining of the word that has been adopted as the title of this book.

Inspiration for waterways improvement reached new heights in 1935 when J.F. Pownall advocated a national waterways scheme in an article published in *Modern Transport*. Later, in 1942, Pownall issued a booklet setting out his idea of a Grand Contour Canal. It was a project that involved a new canal network made at the 310ft contour that united London and Bristol through the Midlands with the North West and North East and extended as far north as Newcastle-upon-Tyne.

Any hopes of a national network receded with the onset of the Second World War in 1939. However waterways came to be controlled and supported by the Government and under the direct responsibility of the Ministry of Transport. A new urgency came into being for keeping all transport routes open. Movement of commodities such as coal and oil became particularly important.

River traffic on the Severn was singled out for improvement with the opening of Nelson Wharf and a transit shed constructed along the river bank at Stourport, south of the power station, on land leased from the Severn Carrying Company. There was also a new jetty built at North Quay, Worcester, at a cost of £3,035 which was completed in May 1944. Making the jetty was done as an emergency measure and intended to transfer coal from water to rail, but was never used.

CHAPTER 10

CANAL DECLINE
AND RESTORATION

The 1948 Transport Act brought many of the remaining independent waterways and the sur-viving railway-owned navigations under the control of the British Transport Commission. The independent waterways passed immediately to the Docks & Inland Waterways Executive, others were transferred from the Railway Executive between 1948 and 1950. Under the Docks & Inland Waterways the ownership was rationalised with the English waterways passing under the direct control of one of four regions. With this Executive's abolition they were controlled by a new organisation, British Transport Waterways.

At first every attempt was made to maximise trade on the waterways, but this vision was soon replaced by one of economy. Orders for abandonment were applied for as little-used water-ways were closed. The Birmingham Canal lost some 60 miles of canal, most notably the Ogley to Huddlesford section that passed through Lichfield, the Wyrley Bank, parts of the Cannock Extension and parts of the Old Main line at Ocker Hill. The former Staffordshire & Worcestershire Hatherton Branch faced a similar fate. In the East Midlands, the Derby Canal finally succeeded in obtaining an abandonment of the Swarkestone and Sandiacre lines during 1964 and the Nottingham Canal was closed between Langley Mill and Lenton.

The Trent & Mersey remained a busy working waterway, dealing in particular with pottery and salt traffic. Salt extraction had some unfortunate side effects. Subsidence, in particular, affected the waterway in places. At Marston, the canal was diverted into a new channel.

A length of 1750ft of new canal was cut between 1957 and 1958 that was lined with concrete and steel piling. George Dew & Co. Ltd of Oldham was given the work by B.W. North Western Division. The cost of the contract and land purchase amounted to £30,000.

Another piece of work involved the double locks at Thurlwood near Rode Heath. Subsidence came to affect both locks. The lock by the towing path was rebuilt with bricks and masonry in the standard fashion. The other was singled out for a unique experiment. It was to be made of steel and set in a sealed chamber, where the option of jacking up was possible should further subsid-ence occur. Guillotine gates were provided at each end in a prefabricated structure installed by the contractors, Sir William Arrol & Co. of Glasgow.

Improvements to the River Trent included the opening of a group of large flood control sluices at Holme Lock in Nottingham in 1948 and the subsequent rebuilding of Newark Town Lock in 1952. River improvements on the Soar led to the diversion and replacement of Redhill and Ratcliffe Locks.

Road improvement often had an effect on canal infrastructure. At Dudley Port (A461) the orig-inal aqueduct, Rylands, was replaced in the 1960s with a new concrete structure. Another concrete aqueduct, complete with paving slabs for the towing path, was built across the north-bound car-riageway of the M5 at Ray Hall, near Tame Bridge, adding to the variety of the aqueducts along the Tame Valley Canal.

Motorway building had access problems in the concentrated road, rail and canal network that existed in places north of Birmingham. Planners decided that the best route for the M5 through

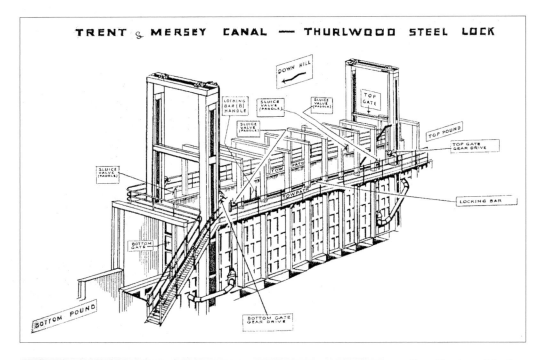

Above: Thurlwood Steel Lock was constructed on the Trent & Mersey to replace the existing one of the paired locks that had been most affected by subsidence. This lock was opened for traffic on 19 May 1958, but was not favoured by boatmen who preferred to use the adjacent conventional lock.

Left: Soar Navigation – the lock at Radcliffe; used and disused lock chambers are seen side by side. (Author)

Oldbury was along an elevated section. Part was carried over the Old Main Line of the Birmingham Canal from Spon Lane towards Titford Locks. Building the concrete support pillars led to a diversion of the canal into a new channel near Chances Glassworks. This was the second time the canal had been rerouted here. The first time was when the New Main Line and Stewart Aqueduct were made.

New feeder roads were constructed to serve the motorway network. The making of one, Telford Way at Smethwick, thankfully diverted traffic from Galton Bridge onto a new parallel road. Yet in making this road an embankment and tunnel was built over the New Main Line west of Galton Bridge. This tunnel was formed with a concrete arch, but restricted the channel and only retained the north towpath.

Space is at a premium in this transport corridor. The elevated section of the M5 motorway crosses the Stour Valley Railway, which in turn crosses the Old Main Line and this crosses the New Main Line at the aqueduct. There are therefore four generations of transport on four levels at this spot. (Author)

The M5 motorway is carried on a raised section over the Birmingham Canal Old Main Line at Oldbury. A section of canal was diverted onto a new concrete-lined course so that the supporting pillars would not obstruct the navigation. (Author)

A major civil engineering project on the Worcester & Birmingham Canal was making a new cut across Coopers Hill near Alvechurch in conjunction with construction of the M42 motorway. The cost of making a motorway embankment was more than providing a canal diversion, so the canal was moved and the old canal route became a waterway cul-de-sac. The deviation of the canal was done between 1984 and 1985. Dr Alan Robertson, vice-chairman of the British Waterways Board, formally opened the route on 9 March 1985.

In Birmingham, road improvements at Sandy Lane led to the diversion of the canal on the Camp Hill Flight of locks on the Grand Union (Warwick & Birmingham) Canal in 1990. Two of the original locks were cut down and filled in as the canal was diverted from the Coventry Road Bridge through a new lock, under the new dual carriageway bridge, into a new basin and then the second new lock before the original course was resumed.

With the building of the M6 Toll motorway provisions were made for the restoration of the Lichfield Canal with the supply and erection of a steel aqueduct at Brownhills. The making of the M6 Toll also affected the route of the Birmingham & Fazeley Canal. Curdworth Top Lock (built by John Pinkerton) was removed and the lock cottage demolished. The canal was cut back and a new lock constructed south of the M6 Toll over-bridge.

New road systems serving Selly Oak and the Queen Elizabeth Hospital led to contractors cutting through the embankment of the Worcester & Birmingham Canal north of Selly Oak (2009–10). The bed was dug out revealing what had been done by Morecroft & Co. when the embankment was raised. The canal was diverted onto a narrow channel and a temporary lift bridge erected over the channel for contractors' vehicles. Contractors Birse had completed a new

Above: The original route of the locks was in a straight line under the railway bridge. The altered course was diverted to the right in this view. (Author)

Left: The new lock at Camp Hill on the Warwick & Birmingham, as constructed for British Waterways as part of the Sandy Lane road–widening scheme. (Author)

Below: The construction of a new bypass road at Selly Oak has led to a temporary diversion of the Worcester & Birmingham Canal and the provision of a contractors' lift bridge, which is normally left raised to allow boats to pass, and is lowered for the use of the contractors building the new aqueduct. (Author)

concrete aqueduct by December 2010, while during January 2011 earth-moving equipment had begun to dig out the spoil underneath the structure.

The 1960s were a period of awakening for canal restoration. Growing interest in waterways for leisure use was generating interest in restoration of closed waterways. In 1964 the Lower Stratford-upon-Avon Canal was reopened. Credit for this restoration has been principally with David Hutchings. His next project was the restoration of Upper Avon between Stratford and Evesham that would open up a new navigation route to the Severn. Support and finance took time to arrange and it is further credit to David for achieving it.

There were several restoration projects then in progress which included parts of the Kennet Navigation, the Peak Forest and Caldon Canal. A key restoration at this time was the Stourbridge Canal and in particular the Stourbridge 16 Lock Flight that was organised by David Tomlinson of the Staffordshire & Worcestershire Canal Society. Restoration by volunteers was a part-time occupation. They attended at weekends and occasionally at other times. David devoted nearly three years to the task and was aided by other society members and Midland members from the Inland Waterways Association (IWA).

From 1966 IWA members started to take part in organised work parties that went off to the different sites. They aided the Stourbridge Lock restoration and it was considered a key restoration; the success or failure of the restoration movement was seen to depend on the successful opening of these locks.

Volunteers worked as eighteenth-century navvies aided by modern plant. They moved mud by wheelbarrows, grappled with a host of items deposited in the canal and repaired the infrastructure. The IWA recorded much of the work in a publication initially known as *Navvies Notebook*. An extract from issue 4, March 1967, graphically describes the work done at Lock 10:

> Each skip brought from the depths of lock brought with it much of the vandals work and mud of the last 15 years. The incline up past the lock to the tip was stiff and assistance was needed. This was provided by a grubby length of rope wound around the front axle of the wheel barrow and then with one pulling and one pushing, a run at the bank. Many a good navvie floundered here! The tip grew, steadily the mud was bitten back until the light gave out and the gear was stowed away under the lock cottage.

The Stourbridge Canal reopened in May 1967, in a classic case of 'job done'. Preparations for the Avon project proceeded steadily. Ground paddle and gate paddle gear was reclaimed from the abandoned Runcorn Lock Flight, courtesy of the owners of the Manchester Ship Canal.

Reopening of the Lower Avon to Evesham in 1964 provided incentive for restoring the Avon up to Stratford. During 1969 the Upper Avon restoration team took over the disused Harvington Station which was repaired and served as David Hutchings' home and office. They planned to restore certain locks and built new ones. It was a challenge that involved considerable new construction.

Dredging and cutting new channels proved to be an essential part of the making of the new navigation. All weirs south of Stratford (that is those at Lower Harvington, Upper Harvington, Cleeve, Bidford, Bidford Grange, Lower Welford, Upper Welford, Lower Luddington and Upper Luddington) had either been lowered or demolished by either the Severn River Authority or through the natural process of decay. Only the weir at Stratford-upon-Avon was left intact. Those weirs that had been repaired or replaced were set at a lower level to suit the needs of land drainage.

Ten locks and weirs were initially proposed by the Trust and the method of construction chosen was of an economical and practical nature. Steel piling was generally preferred to extensive concrete walling as was adopted for the new Trent Locks. Once piled, the piles were covered with a concrete slab:

PROPOSAL FOR NEW LOCKS ON UPPER AVON 1969

Location	Weir	Lock Site	Lift
Offenham	existing	new	2ft 2in
Harvington	existing	existing	5ft 5in
Marcliffe	new	new	3ft 9in
Barton	new	new	3ft 5in
Bidford Grange	new	new	2ft 5in
Lower Welford	new	existing	3ft 0in
Upper Welford	existing	existing	5ft 5in
Luddington	new	existing	3ft 5in
Stour	new	existing	4ft 0in
Stratford	existing	existing	7ft 5in

Navvies Notebook, No. 15, November 1968

Waterway construction entered a new phase with the co-operation of sappers belonging to the Royal Engineers from Belfast. They were called on, from time to time, to use explosives and blast rock away. The restoration team's first project was at Harvington Old Lock. Work began in May 1969 and the working party comprised volunteers from Gloucester Prison working under the supervision of a team from the Upper Avon Trust. What remained of the old lock chamber was removed with explosives and then steel piling commenced. This job was finished in eight weeks (July 1969). The work party then transferred to Marcliffe Lock site where the lock chamber had been blasted out of the hard marl, again with the help of the sappers.

Finance for making the locks was achieved through sponsorship. Work on Offenham Lock was sponsored by George Billington, who was terminally ill, and through his contributions this lock became known as George Billington Lock. Similar re-naming happened throughout the navigation. Marcliffe Lock was subsequently renamed IWA Lock, whilst Harvington became Robert Aickman Lock.

Piling George Billington Lock was conducted during November and December 1969, lock gates hung, and the lock cuts either end of the chamber dug out. Dredging the river was also commenced and some 50,000 cubic yards of spoil excavated, dumped and spread or carted away before the harshness of winter stopped further work until the spring.

Work resumed in 1970 with more dredging and the demolition of weirs at Lower Harvington and Cleeve. The Upper Avon Navigation was thus methodically and gradually opened. By June 1970 boats were able to navigate between Evesham and Cleeve and during November 1970 had reached Bidford-on-Avon. Permission was granted by the Severn River Authority to construct a new weir at Marcliffe. The lock cuts at Marcliffe required the sappers' attention to blast away rock. A deep channel was made through one arch of Bidford Bridge for the navigation.

In October 1970 the working party moved on towards Barton for the construction of a new lock, Pilgrim Lock (paid for by the Pilgrim Trust). This marked the start of Phase II. At Pilgrim Lock the walls of the chamber were made with hollow concrete blocks stacked dry off a concrete chamber floor. Each wall was held back by six anchors. The end walls were formed of sheet steel piling and the block walls reinforced with steel bars and back filled with concrete. The piecemeal acquisition of second-hand materials continued with a pair of ex-Thames Conservancy gates acquired as top gates for Pilgrim Lock. Two gates, formerly of Runcorn, were used for the bottom gates.

Dredging continued towards Welford during 1971 and a decision not to proceed with locks at Barton or Lower Welford made. Work piling Welford Lock started following the delivery of piles to a newly made wharf beside the Four Alls public house at Binton Bridges.

Piling was conducted by the piling gang at Upper Welford, now designated W.A. Cadbury Lock, from April 1971. They then transferred to Luddington and finally Stratford. Excavations at Stratford Lock were the deepest undertaken. Here a single lock was to replace the former staircase pair that had existed there. The dig went to a depth of 25ft for a chamber depth of 11½ft. Making this lock incurred various problems. Part of the lock wall collapsed, which led to the team fitting steel beam strengthening for the sides and above the chamber. Stratford Lock was completed during October 1971.

Construction of a lock at Barton was reconsidered and work stated in May 1972. This lock was placed on an island, requiring the piling and making of three walls and was longer than other locks on the river. The length was increased in case the Severn River Authority decided to erect a sluice gate there. Work was carried out with the assistance of volunteers from Hewell Grange Borstal. The bed of the lock was placed on hard marl. Photographs of the lock during construction show two lock walls piled from wing wall through the chamber to the other wing wall, capped with concrete. The third wall formed the barrier between the lock and river. A concrete slab formed the base of the lock. Barton Lock was completed in July 1972 and was named E.H.Billington Lock.

Cutting through the rock outcrops between Binton and Luddington, along with obstructions at the mouth of the River Stour, were the next challenge. Access for plant proved particularly difficult to arrange. Funds were also needed to complete the restoration and £25,000 was requested by public appeal.

By the summer of 1973 work remaining included the making of Luddington Weir and cutting through the slab at the junction with the Warwickshire Stour. Finally, after five years of graft, the navigation was opened between Stratford and Evesham by HRH Queen Mother in June 1974.

All canal restoration schemes were thrown into turmoil in the winter of 1971, when the Government proposed to dispose of British Waterways' responsibilities and distribute them between ten new regional water authorities. Fortunately protest from enthusiast groups and organisations led to a reconsideration in policy. Restoration of several canals went ahead with six formal openings made in the year 1974. Those that joined the Upper Avon as navigable waterways in this year were the Ashton, BCN (Titford Canal), Caldon, Grand Western and Lower Peak Forest canals. The Ashton, Caldon and Lower Peak restorations were achieved with the co-operation of British Waterways and local authorities.

For the Caldon this was a particular achievement. The section between Etruria and Endon had retained a navigation of sorts, but the rest was disused. A feature of the Froghall end was the pipe laid along the centre of the canal to supply Thomas Bolton's copper works. A rally organised by the Inland Waterways Protection Society at Consall Forge on 19 May 1963 was attended by speakers, which included David Hutchings, who presented the case for restoration. The rally consisted mainly of canoes as no other boats could reach there. Restoration of the Caldon included the complete rebuilding of a lock at Chesterton.

Cosmetic improvement of a derelict part of the Droitwich Canal in Vines Park provided an incentive for putting the Barge Canal back into use. The Droitwich Dig, of 27–28 October 1973, gathered together the largest number of volunteers then ever assembled at a restoration site. It proved to be a wet weekend that so often occurs at organised events, yet the volunteers laboured together to dig out the mud, earth and rubbish from the top four barge locks (Ladywood Top–Portershill). So started one of the longest canal restoration projects and added another chapter to the Droitwich Canals saga. The Barge Canal had last been used in 1918 and both the Junction and Barge Canals had been abandoned in 1939. The Droitwich Canal Trust was formed and they invested in a second-hand 2ft-gauge locomotive, light railway track and skips purchased in 1976. Using the railway they began in earnest with reclaiming the disused waterway.

Volunteers made regular trips to the canal locks during the 1970s, gradually working south towards Hawford. So much was achieved, but there were three major obstacles to be overcome:

1   The repair of the Junction Locks
2   The making of a navigable passage under the M5 motorway
3   The making of a navigable passage under the A449

With these in place a boating ring could be created. Financing such a scheme was beyond simple hard work. Business plans, land purchase and suitable funding were required. Once the section from Vines Park to Ladywood was restored and barge locks repaired, further work stopped and the locks were recovered to prevent vandalism and delay deterioration of the structures. From year to year finance was sought to complete the job. A legacy from the late Neil Pitts enabled the Waterways Recovery Group to restore the top three locks at Hanbury in the years 2001 and 2002. Finally a £12 million finance scheme was put together that enabled the work to proceed. The partnership featured the Droitwich Canal Trust, British Waterways, the Waterways Trust and local councils. Funding was provided by Advantage West Midlands, the Heritage Lottery Fund and local authorities.

Halcrow surveyed the route and produced the plan for the revised navigation. Morrison Construction was engaged to build four new locks as well as the canalisation of a stretch of the Body Brook. A public appeal raised money to restore the barge lock at the Vines in 2008. Morrison Construction proceeded with the work during 2008 and 2009. Using the modern motorway-making tool, the digger, a new channel was cut through to join up with the Body Brook. A new bridge was also constructed to carry the Rugby Club access road over the canal.

From this bridge the canal curved round to the top of the fourth lock. Locks 4 and 5 were made in the concrete and form a staircase pair. They are the first new 'staircase pair' to be built in the Midlands since Bascote on the Grand Union Canal. Initially three separate locks were at first considered, but the staircase was built as an economy measure. A short distance below Lock 5 the canal drops again through Lock 6 to the level of the Body Brook. This brook enters the navigation here and in effect from here becomes the Body Brook Navigation. The brook culvert under the M5 motorway is the conduit for boats to pass under the motorway. Headroom is somewhat restricted, although it is said to be higher than that at Dudley Canal Tunnel.

The Body Brook course is also used to take the navigation under Impney Road Bridge and from there turns towards the road and the original canal course. Any surplus water from the Body Brook is allowed to pass over a weir and flow into the Salwarpe. The navigation then follows a widened waterway towards Lock 7. Here construction has presently ceased awaiting British Waterways to gain access and dredge a 500m section of the Salwarpe for boats to reach the Barge Canal.

Planned work includes straightening the river and putting down a towpath. Certain buildings alongside will be demolished and the banks raised out of the flood plain to create new strips of building land. Funding for this part required a partnership with a developer for new houses along the route. Finishing the Droitwich Junction Canal encountered yet another hurdle, when the original partners pulled out of the arrangement.

Complete reopening of both waterways was anticipated to take place in 2010, but only the Barge Canal link through to Hawford was finished. With the passage under the A449 accomplished through cut-and-cover construction, the way for the final opening of the Barge Canal became possible. A cavalcade of boats ascended from the Severn on 11 September 2010. Navigation was limited to water extraction from the Salwarpe and this extraction was also restricted to certain dates and times by the Environment Agency.

Once the Junction Canal is opened, a pipe will convey water from above Lock 7 through to the canal above Lock 8. A causeway also remained across the Droitwich Junction Canal below Lock 5 to permit the carriage of spoil once the straightening of the Salwarpe is commenced.

The Droitwich Canal belongs to a group of waterway restorations where new lengths were required to complete the route. Diversions have been planned on unfinished restorations for the Grantham, Lichfield and the Shrewsbury & Newport canals. Perhaps the most ambitious is the Shrewsbury & Newport that has considered locking down to the River Severn as an alternative to the difficult, and probably impossible, restoration of the existing route crossings of the A5.

Abandonment of the Grantham Canal was agreed in 1936, although this waterway had closed to trade in 1929. The Grantham Canal Restoration Society was founded in 1970 with the object to restore the navigation of the canal to full use. They faced many problems, yet reconstruction of sections and locks ensued and parts were opened up for the use of craft such as trail boats. Restoration by such means is rich in volunteer labour, but frequently poor in finance when major obstacles such as dropped bridges and new roads have to be passed. The Grantham Navigation Association was formed in 1992 to promote liaison with local authorities and other grant-awarding bodies. New road building such as the A52 trunk road and the other dropped bridges on the urban section at the Nottingham end led the Society to consider options on how to restore this

The three locks on the Droitwich Junction Canal descend in a line to the Body Brook, which meets the canal below Lock 6. The former brook channel has been widened and deepened by the contractors through to the M5 motorway. (Author)

The Body Brook navigation runs from below lock 6 under the motorway and Impney Road through to the River Salwarpe. Water from the brook is allowed to run over a weir into the Salwarpe, whilst the canal is again diverted close to the original canal bed to Lock 7. In the final piece of restoration the spoil between Lock 7 and the Salwarpe needs to be dug out and the river deepened as far as the barge lock (Lock 8) at Vines Park. (Author)

section. The favoured option has become the diversion of the navigation along the Polser Brook and to use the existing culvert under the A52 to join the Trent near Radcliffe. The proposed route included three new locks at the junction with the existing canal and new locks at Holme Pierrepont. It is a similar route to the first proposed line for the Grantham from the Trent.

Active restoration is under way at the Lichfield Canal and the separate Hatherton Canal that is the combined aim of the Lichfield & Hatherton Trust. Most progress has been made on the Lichfield Canal where volunteers have restored locks and short sections of the Ogley Flight of the former Wyrley & Essington Canal. Public appeals have raised funds to complete the Brownhills steel aqueduct over the M6 Toll. One aim is the complete restoration of the Ogley Locks and the navigation between the Wyrley & Essington and the Coventry Canal. Several alterations to the old line were required.

The first deviations from the original route were made in 1997–98 at Darnford Lane, where the old lock was abandoned and a new course cut towards the lane. A lift bridge was installed on the restored canal adding a new feature to the navigation. Work then transferred to Tamworth Road and the locks beside the road. Rebuilding Locks 25 and 26 has occupied a long period. The dedication of the volunteers has resulted in the making of another new feature there. This is a circular bywash weir and drop shaft at Lock 25, which was completed in 2010.

The Trust has a long-term timetable for restoration, thinking and planning in terms of decades rather than years. They negotiate with the different local authorities as land becomes available, and deal with the unplanned as well as the planned. The making of the Lichfield Bypass was viewed as a long-term solution for taking the canal around the filled-in section east of Lock 19. When the plans for making this road were about to be implemented, a strip of land, which the Trust intended for a diversion of the canal, was reduced in size. This act led the Trust to finance a culvert under the Birmingham Road, at short notice.

Between Gloucester and Hereford, the Hereford & Gloucester Canal Trust also expresses a long-term view for restoration, slowly and methodically acquiring parts along the length of the disused canal. They face a considerable challenge as parts were converted into a railway. But with the conversion other parts of the canal, including the three tunnels, have survived. Sections have now been put back into water, but only a short section at Over has been fully restored. The purchase of the Lanthony barge lock site on the Severn has become part of the project that will eventually bring boats back onto the canal.

Sporadic bursts of restoration have been conducted for and by the Lapal Canal Trust. Their ambitious aim is to restore navigation along Dudley No.2 Canal from Selly Oak to Hawne Basin including the Lapal Tunnel. The only visible part of this scheme so far has been the making of the isolated concrete-lined section on the embankment through Leasowes Park.

At Stafford, a group called the Stafford Riverway Link plans to restore the Sow Navigation. They intend to reopen the junction with the Staffordshire & Worcestershire, build a new aqueduct over the Penk and rebuild the lock down to the Sow. It is also intended to restore the canal basin at Forebridge, Stafford, that was made when the navigation first opened in 1816.

Modern restoration schemes involve detailed engineering reports and business plans to proceed with the sanction of local authorities and funding. There is also a minefield of new regulations. It is an uphill battle that involves a different sort of commitment from those interested in restoration. The Derby & Sandiacre Canal Society face this challenge. With the route through Derby from Swarkestone lost to new roads, another link across the Derwent to the Sandiacre line has been contemplated. A survey made by W.S. Atkins broke the restoration down into fifty-eight projects. The Derby & Sandiacre Canal Trust was established and during 2003 this Trust started to tackle

A concrete linked section for the Dudley Canal in Leasowes Park, Halesowen, was completed although it is presently not joined to the canal network. (Author)

British Waterways embarked upon restoring Mart Lane Basin at Stourport on the Staffordshire & Worcestershire, constructing a new bridge that was wide enough for narrowboats to pass. The original bridge had been made wide enough for barge transit. (Author)

the easier work at Swarkestone, Borrowash and Hopwell Road. They have purchased sections of waterway and have intentions to purchase the remainder. The diversion planned includes a new canal across Pride Park from Wilmorton, incorporating a culvert under Wilmorton College and an aqueduct over the Derwent.

Our present waterway network is a mix of working and disused navigations. Within the Midlands region most is currently the responsibility of British Waterways, the sole survivor of the 1948 transport nationalisation plan. The rest are in private ownership. With each year there is the potential of new canal and river work being done, whilst the continuing maintenance of eighteenth- and nineteenth-century navigations draws on the skills of both British Waterways and volunteer groups. It is a remarkable fact that waterway improvement still challenges and tests the ability of the modern engineer. Perhaps the best recent example is the Falkirk Wheel although the Droitwich Junction Canal must also rate highly in the list of modern engineering innovation.

REFERENCES

ARCHIVE SOURCES

(a) Archives and Local History, Sixth Floor, Birmingham Library – Collections include Boulton & Watt, MS 86 (Birmingham Canal)

(b) Derby Library – Derby Canal Minutes

(c) Leicester Archives, Wigston – Leicester Flood Works Committee

(d) Nottingham Archives, Nottingham – Borough of Nottingham Trent Navigation Committee Minute Book Ca CM 87/1

(e) National Archives, Kew:

Ashby Canal (Rail 803)

Birmingham & Liverpool Junction Canal (Rail 808)

Birmingham Canal Navigations, Proprietor Minutes, reports and accounts (Rail 810)

Coventry Canal (Rail 818)

Cromford Canal (Rail 819)

Droitwich Canal (Rail 822)

Dudley Canal (Rail 824)

Erewash Canal (Rail 828)

Grand Junction Canal (Rail 830)

Grand Union Canal (Old) (Rail 831)

Grand Union Canal (New) (Rail 832)

Grantham Canal (Rail 833)

Leicester & Northampton Union Canal (Rail 847)

Leicester Navigation (Rail 848)

Loughborough Navigation (Rail 849)

Nottingham Canal (Rail 854)

Oxford Canal (Rail 855)

Severn Commissioners (Rail 863)

Staffordshire & Worcestershire Canal (Rail 871)

Stratford-upon-Avon Canal (Rail 875)

Trent Navigation Company (Rail 879)

Warwick & Birmingham Canal (Rail 881)

Warwick & Napton Canal (Rail 882)

Worcester & Birmingham Canal (Rail 886)

Wyrley & Essington Canal (Rail 887)

After Nationalisation Papers (AN)

(f) Staffordshire Archives Service, Lichfield

(g) Staffordshire Archives Service, Stafford – Paget papers MSS D603, Staffordshire & Worcestershire MSS D3186

(h) Warwick Archives – CR1590 Coventry, Grand Union and Oxford Canal MSS

(i) Waterways Museum, Gloucester – various, including BCN, Nottingham Canal and River Trent

(k) Worcester Archives – Droitwich Canal Tolls

ARTICLES

'The Navigation of the Avon', Percy G. Feek, *Birmingham Archaeological Society Transactions*, vol.36, November 1910

'Saltways of Droitwich District', Revd William Thomas Whitley, *Birmingham Archaeological Society Transactions*, vol.49, 1923

'Saltways', F.T.S. Houghton, *Birmingham Archaeological Society Transactions*, vol.54, 1932

'Making of the Leicestershire Canals (1766–1814)', A. Temple Patterson, *Transactions of the Leicestershire Archaeological and Historical Society*, vol.27, 1951

'Railways of the Leicester Navigation', Robert Abbot, *Transactions of the Leicestershire Archaeological and Historical Society*, vol.34, 1958

'Ashby-De-La-Zouch Canal and its Railways', C.R. Clinker & Charles Hatfield, *Transactions of the Leicestershire Archaeological and Historical Society*, vol.31, 1955

'Report on the History of the River Leen, near Nottingham', H.R. Potter, Senior Hydrology Assistant, Trent River Board, Unpublished paper, April 1962

'The Grantham Canal and Belvoir Castle Tramway', Ken Cheetham and Nigel Wood, *East Midlands Group, Railway and Canal Historical Society*, 1989

'The Birmingham and Liverpool Junction Canal: Planning and Construction in the Norbury District (Part I)', Edwin Shearing, *Journal of the Railway and Canal Historical Society*, No.146, vol.30, July 1990

'The Birmingham and Liverpool Junction Canal: Planning and Construction in the Norbury District (Part II)', Edwin Shearing, *Journal of the Railway and Canal Historical Society*, No.146, vol.30, November 1990

'Cast Iron Canal Aqueducts', Edwin Shearing, *Journal of the Railway and Canal Historical Society*, No.149, vol.30, November 1991

'Voices along a forgotten waterway (Nottingham Canal)', Keith Taylor, *Waterways World*, June 1994

'The Promotion of the Grantham Canal', W.M. Hunt, *Journal of the Railway and Canal Historical Society*, No.163, vol.32, March 1996

'Burton's lost link with the Sea', Robert Hamilton, *Waterways World*, February 1999

'The canals of England and Wales – The future they never had', Tony Burnip, *Waterways Journal*, the Boat Museum Society, May 1999

'The Building of the Macclesfield Canal', Graham Cousins, *Journal of the Railway and Canal Historical Society*, No.173, part 2, vol.33, July 1999

'Construction of canal locks', Brian Lamb, *Journal of the Railway and Canal Historical Society*, No.173, vol.33, July 1999

'How a canal almost came to Ludlow', Bryan Heatley, *Journal of the Railway and Canal Historical Society*, No.177, vol.33, November 2000

'The Macclesfield Canal – the Early Years', Graham Cousins, *Journal of the Railway and Canal Historical Society*, vol.33, July 2001

'Foxton Revisited', David Turnock, *Journal of the Railway and Canal Historical Society*, No.181, vol.34, March 2002

'The Archaeology of Navigation on the Upper Severn', Neil Clarke, *Journal of the Railway and Canal Historical Society*, No.185, vol.34, July 2003

'Bullbridge Aqueduct: the Cromford Canal and the North Midland Railway', John Rapley, *Journal of the Railway and Canal Historical Society*, No.186, vol.34, November 2003

'Navigation of the River Teme', Pat Jones, *Journal of the Railway and Canal Historical Society*, No.194, vol.35, March 2006

'Historical Profile, Staffordshire and Worcestershire Canal', Ian Langford, *Narrowboat*, spring 2006

'The River Teme and Other Midlands Navigations', Peter King, *Journal of the Railway and Canal Historical Society*, No.195, vol.35, July 2006

'Single Barrier Navigation Structures', Pat Jones, *Journal of the Railway and Canal Historical Society*, No.198, vol.35, July 2007

'The Ketley Canal' Paul Luter, *Journal of the Railway and Canal Historical Society*, No.199, vol.35, November 2007

'Canal Reservoirs in Great Britain', D Henthorn Brown, *Proceedings of the Institution of Civil Engineers, Engineering History and Heritage*, No.162, May 2009

'William Reynolds and the East Shropshire Tub Boat System', Neil Clarke, *Journal of the Railway and Canal Historical Society*, No.206, vol.36, July 2009

'Canal contractors 1760-1820', Peter Cross-Rudkin, *Journal of the Railway and Canal Historical Society*, No.207, vol.36, March 2010

BOOKS

Canals and Traders, Edwin A. Pratt, P.S. King & Son, 1910

The Canals of South Wales and the Border, Charles Hadfield, University of Wales Press and Phoenix House Ltd, 1960

Waterways to Stratford, Charles Hadfield & John Norris, David & Charles, 1962

Canals of the West Midlands, Charles Hadfield, David & Charles, 2nd edition 1969

Canals of the East Midlands, Charles Hadfield, David & Charles, 2nd edition 1970

The Nutbrook Canal, Peter Stevenson, David & Charles, 1970

Lost Canals of England and Wales, Ronald Russell, David & Charles, 1971

The Grand Junction Canal, Alan H. Faulkener, David & Charles, 1972

The Leicester Line, Philip A. Stevens, David & Charles, 1972

A Towpath Guide to the Staffordshire and Worcestershire Canal, J. Ian Langford, Goose & Son, 1974

The Grantham Canal Today. A brief history and guide, Chris Cove-Smith, Grantham Canal Restoration Society, 1974

The Melton Mowbray Navigation, M.G. Miller & S. Fletcher, Railway & Canal Historical Society, 1984

The Oxford Canal, Hugh J. Compton, David & Charles, 1976

The Trent and Mersey Canal, Jean Lindsay, David & Charles, 1979

The Industrial Revolution in Shropshire, Barry S. Trinder, Phillimore & Co. Ltd, 1981

The Warwick Canals, Alan H. Faulkener, Railway and Canal Historical Society, 1985

The Shropshire Union Canal-A Towpath Guide to the Birmingham and Liverpool Junction Canal from Autherley to Nantwich, Jonathan Morris, Management Update Ltd, 1991

Josiah Wedgwood 1730-1795, Robin Reilly, Macmillan, London, 1992

A guide to the Anderton Boat Lift, David Carden and Neil Parkhouse, Black Dwarf Publications, 2002

Portal to Portal – A short history of Butterley Tunnel, Des Greenwood, 2003

Birmingham and Black Country Canalside Industries, Ray Shill, Tempus Publishing, 2005

The Worcester and Birmingham Canal – Chronicles of the Cut, Revd Alan White, Brewin Books, 2005

CANAL SOCIETY JOURNALS

Boundary Post, Birmingham Canal Navigation Society

Broadsheet, Staffordshire & Worcestershire Canal Society

Cut Both Ways, Lichfield & Hatherton Canals Restoration Trust

Navvies Notebook (later *Navvies*), Inland Waterways Association

The Legger, Dudley Canal Trust

The Packet, Derby and Sandiacre Society

The New Wych, Droitwich Canal Trust

Tunnel Vision, The Lapal Canal Trust

Waterways, Inland Waterways Association

CANAL SOCIETY RESEARCH GROUP PUBLICATIONS

Railway & Canal Historical Society, Modern Transport Group (2008–date)

Railway & Canal Historical Society, Waterways History Group (1999–date)

Developers have brought mixed blessings to the canalside. Heritage has both been lost and preserved through a wide range of architectural design, experiment and misadventure. Structures like the footbridge over the Coventry Canal perhaps belong amongst the category of better designs, even if the heritage destruction of the former Daimler car factory was achieved in the process. (Author)

NEWSPAPER SOURCES

Aris's Birmingham Gazette
Berrow's Worcester Journal
Birmingham Daily Post
Bristol Mercury
Derby Mercury
Leicester Chronicle
Leicester Herald
Leicester Journal
Midland Counties Herald
Nottinghamshire Guardian
Jackson's Oxford Journal
Sheffield Independent
The Times
Warwick & Warwickshire Advertiser
Worcester Chronicle
Wolverhampton Chronicle

PERIODICAL SOURCES

Archive
Canal Boat
Canal and River Boat
Narrow Boat
Waterways Journal
Waterways World

PRINTED SOURCES

Calender Rolls – Patent
Calender Rolls – State Papers

INDEX

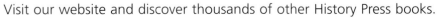

Visit our website and discover thousands of other History Press books.

www.thehistorypress.co.uk